The Economics of Work and Pay

The HarperCollins Series in Economics

Allen
Managerial Economics

Binger/Hoffman
Microeconomics with Calculus

Bowles/Edwards
Understanding Capitalism

Branson
Macroeconomic Theory and Policy

Browning/Zupan
Microeconomic Theory and Applications

Burgess
The Economics of Regulation

Byrns/Stone
Economics

Caniglia
Statistics for Economics

Canterbery
The Literate Economist: A Brief History of Economics

Carlton/Perloff
Modern Industrial Organization

Caves/Frankel/Jones
World Trade and Payments

Cooter/Ulen
Law and Economics

Ehrenberg/Smith
Modern Labor Economics

Ekelund/Tollison
Economics

Filer/Hamermesh/Rees
The Economics of Work and Pay

Fusfeld
The Age of the Economist

Gordon
Macroeconomics

Gregory/Ruffin
Economics

Gregory
Essentials of Economics

Gregory/Stuart
Soviet and Post-Soviet Economic Structure and Performance

Hartwick/Olewiler
The Economics of Natural Resource Use

Hogendorn
Economic Development

Hughes/Cain
American Economic History

Hunt
History of Economic Thought

Hunt
Property and Prophets

Husted/Melvin
International Economics

Kohler
Statistics for Business and Economics

Krugman/Obstfeld
International Economics: Theory and Policy

Kwoka/White
The Antitrust Revolution

Laidler
The Demand for Money

Lardaro
Applied Econometrics

Lipsey/Courant/Purvis/Steiner
Economics

McCafferty
Macroeconomic Theory

McCarty
Dollars and Sense

Melvin
International Money and Finance

Miller
Economics Today

Miller/Benjamin/North
The Economics of Public Issues

Miller/Fishe
Microeconomics: Price Theory in Practice

Mills/Hamilton
Urban Economics

Mishkin
The Economics of Money, Banking, and Financial Markets

Petersen
Business and Government

Phelps
Health Economics

Ritter/Silber
Principles of Money, Banking, and Financial Markets

Ruffin/Gregory
Principles of Economics

Ruffin
Intermediate Microeconomics

Salvatore
Microeconomics

Sargent
Rational Expectations and Inflation

Scherer
Industry Structure, Strategy, and Public Policy

Schotter
Microeconomics: A Modern Approach

Sherman/Kolk
Business Cycles and Forecasting

Studenmund
Using Econometrics

Su
Economic Fluctuations and Forecasting

Tietenberg
Environmental and Natural Resource Economics

Tietenberg
Environmental Economics and Policy

Zerbe/Dively
Benefit-Cost Analysis

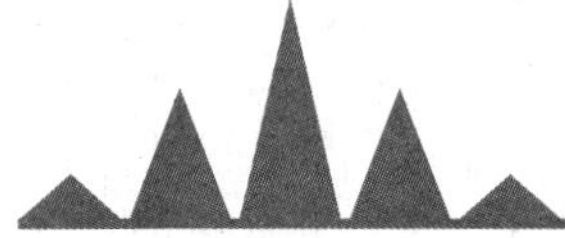

THE ECONOMICS OF WORK AND PAY

SIXTH EDITION

Randall K. Filer

Hunter College and the Graduate Center of the City University of New York
CERGE EI–Prague

Daniel S. Hamermesh

University of Texas, Austin

Albert E. Rees

Late, Princeton University

HarperCollins*CollegePublishers*

Executive Editor: *John Greenman*
Project Editor: *Elizabeth LaManna*
Senior Design: *John Callahan*
Cover Designer: *Sarah Johnson*
Art Studio: *Paul Lacy*
Electronic Production Manager: *Su Levine*
Desktop Administrator: *Laura Leever*
Manufacturing Manager: *Willie Lane*
Electronic Page Makeup: *Interactive Composition Corporation*
Printer and Binder: RR Donnelley & Sons Company
Cover Printer: New England Book Components, Inc.

The Economics of Work and Pay, Sixth Edition

Library of Congress Cataloging-in-Publication Data

Filer, Randall Keith.
The economics of work and pay/Randall K. Filer, Daniel S. Hamermesh, Albert E. Rees. —6th ed.
p. cm.—(HarperCollins series in economics)
Rev. ed. of: Economics of work and pay/Daniel S. Hamermesh. Albert Rees. 5th ed. 1993.
Includes bibliographical references and index.
ISBN 0-673-99474-0
1. Labor economics. I. Hamermesh, Daniel S. II. Rees, Albert, III. Hamermesh, Daniel S. Economics of work and pay. IV. Series.
HD4901.H18 1996
331—dc20 95-40602
CIP

96 97 98 9 8 7 6 5 4 3 2

CONTENTS

PART FOUR INTERNAL LABOR MARKETS 329

CHAPTER 9 Effort, Wages, and Job Structure 331

CHAPTER 10 Job Amenities and Employee Benefits 372

PART FIVE UNIONIZED LABOR MARKETS 411

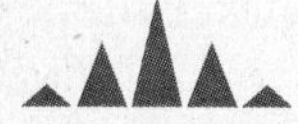

To the Instructor

This edition of *The Economics of Work and Pay* represents a major revision. In addition to updating the facts and references, the entire text has been rewritten and reorganized. As in past editions, it assumes only that the student has taken an introductory course in microeconomic principles and is able to handle graphical analysis. At most, a little algebra is used. While an introductory course in macroeconomics may be useful in understanding certain topics, it is not essential.

STRUCTURE OF THE BOOK

The introductory section "To the Student" provides an overview of labor economics and a guide to studying it. The text itself is divided into six major sections, each containing chapters linked to one broad topic. The first two sections follow the standard distinction in economics between households and businesses. Part One discusses the quantity and quality of labor that households decide to supply to the market, that is, how people choose to allocate their time between home and work. The major questions deal with how the value of individuals' time at home and in the labor market affects these decisions, including choices about how much formal and informal education and on-the-job training they choose to acquire.

Part Two discusses businesses' demand for workers. The main issues are how a higher cost of labor affects this demand and how businesses choose between hiring more workers and having their existing workers put in longer hours.

Parts Three through Six build directly on the first two sections by bringing labor supply and labor demand together in a variety of ways. Keeping in mind that in labor markets, as in other markets, outcomes are the result of interactions between suppliers and buyers, the emphasis here is on the simultaneous behavior of households and businesses. Part Three focuses on external labor markets and examines such issues as employment, unemployment, vacant jobs, job search, and the movement among jobs, geographic areas, and occupations.

Part Four, which analyzes the labor market within firms, examines how pay is structured to bring forth effort. It also focuses on how and why workers and firms determine the division of compensation among pay, employee benefits, and working conditions.

In Part Five we discuss the most important single private institution affecting outcomes in the labor market—trade unions. Why workers join unions as well as how these organizations affect pay, working conditions, and productivity are the primary questions explored.

Part Six examines the aggregate economy. It focuses on how the decisions of individuals and firms studied in the first five sections generate overall outcomes in the economy. Among the areas studied are the earnings achieved by members of various groups and whether evidence of discrimination in labor markets exists. We also discuss the impact of labor-market decisions on the distribution of earnings and the extent of poverty, and the macroeconomic effects of cyclical variation in aggregate demand. While the first five sections generally treat the labor market as at most tangentially affected by and having little impact on aggregate fluctuations, here we demonstrate how macroeconomic fluctuations can begin in the labor market, and how labor markets themselves react to changes in aggregate demand.

While we believe the entire book can be covered in a one-semester course, instructors teaching a quarter-long course or those who wish to present the material more slowly have a great deal of flexibility. Chapters 1 through 4 form the basic core of the book. It would be difficult to understand the material that follows if these chapters are omitted. After Chapter 4, instructors have the freedom to pick and choose what they would like to cover. Chapter 5 is optional for those who would like to present additional material on labor demand. It is perhaps best to treat Parts Three, Four, and Five as organic units, covering all or none of the chapters in each section. The three chapters in Part Six can each stand alone, although Chapter 16 will be more easily understood if Part Three has been covered.

CHANGES IN THIS EDITION

The changes to the sixth edition of *The Economics of Work and Pay* extend throughout the book and involve far more than the usual updating of facts and references. We have attempted to use our own and others' experiences in teaching labor economics to present the material in a way that is simultaneously accurate, accessible, and involving to the student. This has meant a major rewriting and reorganizing of the text as well as extensive changes in presentation. All of the artwork is new and is now in two colors to enhance clarity. One-third of the policy issues illustrating how economic principles can be used to analyze real-world situations are also new. There are more than twice as many end-of-chapter questions.

As in previous editions, we intermix theory with the often substantial econometric evidence relating to it. In this edition, several hundred new scholarly works are cited, many of which replace studies whose results are based on out-of-date data or that are no longer the best available on the topic. We have attempted to present all sides of controversial issues. On the other hand, where we believe the evidence points to a resolution of previously disputed topics we have not hesitated to say so. It is important for students to learn that the scientific method does eventually yield answers, and that not all opinions can be supported equally. Empirical results are referenced specifically, as are the sources of data presented in the tables.

The emphasis on international comparisons introduced in the previous edition has been expanded. The increasing interconnectedness of the world economy demands this focus, while the increasingly shared research interests of labor economists around the world and the growth of sources of comparable data make it possible.

The ancillary materials have also been totally revised and expanded. The Study Guide, completely new with this edition, is an essential companion to the text. It contains definitions of the key words, and provides a framework for studying each chapter. The answers to selected end-of-chapter questions, as well as more questions and problems that students can use to check their understanding, are also included. In addition, the Study Guide contains important supplemental material, including an explanation of regression analyses and a list of locations where students can search for data and source material for term papers or to increase their knowledge in specific areas of labor economics. There is also a new Instructor's Manual.

Finally, there has been a change in authorship with this edition of *The Economics of Work and Pay.* Al Rees, one of the founders of modern labor economics, died on the day the fifth edition was released. He remains listed among the authors for a simple reason. This book was originally written because Al had a specific way he believed labor economics should be taught. His emphasis on uncompromising theoretical rigor evaluated in the light of the latest empirical work continues to guide our own teaching. Whenever we had doubts about how to present a specific topic or evaluate a specific study we would e-mail each other: "What would Al have said here?" Thus, his spirit very much pervades this book. Randy Filer, who joins this edition as a coauthor, was Al Rees's last dissertation student and teaching assistant at Princeton before Al became president of the Sloan Foundation. There is, therefore, a symbolic passing of the torch with this edition. We only hope that in it we have been able to convey some of the intellectual passion for economics in general and labor economics in particular that made Al Rees such an inspiring teacher and that, because of this, future generations of students will be motivated to follow not only in his footsteps, but also to take up his challenge to advance our understanding of the way the labor market operates and its impact on us all.

ACKNOWLEDGMENTS

No textbook is an individual effort. We owe debts of gratitude to Linda Friedman-Moskowitz and Elka Munizaga for tracking down references and updating statistical data. The staff of the Social Science Reference Center in

Princeton's Firestone Library were especially helpful in locating the most difficult items. Steve Allen, Nevila Konica, and Irena Dushi contributed to the end-of-chapter questions. Barbara Forbes performed an invaluable service by carefully reading each sentence in the book for both form and content.

This text has benefited greatly from the comments and criticisms of our colleagues and friends. Previous editions were aided by comments from

Steven Allen, North Carolina State University
Terry Ashley, Auburn University
Peter Barth, University of Connecticut
Melvin Bers, SUNY Albany
Charles Blake, Kettering, Ohio
Francine Blau, Cornell University
George Borjas, University of California, San Diego
Charles Brown, University of Michigan
Christopher Bruce, University of Calgary
Glen Cain, University of Wisconsin
Barry Chiswick, University of Illinois, Chicago
Henry Farber, Princeton University
T. Aldrich Finegan, Vanderbilt University
George Greenwade, Sam Houston State University
John Hambleton, San Diego State University
Alan Harrison, McMaster University
James Johannes, University of Wisconsin, Madison
George Johnson, University of Michigan
Duane Leigh, Washington State University
H. Gregg Lewis, late of Duke University
Thomas Michl, Colgate University
Jacob Mincer, Columbia University
Olivia Mitchell, Cornell University
George Neumann, University of Iowa
Ronald Oaxaca, University of Arizona
Donald Pearson, Eastern Michigan University
L. Wayne Plumly, Valdosta State College
Tod Porter, Youngstown State University
James Ragan, Kansas State University
Sherwin Rosen, University of Chicago
Robert Ross, Bloomsburg University
Frank Stafford, University of Michigan
Joe Stone, University of Oregon
Barry Stregevsky, Central Michigan University
Michael Taussig, Rutgers University
Stephen Trejo, University of California, Santa Barbara
Donald Williams, Kent State University
John Wolfe, Michigan State University
Stephen Woodbury, Michigan State University

The sixth edition has been aided by additional comments from many of the above as well as the following:

Orley Ashenfelter, Princeton University
Eli Berman, Boston University
Brent Bratsberg, Kansas State University
James A. Dyal, Indiana University of Pennsylvania
Linda Edwards, City University of New York
Dale Mortenson, Northwestern University
Derek Neal, University of Chicago
Robert Sandy, Indiana University–Purdue University, Indianapolis
Edwin A. Sexton, Virginia Military Institute
Walter Wessels, North Carolina State University

None of these scholars is in any way responsible for our conclusions. To each, however, we are deeply indebted.

RANDALL K. FILER

DANIEL S. HAMERMESH

To the Student

LABOR AS A SUBFIELD OF ECONOMICS

You are about to embark on the study of labor economics. Perhaps more than any other subfield of economics, labor economics deals with issues that directly affect each of us. Labor markets exist in all economies, no matter how primitive or how advanced. Most of us spend far more of our lives at work than we do in any other activity. What we can do when we are not working is largely determined by the incomes we earn from our jobs.

Some things that are a part of labor economics are obvious, while others may seem surprising at first. As the title of this book implies, labor economics encompasses work and pay. Questions we will be examining include:

Who decides to work and who stays at home?

How do individuals decide on the division of their time among work, play, and investment in skills?

What determines how much and what type of education people decide to obtain?

How do firms decide which workers to hire and how much to offer to pay them?

What is unemployment and why does it exist?

Why are some workers paid by the hour while others make a fixed salary, and still others are paid only for what they produce?

Why do some sports and movie stars or top executives make enormously high salaries?

Why do trade unions exist and who do they help or hurt in an economy?

Are some groups discriminated against in the labor market, and what has been the effect of programs designed to alter labor market outcomes?

Who is helped and who is hurt by government programs such as minimum wages, occupational safety laws, and unemployment insurance?

Labor economics is not a course in industrial relations or personnel management. These fields have as their main focus the relationship between a specific employer and its workers or their union. While labor economics is based on behavior by these small units, its purpose is to develop general principles about the behavior of broader groups and the economy as a whole.

Labor economics has evolved as a special field in large part because labor markets are very different from other economic markets. Unlike transactions in most markets, which are brief and impersonal, a job involves an ongoing personal relationship between an employer and an employee. While producers of commodities have comparatively little interest in their products once they are sold, workers care a great deal about how they are employed by those to whom they sell their labor services.

The focus on studying the behavior of workers and firms means that labor economics also examines a wide variety of government policies. Policies directly affecting working conditions or pay, such as minimum wage requirements, affirmative action, payroll taxes, and workplace safety, impinge on labor markets. Less obvious, but no less important, are policies such as unemployment insurance and subsidized day care that may be perceived as affecting workers only outside the workplace, but nevertheless may change the amount they work or are paid.

For all these reasons, labor economics is the branch of economics most concerned with the lives of every citizen and the policies that affect us all in ways that either improve or reduce our well-being.

HOW TO STUDY FROM THIS TEXT

Prior Knowledge

The analysis in this text is the next step beyond the material covered in a principles of economics course, and no additional preparation is required. The ideas from your principles class that you will encounter most often in this text are as follows:

1. The marginal principle: engaging in an extra bit of any activity such as buying another beer, making a concrete road a little thicker, or studying a little longer only so long as the extra benefits are sufficient to cover the extra costs.
2. Discounting: marking down future values to relate them to current values in recognition that money in the future is not worth as much as money today.
3. Opportunity costs: measuring the real cost of any action by the value of the resources, including time, devoted to it in their next best alternative use.
4. Elasticity: relating the percentage change in one thing to a 1 percent change in something else that affects it.
5. Supply and demand curves: showing the relationships between quantities and prices and what causes those relationships to shift.

LEARNING THE LANGUAGE

As in any field, labor economics has a set of terms you need to learn in order to analyze issues and speak intelligently about the concepts. In this book we have placed the essential terms in boldface in the text as well as listing them in Key Words at the end of the chapter where they first occur. All key words are defined in the separate Study Guide that accompanies the text.

Learning the precise definition of terms is particularly important in labor economics because many words common in everyday speech are used by economists as technical terms with very specific meanings that may differ from common usage. Students often find this confusing. For example, key terms such as *utility* or *efficiency* have precise scientific meanings as they are used in economics that are only somewhat related to their casual usage. Exact knowledge of the definitions allows clear thinking about the economic concepts you will be analyzing and learning to apply to new situations.

The importance of using terms correctly is illustrated by the following newspaper headline: "Demand exceeds supply of jobs." This headline implies that workers are demanding and businesses are supplying jobs. No economist would ever make this statement. Under normal circumstances, jobs are not bought and sold. Workers supply a service that businesses demand. The service being exchanged (and only goods and services can be exchanged) is the service of workers' time. Even though readers may understand this headline, an accurate headline would read, "Supply exceeds demand for workers."

APPROACHING THE MATERIAL

Professional economists typically approach their work through the use of the scientific method, and we have attempted to replicate this approach in presenting the material in this text. Scientists follow a logical sequence in analyzing problems, whether in economics or physics. Typically, advances in knowledge occur in a three-step process:

1. A phenomenon of some kind grabs a researcher's attention as being interesting and not well understood.
2. Theoretical models are developed that attempt to explain the observed reality. These models are used to derive predictions about the behavior of the phenomenon we should expect to see in the real world.
3. These predictions are tested by careful experimentation and observation to see if the theory can, indeed, explain reality beyond the facts used to develop it.

If the predictions are valid, then the theoretical model becomes generally accepted until it fails to explain an observed phenomenon or until a competing theory does a better job of explaining the observed reality. If the predictions are not supported, the theoretical models are revised and the process begins again. Eventually, it is hoped, our theoretical understanding approximates the underlying reality.

Labor economists' attention is often drawn to an area because they see some pattern or trend in data about work or pay. We frequently introduce a topic by presenting recent data. While these data are important in their own right, you need not memorize every detail. Instead, you should learn approximate magnitudes, what trends have taken place, and how outcomes differ among countries. For example, it is not necessary to memorize that in 1954 the labor force participation rate among white women was 33.3 percent while in 1994 it was 58.9 percent. It is important, however, that you know that nearly three-fifths of adult women are now working, substantially more than in the past.

We then present the theoretical models developed by economists in an attempt to understand these data. These models are often originally expressed as mathematical relationships. Despite the trend toward labor economics (and economics in general) becoming increasingly mathematical over the past several decades, the basic ideas can be understood without requiring detailed mathematical knowledge or ability. The level of mathematics used in this text does not go beyond what is taught in a high-school algebra course.

Nearly all the ideas economists originally developed using higher math can also be shown graphically. Since these graphs are usually easier for undergraduates to understand, we rely heavily on graphical expositions of the major ideas in this text. This means that you need to understand slopes, intercepts, and tangencies. You must also know what it means when we say that a line or curve shifts, how variables not listed on the axes of a graph are "held constant" along a curve, and how the curve is altered when they change. You should be familiar with these skills from your principles of economics course.

Once again, memorization is not the best way to study the graphical analysis. You should, instead, be able to re-create any graph in the book from first principles. This ability will not only establish your mastery of specific points made in the text, but also will enable you to analyze different but related situations not covered here.

In economics, verification of theory typically cannot take place through laboratory experiments. It must, instead, be accomplished through real-world observation. The evidence that convinces labor economists that a theory is correct or some effect has a particular magnitude typically relies on careful and repeated hypothesis testing, as well as the measurement of behavior at different times and in many countries.

While some of this evidence comes from examining the response of economic agents to changes in the world around them, such as the introduction of a new law, much of it comes from econometric research using various data sets and statistical methods to examine economic behavior. The most common statistical technique is multivariate regression. It is not necessary to have completed a course in statistics or econometrics to understand the evidence we present in this text. You may find, however, that you are more comfortable evaluating it and reading the original research when you want to go beyond the text if you have some understanding of the techniques used. The Study Guide contains a basic introduction to regression analysis that you may find helpful.

Since the analytical techniques presented here are generally applicable to any labor market, many examples and much of the raw data presented cover a wide range of countries. This is partly because the increasing interconnectedness of the world economy means that no country can be studied in isolation. Important phenomena frequently are understood better when analyzed in light of the divergent experiences of countries with different legal systems, historic backgrounds, and government policies. The range of experiences is so much greater worldwide than within any single nation that international examples can often illustrate an idea better than an example from one particular country.

While much of the evidence summarized and even some of the raw data may seem old, this situation is in part the necessary result of how research is done. It often takes four or five years from when an economist begins a study until the research results are publicly available. Data on which a study is based have often been collected previously by some government or private agency. Thus, a study published in 1995 may rely on data collected in the late 1980s. Moreover, many topics of interest may not have been studied in recent years, because once a consensus is reached in the profession it is not particularly interesting simply to verify that the situation has not changed.

In working to understand the empirical evidence presented in this text you should strive for a good understanding of the approximate sizes of the effects of various factors on outcomes of interest. You also need to be familiar with the impacts of particular policies, and the general facts about behavior in the labor market. Knowledge of these magnitudes should enable you to take an applied problem and produce your own analysis of the direction and size of the effects of any change in government policies or other factors that might alter labor market outcomes.

The requirement for verifying theoretical models means that not all ideas are equally valid. An analysis is accepted only when it is both logically consistent and has been confirmed by carefully constructed empirical research. If a theory is not falsifiable (that is, if there is no possible way that empirical research could fail to confirm it), then that theory is of little use.

Economics is a positive science. It asks questions about what is and what would happen if, not about what ought to be. The role of an economist is to say that if a specific occupational safety rule is adopted, there will be so many fewer injuries each year, employment will be reduced by so much, and wages will go down and prices up by a certain amount. Whether, on balance, these effects indicate that the rule should or should not be adopted is not the province of the professional economist. In these sorts of normative questions, the economist has no more of a claim to expertise than any other citizen.

APPLYING THE CONCEPTS

Labor economics, like all of economics, is not just a body of facts or a set of analytical methods. It is more than anything else a way of thinking about behavior and its effects on real-world outcomes. To encourage this way of thinking, we give numerous examples illustrating the major conceptual points in the text and present policy issues set apart from the body of the text to show how the theoretical principles are applied to the real world. Many of these discussions present important labor market policy problems that are continuously in the news.

These policy issues can often provide you with ideas that can be developed into a term paper. Additional support for term papers can be gleaned from the numerous references throughout the text to the professional literature in particular areas. The Study Guide contains a discussion of how to find both analytical research and raw data that will be useful for your term papers.

While we have sought out interesting policy issues and applications from around the world, the best examples are the ones you develop yourself. One of the best ways to study the material in this book is to generate your own examples of the main concepts we discuss. This type of active introspection is an important aid to understanding economic analysis. If you understand how to use a general theory to gain insight into specific situations in your life, it is likely that you really understand the theory. You should approach the material with a sense of play and exploration, asking yourself, "Where else might this principle apply?"

This mode of study means that an economics text cannot be read like a novel. If you are reading the material quickly, it is unlikely that you are thinking carefully about it or giving it time to sink in. Allowing yourself time to get involved with the ideas will vastly improve your comprehension and make the entire learning experience more enjoyable. Active reading is the key. Read each section and try to rephrase it in your own words. Then put the book aside and see if you can recall the material, re-create the arguments, and apply them in different situations. As a general rule, you should plan on spending at least three hours studying the text for each hour you spend in lectures.

At the end of each chapter are questions and problems designed to reinforce this approach. They require you to apply the theoretical concepts introduced in the chapter, and often to integrate several major points. Answering the questions and problems is a good way to make sure you understand the material in the chapter. Possible answers to many end-of-chapter questions are provided in the Study Guide, as are additional questions of various types that you can use to check your understanding of the material.

If you study this material by thinking about it actively, you will know the major facts describing labor markets when you have finished this textbook. You will also know the roles of the main institutions and policies affecting labor markets, as well as understanding the theories economists have created to explain the world around us. Most important, because the techniques used here are applicable with appropriate changes to topics other than those discussed in the text, you will be able to analyze and understand other, often new, labor market issues as you confront them as a worker and as a citizen.

Randall K. Filer

Daniel S. Hamermesh

Part One

LABOR SUPPLY

The first section of this book examines the supply of labor. Although it has similarities with analyses of the supply of other factors of production or of outputs, the study of labor supply is different in fundamental ways. Most of these stem from the fact that the person who supplies labor is more closely connected with that supply than the producer of a commodity. Chapter 1 considers who among the potential work force actually decides to provide labor to the market. Chapter 2 investigates how much labor each worker will decide to supply. Finally, Chapter 3 discusses the quality of the labor provided by workers in terms of the skills that it embodies.

1

LABOR FORCE PARTICIPATION

THE MAJOR QUESTIONS

- ▲ What determines who seeks work and who does not?
- ▲ How do we measure the number of "work-seekers?"
- ▲ What are the differences by age, race, sex, and other characteristics in the probability that a person is working or seeking work?
- ▲ How have these differences changed over the years?
- ▲ How have government policies affected labor participation decisions of various groups and influenced changes in these decisions over the years?

THE MEANING OF LABOR SUPPLY

These questions refer to **labor supply**. For 18th- and 19th-century economists, the discussion of labor supply concerned forces that determined the size of the working-age population and the effect of changes in real wages on population growth. The questions posed above were considered of little importance, since it was assumed that virtually everyone old enough and healthy enough to do any useful work toiled the entire day.

Modern labor economists reverse this emphasis. We define labor supply as the amount of effort offered by a population of a given size. We pay little attention to changes in the size of the population resulting from birth rates (fertility) and death rates (mortality), leaving the study of these factors to **demography**, a separate discipline that combines economics, sociology, and mathematics.[1]

It is important to recognize, however, that demographic changes have a significant impact on labor supply. Between 1980 and 1990 the labor force

---

[1]For a discussion of some of these issues, see Randall J. Olsen, "Fertility and the Size of the U.S. Labor Force," *Journal of Economic Literature* 32: 60–100 (1994).

between ages 16 and 64 grew by a total of 17 percent in the U.S. and Canada. Almost 10 percentage points of this change were due to the difference between the number of people reaching age 16 and the number exiting the labor force after age 64. The remaining 8 percentage points occurred because of international migration and increased labor force participation among all age groups.

Several additional areas where issues of current or past fertility play an important role in labor economics will be discussed in this book. Among these are the effect of wages on fertility, the impact of child care costs on female labor force participation, and the effect of the relatively large "baby boom" cohort on labor mobility and internal labor markets. Furthermore, changes in the age structure of the population brought about by changing birth rates have an impact on such issues as the normal rate of unemployment and the funding of the Social Security system. Changes in population resulting from immigration also have important economic determinants and impacts which will be discussed later.

The amount of labor supplied by a given population has four components.

1. **Labor force participation rate** (LFPR) The percentage of the population engaged in or seeking gainful employment. This component has been studied extensively. Today we understand a great deal about why different groups are more or less likely to be working or seeking work and how government programs affect participation. In this chapter we discuss the various factors that determine participation.
2. **Hours of work** The number of hours people wish to offer per day, per week, or per year while they are in the labor force. This aspect of labor supply is treated in Chapter 2.
3. **Effort** The intensity (either physical or mental) that people put into each hour or day at work. The discussion of this factor is begun in the last section of Chapter 2 and continued in more detail in Chapter 9.
4. **Skill** The level of natural ability and training that workers bring to their jobs. This important topic is the subject of Chapter 3.

Although we separate these four components of labor supply for discussion, they are not independent of each other. Many of the same forces that affect one affect others. Together these components make up the amount of labor—**total work effort**—available for the production of goods and services to be sold in the marketplace.

THE LABOR FORCE

The **labor force** is the number of people who are working for pay or profit or who are unemployed during any part of a defined period of time. In the United States, the labor force is measured once a month for a **reference week**, that is, the week containing the 12th day of the month. In the week following this reference week, people in nearly 60,000 households in 700 geographic areas are interviewed by the U.S. Bureau of the Census. These interviews form the **Current Population Survey (CPS)**, the basis for calculating unemployment and other labor force statistics.

Households chosen for the CPS reflect the principal characteristics of the population as measured in the most recent decennial census. The same household is included in the survey for four consecutive months, removed for eight months, and then included again for a final four consecutive months. This pattern improves estimates of changes from month to month and year to year by enabling comparisons based on at least some of the same individuals and households.

In the U.S., a person is deemed to be **employed** if he or she worked one hour or more for pay during the reference week or did 15 hours or more of unpaid work in a family business or farm. Those absent from work because of vacation, illness, bad weather, or strikes and lockouts are also counted as employed, but in the separate subcategory "with a job but not at work."

The **unemployed** are those who have no job but were available for work during the reference week and have looked for work during the preceding four weeks using one or more of a specific list of methods. Also included as unemployed are those who are temporarily laid-off from a job to which they expect to be recalled, or who are waiting to report to a new job within the next 30 days.

People under the age of 16 are not included in the population surveyed. As far as the CPS is concerned, a 15-year-old who is working for pay is not employed. On the other hand, a 95-year-old who is neither looking for work nor currently working is included in the survey but is categorized as out of the labor force. Being in school does not preclude someone 16 or over from being counted as in the labor force. People who are institutionalized in prisons, mental institutions, and the like are not counted at all.

Separate data are kept on the **civilian labor force** and the **total labor force**, which also includes military personnel living in the U.S. Because the military currently represents less than 2 percent of total employment, the differences in percentage terms between the two concepts are very slight. In this book, only the behavior of the civilian labor force is discussed.

Analysis of the CPS enables the labor force participation status of each civilian aged 16 or more who is not institutionalized to be determined. Labor force participation is an all-or-nothing matter. For purposes of the CPS, a person is either in the labor force or out of it. Answers to the CPS questions enable the **population over age 16,** P, to be divided into employed, E, unemployed, U, and **out-of-the-labor force**, O, such that

$$P = E + U + O.$$

The labor force, L, consists of those who are employed or unemployed

$$L = E + U.$$

The labor force participation rate, $LFPR$, usually expressed as a percentage, is

$$LFPR = 100 \times (\frac{L}{P}).$$

The **unemployment rate**, *UR*, also measured as a percentage, is

$$UR = 100 \times (\frac{U}{L}).$$

Because the CPS interviewers also record age, sex, race, ethnicity, marital status, and education the government publishes information on participation classified by these criteria. Information on labor force participation by location has been collected in the decennial Census of Population, at least through 1990. Taken together, the data in the CPS and the census enable analysts to calculate labor force participation rates for a variety of population groups and to examine their determinants.

LFPRs by age and sex for a recent year are shown in Table 1.1. These rates are based on a civilian noninstitutional population of 196 million people aged 16 or more, of whom 94 million are men and 102 million are women. Large variations in LFPRs among groups are immediately apparent. The participation rate is generally higher for men than for women. Within each sex there is substantial variation by age, with the age patterns for men and women somewhat different.

INDIFFERENCE MAPS

To analyze labor supply it is often helpful to use **indifference maps** like the one in Figure 1.1. Indifference maps show a consumer's hypothetical preferences between two things. As generally drawn, more of each thing makes the consumer happier. The customary use is to examine the consumer's choice between, for example, CDs and pizzas. In labor economics, however, indifference maps are used to show a typical worker's preferences for **leisure** (mea-

TABLE 1.1 CIVILIAN LABOR FORCE PARTICIPATION RATES BY AGE AND SEX, 1994

Age	Males	Females
16–19	54.1	51.3
20–24	83.1	71.0
25–34	92.6	74.0
35–44	92.8	77.1
45–54	89.1	74.6
55–64	65.5	48.9
65+	16.8	9.2

Source: *Employment and Earnings*, January 1995, p. 164.

POLICY ISSUE

YOU ARE WHAT YOU ASK

Statistics often give the impression of being precisely measured. After all, things like the unemployment and inflation rates are reported with decimal points, implying that they are accurate to at least a 10th of 1 percent. It is important, however, to remember that figures derived from any survey depend on the questions asked.

In January 1994 the Labor Department officially changed the questions asked in the CPS to take into account changes in the structure of jobs and families since the last revision 25 years earlier. The old survey, for example, had started with the following two questions:

1. What were you doing most of last week . . .
   a. . . . working or something else?
   b. . . . keeping house or something else?
   c. . . . going to school or something else?
2. Did you do any work at all last week, not counting work around the house?

When asking Question 1, the interviewer was supposed to pick *one* option to complete it. In practice, most adult men were asked Option a, whereas adult women were asked Option b. The problem arose with respect to unemployed women who would likely answer "keeping house" to Question 1, and "no" to Question 2. Interviewers apparently did not ask the women if they were looking for work, and these women were classified as out of the labor force rather than unemployed, thus undercounting the number of women in the labor force. When the questions were revised to leave out the first question and explicitly ask all respondents about their job search behavior, the reported unemployment rate for adult women increased. The revised questions were tested by asking them along with the old ones from September 1992 to August 1993. During this period unemployment among women measured 6.0 percent using the old set of questions but 6.8 percent when the new set was substituted.

Similarly, the old CPS asked workers "Are you on layoff from a job to which you expect to return?" Traditionally, a *layoff* was a temporary situation when, for example, new equipment was installed or models changed on an assembly line and workers were given a definite date when they could expect to return. Such workers were counted as unemployed whether they were looking for work or not. Over time, however, the term *laid-off* has come to mean a polite way of saying fired. Thus, people who were really fired (and therefore should have been looking for work to be counted as unemployed) were erroneously included among the unemployed even without job search since they said they were laid-off.

It is also important when making comparisons across countries, as well as over time, to be sure that the questions used to measure an economic concept are the same and are understood to have the same meaning. Several countries (Canada in particular) have had surveys like the CPS for 40 years or more. Until the 1970s most other industrialized nations relied instead on counting the number of people receiving unemployment benefits or registering for work with government employment offices. Since that time, household surveys of employment status similar to the CPS but adapted to the specific needs of the country have been adopted by most developed nations. This situation makes cross-national comparisons of labor force employment statistics more solidly based today than they were before the 1980s. Differences in exact definitions or the wording of questions, however, mean that such comparisons must still be made with great care and understanding of the situation in each country.

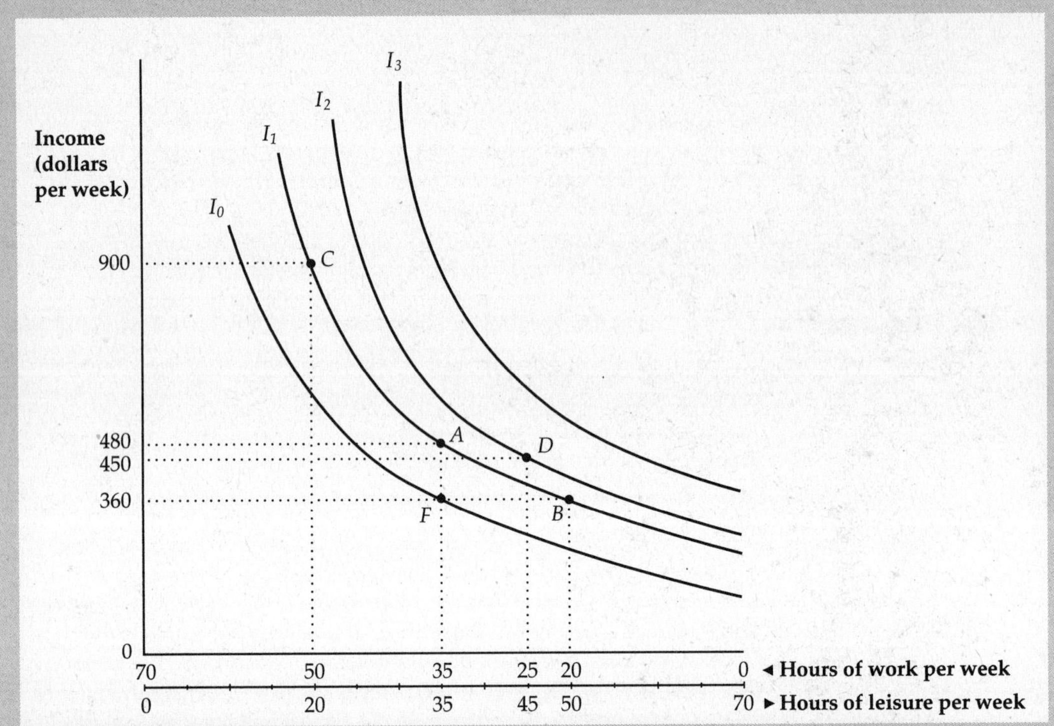

FIGURE 1.1 WORKERS' PREFERENCES FOR INCOME AND LEISURE
Indifference curves such as I_0 show all combinations of income and leisure that result in an equal level of satisfaction for a particular individual. This consumer is equally well-off at point *A* or at point *B*, which has less income but more leisure (less work).

sured on the horizontal axis) and **income** (on the vertical axis). *Income* can come from any source but is usually obtained partly by working, which produces money income or the ability to buy market goods. The term *leisure* denotes all activity except work in the labor market. Thus, for any individual, hours of leisure and hours of work must add up to the total number of hours available.

In Figure 1.1, where the total time available to the worker is a week, the sum of leisure hours plus work hours cannot exceed 168, the total number of hours in a week. Looking at the horizontal axis where hours of work are measured from *right to left*, the scale has been arbitrarily cut off on the left at 70 hours, since very few people choose to work more than 70 hours per week. The other 98 hours not shown on the far left might be considered *required leisure* to be used for such things as sleeping, eating, and bathing. Thus, the amount of discretionary leisure, which is measured from *left to right* on the horizontal scale, is 70 minus the actual number of hours worked.

Indifference maps contain an infinite number of **indifference curves**, only four of which are shown in Figure 1.1. Each indifference curve shows all the hypothetical combinations of two things where the worker considers herself equally well-off. The arbitrarily selected indifference curves in Figure 1.1 each represents a different level of satisfaction or **utility**. As labeled in Figure 1.1, the higher the number of the curve (I_0 to I_3), the greater the worker's satisfaction (i.e., $I_2 > I_1 > I_0$). For a given individual, two indifference curves cannot cross because at the point of intersection the same combination of goods and leisure would apparently yield two different levels of satisfaction—an impossible result.

Along each indifference curve such as I_1, points like *A* and *B* represent combinations of leisure and work that give the worker equal utility. Each curve is convex to the origin, that is, it bows in. What does this mean? Looking along curve I_1 tells us that the worker is equally happy working 20 hours per week for an income of $360 per week (point *B*), or working 35 hours per week for an income of $480 per week (point *A*). To maintain equal satisfaction when adding 15 hours to a 20-hour work week, the individual in Figure 1.1 requires only $120 more (the difference between $360 and $480). If the work week is increased by another 15 hours from 35 to 50 hours, however, the worker requires an additional $420 dollars for an income of $900 (point *C*) to remain equally satisfied.

In other words, along an indifference curve workers must be paid increasingly large amounts to get them to give up their increasingly scarce leisure time. Intuitively, this makes sense. Workers with very little leisure time devote it to the activities most critical to them. They need to be paid a lot to part with each such hour. On the other hand, workers with a lot of leisure time probably devote some hours to activities that are relatively unimportant to them. They are willing to give up some of these hours for a small increase in income.

Remember that indifference curves such as I_3 and I_2, lying above and to the right of I_1, represent higher levels of satisfaction, or, in utility terms, $I_2 > I_1 > I_0$. Therefore, point *D* on indifference curve I_2, where the worker has $450 for a 25-hour work week, is preferred to all points on curve I_1. More hours are worked than at point *B*, and less income is received than at point *A*, but the combination of income and hours at point *D* is preferable to either *A* or *B* (or to any other points along I_1).

As mentioned earlier, along any indifference curve such as I_1 in Figure 1.1, the total level of utility is constant. For example, in moving from point *A* to point *B*, the change in utility must be zero. From this fact, the *slope* of an indifference curve—the rate at which the individual is willing to trade income for additional leisure—can be inferred. Movement from *A* to *F* in Figure 1.1 results in a loss of $120, where each dollar yielded some additional utility, called the **marginal utility** of income, or $MU_\$$. Moving from *F* to *B*, however, compensates for this loss by adding 15 hours of leisure, each hour of which provides some additional utility, called the marginal utility of leisure, or MU_L. In utility terms, the move from *A* to *B* can be broken down into

$$A \rightarrow F + F \rightarrow B = A \rightarrow B = 0.$$

This can be rewritten as

$$MU_\$ \times AF + MU_L \times FB = 0.$$

Rewriting this equation to solve for the ratio AF/FB,

$$AF/FB = -MU_L/MU_\$ = MRS_{L\$}$$

where $MRS_{L\$}$ is the **marginal rate of substitution** of leisure for income, the rate at which individuals are willing to trade off income for additional leisure. The absolute value of the slope of the indifference curve is the ratio of the utility (satisfaction) obtained from an extra unit of leisure to the utility obtained from an extra unit of income. This absolute value is lower when the individual is already enjoying a lot of leisure (*to the right* in Figure 1.1). This makes sense: The extra satisfaction from another hour of leisure will be low when the amount you are already consuming is already high.

Indifference maps by themselves do not tell us anything about the decisions a worker will make. To do this, we also need to know the opportunities available to the worker, which are represented by a **budget line.** Figure 1.2

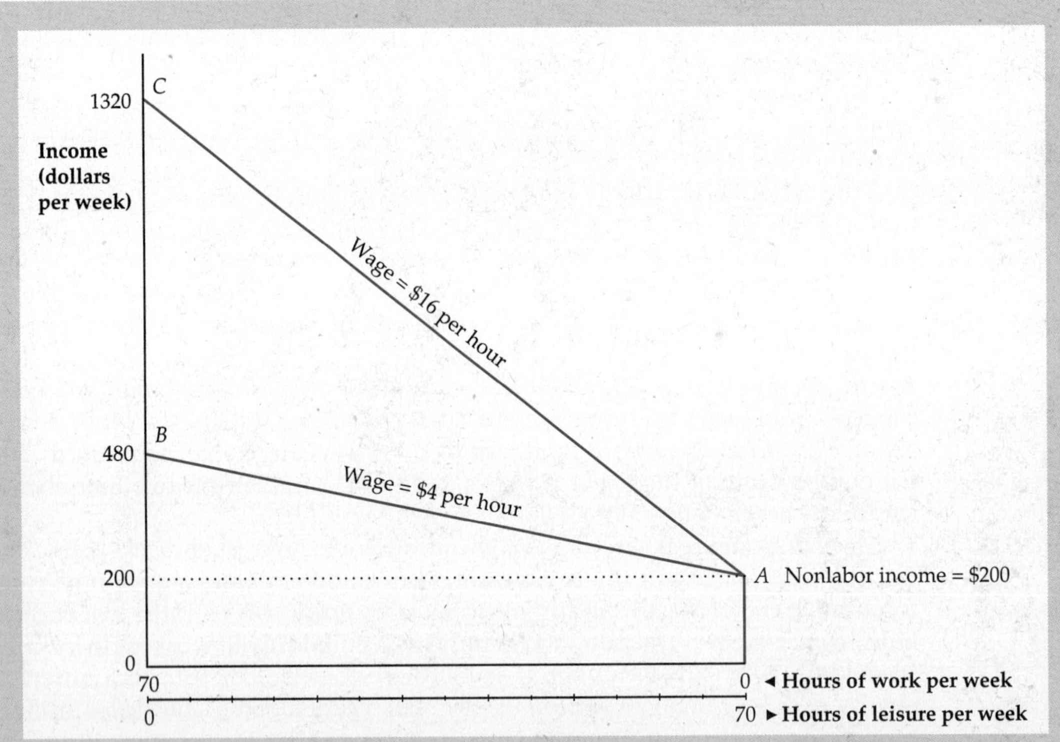

FIGURE 1.2 TWO BUDGET LINES

As workers give up more hours of leisure in order to work, their income available to purchase goods increases. The absolute value of the slope of the budget line is determined by the wage rate while the distance $0A$ represents nonlabor income.

shows two different budget lines for a worker with a **nonlabor income** of \$200 a week (0*A*) even if he works no hours. This nonlabor income could be from investments, charity, a public support program, or the earnings of other family members. We assume, for the moment, that this worker is free to choose as many hours as he wants at a constant hourly wage rate. The wage rate is the absolute value of the slope of the budget line. One such wage rate of \$4 per hour is represented by the slope of the line moving left from *A* to *B*. Working 70 hours per week yields earnings of \$280. Adding the \$200 of nonlabor income gives a total income of \$480 (point *B*). The height of this budget line above the horizontal axis measures the sum of the income in dollars per week earned by working that many hours, plus nonlabor income of 0*A* = \$200. If the worker works 69 hours instead of 70 hours, only \$276 is earned, and total income is \$476. In general, then, each additional hour of leisure reduces income by the wage rate *w*, (in this case by \$4). This drop in income when an additional hour of leisure is consumed measures the price of leisure.

Budget line 0*AC* represents a higher wage of \$16 an hour. Here the worker would receive \$1320 (\$16 times 70 hours plus \$200 in nonlabor income) if she worked 70 hours a week. If she chooses to work only 69 hours, the additional hour of leisure costs her \$16; hence the greater slope to the budget line.

LABOR FORCE PARTICIPATION DECISIONS

THE INDIVIDUAL

We have drawn the indifference maps and budget lines as if the entire process of choice involved one individual acting alone. Recall from the discussion of the CPS that in reality we are dealing with households in which each member may be in or out of the labor force. Whether an individual seeks work is a complex choice likely to involve the entire household. We will, however, start with the simplest case, that of a one-person household, and then consider how the decisions might be different if the worker were a member of a larger unit.

The individual's choice of whether or not to work can be seen in Figure 1.3, which combines her indifference map from Figure 1.1 with her budget lines from Figure 1.2. Remember that even if no hours are worked, the worker shown here receives nonlabor income of 0*A* = \$200, which allows her to buy some things without working. Like all workers, she seeks the combination of income and leisure that gives her the greatest satisfaction (highest utility). This combination lies on the indifference curve that is as far up and to the right as her situation will allow. With a wage of \$4 per hour, the worker can do better than I_0 (part of budget line *AB* is higher and to the right of I_0) but cannot improve on I_1. Any better indifference curve is simply unavailable to people with this wage rate and nonlabor income because it is always above

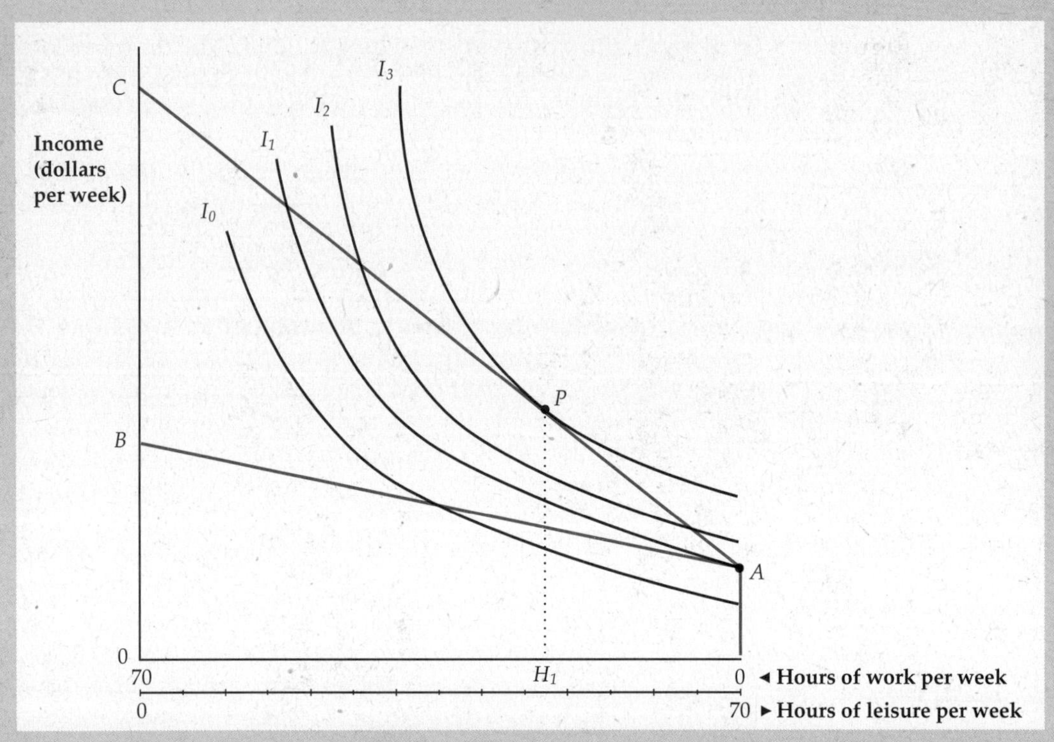

FIGURE 1.3 DETERMINATION OF LABOR FORCE PARTICIPATION
An individual will join the labor force if the slope of her budget line exceeds her reservation wage (slope of the indifference curve I_1) at point *A*. This individual will work if she faces budget line *AC* but be out of the labor force if her budget line is *AB*.

their budget line and, hence, not feasible. The best they can do is earn nothing from working, spend all their time enjoying leisure, and not participate in the labor force. Point *A* in Figure 1.3 indicates this combination of leisure and income.

At point *A* the absolute value of the slope of indifference curve I_1, $MRS_{L\$}$, shows how much money the workers would require to be willing to give up one hour of leisure when they are not working at all. This amount of extra earnings is called the **reservation wage,** w^*.[2] The reservation wage is the

[2]This concept goes back at least as far as Jacob Mincer, "Market Prices, Opportunity Costs, and Income Effects," in Carl Christ (ed.). *Measurement in Economics*, Stanford, Calif.: Stanford University Press, (1963). This approach to analyzing participation decisions was developed and placed in a framework that allows one to infer the value of the reservation wage by Reuben Gronau, "The Intrafamily Allocation of Time: The Value of the Housewives' Time," *American Economic Review* 63: 634–651 (1973), and James Heckman, "Shadow Prices, Market Wages and Labor Supply," *Econometrica* 42: 679–694 (1974).

value of leisure if the person is not working (i.e., is out of the labor force). As Figure 1.3 is drawn, the reservation wage exceeds the market wage. (Indifference curve I_1 is steeper than the line *AB*.) Remember that the absolute value of the slope of the budget line at *A* is *w*. Thus, the worker will not participate in the labor force if $MRS_{L\$} = w^* > w$. In other words, if the extra utility lost giving up the 70th hour of leisure is greater than the wage rate obtained from the first hour of work, the potential worker will opt not to enter the labor force.

What induces workers to give up some leisure time in order to enter the labor force? If the wage rises to $16 per hour, so that the line *AB* rotates clockwise to *AC*, the wage will exceed the reservation wage. Now at point *A* along I_1 w^* is less than *w* because *w* has risen. Market work pays more than the value of the 70th hour of leisure. Workers will enter the labor force, working H_1 hours per week. The highest attainable indifference curve is now I_3; they choose *P*, the point at which *AC* is tangent to I_3. In other words, people will be in the labor force whenever their wage rate exceeds their reservation wage. The condition for participating in the labor force is

$$w^* < w.$$

At point *P* the worker's behavior represents an **interior solution** with positive hours of work as opposed to the **corner solution** at point *A* where wages were lower. There the worker's decision was constrained by the fact that she could not reach the point where an indifference curve was tangent to budget line *AB* because she cannot work less than zero hours per week.

Abstracting from differences in reservation wages, individuals with high (potential) wage rates are more likely to be in the labor force. In other words, as a group, they will have a high labor force participation rate. Looking at the flip side and abstracting from differences in wage rates, groups of people with low reservation wages are also more likely to be in the labor force. The low reservation wage suggests that they do not value leisure time very highly. Conversely, people with many hobbies or outside interests place a high value on their leisure time (have a high reservation wage) and are less likely to be in the labor force. These differences in tastes will be reflected in the shapes of the individuals' indifference maps.

Analysis of the type we have just done using Figure 1.3 is called **comparative statics**. In such analyses, various states are compared to see how the economic equilibrium changes when some factor is altered. In Figure 1.3 we saw that for an individual who is not participating in the labor force, increasing the market wage will eventually lead to a decision to work. If you don't believe this, try drawing a normal, convex indifference curve map and see if you can find some wage (perhaps a very high one) that will induce the individual to provide at least some hours of work.

In comparative static analysis, we do not investigate the dynamics of how individuals get from one equilibrium to another (from point *A* to point *P* in Figure 1.3). These changes may take some time to complete and are generally interesting in and of themselves. We will focus on them in greater detail in later chapters when we discuss institutional aspects of the labor market.

In addition to wage rates, what other factors might change and alter an individual's decision about whether to participate in the labor market? Perhaps the most obvious candidate is the individual's nonlabor income. Does an increase in nonlabor income make a person more or less likely to work? The answer lies in how that person regards leisure. If leisure is a **normal good** (that is, if a consumer wants to purchase more leisure as his income rises), then the individual's reservation wage will increase and his indifference curve will be steeper at higher levels of nonlabor income. Figure 1.4 shows such an indifference map. In this and subsequent figures, we do not label the vertical axis with specific dollar figures, nor do we label the number of work or leisure hours on the horizontal axis. The absolute values of the slopes of lines such as *AB* and *DE* still indicate *w*, the wage rate that the worker can obtain. In Figure 1.4, with low nonlabor income (budget line *AB*) the individual opts to participate at point *P*. When nonlabor income increases, with no

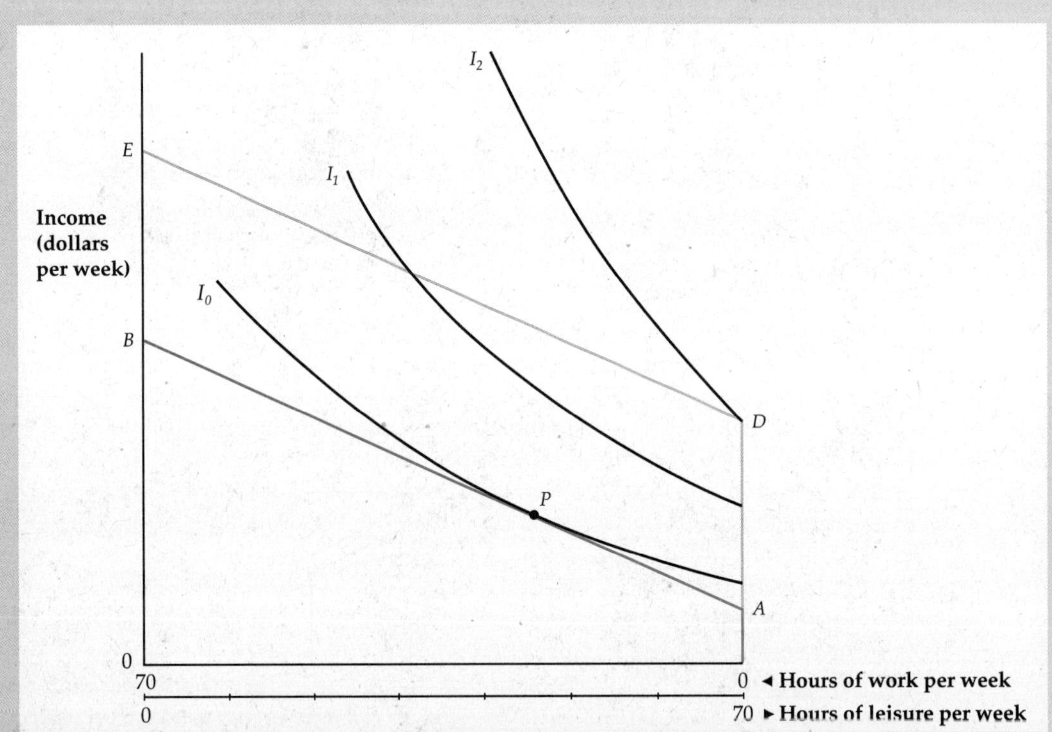

FIGURE 1.4 EFFECT OF A CHANGE IN NONLABOR INCOME ON LABOR FORCE PARTICIPATION

If leisure is a normal good, indifference curves become steeper and reservation wages increase as nonlabor income rises. Thus, at the wage rate equal to the slope of *AB* or *DE*, this individual will work if his nonlabor income is 0*A* but not be in the labor force if it is 0*D*.

change in the wage rate (the slope of budget line *DE* is the same as that of *AB*), it is now so much more attractive to increase the consumption of leisure so much that hours of work fall to zero.

CONSTRAINTS ON POSSIBLE HOURS

So far, the discussion has proceeded as if individuals who participate in the labor force could work as many or as few hours as they wished. Although, as we will see in Chapter 2, there is much more flexibility than is commonly believed, few people have complete freedom over the number of hours they work. The most extreme assumption is that there is no choice. In Figure 1.5, for example, workers are offered the choice of working 40 hours or not working at all. Examine first the decision of a worker with a low market wage

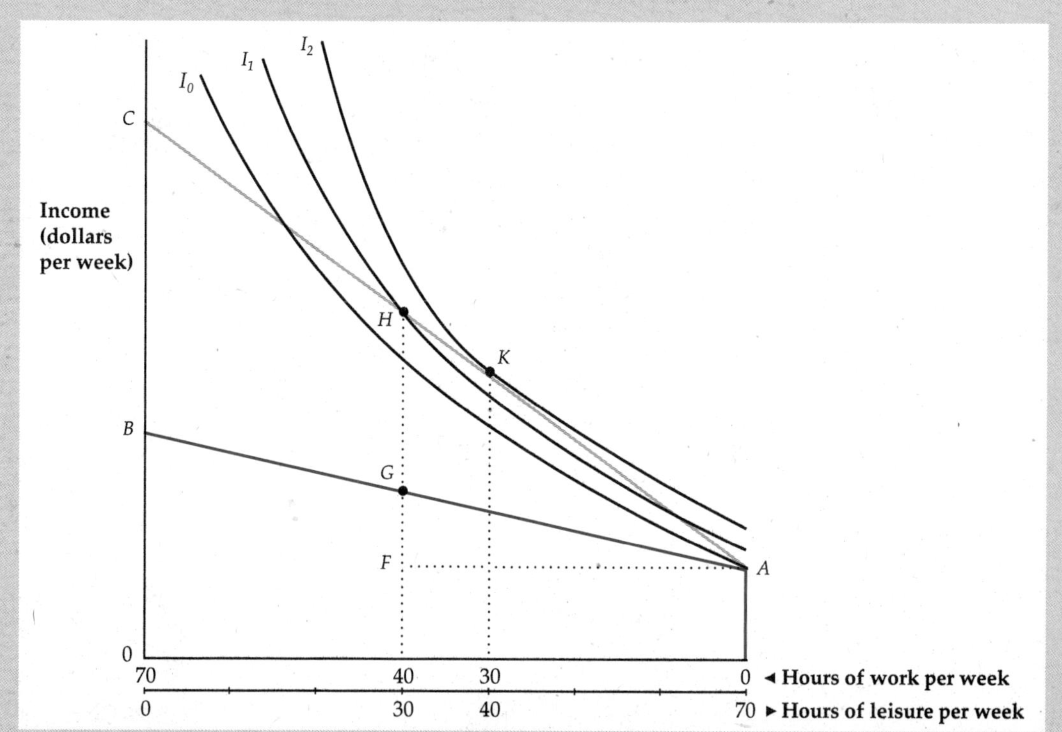

FIGURE 1.5 LABOR FORCE PARTICIPATION WITH AN HOURS CONSTRAINT
Forcing this individual to work a fixed number of hours or none at all will lower utility from I_2 to I_1, but will not change the rule that the market wage must exceed the reservation wage for her to participate.

shown by budget line AB. Keeping in mind that this worker still has nonlabor income of $0A$, he has a choice of working and earning an amount FG or not working at all (point A). Since indifference curve I_0 is the highest he can attain, he chooses not to participate in the labor force. The slope of I_0 at point A, with an absolute value of w^*, exceeds the absolute value of the slope of the line AGB, which is the earnings gain per hour when the worker offers 40 hours of labor instead of zero.

A worker with a higher wage rate (so that her budget line is AC) has a choice of not working (point A) or working 40 hours and earning amount FH. As shown in Figure 1.5, this worker would prefer to be at point K and work 30 hours per week. Since this is not possible, she will choose to participate and work 40 hours per week at point H. Her utility at H (I_1) is still greater than at A (I_0) even though the worker is working more hours than at her highest utility (point K on I_2). As in Figure 1.3, the condition for participation is that $w^* < w$, so that an increase in the market wage rate increases the likelihood of participation. So, too, anything that decreases the reservation wage (makes the indifference curves flatter at zero hours of labor supplied) increases the likelihood that people will choose to participate.

THE INDIVIDUAL WITHIN A HOUSEHOLD

Let us now consider households with more than one person. While the fraction of Americans living in families has declined, families—households with people related by blood or marriage—still contained 85 percent of the U.S. population in 1993. The presence of other family members, their earning power, and requirements for support affects each person's reservation wage and, thus, each person's choice about whether to participate in the labor force.

To model the precise effect, it is necessary to consider how decisions are made in the household. The simplest case is when a single set of preferences about how much each household member should work and consume is held in common by all members of the household. In traditional societies, the preferences of the head of the household simply may be adopted by all the other household members. An alternative is for the members to selflessly act as a single unit with one set of preferences derived by negotiation among themselves. In either case, there exists a well-defined indifference map for each member of the household and a consistent set of preferences incorporating the decisions of other household members.

Analysis of this simple case is identical to that in Figure 1.4. As we saw earlier, this figure shows what happens to an individual's decision when nonlabor income increases. Now assume that the figure shows the single indifference map *of the household* defined over family income and hours of work (and thus hours of leisure) for one member of that household, say, a teenage son. Initially nonlabor income and earnings by other household members bring in $0A$ dollars per week. This low amount is such that the reservation wage characterizing the time of the teenage son makes it attractive to the family to have him in the labor force. The household's satisfaction is highest if he works H_1 hours.

Now assume that his father or mother obtains a better job, so that the household's other income rises from $0A$ to $0D$. The budget line describing choices about the son's time becomes $0DE$. With this new budget line, the household's highest utility is achieved at point D, with the son out of the labor force. The son's reservation wage has risen because his parents are earning more. Even though his wage rate has not changed, the household decides that he should leave the labor force, because the marginal utility the family obtains from his extra earnings has fallen relative to the value they attach to his time at home.

Many factors can affect the distribution of who works in a household. (You might test your understanding by trying to draw the appropriate changes in indifference maps and/or budget lines.) The addition of a young child to the household affects the reservation wages of the adults by sharply increasing the value of their time spent at home (the slope of their indifference curves). Because of this increase, one of the adults who had been in the labor force may drop out. The value of his or her time at home suddenly exceeds the market wage. As children grow up they require fewer hours of care, so the value of the adults' time at home decreases. An adult who had left the labor force might then return to it. Historically, in most industrialized countries the wife's behavior has been most affected by the birth of a child, so that if any member of a household drops out of the labor force it has been the mother. This phenomenon is partly cultural and, as attitudes change and the market wages of women approach those of men, we might expect to see different patterns of behavior. Perhaps more men will be out of the labor force caring for children or perhaps more teenagers will drop out of the labor force to provide after-school care for their younger siblings.

The reservation wage when young children are present is also affected by the availability of substitutes for parental time spent caring for them. The presence of a nearby relative for baby-sitting, low-priced and convenient day-care centers, or inexpensive domestic help all reduce the likelihood that one spouse will be out of the labor force to care for small children. Moreover, the existence of automatic washing machines, microwave ovens, and fast-food restaurants, all of which reduce the time spent on household chores, also lowers the reservation wage and increases the likelihood of participation.

An increase in the household's resources such as an inheritance that substantially increases nonlabor income (unaccompanied by any other change in opportunities) will usually reduce the number of household members who work. It might lead the family to decide that a teenage son should stay in school, or an elderly grandparent should retire, or a working spouse should become a full-time homemaker. One study found that among married couples in the early 1980s, an increase in inheritances of \$350,000 increased the probability that one spouse would be out of the labor force by 0.128 and that both spouses would not work by 0.013. Another study found that inheritances had essentially no impact on the labor supply of men but that each

$10,000 a couple inherited reduced the probability that the wife in that couple would work by 0.2 percent.[3]

The values attached to other nonmarket alternatives also affect the household's decisions. For example, if either a spouse or a teenager must work to maintain the family's customary living standard, and if both could earn the same market wage, how would the family choose which one works? One set of considerations is the extent to which the teenager's additional schooling could augment his or her future earnings compared to the costs of the spouse's absence from the home now.

PARTICIPATION RATES—THE EFFECT OF AGE, SEX, AND RACE

PRIME-AGE MALES

Prime-age males are generally defined as men between the ages of 25 and 54, although the term is sometimes applied to men 25 to 44 or 35 to 44 only. If a household includes an able-bodied prime-aged male who has completed his formal schooling and not yet reached retirement age, it is almost taken for granted in industrialized societies that he is participating in the labor force. In 1993 the labor force participation rate of married men (with wife present) between the ages of 35 and 44 was 96.1 percent. Presumably most of the remaining men were disabled. Even a married man with enough income from property to escape the necessity of working would likely have reported himself as employed in managing his investments.

Although the labor force participation rate of married men in the prime age groups is very high, it is still possible to find differences in the rates for different population categories. For example, the participation rate among white men is higher than among nonwhites. Participation rates also increase with the number of years of school completed.[4] Both of these effects correspond to differences in market wages, which are higher for whites than for nonwhites, and increase with education in both groups.

We might expect participation rates to be lower for single men, who do not have spouses on whom they can rely to take care of domestic responsibilities. Their reservation wage may be greater than that of otherwise identical married men, because they must arrange for cooking, cleaning, and so on. Also, the hourly wage rate of single men is around 10 percent less than that of married men who appear to be identical along all other economic dimen-

---

[3]Douglas Holtz-Eakin, David Joulfaian, and Harvey S. Rosen, "The Carnegie Conjecture: Some Empirical Evidence," *Quarterly Journal of Economics* 108: 413–435 (1993), and David Joulfaian and Mark O. Wilhelm, "Inheritance and Labor Supply," *Journal of Human Resources* 29: 1205–1234 (1994).

[4]William Bowen and T. Aldrich Finegan, *The Economics of Labor Force Participation*, Princeton, N.J.: Princeton University Press (1969), p. 45.

POLICY ISSUE

DIVORCE LAWS AND LEISURE WITHIN MARRIAGE

The determination of the number of hours work and leisure for members of a multiperson household becomes much more complicated when the members act independently, even if they take into account the welfare of other household members. Consider a two-person household. To the extent that income is shared within the household, the amount earned by one partner is the nonlabor income for the other partner. Thus, a wife's decision about whether or not to work depends on the income of her husband. The husband's income, however, depends on whether and how much he decides to work, which depends on his wife's income. The eventual outcome in such a household will depend on bargaining between the two parties.

To take a simple example, each partner might prefer to consume a great deal of leisure, while the other partner worked many hours and brought in a great deal of income. Clearly, there would have to be negotiation to decide the actual combinations of income and leisure for each partner. Economic theory suggests, however, that the outcome of this negotiation can never leave one partner worse off than if the union were dissolved and each partner were simply to reach the highest utility they could on their own (taking into account the loss of any satisfaction derived from the partnership). Thus, any alteration in divorce laws that improves the economic position of one partner following divorce should improve the bargaining power of that partner within the marriage, leading them to consume a greater share of the household's leisure.[5]

The trend toward mutual no-fault divorce, coupled with changing expectations of women's roles, has resulted in a sharp decline in the probability of women being awarded alimony. This outcome might be expected to lower women's post-divorce income (and utility) and, all other things being equal, reduce their bargaining power within the marriage. This leads to a prediction that reducing the probability of alimony would cause married women to work more and consume less leisure. (Of course, as we will see, many other factors also cause changes in the labor supply decisions of married women.)

sions we can measure.[6] Finally, single men obviously do not face as much pressure to contribute to the support of others as married men. In 1993 the labor force participation rate of men between the ages of 35 and 44 who were widowed, divorced, or separated was 89.6 percent, 6.5 percent less than among married men, while among men who had never married it was only 84.5 percent. The same patterns hold for men at every age.

These facts do not necessarily imply that being single causes a lower rate of participation. Rather, the same underlying factors that lead some single men to drop out of the labor force might also have contributed to their not

---

[5]H. Elizabeth Peters, "The Importance of Financial Considerations in Divorce Decisions," *Economic Inquiry* 31: 71–86 (1993); Notburga Ott, *Intrafamily Bargaining and Household Decisions,* Berlin: Springer-Verlag (1992).

[6]Sanders Korenman and David Neumark, "Does Marriage Really Make Men More Productive?" *Journal of Human Resources* 26: 282–307 (1991).

being married. Perhaps some men do not like to be tied down, either by a job or a spouse. On the other hand, perhaps women can tell which men are likely to be poor providers and avoid marrying them. Finally, freedom from family responsibilities may make single men more likely to alternate periods of intensive work with periods of nonmarket activities such as travel or study.

In recent years there has been a noticeable decline in the labor force participation rate of prime-age males, especially among lower-income (i.e., less educated and minority) males. How much of this decline is due to decreased market wages and how much is due to increased reservation wages is a matter of substantial controversy. Reservation wages may have increased either because of expanded nonmarket earnings potential from illegal activities such as dealing drugs, or because of greater access to nonlabor income from increased provision of public assistance to males as well as females.

PRIME-AGE FEMALES

The single most important U.S. labor market development of this century has been the growth in the percentage of adult women who are working or seeking work. As Table 1.2 and Figure 1.6 show, this growth has been tremendous in every age category and demographic group, leading to what one author has called "the subtle revolution."[7] The growth began prior to World War II, but it continued and may even have accelerated between 1965 and 1980. Around 1980, the growth in labor force participation seemed to stop for the youngest group of women. Growth continued at older ages because different groups of women fall into each age range at different periods of time. At every age, the maximum rate of female labor force participation seems to be reached when the cohort born between 1955 and 1960 reaches that age. These maximum rates are still well below those of men in the same age categories in the U.S.

A very strong positive relationship exists between educational attainment and the likelihood of married women being in the labor force. This relationship reflects the higher market wage available to more educated workers, as well as access to more interesting and challenging jobs. Since women in the U.S. receive the same amount of formal education as men (among women aged 25 or more in 1991, the median educational attainment was 12.7 years while among men it was 12.8 years), educational differences are not likely to explain the gender difference in labor force participation rates.[8]

The explanation probably lies in current attitudes about responsibilities for domestic chores. Wives are generally expected to bear most of the burden of child care and household maintenance, even if they are working. The value

---

[7]Ralph Smith (ed.). *The Subtle Revolution: Women at Work*, Washington: Urban Institute, (1979).

[8]Changes in the wording of questions in the CPS mean that median years of education cannot be computed after 1991. In 1993, however, 81 percent of men 25 or older had completed high school as opposed to 80 percent of women.

TABLE 1.2 LABOR FORCE PARTICIPATION OF WOMEN BY AGE, 1955–1994

	Age			
Year	20–24	25–34	35–44	45–54
1955	45.9	34.9	41.6	43.8
1960	46.1	36.0	43.4	49.8
1965	49.9	38.5	46.1	50.9
1970	57.7	45.0	51.1	54.4
1975	64.1	54.6	55.8	54.6
1980	69.0	65.4	65.5	59.9
1985	71.8	70.9	71.8	64.4
1990	71.6	73.6	76.5	71.2
1994	71.0	74.0	77.1	74.6

Source: *Employment and Training Report of the President*, 1981, Table A–5; and *Employment and Earnings*, January 1986, p. 154, January 1991, p. 164, and January 1995, p. 164.

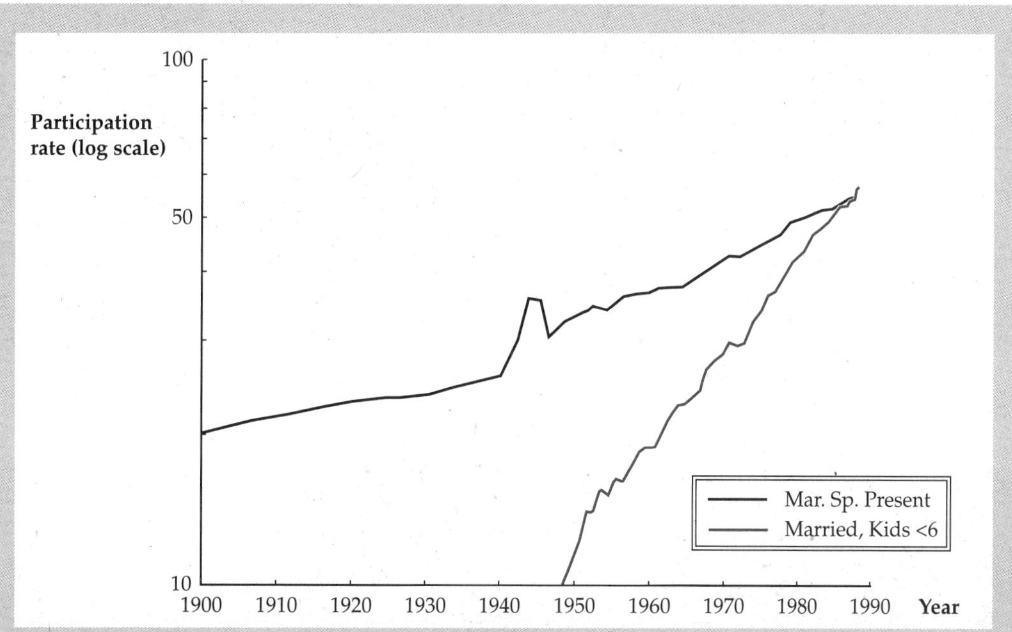

FIGURE 1.6 LABOR FORCE PARTICIPATION OF WOMEN: 1900–1988
Married women's labor force participation has risen throughout this century. The increase has been especially great since World War II among women with young children.

Source: Randall J. Olsen, "Fertility and the Size of the U.S. Labor Force," *Journal of Economic Literature*, 32 (1994) p. 94.

TABLE 1.3 WOMEN'S AND MEN'S HOURS PER WEEK, AT HOME AND IN THE LABOR MARKET

	Home		*Market*	
	Early	More Recent	Early	More Recent
United States				
1965, 1981: Women	41.8	30.5	18.9	23.9
Men	11.5	13.8	51.6	44.0
U.S.S.R.				
1965, 1985: Women	31.5	27.0	43.8	39.3
Men	9.8	11.9	54.6	53.8
Denmark				
1964, 1987: Women	30.1	23.1	13.3	20.8
Men	3.8	12.8	41.7	33.4
Japan				
1965, 1985: Women	31.5	31.0	33.2	24.6
Men	2.8	3.5	57.7	52.0

Source: F. Thomas Juster and Frank Stafford, "The Allocation of Time," *Journal of Economic Literature* 29 (1991), Table 3.

of their output at home is very large. One study estimates that the value of the services produced in the home, mostly by housewives, exceeded two-thirds of a typical family's after-tax money income.[9]

Table 1.3 presents data on women's hours of work in four industrialized countries for which comparable data are available. In 1965, the average woman in the U.S. worked 42 hours per week (nearly 6 hours per day) in the home, a figure that dropped to 4.5 hours per day by 1981. There were smaller declines but from a lower starting level in the U.S.S.R. and Denmark. In the U.S. and Denmark, average hours of market work increased for women, mostly because more women were working, not because women worked more hours. Japan is an obvious exception, with market work by women declining while work at home stayed about the same. This situation likely represents a return to normality from the severe labor shortage and abnormal age-structure of the population that prevailed in Japan in the aftermath of World War II.

The total hours women worked at home and in the market fell in every country except Denmark (where they were unusually low to begin with). Among men, time spent in household chores has risen slightly in these countries, but it is still far less than that spent by women. By 1985, the sum

[9]Reuben Gronau, "Home Production: A Forgotten Industry," *Review of Economics and Statistics* 72: 412 (1980).

of time spent in home and market work did not differ much between men and women in any of the four countries, meaning that both sexes devote roughly the same amount of time to leisure. One reason may be that the leisure time of husbands and wives is complementary since spouses enjoy spending time together. With the exception of Denmark, leisure time has increased for both sexes.

Given the attitudes implied by the comparison of home and market time by sex, we should not be surprised that changes in domestic circumstances have far greater effects on women's labor force participation rates than on men's. As a woman's husband earns more, her reservation wage increases, and her likelihood of participating in the labor force declines. Even in data from the 1950 census, among women with the ability to earn the same wage, those whose husbands earned more were less likely to be in the labor force.[10] Data on recent mothers from the CPS between 1979 and 1988 show that, adjusted for numerous other factors, increasing a husband's earnings from the average level by 10 percent lowered the probability that the wife would participate in the labor force by 7 percentage points. Among Japanese women in 1975, each 10 percent increase in earnings by the husband reduced the likelihood of participation by 2 percentage points (about 7 percent of the mean). The interdependence of wives' and husbands' participation decisions is most pronounced among couples with preschool children.[11]

Additional children in the home raise the wife's reservation wage and lower her likelihood of being in the labor force. Data for 1976 show that having a child under age 6 reduces the wife's likelihood of being in the labor force by nearly 20 percent after controlling for other factors. The more educated the wife, the less likely it is that young children will deter her from participating in the labor force. Either her education makes her a more efficient household worker, thus lowering her reservation wage, or her higher market wage enables her to purchase substitutes for her own time at home.

The effect of children on labor supply has become less pronounced over time. Among women with children under age 1, only 20 percent were in the labor force in 1971 but nearly 40 percent were in 1987. Unlike the period prior to the 1970s, the presence of children aged 6 or more currently has a very small impact on a woman's likelihood of working. Lower prices for domestic help and cheaper day care, both substitutes for wives' time, also

---

[10]Jacob Mincer, "Labor Force Participation of Married Women," in H. Gregg Lewis (ed.). *Aspects of Labor Economics*, Princeton, N.J.: Princeton University Press, (1962).

[11]Arleen Leibowitz, Jacob Klerman, and Linda Waite, "Employment of New Mothers and Child Care Choice," *Journal of Human Resources* 27: 112–133 (1992); M. Anne Hill, "Female Labor Supply in Japan: Implications of the Informal Sector for Labor Force Participation and Hours of Work," *Journal of Human Resources* 24: 143–161 (1989); Shelly Lundberg, "Labor Supply of Husbands and Wives: A Simultaneous Equations Approach," *Review of Economics and Statistics* 70: 224–235 (1988).

increase the likelihood of married women participating.[12] Husbands' labor force participation is far less sensitive to differences in wives' market wages or to the presence of young children. As we have seen, the participation rate of married men above age 25 and not yet close to retirement age is nearly 100 percent and therefore cannot differ greatly with family circumstances.

Black women are somewhat more likely to be in the labor force than white women. Much of this difference is because black women are less likely to be married. For those who are married, a substantial part can be explained by the difference in husbands' incomes.[13] The lower wage rates earned by black men reduce their wives' reservation wages and increase their wives' labor force participation rates. A greater prevalence of extended-family living arrangements also provides black women with a ready source of child care in the form of grandparents living at home.

Hispanic women have a relatively low participation rate, perhaps due to cultural differences as well as to their lower educational attainment, which reduces their market wage relative to their reservation wage.[14] The labor force participation rates of Hispanic women have increased even more rapidly than those of all women during the 1980s (nearly 1 percentage point per year) as their educational attainment has increased and as recent immigrants have become more acculturated.

What explains the tremendous growth in participation among women since World War II? As we have seen, this growth implies that more women are now finding that their market wage exceeds their reservation wage. Such a change could occur either because market wages increased or reservation wages fell.

Market wages have risen substantially for women in recent years. One possible reason is the tremendous increase in women's educational attainment since the 1950s. The median years of schooling for women 25 or more rose from 9.6 in 1950 to 12.7 in 1991. The most rapid growth in women's education, however, was before 1970 (when the median number of years of schooling was already 12.1), whereas participation has risen most rapidly since 1970. Moreover, the increase in women's education levels over time is less than that which occurred for men. Changes in educational attainment, therefore, are not a very good explanation of the rapid rise in participation. Affirmative action laws as well as changes in employers' and employees' attitudes that were partly a result of the women's liberation movement are better explanations, since they date from the late 1960s when participation rates began their rapid rise.

---

[12]Liebowitz, Klerman, and Waite, "Employment of;" John Cogan, "Labor Supply with Costs of Labor Market Entry," in James Smith, (ed.). *Female Labor Supply: Theory and Estimation*, Princeton, N.J.: Princeton University Press, (1980), p. 348; Orley Ashenfelter and James Heckman, "Estimating Labor Supply Functions," in Glen Cain and Harold Watts (eds.). *Income Maintenance and Labor Supply*, Markham, Chicago, (1973); David Blau and Philip Robins, "Child-Care Costs and Family Labor Supply," *Review of Economics and Statistics* 70: 374–381 (1988).

[13]Cordelia Reimers, "Cultural Differences in Labor Force Participation among Married Women," American Economic Association, *Papers and Proceedings* 75: (1985), Table 3.

[14]Reimers, "Cultural Differences."

There are several reasons why women's reservation wages may have fallen in recent years. Changes in husbands' incomes are one factor. As Table 1.2 shows, the biggest increases in participation rates since 1955 have been among women aged 25 to 34, with the sharpest increase occurring between 1975 and 1985, a period when earnings of young husbands grew relatively slowly after adjusting for inflation.[15]

The decline in birth rates from the 1960s through the early 1980s has also made it much easier for married women to participate in the labor force. With the total fertility rate per adult female down from 3.6 children in 1955 to 2.1 in 1988 (up a bit from its low of 1.8 in the mid-1970s), it is not surprising that more women in their childbearing years are working. The causation may go the other way, however. Perhaps women are having fewer children because of an increased commitment to the labor market. Evidence suggests, however, that even when reverse causation is accounted for, the number of children has a powerful effect on women's labor force participation.[16]

An additional part of the increase in women's labor force participation is explained by married women entering the labor market to acquire experience that may be useful should they later be divorced, an important factor during an era when divorce rates have risen so rapidly that, by the 1990s, over 40 percent of first marriages end in divorce.[17]

Other less easily quantifiable factors may account for the rest of the increase in participation. Technological changes have led to the expansion of industries and occupations that have historically provided the most jobs for women. The standard work week has been shortened, making part-time participation easier. The availability of products that reduce the amount of work required in the home may make it easier for a wife both to hold a job and care for a house. Dishwashers were essentially unknown in 1953; by 1990, 45 percent of U.S. homes had them. Similar growth occurred in automatic washing machines (to 76 percent) and clothes dryers (to 69 percent).[18] In addition, a more positive attitude among women toward careers may be important.

---

[15]Finis Welch, "Effects of Cohort Size on Earnings," *Journal of Political Economy* 87: S65–S98 (1979); Mark Berger, "Effects of Cohort Size on Earnings: A Reexamination of the Evidence," *Journal of Political Economy* 93: 561–573 (1985).

[16]Glen Cain and Martin Dooley, "Estimation of a Model of Labor Supply, Fertility, and Wages of Married Women," *Journal of Political Economy* 84: S179–S200 (1976); Belton Fleisher and George Rhodes, "Fertility, Women's Work Effort and Labor Supply," *American Economic Review* 69: 14–24 (1979); Mark Rosenzweig and Kenneth Wolpin, "Life Cycle Labor Supply and Fertility," *Journal of Political Economy* 88: 328–348 (1980).

[17]James Smith and Michael Ward, "Time-Series Growth in the Female Labor Force," *Journal of Labor Economics* 3: S89 (1985); William Johnson and Jonathan Skinner, "Labor Supply and Marital Separation," *American Economic Review* 76: 455–469 (1986).

[18]Glen Cain, "Women and Work: Trends in Time Spent in Housework," University of Wisconsin, IRP Discussion Paper No. 747–784, (April 1984); U.S. Energy Administration, *Housing Characteristics: 1990* Washington, D.C.

DIFFERENCES BY AGE

Table 1.1 showed large differences in labor force participation by age group. Among men and to a lesser extent among women, the pattern is shaped roughly like an upside-down U. This shape is predicted by the **life cycle theory** of labor supply. When people are young and inexperienced, their market wage is likely to be low, providing limited incentive to participate in the labor force. Moreover, time spent in the labor force must be traded off against time spent in school that will produce a higher wage to benefit them over a working life that could last 40 or 50 years. As we will see in Chapter 3, it makes sense for most people to reduce their labor force attachment and go to school even after the age of compulsory school attendance. At the other end of the life cycle, people's market wages are likely to be growing very slowly or even declining in real terms as their capacities deteriorate. At the same time, the relative utilities of working and leisure may be shifting as they find their jobs harder to do. Knowing that these effects will occur, they will accumulate wealth during their working lives through saving, Social Security, and other retirement plans to make it possible for them to consume more leisure. Thus, we should expect older people to have lower labor force participation rates than people in their 30s and 40s.

The life cycle theory of labor supply makes an even stronger statement about how participation at one point in one's life is affected by market wages at other points. It says that people will increase their likelihood of participating during times when their wages are unexpectedly high, and that this additional participation will reduce their participation at other times. In other words, people will seek a certain amount of participation over their entire lives, but will concentrate it in those times when the difference between the market and the reservation wages ($w - w^*$) is greatest. While evidence indicates that some of this **intertemporal substitution** does occur, older men who have had a period of unexpectedly high wages earlier in their lives do not appear to work much less than similar men who did not have an earlier period of high wages.[19]

YOUTH

Labor force participation rates among 16- to 24-year-olds are strongly influenced by decisions about leaving school. As the last two columns in Table 1.4 show, in industrialized countries generally, the overwhelming majority of youth aged 16 to 19 and 20 to 24 who are not in school participate in the labor force. Their labor force participation both is strongly affected by and

[19]David Card, "Intertemporal Labor Supply: An Assessment," in Christopher Sims (ed.). *Advances in Econometrics—Sixth World Congress*, Vol. II, Cambridge: Cambridge University Press, (1994).

POLICY ISSUE

SUBSIDIES FOR DAY CARE

The fact that young children deter labor force participation by married women, partly because of the cost of finding alternative child-care providers, has led to calls for subsidization of child care, particularly for single mothers who might otherwise receive public assistance.

The effect of needing to obtain child care on mothers' labor force participation is shown in Figure 1.7 (page 29), a modified version of Figure 1.4. In this example, if child care were costless, the woman would face budget line *0AE* and work H_1 hours per week, reaching indifference curve I_2. The distance *AC* is the sum of the **fixed costs of child care**. Even if the woman works just one hour per day she must incur the costs of transporting the child to a baby-sitter, for example. Thus, if she works only a little bit, her net income drops from 0*A*, if she did not work, to 0*C*. Moreover, the more she works, the more she must pay for child care, since most baby-sitters charge by the hour and child-care centers also charge more the longer the child stays. Thus, hourly wages net of child-care costs are lower for a woman with children than for the same woman without children. The market wage with children is shown by the slope of *CB*. This slope is less than the slope of *AE*, which measures her wage before accounting for these **variable costs of child care**. In this situation, I_0 (at point *Q*) is the highest indifference curve she can attain if she works, while if she drops out of the labor force her utility increases to I_1 at point *A*. Clearly she will choose not to participate in the labor force.

The costs of child care can be substantial. In 1991, 35 percent of working mothers with children under 15 made cash payments for child care. Families that paid for child care averaged payments of $275 a month. Unmarried women paid even more. Among women making child-care payments, these averaged 7 percent of household income. Among poor women who paid for child care, average payments were over 26 percent of their total household income. In 1986, working women with preschool children paid an average of $1.86 per child per hour for nonparental child care. After adjusting for inflation, these costs represent over half the earnings of a minimum-wage worker. Estimates from about the same time suggest that the fixed costs of child care may average about $100 a month.[20]

Free or subsidized day care, if it is available, can change the situation. The impact will depend on how it is structured. If the subsidy pays both the fixed and variable costs, then a parent's optimal decision will return to point *P*. Suppose, however, that the subsidy is either a fixed grant or a fraction of the actual expenses of child care. It is clear that a lump-sum grant must be at least as large as the fixed costs of child care (*AC*) if it is to induce any labor force participation. Such a grant is shown by the dashed budget line *AF* in Figure 1.7. Here the lump-sum grant will induce work, but with fewer hours than at point *P*.

A subsidy that pays a portion of the variable costs of child care is more valuable the more a women works. This will shift the incentive toward working longer hours. In Figure 1.7

---

[20]Lynne Casper, Mary Hawkins, and Martin O'Connell, "Who's Minding the Kids?" U.S. Department of Commerce (1994); V. Joseph Hotz and M. Rebecca Kilburn, "The Demand for Child Care and Child Care Costs," University of Chicago, unpublished paper, (December 1991); David C. Ribar, "A Structural Model of Child Care and the Labor Supply of Married Women," *Journal of Human Resources* 27: 134–165 (1992).

budget line *CG* represents a subsidy of 100 percent of the variable costs of child care, but none of the fixed costs. It is clear in Figure 1.7 that either form of subsidy *can* induce a woman with children to enter the labor force. They will differ, however, in the number of hours of labor she will want to supply. In the U.S., the major form of child-care subsidy is an income tax credit equal to 20 percent (or more for low-income families) of a family's expenditures *up to a fixed maximum*. This is the equivalent of a fixed grant to women who work many hours, since their expenditures exceed the maximum, and a variable one to women who work fewer hours and spend less on child care.

Although day care is rarely free, day-care programs have expanded greatly in the United States. In 1987, 5 million children under age 5 were cared for outside their own home. In part, this is the result of the expansion of day-care centers receiving at least partial government funding. In part, the centers were also a response to changes in other incentives that have led to an increase in mothers' labor force participation. The evidence suggests that expansion of subsidies for child care would increase the rate at which younger women participate in the labor force. It remains a subject for social debate whether this increase (and the resulting change in how children are raised) is desirable public policy.

affects their living arrangements. A recent study found that 58 percent of men aged 19 to 24 who worked lived at home, while 72 percent of those who did not work lived at home. The working young adult living at home has become increasingly common, however. In the U.S., 15 percent of all men 25 to 34 live with their parents. Among young adults the parents' home provides insurance should they be unable to find work.[21]

Even among those in school, there is substantial participation on a part-time and part-year basis (after school, on weekends, and during vacations) in English-speaking countries, although not in continental Europe. In Australia, Britain, Canada, and the U.S., around two-fifths of the students aged 16 to 19 are in the labor force, as are over half of the students aged 20 to 24. These participation rates reflect averages over the calendar year that include high participation in the summer and lower participation during the school year. Thus, in the United States, in August 1994, 60.2 percent of youths aged 16 to 19 participated, while, in November 1994, only 49.5 percent participated.

One might expect lower participation rates by students from higher-income families. As we discussed earlier, they may be better able to afford to devote full time to their studies. Data for students 19 and 20 years old show that weeks worked, and presumably also participation rates, were lower among those from upper-middle–income families than from low–income

---

[21]Marjorie McElroy, "The Joint Determination of Household Membership and Market Work: The Case of Young Men," *Journal of Labor Economics* 3: 305 (1985); *New York Times*, (June 16, 1991), p. A10.

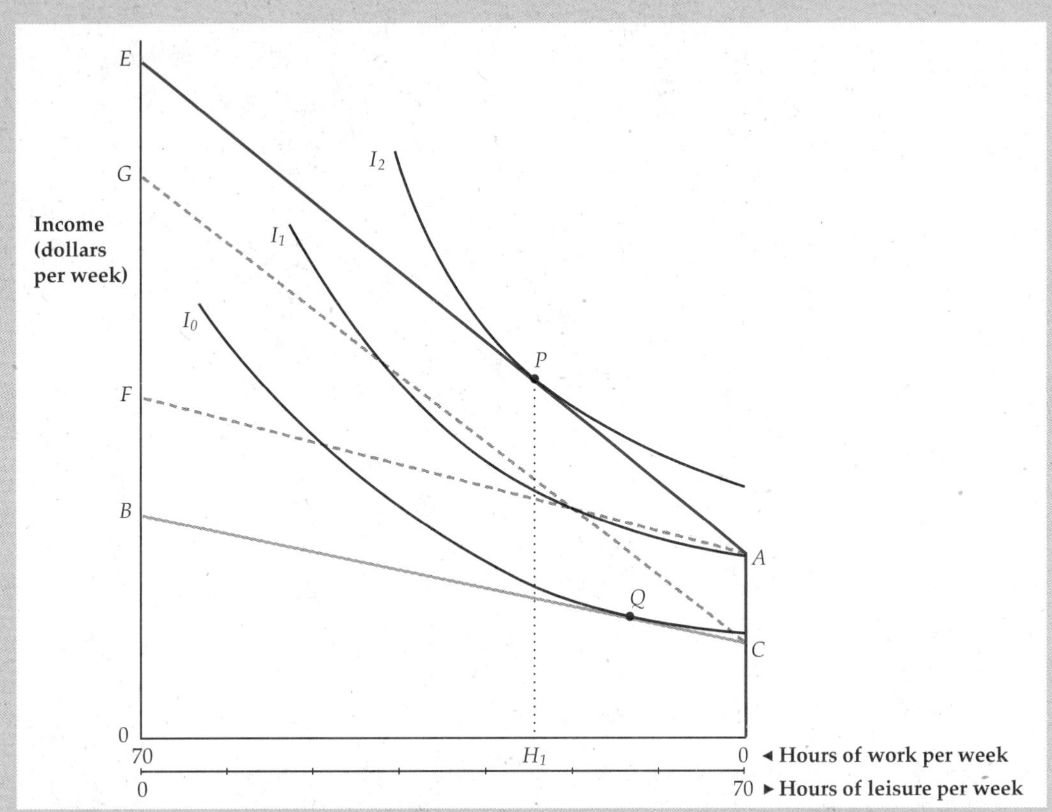

FIGURE 1.7 COSTS OF WORK AND LABOR FORCE PARTICIPATION

Both the fixed costs (distance *AC*) and variable costs (the change in slope from *AE* to *CB*) of working will lower the probability a person will enter the labor force, since it is likely that point *A* will be on a higher indifference curve than point *Q*. Subsidies that pay all or part of these costs (such as for child care) will encourage participation, with those that pay a fixed amount encouraging part-time work while those that pay a variable amount encouraging full-time work.

families, after adjustment for differences in race, high school achievement, and other effects.[22]

As Table 1.4 shows, there has been a very sharp upward trend in the U.S. since 1960 in the participation rates of youth still in school. (The upward trend among youth not in school is chiefly due to the increased participation of young women discussed above.) This trend is especially strong among high

[22]Robert Meyer and David Wise, "High School Preparation and Early Labor Force Experience," in Richard Freeman and David Wise (eds.). *The Youth Labor Market Problem: Its Nature, Causes and Consequences*, Chicago: University of Chicago Press, (1982), Table 9A.1.

TABLE 1.4 LABOR-FORCE STATUS OF YOUTH, BY AGE AND ENROLLMENT STATUS, UNITED STATES 1955–1994, AND SELECTED COUNTRIES, 1991

United States (Labor Force Participation Rate)

	In School				*Not in School*	
	Males		*Females*		*Both Sexes*	
Year	16–19	20–24	16–19	20–24	16–19	20–24
1955	39.2	41.7	22.9	42.0	71.9	67.1
1960	34.6	44.2	26.5	40.6	71.1	69.3
1965	36.8	49.0	26.9	39.6	71.8	69.8
1970	40.5	51.2	34.8	50.5	70.4	74.1
1975	41.9	51.2	40.3	55.1	74.8	78.9
1980	45.2	55.3	42.5	59.0	77.6	83.0
1985	42.1	54.0	42.3	57.7	71.9	83.7
1990	43.9	57.6	43.5	59.9	70.9	83.8
1994	43.3	59.8	44.8	61.8	69.2	83.0

Selected Countries (Employment/Population Ratio) (1991)

	In School		*Not in School*	
	Both Sexes		*Both sexes*	
	16–19	20–24	16–19	20–24
Australia	27.9	50.4	71.0	76.0
Canada	38.8	38.9	55.9	70.5
France	0.1	8.2	49.6	71.3
Germany	2.5	11.6	77.7	85.0
Spain	3.2	10.7	63.5	63.5
United Kingdom	38.1	19.7	75.8	75.5
United States	34.6	54.9	56.0	72.9

Sources: Calculated from *Employment and Training Report of the President*, 1981, Table B–9; *Employment and Earnings*, January 1986, p. 160, January 1991, page 190, and January 1995, pp. 170–171; OECD, *Employment Outlook*, 1994, Table 1.20.

school women and college-age youth of both sexes. Better market opportunities do not provide the answer. The weekly earnings of full-time workers aged 16 to 24 fell between 1967 and 1985 from 80 to 66 percent of the economy-wide average, and have risen only slightly since then. This drop suggests that postponing entry into the labor force should be more desirable. Moreover, unemployment rates among youth rose dramatically during this period, reaching a peak of 23.9 percent in the recession of 1982 but still at 17.6 percent in 1994. Thus, both falling wages and rising unemployment imply that market opportunities were decreasing.

The answer must, therefore, lie on the reservation-wage side of the participation decision. Smaller family sizes since the early 1970s mean that fewer teenagers and young adults must stay home after school to help care for younger children in the household. The value of their time at home, which determines their reservation wage, has dropped. Greater flexibility in the scheduling of classes and the increased possibility of being a part-time student also make it easier for youth to work and remain in school. Grade inflation and decreased expectations of teachers in the amount of homework and study outside of class may also have decreased the value of time spent out of the labor force. Abolition of the draft has removed the incentive for young men to attend school full-time as a way of obtaining deferments that kept them out of the military. Increases in the costs of attending college that have outpaced inflation may also have induced more students to work part-time to finance their education. All of these factors have led university students to mix study and work to a greater degree than before and to spend more years in college than their parents.

OLDER PEOPLE

In 1994 the participation rate of American men aged 65 and over was 16.8 percent, versus 65.6 percent among men 55 to 64. Among women, the comparable figures were 9.2 and 48.9 percent. Although we often think of people retiring at age 65, Figure 1.8 shows a steady decline in male labor force

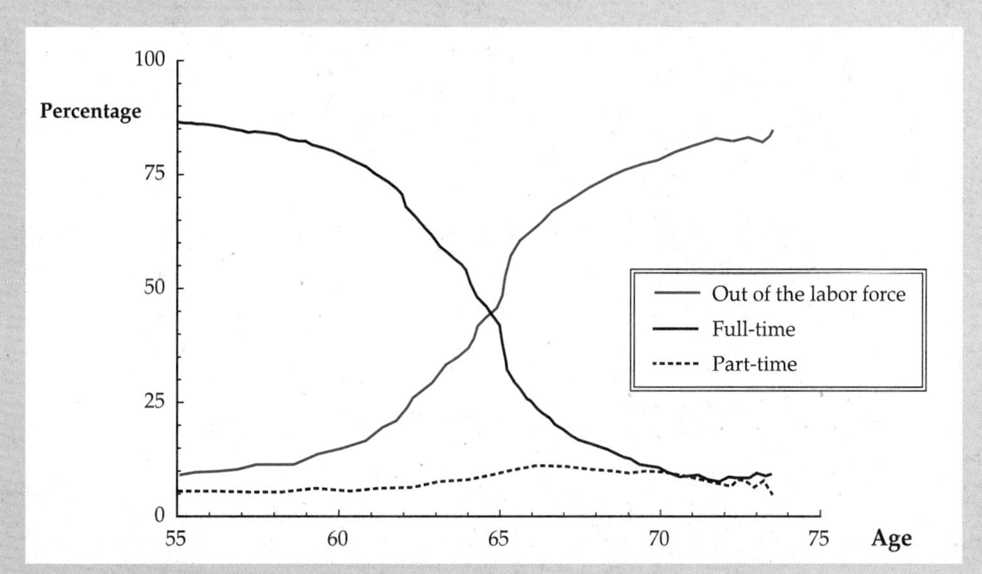

FIGURE 1.8 MEN'S LABOR FORCE STATUS BY AGE

The probability of participation falls continually from age 55 through the early 70s although some men retire before 55 and some work well into their 70s. There is a slight increase in the probability of part-time work among older men.

Source: David M. Blau, "Labor Force Dynamics of Older Men" Econometricia 62 (1994) p. 122.

participation starting in the late 50s and continuing until the early 70s. A major factor contributing to this sharp drop is the existence of pension plans offering substantial incentives to retire, often at age 65. Examination of over 1000 company pension plans showed that workers who stay beyond the normal retirement age are penalized in the form of lower lifetime incomes.[23] Eligibility for a pension raises the reservation wage by providing an alternative source of income that raises the value of time spent at home.

Even among people eligible for pensions, other factors affect the reservation wage, thus changing the likelihood of labor force participation. The most important factor is education. Among men aged 62 to 64 who were interviewed in the March 1973 CPS, each extra year of schooling increased the likelihood of being in the labor force by 1 percentage point, after adjustment for numerous other differences. The effect was even more pronounced, 2 percentage points, among men aged 65 to 70.[24] College graduates are close to the peak of their earning power after age 55, whereas the earnings of those with little education whose jobs depend more on physical strength and stamina are more likely to have declined. Bad health also reduces participation rates among older people by reducing market wages and raising reservation wages. Among men aged 58 to 71, those in poor health are far less likely to be working.[25]

An interesting question is whether older men with working wives are more or less likely to work. Put differently, does a wife's market work have any effect on a husband's reservation wage except through the increased income the wife provides? The issue is whether the leisure time of older husbands is a complement to or a substitute for the leisure time of their wives causing them to consume leisure together or apart. If his wife works, an older husband may have to bear more of the burden for household chores. The greater usefulness of time spent at home should reduce his likelihood of being in the labor force. On the other hand, he may find that time spent at home when his wife is away is not very enjoyable. This would lower his reservation wage. The evidence shows that an older man is less likely to be working if his wife is not working, implying that the leisure time of an older husband and his wife are complements.[26]

There have been sharp downward trends in the participation rate of older workers. Early in this century, more than 60 percent of men over age 65 were

---

[23]Laurence Kotlikoff and David Wise, "Pension Backloading, and Old Age Work Disincentives: Is the Subsidy to Private Pensions Worth the Price?" *Tax Policy and the Economy* 2: 161–196 (1988).

[24]Anthony Pellechio, "Social Security and the Decision to Retire," National Bureau of Economic Research, Working Paper No. 734, (1981).

[25]Gary Burtless and Robert Moffitt, "The Joint Choice of Retirement Age and Hours of Work," *Journal of Labor Economics* 3: 209–236 (1985).

[26]Donald Parsons, "The Decline in Male Labor Force Participation," *Journal of Political Economy* 88: 117–134 (1980).

TABLE 1.5 LABOR FORCE PARTICIPATION OF OLDER PERSONS, 1955–1994

	Age and Sex			
	Men		Women	
Year	55–64	65+	55–64	65+
1955	87.9	39.6	32.5	10.6
1960	86.8	33.1	37.2	10.8
1965	85.6	28.0	41.1	10.0
1970	83.0	26.8	43.0	9.7
1975	75.8	21.7	41.0	8.3
1980	72.3	19.1	41.5	8.1
1985	67.9	15.8	42.0	7.3
1990	67.7	16.4	45.3	8.7
1994	65.5	16.8	48.9	9.2

Sources: *Employment and Training Report of the President*, 1981, Table A-5; and *Employment and Earnings*, January 1986, p. 154, January 1991, p. 164, and January 1995, p. 164.

in the labor force. Now it is less than 20 percent. A similar but less pronounced decline has occurred for men between the ages of 55 and 64. Among women, participation rates have fallen for those over 65 but risen for those between 55 and 64, probably in response to changes in tastes and preferences as different cohorts have entered this age group.

In some ways the decline in labor force participation among older workers is quite puzzling. **Cross-sectional** research done at one point in time has identified many factors that affect the participation rate of older men. Almost all of these have been changing in such a way as to imply that the elderly should be *more* likely to work today than in the past. Their real wages have not only increased in absolute terms but also relative to those of the average male. This result partly reflects the greater educational attainment of older men today as compared to their fathers' generation at the same age. (In 1950 the average male aged 55 to 64 had attained only 8.4 years of schooling while today it is well over 12 years.) The downward trend has also not been caused by declining health. Life expectancy among males aged 55 increased from 16.9 years in 1950 to over 22 years today. Today's older male can look forward to a longer and healthier future than could older men in previous generations.

There is one factor affecting the participation of older workers in the cross section that has changed dramatically over time in a direction that should reduce their participation. In 1950, 26 percent of private sector workers were covered by a pension plan other than Social Security. By 1993, over 60 percent of private sector workers were employed by firms with pension plans. While some of these workers may not have been covered because they worked too few hours or had not been at the firm long enough, half of all full-time private sector workers were covered. (An additional 6 percent did not know whether they were or not!)

There is an important issue of causality here. Workers who expect to retire at an early age will provide for this rationally by increasing the fraction of their earnings capacity they opt to take as pensions rather than as wages while they are working.[27] Thus, the size of a worker's pension is not an exogenous determinant of retirement, but rather endogenously depends on when that worker plans on retiring.

Some economists point to the sharp increase in Social Security retirement benefits as the main cause of the decline in older men's participation rates. Benefits have been liberalized substantially since the inception of the program in the late 1930s, and an increasing fraction of older workers has become eligible. Covered workers aged 65 and over have been eligible for benefits throughout the life of the program, but in 1956 (1961 for men) women workers aged 62 also became eligible for reduced benefits. In addition, full indexation of Social Security benefits has reduced the risks of earlier retirement that might arise from unexpected inflation eroding living standards.

Labor economists have devoted substantial effort to measuring the impact of Social Security benefits on retirement. While there is still some controversy over the issue, an emerging consensus is that its contribution to the downward trend in labor force participation among older people is very small. Especially convincing evidence is provided by a **natural experiment**—an unexpected change in the law. The 1977 Social Security amendments unexpectedly reduced benefits for people born after 1917 compared to otherwise identical people born earlier. Despite this reduction, the decline of labor force participation among men born after 1917 was about as rapid as that among men born just a year earlier.[28]

In comparing the labor force participation behavior of men at various ages, it appears that no fundamental difference exists in the forces that have shaped the behavior of older and younger men. Work has become less attractive relative to nonmarket activities for all groups. Since young men are not eligible for Social Security pensions, the root cause must lie elsewhere.[29]

---

[27]Randall K. Filer and Peter A. Petri, "A Job-Characteristics Theory of Retirement," *Review of Economics and Statistics* 70: 123–129 (1988); Randall K. Filer and Marjorie Honig, "A Model of Endogenous Pensions in Retirement Behavior," Hunter College Economics Working Paper No. 94–8, (December 1994).

[28]Alan Krueger and Jörn-Steffen Pischke, "The Effect of Social Security on Labor Supply, A Cohort Analysis of the Notch Generation," *Journal of Labor Economics* 10: 412–437 (1992); Burtless and Moffitt, "The Joint Choice;" Alan Gustman and Thomas Steinmeier, "The 1983 Social Security Reforms and Labor Supply Adjustments of Older Individuals in the Long Run," *Journal of Labor Economics* 3: 237–253 (1985) find similarly small effects of Social Security benefits on retirement.

[29]Franco Peracci and Finis Welch, "Trends in Labor Force Transitions of Older Men and Women," *Journal of Labor Economics* 12: 210–242 (1994).

POLICY ISSUE

CUTTING OFF DISABILITY BENEFITS

Since 1960 people of any age who are disabled have been eligible for benefits under the Social Security system. These disability insurance payments to over 5 million disabled workers or their spouses and children totalled $34.5 billion in 1993 and are administered under strict standards. The level of the disability payment is related to the Social Security retirement benefit that the person would receive were he or she of retirement age. The benefit is a smaller fraction of the worker's full-time wage, the higher that wage was.

Certifications of disability are often for an "occupational disability," implying the workers are no longer physically able to work in their previous occupations. After nearly doubling in the 1970s, the number of disabled workers receiving payments dropped from 2.9 million in 1980 to 2.6 million in 1984, then rose again to 3.5 million in 1992. Part of the reason for this turnabout was the Reagan and Bush administrations' efforts to redefine occupational disability and require that beneficiaries continue to demonstrate their medical inability to work. This policy led to many lawsuits in which workers sought to overturn their disqualification. Perhaps the most significant was a New York State suit, which ruled that heart disease was a disability sufficient to qualify the victim for benefits.[30]

Why would someone who becomes partly disabled want to avoid participating in the labor force when the need for income has, if anything, increased? The effect of disability insurance on the choice of whether or not to participate is shown in Figure 1.9. In the absence of disability benefits partly disabled workers, who can earn a wage shown by the slope of the line *AB*, will choose to work H_1 hours. Participation in the work force is the best choice since point *P* on indifference curve I_1 yields the highest level of satisfaction given the budget line 0*AB*. Although they might like to stay at home, their nonlabor income 0*A* is insufficient to raise the reservation wage above the market wage. (I_0, along which $w > w^*$ at *A*, yields lower satisfaction than I_1.)

When a disability insurance program is started that forbids beneficiaries to earn anything, the individual receives an additional *AG* of nonlabor income, *but only if that person leaves the labor force.* Should potential recipients drop out? For people in Figure 1.9 whose budget line is 0*AB*, the answer is "yes." They achieve a higher level of satisfaction at point *G* on I_2 than by working H_1 hours. The combination of benefits and additional leisure makes participation less attractive.

This diagram describes the direction of the program's effect, but we must rely on statistical research to gauge its size. Research suggests that disability insurance has accounted for as much as one-fourth of the decline in older men's participation. The effects are more pronounced among workers who earned low wages when they worked.[31] Figure 1.9 leads us to expect this result. High-wage workers face the budget line 0*AE* if they do not accept benefits, but would obtain 0*G* if they do accept benefits. Clearly, they are better off working since they can achieve an indifference level of I_3 at point *Q*, as compared to I_2 at point *G* if they do not work.

---

[30]*New York Times*, (June 28, 1990), p. B11.

[31]Parsons, "The Decline"; John Bound, "The Health and Earnings of Rejected Disability Insurance Applicants," *American Economic Review* 79: 482–503 (1989); Bound and Timothy Waidmann, "Disability Transfers and the Labor Force Attachment of Older Men: Evidence from the Historical Record," *Quarterly Journal of Economics* 107: 1393–1419 (1992); Robert Haveman, Philip de Jong, and Barbara Wolfe, "Disability Transfers and the Work Decision of Older Men," *Quarterly Journal of Economics* 106: 939–950 (1991).

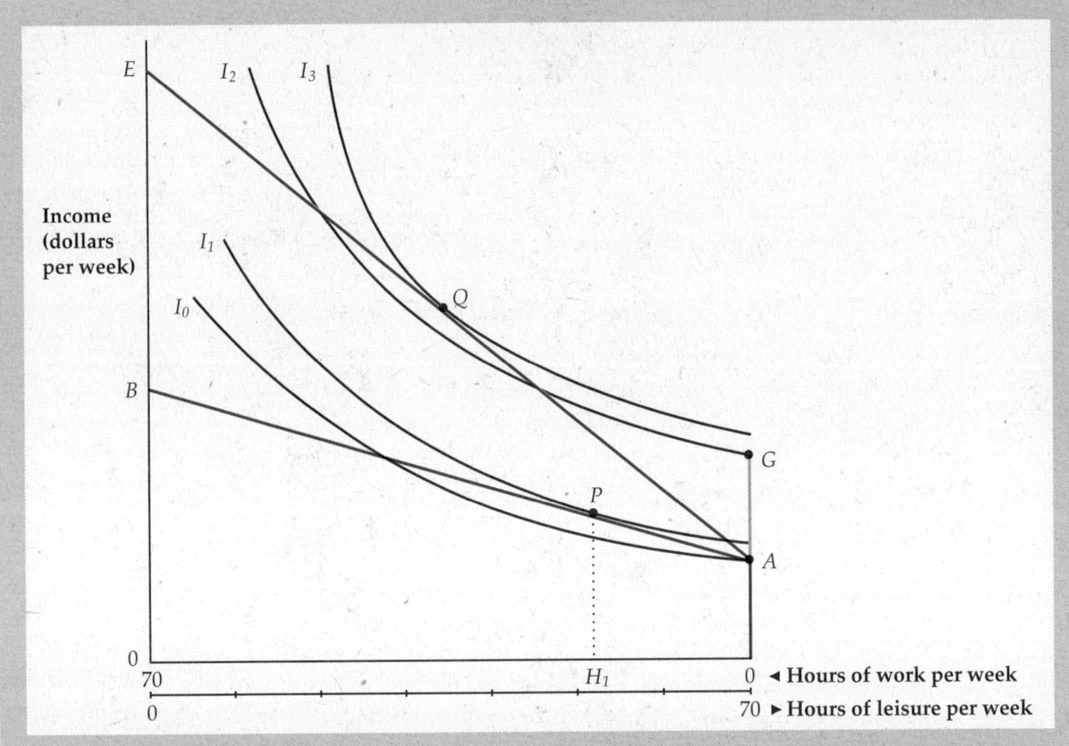

FIGURE 1.9 THE EFFECT OF DISABILITY BENEFITS OF PARTICIPATION
Eligibility for disability benefits of the amount *AG* will cause low-wage workers with budget line *AB* to drop out of the labor force but will not effect high-wage workers with budget line *AE*.

DIFFERENCES BY RACE AND ETHNICITY

As can be seen in Table 1.6, participation rates also differ by race. They are lower for black men than for white men at all ages. Among black men over 20 in 1994, the participation rate was 72.5 percent, as compared to 77.3 percent for white men. Among ethnic groups for which data from the CPS are published, Hispanic adult men were most likely to participate with 82.5 percent in the civilian labor force in 1994. Among women, a somewhat higher percentage of adult blacks than whites were in the labor force, while participation rates for Hispanic women were lower than for either black or white women. Among both youth in school and those who are not, participation rates are substantially higher among whites than among blacks. In 1994 white males 16 to 19 years old were 17 percentage points more likely than blacks to be in the labor force. Among young women, this difference was 19 percentage points.

The trends in Table 1.6 point up an especially disturbing change in the U.S. labor market—the sharp decline in the labor force attachment of young

TABLE 1.6 LABOR-FORCE PARTICIPATION RATE BY RACE, SEX AND AGE, 1955–1994

	White				*Black*			
	Males		*Females*		*Males*		*Females*	
Year	16–19	20+	16–19	20+	16–19	20+	16–19	20+
1955	58.6	87.5	40.7	34.0	60.8	87.8	32.7	47.5
1960	55.9	86.0	40.3	36.2	57.6	86.2	32.9	49.9
1965	54.1	83.9	39.2	38.0	51.3	83.7	29.5	51.1
1970	57.5	82.8	45.6	42.2	47.4	81.4	34.1	51.8
1975	61.9	80.7	51.5	45.3	42.6	76.0	34.2	51.1
1980	63.7	79.8	56.2	50.6	43.2	75.1	34.9	55.6
1985	59.7	78.5	55.2	54.0	44.6	74.4	37.9	58.6
1990	59.4	78.3	55.4	57.6	40.6	73.8	36.7	60.0
1994	57.7	77.3	55.1	59.2	40.8	72.5	36.3	60.9

Source: *Economic Report of the President*, 1991, Table B-37, 1995, Table B-38.

black males as well as the smaller but still significant decline in older black male participation relative to that of white males. The lack of trend in participation among young whites and black females is the result of longer school attendance being offset by the greater propensity to work while in school that we saw in Table 1.4.

What is striking is the change in the relative participation rates of blacks and whites over the past four decades. Simple economic theories are not particularly successful in explaining this phenomenon. Since it is logical to assume that discrimination against blacks was greater prior to the Civil Rights Act of 1964, it is interesting that up until 1965, participation rates for young black males were as high or higher than for whites. They plunged relative to white rates during the following decade and have remained at about two-thirds of the white rate since 1975.

There is no consensus on why this trend occurred. Possibilities include rising relative unemployment rates for young black males (caused in large part by the decline of Southern agriculture as a source of employment as well as increased coverage by minimum wage laws), or changing family structures that have removed older, working male role models from many inner city households. Some have blamed the large increase in welfare programs in the late 1960s and early 1970s that reduced the necessity for young parents to marry and support their children.[32]

[32]Charles Murray, *Loosing Ground: American Social Policy, 1950–1980*, New York: Basic Books, (1984).

PARTICIPATION RATES—THE OVERALL TREND AND SOME INTERNATIONAL COMPARISONS

For all workers combined, labor force participation rates were basically unchanged between 1950 and 1970. Increases in the participation rates of women roughly offset the decreases for men. As Table 1.7 shows, since 1970 the more rapid upward trend in female labor force participation has dominated the declining participation of older men. Overall, the civilian labor force participation rate for both sexes has risen from 59.2 percent of the noninstitutional population in 1950 to 66.6 percent in 1994.

Many of the trends and demographic differences noted in the United States are also present in other developed countries. Table 1.8 presents international comparisons of labor force participation that exclude the population aged 65 or more (which explains why the rates for the United States are much higher in Table 1.8 than in Table 1.7). Not surprisingly, the comparisons show that other major industrialized nations have also had an increase in female labor force participation. Indeed, studies of participation in these countries suggest a similar mix of causes as in the United States, including fertility declines and increased access to labor-saving devices. In Sweden, for example, child care subsidies, which are very generous and widespread, are a major reason for one of the highest female participation rates in the industrialized world.[33]

Despite similar *trends* in participation rates, there is little sign of a *convergence* in these rates among developed economies. In France and Germany, the increase in female participation has not been sufficient, as it has in the United States, to offset the decline in male participation and increase the total participation rate. The trends are sufficiently diverse that the range in aggregate participation rates in 1993 across countries is larger than it was in the 1960s. Part of this diversity is due to differences in the age structure of the populations. Countries with relatively few youth or elderly exhibit higher participation rates. The great diversity in the face of often similar trends and cross-sectional differences suggests the importance of various persistent factors that affect participation. Among these are the structure and level of income taxes and government benefit programs as well as cultural differences across societies.

THE DYNAMICS OF PARTICIPATION

It is important to realize that group participation rates do not apply to particular individuals. For example, a 74 percent participation rate for females aged 25 to 34 does not mean that each woman in this age group will be in the

[33]"Trends in Women's Work, Education and Family Building: Proceedings of the Conference, Chelwood Gate, Sussex, England, May 31–June 3, 1983," *Journal of Labor Economics* 3: Number 1, Part 2: S1-S396 (1985); Siv Gustafsson and Frank Stafford, "Daycare Subsidies and Labor Supply in Sweden," *Journal of Human Resources* 27: 204–230 (1992).

TABLE 1.7 CIVILIAN LABOR FORCE PARTICIPATION RATE BY SEX, 1950–1994

Year	Both Sexes	Males	Females
1950	59.2	86.4	33.9
1955	59.3	85.4	35.7
1960	59.4	83.3	37.7
1965	58.9	80.7	39.3
1970	60.4	79.7	43.3
1975	61.2	77.9	46.3
1980	63.8	77.4	51.5
1985	64.8	76.3	54.5
1990	66.4	76.1	57.5
1994	66.6	75.9	58.9

Source: *Economic Report of the President*, 1995, Table B–38.

TABLE 1.8 LABOR FORCE PARTICIPATION RATES, INDUSTRIALIZED COUNTRIES, 1966 AND 1993, PERSONS 15–64[a]

	Year and Group					
	Total		*Male*		*Female*	
	1966	1993	1966	1993	1966	1993
Australia	68.1	73.9	93.6	85.0	42.0	62.5
Canada	63.5	72.2	89.4	78.9	38.0	65.4
France[b]	69.2	66.7	89.9	74.7	48.9	58.7
Germany[b]	70.1	68.4	93.8	78.9	48.4	58.6
Japan	72.0	75.9	88.6	90.1	56.2	61.7
Sweden	75.0	78.5	93.1	80.3	56.5	76.5
United Kingdom	73.4	73.9	95.7	83.3	51.4	64.3
United States	68.7	76.8	91.2	84.5	46.8	69.1

[a]Except 16–64 for United States.

[b]1992.

Source: OECD, *Labor Force Statistics*, selected issues; OECD., *Employment Outlook*, 1994, Tables I and J.

labor force 74 percent of the time. Neither does it mean that 74 percent of women in this age group are in the labor force all the time while the other 26 percent never participate. The correct situation lies somewhere between these two extremes. In a sample of American women who were 24 to 30 at some point between 1968 through 1985, only 25 percent were in the labor force at least 90 percent of the time. On the other hand, nearly 90 percent participated in the labor force at least some of the time during this six-year age interval. The average participation rate in each year was around 60 percent.[34] Some people are always in the labor force, others never participate, and still others participate at some times and not at others.

The magnitude of these flows into and out of the labor force is even more striking when one considers the entire population. In a typical month in 1988 in the United States, 6 percent of all adult men who had been out of the labor force in the previous month were participating, as were 5 percent of the women. In a typical month in 1981 to 1983, nearly 20 percent of the teenagers who had not been in the labor force in the previous month were participating.[35]

These flows partly reflect the behavior of seasonal workers and students who enter and leave the labor force on a regular basis. They also reflect changes in the reservation wages and other variables that affect the decisions of nonseasonal workers. For example, workers who expect higher wages in the future are more likely to move into the labor force and less likely to move out of it.[36] Merely looking at participation rates for entire demographic groups masks the dynamics of participation within these groups. Underlying the broad averages is a substantial commitment to the labor market by many people who, while they may not be in the labor force in a particular month, do participate in most months of most years.

THE EFFECT OF CHANGES IN DEMAND

We now turn to the effect of demand for labor on labor force participation decisions. The question is one of **time-series** variation in participation. Discussion of this topic began in the 1930s with the emergence of the so-called **added-worker hypothesis**. This view holds that when the usual breadwinner is unemployed other household members enter the labor force in an effort to maintain the family's income. Thus, labor force participation rates should rise as unemployment rises. The added-worker hypothesis, therefore, implies that unemployment rates are overestimated in recessions since creating one new job might reduce the number of unemployed by two or more people.

The contrary view, known as **discouraged-worker hypothesis**, holds that looking for work in conditions of general unemployment becomes so disheartening that some of the unemployed give up and withdraw from the

---

[34] Audrey Light and Manuelita Ureta, "Gender Differences in Wages and Job Turnover among Continuously Employed Workers," American Economic Association, *Papers and Proceedings* 80: 293–297 (1990).

[35] Donald Williams, "Employment in Recession and Recovery: A Demographic Flow Analysis," *Monthly Labor Review* 108: 35–42 (1985).

[36] Kenneth Burdett, Nicholas Kiefer, Dale Mortensen, and George Neumann, "Earnings, Unemployment and the Allocation of Time Over Time," *Review of Economic Studies* 51: 559–578 (1984).

labor force. In addition, some people who would ordinarily enter the labor force do not do so. The size of the labor force, therefore, varies in the same direction as demand rather than in the opposite direction.

The CPS attempts to measure the number of discouraged workers by counting those who have not looked for work in the past month and who list as the primary reason a belief that no jobs are available. The official definition in other countries differs. In Canada, for example, to be counted as discouraged a person must have looked for work in the past six months. Excluding discouraged workers implies that unemployment is underestimated and that we should also include an additional group of **hidden unemployed**, who would be looking for work if they did not regard the search as hopeless.

On average during the 1980s the number of people counted as discouraged in the CPS averaged about 15 percent of the number counted as unemployed. This is substantial (about 1 million people), but in 1993, it would have raised the labor force participation and unemployment rates by less than 1 percentage point, increasing the unemployment rate, for example, from 6.7 to 7.5 percent. In countries where the definition is more stringent (Canada, for example) the number of people counted as discouraged is an even smaller fraction of the adult population and of measured unemployment. In Japan, which uses a definition like the U.S. and where measured unemployment is very low, almost as many workers are counted as discouraged as are counted as unemployed.[37]

This discussion shows that reductions in the demand for labor have two effects on the worker's choice about whether or not to participate. The added-worker hypothesis implies that reduced aggregate demand directly lowers the income of family members who lose their jobs or are put on short workweeks. As in Figure 1.4, this also reduces the nonlabor income of other family members who are not currently in the labor force, lowering their reservation wages since there is now less income from other sources to support the household.

If all families had large holdings of liquid assets or could borrow easily at the going rate of interest, a temporary reduction in earned income might have only negligible effects on labor force participation. The family's usual standard of consumption could be maintained by drawing down assets or by borrowing. The typical working family, however, has only limited liquid assets or ability to borrow. Interest rates on cash loans to such families, when they are available, are typically very high. Unemployment insurance benefits, for those eligible to receive them, usually cover no more than half the income lost.

Under these conditions, an increase in labor force participation by other family members is an important alternative means of adjustment to unemployment even when it is expected to be temporary. That people react

[37]OECD, *Employment Outlook*, (1994), Table 1.4.

this way is suggested by the fact that in 1993, 68 percent of families with one unemployed member had at least one other family member working full-time.

The discouraged-worker hypothesis stresses the importance of the reduction in market opportunities, even in good times, for people in the labor force. During reductions in labor demand, the jobs still available are likely to be lower paid or less attractive than before. If they can be found at all, it is only after a longer and more costly search. These factors will tip the scales in favor of the nonmarket activity for some people trying to decide whether to stay in school or remain full-time homemakers instead of seeking employment. Elderly workers who lose their jobs when unemployment rates are high are also more likely to accept early retirement than if the chances of finding suitable new positions were better.

Clearly, both the added-worker and the discouraged-worker effects can be present at the same time, either for different households or for different members of a particular household. The question is which effect predominates? There is evidence that economic hardship encourages some people to enter the labor force who otherwise would not have participated. In one sample, only 7 percent of wives whose husbands were employed entered the labor force in a particular month, compared with 9 percent of wives with unemployed husbands. Women whose husbands cannot work as many hours as they want are also more likely to participate in the labor force.[38] On the other hand, difficulty in obtaining jobs induces other workers to leave the labor force. The number of people reporting they were out of the labor force because they could not obtain a job fell from 1.6 million in the recession year 1983 to 859,000 in the boom year 1989.

The net effect seems to be that the discouraged-worker effect predominates. Table 1.9 shows one recent set of estimates of the sensitivity of labor force participation rates to unemployment for men and for women. An increase of 1 percentage point in the unemployment rate of men 35 to 44 causes a 2 to 5 percent decline in the participation rates of all teenage groups. It causes smaller but still significant declines in participation rates of white and Hispanic women, but has very little effect on those of other groups. Another study found that in Britain married women's participation drops when unemployment increases, but married men's participation is almost unaffected.[39] The evidence makes it clear that the responsiveness of participation to the business cycle is greatest among those groups whose participation rates are lowest on average.

---

[38]Shelly Lundberg, "The Added Worker Effect," *Journal of Labor Economics* 3: 11–37 (1985); Tim Maloney, "Employment Constraints and the Labor Supply of Married Women," *Journal of Human Resources* 22: 51–61 (1987).

[39]Ian Molho, "A Time-Series Study of Household Participation Decisions through Boom and Slump," *Oxford Economic Papers* 38: 141–159 (1986).

TABLE 1.9 ESTIMATED SENSITIVITY OF LABOR-FORCE PARTICIPATION TO UNEMPLOYMENT, 1973–1984[a]

Ethnic Group and Age	Men	Women
White, 16–19	–2.1	–1.6
Black, 16–-19	–5.4	–5.6
Hispanic, 16–19	–3.6	–2.8
White, 20+	–0.2	–0.7
Black, 20+	–0.01	–0.2
Hispanic, 20+	–0.2	–0.6

[a]The estimated sensitivity is the percentage change in the labor-force participation rate associated with a 1 percentage point increase in the unemployment rate of men aged 35–44.

Source: Based on Gregory de Freitas, "A Time-Series Analysis of Hispanic Unemployment," *Journal of Human Resources* 21: 34–35 (1986).

Although the discouraged-worker effect is dominant, the seriousness of the problem should not be exaggerated. Only half of those who claimed to be discouraged workers bothered to look for work within the previous 12 months. Of the people who reported themselves discouraged workers between 1979 and 1983, only 31 percent had worked at all in the previous 12 months. Most importantly, of the nearly 1.7 million people who claimed to be "discouraged" during the bottom of the 1981–82 recession, nearly half were out of the labor force a year later but did not claim to be discouraged.[40] The conclusion is that, while rising unemployment does reduce the size of the labor force, most of the fairly small reduction occurs among people who do not have much attachment to the labor market in the first place.

SUMMARY

Labor force participation—the choice of whether or not to work or seek market work—is based on a comparison of market opportunities and the benefits of staying at home. The choice can be analyzed by converting it to a comparison of people's market wages and their reservation wages. Using this framework, we can explain a number of differences in labor force participation rates (the fraction of persons aged 16 and over in a particular demographic group who are in the labor force). These include: (1) why women with young children, especially those who lack access to child-care facilities or who have less education, are less likely to be in the labor force; (2) why youth who are in school are less likely to be in the labor force; (3) why there is a sharp

[40]Paul Flaim, "Discouraged Workers: How Strong Are Their Links to the Job Market?" *Monthly Labor Review* 107: 8–11 (1984).

decline in participation rates among older workers; and (4) why participation rates are higher among the better educated.

This approach explains increases in female labor force participation, the major labor force trend of the past 40 years in the U.S. and most other industrialized countries. This trend results from a combination of reductions in the reservation wages of married women, which stems from a decline in birth rates and a growth of good substitutes for housewives' time at home, and the rising real wages women can obtain by working in the market.

Theoretical modeling of participation also enables us to understand the effects of several government policies. Subsidies for day care, for example, are clearly designed to increase participation. Numerous programs that transfer nonlabor income to recipients, such as welfare, Social Security retirement benefits, and disability insurance, are likely to reduce participation rates. The actual effects of each program must be carefully and specifically evaluated, but the basic framework we have outlined should underlie any such evaluation.

APPENDIX

Combining Income and Leisure

The analysis of labor force participation in this chapter and hours of work in Chapter 2 follow the traditional approach of dividing activity into market work and all other activity, which is called *leisure* for convenience. An alternative approach that gives greater generality at a cost of greater complexity notes that both work and consumption take time, with leisure being the time used to enjoy consumption.[41] In this framework, satisfaction is produced by activities that combine two inputs: time and purchased goods. These activities can be classified by whether they are relatively **time-intensive** or relatively **goods-intensive**. Work can be viewed as an activity that yields more goods than it uses and typically produces negative satisfaction. The price of an activity depends on (1) the relative amounts of time and purchased goods taken to produce it, and (2) the prices of those goods and the value of the time (i.e., the market wage) of the person doing the consumption. The outcomes of events such as increasing wages can then be analyzed in terms of their effects on time-intensive and goods-intensive activities, rather than simply on the amount of labor and leisure.

Classifying satisfaction-producing activities into those that are relatively time-intensive and those that are relatively goods-intensive is not as easy as it might appear at first. Listening to Mahler's Third Symphony takes 90 minutes (there is no satisfactory way of listening to it more quickly) and requires the purchase of a CD player and two discs, the cost of which will be amor-

[41]Gary Becker, "A Theory of the Allocation of Time," *Economic Journal* 75: 492–517 (1965).

tized over many years of listening and will amount to at most a few pennies each time the symphony is played. Thus, this activity is relatively time-intensive. So is sleep, on which we spend nearly one-third of our time. (The hourly cost of a bed and linens purchased for $1000 and used for 10 years is about 3 cents.) Conversely, automobiles can be quite goods-intensive. A typical car that costs 50 cents a mile to operate (including gas, repairs, and depreciation), will cost $15 an hour if driven at 30 miles per hour.

When it comes to broader commodities the classification is less clear. Is a one-week vacation relatively time-intensive or goods-intensive? It is time-intensive if you spend it tenting at a lake in a nearby national park. It may be relatively goods-intensive if you spend it flying to Paris on the Concorde, staying at the George V, and eating at three-star restaurants.

Despite the potential ambiguity, this extension of standard labor force participation theory enables the derivation of predictions that do not emerge from traditional theory. Consider, for example, the effect of a rise in wages offset by a fixed-amount (lump-sum) tax on workers. Traditional theory predicts only that this would induce more labor force participation, since the wage is increased while household income and the reservation wage are unchanged. The extension of standard theory allows us to examine the effects this change has on the activities workers undertake. The change in circumstances will encourage reductions in all time-intensive activities, not just the broad category *leisure*. Thus, it will presumably lead to activities that use more market goods such as eating in restaurants being substituted for time-intensive activities like cooking at home. This approach also says something about how people spend their time away from work. Given the same total income, people with high wages and low nonlabor income spend their non-market time doing things that are relatively goods-intensive. Compare two people with the same income, one living off an inheritance and the other a highly paid executive. The wealthy person will consume time-intensive commodities while the executive will consume goods-intensive commodities.

A few attempts have been made to study various activities to see which ones are complements to (consumed with) leisure, and which are substitutes for (consumed instead of) leisure. For example, people with higher wages do sleep less and spend less time personally fixing up their houses.[42]

What does this extended theory say about how consumption patterns change as the value of people's time increases? With higher and higher earned income and thus greater command over goods, but with no more time available to spend their incomes, people will substitute goods-intensive activities for time-intensive ones. Thus, economic theory predicts why medieval lovers

---

[42]Michael Abbott and Orley Ashenfelter, "Labour Supply, Commodity Demand and the Allocation of Time," *Review of Economic Studies* 43: 389–412 (1976); Jeff Biddle and Daniel Hamermesh, "Sleep and the Allocation of Time," *Journal of Political Economy* 98: 922–943 (1990); Peter Kooreman and Arie Kapteyn, "A Disaggregated Analysis of the Allocation of Time within the Household," *Journal of Political Economy* 95: 223–249 (1987).

woo in person with sonnets and ballads while moderns send greeting cards and singing telegrams. In an entertaining popular account of these effects, one author has referred to them as problems of the "harried leisure class."[43] Alternatively, people will pay others to engage in a wide variety of surrogate household production that is uneconomic for the person whose value of time is high and increasing. Hiring fashion consultants to shop for executives' wardrobes, arranging to have laundry collected and returned at the train station on one's commute, and buying gourmet dinners delivered to the door are good recent examples of markets responding to these new demands.

QUESTIONS AND PROBLEMS

1.1 The following data were obtained from the December 1994 CPS:

Noninstitutional population 197,765
Men employed 67,292
Men unemployed 3,767
Women employed 57,437
Women unemployed 2,922
Men out of the labor force 23,792

Compute the following labor force statistics:

a. Labor force participation rate.
b. Unemployment rate.
c. Unemployment rate of men.
d. Labor force participation rate of women.
e. Number of persons not in the labor force.

1.2 Classify the following people by labor force status:

a. Paul, who has not earned any money in the past year because he has been working at home writing a software package that he expects to market when he finishes it next year.
b. Jim, a lawyer who has taken a seven-month leave of absence without pay from his law firm in order to travel around the world.
c. Frances, who has quit her job in order to return to school full time.
d. Matthew, a college student who is working without pay as a summer intern for a United States senator.
e. Madeleine, who does 20 hours per week of unpaid volunteer work for local charities.

1.3 Many authors have suggested that a revolution in work habits is being produced because people can accomplish their work using computers installed in their homes. Assume that the hourly wage is not changed

[43] Staffan Linder, *The Harried Leisure Class*, New York: Columbia University Press, (1970).

by this revolution. Analyze the likely effects on the labor force participation rate overall and by sex and marital status.

1.4 Fred receives \$100 per week in dividends and interest from his vast financial empire. He is just as happy if he works one hour per week to raise his income to \$105 or works two hours a week to raise his income to \$112 as he is when he does not work at all.

a. What is Fred's reservation wage? (Use a graph in your answer.)
b. Suppose you offered Fred a job at \$5.50 per hour. Would he take it?
c. If dividend rates fall because of a recession, what will happen to Fred's reservation wage?

1.5 Recently Congress considered bills to require employers to give workers paid paternity and maternity leave. Such laws already exist in most European countries, and many states have passed their own variants. Analyze the effect of such legislation on the labor force participation rates of married women and married men by graphing the effects of the proposal on the budget lines facing typical individuals and discussing the results.

1.6 In discussing subsidies to child care, we saw that the major subsidy in the U.S. is an income tax credit for a portion of a family's expenditures. In 1994 the maximum expenditure eligible for this credit was \$2,400 for one child and \$4,800 for two or more children. The rate of the credit depends on the family's income and ranges from 30 percent for incomes less than \$10,000 a year to 20 percent for those over \$28,000. Suppose that there is only one intermediate rate of 35 percent for incomes between \$10,000 and \$28,000. Mary is a single parent with one child whose skills will only allow her to obtain a minimum wage job paying \$4.25 an hour. She receives \$800 a month in child support from her former husband. If she works she must pay \$50 a week in fixed costs and \$1.00 an hour for each hour she leaves her child in day care. Assuming that the work year is 50 weeks long, graph Mary's budget constraints with and without the child-care tax credit. What effect is this credit likely to have on her labor force participation?

1.7 Alice, who lives in New Jersey, is recently divorced and was awarded support of A dollars per week from her husband.

a. The highest wage she can find in New Jersey is M dollars per week. Her utility function is such that she prefers not to take this job, but she would be happy to work 40 hours per week at a wage of $2M$ dollars. Draw Alice's budget line and her utility function.
b. By expanding her search to New York, Alice can obtain much higher wage offers than in New Jersey. Given that she has a house in New Jersey, however, she will have to pay B dollars per week for commuting and spend 10 hours per week travelling.

Draw the budget line that will leave Alice indifferent between taking the job in New York and staying at home in New Jersey.

1.8 During the shift from communism to market economies in Eastern Europe, a wide divergence in the pattern of female labor force participation arose. Women's labor force attachment was among the highest in the world in all countries in the region prior to 1990. Since then, it has fallen drastically in some countries (notably the Czech Republic and Albania) but remained virtually unchanged in others (such as Romania and Bulgaria). At first it seems odd that the largest decreases have been in the richest and poorest countries in the region. How can you explain this observation?

1.9 The U.S. determines if an individual is unemployed on the basis of a series of questions regarding whether he has worked or looked for work in recent weeks. Some other countries base this determination on registration with a state employment agency. Alternatively, many politicians advocate that it be based simply on whether an individual claims that he would like to work. Discuss the advantages and disadvantages of changing the official U.S. definition to each of these alternative concepts.

1.10 We have seen that labor force participation rates are lower for black men than for white men. This might be due to differences in preferences or differences in opportunities. Draw the budget lines and indifference curves for blacks and whites that illustrate these two possibilities. How would you attempt to distinguish between them empirically?

KEY WORDS

added-worker hypothesis
budget line
civilian labor force
comparative statics
corner solution
cross section
Current Population Survey (*CPS*)
demography
discouraged-worker hypothesis
effort
employed (*E*)
fixed costs of child care
goods-intensive
hidden unemployed
hours of work
income
indifference curve (*I*)
indifference maps
interior solution
intertemporal substitution
labor force
labor force participation rate (*LFPR*)
labor supply
leisure
life cycle theory
marginal rate of substitution (*MRS*)
marginal utility (*MU*)
natural experiment
nonlabor income

normal good
out-of-labor force (O)
population over age 16 (P)
reference week
reservation wage (w^*)
skill
time-intensive
time series
total labor force
total work effort
unemployed (U)
unemployment rate (UR)
utility
variable costs of child care

2

Hours of Work and Hours of Effort

THE MAJOR QUESTIONS

- ▲ How much time do workers spend at their jobs?
- ▲ What has happened over time to hours of work in the U.S.?
- ▲ How does labor economics explain both time-series and cross-sectional differences in work hours with a simple theoretical apparatus?
- ▲ What explains why some people work overtime, while others work part-time, and still others moonlight?
- ▲ How do income taxes affect incentives to work?
- ▲ How does welfare influence incentives among low-wage people? More generally, how do a variety of government programs affect hours of work?

VARIATION IN HOURS OF WORK

In addition to the number of people in the labor force, the amount of labor supplied to the economy depends on the number of hours per time period workers are willing to work. We need to distinguish among three concepts of hours supplied: (1) hours paid for, which include paid holidays and vacation time; (2) hours spent at the workplace; and (3) hours spent actually working. The amount of time *actually spent working* rather than preparing to work or relaxing determines the amount of labor available for production. The supply aspects of hours spent at the workplace have been widely studied and receive most of the attention in this chapter. Economists are increasingly studying workers' efforts on the job, however, and the last part of this chapter and much of Chapter 9 discuss this aspect of labor supply.

Before turning to the theory of hours of work, let us look at a few facts. First, there clearly has been a long-term decline in average hours at the workplace. The data in Table 2.1 show that this decline was very rapid in the

TABLE 2.1 AVERAGE FULLL-TIME HOURS OF WORK PER WEEK IN MANUFACTURING AND PRIVATE NONFARM INDUSTRY, SELECTED[a] YEARS, 1900–1993

Year	Manufacturing[b]	Private Nonfarm Industry[c]
1900	55.0	—
1910	52.2	—
1920	48.1	—
1929	48.0	—
1939	37.3	—
1948	38.8	40.0
1957	37.8	38.8
1969	38.0	37.7
1979	37.2	35.7
1993	37.0	34.5

[a]The years shown were chosen to avoid recession years.

[b]Average of hours per week actually spent at the workplace (not hours paid for) so that an increase in paid leave time such as holidays and vacations results in a reduction of the average workweek as measured in this series.

[c]Average hours per week paid for.

Sources: For manufacturing, 1900–1957, Ethel Jones, "New Estimates of Hours of Work per Week and Hourly Earnings, 1900–1957," *Review of Economics and Statistics* 45: 375 (1963); for 1969–1993, *Economic Report of the President,* 1994, Table B–45, linked to Jones, op.cit., using U.S. Chamber of Commerce, *Employee Benefits,* selected years.

United States between 1900 and 1940, mainly because of reductions in the length of the **standard workweek.** Since 1940 the standard workweek in manufacturing has not been reduced significantly, but average hours at work have continued to fall, though more slowly. Taking years of roughly comparable demand pressures, we find that CPS data from 1963 show that the average workweek (among all workers) was 39.6 hours in the survey week; in 1994 it was only 39.2 hours. There is evidence that the failure of reported hours to fall may be due to reporting errors in the CPS. Many workers apparently just give the standard workweek when asked how long they work rather than their actual hours. Thus, between 1965 and 1981 CPS data showed only a 2.7 percent decline in workweeks for men aged 20 to 65, whereas time diaries that asked men to actually account for what they were doing each minute of the day showed a 13.5 percent decline.[1]

---

[1]F. Thomas Juster and Frank Stafford, "The Allocation of Time: Empirical Findings, Behavioral Models and Problems of Measurement," *Journal of Economic Literature* 39: 471–522 (1991).

TABLE 2.2 INTERNATIONAL COMPARISONS OF WORK SCHEDULES

	Actual Weekly Hours of Full-Time Employees, 1988	Annual Hours of All Employees, 1970	Annual Hours of All Employees, 1993
United States	39.4	1889	1776
Canada	38.0	1890	1719
France	40.3	1962	1666[b]
Germany	39.9	1949	1588
Japan	46.8[a]	2201[c]	1965[b]
Sweden	37.6	1641	1507

[a]Includes part- and full-time workers.

[b]Data for 1992.

[c]Data for 1973.

Source: OECD, *Employment Outlook,* 1990, Tables 1.4, 1.6, 1994, Table B.

The second important fact is that the level of hours (both hours paid for and hours spent at work) in the U.S. is similar to other developed nations. Table 2.2 shows that for major industrialized countries with comparable data, workweeks of about 40 hours are fairly typical. Unlike the U.S., there have been declines in the reported workweek in other countries since 1950. Average workweeks fell nearly 30 percent between 1950 and 1987 in Germany and Sweden, and around 15 percent in France and Britain.[2] As seen in Table 2.2, however, these reductions were sufficient only to bring the average workweek for full-time workers in line with that of the U.S.

The third important fact is that at any given time, there is substantial variation in the hours worked by different members of the labor force. Table 2.3 gives the percentage distributions of hours worked at all jobs in May 1994. Although 36 percent of workers in all but the agricultural sector reported working exactly 40 hours, the prevailing standard workweek, many people worked much less or much more. Why is the 40-hour workweek a standard? One answer is that, in the U.S. at least, labor laws require that many workers be paid overtime for every hour above 40. It is more likely, however, that the law was written to reflect the standard week: 40 hours is exactly five 8-hour shifts. Since much of the economy needs to operate 24-hours a day, standard shifts must be divisible into 24. In fact, the decline in average workweeks shown in Table 2.1 occurred as more factories shifted from 12-hour days to 8-hour days, not as the average day became shorter in all factories.

The common view is that employers establish hours and that workers must accept them if they are to have jobs. This demand-dominated view con-

[2]John Owen, "Work-Time Reduction in the U.S. and Europe," *Monthly Labor Review* 111: 42–45 (1988).

TABLE 2.3 PERCENT DISTRIBUTION OF HOURS OF WORK PER WEEK, MAY 1970 AND MAY 1994, NONAGRICULTURAL INDUSTRIES

Hours of Work	May 1970		May 1994	
1–14	6.1	22.0	5.0	24.6
15–29	10.2		12.4	
30–34	5.7		7.2	
35–39	7.1	50.1	7.6	43.5
40	43.0		35.9	
41–48	12.1	27.9	12.2	31.9
49–59	8.8		11.4	
60+	7.0		8.3	
Total at work	100.0		100.0	

Sources: *Employment and Earnings,* June 1970, Table A–22; June 1994, Table A–27. The figures are obtained from household interviews in the Current Population Survey.

tains an important element of truth, but the reality is more complicated. Employers must compete to attract and keep workers. If the hours they offer differ too much from what their workers want, they will lose employees to other firms willing to offer a schedule more compatible with the workers' desires. The substantial decrease in hours shown in Table 2.1 did not occur because firms wanted their employees to work fewer hours. Rather, as incomes rose over time, workers wanted to consume more leisure, and competitive pressure forced firms to accommodate this wish.

The importance of supply forces is also illustrated by the existence of nonstandard schedules. Many people want to work only part-time because of commitments at home or school, and many succeed in finding regular part-time jobs. In some cases workers may take full-time jobs because they cannot find part-time jobs. In other cases employers create part-time jobs when they cannot find full-time employees. For example, they staff one full-time position with two half-time workers.

Just as there are people who want to work less than the standard workweek, there are others who want to work more. Some of those who want more income than they can get from a single job with a standard workweek hold two or more jobs at once. In Table 2.3 multiple jobholders are included among those working long total hours. Others choose occupations or employers that allow the flexible scheduling of their weekly hours of work.

We will analyze the determinants of these departures from the standard workweek later in the chapter, but first let us consider the supply forces that influence the length of the standard workweek itself.

POLICY ISSUE

LAZINESS AND INTERNATIONAL COMPETITIVENESS

A major concern among American businesspeople and politicians is the fear that the nation has lost its "competitiveness" with other industrialized economies, that it cannot produce efficiently and is destined for continued relatively slow economic growth. Is the problem due to a decline in the American work ethic? Are Americans no longer willing to work hard? Table 2.1 showed that the average workweek had become shorter in the U.S. Since we saw an even greater downward trend in Europe, are Americans any lazier than residents of other industrialized countries?

The second and third columns of Table 2.2 show the total hours worked in two different years by all employees in a number of countries. To find the **total number of hours worked** in a country, this figure is multiplied by the size of the labor force. For the U.S. in 1993, this calculation yields

$$1776 \times (193.5 \textit{ million} \times .663) = 227.8 \textit{ billion hours},$$

where 193.5 million is the population aged 16 and over and .663 is the fraction who were in the labor force. Similar calculations could be made for other countries. It is worth noting, however, that except for Japan, where hours worked per year are much higher, the U.S. ranks fairly high in hours worked per employee. The data in Table 1.8 show that the overall participation rate in the U.S. is not unusually low. Sweden, whose workers put in the fewest hours among countries listed in the table, has the highest participation rate so that total hours are not especially low relative to population size.

Part of the confusion is that the press has not been particularly careful in its reporting on worker productivity. American labor force productivity, whether measured as output per worker or output per hour is the highest in the world, 25 percent higher than Germany's, 40 percent higher than the U.K.'s, and more than 60 percent greater then Japan's. Only occasionally is there any industry where workers in another country are more productive than those in the U.S. One example is the restaurant industry in France, an area Americans might be willing to concede.[3] What is true is that the *rate of growth* of productivity in some other countries has exceeded the rate of growth in the U.S. This is not surprising, since it is always harder to forge the path than to follow behind.

THE THEORY OF CHOICE OF HOURS OF WORK

In Chapter 1 we analyzed how a rational decision maker chooses *whether or not to participate* in the labor force. Here we use the same mechanism to analyze how such a decision maker chooses the *number of hours* to supply. As in the discussion of labor force participation, we first assume that workers can earn a fixed wage rate for each hour they choose to work, and that the num-

[3]Dirk Pilat and Bart van Ark, "Productivity Leadership in Manufacturing, Germany, Japan and the United States, 1973–1989," University of Groningen (1992); McKinsey Global Institute, *Service Sector Productivity*, Washington: McKinsey Global Institute (1992).

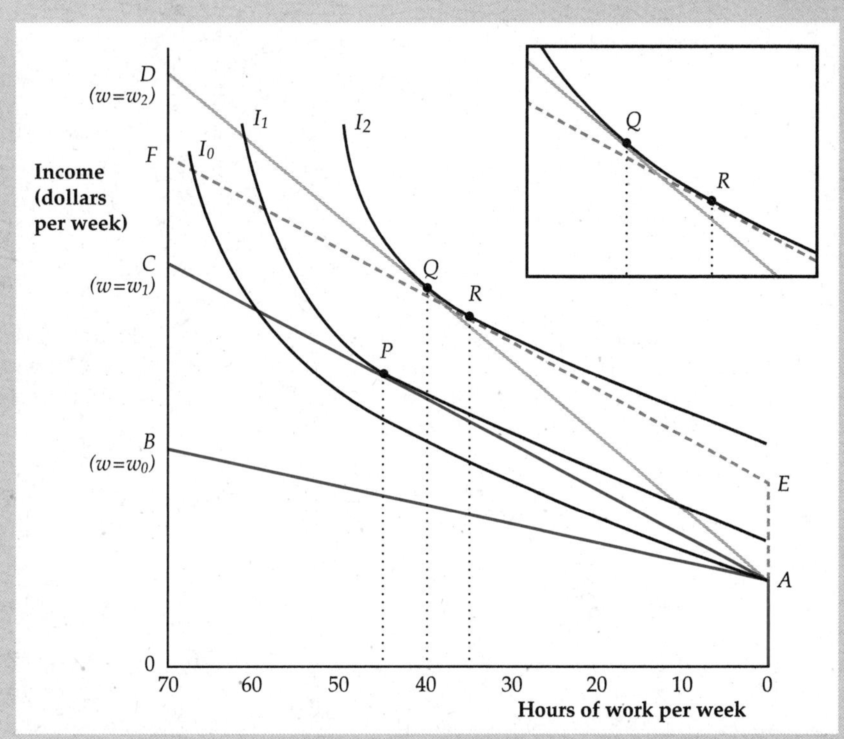

FIGURE 2.1 THE CHOICE BETWEEN INCOME AND HOURS OF LEISURE

Workers' utility is maximized where one of their indifference curves is tangent to their budget line. Point *P* shows the best combination available to a worker with wage w_1 and nonlabor income 0*A*. If the wage rises to w_2, the worker's move to his new maximum at point *Q* consists of an income effect that reduces the hours of work from *P* to *R* and a substitution effect that increases them from *R* to *Q*.

ber of hours chosen is entirely at their discretion. Later we will relax these assumptions.

Consider Max I. Mizer, whose opportunities are depicted in Figure 2.1. As we saw in the previous chapter, at a wage rate w_0, which is lower than his reservation wage, he chooses to supply zero hours since the best attainable combination of income and leisure would be at point *A*. With a wage rate of w_1 per hour, he is free to choose any combination of hours and income along the budget line 0*AC*. Max's tastes are summarized by his indifference map, from which three indifference curves are shown in Figure 2.1. Given the wage rate w_1, Max will maximize utility at *P*, where *AC* is tangent to I_1, and supply 45 hours of work a week. At this point $MRS_{L\$} = w_1$. The wage rate exactly equals the amount Max requires to give up another hour of leisure.

Any other point on AC lies on a lower indifference curve and therefore represents a less satisfactory position.

If the wage rate now rises to w_2 so that Max can choose points along $0AD$, his new optimum is at Q, where AD is tangent to the higher indifference curve I_2. At this point he is still operating where the marginal rate of substitution equals the wage rate, but now the higher wage rate persuades him to consume more leisure, so Max chooses to reduce the number of hours he supplies to 40.

Although we cannot read an individual's supply curve of hours in terms of wage rates directly from Figure 2.1, we can use the figure's results to find this curve. We know that at wage rate w_0 Max supplies zero hours, while at w_1 he supplies 45 hours, and at w_2, 40 hours. If we draw a different line for each possible wage rate, we could determine the number of hours offered at each wage. Taking these three combinations of wage rates and hours we have derived already from Figure 2.1, and assuming that we have derived the other intermediate combinations, we might find Max's labor supply curve looking like the one in Figure 2.2. This supply curve implies that he offers more

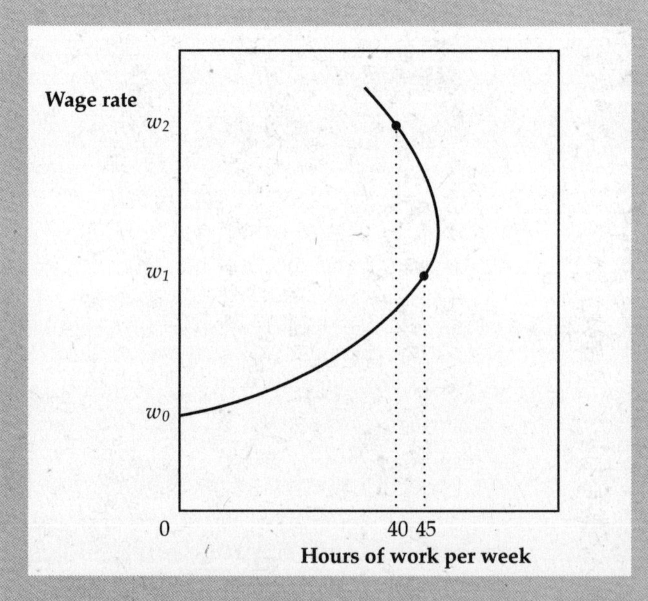

FIGURE 2.2 SUPPLY CURVE OF HOURS PER WEEK

Low-wage workers respond to wage increases by offering more hours of labor. When wages rise above some level, however, many workers will respond to even higher wages by cutting back on the hours they work so as to be able to purchase more leisure.

hours as the wage rate rises up to or slightly beyond w_1. Further increases in the wage rate decrease the number of hours offered. At wage rates above this level, Max's supply curve is **backward-bending**.

The supply curve in Figure 2.2 may seem strange, since most supply curves have a positive slope throughout. Why is this one different? The answer lies in the fact that to supply labor, workers must give up something they like—leisure. The supply curve of labor (the demand for leisure) can have a negative slope because a rise in the price of leisure (the wage rate), which by itself makes workers consume less leisure, also raises their incomes, which may lead them to consume more leisure.

The effect of the wage rate increase from w_1 to w_2 in Figure 2.1 can be decomposed into two distinct responses by drawing a line parallel to *AC* that is tangent to I_2, the indifference curve Max reaches at the higher wage w_2. This line *EF* is tangent to I_2 at point *R*. The distance between *AC* and *EF* is the amount of nonlabor income Max would need to be as well-off as he is after the wage increase, *if* there had been no change in the wage rate (the return to giving up each additional hour of leisure). Since *AD* is steeper than *AC* (or *EF*), leisure is now more expensive in terms of earned income. This means that *R* must lie to the right of *Q*. As the figure is drawn, the wage increase reduces the hours Max supplies from 45 to 40. The equivalent increase in nonlabor income would reduce them to 35.

The horizontal distance from *P* to *R* is the **income effect** of the wage change on hours of work. An income effect shows what the response of hours worked would have been had the higher indifference curve reached after a wage increase (I_2 in Figure 2.1) been achieved solely by an increase in nonlabor income without changing the wage rate. In this example, if Max's rise in utility came because of an inheritance or a large gift, he would choose to work 10 less hours a week, so the income effect is –10 hours per week.

The horizontal distance from *R* to *Q* is the **substitution effect**. The substitution effect shows the change in hours that occurs when wage rates change (changing the slope of the budget line), but the worker's nonlabor income is modified sufficiently to keep his utility constant (keep him on the same indifference curve). In this example, at the higher wage rate, Max's utility is maintained if he consumes 5 more hours of leisure a week, so the substitution effect is +5 hours per week.

The sum of the income and substitution effects, the horizontal distance from *P* to *Q*, is the total effect of the wage change on hours of work. Summarizing the impact of a change in the wage rate in terms of Max's decisions:

$$P \to Q = P \to R + R \to Q$$

or

Total effect = Income effect + Substitution effect.

Theory predicts that the substitution effect must be positive, involving a move to the left in Figure 2.1. When a good (leisure) becomes more expensive we buy less of it. Increased wages increase the **opportunity cost** of each unit of leisure consumed. If leisure is a normal good, so that a worker wants to consume more leisure as his income increases, then the income effect on hours worked will be negative. As long as leisure is normal (a very reasonable assumption), point *R* must lie to the right of point *P*.

There is no theoretical relationship between the positions of *P* and *Q*, however. As drawn in Figure 2.1, *Q* lies to the right of *P*. This implies that the income effect dominates the substitution effect, and Max values additional leisure so much that the extra purchasing power generated by a rise in the wage rate from w_1 to w_2 more than offsets the incentive that the increased wage rate gives him to reduce his consumption of leisure.

For other workers, *Q* might lie to the left of *P*, implying that the substitution effect dominates the income effect. Consider Maxine, whose response to a wage increase is shown in Figure 2.3. She has the same nonlabor income,

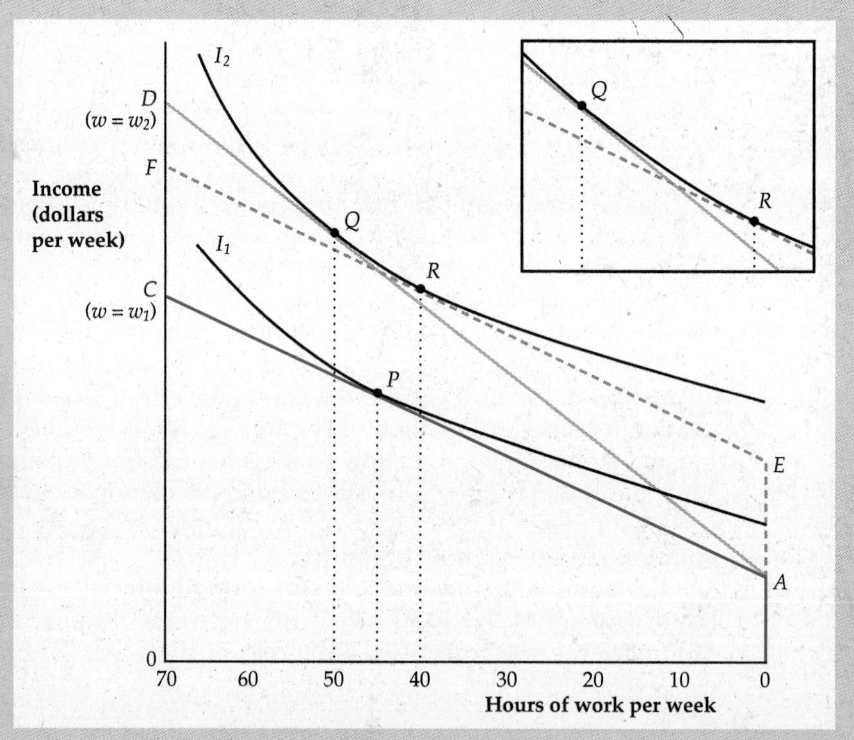

FIGURE 2.3 AN ALTERNATIVE RESPONSE TO CHANGING WAGES
The shape of some workers' indifference curves will mean that the substitution effect between *R* and *Q* will be larger than the income effect between *P* and *R*. For these workers, hours of work will increase when wages rise.

$0A$, and faces the same initial wage rate, w_1. Like Max, when faced with the budget line $0AC$ she chooses to supply 45 hours, since at point P her $MRS_{L\$}$ equals the wage rate w_1.

When the wage rate rises to w_2, Maxine finds that her best choice on the new budget line $0AD$ is at point Q, where her $MRS_{L\$}$ on the higher indifference curve I_2 equals the new wage rate, w_2. Unlike Max, the rise in the wage has induced her to supply more hours. The reason is that the income effect of the increased wage ($P \rightarrow R$) is only –5 hours for her. Higher nonlabor income would induce her to work less, but not very much less. The substitution effect for her ($R \rightarrow Q$) is +10 hours. At the same level of satisfaction, I_2, an increase in the wage rate leads her to work much longer. The net impact ($P \rightarrow Q$) is positive because the positive substitution effect outweighs the small, negative income effect.

Unlike Max, Maxine places only a small value on additional leisure compared to additional income; when the wage rises, she is willing to work more. Unlike Max, her supply curve is not backward-bending over the range of wage rates between w_1 and w_2. Instead, it slopes upward steadily; as the wage rises from w_0 to w_1 to w_2, her hours increase from 0 to 45 to 50.

As these two examples show, nothing *requires* that individual preferences (indifference maps) be such that the supply curve is backward-bending or upward-sloping. The only requirement is that the substitution effect be positive. Whether the income effect is actually negative, and whether it is big enough to offset the positive substitution effect, are empirical issues.

Labor economists have paid tremendous attention to these issues. Table 2.4 gives our best estimates of the size of these effects based on a summary of results from many studies of how labor supply decisions are affected by

TABLE 2.4 ESTIMATES OF LABOR SUPPLY ELASTICITIES[a] FOR MEN AND WOMEN

	Total Effect	Substitution Effect	Income Effect
Men			
Medium	0	0.10	–0.10
High	0.10	0.50	–0.40
Low	–0.10	–0.05	–0.05
Women			
Medium	0.80	1.00	–0.20
High	1.35	1.65	–0.30
Low	0.45	0.50	–0.05

[a]The range of the elasticities is the interquartile range of the set of estimates.

Source: Based on Mark Killingsworth, *Labor Supply*, New York: Cambridge University Press, 1983, Table 4.3.

changes in wage rates when other factors are held constant. The estimates are presented as **elasticities of labor supply**—percentage responses of hours supplied to 1 percent increases in wages or nonlabor income. These average estimates mask a wide variation in the underlying studies stemming from differences in data used, estimation techniques, and the demographic composition of the groups being studied. Most empirical studies of hours of work find that the substitution effect is positive as theory predicts it should be. Most have also found that income effects are negative, implying that for most people leisure is a normal good.

Empirical elasticities of hours supplied differ significantly by sex. Income effects may be slightly more negative for women than for men. The big difference, however, lies in substitution effects, which are far more positive for women. Among women the total elasticity is positive, implying that for the average woman the supply curve is always upward-sloping. The total elasticity of hours supplied by men is approximately zero. This means that for the average man the supply curve in Figure 2.2 would be nearly vertical around the going wage rate.

The difference in supply elasticities by sex implies that nonmarket activities are a more attractive option for women than for men. Thus, when nonlabor incomes rise, women reduce hours worked by a greater amount. Similarly, when wages fall, they are more willing to shift time from paid labor to nonmarket activities.

Remember that Figures 2.1 and 2.3 (as well as the estimates in Table 2.4) are comparative static analyses. They describe two equilibria, but not the process by which a worker moves from one to the other. As such, they may give the impression that an increase in the wage rate or in nonlabor income produces an *immediate* change in hours supplied of the size shown. This is inaccurate. Like much other behavior, people's labor supply is based partly on habit and institutional arrangements. A change in the regular hourly wage rate affects their behavior only slowly. It takes time before people realize that a wage change is permanent, and more time to adjust to the new set of circumstances facing them. Estimates are that it takes from two-and-one-half to four years before half of the eventual labor supply response to a change in wage rates occurs. One reason is that employers schedule hours for an entire group of workers and cannot alter just one worker's schedule. Workers find it much easier, therefore, to change their hours by changing jobs instead of trying to alter their supply of labor within the same job.[4]

---

[4]Richard Freeman, "Employment and Wage Adjustment Models in U.S. Manufacturing, 1950–1976," *Economic Forum* 11: 1–27 (1980); Edward Kalacheck, Fredric Raines, and Donald Larson, "The Determination of Labor Supply: A Dynamic Model," *Industrial and Labor Relations Review* 32: 367–377 (1979); Joseph Altonji and Christina Paxson, "Labor Supply, Hours Constraints, and Job Mobility," *Journal of Human Resources* 27: 256–278 (1992).

POLICY ISSUE

DUNNING DELINQUENT DADS

A series of legal reforms in recent years have increased the role of the federal and state governments in ensuring that child support ordered by courts is actually paid. Perhaps the most important reform allows wages to be garnisheed to recover overdue child support. Evidence suggests that these reforms have increased the fraction of ordered child support actually paid.[5] An economic question is what effect does increased enforcement have on labor supplies?

For men, garnisheeing wages is equivalent to a tax on their earnings. If earnings are reduced by a fixed amount no matter how much the man earns, the reduction produces a pure income effect on their hours of work. As we saw in Table 2.4, the consensus estimate is that income effects for men are very small, perhaps −.10. If, instead, earnings are reduced by a fixed percentage, both income and substitution effects are induced since the reduction is equivalent to a cut in the wage. Since Table 2.4 shows that the best estimate of the total supply elasticity for adult men is close to 0, no matter how the garnisheement is structured, men's labor supply should be affected only slightly.

For the divorced mother, added child support represents an increase in unearned income. As Table 2.4 shows, among women income effects are larger and this transfer from her ex-husband will reduce her working hours. One study of women based on the April 1979 and 1982 CPS indicates that a $1000 increase in child-support payments (a 60 percent increase) reduced the supply by 2 percent.[6] Thus, the overall impact of increased child support will be to reduce the aggregate supply of labor to the economy but to increase the amount of time divorced mothers spend with their children.

LABOR SUPPLY IN MORE THAN ONE PERIOD

So far we have treated the worker as if he made all his decisions with respect only to the current period. In fact, workers often take their entire lifetime earnings into account. We can save out of today's earnings in order to work less or consume more in the future. To some extent we can also borrow from future earnings to consume today, as anyone who has used their credit card to finance a trip around the world can attest. In Chapter 3 we will see why workers are willing to sacrifice both work and consumption today to invest in obtaining higher wages in the future.

Imagine Max and Maxine each receives a wage increase of $10 an hour. Max believes that this wage increase is permanent and will last for as long as he continues to work. Maxine, however, believes that her wage increase is temporary and will last only a short time. Perhaps there is unusually high

---

[5] Freya Sonenstein and Charles Calhoun, "Determinants of Child Support: A Pilot Survey of Absent Parents," *Contemporary Policy Issues* 8: 75–94 (1990).

[6] John Graham and Andrea Beller, "The Effect of Child Support Payments on the Labor Supply of Female Household Heads," *Journal of Human Resources* 24: 664–688 (1989).

demand for her services right now because of special developments in the product market, as would be true for a carpenter in South Florida just after a hurricane. Even though the wage changes in Figure 2.1 and 2.3 would look the same for both Max and Maxine, our understanding of income and substitution effects leads to a prediction that their labor supply responses will differ by far more than any differences in their utility functions might predict.

Max's wage increase has made him much wealthier because it represents a considerable increase in his **permanent income**. As such, it will have a relatively large income effect since he will want to consume some of this added wealth as additional leisure. Since wages are higher in every period, it does not matter when he consumes this leisure and he will spread it out over his lifetime.

Maxine, on the other hand, knows that if she doesn't "make hay while the sun shines" today, her wage will revert to its lower level soon. Her wage increase represents **transitory income**, and therefore not much of an increase in her wealth. Thus, her labor supply response will be almost entirely a substitution effect and she will work as many hours as she physically can during this period, deferring consumption of leisure to the future when it costs her less in terms of lost wages.

For most workers wages increase with age. This increase can be anticipated in advance, however, so workers do not feel any wealthier when it actually occurs. This behavior suggests that anticipated wage increases coming with experience do not have much if any income effect. The **intertemporal elasticity of labor supply**, which assumes that known future wage increases are already accounted for in an individual's utility, implies that when these increases happen the individual will stay on the same indifference curve (moving from $R \rightarrow Q$ in Figure 2.1 or 2.3). Intertemporal elasticities are generally found to be larger than conventional ones, since there is no negative income effect to offset the substitution effect.[7]

GOVERNMENT PROGRAMS AND THE SUPPLY OF HOURS

The decomposition of a wage change impact into income and substitution effects is not merely an expositional device. It allows us to examine both general economic issues and specific policy matters. Many states offer grand

---

[7]G. Ghez and G. Becker, *The Allocation of Time,* New York: Columbia University Press for NBER, (1975); J. MacCurdy, "An Empirical Model of Labor Supply in a Life-Cycle Setting," *Journal of Political Economy* 89: 1050–1085 (1981); J. Hotz, F. Kydland, and G. Sadlacek, "Intertemporal Preferences and Labor Supply," *Econometrica* 56: 335–360 (1988); K. Shaw, "Life-Cycle Labor Supply with Human Capital Accumulation," *International Economic Review* 30: 431–456 (1989); F. Jiang and S. Polachek, "Investment-Dependent Labor Supply Over the Life-Cycle," *Research in Labor Economics* 12: 245–267 (1991).

prizes in the state lottery that pay the winners substantial sums each year for many years. These represent a large addition of unearned income to the person's resources. Given the negative income effects that the estimates in the third column of Table 2.4 suggest exist, typical workers should reduce their supply of hours. If the income effect is sufficiently large, or the lottery prize is sufficiently generous, they may drop out of the labor force entirely. Now we turn to more significant policies that affect labor supply decisions for a large number of people.

TAXES

The most important application of labor supply theory has been to assess the effects of government programs that tax income earned by or transferred to households. So far we have treated the individual's budget line as having a constant slope with an absolute value equal to the market wage. If tax rates were constant, no matter how much people earned the budget line would be flatter just as if the wage rate were lower. In symbolic terms, if t is the tax rate, the slope of the budget line would have an absolute value $(1 - t)w$. This how much more a worker could earn by working an extra hour. The rest of her earnings (tw) would be taken by the government in higher taxes.

In most industrialized countries the tax rate on income is not constant. Instead, income tax is progressive, with tax rates rising as incomes rise. To simplify the analysis, assume there are only three tax rates. This case is shown by the budget line $0ABCD$ in Figure 2.4. Along the segment AB people retain most of their earnings. If they increase their hours of work by moving to the left of B, the tax rate rises, and the reward for more work is reduced. If they increase effort still further, to the left of C, the tax rate is higher still, and the net reward to an additional hour of labor is even less.

As is always the case, the taxpayer/worker will seek the highest attainable point on the budget line $0ABCD$. The position of that point depends on the person's preferences for income and leisure. What is interesting is how people might react to a change in the tax structure. Suppose there were only one tax rate—what is often called a **flat tax**. Most proposals for such tax reform often involve a single low rate but disallow many deductions from what is taxed to keep revenue unchanged. With a flat tax rate, this elimination of deductions reduces the income available to a consumer by the same amount at each income level and can therefore be represented as a reduction in nonlabor income from $0A$ to $0E$ in Figure 2.4. The lower rate would mean, however, that their take-home pay from each extra hour of work would rise and would not diminish if they worked more hours. For simplicity, we assume that the tax rate of all earnings in the flat tax situation is the same as the first tax rate under the initial tax system with three rates. If so, the new budget line facing the typical taxpayer/worker is $0EF$ (parallel to $0AB$).

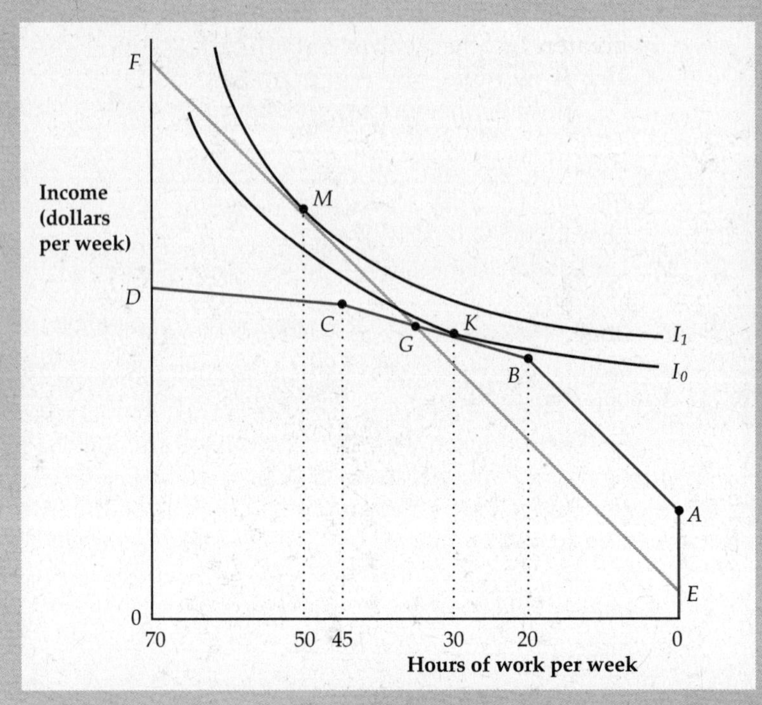

FIGURE 2.4 CHANGING FROM A PROGRESSIVE TO A FLAT TAX

By removing marginal disincentives to work, a revenue-neutral flat tax that alters the budget line from 0*ABCD* to 0*EGF* could induce a substantial increase in hours worked as the consumer's optimal combination of goods and leisure shifts from point *K* to point *M*.

How much will taxpayer/consumers wish to work when faced with the new tax structure? If they were not working much before, so that they were on segment 0*AB* under the old law, the tax change would not affect the wage rate they face. The only change is a reduction in after-tax nonlabor income of the amount *AE*. For these workers there is only an income effect. Since income effects on hours of work are usually negative, taxpayers will choose to supply more hours to the market under the flat tax.

For people who had initially worked more hours than at point *B*, the analysis is more complex and depends on individual circumstances. Consider people whose indifference curves are not shown in Figure 2.4 who had chosen point *G* before the tax change. For them, the tax change has no income effect since at point *G* their income is the same under either tax situation. An indifference curve that just touched the line segment *BC* at point *G* would not be the highest attainable once the budget line changed to 0*EF*. Instead, a higher indifference curve that touched the line segment *EF* to the left of point

G could be attained. The only effect is that the return to an hour of work is greater. In other words, only the substitution effect exists for them. They will clearly increase their hours of work.

Among other people, the effects are less clear-cut and depend on the relative importance of the income and substitution effects that are produced when the return to an hour of work changes. In some cases, small changes in the returns to work can produce huge changes in hours supplied. Consider people in Figure 2.4 who achieved the highest utility, I_0, at point K along BC. Under the changed tax system they find that their highest utility is achieved at point M on I_1, a higher indifference curve that was not feasible for them under the old tax system. Although only slightly better-off (the change from I_0 to I_1 is small), they greatly increase their hours supplied. This effect occurs because the flat rate tax situation makes available a ranges of choices, the area DFG, that these workers find very attractive.

TRANSFER PAYMENTS

In 1993 federal and state governments transferred $836 billion (roughly 13 percent of Gross National Product) to families and individuals. Among the many programs providing transfers that can affect the labor supply of recipients are Social Security, unemployment insurance, and welfare. The largest welfare program is **Aid to Families with Dependent Children (AFDC),** which in 1993 provided $22 billion to low-income households.[8] Under the program's regulations the amount of an AFDC grant is reduced when recipients earn income, giving an **implicit tax rate**, which was close to 100 percent by the early 1990s, on earned income.[9]

The situation faced by someone potentially eligible for AFDC is depicted in Figure 2.5. Such a low-income individual is unlikely to have much nonlabor income and is unlikely to earn enough to pay income taxes even if he or she did work full-time. Without a welfare program, the budget constraint faced by the individual is shown by $0AB$ in Figure 2.5. The worker will opt to work H hours at point P. With an AFDC grant of AC dollars and a 100 percent implicit tax rate, the recipient's budget line becomes $0CDB$. This individual, whose indifference map is represented by I_0 and I_1, will decide to drop out of the labor force and collect the welfare grant of AC. Of course, an individual

---

[8]In some states AFDC payments are only available to unmarried mothers and their children. Other states, worried about the incentive this policy creates for marriages to break up (or never form), also provide AFDC payments to low-income families containing unemployed fathers.

[9]In fact, given that most AFDC recipients also participate in other transfer programs such as food stamps and housing subsidies, the implicit tax rate for many families can exceed 100 percent. See Gary Burtless, "The Economist's Lament: Public Assistance in America," *Journal of Economic Perspectives* 4: 57–78 (1990); Robert Moffitt, "The Incentive Effects of the U.S. Welfare System: A Review," *Journal of Economic Literature* 30: 1–61 (1992).

POLICY ISSUE

IT'S ALL IN HOW YOU COUNT

Under current deficit reduction rules, Congress is required to "pay for" every dollar of lost revenue resulting from tax cuts with an offsetting dollar of spending cuts. Projections of the revenues to be gained from tax increases are used to forecast future deficits and predict the amount of money potentially available to fund increased spending. Both the Treasury Department and the Congressional Budget Office (CBO) have traditionally predicted the effect of tax law changes through the use of what is known as **static scoring**. Suppose that income tax rates were increased. Static scoring assumes that every worker continues to work exactly the same number of hours and makes revenue projections by simply multiplying current incomes by the new rates.

As Figure 2.4 makes clear, assuming that workers and consumers do not respond to tax changes violates basic economics. This error has led many analysts to call for a change to **dynamic scoring** under which responses to tax changes are taken into account. Perhaps the fallacy of static scoring is best seen in a request that Senator Robert Packwood made to the CBO in 1989. When asked what the impact would be of taxing all income over $200,000 at a 100 percent rate, the CBO responded that revenues would rise by $104 billion in the first year and $204 billion in the next year. See if you can draw an indifference map and a set of budget lines with a 100 percent tax on earnings over $200,000 a year that do not produce a decrease in revenue rather than an increase of hundreds of billions of dollars.

Of course, the impact of more realistic changes depends on whether a worker is on the forward or backward sloping part of their labor supply curve. Hours of work for a particular worker might change in either direction, and the total effect on the economy would depend on which workers are on which parts of their labor supply curve as well as just how the tax change is structured. Given the elasticities in Table 2.4, we might expect most changes to have relatively small impacts on labor hours. Studies of income taxation in the United States, France, Italy, the Netherlands, and Sweden using data from the early 1980s suggest that it has little impact on hours supplied by men, and a larger, though still not huge, effect on women's labor supply. For example, estimates for the U.S. suggest that income taxes reduce men's labor supply by only 3 percent but women's by at least 10 percent.[10] Of course, a finding that labor supply is reduced only a small amount by higher taxes does not imply that government revenues are unaffected. One study found that higher taxes result in a substantial shift of work time from the legal, reported economy to the **underground economy**.[11] It is also likely that other areas of the economy, such as the realization of capital gains, are far more affected by tax incentives than labor supply.

---

[10] "Special Issue on Taxation and Labor Supply in Industrial Countries," *Journal of Human Resources* 25: 313–558 (1990), including Robert Triest, "The Effect of Income Taxation on Labor Supply in the United States."

[11] Thomas Lemieux, Bernard Fortin, and Pierre Fréchette, "The Effect of Taxes on Labor Supply in the Underground Economy," *American Economic Review* 84: 231–254 (1994).

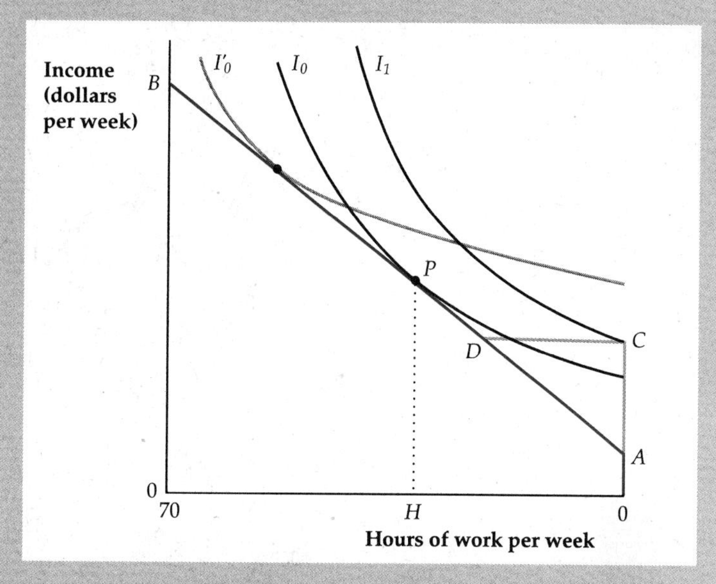

FIGURE 2.5 AN AFDC GRANT WITH A 100 PERCENT TAX RATE

Providing welfare benefits equal to *AC* but taxing these benefits at a 100 percent rate when income is earned creates budget line 0*CDB*. Given this budget line, many individuals will reach their highest possible utility at point *C*.

with a different set of preferences, represented by the dashed indifference curve I_0' would not respond to the offer of a welfare grant.[12]

An obvious solution to the problem depicted in Figure 2.5 is to reform the welfare system by reducing the implicit tax on earnings. Such a goal has been behind many calls to replace all current welfare programs with a **negative income tax**. A negative income tax would work by offering every family a basic or **guaranteed income** even if they did not work, and then reducing this grant by an implicit tax rate for each dollar of earned income. In order to avoid the problem depicted in Figure 2.5, the proposed implicit tax rate was much less than 100 percent. Despite an impressive array of advocates, including Presidents Nixon, Ford, and Carter, the U.S. has never adopted a negative income tax. Why not?

---

[12]Do not be confused by the fact that indifference curve I_0' crosses indifference curve I_0. Indifference curves cannot cross *for a given individual*. Unless two individuals have exactly the same tastes and preferences, indifference curves for different individuals *must* cross.

The answer lies in the fact that the numbers cannot add up. Since a negative income tax is supposed to replace all current welfare programs, we certainly would want the base grant to be large enough to support a family who could not work. Suppose we made this grant equal to the poverty level for a family of four ($14,335 in 1992). To avoid disincentives to work, the tax rate should not be too high. Suppose we really stretched and made it 40 percent, about the highest rate applied to the richest Americans. These terms would mean that a family would be getting a subsidy (and not paying any income tax) if their earnings were less than $35,838 ($14,335/.4), a point known as the **break-even point**. But in 1992 the *median* income of all American families was only $35,776. Thus, with reasonable conditions, half of all American families would be "on welfare" under this negative income tax. It is doubtful that the remaining workers would be willing to pay sufficient taxes to finance these benefits plus all the other activities of government.

Clearly, the guaranteed benefit would have to be considerably lower, the tax rate considerably higher, and/or many families ruled ineligible. In any of these cases, the negative income tax would quickly come to resemble the current welfare system.

NONSTANDARD WORK SCHEDULES

Throughout this chapter we have discussed individuals' choices about hours as if there were a single worker whose preferences determined the workweek. As Table 2.3 has shown, in the U.S. there is a substantial clustering of workers around 40 hours, which has come to be viewed as the standard work-

POLICY ISSUE

THE END OF WELFARE AS WE KNOW IT

Another possible way of reforming the welfare system is to adopt some form of "workfare," where recipients have to work for their grant. Figure 2.6 shows how one such workfare system might work. Budget line *OAB* shows the income/hours options for someone who worked a minimum wage job. The workfare program would guarantee anyone who asked for one a government job where he or she would work *H* hours per week and receive a grant of *CD* dollars. The grant *CD* is somewhat less than what the person would earn if he worked *H* hours at the minimum wage. Anyone who received a welfare grant would have to work *H* hours for the government but then could work additional hours at the minimum wage. Therefore, the slope of the segment *DE* is the same as *AB*. Clearly, unlike Figure 2.5, no person who could find a job in the private sector would ever find it optimal to accept the welfare grant. Thus, the workfare program would automatically be restricted only to those who really needed it. Of course, this would not be true if workfare recipients also received additional benefits such as medical care, subsidized child care, or preference for public housing that were not available to workers not on welfare. Can you draw what the budget lines might look like in this situation?

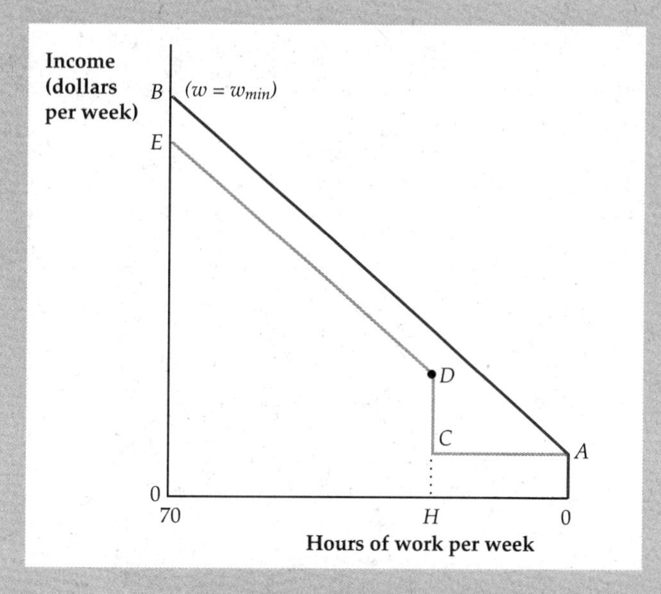

FIGURE 2.6 A WORKFARE BUDGET CONSTRAINT

If *H* hours of work are required in return for a welfare grant of *CD* dollars (less than *H* times the minimum wage), then budget line 0*ACDE* ensures that only those who cannot find a job will accept the welfare payment.

week. Yet, as the table also makes clear, 32 percent of the labor force supplies more than 40 hours per week and 25 percent supplies less than 35 hours. In part, this diversity reflects differences in individuals' tastes. In part, it results from the rewards to choosing alternative patterns of hours to supply.

LONG WORKWEEKS AND OVERTIME

Many of those working more than 40 hours per week (and a few working less than this) are working **overtime** or extra hours beyond those regularly scheduled on their jobs. In recent years roughly 10 percent of full-time employees in a typical week receive extra pay for working overtime. If we focus on the supply response, this extra pay reflects premium rates that reward workers' willingness to work long hours. On the demand side, overtime can be viewed as a penalty on employers, as we will see in Chapter 5. In the U.S. overtime is almost always paid at 1.5 times the straight-time rate because of provisions in the **Fair Labor Standards Act of 1938**. The practice differs in other countries. For example, in Britain 1.25 and 1.33 times the

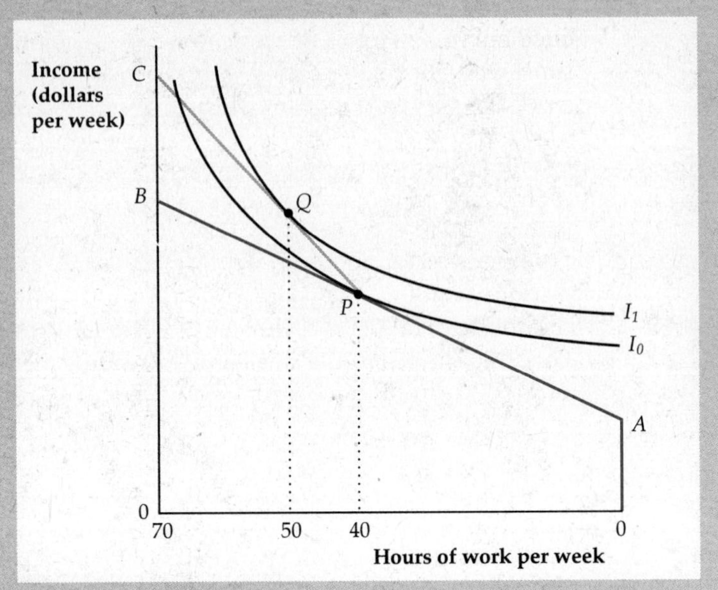

FIGURE 2.7 THE CHOICE OF OVERTIME HOURS

A premium for overtime work produces a large substitution effect relative to the income effect. This is likely to create a substantial impact on hours worked. Workers who opted to work 40 hours a week at point *P* without the overtime premium would never choose that number of hours if they were offered overtime pay.

straight-time rate are often used, while in Australia overtime premiums are more like those in the U.S.

Figure 2.7 shows the worker's response to overtime premiums under the assumption that they can freely choose the amount of overtime they work. They can earn a straight-time wage w_0 for each hour worked, shown by the slope of *AB*. Let us assume that if no overtime were paid, workers would achieve the greatest satisfaction along I_0, at point *P*, working 40 hours per week. If an overtime premium of time and a half beyond 40 hours is introduced and overtime work is freely available, they could choose any combination of income and leisure along the lines 0*APC*. Point *P* would no longer be the best they could do, because their $MRS_{L\$}$ is now less than what the market would pay for another hour of work, $1.5w_0$ in this example. Since the pay for the extra hour exceeds their reservation wage, they would move to where their

$$MRS_{L\$} = 1.5w_0$$

choosing point Q on indifference curve I_1, which is higher than the indifference curve I_0. Hours of work now rise from 40 to 50. Premium pay for overtime will call forth more hours of work from anyone who initially chose to work the standard workweek. A very small increase in the premium above the standard rate produces only a positive substitution effect on hours supplied. In general, since there is no increase in wages for the first 40 hours worked each week, an overtime premium has a larger substitution effect relative to its income effect than an increase in the base wage of the same amount.

It should be obvious from Figure 2.7 that, in the presence of overtime, no worker would ever opt to work exactly the standard workweek since no convex indifference curve can ever be tangent to budget line $0APC$ at point P. This finding provides strong evidence that the actual workweek is, at least in part, set by interaction between workers and employers.

LONG WORKWEEKS AND MOONLIGHTING

While some people who want to work more than the standard workweek can work overtime, others may not have this opportunity on their main job. **Moonlighting** or working at two jobs is an option for some workers who do not value leisure very highly and cannot work as long as they would like on their first job. Table 2.5 shows that moonlighting is not very widespread in the U.S., but showed a sharp increase during the late 1980s among women.

POLICY ISSUE

CAN AN OVERTIME LAW HAVE ANY EFFECT?

Figure 2.7 probably reflects what Congress thought it could accomplish by passing a law requiring time-and-a-half for work in excess of 40 hours a week. Indifference curve I_1 lies above indifference curve I_0, and the worker is made better-off by the overtime premium. For this result to occur, however, workers must be free to choose their hours, rather than having to accept a job that sets both hours of work and pay.

Suppose that budget line $0AB$ in Figure 2.8 represents the world without any attempt by government to impose an overtime premium. Workers would pick point P on indifference curve I_0, working H hours per week and receiving a total income of M dollars per week. Now suppose that Congress passes a law requiring a 50 percent overtime premium. All the employer has to do is reduce the base wage by a little bit, so that the new budget line, $0ACD$ passes through point P. Of course, given a free choice, the worker would now like to work H' hours at point Q. If the employer offers only H hours, however, the worker will end up at point P with income M, and passage of the law would have changed nothing.[13]

---

[13] Stephen Trejo, "Compensating Differentials and Overtime Pay Regulation," *American Economic Review* 81: 719–740 (1991).

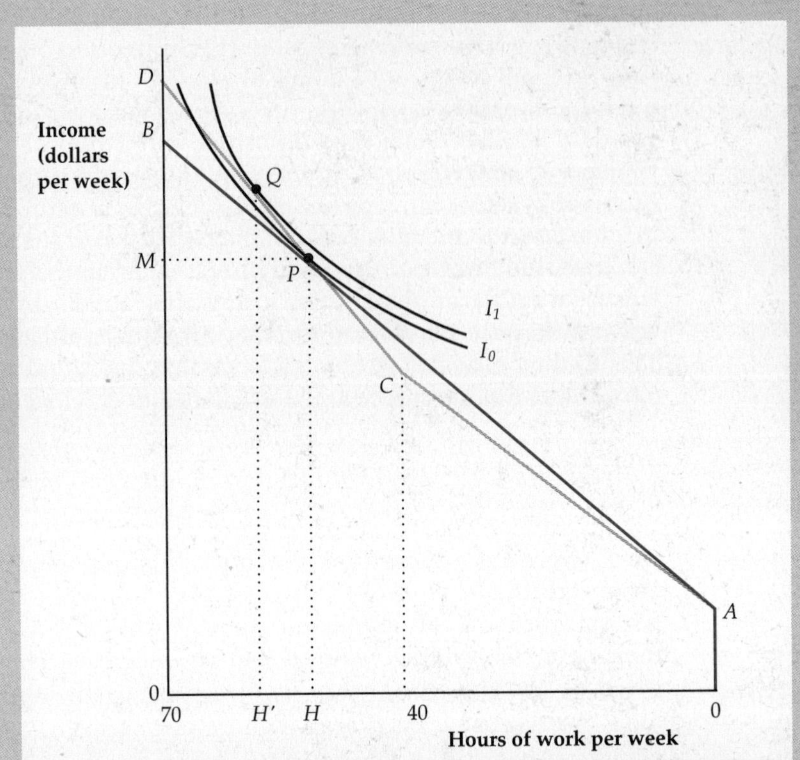

FIGURE 2.8 AN OVERTIME PREMIUM WITH NO EFFECT
If firms and workers can sign contracts that stipulate both wages and hours of work, they can respond to the introduction of an overtime premium by reducing base wages but fixing the hours of work. This results in the worker having the same utility and the firm the same labor cost as without the premium.

In 1970 women were much less likely than men to hold two jobs. Today there is only a small difference by sex. Why might this have occurred?

Consider the people whose behavior is described in Figure 2.9. If they could choose their hours freely at the wage on their main jobs, they would be able to choose any point along the line $0AB$. Given their preferences, the highest indifference level attainable is at point P along indifference curve I_2. If their employers do not offer more than 40 hours of work, the best they can do on their current jobs is to work 40 hours at point Q, attaining a level of satisfaction indicated by indifference curve I_0. At point Q, $MRS_{L\$}$ is less than w (the slope of $0AB$), and workers would be more than willing to give up the additional hour of leisure to obtain a wage of w.

TABLE 2.5 PERCENTAGE OF MOONLIGHTERS AMONG THE EMPLOYED, UNITED STATES, 1970–1994

Year	Total	Men	Women
1970	5.2	7.0	2.2
1975	4.7	5.8	2.9
1980	4.9	5.8	3.8
1985	5.4	5.9	4.7
1991	6.2	6.4	5.9
1994	5.9	5.9	5.9

Sources: John Stinson, "Multiple Jobholding Up Sharply in the 1980s," *Monthly Labor Review* 113: 3–12 (July 1990); U.S. Bureau of Labor Statistics, *News*, USDL 91–547 (1991); *Employment and Earnings*, January 1995, p. 206.

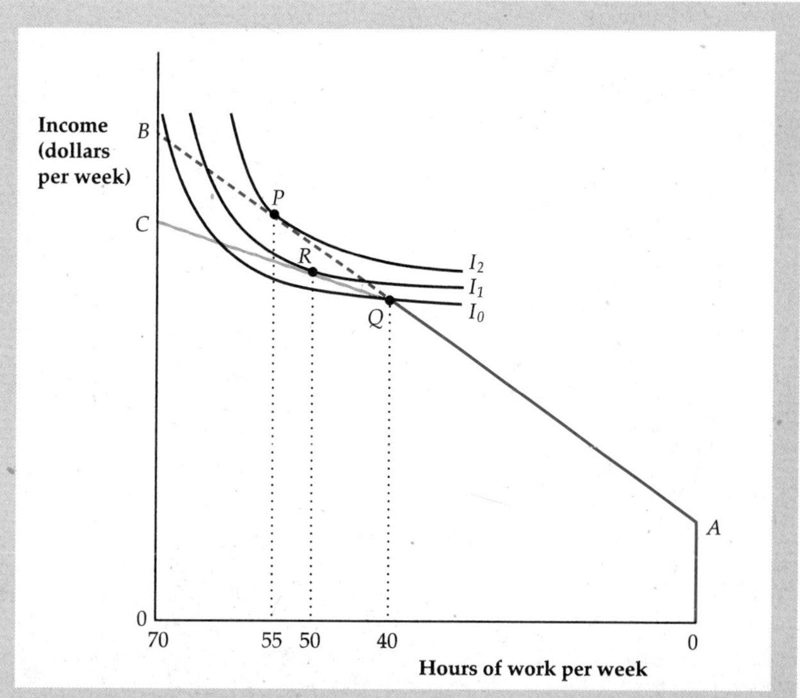

FIGURE 2.9 THE DECISION TO MOONLIGHT

Even though wages on a second job may be much lower than on their main job (the slope *QC* is less than *AQ*), workers constrained in how many hours they can work on their main job may be better off moonlighting at point *R* than only working the constrained number of hours on their primary job at point *Q*.

What if second jobs become available that offer workers as many hours per week as they wish, but at wage rate w_1, lower than the rate they receive on their primary jobs? The budget line then becomes $0AQC$ with the segment QC having a smaller slope than QB because w_1, the wage on the jobs at which they can moonlight, is less than w, the wage on their primary jobs. This is a reasonable assumption. Among one sample of American men in 1984, the average wage on their secondary jobs was $4.46 an hour, barely half of the wage on their primary jobs of $8.84 an hour.[14]

To achieve the highest satisfaction, individuals whose preferences are depicted in Figure 2.9 will choose point R and attain an indifference level, I_1, greater than the I_0 attainable without moonlighting. Although they are not as well-off as if their primary employers allowed them to work 55 hours at the regular straight-time wage rates, their weak desire for leisure makes them better off moonlighting than not. Other individuals, whose indifference curves are not shown, might work 55 hours if they could obtain a wage w, but offer only 40 hours if they can only obtain w_1. Thus the inability to earn as high a wage on the second job adds to the clustering of hours worked around 40 that we observed in Table 2.3.

A number of different factors affect the probability that a worker will moonlight. Data for some developing countries (such as the Ivory Coast and Peru) for the mid-1980s show that people are more likely to moonlight when the wage rates on their main jobs are reduced. Among a sample of men in the U.S. in 1984, a lower wage rate on the second job, a higher wage rate on the primary job, longer hours on the primary job, and increased wife's earnings all decreased the number of moonlighting hours.[15] Each of these four effects is predicted by the analysis in Figure 2.9. For example, an increase in a wife's earnings produces a negative income effect that lowers hours of work by her husband.

How can the upward trend in moonlighting rates among women and their convergence toward the behavior of men be explained? In part, it results from the relative decline in male earnings (see Chapter 14) but, more importantly, from the growing number of women without a spouse present (and, thus, no other earnings in the household). The latter change produces a negative income effect that increases the supply of labor. More generally, the increase in moonlighting among women reflects the same kind of convergence in labor supply between the sexes that we saw for the U.S. in Table 1.7.

Of course there are other reasons why an individual might choose to moonlight. The second job might be higher paying but not always available

[14] Jean Kimmel and Karen Smith Conway, "A Duration Model of Moonlighting," W. E. Upjohn Institute for Employment Research, Photocopy (1994).

[15] Jacques van der Gaag, Morton Stelcner, and Wim Vijverberg, "Wage Differentials and Moonlighting by Civil Servants: Evidence from Côte d'Ivoire and Peru," *The World Bank Economic Review* 3: 67–95 (1989); Pramila Krishnan, "The Economics of Moonlighting: A Double Self-Selection Model," *Review of Economics and Statistics* 72: 361–367 (1990).

(or not available at all without the credentials provided from the first job), such as a professor who offers expert court testimony in her off hours. Alternatively, the second job may provide consumption rewards but insufficient income to pursue full-time. An obvious example is the actor who is not successful enough to give up his "day job" as a waiter. The evidence is that, although other factors play a part, constraints on the number of hours individuals can work on their main job is the major reason for moonlighting.[16]

SHIFT WORK, FLEX-TIME WORK, AND PART-TIME WORK

The supply of hours depends not only on the number but also on the pattern of hours during the workweek. Many jobs must be covered 24 hours a day. Examples include police, fire, and medical workers; broadcasters; and electric power plant operators. In other industries, large investments in capital dictate multiple shifts. It is simply too expensive, for example, to leave a multibillion dollar automobile assembly line idle for two-thirds of every day. In some continuous-processing operations, such as steel mills and petroleum refineries, it is necessary for the plant to operate 168 hours a week. In general, workers are reluctant to work night shifts or weekends and must receive extra compensation to persuade them to do so. Another undesirable work situation is the split shift, often used in fast-food restaurants, in which a worker works several hours during the lunchtime rush and several more at dinnertime.

Such strange work schedules are much more common than one might suspect. In the U.S., only about 75 percent of manufacturing workers regularly work day shifts. About 15 percent regularly work evening or night shifts, while the rest work rotating shifts. When shift-work exists in an organization, this work is often shared among workers. Thus, among service workers in 1991, only 57 percent always worked a day shift, while 15 percent always worked an evening shift, and 9 percent a night shift. The remaining 19 percent worked variable shifts on either a regular or irregular rotation.

In some cases this pattern of labor supply may accord with workers' preferences. In particular, by working different shifts parents can avoid having to pay for child care. In other cases, the need for shift work occasioned by employers' requirements necessitates payment of premium rates for undesirable shifts. In the United States these premiums are fairly low. Among manufacturing workers in the May 1985 CPS, the average premium for shift work was only 8 percent. Premiums for the night shift only were a bit higher, 10 percent. Unlike overtime premiums in most industries, these shift premiums are generally set too low to overcome worker aversion to night and split

[16] Karen Smith Conway and Jean Kimmel, "Male Labor Supply Estimates and the Decision to Moonlight," Department of Economics, University of New Hampshire, Photocopy (1994).

shifts. Thus, in the absence of rotation, these shifts are staffed by workers with the least seniority or those at the greatest disadvantage in the labor market. For example, in the May 1985 CPS the average shift worker had nearly two years less seniority than the average daytime worker. In other countries, shift premiums are often larger than they are in the U.S. In France second-shift workers receive about 10 percent higher pay while night-shift workers can earn as much as 30 percent more.[17]

Related to shift work, but stemming more directly from workers' preferences, is **flex-time**. This takes such forms as longer workdays in a four-day week, four long and one short workday, or late starting and finishing times. The first example is an obvious way of minimizing the fixed costs of attending work, including commuting and the fixed component of child care that we discussed in Chapter 1, as well as allowing workers to bunch their leisure time.[18] According to the CPS, in 1991 over 15 percent of all workers could vary the time they began and ended work. This was an increase of almost 3 percentage points since 1985. A large fraction of these people are managers, professionals, and sales workers who are not paid by the hour, but more than 7.5 percent of production workers in manufacturing, construction, and transportation also have flexible schedules. One survey of 1034 U.S. firms found that 60 percent offered some form of flexible scheduling. Another survey found that almost a quarter of employees eligible for flexible schedules take advantage of this opportunity.[19]

Working the standard workweek or longer on one job is the apparent preference of most labor force participants. As shown in Table 2.3, however, a large and increasing fraction of workers work less than the 35 hours per week considered full-time in the U.S. Substantial increases in the share of workers who work part time have also occurred in West European countries, also in large part because of labor supply decisions resulting from women's desire to combine work and family responsibilities. For example, between 1975 and 1991 the share of part-time workers among all workers increased from 8.2 percent to 12.3 percent in France, 17.1 percent to 23.1 percent in the U.K., and 8.7 percent to 32 percent in the Netherlands. Of the 24.6 percent of workers in the U.S. who work part-time, most did not want or could not accept full-time jobs. Similarly, in Australia the majority of part-time workers

[17]*Monthly Labor Review*, 108: 7 (December 1985); Peter Kostiuk, "Compensating Differentials for Shift Work," *Journal of Political Economy* 98: 1054–1075 (1990); Horst Entorf and Francis Kramarz, "The Impact of New Technologies on Wages: Lessons From Matching Panels of Workers and Their Firms," Paris: INSEE Discussion Paper No. 9407 (1994).

[18]Rebecca Blank, "Simultaneously Modeling the Supply of Weeks and Hours of Work among Female Household Heads," *Journal of Labor Economics* 6: 177–204 (1988).

[19]U.S. Bureau of Labor Statistics, *News* USDL 92–491 (1992); Jaclyn Fierman, "Are Companies Less Family-Friendly?" *Fortune* pp: 64–68 (March 21, 1994).

were not seeking full-time work.[20] The fraction of the American labor force voluntarily at work part-time grew rapidly from the early 1950s until 1970 but has been remarkably constant since then at around 13 percent.

Relatively few married men or prime-age women (25 to 54 years old) without young children are part-time workers. The part-time work force consists disproportionately of women with young children, teenagers, and older workers. Seventy-two percent of teenage nonfarm employees worked part-time in 1994, as did 35 percent of workers 55 or older, but only 13 percent of men 25 to 54 voluntarily worked part-time schedules.

Even accounting for the impact of demographic forces, purely economic forces play a major part in the choice to work full- or part-time. One study suggests that a 1 percent increase in the hourly wage for part-time work would induce a 5 percent increase in the supply of part-time workers relative to the number of full-time workers.[21] This response seems large. It reinforces the observation that hours of work supplied by people with a relatively loose attachment to the labor force are responsive to changes in the returns to work. It also suggests why part-time workers are paid a much lower wage rate (16 percent lower for American workers, 10 percent for Canadian workers in the early 1980s) compared to otherwise identical full-time workers. Workers with loose attachments to the labor force are likely to enter and leave it often, involving additional hiring and training costs for employers.[22]

THE SUPPLY OF EFFORT

So far the discussion of labor supply has referred to scheduled hours (hours paid for) or to hours spent at the workplace. Each hour at work has been treated as if it measured the same amount of effort being offered, and thus the same **effective supply of labor.** In reality this may not be the case. If workers' attendance at the workplace is erratic, their productivity per hour on the job will be less than that of otherwise identical workers. The employer may be forced to maintain a larger work force merely to prevent operations from being slowed down by an unexpectedly large number of absentee workers on a particular day.

---

[20] Frederike Maier, "Institutional Regimes of Part-Time Working," in Günther Schmid (ed.). *Labor Market Institutions in Europe,* Armonk NY: M. E. Sharpe (1994); Peter Dawkins and Keith Norris, "Casual Employment in Australia," *Australian Bulletin of Labour* 16: 156–173 (1990).

[21] John Owen, *Working Hours,* Lexington, Mass.: Heath, p.: 67 (1979).

[22] B. F. Kiker and Blaine Roberts, "The Durability of Human Capital: Some New Evidence," *Economic Inquiry* 22: 269–281 (1984); Wayne Simpson, "Analysis of Part-Time Pay in Canada," *Canadian Journal of Economics* 19: 798–807 (1986).

POLICY ISSUE

THE EARNINGS TEST FOR SOCIAL SECURITY

The design of the Social Security retirement program provides a partial explanation of why part-time work is common among the elderly. It also provides an opportunity to test the extent to which workers treat earnings at different periods in their lifetime as substitutes. In 1994, workers between 65 and 69 who were eligible for Social Security could earn up to $11,160 per year without losing any retirement benefits, but had to give up $1 for each $3 earned beyond that. After their 70th birthday, workers' benefits were unaffected by their earnings. More importantly, benefits given up because a worker earned more than the allowable amount were returned to him (with interest) in the form of higher benefits after he turned 70. What does labor supply theory predict about the behavior of those subject to the earnings test?

If workers act without regard to future income (called **myopic workers**), the implicit tax rate in this **earnings test** represents a cut in their wages. Without Social Security benefits, their budget line is like 0*AB* in Figure 2.10, where we assume the budget line already accounts for income taxes on earnings. With Social Security and the application of the earnings test, the budget line shifts to 0*CDEB*. The segment *CD* is parallel to *AB*, because workers can earn income at their usual wage rate w_1 and keep each dollar earned. To the left of point *D* workers' earnings exceed $11,160 and each additional dollar earned yields only 66 ⅔ cents of income, reducing the slope of *DE* to two-thirds that of *AB* or *CD*. To the left of point *E* the worker earns more than $33,480 (three times $11,160) and receives no benefits.

Myopic workers who achieve their highest indifference level at point *P* along I_0 are induced by the presence of the earnings test to change their behavior when they become eligible for benefits. The return to extra hours of work beyond H_1 is cut by a third, and their incomes are also higher because of the benefits *DF* paid if they work only H_1 hours. The first change induces a substitution effect that reduces work hours. The second induces an income effect in the same direction. Together they lead workers to a higher indifference level, I_1, where they are better off than before but work fewer hours, perhaps even part-time.

Now consider the impact of the earnings test on forward-looking workers who optimize over several periods and know that if their benefits are reduced today, they will increase in the future. For these workers there is no income or substitution effect. The only thing that has changed is the timing of their income, not its amount. Their behavior should not be altered at all.

Although increasing future benefits in response to present reductions for earnings over the maximum may be fair on average, it will not be fair to every person. People who live longer than average will actually gain because they will receive the higher future benefits for longer, while people who die relatively soon will lose since they will not live long enough to get all their deferred benefits back. Interestingly, some research has found that men, who tend to die younger, do reduce their hours of work in response to the earnings test, while women, who live longer and would benefit from deferring benefits, do not reduce hours.[23]

---

[23] Cordelia Reimers and Marjorie Honig, "Responses to Social Security by Men and Women: Myopic and Far-Sighted Behavior," *Journal of Human Resources* 31: forthcoming (1996).

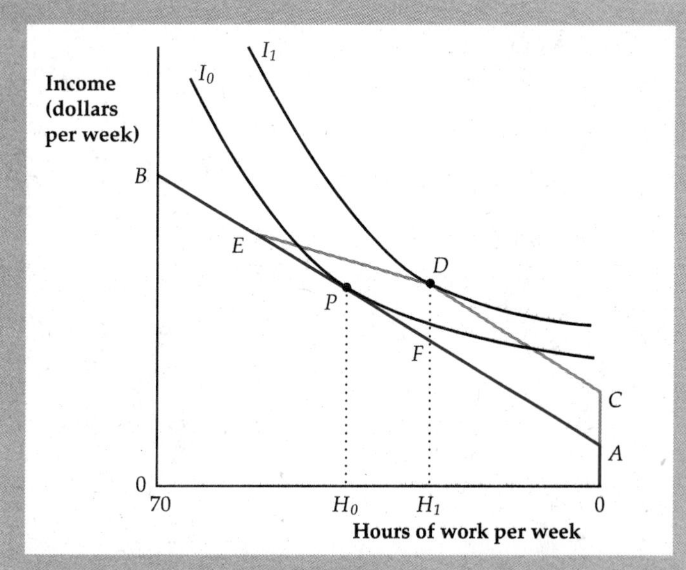

FIGURE 2.10 THE EFFECT OF A SOCIAL SECURITY EARNINGS TEST FOR MYOPIC WORKERS

If workers do not take into account future benefit increases in response to reductions in current benefits when they have an earned income greater than H_1w, they will perceive their budget constraint to be 0*CDEB*. This will cause many workers to reduce their hours of work to H_1 or less.

Table 2.6 shows that paid sick leave accounted for over 1 percent of wage and salary costs. Estimates of total absenteeism in 1994 (both paid and unpaid) based on the CPS were 4.2 percent of scheduled work hours. As the table indicates, the costs of paid vacations and holidays are large and growing rapidly. As the income effect of their increased real wage rates induces them to consume additional leisure, Americans have chosen to take a growing fraction of their leisure in the form of paid sick leave, vacations, and holidays rather than as reductions in the standard workweek or as reduced labor force participation. European countries generally offer even greater time off for vacations, holidays, and sick leave, as their shorter work years shown in Table 2.2 suggest.

Illness and pressing personal business are common reasons for absenteeism. Workers whose health is worse are more likely to be absent. The requirement of a fixed work schedule is also associated with a greater likelihood of being absent. For example, a plant that was put on flex-time saw a sharp reduction in absenteeism. Economic factors are important as well. To the extent that the labor supply curve is upward-sloping, absenteeism will be

TABLE 2.6 PAID TIME NOT AT WORK AS A PERCENT OF WAGE AND SALARY COSTS, 1929–1993

	1929	1955	1965	1975	1985	1993
Vacation	0.3	3.0	3.8	4.8	5.2	5.6
Holidays	0.3	2.0	2.5	3.2	3.5	3.1
Sick leave	0.1	0.8	0.8	1.2	1.3	1.3
Other time paid but not worked	0.0	0.1	0.2	0.2	0.3	0.4

Source: U.S. Chamber of Commerce, *Employee Benefits,* Washington, D.C.: Chamber of Commerce, 1986 p. 30; (1994) p. 15.

lower where the wage rate is higher. Accounting for the presence of paid time off, and holding skill level constant, the absentee rate in one sample of American workers decreased by 5 percent for each 10 percent increase in the wage rate. Among Australian workers from the 1960s through the 1980s a 10 percent increase in wages lowered the absentee rate by 6 percent. Among inner-city American youth economic factors such as wage rates and opportunities for advancement not only were significant determinants of absenteeism but were found to be as important as personal characteristics such as grades and participation in criminal activities.[24]

Hours away from work are easy to identify. At least as important, but far harder to measure, is effort while at work. This complex issue gets to the heart of the interaction between management and workers. It relates to personnel administration and employers' attempts to elicit greater effort from their workers. Economic determinants of effort are a major focus of attention in the crucial area of **internal labor markets,** the subject of Chapter 9. As with hours per week or per year, changes in wage rates should also affect the supply of effort.

SUMMARY

Hours of work in developed nations have been decreasing since 1900. In the U.S. the rate of decline has slowed since World War II, while in Europe it continued rapidly through the 1970s. This decrease reflects the long-run pre-

[24] Steven Allen, "An Empirical Model of Work Attendance," *Review of Economics and Statistics* 63: 77–87 (1981); Dan Dalton and Debra Mesch, "The Impact of Flexible Scheduling on Employee Attendance and Turnover," *Administrative Science Quarterly* 35: 370–387 (1990); Peter Kenyon and Peter Dawkins, "A Time Series Analysis of Labour Absence in Australia," *Review of Economics and Statistics* 71: 232–239 (1989); Ronald Ferguson and Randall Filer, "Do Better Jobs Make Better Workers? Absenteeism from Work Among Inner-City Black Youths," in Richard Freeman and Harry Holzer (eds.). *The Black Youth Employment Crisis,* Chicago: University of Chicago Press for NBER (1986).

dominance of the income effect of higher wage rates on the demand for leisure over the substitution effect. At a given point in time, higher wage rates elicit a greater supply of hours from most workers, although the effects are generally rather small. They are greatest among married women with young children, younger workers, and workers nearing retirement. For these groups both income and substitution effects differ significantly from zero, with the substitution effect being the larger of the two. Among prime-age men and increasingly among prime-age women, the income and substitution effects of higher wage rates are both very small so that the elasticity of their labor supply is approximately zero.

Changes in tax systems and transfer programs have the potential to affect the labor force participation and hours supplied by workers. The particular effects depend on the nature of the program, especially how it affects the budget line that shows the choices workers face. In general, the impacts of tax and transfer programs on labor supply are smallest on workers for whom the income and substitution effects of higher wage rates are smallest—those people whose labor supply is the least elastic.

Fewer than half of workers in the U.S. work exactly 40 hours a week. Part-time work and moonlighting are not uncommon and are affected by variations in wage rates paid for part-time work or for second jobs. Among people with a scheduled standard workweek, many work overtime. The greater the extra pay, the more workers will seek it. Absenteeism, unscheduled work breaks, and variations in effort while at work increase the difference between hours paid for and the actual supply of work effort. These, too, are reduced when the earnings loss they produce rises. Together with the declining average length of the workweek, the fact that paid leisure such as holidays and vacation time has been growing in importance provides further evidence that income effects from higher real wages dominate substitution effects.

QUESTIONS AND PROBLEMS

2.1 Graph Maxine's labor supply curve, using the approach used in the text to graph Max's labor supply curve.

2.2 Draw the indifference map for Maximilian, who reacts to an increase in the wage rate with a *positive* income effect, and show his utility-maximizing choice of labor supply at two different wage rates. Then use this graph to draw his labor supply curve.

2.3 Several years ago a number of people proposed a credit income tax. Each person would receive a $2000 grant no matter what. To pay for this the average tax rate on labor income would rise from the current 15 percent to 20 percent. Assume that the tax rate is the same on all workers (i.e., the tax is not progressive now or after the proposal is instituted). Analyze how typical workers' labor force participation rates and hours supplied would differ before and after the imposition of this proposal. Also, discuss how the effects would differ between men 25 to 54 and all persons 55 to 64.

2.4 Under the tax law in effect in 1994 there is an earned income tax credit for low-wage workers—extra income is given to them by the federal government under certain circumstances. There is no credit if nothing is earned. The credit peaks at $2,528 when the worker has earned around $9,000, and is phased out completely if the worker earns $25,000 or more per year. Assuming the worker faces no other taxes, graph the budget line that the credit creates for a typical worker earning w per hour. Analyze how the imposition of the credit affects hours of labor supplied. Assuming that substitution effects are larger than income effects for the typical low-wage worker, is it necessarily so that the credit increases hours of work for all those who are eligible? Why or why not?

2.5 Graph the typical worker's indifference map for income and leisure between 9 A.M. and 5 P.M. Using what you have learned about premium pay for shift work, graph the same worker's indifference map for income and leisure between 1 A.M. and 9 A.M. How does the worker's reservation wage differ in the two situations? What are the differences between the magnitudes of the income and substitution effects produced by increased wage rates in each of the two periods?

2.6 John has preferences over income and leisure represented by the following utility function:

$$U(I, L) = I^2 * L,$$

where I is income and L is leisure.

a. Under what terms will John be willing to trade off one hour of leisure for additional income?

b. The market wage rate is 1, and John doesn't have any unearned income (so that $I = H$, where H is number of hours worked). Find his "desired" (i.e., utility maximizing) number of hours worked per day ($L + H = 24$). Is your result a surprise? If yes, what do you think drives John's desired number of hours worked?

c. Suppose that under current law, John is not allowed to work more than 8 hours per day. Given this law, how many hours will he work? What will be the value of his utility? Compare this value with the utility-maximizing value without any law that constrains the number of hours he can work.

d. Given your answer to part (c), what might be the economic justifications, if any, for a law that constrains how many hours someone can work?

2.7 There is a great deal of evidence that the fraction of total available time spent by the adult population in market work has decreased during this century in almost every industrialized country. This decrease has been greater for hours worked by those in the labor force than for labor force participation rates. These changes have occurred at the same time as the largest sustained increase in real wages the world has ever seen. How can you reconcile these trends given the evidence that men's labor supply curves have a slope that is close to zero and may even be positive?

2.8 At any point in time, the higher the husband's income in a family, the lower the labor supply of the wife. Over the past 40 years men's wages have risen considerably, especially for more educated men. At the same time, however, married women's labor supply has also risen, most dramatically for women married to highly educated men. What factors might explain this apparently anomalous pattern? Illustrate as many of these as you can with appropriately shifted budget lines and indifference curves.

2.9 Define a "workaholic" as someone for whom work makes a positive contribution to utility independent of any income it generates. Draw the indifference curves for such an individual. Where will her optimum leisure/income point be given a nonlabor income of $\$Y$ and a wage rate of $\$w$ per hour?

2.10 Consider the impact of a wage increase of 10 percent on the labor supply behavior of male workers. Will the effect on hours worked be different for young and prime-aged men? Why or why not? What about for married and single men? High school and college educated men?

KEY WORDS

Aid to Families with Dependent Children (AFDC)
backward-bending supply curve
break-even point
dynamic scoring
earnings test
effective supply of labor
elasticity of labor supply
Fair Labor Standards Act of 1938
flat tax
flex-time
guaranteed income
implicit tax rate
income effect
internal labor market
intertemporal elasticity of labor supply
moonlighting
myopic workers
negative income tax
opportunity cost
overtime
permanent income
standard workweek
static scoring
substitution effect
total number of hours worked
transitory income
underground economy

THE SUPPLY OF SKILL: INVESTMENT IN HUMAN CAPITAL

THE MAJOR QUESTIONS

- ▲ How do people obtain skills that make them productive at work?
- ▲ How has the amount or level of skill changed over time in developed economies?
- ▲ How do economic factors affect decisions about how much skill to acquire?
- ▲ What are the costs of acquiring skills in each of several different ways?
- ▲ What are the benefits or returns to skills acquisition?
- ▲ Do the things we assume increase skills (such as more education or training) truly increase a worker's productivity?

AN OVERVIEW

The effective labor supply provided by a worker is a function not only of the hours she works and the effort she expends each hour, but also of the talents and skills she brings to the job. All of us have certain natural or inborn talents and abilities, but many skills that are valuable in the labor market are acquired through either schooling or experience. Experience can provide formal or informal on-the-job training. Both schooling and on-the-job training are forms of investment in **human capital**. Human capital is defined as all acquired characteristics of workers that make them more productive. Other forms of investment in human capital include expenditures to improve workers' health, time spent acquiring information about jobs, and the costs of migration to a labor market where employment opportunities are better.

Most of the discussion that follows treats schooling as if it always involved the acquisition of skills. Whether this view is correct is the subject of much debate to which we turn later in the chapter. Even if only partly valid, it suggests society should analyze the importance of human capital to help determine how much of its resources to devote to schooling and training relative to investment in other areas, such as research and development or physical capital (structures and machines). The analysis helps us consider who should pay for investment in schooling—students and their parents or society. Also, it enables us to understand some causes of differences in wage rates among workers.

The growing importance of skills in the labor market is suggested by the changes in the distribution of workers among occupations shown in Table 3.1. The definitions of certain broad occupational categories in the United States were changed in 1983, so we cannot make all the comparisons of interest. Moreover, the data for the U.S. and Canada are not strictly comparable, but the important patterns are obvious nonetheless. Since the 1950s there has been a sharp decline in the proportion of farm and factory workers and a striking growth in white-collar occupations, especially professional and technical ones. Going back further in history makes the trends even clearer. In 1900, for example, less than 5 percent of workers were in professional or technical occupations.[1] Similar trends have occurred in other industrialized countries.

Another way of looking at the growth of skills is illustrated in Table 3.2, which gives the educational attainment of the American labor force for various years. These data provide a measure of the level of schooling workers bring to their jobs. They show that in 1993 the average adult was over 3.3 times as likely to have graduated from high school and over 4.7 times as likely to be a college graduate than in 1940. Clearly, measuring skill by formal schooling leads to the conclusion that the skill embodied in American workers has grown over time.

THE NATURE OF HUMAN CAPITAL

In economic history the proposition that investments in training are similar to investments in machinery goes back to the 18th century. The point was best expressed by Adam Smith, who wrote in 1776:

> When any expensive machine is erected, the extraordinary work to be performed by it before it is worn out, it must be expected, will replace the capital laid out upon it, with at least the ordinary profits. A man educated at the expense of much labor and time to any of those employments which require extraordinary dexterity and skill, may be compared to one of those expensive machines. The

[1]Gertrude Bancroft, *The American Labor Force: Its Growth and Changing Composition,* New York: Wiley, (1958), Table D–2.

TABLE 3.1 PERCENT DISTRIBUTION OF WORKERS BY MAJOR OCCUPATION GROUP, SELECTED YEARS, U.S. AND CANADA

	Canada		*United States*	
	1951	1993	1958	1994
Professional and technical	7.3	18.0	11.0	17.3
Managers	7.9	12.9	10.8	13.3
Clerical	11.0	15.6	14.5	15.1
Sales	6.6	9.7	6.3	12.0
Craft, laborers, and related	38.2	24.7	37.0	25.5
Service workers	8.6	14.2	11.9	13.7
Farming, mining, and related	20.4	5.0	8.5	2.9
Total	100.0	100.0	100.0	100.0[a]

[a]Numbers add to less than 100.0 due to rounding.

Sources: International Labour Organization, *Year Book of Labour Statistics*, retrospective edition, (1990), Table 2, and (1994), Table 2B; *Handbook of Labor Statistics*, BLS Bulletin No. 2175, Table 16; *Employment and Earnings*, January 1995, p. 174.

TABLE 3.2 EDUCATIONAL ATTAINMENT OF ADULTS 25 OR OLDER: 1940–1993

	Percentage with High School Degree or More			*Percentage with College Degree or More*		
	Total	Male	Female	Total	Male	Female
1940	24.1	22.3	25.9	4.6	5.4	3.7
1950	33.3	31.5	35.1	6.0	7.1	5.0
1960	41.0	39.4	42.5	7.7	9.6	5.8
1970	55.2	55.0	55.4	11.0	14.1	8.2
1980	68.6	69.2	68.1	17.0	20.9	13.6
1990	77.6	77.7	77.5	21.3	24.4	18.4
1993	80.2	80.5	80.0	21.9	24.8	19.2

Source: U.S. Bureau of the Census, *Current Population Reports*, Series P–20 (1994).

> work which he learns to perform, it must be expected, over and above the usual wages of common labor will replace to him the whole expense of his education, with at least the ordinary profits of an equally valuable capital. It must do this too in a reasonable time, regard being had to the very uncertain duration of human life, in the same manner as to the more certain duration of the machine.[2]

Investing in either a skill or a machine requires sacrificing consumption today in order to increase output in the future. Although this point has been

[2]Adam Smith, *The Wealth of Nations*, New York: Random House, (1937), Book 1, Chapter 10.

recognized by economists since Smith, precise analysis of the nature and role of human capital began only around 1960.[3]

Markets for human capital differ from those for physical capital in that human capital is always rented rather than sold. Since you cannot own other people, the only allowable contract is for their labor for a limited period. The fact that the market is for the services of the capital rather than for the capital itself is a major reason why most investment in schooling is made by students and their families or governments and nonprofit institutions such as foundations and universities. Commercial interests invest very little in schooling since they would have a difficult time ensuring that they receive the return on their investment.

Some economists assert that the inability to transfer property rights in human capital (that is, the prohibition of slavery) inhibits the development of a commercial market for investment in people. This idea suggests that losses through default will be higher on loans without collateral to finance college education than on loans with physical or financial collateral, and may account for the remarkably high default rate on student loans (over 17 percent in 1991).

No stock market for investment in people has developed. Such a market might involve loans to students that would be repaid as a fraction of the students' earnings after graduation rather than as a fixed amount of principal plus interest. The difficulty with such a plan is obvious and involves what is known as *adverse selection*. Students who expect high earnings would choose to avoid the plan and finance their education some other way (perhaps by savings or conventional loans). Only students with the poorest earnings prospects would choose the plan. Despite this drawback, Yale University once offered students a plan like this, while a bill to make federally guaranteed student loans repayable on this basis was introduced into the United States Senate in 1991 and Australia has adopted a similar policy nationwide.[4]

Skills acquired through schooling beyond the legally required minimum are supplied by people who voluntarily pay the additional cost in return for higher income or satisfaction in later years. Since decisions about schooling are based largely on economic factors, an increase in the supply of skills acquired through schooling requires that: (1) private costs be reduced; (2) earnings of those who obtain extra schooling be increased; or (3) nonmonetary rewards (such as the prestige or satisfaction) of work that uses the skills obtained through extra schooling be increased.

---

[3]See especially T. W. Schultz, "Investment in Human Capital," *American Economic Review* 51: 1–17 (1961), and Gary Becker, *Human Capital: A Theoretical and Empirical Analysis, with Special Reference to Education,* New York: National Bureau of Economic Research, (1964).

[4]102nd Congress, S. 1562. The economics of this type of plan are analyzed by Karl Shell, Franklin Fisher, Duncan Foley, and Ann Friedlaender, "The Educational Opportunity Bank: An Economic Analysis of A Contingent Repayment Loan Program for Higher Education," *National Tax Journal* 21: 2–47 (1968), and by Marc Nerlove, "Some Problems in the Use of Income-Contingent Loans for the Finance of Higher Education," *Journal of Political Economy* 83: 157–183 (1975). The idea stems from Milton Friedman, "The Role of Government in Education," in Robert Solo (ed.). *Economics and the Public Interest,* New Brunswick, N.J.: Rutgers, (1955).

AGE-EARNINGS PROFILES

To study the effect of investment in human capital on earnings, economists use **age-earnings profiles**, which show average hourly or annual earnings for people of different ages who have had the same amount of schooling. Age-earnings profiles for five levels of schooling are shown for the United States in 1993 in Table 3.3. These figures are for year-round, full-time, male workers only, so that much of the effect of education on time spent not working is excluded. In other words, effects of education on labor force participation rates and unemployment rates are ignored. Its effect on hours are not entirely removed from the data, however, since education may affect the number of hours worked by full-time workers if it alters the amount of overtime a worker puts in. Part of the higher earnings of those with postgraduate degrees may be due to the long hours that professionals like lawyers and accountants (at least at tax time), work every week.

Using a **synthetic cohort** composed of people of different ages interviewed in the same year poses serious problems for analyses of how women's earnings change with age and education. There have been such vast changes in women's attitudes and attachments to the labor force over the past decades that it is inherently misleading to compare the earnings of 50-year-old women who grew up in a different era with those of postliberation generations. Thus, in order to enable us to focus on education and experience effects, Table 3.3 contains figures only for men, a group whose attitudes toward work and attachment to the labor force have remained relatively constant in recent decades.

There is nothing unusual about the data in Table 3.3. Similar results are observed in other developed economies, as Table 3.4 shows for the Netherlands in 1987. In both tables people with more education earn more at each age.

We can illustrate the relationships between these profiles and demonstrate their individual features by graphing them. Figure 3.1 graphs the age-

TABLE 3.3 MEAN EARNINGS OF YEAR-ROUND, FULL-TIME, MALE WORKERS BY AGE AND YEARS OF SCHOOLING, UNITED STATES, 1993

	Years of School Completed				
Age in 1994	<12	12	13–15	16	>16
<25	$14,172	$16,276	$17,976	$24,062	NA
25–34	18,648	24,641	28,333	38,494	46,133
35–44	21,716	30,473	35,566	46,942	59,501
45–54	23,220	33,593	39,716	51,909	63,693
55–64	25,065	31,241	38,630	51,200	59,150
>65	18,484	23,904	30,246	46,124	57,914

Source: Calculated from the March 1994 Current Population Survey, Public Use Data File.

TABLE 3.4 AVERAGE NET INCOME OF MALE WORKERS BY EDUCATIONAL ATTAINMENT, THE NETHERLANDS, 1987

Age	Basic and Special Education	Second Level Lower Stage	Second Level Higher Stage	Third Level Lower Stage	Third Level Higher Stage
25–34	27[a]	28	33	34	38
35–44	29	31	36	45	55
45–54	27	32	41	49	65
55–64	28	29	41	47	—

Source: Central Bureau of Statistics, *Statistical Yearbook of the Netherlands,* 1990, The Hague.
[a]Figures given in units of 1000 guilders.

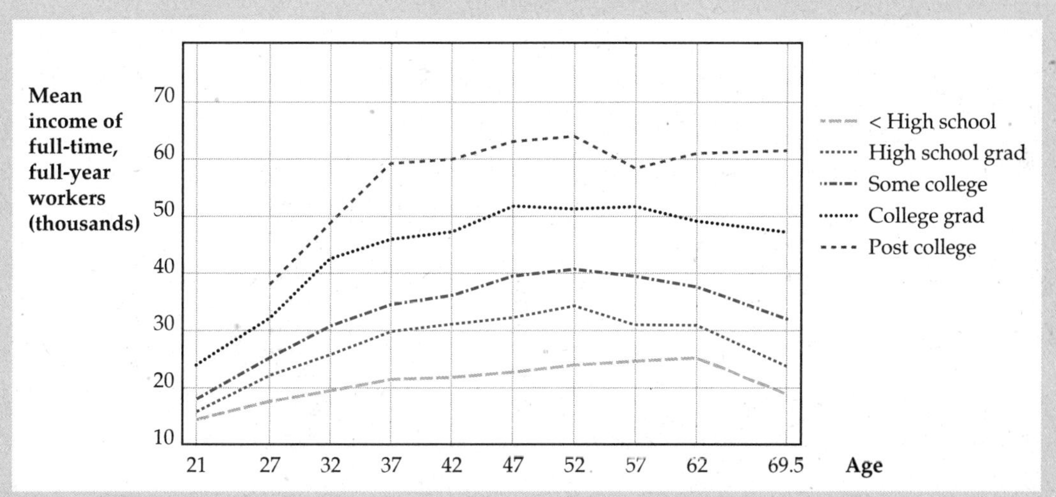

FIGURE 3.1 AGE-EARNINGS PROFILES FOR U.S. MALES IN 1993
Age-earnings profiles are higher for workers with more education throughout their working lives. For each level of education, they increase rapidly at the start of the career due to investments in on-the-job training.

earnings profiles for U.S. workers. Cross-section age-earnings profiles, like those shown in Figure 3.1, typically have a shape like a rotated letter J. Three crucial features that stand out in Figure 3.1 and Tables 3.3 and 3.4 comprise the set of facts that human capital theory is designed to explain:

1. More educated workers occasionally start out with lower earnings than those with less education, but quickly overtake the less educated and enjoy higher earnings on average for the rest of their work lives.

2. People with more education typically have age-earnings profiles with *later peaks*. In Table 3.4 the peak for the lowest level of education is at 35 to 44 years; for the highest level, at 55 years or more.
3. People with more education have *steeper* age-earnings profiles than those with less education. Age-earnings profiles "fan out" as workers age (at least until the oldest working ages), as Figure 3.1 shows. Increasing education levels over time is a major reason why more recent cohorts have a more rapid growth of earnings than earlier cohorts.

Cross-section profiles like those in Figure 3.1 seem to suggest that a worker's earnings decline after middle age. This statistical artifact arises because the figures are generated using a synthetic cohort. Within each actual **cohort** (a group of workers born in the same year) earnings typically continue to rise throughout a worker's life. The rate of increase is slower for older workers than for younger ones, and each successive cohort starts at a higher level of earnings when they enter the labor force since their human capital is of a more recent vintage.

These facts could produce the hypothetical pattern shown in Figure 3.2 for three cohorts of workers born in 1940, 1950, and 1960. This figure is a stylized version of the growth patterns in earnings observed over shorter peri-

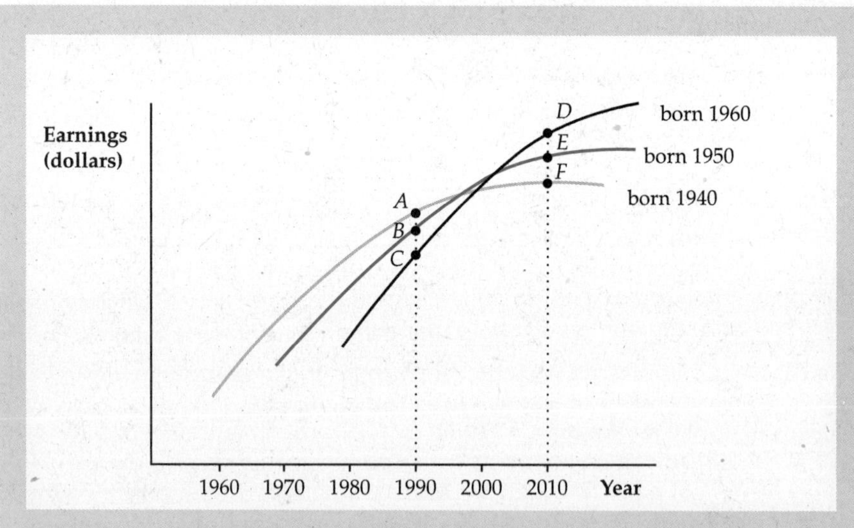

FIGURE 3.2 AGE-EARNINGS PROFILES FROM SYNTHETIC COHORTS

Even if the earnings of every actual cohort increase continuously throughout the work life, in the synthetic cohort created from a cross-section taken in a given year, such as 2010, it may look like earnings decrease for older workers.

ods of time for different cohorts in the U.S.[5] Here and throughout this chapter we are talking about changes over the lifetime in **real earnings**. Inflation-induced changes are assumed to be removed from all the effects we discuss.

Earnings rise throughout the work life of each cohort in Figure 3.2. Viewed in 1990, the members of the oldest cohort earn *A*, exceeding the earnings *B* and *C* of the younger cohorts. This pattern is consistent with the data in Tables 3.3 and 3.4 showing higher earnings for 50-year-olds than for 40- and 30-year-olds at most levels of education. In 2010, even though each worker's earnings have risen through time, workers in the youngest cohort (born in 1960) earn *D*, more than *E* earned by those in the 1950 cohort, and more than *F* earned by those in the 1940 cohort. In 2010, 50-year-olds earn more than 60-year-olds, who earn more than 70-year-olds. This, too, is roughly consistent with many features of the cross-section age-earnings profiles shown in Figure 3.1 and Tables 3.3 and 3.4. Thus, even though an individual worker's earnings may not actually fall once he gets past a certain age, the cross-section age-earnings profiles can slope down.

SKILLS ACQUIRED AT SCHOOL

DECIDING TO INVEST IN EDUCATION—USING AGE-EARNINGS PROFILES

Stylized versions of age-earnings profiles for high school and college graduates are shown in Figure 3.3. Dollar figures such as money earnings and the **out-of-pocket costs** of education to the individual (tuition, books, and so on) are measured on the vertical axis. Age is measured on the horizontal axis. For simplicity's sake we will discuss a hypothetical decision faced by a typical student who leaves high school at age 18 and must decide whether to go directly to college. In reality, an increasing number of students are starting college at older ages. For these students, Figure 3.3 would have to be modified to begin at the age of enrollment. In this illustration we will also assume that the student finishes college in four years, although the analysis presented could easily be adapted to those who take longer.

Max enters the labor market at age 18 on graduation from high school and works until retirement (say, at age 65). Maxine attends college, incurring out-of-pocket costs for four years. These costs are shown by the left part of the earnings curve for a college graduate, which lies below zero on the vertical axis. In addition, Maxine has **forgone earnings** equal to the amount Max made that she too could have earned had she entered the labor force at 18. These areas, labelled "Out-of-Pocket Costs" and "Forgone Earnings" sum to

[5]See Giora Hanoch and Marjorie Honig, " 'True' Age-Earnings Profiles Adjusting for Censoring and for Period and Cohort Effects," *Review of Economics and Statistics* 67: 383–394 (1985).

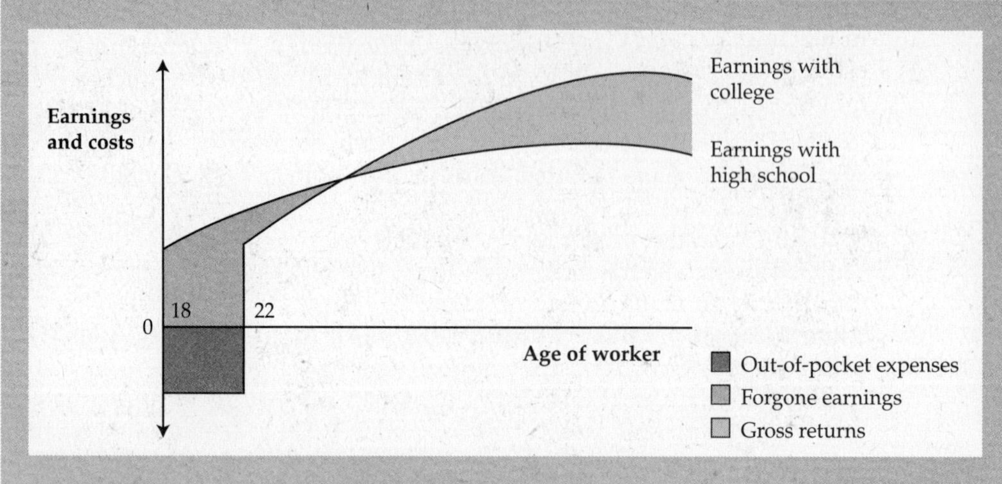

FIGURE 3.3 INVESTMENT IN SCHOOLING
For investment in education to be economically worthwhile, the present discounted value of the higher earnings derived from the education must exceed the present discounted value of the direct cost of the schooling plus the opportunity cost of the earnings forgone while in school.

the total cost of Maxine's investment in college education. In practice, earnings from jobs during vacations and part-time jobs during the school year may reduce these costs. The cost of subsistence while in school should not be included as a cost, unless subsistence is higher when enrolled in college. To count both subsistence and forgone earnings would be double counting, since Max has to pay his subsistence costs out of his earnings.

As Figure 3.3 is drawn, Maxine's earnings on entering the labor market do not immediately equal Max's. Max has been receiving on-the-job training since age 18, which, as we discuss later in this chapter, also affects the age-earnings profile. The forgone earnings associated with attending college might, therefore, extend beyond the years in college. Although this pattern is common, it is not a necessary feature of the diagram, which could have been drawn so that Maxine's earnings were greater than or equal to Max's from the time of her entry into the labor force.

At some time after entry into the labor force Maxine's earnings overtake and surpass Max's. After this **overtaking point**, Maxine's earnings remain higher for the rest of their work lives. The area to the right of the overtaking point that lies below Maxine's profile but above Max's, is the **gross return** to college education. If overtaking did not occur the gross return on the investment in schooling would be negative and there would be no economic reason to attend college.

Even if the gross return is positive and larger than the forgone earnings and the out-of-pocket costs, the investment still may not be worthwhile because the returns to college come at a later point in the work life. If Maxine had opted not to go to college, she could have taken the amount she invested in her human capital and invested it in something else such as stocks or real estate. For college to make sense as an investment, the gross returns must exceed the returns available from alternative investments.

There are two alternative ways that this comparison is frequently made. In the first method, both the costs and gross returns are discounted back to the age of enrollment (here assumed to be 18). The appropriate interest rate to use to calculate the **net present value (NPV)** of the investment at age 18 is the rate r at which the student can borrow to finance an education. In deciding whether to make the investment in college education, an individual who seeks to maximize lifetime net income will undertake the investment if it has a positive present value.

Formally, the net present value is

$$NPV = \sum_{i=18}^{T} \frac{Y_i^C - Y_i^H}{[1+r]^{i-18}}$$

where NPV = present value at age 18
i = age
T = the age at which the worker dies (or the latest age of any work)
Y^H = earnings if the worker stopped education after high school
Y^C = earnings with a college education.

Y^C is net of the cost of tuition, books, and so forth. These costs may make Y^C negative during the college years and, as discussed above, Y^C may be less than Y^H not only during the college years but also during the first few years the college graduate is in the labor force. Both Y^C and Y^H may be zero in later years after the worker retires, although there may be a difference in the age at which high school and college graduates retire. In short, the NPV is equal to the sum of discounted differences in the monetary returns from going to college as opposed to entering the labor market after high school at age 18.

Calculating NPV allows the comparison of dollars today with dollars in the future. To be comparable to $1.00 today, more than $1.00 is required in the future. Even after accounting for inflation, one must make up for the interest one can earn if today's funds are invested in alternative ways. The higher the interest rate, the smaller the present value of investing in college. As long as the interest rate is positive, the denominator in the NPV formula will get larger as the worker's age (i) increases. Thus, since it will be discounted (divided) by a larger number, a dollar earned further in the future will be worth less today than a dollar earned sooner. For example, at a real interest rate of 2 percent (about right for the U.S. over the long run), $1.00 earned five years from now is worth $0.91 today, since if you put $0.91 into the bank at 2 percent interest you would end up with $1.00 in 5 years. Similarly, $1.00 earned 10 years from now is worth only $0.82 today while $1.00, 25 years from now is worth only $0.61 today.

NPV can be negative at high interest rates even if total costs are much smaller than gross returns. The costs all occur before the returns begin, so

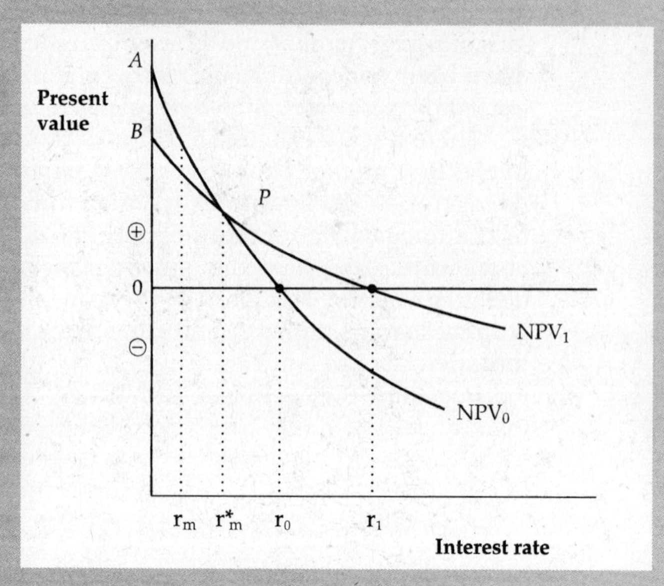

FIGURE 3.4 THE PRESENT VALUES OF TWO INVESTMENTS

The net present value (NPV) of an investment declines as the market interest rate increases. The speed of this decline depends on the timing of the stream of returns. The returns generating stream NPV_1 occur earlier than those generating NPV_0. The interest rate that makes the NPV of an investment equal to zero is the internal rate of return (IRR) for that investment.

the returns are discounted heavily. Figure 3.4 shows how the *NPV* of an investment changes as the interest rate changes. Let us first examine curve labelled NPV_O, which shows the NPV of one possible educational investment plan (e.g., attending college followed by law school as opposed to entering the labor force after high school). We will discuss curve NPV_1 later. Since the interest rate along the vertical axis is zero, the distance $0A$ measures the difference between undiscounted returns and undiscounted costs $(\Sigma(Y^C - Y^H))$. As the interest rate (r) increases, the value of returns to the investment falls since they occur in the future. At higher interest rates, the costs (which occur early on) assume more relative importance since the opportunity costs of not investing elsewhere the money spent on education are larger.

At some interest rate (labelled r_0 on curve NPV_0 in Figure 3.4) the *NPV* of the investment will be zero. This interest rate is known as the **internal rate**

of return (IRR).[6] At the IRR, the costs and returns are exactly equal after discounting. As always, we are discussing real rates. The effects of inflation have been removed by subtracting the inflation rate from the nominal interest rate.

In general, an investment makes sense if the NPV is greater than zero or the IRR is greater than the market interest rate. Why did we compute both measures? The answer is because students do not simply make a choice about one possible educational investment. Rather, they must choose among many different options. A student graduating from high school could enter the labor force; go to a two-year college for a technical degree; go to a four-year college to major in English, engineering, or economics; be a pre-law or pre-med student; or plan on getting a divinity degree. How should these options be compared? One possibility would be to pick the option with the highest NPV. Another option would be to pick the option with the greatest IRR. Unfortunately, these two options often give different answers.

Return to Figure 3.4 and consider an alternative educational investment shown by curve NPV_1, say training as an accountant rather than as a lawyer. This option has lower total lifetime earnings net of investment costs (point *B* is below point *A*), but a higher internal rate of return. This situation would occur if option 1 had higher earnings earlier in life when the effect of discounting is small but lower earnings later in life that are heavily discounted. If the market rate of interest were r_m, then option 0 would have a higher NPV even though option 1 had the greater IRR.[7]

The answer to which investment (a law or an accounting degree, in this example) is better depends on an assumption about what the worker with the higher earnings earlier in the work life will do with those earnings. Using the IRR assumes that this worker would reinvest the difference in earnings at the same high rate of interest. In fact, as we will see below, rates of return on education are typically higher than on other investments. Once a worker has picked a career and obtained the type and level of education needed for that career, she is unlikely to be able to earn as much on future investments. If she can only earn the market rate of interest (r_m), then picking the investment with the highest NPV is the most appropriate alternative.

A NUMERICAL EXAMPLE

Consider a potential investment program of attending law school for three years beginning immediately after college graduation at age 22. We assume

[6]There is no unique internal rate of return. Instead, there are as many values of r that make NPV = 0 as there are sign changes in the stream of costs and returns. Usually, though, only one calculated value of r is economically reasonable.

[7]If the market rate of interest were r_m^* or higher then there is no conflict and option 1 is clearly preferable.

that the college grad will work until age 68 whether or not she chooses to attend law school. If she does not go to law school, we assume, for simplicity, that she will earn \$21,000 per year after taxes in every year of her work life. (As is customary, we consider only real earnings and real rates of return and interest. Any inflation that occurs washes out of the calculations.) If she goes to law school she will have out-of-pocket costs of \$9,000 per year for tuition, books, and other expenses. Moreover, for the three years of school she will forgo \$21,000 per year of after-tax earnings.

What is the minimum after-tax earnings she must receive each year in her law career to make the investment worthwhile—to make the present value of the investment greater than or equal to zero? We can apply the present value formula to this case and calculate

$$NPV = \sum_{i=22}^{24} \frac{0 - 30{,}000}{[1+r]^{i-22}} + \sum_{i=25}^{68} \frac{Y^L - 21{,}000}{[1+r]^{i-22}}$$

where Y^L is her earnings as a lawyer beginning with her graduation at age 25. The first summation shows the discounted costs of the investment, equivalent to the sum of the out-of-pocket costs and forgone earnings in Figure 3.3; the second shows the discounted gross returns on the investment.

With a higher real rate of interest, the earnings generated by the investment, Y^L, must be greater to justify undertaking it. Table 3.5 shows the required annual after-tax earnings necessary to justify the investment at various real interest rates. With low real interest rates, the law degree need only offer wages slightly above those available to the fresh college graduate to make it worthwhile. With a real rate of 14 percent, however, substantially higher wages are required to justify the investment.

EMPIRICAL EVIDENCE ON INCENTIVES TO INVEST

Estimates of returns to education vary considerably depending on the data used, period analyzed, and assumptions made, but several consistent patterns emerge:

TABLE 3.5 ANNUAL EARNINGS NEEDED TO MAKE THE INVESTMENT IN LAW SCHOOL PAY OFF

Real *r*	After-Tax Annual Earnings Required	Percent Increase Over College-Graduate Earnings
2 percent	\$24,160	15.0
5 percent	26,350	25.5
8 percent	29,065	38.4
11 percent	32,140	53.0
14 percent	35,490	69.0

POLICY ISSUE

HUMAN CAPITAL IN DIVORCE

Today, with many marriages ending in divorce and with more and more women working in the labor force, courts are increasingly asked to decide not the proper amount of alimony for a nonworking woman, but how to fairly divide the assets of a married couple. Typically, this division is based on such factors as who earned the income that paid for the assets.

Division of physical assets such as stocks, bonds, or a house is fairly simple. Typically, however, young couples have invested far more in human capital than in physical capital. We tend to go to school early in our lives so that there will be a longer period to reap higher earnings. Even if a young couple has purchased a house, in the early years they are primarily paying interest, and their equity value is likely to be quite small. Thus, in many divorces, the key issue is how to value and divide the human capital assets acquired in a marriage. Perhaps one partner has worked and supported the other through medical school. Unlike stocks and bonds, a medical degree cannot be sold and the proceeds divided. Yet the value of this asset may be enormous. Suppose that going to medical school increases Max's earnings by $60,000 a year over what he would have made had he simply gone to work after college. With a 35-year work life and a 2 percent real interest rate, the present value of these extra earnings would be $1,499,918.

How should this asset be divided? If the rate of return on human capital were the same as on physical capital, the court could simply return to Max's wife half of what they have invested (medical school tuition plus lost earnings) and let her invest this in the stock market. As we will see, however, human capital typically earns a greater rate of return than physical capital. Should the court award Mrs. Max $749,959 now? How could Max come up with that much cash? Should she be awarded $30,000 a year for the next 35 years? How would you feel about having to send a check to your ex-spouse for 35 years? Would there be incentives for Max to declare bankruptcy?

1. Real rates of return on education are generally higher than those for investments in physical assets. A range from 5 to 15 percent for college seems reasonable as opposed to a real interest rate of less then 3 percent.[8] While some of this difference is due to the riskiness of education as opposed to bonds, a large part may reflect capital constraints. Despite the tremendous loan money available for college study, the fact that it is hard to use a college degree as collateral (it cannot be repossessed!) may limit lending for education below the optimal level.
2. Rates of return have varied substantially over time. The average earnings of college graduates were 40 to 45 percent more than those of the typical high school graduate in the 1960s, fell to only 34 percent more in the late 1970s, but have risen to over 50 percent more in the early 1990s. At least part of the apparent increase in returns to college for young workers represents a change in what students learn in college.

---

[8]George Psacharopoulos, "Returns to Education: A Further International Update and Implications," *Journal of Human Resources* 20: 583–604 (1985); Becker, *Human Capital,* and Jacob Mincer, *Studies in Human Capital,* Aldershot, U.K.: Elgar, (1993).

Increasing math skills among women and shifts in choice of major among men may have accounted for about a quarter of the increase in relative earnings of new graduates in the 1980s. The remainder, however, represents increases in returns to given levels of skills.[9] These comparisons are not true rates of return for a number of reasons. They ignore college costs, which have risen faster than inflation in recent years, and do not account for the fact that the average college graduate currently in the labor force is younger than the average high school graduate since college enrollment rates have risen over time. Nevertheless, they are highly reflective of the pattern in returns.

3. Part but not all of the variation in returns over time is related to the business cycle.[10] In a recession, the wages and opportunities available to high school graduates typically fall more than those for college graduates. This lowers the costs of college since the forgone earnings are less. It also affects estimates of the return because the apparent difference in earnings derived from current data is larger. Of course, this effect would not be meaningful for any student making the decision of whether to enter college since he could expect to work during both recessions and booms for the rest of his life. Thus, he should base his decision on the average pattern of high school versus college earnings over the business cycle, not what exists at any given moment.
4. Returns vary according to the level of education. They are higher for lower levels than for college or graduate school. For example, each year of elementary school may provide a return as high as 22 percent, while each year of high school might yield about 15 percent. Estimated returns to each year of college are rarely over 10 percent. In large part this is because the costs of education increase drastically as students get older. Remember that for college students most of the costs of education consist of forgone earnings. These are likely to be very small for the typical elementary school student.
5. Within each level of education there appear to be "bonus" returns for finishing the degree and obtaining a diploma. Called **sheepskin effects**, these returns cause some to question whether the higher earnings of college graduates really represent greater human capital, since it is hard to argue that students learn more in their senior year than in their ju-

---

[9]Lawrence Mishel and Jared Bernstein, "Declining Wages for High School and College Graduates," Briefing Paper, Washington D.C.: Economic Policy Institute, (1992); John Bound and George Johnson, "Changes in the Structure of Wages in the 1980's: An Evaluation of Alternative Explanations,"*American Economic Review* 82: 371–392 (1992); Jeff Grogger and Eric Eide, "Changes in College Skills and the Rise in the College Wage Premium," *Journal of Human Resources* 30: 280–310 (1995).

[10]Thomas Kniesner, Arthur Padilla, and Solomon Polachek, "The Rate of Return to Schooling and the Business Cycle," *Journal of Human Resources* 13: 274–275 (1978), J. Peter Mattila, "Determinants of Male School Enrollment: A Time-Series Analysis," *Review of Economics and Statistics* 64: 242–251 (1982).

nior year. One study estimated that the return to each year of college if you did not finish was 5 percent, but the return to the final year was 14 percent. Similarly, the return to one year of graduate school was near zero, but the return to a graduate degree was considerably higher. Other studies found that students with a bachelor's degree earned between 19 and 21 percent more than those with 16 years of schooling but no degree. Recent evidence indicates, however, that the sheepskin effect may be minor if the amount of education is properly measured. If education is measured by the number of credit hours passed rather than years attended, degree recipients did not earn significantly more than nonrecipients with the same number of credits.[11] If there is a bonus for completing a program, it probably reflects personal attributes, such as the determination needed to finish tasks, that are valued by employers and are more likely to be present among graduates than among dropouts. The effects of such personal attributes on the true rate of return to education are discussed below.

A number of difficulties are involved in estimating the returns to educational investments. The next several sections will discuss several factors that may introduce systematic **biases** into estimates of the rate of return (or net present value) of educational investments. We first examine reasons why estimates of the return to education may be biased downward (too low).

PROPER MEASURES OF COSTS

It is important to be sure that the cost figures used are actually the amount invested. College budgets contain expenditures for other activities such as the research conducted by faculty members, and therefore overestimate the resources devoted to human capital production by colleges.[12] Much of what is spent by students for college, on the other hand, may actually be expenditures for consumption rather than investments in education. While dorm and cafeteria fees are excluded from cost estimates as subsistence, much of what is included as general college fees should probably also be excluded. How

---

[11]Thomas Hungerford and Gary Solon, "Sheepskin Effects in the Returns to Education," *Review of Economics and Statistics* 69: 175–177 (1987); Dale Belman and John S. Heywood, "Sheepskin Effects in the Returns to Education: An Examination of Woman and Minorities," *Review of Economics and Statistics* 73: 720–724 (1991); David Jaeger and Marianne Page, "Degrees Matter: New Evidence on Sheepskin Effects in the Returns to Education," University of Michigan Population Studies Center Research Report No. 94–307 (1994); Jin Heum Park, "Estimation of Sheepskin Effects and Returns to Schooling Using the Old and New CPS Measures of Educational Attainment," Princeton University Industrial Relations Center Working Paper No. 338 (1994); Thomas J. Kane and Cecilia Elena Rouse, "Labor Market Returns to Two- and Four-Year College: Is a Credit a Credit and Do Degrees Matter," *American Economic Review,* 85: 600–614 (1995).

[12]Of course, these research activities should generate returns elsewhere through higher productivity, new innovations, or improvements in culture and other areas of life.

much would you pay (over and above the charge for dorm room and cafeteria) for a full year of idyllic existence on a green, parklike campus with movies and live entertainment every night, a great gym, and lots of young people to hang out with? Ideally the costs of the "summer camp" aspects of college life should be subtracted from total college costs to derive an estimate of investment in education. The costs of the college gym and swimming pool are subsistence costs just as much as membership in a health club would be for someone who did not enroll in college. To the extent that any improper costs are included in the estimates, rates of return will be underestimated.

NONWAGE RETURNS

So far we have described the value of the skills acquired in school solely in terms of earnings. There are other increases in compensation that make schooling attractive and may cause estimates of the rate of return to education to be too low. Workers with more education receive a higher portion of their compensation in the form of employee benefits such as pensions or insurance plans. In addition, education improves the conditions under which workers do their jobs. More education permits workers to avoid repetitious and physically dangerous work. As will be seen in Chapter 10, these more attractive working conditions available to the more educated worker are obtained at the price of a somewhat lower wage than the educated worker could earn on a less attractive job. This creates a lower apparent return to schooling than if all aspects of compensation were included. Accounting for better job conditions obtained by more educated workers raises the rate of return to schooling by over 1 percentage point.[13]

More education should also lead to better health and thus greater longevity, as better-educated people are more aware of behaviors that contribute to good health. Death rates are slightly lower among more educated older people, independent of any effects of higher income or greater wealth.[14] Although a monetary value cannot easily be placed on the improved health caused by greater education, concentrating on the monetary return to schooling may lead to underestimating its total benefit to the individual.

Even such apparently casual formal learning as noncredit adult education increases people's productivity at home. Increased education of parents, especially the parent who spends more time at home, raises the return to schooling for their children. It enables parents to educate their children more effectively before the children start regular school, improving their perfor-

---

[13]Robert E. B. Lucas, "Hedonic Wage Equations and Psychic Wages in the Returns to Schooling," *American Economic Review* 67: 549–558 (1977); Robert Haveman and Barbara Wolfe, "Schooling and Economic Well-Being: The Role of Nonmarket Effects," *Journal of Human Resources* 19: 377–407 (1984).

[14]Paul Menchik, "Economic Status as a Determinant of Mortality Among Black and White Older Men: Does Poverty Kill?" *Population Studies* 47: 427–436 (1993).

mance in school and raising the returns on their time spent at school.[15] Thus, additional education in one generation spills over to improve the economic status of the next generation.

We turn now to reasons why the estimated rate of return on human capital investments may be biased upward or overstated.

LOSS OF LEISURE

Since investment in human capital raises wages, it also raises the price of leisure. As we saw in Chapter 2, for most workers the result is that they work more hours each week. Indeed, if investments in human capital earned the same rate of return as other investments, they would not change the worker's wealth. Any increase in income resulting from human capital investments would be offset by a loss of income from other forgone investments. In this case, there would be no income effect and the substitution effects induced by the increased wage rates associated with greater human capital would inevitably cause an increase in hours worked.

This result implies that part of the increased earnings we observe after an investment in human capital does not represent an increase in the welfare or utility of the worker. Rather, it is offset by a loss in utility resulting from the decreased consumption of leisure. Estimates of the monetary rate of return on these investments will, therefore, overstate the true impact on workers' utility.[16]

ABILITY BIASES

Perhaps the most serious difficulty with estimates of the rate of return to schooling arises with respect to **ability biases**. The question we really would like to answer is what would happen to the earnings of a particular individual if he or she obtained more education. This situation can never be observed, since, by definition, one person cannot at the same time have two different levels of education. Thus, estimates of rates of return typically compare earnings of those who obtained a college degree, for example, with earnings of a *different* group of people who stopped their schooling after high school.

The problem arises because the people in these groups are inherently not the same. There is some reason why those in one group went to college while those in the other did not. Perhaps the college students are smarter, more

---

[15]John Wolfe, "The Impact of Family Resources on Childhood IQ," *Journal of Human Resources* 17: 213–235 (1982); Frank Stafford, "Women's Work, Sibling Competition and Children's School Performance," *American Economic Review* 77: 972–980 (1987). The evidence on noncredit education is in Hope Corman, "The Demand for Education for Home Production," *Economic Inquiry* 24: 213–230 (1986).

[16]C. M. Lindsay, "Measuring Human Capital Returns," *Journal of Political Economy* 79: 1195–1215 (1971).

motivated, harder working, or simply better at winning the favor of teachers who write letters of recommendation. Most factors that make people more likely to go to college would also yield higher earnings even if they had stopped their education after high school. If the earnings of actual high school graduates who enter the work force are lower than what the earnings of college students would have been had they not gone on to college, then the comparison being made to estimate the rate of return to college is inherently unfair.

Economists have attempted to remove ability biases from estimates in the rate of return to education in a number of ways. The earliest studies tried to control directly for differences in ability by including measures such as IQ. The problem with this technique was that it was never possible to find measures that could account for all the possible differences, such as motivation, between students who left school with different levels of education.

For this reason, later studies have tried to find **natural experiments** that might result in students getting different levels of education for reasons outside of their control. Two obvious such experiments are based on the students' date of birth. Compulsory attendance laws typically require students to remain in school until a certain age. This might occur at the beginning of grade 10 for students born early in the school year, but late in the same grade for other students. During both World War II and the Vietnam War, students were drafted into the army according to their birth date, a situation that also caused some students to alter their education plans for reasons other than their own. Finally, some researchers have examined the effect of differences in education for identical twins who presumably should have similar native abilities. All these studies conclude that the size of the ability bias is likely to be fairly small.[17]

PRIVATE VERSUS SOCIAL RETURNS

All discussion so far has centered on the **private rate of return** to individuals choosing to invest in education. Society and the government representing it would not make the same calculations that we have presented in deciding whether to devote more resources to education. Both the costs and the returns to society will differ from those to the individual.

---

[17]McKinley Blackburn and David Neumark, "Omitted-Ability Bias and the Increase in the Return to Schooling," *Journal of Labor Economics* 11: 521–544 (1993); Joshua Angrist and Alan Krueger, "Does Compulsory School Attendance Affect Schooling and Earnings," *The Quarterly Journal of Economics* 106: 979–1014 (1991); Joshua Angrist and Alan Krueger, "Estimating the Payoff to Schooling Using the Vietnam-Era Draft Lottery," NBER Working Paper No. 4067 (1992); Orley Ashenfelter and Alan Krueger, "Estimating the Economic Returns to Schooling from a New Sample of Twins," *American Economic Review* 84: 1157–1173 (1994); David Card, "Earnings, Schooling and Ability Revisited," in Ronald Ehrenberg (ed.). *Research in Labor Economics* Greenwich, Conn.: JAI Press, (1995).

POLICY ISSUE

CHILD CARE AND INVESTMENT IN HUMAN CAPITAL

In Chapter 1 we discussed the effect of subsidized day care on the labor force participation of adult women. The conclusion was that expanded subsidies would have a positive, although probably not very large, effect in overcoming the fixed and variable costs of participating in the labor force. We also saw that, to some extent, women who work more in the market work less at home. If they are unmarried mothers, or if their husbands do not increase their time spent working at home, including time with young children, the children will receive less attention. This would be a negative side effect of expanded day care *if* more time spent with the children improves their well-being.

While the evidence on this very sensitive issue is by no means clear, and it is too soon to draw hard and fast conclusions, one recent study produced a striking finding. If an educated mother spends more time with her children, these children subsequently spend more time in school and do better in the labor market. If a mother with relatively little education spends more time at home, there is no effect on her children's subsequent achievement.[18]

This result implies that providing subsidized day care to low-income households may have the positive effect of increasing their financial well-being with no detrimental side effects on the children's investment in human capital. The same happy conclusion does not hold for subsidizing the care of children from higher-income households. Taken together, the results give a strong reason for limiting subsidized day care to low-income households.

Social costs would have to be adjusted upward to include expenditures on education by governments and nonprofit institutions over and above expenditures by students and their families. These public costs are likely to be a substantial fraction of total costs, especially for lower levels of schooling when most students are enrolled in public schools and the opportunity costs of forgone earnings are small. Social costs will also exceed private costs by the value of taxes that would have been paid on the forgone earnings. Social benefits are also likely to be larger than private benefits. The social gross returns to schooling are calculated without deducting income and payroll taxes, since society as a whole benefits from the services bought with these taxes. This effect is magnified because the progressive income tax causes the additional returns to society from higher taxes to increase faster than income as more education is obtained. Other social returns to schooling are harder to quantify. Citizens with more education may be better informed voters. They may be less likely to commit crimes, thereby improving the lives of those who were not victimized and reducing the tax dollars everyone must spend on courts and prisons. More educated citizens may benefit society

[18]Linda Datcher-Loury, "Effects of Mother's Home Time on Children's Schooling," *Review of Economics and Statistics* 70: 367–373 (1988).

through their inventions and discoveries. Part of this return is private, since it will increase the income of the inventor. It is likely, however, that this increase in income does not capture the full value of most inventions, leaving a considerable surplus for society. Consider the person who discovers a cure for lung cancer. She will probably become fabulously wealthy. Even if she becomes a billionaire, however, it is likely that people who had cancer would willingly have paid far more than her income for the cure.

Comparing the social returns to the social costs yields an estimate of the **social rate of return** to the investment. Although some studies suggest that the social rate of return to education exceeds the private rate of return, most find that private rates are greater. For example, one British government study found that the social rate of return to university study was about 5 percent while the private rate of return was 22 percent. This may make economic sense since society as a whole should use a lower discount rate than a private individual. It may also reflect public pressure on the part of various interest groups (such as teachers' unions) to invest more than an optimal amount in education.[19]

SCREENING AND SIGNALLING

It has generally been assumed that the higher earnings of more educated people result from education increasing their productivity. If this is not the case, social rates of return to education may be much less than private ones. A diploma, especially one from a school or college with high prestige, may simply be a way of gaining preference for scarce highly paid jobs. The argument is that successful applicants are selected by previous graduates of the same schools or similar ones on the basis of loyalty and friendship rather than on performance. If this **old-school-tie hypothesis** were a good description of reality, the true social rate of return on higher education would be negative. Costs would be incurred by society without a gain in productivity or in employers' ability to find the workers who are inherently more able. Of course, the private return would still be positive since the workers would benefit from the higher salaries attached to these good jobs. The key is that someone would have filled these jobs and earned the higher salaries anyway, but it would have been cheaper for society to allocate them randomly than to spend resources on schooling that did not increase productivity.

A related but more important criticism is that schooling merely sorts individuals with traits that employers find attractive into those jobs that pay higher wages. Four years spent in college may be a way of demonstrating to employers that the graduates have the self-discipline, motivation, and ability

---

[19]Richard Freeman, "The Decline in the Economic Rewards to College Education," *Review of Economics and Statistics* 59: 28 (1977); UK Department of Education, "Top Up Loans, CM 520," London: HMSO (1988); Solomon W. Polachek and W. Stanley Siebert, *The Economics of Earnings,* Cambridge: Cambridge University Press, (1993).

POLICY ISSUE

RAISING THE AGE OF COMPULSORY SCHOOL ATTENDANCE

In the U.S., as in most countries, children must attend school until they reach a certain age. In most states it is age 16, but 9 states require attendance until age 17 and an additional 9 until age 18. Recent changes in these laws have continued a trend toward higher ages of compulsory school attendance.

Do these laws affect the amount of schooling obtained, and should the trend toward higher ages be continued? Perhaps everyone would attend school until age 16 or later even without compulsory attendance laws. One way to answer the question is to look at whether students born in January, February, or March, who are eligible to drop out earlier in the school year because they are older than their classmates, are more likely to stay in school in states that require attendance beyond age 16. In these states "older students" do, in fact, remain in school longer than in other states. The compulsory attendance laws may reduce the drop-out rate by as much as 25 percent. As expected, their effect on boys' decisions about staying in school is greater than on girls'. Since the full-time wage rates for teenage boys are higher than those of teenage girls, the opportunity costs of staying in school are greater for boys.[20]

This evidence suggests that the laws are effective. Whether they increase the amount of skill embodied in the work force is another issue. Standard measurements of the private rate of return on the extra schooling produced by compulsory attendance laws show that it does not differ much from the rate of return on schooling that students undertake voluntarily. Whether students who are kept in school only by the compulsory attendance law detract from their classmates' ability to learn is another question. Without knowing more about the noneconomic impacts of education, we cannot determine what the actual tradeoff is between these two effects.

to perform well on the job. If this **screening hypothesis** is true, the resources devoted to investment in education may produce a high private rate of return, since the investment enables those who acquire the schooling to reap high earnings later in life. The social rate of return may be negative, however. The only socially productive function of schooling in this case is to provide information to employers about which young people will make good workers.

A variant of the screening hypothesis points out how students' decisions about attending college are affected by employers' willingness to pay more to

---

[20]Joshua Angrist and Alan Krueger, "Does Compulsory School Attendance Affect Schooling and Earnings?" *Quarterly Journal of Economics* 106: (1991); Linda Edwards, "The Economics of Schooling Decisions: Teenage Enrollment Rates," *Journal of Human Resources* 10: 165 (1975).

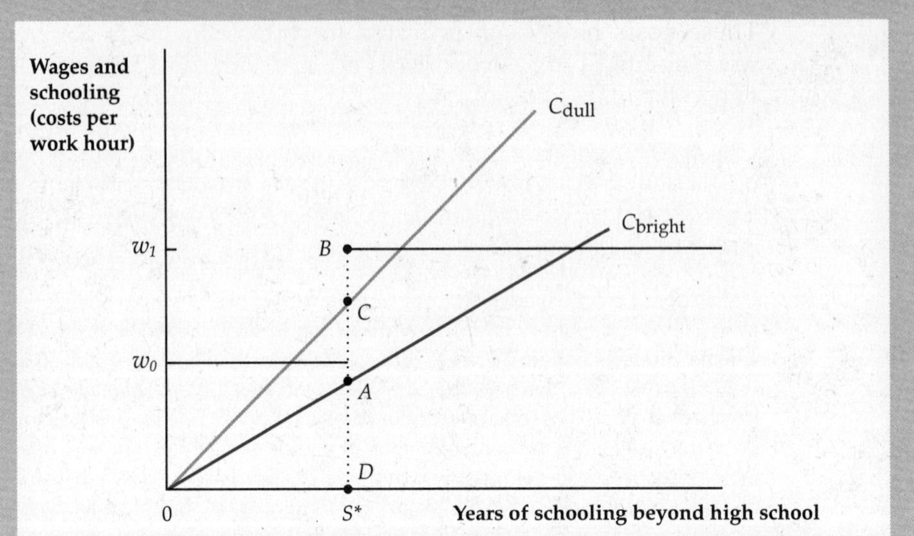

FIGURE 3.5 EDUCATION AS A SIGNAL OF WORKER QUALITY
Paying wage w_1 and requiring S^* years of schooling to be hired ensures that only workers from the more able group apply for the job. It costs these workers *DA* to acquire the necessary schooling, so their net wage is $B - A$, which is greater than the wage w_0 available to those who do not have S^* years of schooling. Less able workers, for whom the cost of S^* years of schooling is *DC*, would find their earnings reduced if they tried for this job, since $B - C$ is less than w_0.

workers who have jumped an educational hurdle.[21] In this view, education functions as a **signal** to employers of people's inherent ability. Consider a world in which there are two equal-sized groups of workers, one of which is naturally less productive (dull) than the other (bright). The dull workers will produce an amount that would justify a wage of w_0 in Figure 3.5. The bright workers will produce an amount justifying a wage w_1, more than w_0, because they are inherently that much more productive. If employers cannot distinguish between workers of the two types, there is no way to keep some less productive workers from obtaining the high-paying jobs. If the employer paid all workers a wage w_1, wages would exceed average productivity. This would mean that the employer would lose money and go out of business.

If it takes the dull workers more effort to succeed in school (the costs of schooling, monetary and nonmonetary, are greater for them), it pays the bright workers to use education as a signal that separates them from the less productive workers. Assume that the dull workers' cost of acquiring school-

[21]Michael Spence, *Market Signaling*, Cambridge, Mass.: Harvard University Press, (1974).

ing is denoted by $0C_{Dull}$ in Figure 3.5, and the bright workers' by $0C_{Bright}$. These costs have been prorated to reflect the costs per hour of expected working life. If employers set a hiring standard of S^* years of schooling and only offer high-paying (wage rate of w_1) jobs to workers who attain this level of schooling, the market for education will be in equilibrium. Dull workers will obtain no post–high school education and will receive a wage of w_0. If they were to obtain S^* years of schooling, they would receive a wage of w_1, but they would also incur a cost of *CD*. Since the difference between returns and costs is *BC*, which is less than w_0, they would not bother with further schooling. The bright workers can acquire S^* years of extra schooling at a cost only of *AD*. If they do so, they earn a gross wage of w_1. Their net wage is the difference between this wage and the costs of their acquiring the education, the distance *BA*. Since this net wage exceeds W_0, it pays them to make the investment in education.

In the world described by Figure 3.5 and by the screening hypothesis more generally, education merely enables employers to separate productive from unproductive workers and prevents the unproductive ones from obtaining jobs that would pay them more than the value of what they produce. Education is productive because it adds to the efficiency of the market by sorting workers into jobs. Without it the bright workers might not obtain the jobs that allow them to be more productive. It is not productive in the sense implied by human capital theory, because it does not add to the ability of an individual worker to produce more. Whether formal education could be a sufficiently efficient signal to justify the resources devoted to it is not clear.

Light is shed upon the screening hypothesis by looking at the schooling decisions of the self-employed. These workers presumably do not need to use education as a screening device because they can assess their own capabilities. The average self-employed person acquires three-fourths as much education beyond high school as the average salaried employee.[22] Assuming people expect to be self-employed at the time they decide how much schooling to acquire, this evidence shows that self-employed individuals believe that acquiring at least some college education provides a direct benefit to them. Their somewhat lower educational attainment may imply, however, that schooling does play a role in screening salaried employees. Similarly, in a very well-designed study, one researcher obtained data on workers' productivity as measured by their output and on their turnover and absentee rates. The major direct effect of a high school education was in reducing absentee and turnover rates. These two studies suggest screening does play a role in informing employers about workers' inherent ability to stick to a job.[23]

---

[22]Kenneth Wolpin, "Education and Screening," *American Economic Review* 67: 956 (1977).

[23]Andrew Weiss, "High School Graduation, Performance and Wages," *Journal of Political Economy* 96: 785–820 (1988).

While it may be important, screening is clearly not the whole story. A variety of evidence shows that education has real effects on productivity. For example, a study of employees within one large corporation found that, after adjusting for the selectivity of the colleges employees attended and the level of degree attained, those who earned a higher grade-point average obtained more rapid rates of salary increase and received higher job-performance ratings. There is also a connection between grades and earnings economy wide. If a higher grade-point average reflects more learning and is not just a more complex signal of the potential employee's ability, this finding is further evidence against the screening hypothesis. Once individual ability is accounted for, students who graduate from selective colleges do not earn significantly more than those who graduate from less selective ones. Since the selectivity of a college is a factor that employers should use as an indicator of ability if college were simply serving as a screening device, this finding provides strong evidence against the screening hypothesis. Achieving a high school degree by taking the general equivalence degree (GED) exam has no effect on earnings beyond what would be predicted by the student's years of schooling. Evidence from developing countries also indicates that schooling is productive independent of any differences in inherent ability among workers. Finally, one study that adjusted for differences among workers in psychological traits such as self-restraint, sociability, emotional stability, and so on found that measurements of the rate of return to college education are only slightly affected by these characteristics.

It is not surprising that education is doing more than merely sorting people with desirable characteristics into higher-paying jobs. Given the large differences in earnings shown in Table 3.3, it would seem highly likely that, were education simply serving as a screen, a cheaper and more efficient way of achieving this outcome could be found. After all, a college education costs well over $100,000 (including opportunity costs) while a battery of psychological tests can be administered for a few hundred dollars.[24]

---

[24]David Wise, "Academic Achievement and Job Performance," *American Economic Review* 65: 350–366 (1975). Interestingly, the benefits of going from the lower to the higher part of one's graduating class are greater if the selectivity of the undergraduate college is greater. See also Paul Taubman and Terence Wales, "Higher Education, Mental Ability and Screening," *Journal of Political Economy* 81: 28–55 (1973); M. Boissiere, J. B. Knight, and R. H. Sabot, "Earnings, Schooling, Ability and Cognitive Skills," *American Economic Review* 75: 1016–1030 (1985), and Randall Filer, "The Influence of Affective Human Capital on the Wage Equation," *Research in Labor Economics* 4: 367–409 (1981); Stephen V. Cameron and James J. Heckman, "The Nonequivalence of High School Equivalents," *Journal of Labor Economics* 11: 1–47 (1993); Linda Datcher Loury and David Garman, "College Selectivity and Earnings," *Journal of Labor Economics* 13: 289–308 (1995).

POLICY ISSUE

TOO MANY M.B.A.s?

The idea that higher earnings of more educated workers may be due to screening has led some to claim that society is spending too much on education. After all, if the only purpose of a college degree is to signal that you are a better worker than someone with a high school degree, the same result could be achieved if you finished the eighth grade and they dropped out after six years of schooling. Meanwhile, thousands of dollars could have been saved by putting both of you to work eight years earlier.

On a more realistic level, it is often said that jobs that used to require a college degree now need an M.B.A., while those that used to require an M.B.A. now need an M.B.A. from a top school, even though the jobs have not changed over time. If true, this "credentialing" effect will cause people to waste time and resources in school. They obviously could have done the job without the extra education since their counterparts in an earlier generation did not need the degree.

Recent research has shown, however, that it is a person's absolute amount of education, not her position in the distribution, that affects earnings. As average levels of education have increased over time, years of schooling have had a consistent positive effect on earnings, while relative position in the distribution of schooling has had little, if any, effect. This finding suggests that the upgrading of degree requirements over time has occurred because jobs with similar titles really are becoming more complex and demanding greater skill.[25]

When all the adjustments are made, the clear conclusion is that investment in education produces rewards in the workplace that make it very competitive with investments in physical capital. Formal education provides skills that add to productivity. Thus, we are correct in equating the growth in educational attainment with an increase in the supply of skill per hour or per labor force participant.

Students' choices about the amount of education they obtain are sensitive to the returns on education derived from its costs and the incremental earnings it produces. One study, which accounted for differences in ability and a wide variety of measures of family background, found that each 10 percent increase in the rate of return induced a nearly 20 percent increase in college enrollment. A nationwide survey of college freshmen found 70 percent stating

---

[25]Eugene A. Kroch and Kriss Sjoblom, "Schooling as Human Capital or a Signal," *Journal of Human Resources* 29: 156–180 (1994).

that to "make more money" was a "very important [reason] in deciding to go to college."[26]

Educated labor is an economic good in that it is scarce. Like other economic goods its supply is responsive to its price. It is reasonable to conclude that the long-run supply curve of educated labor is fairly flat around a true social rate of return that is relatively high even accounting for the risks of investments in education.

THE QUALITY OF SCHOOLING

So far, the discussion has dealt with the *quantity of schooling*. Each particular year of education has been treated as if it were equally productive no matter what other resources were combined with the student's school time to generate the skills that are the outcome of education. The theory of production taught in economic principles classes (and developed further in Chapter 4) implies that time spent in school will be more productive if it is combined with other inputs. According to production theory, better teachers, more classroom aids, and more able fellow students should all raise the rate of return to a year of schooling. Moreover, the rate of return to a year of schooling should be greater if it contains more time, either through longer or more school days or a greater fraction of each day devoted to study.

Do these other inputs really raise the productivity of a year spent in school? Several studies have examined how students' ability affects the rate of return to schooling. The consensus in the literature is that more able students do benefit more (have a higher rate of return) from a year of schooling than less able students.[27]

An even larger effort has been devoted to examining whether spending more on schools improves the quality of education. The evidence suggests

---

[26]Numerous American studies of the relation between the demand for college education and its costs and benefits are summarized by Leonard Miller, "Demand for Higher Education in the United States: A Second Progress Report," in Joseph Froomkin, Dean Jamison, and Roy Radner (eds.). *Education as an Industry*, Cambridge, Mass.: Ballinger, (1976). A British study is Christopher Pissarides, "From School to University: The Demand for Post-Compulsory Education in Britain," *Economic Journal* 92: 654–667 (1982). The specific effect cited in the text is from Robert Willis and Sherwin Rosen, "Education and Self-Selection," *Journal of Political Economy* 81: S32 (1979). The survey results are reported in the *New York Times*, p. 9, (January 29, 1983).

[27]This can be inferred from a variety of studies in the 1970s designed to examine how the correlation of ability with the amount of schooling affects the rate of return. See, for examples, Lee Lillard, "Inequality: Earnings vs. Human Wealth," *American Economic Review* 67: 47 (1977); John Hause, "Ability and Schooling as Determinants of Lifetime Earnings, or If You're So Smart, Why Aren't You Rich?" in F. Thomas Juster (ed.). *Education, Income and Human Behavior*, New York: McGraw-Hill, (1975).

that the effect of additional funds on students' test scores is small,[28] but the key question is what effect do additional inputs have on rates of return to schooling. Examining adults of different cohorts and from different states, one study found that greater spending on teachers' salaries and on reducing student-teacher ratios may increase the rate of return.[29]

POLICY ISSUE

IMPROVING THE PERFORMANCE OF AMERICAN STUDENTS

Between 1967 and 1980 the performance of American students on standardized tests fell by an unprecedented amount, the equivalent of 1.25 grade levels. The decline stopped in 1980, but has not been reversed. This apparent drop in performance occurred at a time when the average quantity of schooling in the U.S. rose slightly, as shown in Table 3.2. One estimate of the effect of this apparent decline in skill suggests that if test scores had not fallen, gross national product (GNP) in the late 1980s would have been 2.7 percent higher ($86 billion per year in 1987).[30]

What can be done to improve this sorry record? In comparative terms, what inputs are lacking in American schools that make schools in other countries generate higher-quality education? The problem is not decreasing resources devoted to education. Per-pupil spending in real terms rose by 3.5 percent per year between 1970 and 1989, far faster than the 1.8 percent annual increase in per-capita GNP. Another input into producing skills through formal education is the time spent in school and at home studying. Table 3.6 shows these inputs for the U.S., Japan, and Korea at various grade levels. The U.S. lags far behind other countries in devoting these crucial resources to education. Not only is the school day shorter, but American students also do practically no homework compared to their Korean and Japanese counterparts.

Although there may be some problems comparing the data across these countries, the striking conclusion is that one crucial input into creating educational quality may be lacking in the U.S. How productive that input is in generating skills (i.e., how much productivity growth would be improved by devoting more time to studying) is unclear. It is difficult to believe, however, that increasing study time would not have a significant effect on the subsequent productivity and earnings of American workers.

---

[28]Eric Hanushek, "The Economics of Schooling: Production and Efficiency in Public Schools," *Journal of Economic Literature* 24: 1141–1177 (1986).

[29]David Card and Alan Krueger, "Does School Quality Matter? Returns to Education and the Characteristics of Public Schools in the United States," *Journal of Political Economy* 100: 1–40 (1992).

[30]John Bishop, "Is the Test Score Decline Responsible for the Productivity Growth Decline?" *American Economic Review* 79: 178–197 (1989).

TABLE 3.6 STUDY TIME BY SCHOOL LEVEL IN THE UNITED STATES, JAPAN, AND KOREA (HOURS PER WEEK)

School Level	U.S.	Japan	Korea[a]
Primary			
In school	25.2	38.2	38.9
At home	1.8	8.3	
Junior high school			
In school	28.7	46.6	58.4
At home	3.2	16.2	
Senior high school			
In school	26.2	41.5	61.4
At home	3.8	19.0	

[a]Total time spent on school work, both in school and at home.

Source: Based on data assembled by Frank Stafford, "Early Education of Children by Families and Schools," in Paul Menchik (ed.), *Household and Family Economics*, Boston: Kluwer (1995).

POLICY ISSUE

GETTING MORE FOR THE SCHOOL DOLLAR

The relatively weak evidence for the effect of added educational expenditures has led many to seek ways of increasing the effectiveness of each dollar spent. One means advocated by some is to adopt a program either of educational vouchers or public school choice. Vouchers would provide the parents of each student with a fixed amount (equal to or less than the amount currently spent by the local public school) to pay tuition at any school of their choice. Public school choice would allow students to opt to attend any public school in their jurisdiction, or perhaps even their state.

Advocates argue that as long as students are forced to go to the local school, these schools have no incentive to be as efficient as possible (i.e., produce the highest rate of return for each dollar spent). With choice, they believe that parents, who want the best for their children, will naturally seek out the most effective schools, causing these schools to expand while the less successful schools will not attract students and will be forced to close. Critics argue that, if it works at all, such a program would only benefit students with the most educated and conscientious parents, leaving the least advantaged students in the worst schools.

Perhaps the best evidence that it is possible to improve the efficiency of American schools comes from a comparison of the results achieved by public and parochial (Catholic) schools in the U.S. In 1992–93 public elementary and secondary schools spent an average of $6059 per enrolled pupil while all private schools combined (including both parochial and independent ones) only averaged $4074 per pupil. Despite this substantial difference in expenditures, several studies have shown that parochial school students are more likely to stay in school, go to college, and earn more after leaving school than public school students who look the same on every characteristic researchers can measure (such as race or family background). Some have argued that this difference occurs because parochial school students are more motivated or different in ways that we cannot measure. Otherwise, why would they or their parents be willing to pay when they could go to public schools for free?

The latest research, using statistical techniques to control for these unobserved differences, finds that attending Catholic schools substantially affects probabilities of further schooling and future wages. Interestingly, these effects are concentrated among minority men from disadvantaged urban areas. It appears that for some disadvantaged students vouchers would increase the gross returns from education while reducing costs, thereby substantially increasing rates of return. Whether they would have offsetting negative effects on social integration remains an issue for further research.[31]

SKILL ACQUIRED ON THE JOB

THE DECISION TO INVEST IN TRAINING

Schooling alone does not explain the growth in real earnings over a worker's career. Since formal schooling usually stops by age 25, if education were the only cause of higher earnings, age-earnings profiles would be flat after that age. Indeed, since human capital like physical capital depreciates over time, earnings would probably drop after leaving school as skills acquired there become obsolete. Investment in **on-the-job training** is the major reason why age-earnings profiles slope upward through much of the work life. Education may reinforce this effect if investments in schooling enable workers to learn better and profit more from later on-the-job training.

On-the-job training varies from formal programs not unlike schools to the simplest forms of learning by doing, observing others, and being reprimanded for mistakes. Since there are substantial economies of scale in conducting formal training programs, they tend to be run mainly by large employers. In 1993, 69 percent of American companies with fewer than 50 employees and over 98 percent of those with more than 50 employees offered formal training in the form of classroom work, seminars, lectures, workshops or audiovisual presentations to their workers. The most common areas for training were sales and customer relations, management, computer skills,

---

[31]J. Coleman, T. Hoffer and S. Kilgore, *Public, Catholic, and Private Schools: The Importance of Community*, New York: Basic Books, (1987); W. Evans and R. Schwab, "Our Lady of the Sacred Heart vs. PS 112: The Relative Efficiency of Catholic and Public Schools," unpublished manuscript, University of Maryland (1993); B. S. Tyler, "An Analysis of Public and Catholic Secondary Education and the Earnings of Men," unpublished dissertation, University of Chicago (1994); Derek Neal, "The Effect of Catholic Secondary Schooling on Educational Attainment," Center for the Study of the Economy and the State Working Paper No. 95, University of Chicago (1994).

and safety issues. The extent of formal training in 1993 was considerably higher than was found in an earlier survey from 1987.[32] On-the-job training of a less formal nature is likely to occur in all types of firms since it takes place while workers are actually on the job.

Where training is clearly a separable activity, its costs can be precisely identified. For example, training an airline pilot to fly a new type of aircraft involves costs that include the pay of the instructor and the trainee, the operating and capital costs of the aircraft, and perhaps the cost of special materials or equipment, such as flight simulators. Where training takes place concurrently with production, the costs may be more difficult to measure. Some of the trainees' time as well as that of their supervisors or coworkers is devoted to training. Output is therefore less than it would be if all workers were fully trained. The use of machinery on which workers are being trained creates higher expenses for capital than if workers already knew their jobs. Similarly, materials may be wasted in scrap or defective products owing to trainees' inexperience.

Although the costs of informal training are generally hard to measure, they probably total much more than those of formal training programs in the workplace. One 1987 study estimated the opportunity cost of on-the-job training in the U.S. as $313 billion (1994 dollars), equal to 11 percent of total compensation (wages and benefits) and 1.3 times the amount spent on elementary and secondary schools.[33]

Whether employers or workers bear the cost of the training depends on the nature of the training provided. Employers will not incur these costs unless they expect enough extra output in the future to provide a rate of return equal to that obtainable on competitive investments. Workers will be unwilling to pay for on-the-job training (usually by sacrificing pay while being trained) unless they can be assured of a higher wage later on. To the extent that these costs are expected to produce enough future benefits to provide a competitive rate of return, employers will offer training and workers will seek training opportunities.

GENERAL AND SPECIFIC HUMAN CAPITAL

In order to understand who pays the costs of on-the-job training, it is helpful to distinguish between two different types of human capital and, therefore, two different types of training. **General human capital** involves skills that are of equal value in many different organizations. An example might be

[32]Ann Bartel, "Formal Employee Training Programs and their Impact on Labor Productivity: Evidence from a Human Resources Survey," in David Stern and Jozef Ritzen (eds.). Market Failure in Training? New Economic Analysis and Evidence on Training of Adult Employees, New York: Springer, (1991); U.S Department of Labor, Bureau of Labor Statistics, News 94–432, Washington, D.C. (September 23, 1994).

[33]Jacob Mincer, "Studies in."

learning a widely used word processing program. **Specific human capital** involves skills that are of value only to a single employer, either because they are a **monopsonist** (the only employer of that type of worker) or because of special methods, routines, and equipment with which workers must become familiar.[34]

This distinction allows us to predict whether the employer or the worker will pay for training. Whoever bears the cost must also expect to receive the return or there will be no incentive to invest. Assume that the productivity of untrained workers would justify a wage rate of w_1 in Figure 3.6. For simplicity's sake, we will assume that training takes place during the first period on the job. While being trained, workers' productivity is reduced and out-of-pocket training costs are incurred. Therefore, the net value to the firm of workers' services during training is only w_0 where the difference $w_1 - w_0$ equals the cost of the training. After training, the worker's higher productivity would be equal to w_2 and would justify this wage if there were no training costs to recover.

Suppose the training produces general human capital. Employers will force employees to pay for this training by paying them only w_0 while being trained. If the firm paid any costs of training (by paying a wage greater than w_0), it would have to receive a return on its investment after the training was completed. The only way it could achieve such a return would be to pay workers less than their productivity (w_2) after training. What incentives would this create for workers and other firms? If the employer pays less than w_2 in an attempt to recover training costs, it would be paying workers less than their productivity. Since the training was general, the workers are more productive at other firms as well, and they would simply seek another job paying w_2. Other employers can use the general training and can offer the worker her full productivity, w_2, since they have no training costs to recover. In this case the current employer must also pay w_2 or the worker will leave the job. In either case (if it pays w_2 or if the employee leaves) the employer cannot recover any of its costs of training and will only be willing to provide it if the employee pays the full cost by accepting a wage of w_0 while being trained. Thus, general training will be financed entirely by workers.

On the other hand, if training is firm-specific, employers have a means of recovering their investment costs. If workers leave the firm after training, the best they can earn is w_1 since the training has no value to other firms. If they stay with their current firm, their employer can pay them only slightly more than w_1 throughout their working lives. The employer can use the excess of productivity over the wage (an amount slightly less than $w_2 - w_1$) to recover his expenditures on training. Thus, the employer can continue to pay the worker a wage of w_1 during training even though productivity is only w_0.

In a more realistic world, an employer must take into account the fact that workers might leave their current job. Perhaps demand conditions will

---

[34]Becker, *Human Capital,* pp. 8–28.

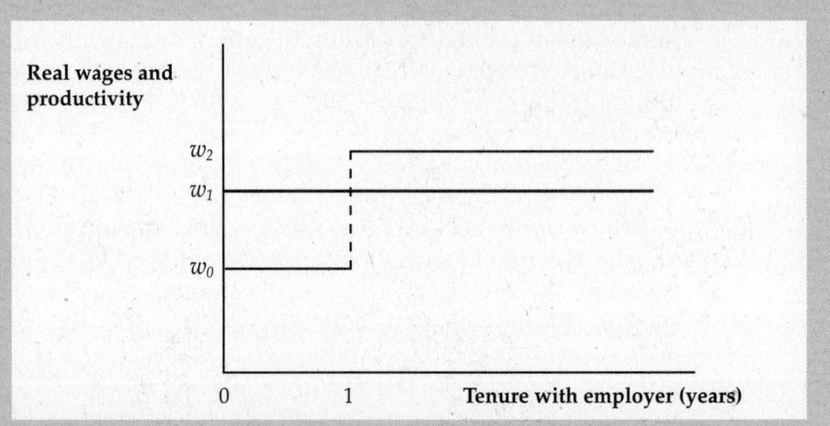

FIGURE 3.6 WAGES AND TRAINING

Workers whose productivity is w_1 without training and w_2 after training but w_0 while being trained can "pay" for their training by accepting wage w_0 during the training period and receiving w_2 after training is completed. Alternatively, they can always receive wage w_1 and let the employer both pay for and receive the benefits from training. The latter option is only available if the training provides specific rather than general human capital. Even in this case, however, employers are likely to require workers to pay for part of their training by accepting lower wages while being trained in return for increased wages later.

make a job at another firm attractive or perhaps they will want to move for personal reasons. In either case, the employer would like to find ways to induce trained workers to remain on their current jobs in order not to lose investments in specific training. The easiest way is to require the worker to share the investment in specific training so that a move on the worker's part would cause the worker to lose his investment. This suggests that the wage paid during training will be less than w_1, even for specific training, and therefore, that wages higher than w_1 will be paid to workers who have received training. Another reason why firms may require employees to pay part of the costs of acquiring specific human capital involves incentives to learn. Since effective training requires participation by the employee, firms that paid all the costs of training (and therefore expected to receive all the benefits) might wonder why their employees (who did not expect any benefit from higher productivity) would bother to learn anything from the training.

How the costs and return to training are divided between firms and workers depends on such factors as the probability that workers will change jobs and how constrained workers are in having resources to invest in training. In any case, the analysis outlined above indicates that workers will pay at least some costs of both types of training, and, therefore, that wages should increase after training. This creates an upward-sloping age-earnings profile as long as training is taking place. Among identical workers, those with lower initial wages have more rapid wage growth so that the present value of income is the same, just as the theory of human capital investment would imply.[35]

General and specific training are really two ends of a continuum rather than alternatives. In most cases a new worker simultaneously acquires some general skills and some that are specific to the firm. Despite our inability to separate the two types of training, the distinction is important for several reasons. It points out that the supply of skill may consist of components not generally useful in the economy as a whole. Firm-specific training provides a reason for different patterns of worker attachment to employers by age, industry, and occupation. It also has implications for the pattern of wage differences among workers.

EVIDENCE REGARDING GENERAL AND SPECIFIC TRAINING

Insight into the division of on-the-job training between general and specific skills can be gained by examining how wages change with workers' **experience** (time worked at all firms) versus how they change with **tenure** (time at the current employer). The effect of firm-specific training can be seen by considering workers who have held several jobs. Any general training acquired through experience with their previous employers will also be useful on their current jobs. Firm-specific training acquired elsewhere, however, does not raise their productivity with current employers. Additional experience raises earnings, as the age-earnings profiles we have discussed make very clear. Additional tenure with the current employer should have an especially large impact, since its effects on wages reflect the returns to both general and firm-specific training. Similarly, any formal company training program undertaken in the current job should have a larger effect on wages than a similar program undertaken before the worker started with the current employer.

Empirical studies confirm these expectations. Training has larger effects on wages if the firm provides it than if the worker takes the training elsewhere. Among adult men in the U.S. between 1968 and 1981, an extra year of job tenure added nearly twice as much to earnings as a year of experience in previous jobs. Similar extra effects of job tenure have been observed in many European countries, and in developing countries such as Mexico, Guatemala, the Ivory Coast, and others.[36] During the transition from communism in

---

[35]David Neumark and Paul J. Taubman, "Why Do Wage Profiles Slope Upwards? Tests of the General Human Capital Model," *Journal of Labor Economics* 13: 736–761 (1995).

[36]Calculated from Jacob Mincer, "Studies in." Somewhat larger effects are implied by estimates in Albert Rees and George P. Shultz, *Workers and Wages in an Urban Labor Market*, Chicago: University of Chicago Press, (1970), pp. 152–156. The estimates for developing countries are from Richard Miller and Mahmood Zaidi, "Human Capital and Earnings: Some Evidence from Brazil and Mexico," Industrial Relations Research Association, *Proceedings* 34: 207–214 (1981); Katherine Terrell, "An Analysis of the Wage Structure in Guatemala City," *Journal of Developing Areas* 2: 405–424 (1989); Victor Levy and John Newman, "Wage Rigidity: Micro and Macro Evidence on Labor Adjustment in the Modern Sector," *World Bank Economic Review* 3: 97–117 (1989).

POLICY ISSUE

GENERAL VERSUS SPECIFIC SCHOOLING

The distinction between general and specific human capital is also helpful in understanding schooling. North American school systems are geared toward providing general human capital. Most American high school students follow a general academic program. In college, while some students may choose a major leading to a specific job (such as nursing), most students choose a broader liberal arts curriculum, and almost all students must meet distribution requirements.

In Europe on the other hand, the educational system is oriented toward producing specific human capital. In Germany, for example, at about age 15 students must choose between a college-preparatory high school program and the more common *arbeitslehre* combination of vocationally oriented coursework and an apprenticeship with a particular firm. If they opt for college, most German students study only one subject, such as math or economics, for their entire college career.

There are clear advantages to each system. Many argue that the German system provides greater incentives for non-college-bound students to stay in school and helps to ease the school-to-work transition. On the other hand, in a rapidly changing world, too much specific training too early exposes students to a risk of their skills becoming obsolete, leaving them with little general human capital on which to fall back. Advocates of the American model argue that workers will have to learn many jobs over their lifetime and the proper role of schools is to teach students how to learn so that they can adapt to whatever changes they may confront. It is interesting to observe, as we will see later, that when German workers become unemployed they typically stay that way far longer than American workers.

Eastern Europe, returns to education (typically general human capital) remained largely unaffected, while those for experience (which provides at least some specific human capital) fell.[37] More direct evidence that only part of training is usable outside the firm offering it is provided by a study of the skills taught in the U.S. military, only half of which were transferable to civilian jobs.[38]

Unfortunately just because workers with longer tenure earn more than those with less tenure does not prove that specific human capital exists. There is another possibility. Consider a group of workers, all of whom start with an employer at the same time. Suppose that some are very well-suited to the job, are very productive, and earn high wages, while others are poorly matched to the job, relatively unproductive, and earn low wages. Over time

---

[37]Alan B. Krueger and Jörn-Steffen Pischke, "A Comparative Analysis of East and West German Labor Markets: Before and After Unification," NBER Working Paper No. 4154 (1992); Edward J. Bird, Johannes Schwarze, and Gert G. Wagner, "Wage Effects of the Move Toward Free Markets in East Germany," *Industrial and Labor Relations Review*, 47: 390–400 (1994).

[38]Stephen Mangum and David Ball, "The Transferability of Military-Provided Occupational Training in the Post-Draft Era," *Industrial and Labor Relations Review* 42: 230–245 (1989).

those in the second group will either be discharged by the employer or will leave for jobs elsewhere that better suit their skills and interests. Thus, as tenure increases, the workers who remain with the employer will consist more and more of high-wage employees, and the average wage will increase with tenure even if no individual worker received training on the job.[39]

Part of the resolution of this argument must be postponed until the discussion of internal labor markets in Chapter 9, but the evidence suggests that lengthier job tenure does increase productivity. Workers who were laid off due to plant closings in the 1980s suffered greater wage losses the longer they had been at their previous jobs, presumably because they had more to lose due to their firm-specific training. Accounting for many hard-to-measure differences in ability, a study of a national sample of U.S. workers followed from 1968 through 1983 found that 10 years of job tenure raised wages 25 percent above those of otherwise identical workers. Another study, which used job satisfaction as a measure to account for differences among workers in how well they fit into their firms, reached a similar conclusion. Finally, the greater wage-loss of high-tenure workers has been shown to exist even after controlling for whether they were in declining industries or regions. Like the relationships between education and wages, and experience and wages, the best evidence indicates that most of the relationship between wages and job tenure reflects the growth of skills.[40]

TRAINING LEVELS OVER THE WORK LIFE

There should be differences in the amount of training that takes place at different points in a worker's life. When employers expect workers to be with the firm a long time, they are more willing to offer training since there is a longer period to receive returns on the investment. Similarly, workers will be more willing to purchase specific training if they expect to stay with the firm longer, or both specific and general training if they are younger. In both cases they have a longer time to reap the returns on the investment. These factors predict that workers spend the highest fraction of on-the-job time learning right after they complete their formal education, and that training declines thereafter. At some point in the work life training will no longer pay since there is not sufficient time left to make the investment pay off. A study of the weekly hours devoted to on-the-job training in the U.S. in 1976 showed a decline from 6.4 hours below age 25 to 4.3 hours between ages 25 and 34,

---

[39]Katharine Abraham and Henry Farber, "Job Duration, Seniority and Earnings," *American Economic Review* 77: 278–297 (1987); Joseph Altonji and Robert Shakotko, "Do Wages Rise with Job Seniority?" *Review of Economic Studies* 54: 437–459 (1987).

[40]Robert Topel, "Specific Capital, Mobility, and Wages: Wages Rise with Job Seniority," *Journal of Political Economy* 99: 145–176 (1991); Joni Hersch and Patricia Reagan, "Job Match, Tenure and Wages Paid by Firms," *Economic Inquiry* 28: 488–507 (1990); William J. Carrington, "Wage Losses for Displaced Workers: Is It Really the Firm that Matters?" *Journal of Human Resources* 28: 435–462 (1993).

to 3.8, 2.2, and 1.1 hours among age groups 35 to 44, 45 to 54 and 55 to 64. Moreover, the fraction of people reporting spending time in training diminished steadily as workers aged. Women, who have shorter expected work lives at each age due to spending more time out of the labor force, receive less on-the-job training than men.[41]

These considerations suggest that the pattern of investment in on-the-job training over the work life is described by a curve like *AA'* in Figure 3.7. The left-hand vertical axis shows the fraction of each year at work that the individual spends in on-the-job training. The worker starts off devoting a substantial fraction of work time to training, but this share declines steadily over time.

This pattern of declining investment in on-the-job training during the work life carries specific implications for age-earnings profiles. The workers' productivity or **earnings capacity** is shown by the curve *CC'*. (Note that dollar amounts are shown on the right-hand vertical axis.) Capacity rises rapidly early in the work life because of the large investment in on-the-job training. It rises much less rapidly as the worker ages, since less is being invested in training. Actual earnings, shown by the curve *BB'*, are also rising, but lie below earnings capacity because the worker is devoting some of her earnings capacity to additional training. Since the worker's investment in training decreases as she ages, the difference between earnings capacity and actual earnings also decreases. The difference is zero at the age when the worker is no longer investing in acquiring new skills (point *F* in Figure 3.7).

Unlike the simplified world we examined in discussing Figure 3.2, it is possible for workers' earnings to actually decline toward the end of their working life. This could occur if the workers' stock of human capital depreciated over time, perhaps because new technologies made their human capital obsolete. At point *D* earnings begin to decrease, since the relatively low level of new investment is no longer enough to offset the effect of depreciation on the stock of skills. Earnings drop more rapidly near the end of the work life, when the stock of skills is still depreciating but is no longer being augmented by additional investment.

The theory of investment in on-the-job training interacts with the theory of investment in formal education to explain the later peak of age-earnings profiles for more educated workers and the fanning out of the profiles for workers with different levels of education in Figure 3.1. More educated workers choose to invest more and longer periods of time in on-the-job training. On-the-job training and formal schooling are apparently complementary. Greater education increases the productivity of on-the-job training, thereby increasing the amount acquired by more educated workers, although some of

---

[41] Frank Stafford and Greg Duncan, "The Use of Time and Technology by Households in the United States," *Research in Labor Economics* 3: 335–375 (1980); Joseph G. Altonji and James R. Spletzer, "Worker Characteristics, Job Characteristics and the Receipt of On-the-Job Training," *Industrial and Labor Relations Review* 45: 58–79 (1991).

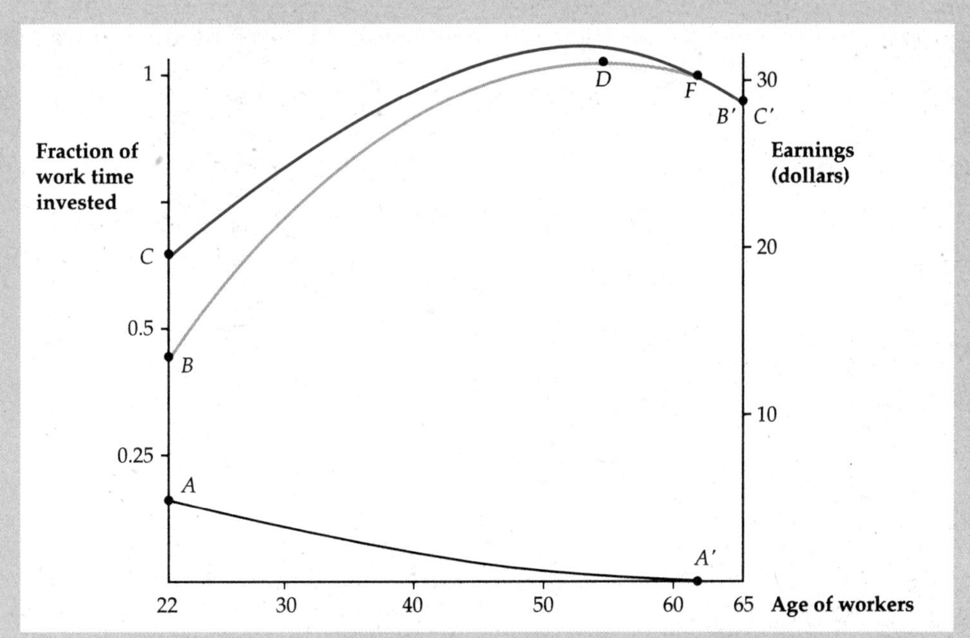

FIGURE 3.7 EARNINGS AND INVESTMENT IN ON-THE-JOB TRAINING
As workers age they have a shorter remaining work life to receive returns on training, so the amount they invest declines along *AA'*. This results in a slower growth of earnings for older workers. The downturn in earnings after point *D* occurs if human capital depreciates.

this difference may be due to workers with more ability acquiring both more education and more training.[42]

Even if more educated workers invested the same amount as other workers in training on the job, however, their earnings would likely peak later in life. Because they usually start their full-time work at a later age, the investment profile *AA'* in Figure 3.7 will produce a peak in earnings capacity and actual earnings at a later age.

THE SOCIAL RATE OF RETURN TO ON-THE-JOB TRAINING

The theory of on-the-job training elegantly describes the optimizing behavior of both workers and employers. Its predictions about age-earnings profiles fit

[42]Altonji and Spletzer, "Worker Characteristics;" Jacob Mincer, *Schooling, Experience and Earnings,* New York: National Bureau of Economic Research, (1974), p. 73.

the observed data well, but just as some observers have objected to the theory of investment in schooling, others have objected to this theory. They argue that age-earnings profiles cannot reflect the effects of productive investment, since experience does not seem to be related to workers' performance as measured by supervisors' assessments. If this is true, we cannot claim that differences in work experience represent differences in the amount of skill supplied to employers.

One study actually found that, adjusting for differences in schooling, workers with more experience in a job category at one large company received worse evaluations than their less-experienced coworkers. Other research has found, however, that workers who participated in more training on the job received better performance ratings.

Direct observations suggest productivity is increased by training. One study measuring the productivity of government employees who search for violations of the Fair Labor Standards Act showed that those with more experience found more violations. Similarly, recruiters for the U.S. Navy steadily increased the number of recruits they signed up each month during their first two years on the job (although thereafter little improvement occurred in monthly productivity). A broad sample of private employers has reported steadily increasing productivity early in workers' stay on the job. Using records from a single company, one study estimated the return to formal training to be 13 percent.[43]

Another line of research examining earnings profiles rather than direct measures of productivity finds similar results. It shows that wages rise especially rapidly during the initial period on the job, exactly the time when workers report themselves undergoing the training required to make them fully competent on the job. This result suggests that there is a relationship between wage growth and investment in on-the-job training.[44]

Based on the available evidence, it seems reasonable to conclude that additional experience represents additional skill that raises workers' productivity. The apparently anomalous finding regarding supervisors' ratings may have been caused by their applying different standards to workers with different levels of experience, or because the study looked at narrowly defined

---

[43]James Medoff and Katharine Abraham, "Are Those Paid More Really More Productive? The Case of Experience," *Journal of Human Resources* 16: 186–216 (1981); Cheryl Maranto and Robert Rodgers, "A Test of the On-the-Job Training Hypothesis," *Journal of Human Resources* 19: 341–357 (1984); Peter Kostiuk and Dean Follmann, "Learning Curves, Personal Characteristics and Job Performance," *Journal of Labor Economics* 7: 129–146 (1989); John Barron, Dan Black, and Mark Loewenstein, "Job Matching and On-the-Job Training," *Journal of Labor Economics* 7: 1–19 (1989); Ann P. Bartel, "Training, Wage Growth and Job Performance: Evidence from a Company Data Base," *Journal of Labor Economics* 13: 401–425 (1995); Alan Krueger and Cecelia Rouse, "New Evidence on Workplace Education," Princeton University Industrial Relations Section Working Paper No. 329 (1994).

[44]Kevin Murphy and Finis Welch, "Empirical Age-Earnings Profiles," *Journal of Labor Economics* 8: 202–229 (1990); James Brown, "Why Do Wages Increase with Tenure?" *American Economic Review* 79: 971–991 (1989).

job categories and more productive workers had been promoted out of the category causing the only workers with a large amount of experience remaining within the category to be the less productive ones.

POLICY ISSUE

IS SUBSIDIZED ON-THE-JOB TRAINING PRODUCTIVE?

In most developed countries the national government offers employers subsidies to cover some costs of on-the-job training. These subsidies may take the form of fixed-amount grants to employers, or they may be paid as wage subsidies during an employee's early years, in recognition of the fact that much training is received early in one's tenure with a particular employer. For most periods since 1962 the U.S. government has offered subsidies to employers to defray the costs of training new workers. These have been either direct subsidies or payments channelled through local agencies under JTPA, the Job Training Partnership Act of 1982, and its predecessor, CETA, the Comprehensive Employment and Training Act of 1973.[45] In 1994 JTPA expenditures totalled $3.6 billion, targeted at training unemployed or very low-wage workers whose prior work records indicated they had not accumulated the skills to guarantee stable employment at a decent wage.

An international comparison that attempted to use comparable definitions of government labor market activities showed that the U.S. spent about 0.24 percent of its 1993 to 1994 GDP on **active labor market policies**, including training, vocational rehabilitation, employment subsidies, and the public employment service. About two-thirds of this amount was spent on various training programs. U.S. spending was less than in most other developed countries. Canada, for example, spent 0.65 percent, France 0.98 percent, Germany 1.58 percent, Italy 0.93 percent, Sweden 2.56 percent, and the United Kingdom 0.52 percent. Among the larger industrialized countries, only Japan, with 0.09 percent, devoted less of its resources to active government intervention in the labor market.[46] Was the American choice reasonable? Do such subsidies increase the amount of human capital embodied in the work force?

The argument for such subsidies rests on several grounds. Unless unemployment is very low, firms are unlikely to offer training to the most disadvantaged, least-educated members of the work force without inducements from the government. Given difficulties in borrowing and the riskiness of investments in training, these workers cannot finance training themselves. Government-subsidized training can provide them with opportunities they would not otherwise receive, allowing them to launch themselves on a path of steady earnings over the rest of their work lives. This argument suggests that the social rate of return to

[45]A thorough description of employment and training programs in the United States through the 1960s and 1970s is provided in Sar Levitan, Garth Mangum, and Ray Marshall, *Human Resources and the Labor Market*, New York: Harper & Row, (1981). More recent information is obtainable from Department of Labor, *Training and Employment Report of the Secretary of Labor*, most recent edition.

[46]Data for 1990 from OECD, *Employment Outlook*, (1991), pp. 238–249.

such training exceeds the private rate of return. Because of the stable employment subsidized training will engender, antisocial behavior by an alienated segment of the work force may be reduced.

The counterargument also has several bases. Those who are offered subsidized training may merely **displace** other workers with similar backgrounds who would otherwise have received the training. While the private rate of return to those receiving the training may be large, the social rate of return is small, because there is little net addition of skills in the work force. In this view the subsidies only shuffle training opportunities around within the low-skilled work force. A second counterargument is that the training will have little value if aggregate demand is insufficient to provide steady jobs for the workers after they are trained. This line of attack suggests that the government would increase the skill level of the population more by maintaining high aggregate demand and thus creating jobs directly.

The relative merits of these arguments cannot easily be discerned in the real world. Economists have attempted to answer only the narrower question of whether those who receive subsidized training increase their earnings sufficiently to justify the government's investment. Substantial effort has been devoted to **cost-benefit analyses** of government subsidized training.

One study dealt with persons trained in 1975 and 1976, whose earnings were observed in 1977 and 1978. It indicated that the program was fairly successful in yielding higher post-training earnings for female participants, especially for white females. Among males there was no evidence of any gain in earnings compared to what otherwise identical males who did not undertake training obtained. Other estimates suggest that the programs did increase the probability that the person trained would remain employed. This was especially true for programs that trained workers outside the plant, but less true for those that subsidized employers to offer training on the job. A series of evaluations of training programs in the 1980s found similar results. One program of subsidized on-the-job training in Maine cost $2019 per participant in 1983 and resulted in increased annual earnings of $941 three years later. On the other hand, a classroom-based program of training AFDC recipients to become home health workers cost $9500 per trainee but only increased earnings by $1121 three years later.[47]

Because the structure of government-funded training programs changes so frequently, it is very risky to use cost-benefit analyses of previous subsidized on-the-job training programs as a guide to the success of current or future programs. These results suggest, however, that the private rate of return to this form of subsidized training may be positive, at least for some groups of workers. Whether the social rate of return is as large is unclear.

---

[47] Lauri Bassi, "Estimating the Effect of Training Programs with Nonrandom Selection," *Review of Economics and Statistics* 66: 36–43 (1984); David Card and Daniel Sullivan, "Measuring the Effect of Subsidized Training Programs on Movements In and Out of Employment," *Econometrica* 56: 497–530 (1988); Judith Gueron and Edward Pauly, *From Welfare to Work,* New York: Russel Sage Foundation, (1991).

OCCUPATIONS—AGGREGATES OF SKILLS

Although the economics of investment in human capital relates to investment in skills, much of the available information on which this theory is tested, like that shown in Table 3.1, relates to occupations. Individuals choose occupations when initiating the process of investing in human capital. Thus, it is important to distinguish between a skill and an occupation.

A **skill** can be defined as the ability to perform a particular task well. An **occupation** is a line of work in which those employed use a particular combination of skills to contribute to the production of some marketable good or service. Some skills are useful in only one occupation (or for personal enjoyment), and may even be the principal requirement for following that occupation (e.g., cutting hair for a barber or flying an airplane for a pilot). We call these occupation-specific skills, and they result from **occupation-specific training**. Others, like the ability to write good prose, are useful in a wide variety of occupations, although they will be more important in some (such as journalism) than in others (such as sheet metal work). Students who have not yet developed a strong preference for a particular occupation or who are uncertain about their prospects in various occupations can hedge by investing in skills with several uses.

Occupation-specific investment represents an important component of an individual's total investments in human capital. One estimate indicates that it is at least as important as firm-specific investment.[48] This finding suggests that individuals may incur substantial losses on their prior investments in human capital when the demand for workers in their occupation declines sharply and unexpectedly. Expected declines (or ones where the probability of decline is known) do not, on average, result in such losses. Workers must have earned higher than normal returns on their skills while they were using them or they would not have chosen to enter these occupations.

Since we cannot directly observe the earnings produced by particular skills, we must use data on earnings by occupation to measure the returns to different types of skills (as distinguished from the quantity of schooling). Age-earnings profiles for different occupations show the expected relationship between the amount of training and the shape of the profile. In those occupations in which more skill is acquired, through both formal schooling and on-the-job investment, the age-earnings profile is both higher on average and much steeper. For example, data from the census show that the average earnings of male professional workers between the ages of 25 and 34 in 1969 rose 196 percent over the next decade; among male sales workers the increase was 171 percent, but among male service workers the increase was only 120 percent. These occupational cohort age-earnings profiles are steeper between ages 25 to 34 and 35 to 44 in the occupations that required more education and training.

---

[48]Kathryn Shaw, "A Formulation of the Earnings Function Using the Concept of Occupational Investment," *Journal of Human Resources* 19: 319–340 (1984).

POLICY ISSUE

ADVANCE NOTIFICATION OF LAYOFFS

Most European countries require employers to inform their workers well in advance (in some cases up to two years) of major layoffs or plant closings. The purpose of these laws is to ease the transition for displaced workers into other jobs or into training programs. In the U.S., bills requiring advance notification were introduced into Congress as early as 1974. In 1988 Congress passed, and the president signed, the Worker Adjustment and Retraining Notification Act (with the snappy acronym WARN). Its opponents argued that such notification interferes with business. Its proponents felt that workers are otherwise unable to plan their lives and would suffer greater losses than without the warning. Is this reasoning correct, or can workers anticipate mass layoffs and plan accordingly?

If a plant closes, workers' prior investments in specific training become worthless. With good information about their employers' financial condition, workers would reduce their investment in firm-specific training during the years immediately prior to the expected plant closing, realizing that the payout period to such investment is shortened. Conversely, if workers have no information about how well the firm is doing, they will continue investing in this type of training until the day the firm closes and then discover that their entire stock of firm-specific training has been rendered worthless.

Evidence suggests that workers in plants that close continue to invest in at least some specific training as the date of the plant's closing approaches. The typical displaced worker in one group studied lost specific human capital valued at nearly $10,000 (1986 dollars). Interestingly, three to five years after job displacements, workers who received advance notice earned approximately 10 percent more than those who did not receive such notice. This effect may not be due to the notice, however, since workers who received notice were more likely to receive other forms of assistance such as retraining, supplemental unemployment benefits, and outplacement assistance.[49]

Thus it might be that advance notification does help workers who would otherwise be surprised by losing their job and suffer greater lost wages. But WARN may produce additional costs for business. There is some evidence that workers who are warned are more likely to quit.[50] They may also try less hard and perform less well on jobs they know they are going to lose anyway. This balance must be considered along with any impact of WARN on businesses' willingness to undertake investment in new plants and equipment.

Other things being equal, young people trying to decide which of two occupations to enter naturally tend to choose the one where the present value of the income stream is higher. Of course, other factors are also important determinants of career choice. Occupations differ not only in their earnings, but also in the conditions under which they are performed. These issues are discussed in Chapter 10. Personal tastes, interests, and the influence of par-

---

[49]Daniel Hamermesh, "The Costs of Worker Displacement," *Quarterly Journal of Economics* 102: 51–76 (1987); Christopher J. Ruhm, "Advance Notice, Job Search, and Postdisplacement Earnings," *Journal of Labor Economics* 12: 1–28 (1994).

[50]Bruce Fallick, "The Endogeneity of Advance Notice and Fear of Destructive Attrition," *Review of Economics and Statistics* 76: 378–384 (1994).

ents, teachers, and friends play major and often controlling roles. People with different personality types sort themselves into occupations that make special use of their characteristics. For example, managers may have greater desires for income than other workers and may be more eager for ascendance over others. Children of doctors are more likely to apply to medical schools than other college graduates.[51]

Despite the importance of tastes and advice, for many students the influence of economic rewards is probably most important. Because tastes change very slowly, economic factors will be especially important in changing the distribution of career choices. A 10 percent increase in the earnings of lawyers relative to earnings of other professionals, for example, raises the number of first-year law students by about 10 percent in a single year and 30 to 40 percent over the long run. Even for very broadly defined occupations, such as "professional" and the others listed in Table 3.1, the elasticities of supply are greater than one.[52]

SUMMARY

Increases in the supply of skill increase the effective supply of labor by making workers more productive. Skill can be acquired formally through education and training programs or informally on the job. All indicators of the skill of the work force, including its occupational mix and the level of education, show that the average skill level in industrialized countries has increased in the past 50 years.

The acquisition of skills in free-market economies is, in large part, the result of optimizing decisions made by current and potential labor force participants. The theory of investment in human capital relates individuals' decisions to the costs (forgone earnings and direct costs) and benefits (higher future earnings) of the investment. Substantial evidence indicates that young people are more likely to acquire human capital through formal education when the costs are lower and the relative earnings of more educated workers are higher. Investment in college education yields a private rate of return even greater than rates of return on physical capital.

Another type of investment in human capital is in skills acquired through on-the-job training. Because there is a longer period over which to amortize the investment, most training occurs early in the work life and early in people's tenure with an employer. This pattern of investment produces the rotated J-shaped profile that characterizes the relationship between age and earnings.

---

[51]Randall Filer, "The Role of Personality and Tastes in Determining Occupational Structure," *Industrial and Labor Relations Review* 39: 412–424 (1986); Bernard Lentz and David Laband, "Why So Many Children of Doctors Become Doctors," *Journal of Human Resources* 24: 396–413 (1989); James E. Long, "The Effects of Tastes and Motivation on Individual Income," *Industrial and Labor Relations Review* 48: 338–351 (1995).

[52]Richard Freeman, *The Overeducated American*, New York: Academic Press, (1976), p. 120; Peter Orazem and J. Peter Mattila, "Human Capital, Uncertain Wage Distributions, and Occupational and Educational Choices," *International Economic Review* 32: 103–122 (1991).

POLICY ISSUE

OCCUPATIONAL LICENSING

Potential entrants are not entirely free to choose some occupations. Instead, they are confronted with state licensing requirements, often consisting of stipulated amounts of training and experience, and often administered by boards of previously licensed practitioners. The list of licensed occupations is long and growing, having increased from about 3 percent of the work force in 1950 to almost 18 percent today. Requirements for licensing are often unusual. In Michigan, for example, hearing-aid dealers have to be licensed. To acquire a license a would-be dealer must have worked for another licensed hearing-aid dealer for at least one year. A licensed barber has to serve a 100-week apprenticeship or spend five years in a combination of apprenticeship and barber college.

Occupational licensing limits entry into the occupation. This restriction, like any constraint on supply, can maintain rates of return to occupation-specific training above what they would be in a competitive market. Average income in professions is associated with the severity of entry restrictions. Thus, average incomes for a profession are lower in states that pass more applicants for licenses to practice that profession. Stricter educational requirements for barbers reduce the number of practicing barbers. Requirements that hospital lab personnel have college degrees raise earnings in that occupation. In states where a lower fraction of dentists pass the licensing exam, fewer students even enroll in dental school. The return on such an education is lower because of the greater probability that the graduate will not get to practice dentistry.[53]

Occupational licensing is almost always depicted as an attempt to preserve reasonable standards of competence in the craft or profession or as a way of protecting the public's health and safety. Occupational licensing legislation, however, raises the problem of distinguishing reasonable standards from unreasonable barriers whose main purpose is to restrict entry. In recent years the trend in the United States toward deregulation of markets has resulted in the easing of occupational licensing laws in many states. This trend will lower the returns to workers in the deregulated occupations and increase consumers' purchasing power. Whether there will be any offsetting negative effects on consumers' health is less clear, but in many occupations, such as barbering, these effects must be small indeed.

Age-earnings profiles have this shape whether we classify workers by level of formal education or by occupation. Occupational choice is partly motivated by considerations of cost and returns to the investment in occupation-specific skills. Gains in earnings from training are especially large if the training is used in the firm that provided it.

Investment in formal education and on-the-job training clearly result in higher subsequent wages. Careful studies relating productivity to these

---

[53]Jeffrey Pfeffer, "Some Evidence on Occupational Licensing and Occupational Incomes," *Social Forces* 5: 102–111 (1974); Robert Thornton and Andrew Weintraub, "Licensing in the Barbering Profession," *Industrial and Labor Relations Review* 32: 242–249 (1979); and William White, "The Impact of Occupational Licensure of Laboratory Personnel," *Journal of Human Resources* 13: 91–102 (1978). See also Simon Rottenberg, "The Economics of Occupational Licensing," in H. Gregg Lewis (ed.). *Aspects of Labor Economics,* Princeton, N.J.: Princeton University Press, (1962); Morris M. Kleiner and Robert T. Kudrle, "Do Tougher Licensing Provisions Limit Occupational Entry? The Case of Dentistry," NBER Working Paper No. 3984 (1992).

investments show that a large proportion of the higher wages received by better trained and more educated workers reflect their greater productivity. Thus human capital investments produce both more skill and higher wages.

SYNTHESIS OF PART ONE: THE SUPPLY CURVE OF LABOR

As we noted at the start of Chapter 1, decisions about labor force participation, hours of work, and investment in human capital are interrelated. For example, individuals who expect to spend their entire lives in the labor force have a stronger economic incentive to invest in education than those who do not. People investing in on-the-job training may work longer total hours than others who regard their training as complete. Workers who have a large investment in human capital retire later than those who do not. All of these many, interrelated decisions are influenced by prevailing wages, the costs of training, taxes on earned income, and the nonlabor income that is available to those who do not work.

We can conclude and summarize the discussion of the supply of labor in the past three chapters by considering several supply schedules. The long-run supply curve of worker-hours to the economy as a whole, shown in Figure 3.8, will probably be backward-bending at the high average real wage levels of

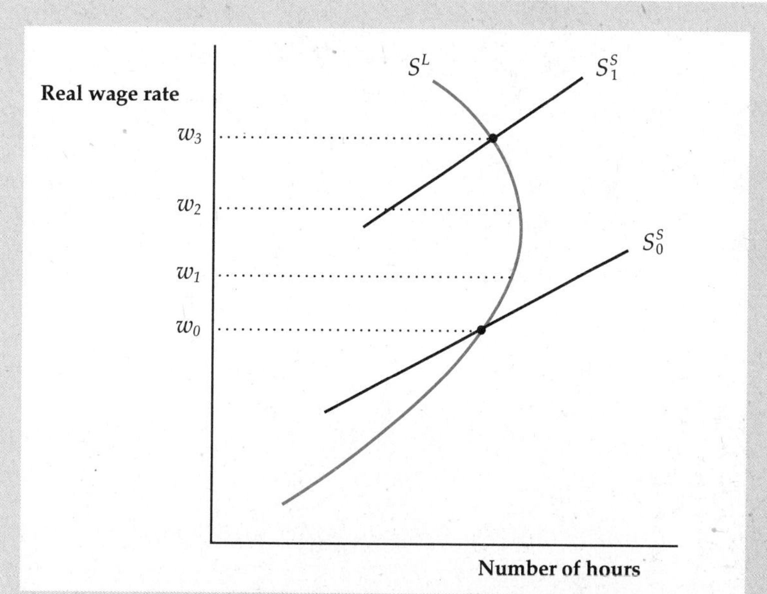

FIGURE 3.8 THE SHORT- AND LONG-RUN SUPPLY OF LABOR TO THE ECONOMY

For the economy as a whole the short-run supply of labor S^S is more elastic than the long-run supply of labor S^L. Income effects will play a greater role in the long run, and the long-run supply of labor is more likely to be backward-bending.

developed countries. With permanent increases in the real wage, from w_2 to w_3, hours of work supplied by a fixed population will decline. Hours actually worked per year are reduced as real income rises over time. While the total labor force participation rate rises slightly and some greater immigration may occur, these increases are not enough to offset the decline in hours worked by those in the labor force. In the long run, the income effect of higher wage rates dominates the substitution effect on the total supply of effort by a population in a developed economy. In developing countries, hours may increase in the long run as the wages rise from w_0 to w_1, giving a labor supply curve that is upward-sloping over some range of wages.

A different picture emerges if we look at short-run supply curves of labor in different countries. Because of discouraged workers and life cycle behavior that leads workers to supply labor at those times in their lives when the returns to work are highest, short-run supply curves like S_0^s and S_1^s slope upward. Temporary increases in real wages cause people to offer even more labor. Similarly, if we relate individuals' average real wage rates to their annual or lifetime labor supply, we find the usual effects. For all but the highest wage groups the supply curve is positively sloped. An increase in the returns to work calls forth more labor, through more hours per year, a greater likelihood of labor force participation, and greater effort per hour on the job. Most individuals' labor supply schedules have shapes like the short-run aggregate labor supply schedules, S_0^s and S_1^s, shown in Figure 3.8.

With respect to more specific labor markets such as those for particular occupations, industries, or geographic areas, relative labor supply schedules (showing how the supply of labor changes with respect to wages assuming that other wages do not change) typically slope upward throughout. Income effects of rising wages may dominate substitution effects for those currently employed in a specific market, thus reducing their labor supply. If wages in one labor market rise relative to those in other markets, however, the overall change in labor supply to the market will largely come through the attraction of workers from other industries, occupations, or regions. Short-run supply will respond less to changes in relative wages than long-run supply, because it will take time for workers to alter their training or residence. For occupations using specialized skills requiring a long training period, like engineering or medicine, the short-run supply curve might be almost vertical, like S^S in Figure 3.9. Among others in which training periods are short and there is little occupation-specific training, the short-run supply curve is much flatter.

The typical long-run supply curve of labor to an occupation looks like S^L in Figure 3.9. It intersects S^S at the point from which some initial change in demand in the occupation causes wages to change. The flattening of the short-run supply curve (the movement from S^S to S^L) arises because an increase in relative wages induces more people to acquire skills specific to the occupation or industry.

While S^L is flatter than the short-run supply curve to the occupation or industry, it is not usually horizontal (perfectly elastic) even in the very long run. It would be perfectly elastic if occupations differed only in the training needed to enter them. Each occupation could then attract an unlimited number of

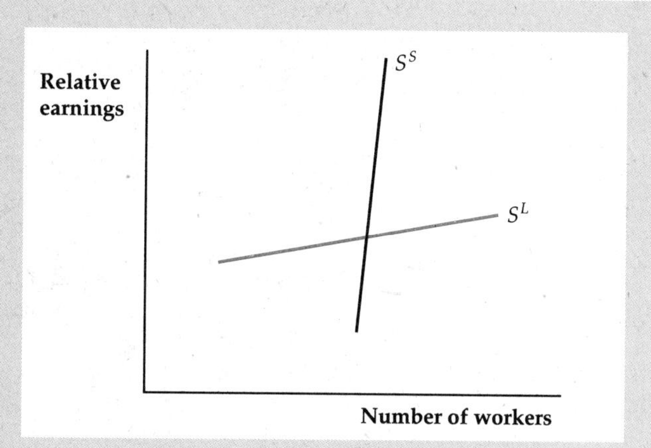

FIGURE 3.9 THE SHORT- AND LONG-RUN SUPPLY OF LABOR TO A SPECIFIC LABOR MARKET

The short-run supply of labor to an industry, occupation, or geographic area will be less elastic than the long-run supply after workers have had an opportunity to relocate or retrain in response to higher relative wages.

entrants by offering lifetime earnings just enough greater than the lifetime earnings of an occupation requiring no training to cover the private costs of training. Occupations differ, however, not only in the amount of training required, but also in their use of scarce innate talents and nonmonetary disadvantages. These disadvantages are evaluated differently by different people, which is sufficient to give the long-run supply curve an upward slope. To the extent that the disadvantages lie in the difficulty of doing the work, they will be least bothersome to people who have the most relevant innate talents or interests. As an occupation continues to expand, it must eventually recruit people who enjoy the work less and who therefore insist on a higher monetary return. This causes S^L, the long-run supply curve of labor to an occupation or industry, to have at least some positive slope.

QUESTIONS AND PROBLEMS

3.1 Graph the age-earnings profiles based on Tables 3.3 and 3.4. Comment on whether they exhibit the three properties described in the discussion of Figure 3.1. If they do not, suggest reasons why not.

3.2 Bob White is a 58-year-old construction worker who earns $16 per hour. While driving his backhoe he hits a gas main that the gas company failed to inform him was present at the construction site. Bob is severely injured and cannot work again. As a consulting economist to Bob's lawyer, what is the present value of the lost earnings that you would recommend seeking from the gas company? Aside from his earnings, what else do you need to know to make the calculation?

3.3 George Jones lives three periods. If he does not become educated he will earn $5000 in period 1, $6000 in period 2, and $7000 in period 3. If he does become educated, he will earn nothing in period 1 and will have to borrow $2000 to pay for tuition and books, but he will earn $10,000 in period 2 and $12,000 in period 3. (No one lives more than three periods, and there is no chance of dying before the end of period 3.) If the market rate of interest is 10 percent per period, should George borrow to make the investment? What is the internal rate of return on this investment?

3.4 Consider the signalling model of Figure 3.6. Analyze how much education will be obtained by dull and bright workers if:

a. Education is costless; or

b. Education costs C_B for both groups.

Comparing your answer to the discussion in the text, what does this imply about the potential effectiveness of educational attainment in signalling employers about the ability of different groups of workers?

3.5 A firm offers two types of one-year training programs to workers. Under each training program, assume the following:

Annual output of workers without training	$20,000
Annual output during training	16,000
Annual output after training	24,000
Materials and supervisory costs per worker during training	5,000

One training program provides skills that can be used in several other firms; the second program provides skills that are useful only at this firm. For each program what are the wages that workers receive during and after training? Also, compare their wages to those of workers who do not participate in either training program. If the worker is going to stay with the firm for only one year after the first program is completed, should that program be undertaken? Would the second program be undertaken in those circumstances?

3.6 Josephine Morgan begins work right after college, earning $20,000. She expects her wage to rise by $400 per year during her first 10 years of work, by $200 per year during the next 10 years, to stay constant during the next 10 years, and to fall by $200 per year during her final 10 years in the labor force. Graph the age-earnings profile that she envisions. Calculate the present value of her investment in on-the-job training, under the alternative assumptions that the appropriate market rates of interest to use in this calculation are 5 and 10 percent.

3.7 Richard, who has just finished high school at age 18, has received a job offer that pays $15,000 per year during first 4 years and $25,000 each year thereafter until he retires at age 58. On the other hand, he can attend college and study economics at a cost of $10,000 per year for tuition plus $15,000 per year for living expenses. If he successfully finishes school and finds a job as an economist his yearly earnings will be $40,000. On the other hand, he might fail out after two years, in which case his earnings will be the same as if he never went to college (including 4 years at $15,000).

a. If Richard believes there is no chance he will fail out of college, will he decide to attend? Assume no psychological costs (i.e., Richard's disutility from learning is the same as his disutility of work) are involved and the market rate of interest is 3 percent. What will be the present value of Richard's college education?
b. How high would the probability of failing out of college have to be for Richard to decide not to enroll?

3.8 Can you use what you know about private and social returns to education to derive a rule for the efficient share of educational costs that should be paid collectively (either through public provision of education or subsidies to students) versus the fraction that students and their families should pay themselves? How do you think this optimal allocation of costs compares with current situation? How does this vary with the grade level of the student? How is it affected by the extent to which education is a screen or a signal?

3.9 Using models of investment in skills, how would you explain the following observations?

a. The rate of increase in wages falls as workers age.
b. Persons with more schooling have steeper age-earnings profiles than persons with less education
c. Returns to majoring in business and engineering are higher for women than for men.
d. There are currently about 25 percent more women than men in college, a dramatic change from 30 years ago when there were twice as many male as female college students.

3.10 You have decided to give a charitable gift of $5 billion to promote "education and training of the least advantaged citizens of the nation." Immediately upon announcing your intention, you are presented with numerous proposals for how to best spend the money. What do you see as the advantages and disadvantages of each of the following proposals?

a. Funding college scholaships for low-income students.
b. Using the funds to guarantee student loans for low-income students who want to attend college.

c. Funding a demonstration program of educational vouchers for elementary school students in several large cities. These vouchers could be spent at any school the students chose, public or private.
d. Providing wage subsidies to employers who agree to hire and train long-term unemployed workers.

KEY WORDS

ability biases
active labor market policy
age-earnings profile
biases
cohort
cost-benefit analysis
displacement
earnings capacity
experience
forgone earnings
general human capital
gross return
human capital
internal rate of return (*IRR*)
monopsonist
natural experiment
net present value (*NPV*)
occupation
occupation-specific training
old-school-tie hypothesis
on-the-job training
out-of-pocket costs
overtaking point
private rate of return
real earnings
screening hypothesis
sheepskin effect
signalling
skill
social rate of return
specific human capital
synthetic cohort
tenure

Part Two

LABOR DEMAND

In this section we turn from studying how individuals and households behave to examining the behavior of employers. Chapter 4 presents the basic theory of the demand for labor in competitive markets. Although we recognize that not all markets are competitive, many are close enough approximations that we can learn a great deal from this analysis. To begin with, we do not distinguish between employees and the hours they work. Chapter 5 examines the demand for labor in noncompetitive markets and studies how employers' demands for workers and hours differ.

4 THE DEMAND FOR LABOR IN COMPETITIVE MARKETS

THE MAJOR QUESTIONS

- ▲ How do businesses decide how many people to employ?
- ▲ How are these decisions affected by changes in wages and other costs of employment?
- ▲ Do employers choose what *types of workers* to hire based on the costs of hiring them?
- ▲ How does technical progress affect employment?
- ▲ How much change in employment occurs as existing businesses grow or shrink, and how much occurs as businesses are born or die?
- ▲ How does the government affect employment decisions by setting a minimum wage rate that employers must pay or mandating various employee benefits?

THE NATURE AND USES OF A THEORY OF THE DEMAND FOR LABOR

The questions above are answered by the theory of labor demand. Much interest in the theory of demand stems from striking differences over time and among countries in patterns of employment. Consider the data in Table 4.1, which shows the distribution of employment by industry in five industrialized economies in the early postwar period and a recent year. In each period the developed economies are similar to each other. What stands out are the immense changes in the industrial distribution of employment that took place over the time period in the table. In every country a decline in employment in manufacturing was accompanied by a large increase in the relative importance of services. The relative stability in the category "Other" in most countries masks a large drop in the fraction of the labor force employed in

TABLE 4.1 PERCENT DISTRIBUTION OF EMPLOYMENT

	Manufacturing	Commerce, Finance, and Real Estate	Construction	Transport, Utilities, Storage, and Communication	Other
United States					
1950	26.0	23.9	6.4	7.8	35.9
1993	16.5	31.3	6.1	7.1	38.9
Australia					
1961	27.6	20.0	9.1	11.0	32.4
1993	14.3	36.8	7.1	7.6	34.2
Canada					
1951	26.0	19.4	6.8	8.8	39.0
1993	14.5	35.4	5.3	7.3	37.4
France					
1954	26.1	17.1	7.1	6.0	43.7
1993	19.6	26.7	6.8	7.3	39.6
W. Germany					
1961	36.5	18.8	8.6	6.4	29.7
1992	30.8	23.4	6.8	6.6	32.4

Source: International Labor Organization, *Year Book of Labour Statistics*, 1945–89, (1994).

agriculture and mining combined with a substantial increase in employment in the public sector.

Anecdotal evidence suggests the extent of differences in employment demand at a single point in time. The role of economic factors in labor demand is clearest when the differences in costs are greatest, as between developed and developing countries. In the United States, a truck that delivers soft drinks to stores is usually operated by one person. In India, similar trucks are said to have a crew of four—a driver, a manager who keeps the records, and two porters who carry the cases into the store. By using a lot of relatively cheap labor, the relatively more expensive truck can spend less time at each stop. The use of resources reflects the differences in the relative prices of labor and capital in the two countries. In China, large rugs are woven on very simple looms by weavers who spend months making one rug. In the United States, the process is mostly mechanized and is much more rapid.

Employers do not usually hire workers without reason. They hire them because customers want a product or service that will be produced by the labor. Thus the demand for labor is almost always a **derived demand**, derived from the demand for the final product. This derivation may be indirect if the labor produces an input into the production of another firm. Thus, the demand for coal miners may be derived from the demand for steel, which is derived from the demand for automobiles and refrigerators.

The basic theory of the demand for labor has changed little since the beginning of this century. It is an application of the **marginal productivity theory** of the demand for any input into production. Inputs into production are known as **factors of production**. Although this theory has been questioned by institutional labor economists and believers in segmented markets, it has survived these attacks because the critics have failed to develop an alternative theory that is as useful in explaining patterns of employment and wages.[1]

The discussion in this chapter maintains three simplifying assumptions:

1. There are no costs of employment other than hourly wages;
2. The productivity of labor is independent of the length of the work-week;
3. There are only two inputs into production—labor and capital.

The first two of these assumptions permit us to express the quantity of labor demanded as employee-hours without worrying about the split between hours per week and the number of employees. Thus we assume that the employer is indifferent between one worker who works 70 hours per week and two workers each of whom works 35 hours, provided that, in both cases, the capital equipment is working 70 hours. We will drop this assumption in the next chapter. Variations in the length of time per week that the capital is working (say, by adding a second or third shift) are not considered as ways of altering the ratio of inputs.

The basic theory and empirical evidence on the demand for labor in competitive markets is considered in this chapter. We will first start by examining the demand for labor of firms that are assumed to last forever. Yet, as plant closings and "going-out-of-business" signs on stores make very clear, businesses do fail. We therefore also examine extensions of the theory designed to explain these phenomena of **job dynamics**.

THE PRODUCTION FUNCTION

All analyses of the demand for labor begin with the firm's **production function**. We assume that the firm is operating efficiently so that the production function shows the maximum amount of output that can be obtained for each combination of labor and capital inputs. It is written as

$$Q = f(K, L)$$

where K and L represent the flow of capital and labor services available to the firm in a given period.

---

[1]Glen Cain, "The Challenge of Segmented Labor Market Theories to Orthodox Theory," *Journal of Economic Literature* 14: 1215–1257 (1976) presents a good comparison of the standard theory to some of the alternatives.

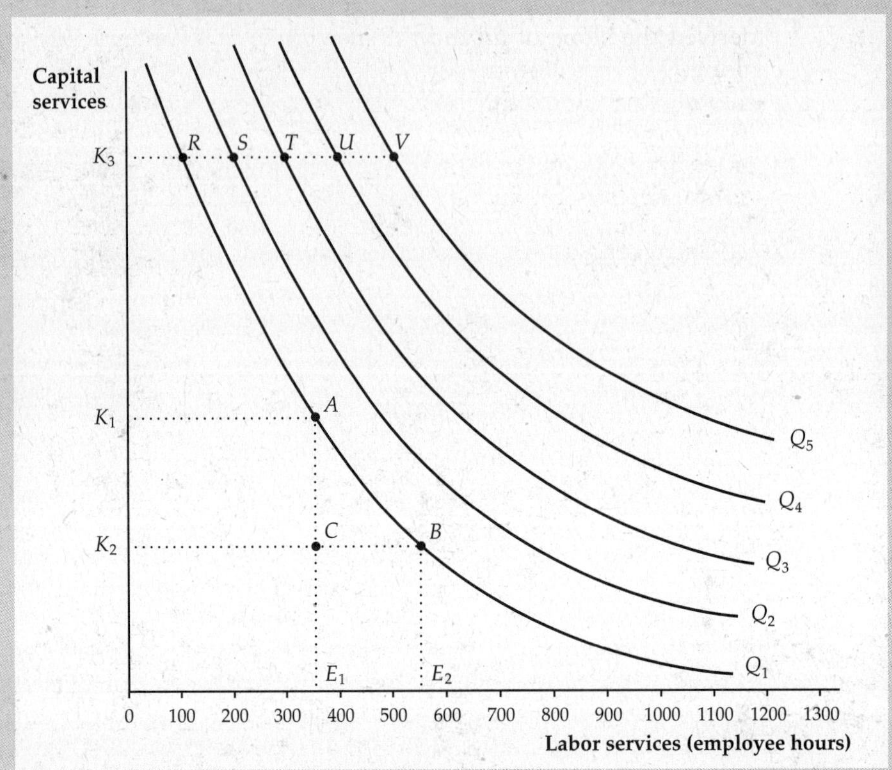

FIGURE 4.1 PRODUCTION ISOQUANTS
Isoquants show all the combinations of inputs, such as points *A* and *B*, that can produce the same amount of output. They are convex because of the diminishing marginal rate of substitution in production. Moving from isoquant to isoquant with a fixed level of capital, such as K_3 generates the short-run total product of labor curve.

In analyzing the demand for labor it is useful to translate the information in the production function into production **isoquants.** Each isoquant (equal quantity) shows all the combinations of *K* and *L* that produce the same amount of output. Figure 4.1 shows several isoquants, labelled Q_1 through Q_5. The properties of firms' isoquants are very similar to those of consumers' indifference curves discussed in Chapter 1. At all points on Q_2 output is greater than at all points on Q_1. The isoquants can be drawn as densely as one likes, but they *cannot* cross. If they did, one point would represent two different outputs, which is not possible if, as the production function implies, the firm is using its inputs efficiently.

The slope of an isoquant can be derived in exactly the same way we derived the slope of an indifference curve in Chapter 1. Moving from A to B along Q_1 keeps output constant. The movement consists of a reduction in capital services, from K_2 to K_1, and an increase in employee-hours, from E_1 to E_2. The reduction in capital services reduces output by the **marginal product of capital services,** MP_K, the amount each unit of capital services produces, times the number of units by which capital is reduced. The addition of employee-hours raises output by the **marginal product of labor,** MP_L, the amount each employee-hour produces, times the additional employee-hours. Since there is no change in output, it must be true, moving along the isoquant Q_1 between points A and B, that in terms of output

$$0 = (A \rightarrow C)\, MP_K + (C \rightarrow B)\, MP_L.$$

Rewriting this equation gives the slope of the isoquant Q_1 as:

$$\frac{AC}{CB} = -\frac{MP_L}{MP_K}.$$

The absolute value of the isoquant's slope (MP_L/MP_K) is the **marginal rate of technical substitution (*MRTS*)** and measures how technically difficult or easy it is to replace one input with the other.

The isoquants are bowed inward. The *MRTS* decreases as more labor is added and capital services are reduced. This represents the principle of **diminishing marginal rate of substitution** in production. The higher the proportion of one factor in the input mix, the more of it the employer would have to add to make up for the loss of one unit of the other factor. For example, with only a few ovens and many workers, it would be very hard for a restaurant to replace an oven with workers since all the ovens would probably be in use constantly. On the other hand, if there were many ovens but few workers to use them, adding another oven would not enable the elimination of many cooks.

THE SHORT-RUN DEMAND SCHEDULE

The **short run** is that time period over which at least one of the firm's inputs is fixed and cannot be changed. Although it is possible for the fixed input to be labor, in general we can assume that it is technology and the business's stock of capital that can least easily be changed. Assume that the amount of capital services available is fixed at some level, say K_3, in Figure 4.1. For some reason (most probably the history of its previous choices about its capital equipment) the firm has on hand machinery yielding only K_3 units of capital services. Because of delivery and installation lags, lack of access to funds to buy machines, or because the rate of return on adding capital equipment would be too low, the firm cannot increase its use of capital services beyond K_3. With technology and capital services fixed, the firm's only choice is about how much labor to use.

TOTAL, AVERAGE, AND MARGINAL PRODUCT CURVES

The **total product of labor** (**TP**—the amount of output produced by K_3 units of capital services and each specific number of employee-hours) can be determined by reading across the isoquants in Figure 4.1. Each level of labor input can be combined with the fixed amount of capital services (K_3) to produce a single level of output. This amount is shown by the isoquant that passes through the point determined by K_3 and the level of labor input. Thus in Figure 4.1, 100 employee hours can produce Q_1 units of output at point *R*, while 200 hours of labor can produce Q_2 units of output at point *S*, and so on up to the Q_5 units of output produced by 500 hours of labor at point *V*.

Figure 4.2 graphs this total product relationship, showing how output changes with the addition of labor inputs holding all other inputs constant. The two halves of Figure 4.2 show how the total product curve would look for two different forms of the production function. Figure 4.2(a) represents a typical production function, while Figure 4.2(b) shows the total product curve for the special case where the production function exhibits **constant returns to scale**. Constant returns to scale mean that if all inputs (labor and capital) are increased by a certain percentage, output increases by exactly the same percentage. In other words, if you double inputs you exactly double the output.

Two important relationships can be derived from the total product curve. The slope of the total product curve is the change in output produced when one extra employee-hour is added. This is the short-run marginal product of labor. Figure 4.3 shows the marginal product *(MP)* curves derived from the total product curves in Figure 4.2. Thus, the level at point *A* in Figure 4.3 is the same as the slope at point *A* in Figure 4.2.

The **average product of labor** (*AP*) measures labor productivity or the amount of output per employee-hour. In terms of the total product curve in Figure 4.2, the *AP* is the *TP* divided by employee-hours. The *AP* at any level of labor input is the same as the slope of a line drawn from the origin to the point on the total product curve that corresponds to that level of labor. Thus the slope of the line *0A* is $((TP_A - 0)/(E_A - 0))$ or TP_A/E_A. Calculating this slope for every point in the total product curves in Figure 4.2 yields the average product curves in Figure 4.3.

Let's examine Figures 4.2(a) and 4.3(a). As drawn, the first employee-hour yields some output, so it has positive marginal and average products. As the *TP* is drawn, however, the second hour of labor yields a greater increment in output, perhaps because two workers employed together can divide up tasks more efficiently. The marginal product lies above the average product, so the average product rises between the first and second units of labor input, pulled up by the increment to output added by the second employee-hour. Additional increments of employee-hours may each be more productive than the first few increments, so that the average product continues rising.

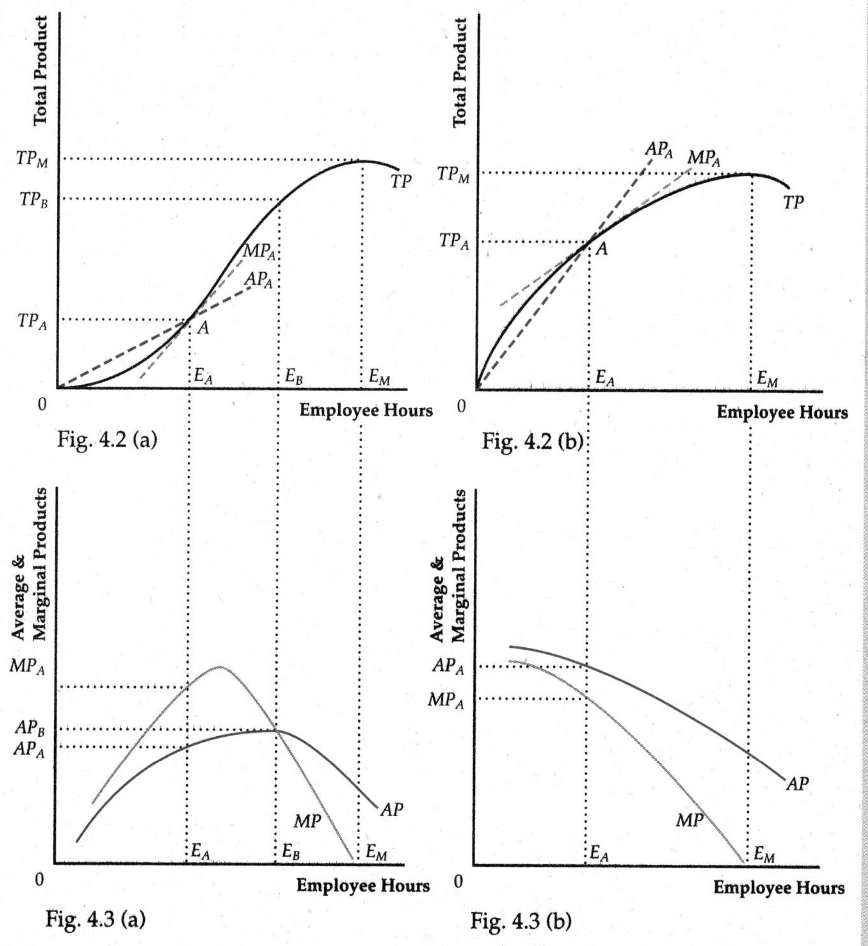

Fig. 4.2 (a)

Fig. 4.2 (b)

Fig. 4.3 (a)

Fig. 4.3 (b)

FIGURE 4.2 TOTAL PRODUCT CURVES

Up to level E_m, total product increases as more labor input is used. Figure 4.2(*a*) shows the total product curve corresponding to a production function with first increasing and then diminishing returns to labor input. Figure 4.2(*b*) corresponds to a production function with constant returns to scale where the return to additional labor input, holding capital constant, is always diminishing.

FIGURE 4.3 AVERAGE AND MARGINAL PRODUCT CURVES

With capital input held constant, the marginal product of labor at any employment level is equal to the slope of the total product curve. The average product of labor at any employment level is equal to the slope of a line from the origin to the point on the total product curve at that level of employment. If the marginal product is below the average product, the average product will be decreasing.

TABLE 4.2 HYPOTHETICAL TOTAL, AVERAGE, AND MARGINAL PRODUCT SCHEDULES

	Output per hour		
Number of Workers	Total Product (Output)	Average Product	Marginal Product
0	0	0	—
1	5	5.0	5
2	12	6.0	7
3	20	6.7	8
4	28	7.0	8
5	34	6.8	6
6	39	6.5	5
7	42	6.0	3
8	44	5.5	2
9	45	5.0	1
10	45	4.5	0
11	44	4.0	–1
12	42	3.5	–2

This effect is shown in Figure 4.2(a) by *TP* rising increasingly rapidly as hours are added beyond the first few. In Figure 4.3(a) $MP > AP$ in the left-hand part of the diagram. When the marginal product exceeds the average product, the average product will increase, just as your grade point average will increase when you receive an A in this course, the *marginal* course in your college career.

At an input of E_B employee-hours in Figure 4.2(a) *AP* begins to decline. At this point the slope of *TP* equals TP_B/E_B and the marginal and average products are equal. Because the average product declines as labor is added beyond E_B, the *MP* in Figure 4.3(a) is drawn below the *AP* to the right of E_B in Figure 4.3(a). The marginal product lies below the average product when the average is falling, just as your low grade in a difficult course (say, physics) will pull down your grade point average and be below that average. The total product curve *TP* in Figure 4.2(a) is rising to the right of E_B, but it is rising increasingly less rapidly than it was up to E_B.

In the special case depicted in Figure 4.2(b), there is never a period when the average product of labor rises as more labor is added to the fixed amount of capital. Thus, the *MP* is always declining and always lies below the *AP* in Figure 4.3(b).

Beyond E_M in Figure 4.2 the total product begins to decline. In a fast-food restaurant, for example, there may be so many workers behind the counter that they get in each other's way and actually decrease the number of burgers produced each hour. The marginal product of labor (the slope of *TP*) is zero at E_M in Figure 4.3. Beyond E_M so much labor is being used relative to the fixed amount of capital services that output could actually be increased by reducing employee-hours. Since output is still being produced, the average product of labor remains positive.

As we have drawn the total product curves in Figure 4.2, the marginal product schedule *MP* slopes downward once the business is using more than a certain amount of labor—(E_B employee hours in Figure 4.2(a) and from the beginning in Figure 4.2(b). This downward slope represents the **law of diminishing returns:**

> As a firm adds more units of one factor to a fixed input of the other, increments to the total product will eventually diminish.

For a production function with constant returns to scale, this diminishing starts with the very first unit of labor input. With a fixed number of grills, each additional worker behind the counter of a fast-food restaurant adds less and less to the output of burgers.

A concrete example of this discussion is shown in Table 4.2, which gives hypothetical total, average, and marginal product schedules for a total product curve such as is drawn in Figure 4.2(a). For convenience, the labor input is measured in number of workers rather than in hours. Reading down the table is equivalent to moving across the horizontal axis in Figures 4.2(a) and 4.3(a). The portion of this line that lies to the left of E_B in Figure 4.2(a) is represented by the first four workers employed. As each of these workers is added, the average product rises until it reaches its maximum when employment is 4. From this point to the point at which employment is 10, total product is rising, but average and marginal products are falling. This part of the table corresponds to the part of the *TP, MP,* and *AP* curves between E_B and E_M in Figure 4.2(a). When more than 10 workers are employed with capital input held constant, output actually falls and, accordingly, the marginal product is negative. This corresponds to points in Figures 4.2(a) and 4.3(a) that lie to the right of E_M.

What happens if the firm has more pieces of equipment and thus access to a greater amount of capital services? With more capital inputs, output is higher at each input of labor. The total product curve would rotate around the origin in Figure 4.2(a) or 4.2(b). Nonetheless, there will still be some labor input beyond which additional employee-hours actually reduce output and the total product declines. It is generally true, however, that at any input of labor the marginal product of an additional hour will be higher than when the firm had access to fewer units of capital services. The slope of the total product curve will be greater at any number of employee-hours. This means that the marginal product of labor is higher at each level of employee-hours. See if you can draw modifications of Figures 4.2 and 4.3 assuming that the firm has an increased amount of capital with which to produce.

PROFIT-MAXIMIZING LABOR DEMAND IN THE SHORT RUN

So far we have only discussed the technical possibilities available to employers. Employers use these possibilities, along with the cost of labor, to determine the quantity of labor they want in the short run. Assume again that the firm has access to K_1 units of capital services, so that it faces a marginal productivity schedule MP_1. We can express marginal productivity in monetary terms, as the **value of the marginal product** (*VMP*). We define the *VMP* as

$$VMP_1 = P \times MP_1,$$

where *P* is the price of output per unit. Since we are assuming in this chapter that the firm operates in a competitive output market, *P* will be constant no matter how much the firm produces. The *VMP* shows how adding another worker or another hour of labor affects the employer's revenue.

Two value-of-marginal-product curves are shown in Figure 4.4 as VMP_1 and VMP_2. Each curve shows the value of marginal product for a fixed amount of capital services K_1 and K_2. Assume the firm has K_1 units of capital available and is confronted with the market wage w_1. If so, it will employ E_1

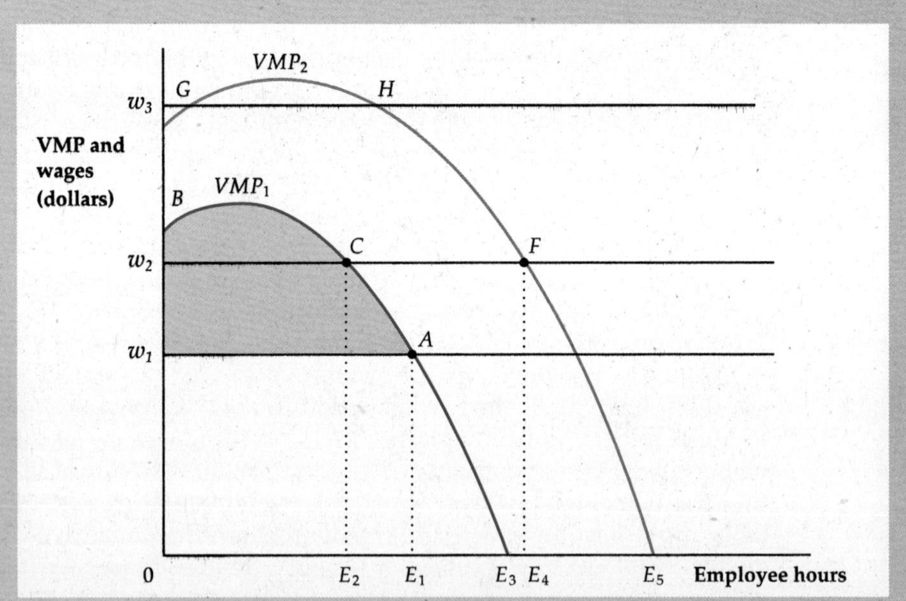

FIGURE 4.4 DETERMINING DEMAND FOR LABOR

Firms employ labor up to the number of hours where the value of the output from the next hour equals the wage rate paid to hire that hour of labor. Raising the wage rate from w_1 to w_2 reduces the amount of labor hired from E_1 to E_2.

hours of labor. The firm will not use more than E_1 hours, because beyond this point the wage paid to hire another hour of labor exceeds the value of its marginal product. Adding employee-hours beyond E_1 would reduce profits.

The value of total output is just the sum of the *VMP* added by each additional employee-hour. In Figure 4.4 it is the area under the value of marginal product curve up to E_1. This whole area $0BAE_1$ is divided into two parts. The **wage bill** or the wage rate times the number of employee-hours used (the rectangular area $0w_1AE_1$) represents that part of the value of output that goes to labor. The remainder of the total value of output (the irregular shaded area w_1BA) represents payments for the services of capital. These include depreciation charges, interest, and profit. In the short run with a fixed input of capital, depreciation charges and interest charges will not vary with changes in wages or the amount of labor used. Thus, changes in the area as the wage rate varies represent changes in profit (that is, in return on capital).

If the wage that the firm must pay rises to w_2 (because of collective bargaining, government decree, or the workings of the market), the employer will make the highest profits at point *C*. At that point the *VMP* of the last worker employed equals the new, higher wage rate w_2. The number of employee-hours demanded falls to E_2. The extra employee-hours between E_2 and E_1 no longer add enough to the firm's revenues to justify their now higher cost. Whether this reduction in labor input is accomplished by layoffs, failure to fill vacancies, or reduced weekly hours will depend on considerations such as fixed employment costs which we leave until the next chapter. If the value of marginal product schedule slopes down, however, as the discussion earlier says it eventually must, the profit-maximizing employer will always adjust to rising wages by reducing labor input.

If the wage drops from w_1, the employer will add employee-hours, but no matter how low the wage falls the firm will not go beyond E_3 employee-hours. Since $VMP_1 < 0$ beyond E_3, employee-hours beyond E_3 subtract from revenue. Even if they cost the employer nothing, they would not be used.

Now assume the firm's fixed amount of capital services increases to K_2 so that the value of marginal product of labor is now depicted by the curve VMP_2 in Figure 4.4. If the market wage the firm faces is wage w_2, it will again employ all employee-hours that add at least w_2 to the value of sales. This means that it will maximize profits at point *F*, employing E_4 employee-hours. Because there is more capital, each hour of labor is more productive. This greater productivity created by the presence of more capital services justifies using more hours at every wage. The same effect on *VMP*, and thus on the firm's demand for labor, would be produced if the price of its product, *P*, were to increase, since *VMP* increases both with more fixed capital and with higher product prices.

Using Figure 4.4, we can derive the amount of labor the employer wishes to use at various wage rates assuming a fixed amount of capital services and a fixed product price and technology. This relationship is the employer's demand curve for labor in the short run. It is the relation between the price of labor services (the wage rate) and the quantity of labor services desired. Note that at some wages (like w_3) there may be two points where the wage rate equals the value of marginal product (points G and H on VMP_2 in Figure 4.4). If you recall how profit is depicted on the diagram, it should be obvious that profit will always be greater at (and the employer will therefore pick) the higher level of labor input (point H). This leads to a general rule:

> The value of marginal productivity (*VMP*) schedule between its peak and the point where $VMP = 0$ is the employer's short-run demand curve for labor.

Since the market consists simply of all the firms, the market demand curve for labor is the horizontal sum of all individual firm's demand curves in the particular labor market, occupation, or industry. Since the curve for each firm slopes downward, the market demand curve must also slope downward.

POLICY ISSUE

CARTER AND BENTSEN ON WAGE SUBSIDIES

In 1977 President Carter proposed stimulating the economy by giving employers a tax credit that would reduce the tax on their profits by an amount equal to 4 percent of their Social Security taxes. The proposal would have reduced payroll costs by only 0.24 percent (since Social Security taxes accounted for 6 percent of payroll cost), and was hardly a major cut in the cost of employing another worker. The extent to which it would have achieved its goal of stimulating employers to increase their use of labor depends on the shape of the labor demand curve. Figure 4.5 shows the economy-wide demand for labor curve (the sum of all individual firm's demand for labor at each wage rate). In order to make the graph readable, please note that Figure 4.5 is *not* drawn to scale. In particular, the changes shown on each axis are far larger than the actual proposal.

The proposed tax credit was equivalent to a cut in the wage rate from w_0 to w_1. Like any other such cut, it would stimulate an expansion in employee-hours demanded, from E_0 to E_1. The size of this expansion depends on the slope of the demand curve or the **elasticity of labor demand**. This wage subsidy would have added $E_1 - E_0$ employee-hours, a clear gain to the economy. But to achieve this the government would be subsidizing employers for every hour of labor they used. To lower the cost of labor to w_1 and induce the small expansion in jobs, the government would have to incur a cost equal to the rectangle w_1w_0CB in Figure 4.5. Most of the subsidy would have been paid to **inframarginal** employment, the E_0 employee-hours that would be demanded even without the subsidy.

In recognition of the small "bang for the buck" this subsidy would have achieved, then Senator Lloyd Bentsen of Texas introduced a **marginal employment tax credit.** As a simplified description, no credit would be given for any employment below what the firm had used the previous year. In Figure 4.5 this means that employers would pay the full cost, w_0, on all hours up to E_0. There would be, however, a large credit for any new jobs. If the firm increased employment beyond E_0, it had to pay only w_2 per hour out of its own funds. In Figure 4.5 it would pay to expand employment from E_0 to E_2, a much larger increase than under the Carter proposal. The cost to the government of this subsidy is shown by the rectangle *HAGF*. It is far less per job created than under the Carter proposal, because the subsidy is not being wasted on jobs that would have existed anyway.

The Carter proposal was quickly dropped, but the Bentsen proposal became law and was in effect from mid-1977 until the end of 1978. Was it effective? Estimates are that it cost the U.S. Treasury $4.8 billion in income tax receipts. One study showed, however, that the New Jobs Tax Credit was responsible for one-third of the expansion in retail and construction employment during its existence. Another indicated that employers who knew about (and presumably used) the tax credit added 3 percent more worker hours during 1977 to 1978 than did otherwise similar employers who did not know about the credit.[2] Of course, we do not know how much of the impact was a real increase in eventual jobs and how much was a shift to 1978 of jobs employers would have added in 1979 anyway.

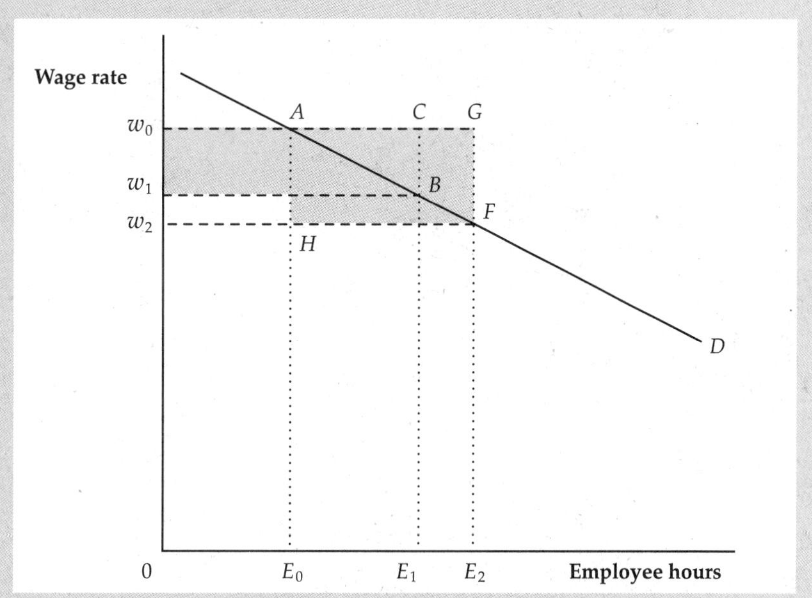

FIGURE 4.5 THE EFFECT OF WAGE SUBSIDIES

A wage subsidy lowers the cost of employing additional labor and increases the amount of labor used. If the subsidy applies only to additional labor above a base level, a given increase in employment will cost the taxpayer less (or a larger increase in employment can be induced for a fixed expenditure on subsidies).

[2]John Bishop, "Employment in Construction and Distribution Industries: The Impact of the New Jobs Tax Credit," in Sherwin Rosen (ed.). *Studies in Labor Markets,* Chicago: University of Chicago Press, (1981); Jeffrey Perloff and Michael Wachter, "The New Jobs Tax Credit: An Evaluation of the 1977–78 Wage Subsidy Program," American Economic Association, *Papers and Proceedings* 69: 173–179 (1979).

THE DEMAND FOR LABOR IN THE LONG RUN

In the short run the firm is limited to using the services of a stock of capital that might not be its best choice under current market conditions. We define the **long run** as the period of time that is sufficient to allow the firm to adjust both labor and capital services to current market conditions. Since it can adjust both, the firm must choose the best combination of these two factors of production.

LONG-RUN COST-MINIMIZING DEMAND

In Figure 4.6 we redraw several isoquants from Figure 4.1. The diagonal line tangent to the Q_1 isoquant at A in Figure 4.6 is an **isocost line** representing a fixed sum, C_1, to be spent in buying inputs. Suppose capital services cost r per unit, and the wage rate is w_1. Then, if the firm spends all its resources on capital services, it can buy C_1/r units. If C_1 is spent entirely on labor, it can buy C_1/w_1 employee-hours. The absolute value of the slope of the budget line is C_1/r divided by C_1/w_1, or just w_1/r. The tangency at A indicates the long-run position of cost-minimizing producers. At this point they produce output Q_1 using the least cost combination of inputs. No lower isocost curve can be attained. At point A the tangency means that the isocost curve and the isoquant have equal slopes, or

$$MRTS = \frac{MP_L}{MP_K} = \frac{w_1}{r}.$$

This fundamental **law of variable proportions** for the choice of two factors of production implies that:

> Factors will be used so that the relative amounts added to output by the last unit of each factor are proportional to their relative costs.

Note that the condition that producers be cost minimizers is much weaker than the condition that they be profit maximizers. It is a necessary but not a sufficient condition. Even organizations not motivated by profits, such as government agencies or nonprofit institutions, will try their best to minimize the costs of producing a given output.

With unchanged **factor prices** (wages and costs of capital), increasing the amount the firm spends will result in a parallel outward shift in the isocost line. Each of these isocost lines will be tangent to only one isoquant. This tangency point shows the maximum output that can be achieved spending the amount represented by the isocost line. Alternatively, it shows the least-cost way of producing each level of output. If we connect the tangency points in Figure 4.6, we will obtain a curve that shows how the amount of labor and capital used will vary with the level of output the firm picks. This curve is called the firm's **expansion path** and is represented by the line $0AX$ in Figure 4.6. To maximize profits the firm not only must produce the level of

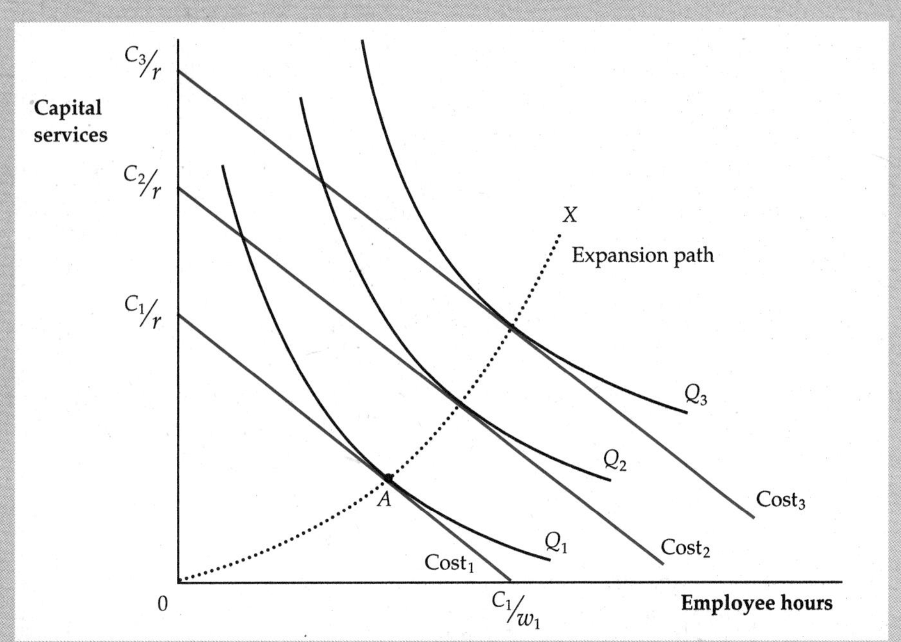

FIGURE 4.6 CHOICE OF THE OPTIMAL COMBINATION OF LABOR AND CAPITAL

In the long run a firm will pick the combination of labor and capital that produces any level of output at the least cost, where an isoquant is tangent to an isocost curve. The locus of all such points gives the firm's expansion path showing how labor and capital inputs will change as output changes.

output it chooses using the least-cost combination of capital and labor (i.e., be on its expansion path), it must also pick the right level of output.

Now consider what happens if the wage rate decreases to w_2 with the price of capital services unchanged at r. The isocost lines will have a flatter slope since any fixed spending would allow the firm to purchase more labor input. If the firm wanted to continue to produce the same level of output (i.e., remain on the same production isoquant), it would now do so by using more labor (the input that has become relatively cheaper) and less capital (the input that has become relatively more expensive). This is shown as the move from point L to point M *along* isoquant Q_1 in Figure 4.7. The firm increases its use of labor from E_L to E_M but reduces the amount of capital it uses. Overall, there is a net saving and isocost curve $Cost_2$ represents a lower total expenditure than isocost curve $Cost_1$ at the old, higher wage. The easiest way to see this effect is by noticing that the new isocost curve intersects the vertical axis at C_2/r, which is lower than C_1/r. Since the price of capital (r) has not changed, this means that C_2 must be less than C_1. The movement from E_L to

E_M is called the **substitution effect in production** and represents the increase in labor inputs that would result from a decrease in wages, *holding output constant*. Substitution effects in labor demand can never be negative in response to a fall in wages. The firm will always use at least as much labor and no more capital to produce a given level of output when wages decrease.

When wages fall, however, the cost of producing Q_1 units of output will also fall. With a lower cost of production, the firm will increase its sales by lowering its price. This change will result in a movement out along the expansion path through point M in Figure 4.7 to a new, higher output level Q_3 that will be produced at point N using E_N units of labor input. The expansion of output that takes place when an input becomes less expensive is called the **scale effect in production**. In nearly all cases the scale effect of a decreased wage rate will be positive. Together this decomposition of the net change in employee-hours in response to a change in the wage rate can be written as:

$$\textit{Total effect} = \textit{Substitution effect} + \textit{Scale effect}$$

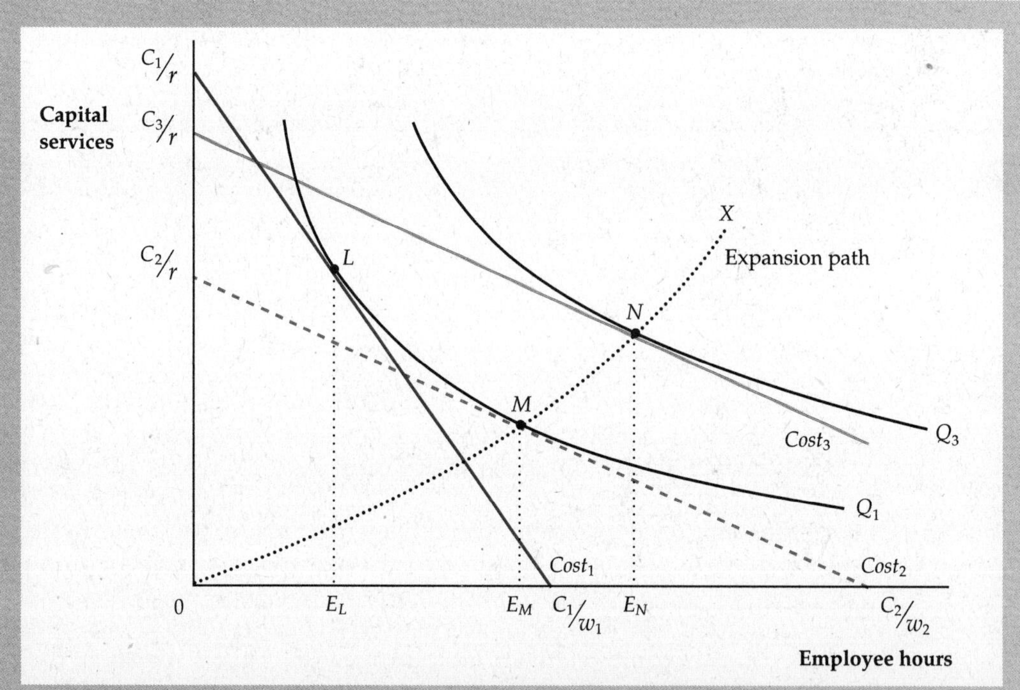

FIGURE 4.7 LONG-RUN ADJUSTMENT TO A CHANGE IN WAGES
When wages fall from w_1 to w_2, firms would produce output Q_1 using more labor and less capital. This movement from L to M produces a substitution effect that increases the amount of labor demanded from E_L to E_M. The lower cost of production reduces the product price and moves the firm from M to N along its expansion path. This creates a scale effect that further increases the demand for labor from E_M to E_N.

or

$$E_N - E_L = [E_M - E_L] + [E_N - E_M].$$

Just as we divided the change in hours supplied when a person's wage rate changes into income and substitution effects in Chapter 2, here we divide the change in employee-hours demanded when the wage rate changes into scale and substitution effects.

SOME EXTREME EXAMPLES OF SUBSTITUTION

The movement in Figure 4.7 is only one of many possible responses employers might have to changes in the relative prices of labor and capital services. Although it is the standard case, some extreme examples are also worth considering. It is possible, though very rare, that even a large change in the relative prices of capital and labor will not change firms' labor input. This situation would occur if it were impossible to substitute capital for labor and inputs must be combined in **fixed proportion.** For example, it takes the labor of four people and the capital services of two violins, a viola, and a cello to produce a string quartet. Adding neither a second viola nor a third violinist will increase the output of music. With the isocost line *DE* and the typical isoquant Q_1 in Figure 4.8(a), the firm will produce at point *A*.

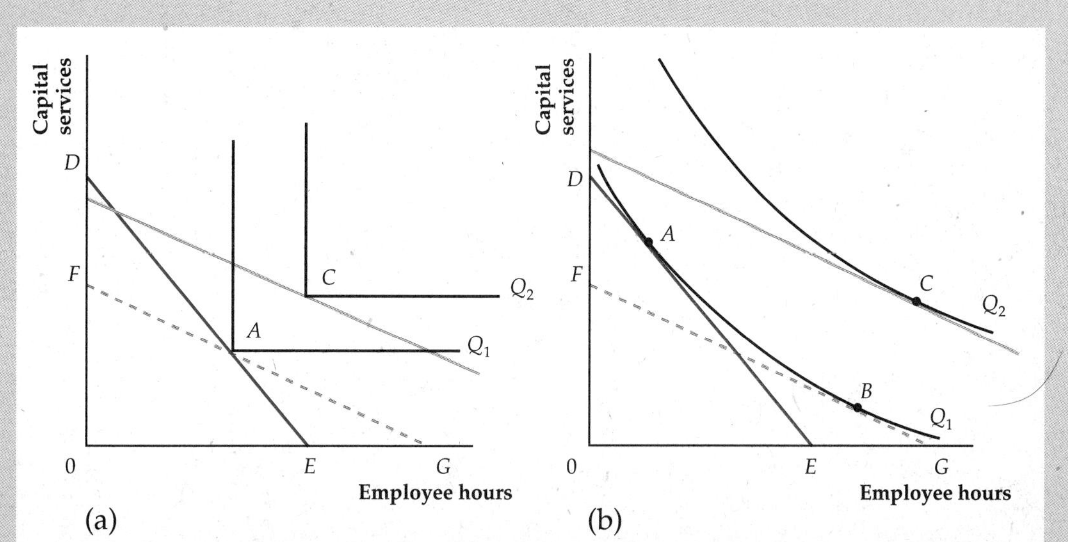

FIGURE 4.8 EXTREME CASES OF SUBSTITUTION POSSIBILITIES

In Figure 4.8(a), capital and labor must be used in fixed proportions so that there is no substitution effect when wages change. Scale effects will cause a move from *A* to *C*. In Figure 4.8(b), it is very easy to substitute between capital and labor, so the substitution effect between *A* and *B* will be large.

What if labor becomes relatively much less expensive in this case? Although the change in the relative prices of inputs shifts the isocost line from *DE* to *FG*, the cost-minimizing employer will not change the mix of capital services and employee-hours used to produce Q_1. In this case the substitution effect is zero; each output can be produced by only one combination of labor and capital. It would never pay to produce the output Q_1 other than at point *A*. Additional labor inputs would not allow any saving on capital inputs, and vice versa. Adding a second cellist would not increase the number of string quartets played. In this situation the demand for labor at a given level of output does not respond to changes in the wage rate. Scale effects still exist, however, so that there will be an increase in output if the lower cost enables the producer to schedule more concerts. Thus, there could be a shift to point *C* on isoquant Q_2.

The nearly opposite case of very easy capital-labor substitution (a very large substitution effect) is shown in Figure 4.8(b). For example, it is fairly easy to replace one laborer driving a leaf-blower with many laborers using rakes. If the budget constraint tilts from *DE* to *FG*, it pays the firm to shift its production of Q_1 from *A* to *B* (in our example, to switch to manual raking). Since labor and capital are very close substitutes, a small change in relative input prices induces a very large change in relative factor use. There will also be a scale effect causing a movement from point *B* to point *C*. Overall, a small wage decrease will cause a very large increase in labor inputs. This means that the long-run demand curve is nearly horizontal.

THE IMPORTANCE OF SUBSTITUTION AND SCALE EFFECTS

Because the firm chooses the amount of labor and capital it uses by setting the *MRTS* equal to the ratio of the wage rate to the price of capital services, there must be a relationship between the relative amounts of labor and capital services used and their relative prices. In particular, the ratio *E*/*K* generally increases as the ratio *w*/*r* decreases. The responsiveness of *E*/*K* to changes in the ratio of the input prices is measured as the **elasticity of substitution**:

$$\sigma = \frac{\textit{Percent change } (E/K)}{\textit{Percent change } (w/r)} \leq 0$$

where the Greek letter sigma (σ) is used as a symbol for the elasticity of substitution. The absolute value of this elasticity is smaller the more curved the isoquants in Figure 4.8. With the fixed factor isoquants in Figure 4.8(a), $\sigma = 0$. The cost-minimizing employer does not change the ratio *E*/*K* no matter how large the change in *w*/*r*. If the isoquants are straight lines, so that capital services and employee-hours are perfectly substitutable, $\sigma = -\infty$.

The elasticity of labor demand is defined as the percentage change in labor demanded in response to a 1 percent change in the wage rate. Because substitution of capital for labor is usually possible in the long run, but by

POLICY ISSUE

SHOULD DEVELOPING COUNTRIES USE WESTERN TECHNOLOGY?

The United States has often financed the export of American technology to developing nations through its programs of foreign assistance. Methods of production that worked well in the United States, in the sense of being able to produce output competitively, were exported with U.S. aid to countries where real wages were far below those in the United States but capital was at least as costly. For example, the United States Agency for International Development (USAID) spent $600 million in Tanzania over a 20-year period. One project it helped fund was a paper mill that closed shortly after opening because its products were twice as expensive as imports.[3] The same agency encouraged agricultural planners and farmers in Africa to adopt mechanized methods of production, including the use of tractors and combines. Did these exports of capital-intensive technologies improve productivity and raise output in the countries the United States "aided?"

Given the vast differences in relative factor prices between the United States and developing countries, it is not surprising that these exports of subsidized technology often did not produce the desired results. Local entrepreneurs, recognizing these difficulties, regularly switched back to older methods that, because of the very low price of labor relative to capital services, allowed them to produce at lower costs. For example, in Sierra Leone bakers abandoned newly installed electric ovens in favor of traditional wood-fired ones. Similarly, clothing firms that used large-scale, capital-intensive technology reported much lower rates of profit than firms that relied on workers using simple sewing machines.[4]

These findings suggest that policymakers may do their citizens no favor by importing technology that looks impressive but is inappropriate given local factor prices. Since real wages have been rising over time in developed countries, it suggests that the most modern means of production may not be appropriate for less-developed countries where wages are still low. Unfortunately local politicians frequently do not want to be seen by their citizens as importing less than the "best" or most modern technologies. Profit-making businesses, however, must respond to the differences in the relative prices of capital and labor. They must choose technology to fit the price structures of input markets in the nations where they operate. Evidence for Swedish and American multinationals suggest they do just that. In countries where labor is relatively less expensive, companies use technologies that rely more on labor and less on capital.[5]

---

[3]*Newsweek,* (June 9, 1986), p. 39.

[4]Enyinna Chuta and Carl Liedholm, *Employment Growth in Small-Scale Industry,* New York: St. Martin's, (1985).

[5]Robert Lipsey, Irving Kravis, and Romualdo Roldan, "Do Multinational Firms Adapt Factor Proportions to Relative Factor Prices?" in Ann Krueger (ed.). *Trade and Employment in Developing Countries,* vol. 2, Chicago: University of Chicago Press, (1982).

assumption is not possible in the short run, the long-run demand curve for labor is usually more elastic than the short-run demand curve. There is never a substitution effect in the short run but unless the isoquants are like the very unusual special case in Figure 4.8(a) there will be a substitution effect in the long run. The substitution and scale effects together determine the long-run elasticity of demand for labor, ε^d. In particular

$$\epsilon_d = s_K\sigma + s_L\eta$$

where s_K and s_L are the fractions of the total value of output accruing to the services of capital and to labor, and eta (η) < 0 is the **elasticity of product demand**.

Alfred Marshall, the great English economist of the late-19th century, summarized the determinants of the elasticity of factor demand in **four laws of derived demand**.[6] The first two follow directly from the formula for ε_d. The demand for labor will be less elastic:

1. The harder it is for firms to substitute labor for capital at a given output, that is, the closer the elasticity of substitution, σ, is to zero; and
2. The closer η, the elasticity of demand for the final product, is to zero.

The first law says that when wages increase the employer would like to replace labor with capital (or some other input) but finds it technologically difficult to do so. This just restates the discussion of the last two sections. Where substitution is easy, employers can respond to a small drop in the wage rate by choosing a technology that uses a lot more employee-hours. The second law implies that wage increases can be passed on to consumers with little loss in the demand for output, and thus in the derived demand for labor.

Marshall's third law states that:

3. The elasticity of demand for labor will be lower if the supply of other factors of production is less elastic.

In the case of an increase in the wage rate, the firm will seek to substitute capital services and other factors of production for labor. In the extreme case, if the supply of these other factors does not expand (the elasticity of supply is zero), no substitution is possible and the substitution effect will be eliminated from the formula for ε_d. If the expansion of the supply of other factors is accompanied by a much higher price for these other factors, the substitution effect will be reduced.

Marshall stated the fourth law of derived demand as:

4. The demand for labor will be less elastic the smaller is s_L.

Marshall's reasoning went like this. Suppose that the wages of musicians comprise 80 percent of the total costs of a symphony concert while the wages

[6]Alfred Marshall, *Principles of Economics,* 8th ed., London: Macmillan, (1923), pp. 241–246.

POLICY ISSUE

UNIONS AND FREE TRADE

Among the most vocal opponents of recent moves toward freer trade such as the North American Free Trade Agreement (NAFTA) or the Uruguay Round of the General Agreement on Tariffs and Trade (GATT) have been U.S. trade unions. It is easy to see why. Consider what happens to the elasticity of demand for domestic labor when a country becomes more open to foreign competition. Now that foreign products can serve as substitutes for domestic products, the elasticity of demand for the output of domestic firms will increase sharply. For example, in the 1960s when foreign competition effectively did not exist, auto and steel companies could pass on union-induced higher wages with very little impact on the demand for their products. With a small drop in product demand the derived demand for labor also dropped only slightly. As the U.S. economy became more open in the 1970s and 1980s, the same higher union wages generated much larger cuts in labor demand because customers could more easily switch to foreign suppliers if employers tried to pass on the wage costs.[7] Thus, moves toward free trade will benefit consumers by limiting unions' ability to extract higher than competitive wages with little loss in employment.

of ushers make up 5 percent of the costs. Now suppose that the wages of musicians rise 10 percent, with other costs remaining constant. To a first approximation, the cost of a concert will increase by about 8 percent and there will likely be a decrease in attendance and the demand for musicians. On the other hand, if the wages of ushers rise by 10 percent, total costs will only increase by about 0.5 percent. With such a small increase there will probably be just about as many people willing to attend the concert and the demand for ushers will not fall much.

Although intuitively appealing, Marshall's reasoning does not go far enough. Another great economist, J. R. Hicks, demonstrated that Marshall's reasoning relied on an implicit assumption about the elasticity of substitution.[8] In our example, it requires that ushers cannot start playing instruments if the wage of orchestra members rises. Hicks proved that if the ease of substituting along an isoquant (σ) *exceeds* the elasticity of demand for the product (η), then the elasticity of demand for labor will be smaller, the *larger* the ratio of labor cost is to other costs. In other words, when the producer can substitute more easily than the consumer, it is an advantage to labor to have a large share in the initial input mix. In this case demand for output and,

[7]Colin Lawrence and Robert Lawrence, "Manufacturing Wage Dispersion: An End Game Interpretation," Brookings Papers on Economic Activity 47–106 (1985).

[8]J. R. Hicks, The Theory of Wages, 2d ed., London: Macmillan, (1964), pp. 241–246.

therefore, the use of labor is not reduced much by an increase in the product price, while substitution in production will be more difficult and expensive if a larger amount of labor needs to be replaced.

These laws will be useful in Chapter 13 when we examine whether a union can achieve a wage increase without causing a substantial loss of employment among its members. They are also helpful in designing wage subsidies aimed at stimulating employment, particularly if those subsidies are to differ by industry, occupation, or geographic area. Indeed, in any case in which the wage of a particular group of workers is to be altered, Marshall's laws aid in identifying the characteristics that will strengthen or reduce the effect on employment.

THE ROLE OF TECHNOLOGICAL CHANGE

The discussion of labor demand in the long run has assumed that technology remains constant. Yet we know that technology does change (where **technology** is defined as the possible ways to combine inputs to produce outputs). Viewed this way, we can think of technological improvements as innovations that offer businesses a wider range of choices about how to produce.

How will technological change affect the individual employer's demand for labor in the long run? With technological change, the isoquant labelled Q_1 in Figure 4.9 moves inward to Q_1'. The typical business can now produce the same amount of output with fewer inputs of capital services and employee-hours. With the ratio w/r that is represented by the isocost curve CD, the employer will now produce the same amount, Q_1, with only E_1' employee-hours, along the new budget line $C'D'$.

As the particular figure is drawn, the shape of the isoquant is also changed by the technological advance. The line $0A$ shows the combinations of E and K that would result in the ratio E/K staying constant. After the technological change, even though w/r stays the same, cost-minimizing employers decrease employee hours more than they cut capital services. In this example the technical change is of the type known as **labor-saving** or capital-using. The same output will be produced with a bigger reduction in labor than capital services. If Q_1 did not change shape as it shifted in, we would call the technical change **neutral**. If it shifted so that relatively more labor was used, the change would be called **labor-using** or capital-saving.

A very good example of labor-saving technical change is the introduction of automatic teller machines in banks. The same number of transactions can be handled with somewhat more capital but much less labor. The cost to the business of producing banking services is cut. Another example is the installation of personal computers and work stations in an office. The same amount of paperwork can be produced with fewer clerical workers (and, presumably, at a lower average cost). We will return to the impact of technical change at the end of this chapter when we discuss the economy-wide aggregate demand for labor.

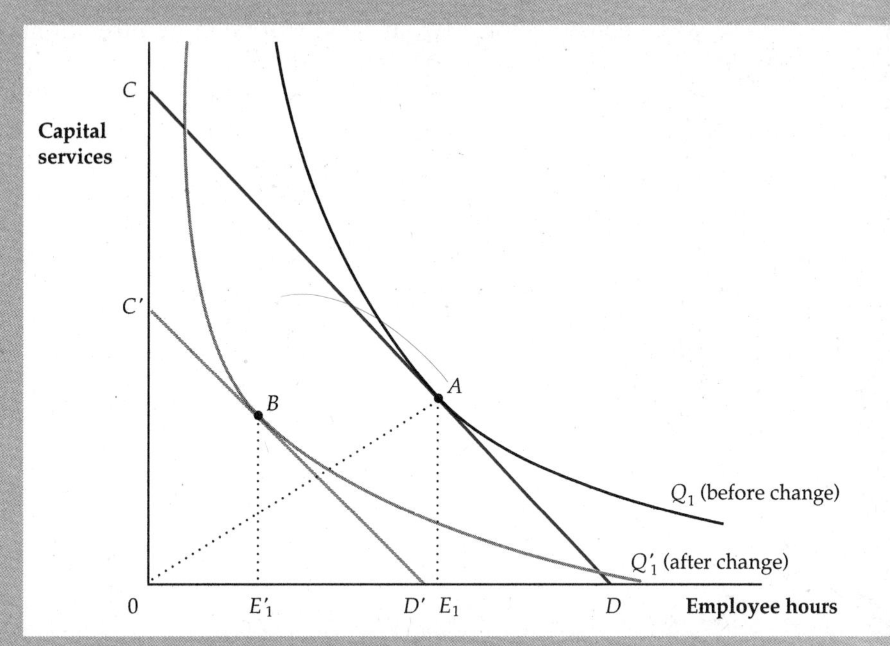

FIGURE 4.9 LONG-RUN LABOR DEMAND AFTER A LABOR-SAVING TECHNICAL CHANGE

Technical change makes it possible to produce the same output using fewer inputs and at a lower cost. If the technical change is labor-saving, as shown here, it will also shift the slopes of the isoquants and increase the ratio of capital to labor in the firm's choice of inputs.

THE BIRTH AND DEATH OF BUSINESSES AND JOBS

Our discussion of labor demand so far has been based on decisions made by an employer who is always in business. Few firms actually last forever. Indeed, many companies survive only briefly, as the turnover of stores at any local shopping mall will show. Thus, it is important in studying labor demand to investigate not only the expansion and contraction of existing employers when wages change but also how wage changes affect the creation and destruction of firms themselves.

Table 4.3 shows a summary of job dynamics for 6 countries in the 1980s and early 1990s. Each entry is the number of jobs created or destroyed per year as a percentage of employment in the previous year. For example, for Canada the table shows that over the 8 years 1983 through 1991 14.5 percent of jobs in one year did not exist the previous year, but of those that

TABLE 4.3 SOURCES OF EMPLOYMENT CHANGES (PER YEAR, AS PERCENT OF TOTAL EMPLOYMENT)

Source of Employment Change	Canada (1983–1991)	Germany (1983–1990)	Sweden (1985–1992)	United Kingdom (1985–1991)	France (1984–1992)	U.S. (1984–1991)
Expansion in existing establishments	11.2	6.5	8.0	6.0	6.7	4.6
Establishment openings	3.2	2.5	6.5	2.7	7.2	8.4
Gross job gains	14.5	9.0	14.5	8.7	13.9	13.0
Contraction in existing establishments	8.8	5.6	9.6	2.7	6.3	3.1
Establishment closures	3.1	1.9	5.0	3.9	7.0	7.3
Gross job losses	11.9	7.5	14.6	6.6	13.2	10.4
Gross employment change (job turnover)	26.3	16.5	29.1	15.3	27.1	23.4
Net employment change	2.6	1.5	1.3	2.1	0.6	2.6

Source: OECD, *Employment Outlook,* 1994, Table 3.1.

did exist the previous year, 11.9 percent disappeared over the next 12 months. Of the 14.5 percent job gains, most were created in existing plants. Of the 11.9 percent job losses, most were also lost in existing plants. This suggests that job dynamics in Canada arose mostly from changes in existing businesses and that the theory presented so far describes most changes in employment.

The Canadian experience is mirrored by the data for Germany, Sweden, and the U.K. also shown in the Table 4.3. Most of the gains and losses of jobs in these countries occurred within continuing establishments. The same is not true for France or the U.S., where a much larger share of the gross increases and losses in jobs occurred because new plants opened or old plants closed.[9]

[9] See also Timothy Dunne, Mark Roberts, and Larry Samuelson, "Plant Turnover and Gross Employment Flows in the U.S. Manufacturing Sector," *Journal of Labor Economics* 7: 48–71 (1989); Randall W. Eberts and Edward B. Montgomery, "Employment Creation and Destruction: An Analytic Review," *Federal Reserve Bank of Cleveland Economic Review,* 30: 14–26 (1994).

The data in Table 4.3 suggest that a theory based solely on continuing businesses is not sufficient to describe many of the changes in employment demand we observe. We also need to explain how economic factors affect the rate at which plants open and close.

Describing the decisions of owners of existing businesses about whether to close is easy. In the *long run* a firm will shut down if the price at which it can sell its products is less than the average cost of producing them ($P < ATC$). This decision rule is discussed in economic principles classes. Firms should close if their costs cannot be covered.

This relationship can be seen in Figure 4.10. The line $0R$ shows how revenue changes with increases in output. Since we are dealing with a competitive firm it is a straight line, with each additional unit of output increasing revenue by the same amount. The curves $0C_1$ and $0C_2$ are two total cost curves, showing how the total cost of production varies with output level. They differ in the wage rate that underlies them. Curve $0C_2$ is based on a higher wage rate. Even after capital is substituted for labor (as in Figure 4.7), higher wages mean higher costs of production at each output level. Suppose that the firm faces wage rate w_1 and total cost curve $0C_1$. With this wage rate, the firm can earn a profit since there are some output levels where the total

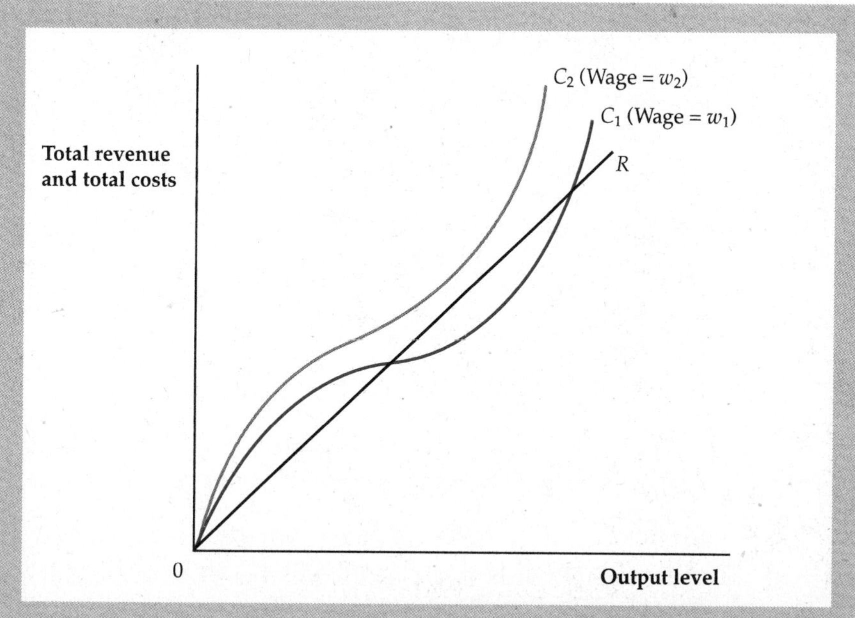

FIGURE 4.10 THE BIRTH AND DEATH OF PLANTS AND FIRMS

Changes in wages will shift a firm's total cost curve and may make it profitable to open or unprofitable to continue to operate a plant. This decision will create large, discontinuous changes in employment between zero and some positive level.

revenue curve lies above the total cost curve. As wages increase, the cost curve will rotate upward. At some wage level costs will become so high (as is the case with cost curve $0C_2$) that there is no output level where the firm can cover its costs. It will now make sense for the firm to close down. Output will fall discontinuously from some positive level to zero. Employment will also drop discontinuously from a positive level to zero.

Figure 4.10 represents the situation for an individual plant. If wages increase by just a little bit, only a few plants will be induced to close down. These are the plants that were just at the margin of losing money before the wage increase. If the wage increase is larger, more plants will no longer be profitable and will opt to close down. While the change in employment for a particular plant that shuts is large relative to the size of that plant, each individual plant is very small compared to the entire U.S. economy. Overall, the reduction in employment from plant closings when wages increase appears fairly smooth and will be greater the larger the size of the wage increase, just as the substitution and scale effects within continuing plants will be greater for larger wage increases. Both effects contribute to the downward-sloping demand for labor curve in the economy as a whole.

The decision about whether to open a business can be analyzed in a similar way. Simply reverse the wage change to go from w_2 to w_1 in Figure 4.10. At lower wages more opportunities will become profitable and more plants (or firms) will be opened. The more wages fall, the more such job creation there will be.

It is important to realize that firms and plants are born and die for many reasons other than changes in wage rates. New technology may replace older methods of production. Changes in consumer tastes may shift the demand for various products. Thus, no matter what the level of wages, there will always be some plants closing and some new ones being established. What changes in wage rates do is to alter the relative balance between plant openings and closings.

DO LABOR DEMAND SCHEDULES REALLY SLOPE DOWN?

Do businesses really make the substitutions implied by the theory of labor demand? Clearly employers do not make explicit estimates of relative marginal products of workers and capital services every time they hire a worker. Most employers are not even familiar with the term *marginal product.* Yet they do make judgments about whether or not new employees are likely to be worth as much as they will cost, and many describe their decisions in exactly these terms.

An analogy is useful in this context.[10] Imagine a driver deciding whether it is safe to pass a truck on a two-lane road when a car is approaching in the

[10]This analogy was suggested by the late Professor Fritz Machlup.

POLICY ISSUE

ARE SMALL BUSINESSES ENGINES FOR CREATING JOBS?

The U.S. government offers substantial incentives to open new businesses and provides aid for existing small business. In 1993 the budget for the Small Business Administration, the agency that provided this aid, totalled $975 million. One of the major arguments for this program is that most new jobs are created by small businesses and that these subsidies are a way of encouraging more rapid growth in the demand for labor, and thus in employment. In his 1993 State of the Union Address, President Clinton proposed "the boldest targeted incentive for small business in history . . . a permanent investment tax credit for the small firms [that have] created such a huge percentage of all the new jobs in our country over the last 10 or 15 years." Is this claim correct?

The widely held belief that small businesses are the major source of job growth comes from a misreading of the actual research. Most research dealing with openings and closings is based on data from plants or **establishments**. Just because an establishment is small, however, does not mean that it is *owned* by a small business. In fact, although small establishments account for a disproportionate share of job creation, the share of new jobs created by small *firms* is about the same as these firms' share of total employment. There is no systematic relationship between net job creation and firm size. Existing medium and large firms do tend to open new plants that are of smaller than average size. In addition, although new small establishments have a larger than proportional impact on job creation, they are also more likely to eliminate jobs through employment reductions or closing altogether. New jobs created in existing large firms are over 15 percent more likely to still exist one year later than those created by small firms. Similar results have been found in other developed economies.[11]

opposite lane. A formal model of the decision involves several different elements, including the speed of the approaching car, how far away it is, the speed of the truck, the rate at which the driver's car can accelerate, and the condition of the road. The driver has neither the ability nor the time to estimate each element separately and to combine them in a formal analysis. Yet millions of such decisions are made correctly every day. A formal model of the process would assist an analyst who was trying to design safer highways or cars, even though it might not describe the driver's conscious thoughts.

Critics of marginal productivity theory often assert that in the short run capital-labor ratios are fixed by technology, so that the short-run marginal

[11]Catherine Armington and Marjorie Odle, "Small Business—How Many Jobs?" *Brookings Review* 1: 14–17 (1982); Bruno Contini and Riccardo Revelli, "The Process of Job Creation and Destruction in the Italian Economy," *Labour* 1: 121–144 (1987); David Evans, "Tests of Alternative Theories of Firm Growth," *Journal of Political Economy* 95: 657–674 (1987); Steven J. Davis, "Size Distribution Statistics from County Business Patterns Data," unpublished paper, University of Chicago (1990); Steven J. Davis, John Haltimanger, Scott Schuh, "Small Business and Job Creation: Dissecting the Myth and Reassessing the Facts," *Business Economics* 29: 13–21 (1994).

product schedule is vertical and raising wages will not reduce the use of labor. No doubt there are cases where this is true, but there are also many where it is not. If the employer is using manual labor to dig a ditch and has only five shovels, each of which can be used by only one worker at a time, it does not follow that the marginal product of a sixth worker is zero. Perhaps the sixth worker could contribute to output by bringing beer for the other five. More realistically, the sixth could add to output by relieving each of the others for 10 minutes every hour, so that the shovels would always be in use while each worker rested 10 minutes per hour. Similarly, the speed of an automobile assembly line can be increased with relatively minor changes in equipment by adding more work stations and providing more relief workers to back up the line when the regular workers fall behind or need to rest.

Much research has measured the slopes of labor demand curves for individual firms or within small industries. Labor demands by airline companies, electric utilities, and trucking companies in the United States; small firms in Latin America; and many others have all been studied. As with any body of empirical research in the social sciences, the estimates differ among the studies. They all show that ε_d is negative, however, and most show that the impact of wage changes is relatively large.[12] Even more research has examined the demand for labor in a single large industry. Studies of such diverse examples as manufacturing in Sweden, Britain, Japan, and the U.S. have all found that long-run labor demand curves slope down.[13]

Table 4.4 (page 167) presents a summary of more than 100 studies of the substitution elasticity. The research suggests that a mid-range estimate is –0.30. The variety of estimates produced by the very large body of research on this subject is also listed in the table. The specific values of scale elasticities have been studied in less detail and vary less, so only a medium value is listed. The studies of scale elasticities indicate that a value of –0.70 seems reasonable. Coupled with the substitution elasticities, this suggests that for a typical firm or small industry the labor demand curve has a substantial negative slope and a wage elasticity of labor demand of –1.0 or slightly higher.

Do businesses' decisions about closing down or opening also respond to changes in labor costs? This issue has been much less widely studied by economists, so the answer to this question must be more tentative. The best

---

[12]Daniel Rich, "On the Elasticity of Labor Demand," *Quarterly Review of Economics and Business* 30: 31–41 (1990); B. Starr McMullen and Linda Stanley, "The Impact of Deregulation on the Production Structure of the Motor Carrier Industry," *Economic Inquiry* 26: 299–316 (1988); and Kim Sosin and Loretta Fairchild, "Nonhomotheticity and Technological Bias in Production," *Review of Economics and Statistics* 66: 44–50 (1984).

[13]John Pencavel and Bertil Holmlund, "The Determination of Wages, Employment and Work Hours in an Economy with Centralized Wage-Setting: Sweden 1950–83," *Economic Journal* 98: 1105–1126 (1988); Stephen Nickell, "An Investigation of the Determinants of Manufacturing Employment in the United Kingdom," *Review of Economic Studies* 51: 529–557 (1984), and Catherine Morrison, "Quasi-fixed Inputs in U.S. and Japanese Manufacturing: A Generalized Leontief Restricted Cost Approach," *Review of Economics and Statistics* 70: 275–287 (1988).

evidence we have is that the wage elasticity of new job creation or destruction via plant openings and closing is also at least −1.0. Support for this conclusion comes from studies as diverse as the close-up examination of coal mines in Kentucky and the widespread effect of wage differences across states and cities on employers' choices about opening new plants.[14]

THE DEMAND FOR SEVERAL TYPES OF LABOR

So far we have examined employers' decisions in choosing between only two factors: capital services and employee-hours. This is clearly an inadequate description of the real world. There are many different kinds of capital services and every worker is at least a little bit different from every other. Even ignoring small, and probably unimportant, differences, some workers are skilled while others are less so. Similarly some are old while others are young. Workers differ by race, sex, education, and other characteristics that are of interest to the public and important for policy. It is an oversimplification to aggregate workers into a single group, since employers do not determine employment this way. Many issues of public policy revolve around employers substituting workers of one type for those of another.

In the simplest extension of our model, businesses use three inputs: capital services, the hours of skilled workers, and the hours of unskilled workers. With three inputs, we must use the isoquant and isocost curve analysis developed earlier even in the short run when capital services are fixed. The employer's decision about how many hours of skilled and unskilled labor to use is shown by the tangency of the budget line *CD* with the isoquant Q_1 at point *A* in Figure 4.11. We begin by assuming that the price of the fixed amount of capital services is low and label the isoquant accordingly. With capital services cheap, the firm will use a lot of these services. Thus, by assumption along the isoquant through point *A* the skilled and unskilled workers have a lot of equipment with which to work.

Now consider the long run when the amount of capital used can be changed. What would happen if the price of capital services rose? We know that the use of any factor will decrease when its price rises, so the firm will use less capital. With less capital, in order to maintain production constant at

---

[14]Dennis Carlton, "The Location and Employment Choices of New Firms: An Econometric Model with Discrete and Continuous Endogenous Variables," *Review of Economics and Statistics* 65: 440–449 (1983); Timothy Bartik, "Business Location Decisions in the United States: Estimates of the Effects of Unionization, Taxes and Other Characteristics of States," *Journal of Business and Economic Statistics* 3: 14–22 (1985); Daniel Hamermesh, "Plant Closings and the Value of the Firm," *Review of Economics and Statistics* 70: 580–586 (1988); Mark Berger and John Garen, "Heterogeneous Producers in an Extractive Industry," *Resources and Energy* 12: 295–310 (1990); Leslie Papke, "Interstate Business Tax Differentials and New Firm Location: Evidence from Panel Data," *Journal of Public Economics* 45: 47–68 (1991).

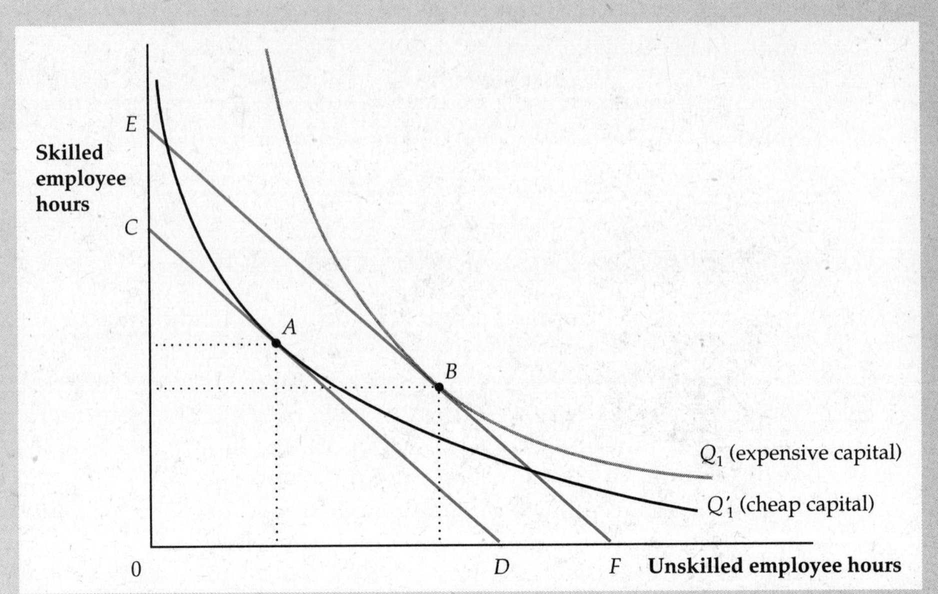

FIGURE 4.11 CHANGES IN THE DEMAND FOR SKILLED AND UNSKILLED LABOR WHEN THE PRICE OF CAPITAL CHANGES

An increase in the price of capital causes a firm to use more labor to produce any level of output. If skilled labor is complementary with capital, it may also cause a shift away from skilled labor toward unskilled labor that is a substitute for both capital and skilled labor.

Q_1 the firm must increase its use of labor. Thus, with high capital costs isoquant Q_1 shifts out and lies above its position with low capital costs. Will it also *tilt* as shown in Figure 4.11? A large amount of research indicates that the typical firm will behave as depicted in Figure 4.11.[15] With the relative prices of skilled and unskilled labor unchanged, firms minimize costs by producing Q_1 at point *B*. They cut their demand for both skilled labor and capital services when the price of capital services rises, and they compensate for these reductions by increasing the use of unskilled workers. Capital and skilled labor are thus **complements in production.** They are used together and when the price of one of them rises firms use less of both. Each is a **substi-**

[15] The initial work is by Zvi Griliches, "Capital-Skill Complementarity," *Review of Economics and Statistics* 51: 465–468 (1969). A good recent illustration of this phenomenon is in Villy Bergström and Epaminondas Panas, "How Robust is the Capital-Skill Complementarity Hypothesis," *Review of Economics and Statistics* 74:540-546 (1992).

TABLE 4.4 ESTIMATES OF LONG-RUN LABOR-DEMAND ELASTICITIES

	Substitution Elasticity	Scale Elasticity	Total Elasticity
Medium	–0.30	–0.70	–1.00
High	–0.75	—	—
Low	–0.15	—	—

Source: Based on Daniel Hamermesh, *Labor Demand,* Chapter 3, Princeton, N.J.: Princeton University Press, (1993).

tute in production for unskilled labor. When either of their price rises, firms use more unskilled labor.

That capital and skilled workers are complements has important implications for a number of issues in public policy and for understanding economic development. It suggests, for example, that investment tax credits and other subsidies for capital investment will stimulate job creation, but that most of the jobs initially created will require skilled workers. Unskilled workers will gain primarily because the overall stimulation of the economy will increase the demand for the products they produce. The ever-increasing mechanization of production that has accompanied economic development has required the simultaneous investment of resources in the development of human capital. Without this investment it seems unlikely that the rising living standards that have accompanied mechanization could have occurred. Investment in human capital would have constrained the returns to investment in physical capital.

We saw in Chapter 3 that both education and experience increase a worker's skill. Thus, it is not surprising that educated workers are substitutes for uneducated labor and complements with capital services. Similarly, research on labor markets in the U.S., Britain, and Australia shows that employers also consider older, more-experienced workers as substitutes for younger, less-experienced ones.[16]

With several types of labor it no longer makes sense to speak of a single long-run demand elasticity for labor. Instead, employers respond differently

[16] Richard Layard, "Youth Unemployment in Britain and the United States Compared," in Richard Freeman and David Wise (eds.). *The Youth Labor Market Problem: Its Nature, Causes and Consequences,* Chicago: University of Chicago Press, (1982); Patricia Rice, "Juvenile Employment, Relative Wages and Social Security in Great Britain," *Economic Journal* 96: 352–374 (1986); Philip Lewis, "Substitution between Young and Adult Workers in Australia," *Australian Economic Papers* 24: 115–126 (1985).

to equal-percentage wage changes for different groups of workers. The evidence generally suggests that employers' responses are greater for workers who embody less human capital. Thus the demand for younger, less-educated, and inexperienced workers is more elastic than that for older, more highly educated, and more-experienced workers. This conclusion implies that any policy that raises the costs of employing less-skilled workers will have a bigger negative effect on their employment than an equal-percentage increase in the cost of employing more-skilled workers. This is an important point since many government interventions in the labor market are supposedly designed to "help" unskilled workers by legislating higher wages or increasing other employment costs by mandating various benefits.

THE EFFECTS OF THE MINIMUM WAGE

The discussion of substitution between workers of different types makes it clear that relative wages are not fixed but instead will adjust to changes in relative demand and supply. Equilibrium will eventually be achieved as long as some external force does not prevent adjustment. One force that might produce a prolonged disequilibrium in the labor market is the imposition of a legal minimum wage above the equilibrium wage, an **effective minimum wage.** Imposed minimum wages exist in many industrialized and most developing countries. In the United States, for example, the minimum wage has been increased under the Fair Labor Standards Act of 1938 from the initial $0.25 to $4.25 after March 1991. Canada has provincial minimum wage laws that, in some cases, mandate fairly high minimum standards. France has a national minimum applying to all workers. Britain has no national law, but agreed-upon minimum wages have been established in some low-wage industries.

The question of interest is how these laws affect the demand for labor and, because of that, how they affect employment. The theory of competitive labor markets predicts that an effective minimum wage will reduce employment, as illustrated by Figure 4.12(a). For ease of exposition, Figure 4.12(a) measures employment in workers rather than employee-hours. The analysis would be unchanged, however, if employee-hours were used instead. As discussed in Chapter 5, the analysis would be much different if the market were not competitive.

The market demand curve is *DD*, and the market supply curve is *SS*. Their intersection determines the competitive wage, w_c, with employment E_c. If a legal minimum wage is set for this market at w_m, employment is reduced to E_m. The reduction in employment is smaller than the excess supply of labor at the minimum wage (the distance *AC*). The excess supply includes both workers displaced from their jobs along with a second component consisting of workers who were not in the labor market before but who are drawn into the market by the prospect of earning the high minimum wage. Of course,

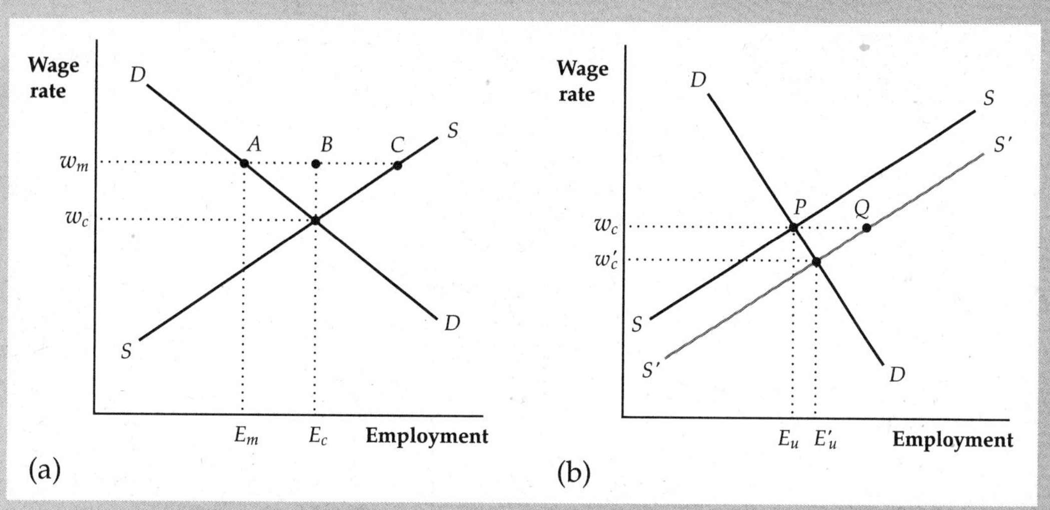

FIGURE 4.12 THE IMPACTS OF AN EFFECTIVE MINIMUM WAGE
A minimum wage above the equilibrium level in a labor market results in an excess supply of labor and unemployment in the covered sector as shown in Figure 4.12(a). The impact on the uncovered sector will *probably* be to shift the labor supply curve to the right, increasing employment and reducing wages as shown in Figure 4.12(b).

the added workers may succeed in finding one of the minimum wage jobs. Thus, the actual workers shut out may be individuals who were previously employed but were replaced by others drawn into the labor force when the wage increased.

The excess supply of labor is dispersed in several ways.[17] Some workers will wait in a queue of unemployed workers seeking the high paying minimum wage jobs. Others may find it optimal to accept employment in the **uncovered sector** (the part of the economy not subject to the minimum wage) while waiting to find a minimum wage job. This sector may be substantial. The 1989 amendments to the federal minimum wage law exempt all employers with annual sales of less than $500,000 from the minimum wage. The labor market for the uncovered sector is shown in Figure 4.12(b), where we assume the equilibrium competitive wage was also w_c. Some workers who were displaced from or do not get jobs in the covered sector enter the uncovered sector, shifting supply out from *SS* to *S'S'* and lowering the wage to w_c'.

The number of workers who shift to the uncovered sector and, therefore, the impact of the minimum wage on wages in that sector and employment

[17] Finis Welch, "Minimum Wage Legislation in the United States," in Orley Ashenfelter and James Blum (eds.). *Evaluating the Labor-Market Effects of Social Programs,* Princeton, N.J.: Princeton University Industrial Relations Section, (1976).

cannot be determined from theory. It depends on which workers actually find a job at the minimum wage and the relative effectiveness of searching for these jobs while unemployed and working in the uncovered sector. Examining Figure 4.12(a), we know that the workers drawn into the labor market by the increase in the minimum wage will either find a job at that wage or remain unemployed while looking for one. The old competitive wage w_C was below their reservation wage or they would have been in the labor market at that wage. Thus, they will be unwilling to accept a job in the uncovered sector at w_C'.[18] The same applies to those workers among the E_0 employed before the imposition of minimum wage whose reservation wage is between w_C' and w_C. Those whose reservation wage is below w_C' would be willing to accept employment in the uncovered sector if such employment did not affect their probability of eventually getting a minimum wage job too adversely.

If all the new workers drawn into the labor market found a minimum wage job and every displaced worker entered the uncovered sector, total employment might rise because of a minimum wage. On the other hand, if many of the workers who did not find minimum wage jobs were the new entrants and/or many of the displaced opted to remain unemployed while searching for a minimum wage job, then total employment would fall. In any case, what is clear is that employment in the *covered* sector will fall when an effective minimum wage is introduced or increased. This loss in employment will consist of a combination of a reduction in workers in current establishments, the closing of some establishments, and the failure of others to open.

The effect of the minimum wage as presented in Figure 4.12(a) will depend on how many workers have their wages raised by the law as well as the magnitude of the mandated increases. These will depend on how many workers are subject to the law and how many of them would have wages lower than the minimum wage without the law. Table 4.5 shows the history of the federal minimum wage since its inception in 1938. As can be seen in the table, the fraction of workers covered by the minimum wage has increased substantially over time. The increase has probably been somewhat less than the table suggests since the data in the third column of the table excludes managerial, supervisory, and technical workers. As we saw in Table 3.1, these categories have been increasing as a share of all workers over time. Even with increases in 1990 and 1991 the ratio of the minimum wage to the average wage has fallen during the past three decades.[19]

---

[18]Technically, this is not true *if* accepting a job in the uncovered sector *increases* their chance of eventually landing a minimum wage job sufficiently. This seems to be an unlikely prospect.

[19]A better measure would be the ratio of the minimum wage to average wages in the entire economy rather than manufacturing only. We use this figure since only manufacturing wages are available prior to the early 1960s. In recent years the average economy-wide wage has been about 90 percent of the average manufacturing wage.

TABLE 4.5 MINIMUM WAGE LEVEL AND COVERAGE, 1938–1995

Date of Change	Minimum Wage	Share of Nonsupervisory Private Industry Employees Covered	*Minimum Wage Relative to Average Wage in Manufacturing*	
			Before	After
October 1938	$0.25	43.4	NA	40.6
October 1939	0.30	47.1	39.6	47.6
October 1945	0.40	55.4	30.8	41.1
January 1950	0.75	53.4	28.7	53.7
March 1956	1.00	53.1	39.3	52.3
September 1961	1.15	62.1	43.1	49.6
September 1963	1.25	62.1	46.6	50.6
February 1967	1.40	75.3	44.8	50.2
February 1968	1.60	72.6	47.6	54.4
May 1974	2.00	83.7	37.8	47.3
January 1975	2.10	83.3	42.7	44.9
January 1976	2.30	83.8	41.7	45.6
January 1978	2.65	85.1	38.5	44.4
January 1979	2.90	85.1	40.8	44.6
January 1980	3.10	86.1	41.7	44.5
January 1981	3.35	86.0	40.1	43.3
April 1990	3.80	87.5	31.4	35.6
April 1991	4.25	88.4	34.2	38.3

Sources: *Statistical Abstract of the United States*, 1994, Table 669; *Employment and Earnings*, various issues.

Whatever the impacts of the minimum wage, we would expect them to be confined to certain segments of the work force. A worker who was getting $3.35 per hour beforehand may well be out of work after an increase to $4.25. Even more likely, in view of the costs of hiring workers (fixed employment costs that are discussed in Chapter 5), a worker who would have been hired for $3.35 will not be hired if the employer must offer a wage of $4.25. On the other hand, a skilled worker earning $20 per hour will not be thrown out of work because the minimum wage is raised from $3.35 to $4.25. In fact, if skilled workers (and capital) are substitutes for unskilled workers, the effect of a minimum wage increase will be to shift out the demand curve for skilled workers and increase both their earnings and employment as businesses attempt to replace the now relatively more expensive unskilled workers with capital and skilled workers. Thus, it is only in the market for low-skilled, inexperienced workers that we should expect to see a negative impact from the minimum wage.

This expectation has led research into the effects of the minimum wage on employment to focus on the demand for teenage workers. Teenagers have

TABLE 4.6 REAL HOURLY COMPENSATION OF U.S. WORKERS, 1960–1994 (1982 = 100)

Year	Total Economy Hourly Compensation	Wages, Full-time Year-round Workers[a]
1960	62.7	87.5
1965	72.7	100.5
1970	85.6	104.8
1975	93.5	107.4
1980	98.1	102.8
1985	100.1	104.1
1990	103.7	104.9[b]
1994	101.8	—

[a]Based on a fixed-weighted average of male and female earnings.

[b]1988.

Sources: Council of Economic Advisers, *Economic Report of the President*, 1995, Tables B–45, B–46; Bureau of the Census, *Current Population Reports*, P–60, selected issues.

not acquired much experience, are not yet well educated, and may have an equilibrium wage below the minimum. In 1987, when increases were under debate, 32 percent of workers aged 16 to 19 earned the then-current minimum wage of $3.35 an hour or less, while just 11 percent of workers between 20 and 24 years old and 5 percent of workers 25 and older did.[20] Moreover, we have seen that the demand for young workers is relatively elastic.

The evidence with respect to the effect of a higher effective minimum wage on teenagers is mixed. Most studies have concluded that the minimum wage has reduced employment among young people in the U.S., especially because of the extension of minimum wage coverage. The estimates vary, but they cluster around a reduction in teen employment below what it would otherwise have been of between 1 and 2 percent for each 10 percent increase in the effective coverage of the minimum wage, defined as the fraction of workers covered times the ratio of the minimum wage to the average wage. Not surprisingly, since their equilibrium wage is somewhat higher, employment of 20- to 24-year-olds is less adversely affected by increases in the minimum. After the U.S. minimum wage was increased from $3.35 to $4.25 an hour between 1989 and 1991, employment of teenaged boys was 7.3 percent below what projections indicate it would have been had the minimum wage remained at $3.35. For teenaged women and blacks, the reductions in

[20]Earl Mellor, "Workers at the Minimum Wage or Less," *Monthly Labor Review* 110: 34–38 (1987).

employment due to the wage increase were 11.4 and 10.0 percent. Similar, but smaller, effects were found for adults who had not completed high school. Among these workers the reductions in employment were 3.1 percent for men, 5.2 percent for women, and 6.7 percent for blacks.[21]

While much of the research on the effects of minimum wages on employment has been in the United States, economists have also examined their effects elsewhere. The impacts of the minimum wage in France and Québec are estimated to be about the same as in the United States. Estimates of the effect on low-wage workers in Britain are also similar, with a roughly 1 percent decline in the employment of young people for each 10 percent increase in the minimum wage.[22]

An additional argument against the minimum wage is that it reduces nonwage benefits from employment. Firms can only afford to pay workers the value of their marginal product. If they are forced by minimum wage laws to pay a higher fraction of this productivity in cash, they will have less available to pay in other ways. Thus, they can be expected to reduce fringe benefits and investments in on-the-job training. As we saw in Chapter 3, workers pay the cost of such training by accepting low wages early in their tenure on the job. With the imposition of the minimum wage, there is a floor to the wage they can be offered. This situation forces employers to bear more of the cost of training, which they will not do if the training is general. There is evidence that both fringe benefits and the amount of on-the-job training are reduced by increases in the minimum wage. In particular, unskilled workers who receive the minimum wage but are prevented by it from paying for general on-the-job training through reduced wages are unlikely to earn higher wages over time and may become trapped in **dead-end jobs.**[23]

A conclusion that minimum wage laws reduce employment and on-the-job training does not dictate the judgment that such a law is undesirable. If

---

[21]Charles Brown, Curtis Gilroy, and Andrew Kohen, "The Effect of the Minimum Wage on Employment and Unemployment," *Journal of Economic Literature* 20: 487–528 (1982); Donald Deere, Kevin M. Murphy, and Finis Welch, "Employment and the 1990–1991 Minimum Wage Hike," *American Economic Review* 85: 232–237 (1995).

[22]Stephen Bazen and John Martin, "The Impact of the Minimum Wage on Earnings and Employment in France," *OECD Economic Studies* 199–221 (Spring 1991); Pierre Fortin, "L'Effet du Salaire Minimum sur les Prix, L'Emploi et la Répartition des Revenus: Le Cas du Québec," *Relations Industrielles* 34: 660–672 (1979); Roger Kaufman, "The Effects of Statutory Minimum Rates of Pay on Employment in Great Britain," *Economic Journal* 99: 1040–1053 (1989).

[23]Walter Wessels, "The Effect of Minimum Wages in the Presence of Fringe Benefits: An Expanded Model," *Economic Inquiry* 18: 293–313 (1980); Jacob Mincer and Linda Leighton, "Effects of Minimum Wages on Human Capital Formation," in Simon Rottenberg (ed.). *The Economics of Legal Minimum Wages,* Washington D.C.: American Enterprise Institute, (1981); Masanori Hashimoto, "Minimum Wage Effects on Training on the Job," *American Economic Review* 72: 1070–1087 (1982); Richard McKensie and Gordon Tullock, "The Minimum Wage: A New Perspective on an Old Policy," in *The Best of the New World of Economics,* 5th ed., Homewood, IL: Richard D. Irwin, (1989); Ralph E. Smith and Bruce Vavrichek, "The Wage Mobility of Minimum Wage Workers," *Industrial and Labor Relations Review* 46: 82–88 (1992).

POLICY ISSUE

COULD THE MINIMUM WAGE INCREASE THE EMPLOYMENT OF YOUTH?

Empirical research in economics typically follows a well-developed pattern. Predictions are derived from theoretical models. Economists then examine real-world behavior of consumers and firms in order to confirm the predictions of the theory.

What happens when the data do not support the theory? Obviously, either the theory was wrong (or at least incomplete), or the empirical test was flawed. Researchers then scramble to revise the theory in ways that are consistent with the new data or to refine the empirical tests to eliminate the inconsistency.

Recently some researchers have claimed to find evidence that increases in the minimum wage might actually *increase* employment among teenagers, in direct contrast with the predictions of standard theory above.[24] Unlike previous studies, which mostly examined variation in minimum wage coverage over time, these studies focused on natural experiments created by differences and changes in state-imposed minimum wages, which may be higher or have more extensive coverage than federal law requires. Two of the most-widely cited new studies used surveys of fast-food restaurants in Texas and New Jersey. One study found that when New Jersey increased its state minimum wage, employment apparently increased relative to Pennsylvania where the minimum wage was unchanged. Another claimed that after California raised its minimum wage in July 1988, employment of young people did not immediately fall relative to other states.

Is there a theoretical mechanism by which increases in the minimum wage might increase employment among low-skilled (young) workers? One possibility, as we will see in the next chapter, is if the local labor market for young workers were a monopsony, characterized by a single buyer of labor. This explanation, however, has several problems. First, it does not seem plausible given the vast number of firms employing teenagers in the U.S. (Keep in mind that fast-food chains like McDonald's consist of thousands of franchisees, each of whom makes his own employment decisions.) In addition, while monopsony behavior is consistent with the employment effects seen in the new studies, it is inconsistent with the apparent effects of minimum wage increases on prices and stock market valuations seen in the same studies.

The failure to find a satisfactory theoretical explanation for results that contrast sharply with the accepted theory has led to a series of attempts to find flaws in the empirical methodology. A number of possibilities have emerged, including:

---

[24]Allison Wellington, "Effects of the Minimum Wage on the Employment Status of Youths: An Update," *Journal of Human Resources* 26: 27–46 (1991); David Card, "Do Minimum Wages Reduce Employment? A Case Study of California, 1987–1989," *Industrial and Labor Relations Review* 46: 38–54 (1992); Lawrence Katz and Alan Krueger, "The Effect of the Minimum Wage on the Fast Food Industry," *Industrial and Labor Relations Review* 46: 6–21 (1992); David Card and Alan Krueger, "Minimum Wages and Unemployment: A Case Study of the Fast Food Industry in New Jersey and Pennsylvania," *American Economic Review* 84: 772–793 (1994); Richard Dickens, Stephen Machin, and Alan Manning, "The Effects of Minimum Wages on Wage Dispersion and Employment: Evidence from the U.K. Wage Councils," *Industrial and Labor Relations Review* 47: 319–329 (1994); Robert Kaestner, "The Effect of Payroll Taxes on Youth Employment," Baruch College, unpublished manuscript (1994).

1. The minimum wage increases studied were announced well in advance. Thus, employers may have adjusted to them prior to when the researchers measured employment levels "before" the increase. For example, in the New Jersey/Pennsylvania comparison, initial employment levels were measured in February of 1992, shortly before the increase took effect on April 1st. The increase was enacted in 1990, however, giving employers ample time to adjust to the anticipated higher wage long before their pre-increase employment was supposedly measured.
2. Employment levels were measured very soon after the increase so that the full impact of the change might not yet have been apparent. For example, in 1990, one to two years after the California increase, the proportion of California teens with jobs fell by 5.6 percent, twice the national average.
3. The data on which the studies were based may be incorrect. When actual payroll records were obtained for a subset of the fast-food restaurants in the New Jersey and Pennsylvania study, they revealed a 4.8 percent decline in relative employment after New Jersey increased its minimum wage.

While the impact of the minimum wage on employment, especially that of young workers will undoubtedly continue to receive a great deal of research and public policy discussion, the best evidence remains that the overall impact of the law is to lower employment of unskilled workers while increasing the earnings of those who are able to get a job. Other research indicates that the minimum wage induces employers to substitute high-productivity young workers for low-skilled ones. These high-productivity workers are drawn into the labor market and drop out of school. Thus, the overall effect of the minimum wage may be to increase unemployment and decrease school enrollment of teenagers.[25]

taking jobs away from young workers means giving them to adults who have more family responsibilities, that may be a reasonable argument for the minimum wage. Raising the minimum wage may raise the incomes of those workers in lower-income households who manage to retain their jobs. To the extent that a more equal income distribution is desirable, the minimum wage contributes to this goal if people who work at the minimum wage are disproportionately in low-income households. Once again the evidence here is mixed. Some recent studies have found that only a small and decreasing percentage of workers at

[25]Alan Reynolds, "Cruel Costs of the 1991 Minimum Wage," *Wall Street Journal*, (July 7, 1992); Daniel Hamermesh," "What a Wonderful World This Would Be," *Industrial and Labor Relations Review* 49: 835–838 (1995); David Neumark and William Wascher, "The Effect of New Jersey's Minimum Wage Increase on Fast-Food Employment: A Re-Evaluation Using Payroll Records," Michigan State University, Department of Economics, photocopy (1995); David Neumark and William Wascher, "Minimum-Wage Effects on Employment and School Enrolment," *Journal of Business and Economic Statistics* 13: 199–206 (1995); David Neumark and William Wascher, "Minimum-Wage Effects on School and Work Transitions of Teenagers," *American Economic Review* 85: 244–249 (1995).

the minimum wage are in households that are below the official U.S. poverty line. On the other hand, it appears that about a third of the workers whose wages were affected by the 1990 to 1991 increases in the federal minimum wage lived in families in the bottom 10 percent of the earnings distribution.[26]

THE DEMAND FOR LABOR IN THE ECONOMY AS A WHOLE

We conclude this chapter by asking what the aggregate demand curve, showing the demand for labor in the economy as a whole, might look like. We construct such a curve by assuming that all wages change in a constant proportion relative to other input prices.

Our earlier discussion of scale effects was based on an increase in wages in one firm or industry only. This might lead one to think that if all wages rise together, there will be no scale effects. This conclusion is not correct. Consider an example in which all wages rise by 10 percent and wages make up half the total costs of production in the coal industry, but only one-fifth of the total costs of production in the oil industry. If cost increases are fully passed on in prices in the long run, the price of coal would rise 5 percent and that of fuel oil only 2 percent, leaving an incentive to use more fuel oil. This means the total number of employee-hours demanded will drop because of the switch to fuel oil.

With a higher relative price of labor, firms will seek to substitute other factors for labor, so that the substitution effect will produce a decrease in the amount of labor demanded. Coupled with the argument above, this effect suggests that when all wages rise together, substitution and scale effects, although smaller than when the wage increase affects only a single firm, are still present. The aggregate demand curve for labor still slopes downward, although it is less elastic than the demand curve for most firms, industries, occupations, or demographic groups.

The aggregate demand curve for labor is derived, like the labor demand curve for each industry or market, under an assumption of constant technology. Technology is continually changing, however. Generally this change is in

---

[26]William Johnson and Edgar Browning, "The Distributional and Efficiency Effects of Increasing the Minimum Wage," *American Economic Review* 73: 204–211 (1983); Richard Burkhauser and T. Aldrich Finegan, "The Minimum Wage and the Poor: The End of a Relationship," *Journal of Policy Analysis and Management* 8: 53–71 (1989); David Card and Alan Krueger, *Myth and Measurement: The New Economics of the Minimum Wage,* Princeton, N.J.: Princeton University Press, (1995).

the direction of increasing the amount of output each worker can produce. In the United States from 1948 to 1975, output per employee-hour in the private business sector rose at the average annual rate of 2.6 percent. Output per hour was twice as high in 1975 as in 1948. Even during the years of slower growth since 1975, output per hour grew at an annual rate of 1.2 percent so that by 1994 it was two-and-three-quarters times as high as in 1948.

What effect does growth in productivity have on the aggregate demand for labor? A naive answer might be that, since it now takes fewer workers to produce each unit of output, demand for labor must fall and technological change will result in unemployment. Indeed, this misperception has led many to resist technological change since the Luddite movement of the early 19th century. It errs in its hidden assumption that the total amount of output in the world is fixed. In fact, growth in output per hour shifts the aggregate demand schedule outward. Even though, as Figure 4.9 showed, it enables each firm to produce the same amount with fewer workers, it also generates greater purchasing power for wage-earners/consumers. Because the demand for labor is derived from the demand for final output, the aggregate demand schedule shifts out even though some individual industries use less labor. Since, as we showed at the end of Part 1, the supply of labor is fairly inelastic in the long run in developed economies, technical improvements will lead to the same or slightly more workers being employed at significantly higher wages in the economy as a whole. (Try to draw the aggregate supply and demand schedules that would represent such a shift due to technological change.)

The best evidence for this argument is given by the fact that over the long run the growth in real wages in every developed economy has closely tracked the growth in labor productivity, while changes in unemployment rates have been unrelated to productivity changes. Thus, it is clear that aggregate labor demand shifted out rapidly enough to absorb the additional output generated by increases in labor productivity and allow for higher real wages. Table 4.6 shows that hourly compensation in the U.S. has increased continually. Rather than being inversely related to technological change, changes in earnings are the results of such changes. Thus, their rate of growth slowed after the mid-1970s when productivity growth slowed. In part, of course, this rate of growth also slowed because the rate of increase of college graduates in the labor force slowed and the composition of workers shifted toward those with less experience and lower earnings as more youth and women entered the labor force.

Although labor-saving technical change shifts the aggregate labor-demand curve out and does not in the long run reduce labor demand in the economy as a whole, its effects are not the same for all groups. In developed economies, at least since the 1940s, technical progress has been **skill-using.** It has therefore raised the rate of return to schooling and on-the-job training. In the aggregate the outward shift in demand has been greater for workers with more skills.[27] The effects are also not the same among industries. Productivity has grown more rapidly in manufacturing than in services. Since consumers tend to increase their relative consumption of services as their incomes grow, this means that workers must shift from manufacturing to service industries.[28] This is the major reason for the long-term trend shown in Table 4.1 toward relatively lower manufacturing employment and relatively more people working in service industries.

SUMMARY

Individual employers' labor demand schedules are downward-sloping. As the wage an employer must pay drops, hiring additional workers becomes profitable. If the wage drops enough, new employers enter the market and add still more to labor demand. If wages rise businesses both reduce their employment and close down, causing labor demand to drop. The demand for particular groups of workers also depends on the wage rates they receive. When the wage of one group rises, employers substitute capital or the hours of workers in other groups for the services of workers who have become more expensive. Even in the economy as a whole the demand for labor is downward-sloping, although not so sharply as for any individual firm, industry, labor market, or group of workers.

The fact that labor-demand schedules slope downward must be remembered whenever we examine the effects of imposing a wage rate change on a group of workers or a particular industry. Wage subsidies, changes in minimum wage rates, and union-imposed wage increases all affect the quantity of labor that employers want to use. The size of the effects depends on many considerations. The major determinants are the substitution effect (the ease with which employers can substitute away from any group of workers whose wage rate is increased) and the scale effect (the ease with which consumers

---

[27] For the United States, see Ann Bartel and Frank Lichtenberg, "The Comparative Advantage of Educated Workers in Implementing New Technology," *Review of Economics and Statistics* 69: 1–11 (1987); Steven Allen, "Technology and the Wage Structure," unpublished paper, North Carolina State University, (May 1994); Jacob Mincer, *Studies in Human Capital*, Brookfield, Vt: Elgar (1993); John Bound and George Johnson, "Changes in the Structure of Wages During the 1980s: An Evaluation of Alternative Explanations," *American Economic Review* 82: 371–392 (1992); Mary T. Coleman, "Movement in the Earnings-Schooling Relationship," *Journal of Human Resources* 28: 660–680 (1993); Eli Berman, John Bound, and Zvi Griliches, "Changes in the Demand for Skilled Labor Within U.S. Manufacturing: Evidence from the Annual Survey of Manufactures," *Quarterly Journal of Economics* 109: 367–397 (1994). For Australia, see Bruce Chapman and Hong Tan, "An Analysis of Youth Training in Australia, 1985–88: Technical Change and Wages," in Robert Gregory and Tom Karmel (eds.). *The Australian Longitudinal Survey: Social and Economic Policy Research*, Canberra: Centre for Economic Policy Research, Australian National University, (1992).

[28] In fact, consumers will shift consumption toward manufactured goods as relative prices fall, but this will in large part be offset by the fact that consumers tend to purchase more services relative to manufactured goods as their incomes rise.

POLICY ISSUE

COMPUTERS AS SKILL-USING TECHNICAL CHANGE

The 1980s have been characterized as the decade of the "computer revolution." In 1984 fewer than 10 percent of establishments reported that they had personal computers. By 1989 this figure had risen to over 35 percent. During much of the 1980s, the quality-adjusted real price of microcomputers fell by 28 percent *a year*. Between 1984 and 1989 the percentage of workers who used a computer at work rose by over 50 percent. Female, white, and more-educated workers are more likely than male, black, or less-educated workers to use computers at work. In 1989 over 58 percent of workers with a college degree used a computer on their job as opposed to only 29 percent of those with a high school degree.[29]

After controlling for a wide variety of factors such as education, experience, race, sex, and so forth, workers who used computers on their job earned between 16 and 19 percent more than otherwise identical workers who did not. Despite the rapid introduction of computers in schools and colleges and the tremendous increase in the supply of workers who could use computers, this premium grew over the decade. Because educated people are more likely to be able to use a computer, the increasing demand for computer skills probably explained over 40 percent of the significant increase in the return to education during this period.

The policy implications are clear. At least during this period (and there is no evidence that it has changed since), employers' demand for computer skills increased far more rapidly than the available supply, increasing the return to those who had such skills. As long as these trends hold, computer training should be a profitable investment for both public and private job training programs. Certainly students who are interested in their postcollege earnings should become as proficient in computer use as they can.

can switch their demands away from employers who attempt to pass the increased wage costs forward through higher product prices).

QUESTIONS AND PROBLEMS

4.1 Suppose the following table represents increases in total output as additional individuals are assigned to work with a piece of machinery.

Number of Workers	Total Output
1	5
2	18
3	36
4	48
5	55
6	60
7	62
8	56

[29] The discussion in this section is based on Alan Krueger, "How Computers Have Changed the Wage Structure: Evidence from Microdata, 1984–1989," *Quarterly Journal of Economics* 108: 33–60 (1993).

Compute the average and marginal products of labor for each additional worker. If the wage rate is $12, and the price of output is $2, how many workers will the employer wish to hire? What if the wage falls to $6? What if it falls still farther to $2?

4.2 Redo Problem 1 under the assumption that the price of output is $3. Graph the short-run labor demand curve under this assumption and under the assumptions made in Problem 1.

4.3 Using the medium estimate of the long-run elasticity of labor demand in Table 4.4, calculate the effects of the following proposals on employment

a. An increase in the Social Security tax rate from 7.65 to 9.0 percent.

b. An increase in the Social Security tax base from $60,000 to $75,000.

Assume that total employment is 120 million, total compensation (labor cost) is $3000 billion, Social Security payroll taxes are $200 billion, and total costs of production are $4000 billion. Indicate in your answer for each proposal how much of the effect on jobs is due to capital-labor substitution, and how much is due to scale effects.

4.4 As a way of equalizing power between large and small employers and reducing the federal deficit, Senator Sam Snort has proposed adding a 5 percent payroll tax on all employees' wages paid beyond the hundredth employee. Draw a demand curve for labor, and show how this proposal would change employers' choices. What would be the effect of a competing proposal that would simply assess a 5 percent payroll tax on *all employees' wages?* Using the medium estimates of substitution and scale elasticities in Table 4.4, and assuming that total employment is 120 million, what would be the effect of this competing proposal, on total employment in the U.S. economy? In answering all of these questions ignore any macroeconomic effects the proposals may produce through their impact on autonomous expenditures.

4.5 Currently there is a limit on workers' earnings for which employers are taxed to finance unemployment insurance in the United States (in 1995, an average ceiling of around $9000 in many states). Proposals have been offered to eliminate the ceiling, that is, make all payroll subject to taxation for this purpose. What would be the effect of this proposal on the relative employment of high- and low-skilled labor? How would it affect the relative amounts of capital services and labor that employers wish to use?

4.6 The evidence cited in the text shows that the impact of the minimum wage in the United States on teenage employment diminished in the 1980s, and that at most each 10 percent higher minimum wage reduces teen employment by 1 percent. That being the case, discuss the effect of a proposal to raise the minimum from $4.25 to $6.00. Consider how the impact of this proposal would be affected by changes in birth rates and rates of college enrollment.

4.7 Suppose a firm has the following production function:

$$y = f(k, l) = k \times l^{1/2}$$

a. What is the marginal rate of substitution between labor and capital in this firm?
b. Given a wage rate w and a price of capital r, what is the fundamental condition for the choice of two factors of production (capital and labor)?
c. How much labor will this firm hire if it wants to produce y units of output?
d. In (c) you found l as a function of w, r, and y. Is this function increasing in y? If so, what is the intuition behind this result?
e. What is the relation between labor demand and price of capital r? Interpret this result.

4.8 What are the effects of an increase in the price of capital on labor demand for a firm that produces output using capital and labor? Use a graph to illustrate your answer, and indicate substitution and scale effects in production. How would you modify your answer if the firm used additional inputs such as energy and raw materials?

4.9 Indicate whether you believe the demand for labor is relatively elastic or inelastic for each of the following groups of workers. Be sure to explain your reasoning. Would your answer differ in the long run as opposed to the short run?
a. Computer programmers
b. Nuclear power plant operators
c. Day-care center attendants
d. Sewing machine operators
e. Economics professors
f. Star basketball centers
g. Reserve ice hockey goalies

4.10 According to the theory of competitive labor markets, will an equal percentage increase in the minimum wage cause a larger or smaller reduction in employment in developed countries than in developing countries? Why would this be so?

KEY WORDS

average product of labor (AP)
complements in production
constant returns to scale
dead-end jobs
derived demand
diminishing marginal rate of substitution
effective minimum wage
elasticity of labor demand (ε_d)
elasticity of product demand (η)
elasticity of substitution (σ)
establishments
expansion path
factor of production
factor prices
fixed proportions
inframarginal
isocost line
isoquant
job dynamics
labor-saving technical change
labor-using technical change
law of diminishing returns
law of variable proportions
long run
marginal employment tax credit
marginal product of capital (MP_K)
marginal product of labor (MP_L)
marginal productivity theory
marginal rate of technical substitution (*MRTS*)
Marshall's four laws of derived demand
neutral technical change
production function
scale effect in production
short run
skill-using technical change
substitute in production
substitution effect in production
technology
total product of labor (*TP*)
uncovered sector
value of the marginal product (*VMP*)
wage bill

Extensions of Labor Demand: Noncompetitive Markets and the Worker–Hours Distinction

THE MAJOR QUESTIONS

- ▲ Are the predictions and evidence in Chapter 4 valid for firms that are not perfect competitors in product markets?
- ▲ How does the demand for labor differ between profit-maximizing businesses and firms that have different objectives?
- ▲ How does the demand for labor change if a business employs a large fraction of the workers in a given labor market?
- ▲ How do nonwage aspects of compensation affect employers' choices about how many workers to employ and how many hours to have them work?
- ▲ How do these costs affect the speed with which employers' adjust the number of workers employed, especially as business conditions change?
- ▲ How do government restrictions, such as premiums for overtime work, affect these decisions?

LABOR DEMAND IN NONCOMPETITIVE PRODUCT MARKETS

The General Case

The simplest way to extend the basic theory is to drop the assumption of perfect competition in product markets. Without perfect competition the firm faces a downward-sloping demand curve for its product. If it employs more labor, it must lower its product price to sell the additional output the extra workers help produce. In this case the demand curve for labor is not $VMP = MP_L \times P$, the value of the marginal product. Instead it is **marginal revenue product**

$$MRP = MP_L \times MR$$

where *MR* is the marginal revenue from selling another unit of product. Perfect competition in product markets is a special case in which marginal revenue product (*MRP*) equals the value of the marginal product (*VMP*) because $MR = P$. Since marginal revenue is always less than price in product markets that are not perfectly competitive, the marginal revenue product must always be less than the value of the marginal product in these markets.

A profit-maximizing employer who has some degree of **market power** (control over the price of its product) but is confronted with a fixed wage will employ labor up to the point where the cost of another hour of labor is equal to the marginal revenue product. In Figure 5.1 this point is where the *MRP* curve cuts the wage w_0, determining employment E_0. Beyond this point, using another hour would increase the wage bill more than it would increase total revenue, thus reducing profits. In this case, the number of hours of

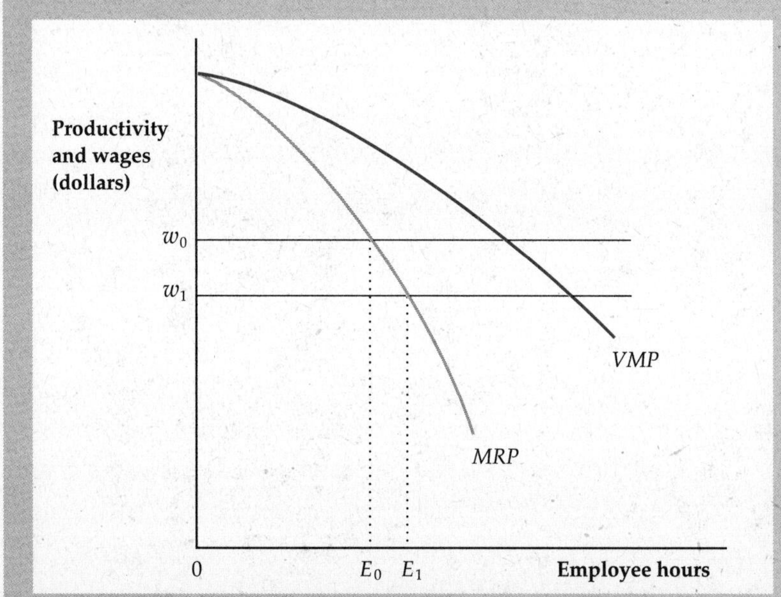

FIGURE 5.1 DEMAND FOR LABOR IN A NONCOMPETITIVE PRODUCT MARKET

When a firm must reduce prices to sell more output, the marginal product produced by additional labor will add less to the firm's revenue than in a competitive industry. The firm will hire labor until the marginal revenue product from an additional hour of labor input is equal to the wage rate. This causes labor demand to be lower and the demand curve to be less elastic than in a competitive industry.

labor used will be less than in a competitive product market. Moreover, because *MRP* is steeper than *VMP*, the short-run demand for labor is less responsive to changes in the wage rate. When the wage falls to w_1, the increase in employment is smaller than if the firm determined its labor demand along *VMP*. Short-run labor-demand elasticities are lower, other things being equal, in noncompetitive firms than in competitive firms that have the same production function.

In the long run, microeconomic theory establishes that firms with product-market power will produce less than they would if the product market were competitive. This behavior means that they will operate on an isoquant closer to the origin in Figure 4.6. If they operate in competitive input markets, however, their decision about how much of each input to use on this isoquant will be unaffected.

Although the analysis of the demand for labor by a profit-maximizing price-setter is a simple extension of marginal productivity theory, one may question whether real-world price-setters behave strictly as profit maximizers. As we will discuss later, when firms enjoy economic profits because of market power, trade unions have an increased ability to force them to share these profits by raising wages and employment levels beyond what would prevail if the firm maximized profits.

Firms with market power may also come under a variety of political and public relations pressures to stabilize employment, restrict profits to reasonable amounts, restrain increases in product prices, and not unduly enlarge their share of the product market. The penalty for not complying, or at least seeming to comply, could be government intervention to diminish or regulate their market power. As a result, the management of a firm with market power might devote some of its profits to paying higher wages or using more labor than a strict profit maximizer. There is some evidence that firms in markets with little competition do pay higher wages than workers could obtain in more competitive industries, but the effect seems to be fairly small.[1]

THE REGULATED FIRM

A firm with some product-market power may be restrained in its ability to make maximum use of this power by the presence of government regulation. For many firms, such as power companies in the U.S., this regulation takes the form of state commissions that must approve price increases. A firm's return on its invested capital is not allowed to exceed a certain limit. While the firm seeks to maximize profits, the commission typically limits only its **rate of return**, defined as the ratio of profits to the firm's rate base (which is

[1]Wesley Mellow, "Employer Size and Wages," *Review of Economics and Statistics* 64: 494–501 (1982); John Heywood, "Labor Quality and the Concentration-Earnings Hypothesis," *Review of Economics and Statistics* 68: 342–346 (1986).

usually about equal to the value of its capital stock, K). For analytical purposes the firm is limited to

$$\frac{Profits}{K} < r^*$$

where r^* is the maximum rate of return it is allowed to earn. Instead of maximizing profits freely in response to changes in the relative prices of employee-hours and capital services, the regulated firm is limited by a ceiling on the ratio of its profits to the present value of the services from its capital.[2]

With a limit of r^* the only way the regulated firm can achieve its stockholders' goal of higher profits is by increasing its capital stock, thus keeping its rate of return at or below r^*. Although using more labor-intensive technology may be the best choice when wages drop relative to the price of capital services, adding labor instead of capital does not add to the rate base. If the choice of technology reduces costs and increases profits, the regulatory commission will force the firm to reduce prices to prevent the rate of return from rising. Choosing a more capital-intensive technology has the advantage of increasing both profits and the rate base. This can avoid an increase in the rate of return, which might be disallowed by the regulatory commission. Since firms facing this type of regulation choose more capital-intensive technologies, a change in the relative price of labor will induce a different rate of substitution of labor for capital than would be undertaken by the typical firm that is free to maximize profits.[3]

NONPROFIT AND LABOR-MANAGED FIRMS

In many firms the profit motive is absent. Universities, many hospitals, charitable organizations, governments, foundations, and other institutions are not governed by the profit motive when they hire workers. To the extent that they seek to produce the maximum possible output for a given budget (which is the same as seeking to minimize costs at each particular output), however, their demand for labor will behave like that of a profit-maximizing firm.

If the nonprofit firm does not minimize costs things are less clear. For example, an elected government official who makes employment decisions may try to maximize his chances of remaining in office by not reducing employment after a wage increase.[4] A university administrator may seek to

---

[2]This argument was first made by Harvey Averch and L. L. Johnson, "Behavior of the Firm Under Regulatory Constraint," *American Economic Review* 52: 1053–1069 (1962).

[3]Michael Crew and Paul Kleindorfer, *The Economics of Public Utility Regulation*, Cambridge: MIT Press, (1986), Chapter 6, discuss the evidence on this issue.

[4]Melvin Reder, "The Theory of Employment and Wages in the Public Sector," in Daniel Hamermesh (ed.). *Labor in the Public and Nonprofit Sectors*, Princeton, N.J.: Princeton University Press, (1975), discusses this and other motivations that might distinguish the labor demand of a governmental unit from that of a private firm.

POLICY ISSUE

DEREGULATION AND EMPLOYMENT

Partly in response to the malaise generated by the rapid inflation of the 1970s, a movement toward **deregulation of industry** swept the U.S. during the late 1970s and early 1980s. This movement resulted in easier entry into such industries as airline transportation, interstate trucking, and long-distance telephone communications, and much more freedom for all participants in these industries to set prices as they saw fit. A major purpose was to increase the extent of competition and, thus, eventually to reduce prices.

The discussion above suggests that deregulation should produce increases in employment in the previously regulated industry, both because an unregulated firm employs more workers than an otherwise identical regulated firm (since the latter will substitute capital for labor), and because the reduced product price will lead to an expansion of output and, thus, a scale effect on employment demand. Offsetting these effects is the need for deregulated firms to increase efficiency through cost cutting in order to meet new competitors. The net effect on previously existing firms is an empirical question to be answered by research. The best evidence is that deregulation did not decrease employment in most industries including airlines, buses, and telephone services. Although employment did decrease in railroads after they were deregulated, this effect was more than offset by a rapid increase in employment in trucking, which was deregulated at the same time.[5]

maintain some traditional balance between junior and senior faculty regardless of changes in the relative costs of employing them. Hospitals may not respond to changes in wages because they also face regulations on entry and on reimbursement for services. In general, however, the evidence shows that nonprofit organizations such as governments, universities, and hospitals respond to increases in the price of labor by reducing employment, and that they substitute one type of labor for another when their relative wages change.[6]

Still other complications are introduced when a firm is managed by its workers, as is the case in many newly privatized firms in Eastern Europe, or when workers have a stake in the firm through employee stock-ownership

---

[5]Wallace Hendrick, "Deregulation and Labor Earnings," *Journal of Labor Research* 15: 207–234 (1994).

[6]Janet Currie, "Employment Determination in a Unionized Public-Sector Labor Market: The Case of Ontario's School Teachers," *Journal of Labor Economics* 9: 45–66 (1991); Howard Tuckman and Cyril Chang, "Own-Price and Cross Elasticities of Demand for College Faculty," *Southern Economic Journal* 52: 735–744 (1986); Gail Jensen and Michael Morrisey, "The Role of Physicians in Hospital Production," *Review of Economics and Statistics* 68: 432–442 (1986).

plans. The goal of a **labor-managed firm** is not clear. It could be to maximize the **wage bill** (wages times employment), or to maximize the number of workers, or something else. The problem is similar to that faced by trade unions, an issue discussed in Chapter 11.

The most reasonable assumption is that workers who direct the policies of a firm seek to maximize their average income net of fixed costs and variable nonlabor costs. With this goal it pays to add new members (equivalent to new employees) only as long as their marginal revenue product is greater than or equal to the net income each member takes from the cooperative. In this case there is no wage rate that the firm takes as given, so there is no standard labor demand curve. The behavior of such firms may vary drastically according to how its workers rule themselves or in response to small variations in external market conditions. Many theories of labor-managed firms even predict apparently perverse behavior. For example, increased product prices may cause these firms to reduce output and employment.

If *any* of a wide variety of assumptions is correct, however, the labor demand of these firms will not differ from that of profit-maximizing firms. Among these assumptions are:

1. The firms operate in a competitive product market;
2. The firms' core members can hire additional "temporary" nonmembers; or
3. Labor-managed firms can rent or lend workers to each other when values of marginal products differ across firms.[7]

Although interesting theoretically, labor-managed firms tend to be relatively rare unless mandated by government policy (as in the former Yugoslavia). They arise in the U.S. mainly as **employee buyouts** of firms in financial difficulty. Many of these firms eventually reconvert to traditional organizations. Some researchers have suggested it is because members have a strong incentive to act like conventional capitalists and replace departing members with nonmembers who will work for a market wage, thereby increasing the surplus to be divided among the remaining members. This result means that their labor-market behavior does not differ from that of conventional firms.[8]

Thus, even though not all firms maximize profits, other motives are equally consistent with the major predictions of labor demand theory.

---

[7]For an excellent and easy to understand summary of the literature on labor-managed firms, see John P. Bonin and Louis Putterman, *Economics of Cooperation and the Labor-Managed Economy*, Chur, Switzerland: Harwood Academic Publishers, (1987).

[8]Hajime Miyazaki, "On Success and Dissolution of the Labor-Managed Firm in the Capitalist Economy," *Journal of Political Economy*, 92: 909–931 (1984); Avner Ben-Ner, "The Life-Cycle of Worker Owned Firms in Market Economies," *Journal of Economic Behavior and Organization* 10: 287–313 (1988).

Therefore, we can safely assume that an increase in the wage rate facing most employers, regardless of industry or firm structure, will eventually reduce the amount of labor they use.

MONOPSONY IN LABOR MARKETS

Many economists are intrigued by the idea that employers might be able to exploit workers who, for one reason or another, are tied to the firm. To examine this issue we restore the assumptions that product markets are competitive and that firms maximize profits. We assume, however, that the firm is a labor market **monopsonist**, meaning that it faces an upward-sloping labor supply curve rather than taking as given a wage set in a competitive labor market. In its simplest form, monopsony refers to a market in which there is only one buyer. We will use it here to include labor markets in which there are only a few employers or employers collude in setting wages.

How prevalent is monopsony in labor markets? The simplest case is the company town with only one employer, a situation once common in the American textile and mining industries and still common in developing countries.[9] Today the importance of such cases is diminishing in developed countries, both because such markets are found largely in declining industries and because better roads and lower costs of auto transportation have reduced the isolation of company towns. It is now practical and even common for American workers to commute 50 or more miles to work, and while the cost of commuting long distances leaves some residual monopsony power to isolated employers, this power is much less than when commuting was more difficult.

Another possible source of monopsony power is collusion or agreements among employers not to raise wages individually and not to hire away each other's employees. There is evidence that such agreements have existed,[10] but they are very difficult to sustain. They are not needed in slack labor markets, where there is no shortage of labor or upward pressure on wages. When labor markets become tight, the temptation for the parties to violate or evade collusive agreements becomes difficult to resist. Once labor is scarce, it is in the interest of each employer to raise its compensation relative to compensation elsewhere. Even if the firms maintain the agreed basic wage scale, they

---

[9] There has been very little study of the amount of employer concentration in labor markets. One work is Robert Bunting, *Employer Concentration in Local Labor Markets,* Chapel Hill: University of North Carolina Press, (1962). Another, James Luizer and Robert Thornton, "Concentration in the Labor Market for Public School Teachers," *Industrial and Labor Relations Review* 39: 573–584 (1986), provides some evidence that monopsonistic exploitation exists where there are few school districts within a geographic area.

[10] For example, Richard Lester, *Adjustments to Labor Shortages,* Princeton, N.J.: Princeton University, Industrial Relations Section, (1955), pp. 46–49.

can increase compensation by upgrading of job titles, paying for unnecessary overtime, or providing enhanced fringe benefits. As with collusion in product pricing, collusion among a small number of employers is easier to maintain than collusion among large numbers.

A third source of monopsony power accrues to an employer who uses highly specialized workers or is the only employer of workers in certain occupations. In this case, however, the power is bilateral. This situation is similar to that of firm-specific training discussed in Chapter 3. The workers have nowhere else to go without leaving the occupation or the area, but the employer has no available labor supply other than the current employees. Attempting to exploit this position will increase the movement of workers out of the occupation with a loss of past investments in worker training.

Figure 5.2 presents a formal analysis of a monopsonist's demand for labor. For a monopsonist we can no longer draw the cost of labor as independent of the amount of labor employed. The downward-sloping *VMP* curve is the same as in the standard case. In this case, the upward-sloping supply curve (*GS*) is measured in number of employees rather than employee hours. The steeper upward-sloping curve *G–MLC* is the **marginal labor cost** (*MLC*) curve, which measures the addition to the wage bill that results from employing an extra worker when all similar workers are paid the same wage, a case known as **nondiscriminating monopsony**. The upward-sloping supply curve indicates that new workers can be hired only at wages that are higher than the wages paid to those already employed. The cost of hiring an additional worker therefore includes both the wage of the new worker and the cost of bringing the wages of everyone the firm already employs up to the new level. For high levels of employment, the second element of this marginal cost can easily exceed the first.

The profit-maximizing employment, E_0, is given by point *A*, where *MLC* and *VMP* are equal. Beyond *A*, employing another worker adds more to total labor cost than it adds to total revenue. The wage corresponding to E_0, is w_0, and is given by the height of supply curve at *B*, *not* the height of *MLC* at *A*, because the supply curve, not the *MLC*, shows how much the firm must pay to obtain E_0 workers.

Although Figure 5.2 is an extension of marginal productivity theory because the value of marginal product is one of the elements determining the wage, here the *VMP* curve is not the labor-demand curve. Monopsonists have no demand curve for labor, in the sense of a simple relation in which quantity demanded depends on the wage, because the monopsonist does not take the wage as fixed by the market. The number of workers demanded depends not only on the height of the supply curve at any level of employment but also on its elasticity. Imagine another supply curve that also passes through *B* but slopes upward more steeply than *S*. The marginal labor-cost curve corresponding to such a supply curve would lie above the one shown in Figure 5.2. Employment would, therefore, be lower than E_0, and the profit-maximizing wage would be below w_0 on the new supply curve.

POLICY ISSUE

MONOPSONY IN BASEBALL

One industry where employers have been able to collude and act like a monopsonist is professional baseball, which Congress exempted from U.S. antitrust laws. Until 1977 professional baseball players worked under the reserve clause. The team that initially employed them reserved an exclusive right to use their services or to trade them to another team or fire them. Since the players' only option was to leave organized baseball (or to play in Japan), team owners had the means to exploit them by paying salaries below what the players added to the teams' revenues (their *VMP*).

In professional sports a player's *VMP* is easy to estimate. It is the revenue from additional ticket sales and higher broadcast fees resulting from each player's performance. Baseball performance is readily captured by numerous statistics such as batting averages, runs batted in, fielding percentages, and (for pitchers) earned-run averages and strikeout-to-walk ratios. These measures for individual players can be related statistically to team revenues. Studies provide strong evidence that before 1977 star players received only a fraction of what they added to their team's revenues.[11]

The reason for this exploitation is clear. Even a small fraction of a star player's *VMP* far exceeded what they could earn in alternative employment. There was no exploitation of mediocre players. Although they were paid relatively little, it was roughly equal to what they added to their team's revenue and the amount they could earn if they left baseball. They could not be exploited since any attempt to do so would have driven them out of the profession.

Following a federal court decision in 1977, each experienced player has had the right to sell his services to the highest bidder. This ruling has resulted in a very rapid rise in average salaries (144 percent between 1977 and 1981 alone, compared to only 51 and 44 percent among professional football and basketball players, respectively, in the same period). A large part of this increase was due to bidding wars for star players. In 1977 the highest salary for a baseball player was $400,000. By 1982, it had risen to $2.5 million. Once a new equilibrium was reached, salaries rose much less rapidly. The maximum salary was "only" $5.1 million in 1994.[12] The salaries of stars rose rapidly to equal their *VMPs*, so that by the late 1980s each $1 difference between two players' *VMPs* produced a $1 difference in salary.[13]

Of course, the move to free agency also had other economic effects. Recall our discussion of investments in training in Chapter 3. The investment in training a baseball player is considerable. A typical major league team might spend several million dollars a year to

---

[11]Gerald Scully, *The Business of Major League Baseball*, Chicago: University of Chicago Press, (1989).

[12]Glen Waggoner, "Money Games," *Esquire* 97: 57 (June 1982).

[13]Paul Sommers and Noel Quinton, "Pay and Performance in Major League Baseball: The Case of the First Family of Free Agents," *Journal of Human Resources* 17: 426–435 (1982); Don MacDonald and Morgan Reynolds, "Are Baseball Players Paid Their Marginal Products?" *Managerial and Decision Economics* 15: 443–457 (1994).

scout and train players, primarily through covering the salaries of minor league players most of whom will never play in the majors. With the reserve clause, this investment resembled specific human capital since if the player became a star he could not sell his talents to other firms. Thus, teams were willing to pay for this investment. With free agency, the training became more like general human capital and any team that attempted to pay a player less than his *VMP* could expect to lose that player to another team. As we have seen, in such a world players themselves can expect to pay for their training, perhaps through substantially reduced minor league salaries or by obtaining training in other ways. For example, the end of the reserve clause should mean that a larger fraction of baseball players attend college where they can receive four years of training at their own expense.

Of course, having been deprived of the reserve clause, baseball owners could be expected to try to recover their investments in players by colluding to restrain salaries. Arbitrators ruled that the owners did this in 1985 and 1986 when they agreed not to bid for the experienced players who were available. The salaries players received when they joined new teams in those years were lower relative to their *VMPs* than those of similarly qualified players who were available in 1984.[14] With the amounts of money involved, collusion is almost irresistible to team owners and is something that the players' association monitors carefully.

In a labor market characterized by competition among employers for workers, the marginal product of labor will equal the wage rate. This is not true in a labor market characterized by monopsony. In Figure 5.2, the value of the marginal product is indicated by the height of the *VMP* curve at *A* but the wage rate is only w_0. In such markets the employer or colluding employers are, in a sense, "exploiting" the workers, since the workers receive a wage less than the value of the marginal product (the distance *AB*).

We can use Figure 5.2 to show that anything that imposes a higher but fixed wage on a monopsonist can sometimes *increase* employment. This is just the opposite of what standard labor demand theory would predict. Examples of imposed wages might be legally required minimum wages or negotiated union contracts. Suppose that a minimum wage is set at w_1 in Figure 5.2, and w_1 is more than the wage w_0 that the monopsonist would have chosen. Marginal labor cost is now equal to w_1 up to point *C*, where w_1 crosses the supply curve. Until employment reaches that level (E_1), additional workers can be hired at the wage already being paid, since hiring them will add only their wage to the wage bill. But at *C* marginal labor cost jumps to *F* on the old *MLC* curve, as shown by the dashed line. The next worker hired must be paid more than the minimum wage, and if this worker is hired,

[14]Thomas Bruggink and David Rose, "Financial Restraint in the Free Agent Labor Market for Major League Baseball: Players Look at Strike Three," *Southern Economic Journal* 56: 1029–1043 (1990).

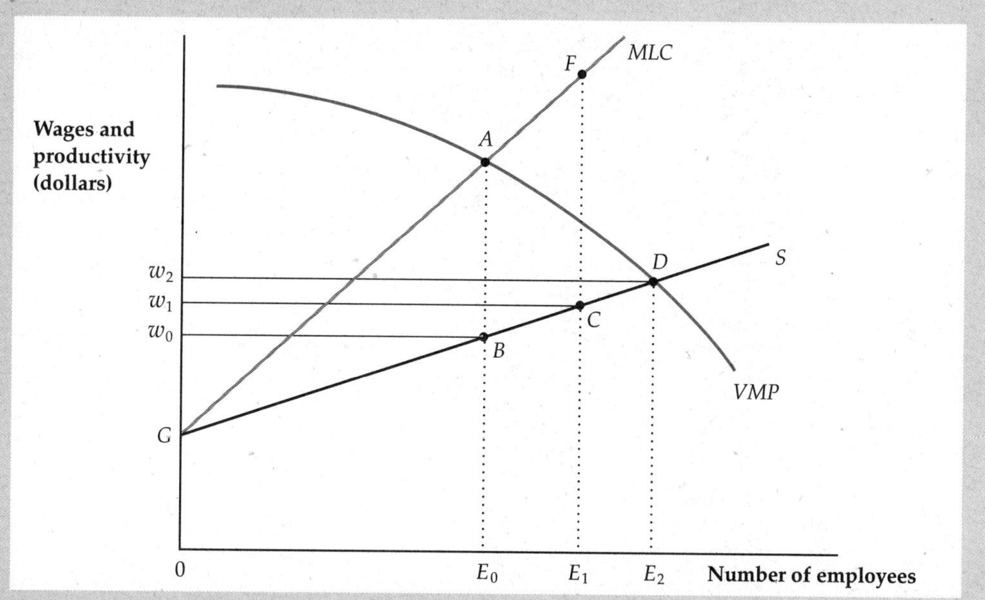

FIGURE 5.2 THE WAGE-EMPLOYMENT DECISION OF A MONOPSONIST
A conventional monopsonist must raise wages when it hires more workers. This creates a marginal cost of labor curve that lies above the supply curve and reduces the amount of labor demanded from the level E_2, where the supply curve intersects the *VMP* (demand curve), that would prevail in a competitive industry to E_0, the level at which the *MLC* curve intersects the *VMP* curve. At this level of employment wage w_0 will be paid. If a higher, but fixed, wage such as w_1 were imposed, the marginal cost would remain constant until E_1 workers were employed and both wages and employment would increase.

everyone previously employed must be paid more as well. If, as in this case, the *VMP* curve passes through the dashed segment *CF*, profit-maximizing employment will be E_1, which is more than the E_0 employed by the monopsonist without the mandated wage. By the same reasoning one can show that an increase in the minimum wage from w_1 to w_2 would increase employment from E_1 to E_2.

After some point raising the fixed wage begins to reduce employment. In Figure 5.2 raising it above w_2 would decrease employment as in the competitive case. The firm would react to rising fixed wages by moving back along the *VMP* curve since the wage would now intersect this curve to the left of *D*. Indeed, if the wage were increased above *A*, employment would be reduced below E_0.

Recall that the above discussion assumes a nondiscriminating monopsony where the employer must pay all workers the same wage. The behavior of a **perfectly discriminating monopsonist** would be much different. Perfect discrimination means that the monopsonist is able to hire each worker at the worker's own **supply price** (the lowest wage at which that worker will accept the job), thus paying different wages to different workers for the same work. Such an employer would maximize profits at *D*, with employment of E_2. This situation is the same as profit-maximizing employment in a perfectly competitive industry with the same supply and productivity conditions. Although the allocation of resources is the same in the two cases, the distribution of income is very different. In the competitive case the wage bill is the rectangle Ow_2DE_2. In the case of the discriminating monopsonist, the triangular portion (Gw_2D) of this rectangle lying above the supply curve becomes part of profit. The wage bill is only the trapezoid $0GDE_2$ lying under the supply curve *S*.

The distribution of income between workers and owners of capital is neither good nor bad, but rather a normative question of how one regards these two groups. Most people would probably prefer that income go to the workers, but it need not be so. Suppose, for example, that the firm is a film studio that acquired monopsony power by having its stars under an exclusive contract. Also suppose that the film studio is owned by an order of nuns that used its profits to support an orphanage. Would you want the orphans to have less to eat so the film stars could have even more income? The key *economic* issue is misallocation of resources, which is absent when a monopsonist is perfectly discriminating.

The possibilities of paying different hourly wages to different individuals doing the same work are probably quite limited for manual workers except through an incentive pay or piecework system. Manual workers have a strong concern for interpersonal equity, as well as a general knowledge of rates of pay. In addition, government regulations make paying different rates for similar work very difficult. Discriminating monopsony may be more possible for professional and managerial workers, where the tradition has been that salaries are confidential and related to individual merit. Where classes of equally productive workers, such as men and women, have different supply schedules, more limited kinds of discrimination are feasible. This problem goes beyond the case of monopsony to the discussion of sex discrimination and is considered at length in Chapter 14.

THE NONWAGE COSTS OF LABOR

So far in the discussion of labor demand we have assumed that the cost of labor to the employer consists only of an hourly wage. Now we drop this assumption and recognize that there are also **nonwage labor costs** that are not proportional to hourly wages. These costs have important implications for the incidence of unemployment by skill level, for the dynamics of employment

POLICY ISSUE

ARE SALARY CAPS EFFICIENT?

We have seen that when firms equate wages with workers' *VMP* economic efficiency is achieved. Is this always the case? One situation where it may not be is in competitive sports, where a number of professional leagues in the U.S now impose salary caps to limit the wages paid to star athletes. Why might these caps be anything other than an attempt to regain the opportunity to exploit labor that owners lost when players achieved free agency?

The answer lies in the nature of competition.[15] Fans do not, in general, care very much about absolute performance. Instead, they care about *relative* performance: does one's team win or lose? A football game is just as exciting to fans if both quarterbacks complete 40 percent of their passes and the home team wins 28 to 25, or if they complete 60 percent of their passes and the home team wins 48 to 42.

When a team owner decides how much to pay a star player, he takes into account only the marginal benefit to his team. Thus, if the star helps the team win more games, it is worthwhile to pay that star a lot. Every game the star helps his team win is a game that some other team must lose, however, which makes the fans and owners of the losing team worse off. Because team owners do not take this **negative externality** into account when deciding how much to pay players, they bid too much for their services from society's point of view. Social welfare would be improved if all teams were limited in their ability to "overpay" star players.

The same analysis can explain why athletic leagues ban drug use by players. Suppose that a drug enhances performance but at a cost of damage to a player's long-term health. If one player took drugs he would gain an advantage and win more contests. In response, all players would have an incentive to take drugs and relative performance would not change. Thus, in the new equilibrium no one would win any more contests but everyone's health would be damaged.

demand, and for the employer's choice between numbers of workers and hours per worker.

TURNOVER COSTS

During the 1990–91 recession, employment of blue-collar workers fell 3.4 percent while that of white-collar workers did not change. Unemployment rates in the two groups were 9.4 and 4.7 percent, respectively, at the cyclical trough in 1991. The best explanation for this pattern is the difference among workers in the level of **turnover costs** or the costs incurred when employees are hired, laid off, or discharged. Hiring costs include the costs of recruitment, screening, and initial training, while termination costs include items such as severance pay and increases in taxes for unemployment insurance.

---

[15] The discussion that follows is based on Robert J. Barro, "Baseball, Drugs and Rational Expectations," *Wall Street Journal,* (October 19, 1994).

For several reasons turnover costs rise as a proportion of total labor cost as the skill level of an employee increases. Much more intensive effort is devoted to hiring highly skilled employees such as professionals or executives than to hiring unskilled workers. This makes sense since mistakes in staffing will be much more costly in jobs involving greater responsibility. Expenses for recruiting (including agency fees or advertising) and for screening are higher for skilled employees. Expenses for travel to interviews may be paid, references are checked more carefully, and more expensive management time is used in interviewing.

Few data are available on the costs of hiring, but those that exist support the assertion that hiring costs increase with skill level.[16] Table 5.1 presents the data from one such study. Recall from Chapter 3 that, like hiring costs, training costs usually vary with skill level. The period spent in learning tasks or specialized on-the-job training before a new employee reaches full effectiveness is typically longer for more skilled workers. A new janitor might be fully trained after two or three days on the job, but a new executive is likely to need months to really learn how an organization functions.

Differences in turnover costs by level of skill make employers more reluctant to lay off skilled than unskilled employees, especially in response to what is perceived to be a temporary drop in product demand (as is the case with most fluctuations over the business cycle).[17] The longer an employee remains with an employer, the longer the period over which initial costs of hiring and training can be amortized. Given that the ratio of hiring and training costs to pay rises with skill level, it may be economical to lay off an unskilled worker during a recession since a replacement can be hired at little cost when demand picks up again. The same is not true for skilled workers. The savings in wages from laying off skilled workers may not be enough to compensate for the substantial hiring and training costs that would have to be incurred when demand revives. Analyses of data for the U.S., the United Kingdom, and Belgium show that the employment of nonproduction workers responds much less to changes in product demand than the employment of production workers.[18] Turnover costs in large part explain the greater stability of employment of skilled workers.

---

[16]J. M. Barron, J. Bishop, and W. C. Dunkelberg, "Employer Search: The Interviewing and Hiring of New Employees," *Review of Economics and Statistics* 67: 43–52 (1985); Employment Management Association, *National Cost Per Hire Survey, 1984,* Raleigh, N.C., EMA, (1985); Bureau of National Affairs, *Personnel Policies Forum*, Nos. 126 and 143.

[17]One of the earliest and best discussions of the issues treated here is Walter Oi, "Labor as a Quasi-Fixed Factor," *Journal of Political Economy* 70: 538–555 (1962).

[18]Matthew Shapiro, "The Dynamic Demand for Capital and Labor," *Quarterly Journal of Economics* 101: 85–106 (1986); Joseph Nissim, "The Price Responsiveness of the Demand for Labor by Skill: British Mechanical Engineering: 1963–1978," *Economic Journal* 94: 812–825 (1984); P. de Pelsmacker, "Long-run and Short-run Demand for Factors of Production in the Belgian Car Industry," in Daniel Vitry and Bernadette Marechal (eds.). *Emploi—Chomage: Modelization et Analyses Quantitatives*, Dijon: Librairie de l'Université, (1984).

TABLE 5.1 AVERAGE SEPARATION AND REPLACEMENT COST BY OCCUPATION, SOUTHERN CALIFORNIA, 1980, IN 1994 DOLLARS[a]

Occupation Group	Separation Costs	Replacement Costs
Production and maintenance workers	$365	$5,300
Office and technical workers	500	3,100
Salaried workers	1,950	14,300

[a]The data were obtained from a survey of 105 firms.

Source: Merchants and Manufacturers Association, *Turnover and Absenteeism Manual*, Los Angeles: M & M Association, (1980).

If, in order not to lose its substantial investment in firm-specific training, an employer retains workers despite a drop in product demand, the employer may be paying these workers more than their *current* marginal product. The decision to retain these workers involves a judgment that in some future period their marginal products will exceed their wages, even though they are lower at the moment. The *VMP* must eventually exceed, rather than simply equal, the wages because the current excess payments must be recovered in the future. This fact is true whether or not the employer's prior investment in the workers' firm-specific training has been fully amortized. This investment is now a sunk cost, and unless the workers' marginal products are expected to exceed their wages in future, the unrecovered initial investment is lost whether they are dismissed or retained. Clearly, the longer a drop in demand lasts, the more convinced employers become of its permanence. As a decline in sales lengthens, increasingly skilled workers are laid off.

THE STRUCTURE OF TURNOVER COSTS

As the discussion above shows, employers do not change their demand for employee-hours immediately upon perceiving that product demand or labor costs have changed. These lags are produced by profit-maximizing employers' responses to the both the level and *structure* of turnover costs. Turnover costs are likely to depend on how rapidly employment levels are being altered.

If a firm seeks to add an extra 1 percent to its work force each month and has been doing so for many months, its hiring costs should not be very great. Work processes will be designed to absorb these new workers, and personnel offices will be set up to handle them. If such a firm suddenly tries to expand by 10 percent, the costs per worker may rise substantially. Production may be seriously disrupted as many new workers are instructed in the plant's operation, and the efficiency of the suddenly overloaded personnel office may decline.

An employer's per-worker cost of reducing employment by an unusually large number may also be higher than when the reductions are a smaller fraction of the work force. Small reductions may be accomplished by attrition, while larger ones may involve layoffs, severance pay, or other costs. An unusually large reduction may create a mismatch between the remaining workers and the skills required for production, resulting in lower output per worker.

These arguments imply that the average cost of adjusting the size of the work force increases with the size of the adjustment.[19] Consider how this affects profit-maximizing employers, such as the one depicted in Figure 5.3(a). Here the wage is assumed to drop from w_0 to w_1. The static theory of labor demand presented in Chapter 4 shows that it would pay to expand employment from E_0 to E_1, where the *VMP* equals the new, lower wage rate. Adding $E_1 - E_0$ workers produces hiring costs, however. Our argument suggests, as shown in Figure 5.3(b), that the average hiring cost is higher the larger the change in employment in each time period (assumed to be a month). If the firm hires all $E_1 - E_0$ workers at once, the per-worker hiring cost is denoted in Figure 5.3(b) by the vertical distance $0C_2$. Total costs of adjustment are thus the whole rectangle $0C_2HJ$.

What if the employer makes only half the adjustment between *A* and *B* in Figure 5.3(a) immediately and waits a month to make the rest? During that first month the *VMP* will not equal the new wage, since employment only expands to E_2 where the *VMP* (point *D*) exceeds the wage (w_1). This will cost potential profits indicated by the triangle *FDB*. The vertical distances in this triangle are the excesses of *VMP* over w_1 for each worker not hired ($E_1 - E_2$). Since fewer workers are being hired per period, however, the hiring cost per worker is now the vertical distance $0C_1$ in Figure 5.3(b). Total hiring costs for the first month are $0C_1GK$. When the adjustment from E_2 to E_1 is made next month, the firm again incurs hiring costs of $0C_1GK$. Since E_2 represented half the total change between E_0 and E_1, the rectangles $0C_1GK$ and *KGIJ* are equal. Together they are less than hiring costs would have been if the adjustment had been made all at once by an amount C_1C_2HI.

Should the firm make the entire adjustment immediately, or should it change employment in two equal monthly increments? The cost savings of waiting (C_1C_2HI in Figure 5.3(b)) can be compared to the forgone profits (*FDB* in Figure 5.3(a)). As the figures are drawn, it pays to wait. Average hiring costs that rise with the number hired may make it optimal for the firm to change employment slowly when factor prices or product demand change. The more rapidly such costs rise with increases in employment (the steeper the slope of the line *CGH* in Figure 5.3(b)), the more profit-maximizing employers will spread out the change in employment.

---

[19] The importance of increasing average costs of adjustment was first pointed out by Charles Holt, Franco Modigliani, John Muth, and Herbert Simon, *Planning Production, Inventories and Work Force*, Englewood Cliffs, N.J.: Prentice Hall, (1960).

For some firms the average costs of adjustment might *decrease* as the size of the adjustment increases. This situation would occur if fixed costs comprise a large part of the adjustment costs. For example, a firm may have to spend the same amount for advertising and interviewing prospective engineers whether it seeks to hire one or a dozen. With fixed costs of hiring, businesses face different incentives from those implied by the analysis in Figure 5.3. Again, however, the employer must consider whether the gains from changing the number of workers exceed the costs of making the change.

Fixed costs may mean that it pays to defer hiring as demand for workers expands until demand has increased enough to justify hiring several workers at once. An employer may opt to forgo the added current income a few additional workers might create in order to divide the fixed costs over a larger number of hires at a later date. Similarly, once workers are being hired it may be rational to hire all the workers the firm *expects* to add in the next several periods at the same time to minimize fixed hiring costs.

Overall, it seems likely that for small levels of adjustment, average costs will fall as the size of the adjustment increases, but that beyond some level adjustment costs per worker will increase as the size of the change in the work force increases. Where this level occurs will be different for different

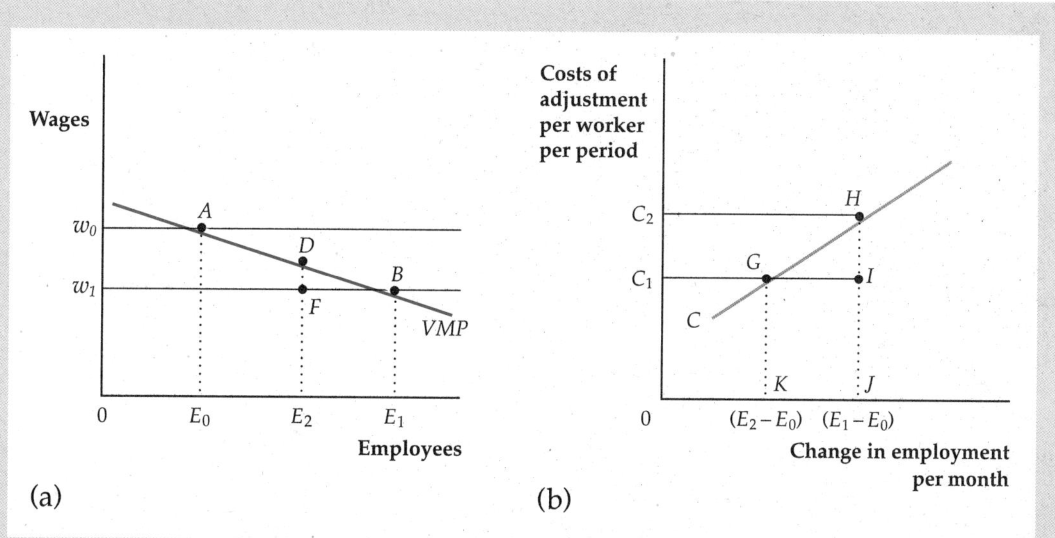

FIGURE 5.3 EMPLOYMENT CHANGES WITH INCREASING COSTS OF ADJUSTMENT
When the costs of adding a worker increases if more workers are added in a given time period, as in Figure 5.3(b), it may pay a firm to spread out a desired adjustment in labor input over several periods. If the firm makes the adjustment from *A* to *B* in Figure 5.3(a) in two periods rather than one, it forgoes profits equal to *DFB* in the first period but saves costs equal to C_1C_2HI in Figure 5.3(b).

firms, but the empirical evidence suggests that it is lower than the adjustment many firms wish to make as demand for their products changes. A very large body of research indicates that it takes three to six months for employers to make half of their eventual employment response to changes in product demand or factor prices they expect to be permanent. One study infers that firms may forgo 2 percent of output by adjusting the employment of their nonproduction workers slowly. Many studies show that adjustment is slower if turnover costs are higher. Research on both the American auto industry and Dutch manufacturing show that adjustment in employment is not entirely smooth. Instead, businesses either make large changes or do not alter employment at all.[20]

To reduce adjustment costs employers can change hours of work rather than employment. The choice between adding workers and adding hours depends on several factors including

1. the quality of workers available to hire (and how much training they will require);
2. the premium that must be paid to current workers to work more hours;
3. whether current workers can increase their hours without lowering their productivity; and
4. perhaps the most important factor, how long the increase in demand is expected to last.

If an increase in demand is expected to be temporary, weekly hours will be increased because the cost of hiring workers and laying them off again will usually be viewed as prohibitive. Some aspects of these costs may be indirect. Employers whose employment is unstable may acquire a bad reputation that could hamper future recruitment or even hurt sales. Employers with a strong social conscience might feel guilty about choosing an unstable employment strategy.

The longer the increase in demand is expected to last, the less important hiring costs become and the stronger the case is for adding workers. This effect explains the consistent tendency of changes in hours of work to occur before changes in employment at cyclical turning points. Hours are increased or decreased while employers are still uncertain about the changes in

---

[20] Daniel Hamermesh, *Labor Demand,* Princeton, N.J.: Princeton University Press, (1993), Chapter 7; Shapiro, "The Dynamic;" Daniel Hamermesh, "Labor Demand and the Structure of Adjustment Costs," *American Economic Review* 79: 674–689 (1989); Gerard Pfann and Bart Verspagen, "The Structure of Adjustment Costs for Labour in the Dutch Manufacturing Sector," *Economics Letters* 29: 365–371 (1989).

demand. Employment is changed in the same direction once the persistence of the demand shift has become clear. In general, turnover costs make employers slower to adjust the number of workers than they are to adjust hours per worker.[21]

PRODUCTIVITY AND EMPLOYMENT ADJUSTMENT

The data in Table 5.2 show that output per worker-hour grew far more slowly during the 12 months before business cycle troughs than during the 12 months afterward. The reason is that businesses respond to the existence of turnover costs by **labor hoarding** during a recession. Despite the fact that lower output levels require fewer workers than in good times, the employer who does not want to lose past investments in specific training or incur hiring costs when the recession is over may not cut employment as much as short-term profit maximization would dictate. Trained workers might be kept busy repairing machinery or cleaning and painting the plant. They can also be allowed to work a little less hard than when product demand is high. A study based on surveys of employers during the 1982 recession indicated that 4 percent of employee-hours could be classified as hoarded labor.[22]

The long-run profit-maximizing behavior implied by labor hoarding means that employee-hours paid for (and hours spent at the workplace) during recessions will overstate the number of employee-hours actually spent producing current output. Labor productivity (i.e., the average product of labor), which is measured as output per hour paid for, thus falls (or rises less rapidly) during a recession. When the recession is over, the opposite occurs. Employers are able to expand output without increasing hours because they can put some of their hoarded labor back to work. Turnover costs dictate the sequence of employers' profit-maximizing responses to a change in product demand: (1) change the amount of effort per worker-hour devoted to actual production; then (2) change hours per worker; and finally (3) change the number of workers.

Using overtime hours is the most common way employers meet fluctuations in product demand. In a survey of employers in the United States in 1986, 91 percent stated they rely on overtime to absorb fluctuations in their organizations' workloads. In recent years employers have also made extensive use of temporary workers when demand is first reviving after the trough of a business cycle. For example, during the first months of the 1992 recovery, some estimates are that almost two-thirds of the new jobs created in the U.S.

[21] Ray Fair, "Excess Labor and the Business Cycle," *American Economic Review* 75: 239–245 (1985).

[22] John Fay and James Medoff, "Labor and Output over the Business Cycle," *American Economic Review* 75: 638–655 (1985).

TABLE 5.2 ANNUAL PERCENTAGE CHANGES IN LABOR PRODUCTIVITY IN THE NONFARM BUSINESS SECTOR, BEFORE AND AFTER BUSINESS-CYCLE TROUGHS, 1961–1991

Trough	Twelve Months Before Trough	Twelve Months After Trough
1961, first quarter	1.1	4.8
1970, fourth quarter	1.7	4.0
1975, second quarter	1.7	4.5
1980, third quarter	0.2	0.9
1982, fourth quarter	0.6	3.8
1991, second quarter	0.4	2.0

Sources: Unpublished data, Bureau of Labor Statistics, for 1961; *Employment and Earnings*, selected issues.

economy were with temporary agencies. In part this may reflect the fact that the 1991 recession was relatively more severe among office workers than previous recessions. Temporary-help agencies have been a traditional way of hiring extra clerical help, while overtime work has been more common on production lines.[23]

In Chapter 2 we discussed overtime from the point of view of the worker. If variations in the amount of overtime worked depended mainly on the supply behavior of workers, we would expect overtime hours to rise in a recession as the income effect created by the loss of labor income when family members became unemployed induced those who were still employed to seek additional pay. In fact, the opposite occurs. During postwar recessions in the U.S., average overtime hours in manufacturing have fallen by roughly 30 percent from cyclical peaks to cyclical troughs. This cyclical decline shows that the main use of overtime is to cushion variations in demand for labor.

THE TRADE-OFF BETWEEN WORKERS AND HOURS

Nothing dictates that employers are always best off if they use their employees exactly 40 hours per week. The evidence in Table 5.3. demonstrates that they may not be. Differences in the length of the average workweek (time paid for) are substantial even among broadly defined industries. If we had presented a much longer table showing differences among smaller, but more diverse industries, the range of hours worked per week would be even greater. Clearly, employers can substitute workers for hours, although work-

---

[23]Katharine Abraham, "Flexible Staffing Arrangements and Employers' Short-term Adjustment Strategies," in Hart, *Employment, Unemployment and Labor Utilization*; "Temporary Workers Were in Big Demand with Firms in 1992," *Wall Street Journal*, (January 29, 1993).

POLICY ISSUE

MAKING LAYOFFS MORE DIFFICULT IN EUROPE

From the late 1960s through the early 1980s European nations adopted a host of policies designed to make it harder for employers to lay off workers permanently. These policies included requirements for government consultation before layoffs (in Germany), subsidies to employers who agreed not to lay off workers (in the United Kingdom), severance pay in addition to usual unemployment benefits (in many countries), and other measures. How did these policies affect adjustment in the labor market?

All of these policies are designed to prevent layoffs during downturns in the demand for products. Consider how this affects the typical firm's employment over the business cycle, as shown in Figure 5.4. The solid curve denotes employment without the policies. Business-cycle peaks are at t_1 and t_3, while the trough is at t_2. In bad times the policies will make employers reluctant to lay off some workers, exactly as they are designed to do. The savings from laying off the marginal workers are no longer greater than turnover costs, which have been increased by the laws. Because of the policies, employment will not drop as far in the recession, perhaps moving along the higher dashed path $C'D'$ instead of the lower CD.

The policies have another effect, however. Faced with the prospect of additional costs when laying off workers, employers will not hire as many workers during the expansions leading up to t_1 and t_3. To do so would be foolish, since the marginal product of the final worker hired could no longer justify the higher costs of laying her off when the recession arrives. This means that employment will not rise as much during boom times. It will move along $F'G'$ instead of the higher FG.[24] In general, the policies will reduce variability in employment over the business cycle by reducing layoffs and hiring.

Overall, the policies will reduce employment for reasons cited in Chapter 4. By imposing a cost on hiring workers, they raise the cost of labor services, inducing employers to substitute other inputs for labor. The net result is that the number of jobs saved in a recession, denoted by the distance $E_r' - E_r$ will be less than the number of jobs *not* created during a boom, denoted by the distance $E_b - E_b'$.

A lot of evidence suggests that these policies reduced cyclical variation in employment. Among ten industrialized countries, those with more stringent employment-security regulations exhibited smaller fluctuations in employment between 1962 and 1986. This behavior was not simply because jobs were protected during recessions. In the European steel industry, for example, the restrictions slowed employers' hiring of new workers. Also, among 22 industrialized countries, employment growth was lower between the 1950s and 1980s in those nations, and at those times, where employment-protection legislation was in effect.[25]

---

[24] This discussion follows from the work of Steve Nickell, "Dynamic Models of Labor Demand," in Orley Ashenfelter and Richard Layard (eds.). *Handbook of Labor Economics*, Amsterdam: North-Holland, (1986).

[25] Giuseppe Bertola, "Job Security, Employment and Wages," *European Economic Review* 34: 851–886 (1990); Susan Houseman, *Industrial Restructuring with Job Security*, Cambridge, Mass.: Harvard University Press, (1991); Edward Lazear, "Job Security Provisions and Employment," *Quarterly Journal of Economics* 105: 699–726 (1990).

The theory and evidence demonstrate that governments and their citizens face a choice when they contemplate enacting employment-protection policies. They must trade off gains from the reduced fluctuations in employment against the costs of lower average employment. In weighing this trade-off they should also recognize that the people who benefit from the reduced variability of employment are not the same ones who lose when fewer jobs on average are created.

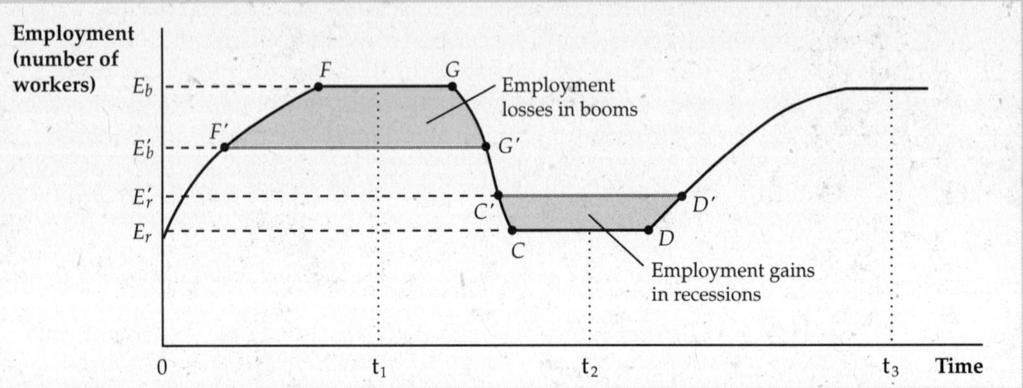

FIGURE 5.4 THE IMPACT OF JOB SECURITY LEGISLATION ON EMPLOYMENT OVER THE BUSINESS CYCLE

By increasing costs of both hiring and firing workers, job security legislation reduces the variation in employment over the business cycle, moving the firm along path *F′G′C′D′* rather than *FGCD*. The loss of employment in the boom will exceed the gain in the recession (*F′FGG′* is greater than *C′CDD′*).

TABLE 5.3 WEEKLY HOURS OF WORK BY INDUSTRY, UNITED STATES, 1994

Industry	Hours
Mining	44.7
Construction	38.8
Manufacturing	46.7[a]
Transportation and public utilities	39.9
Wholesale trade	38.3
Retail trade	28.9
Finance, insurance, and real estate	35.8
Services	32.5

[a]Includes 4.7 overtime hours.

Source: *Employment and Earnings,* (January 1995), Table 50.

ers and hours are not perfect substitutes. A firm that desires to increase employment will not be indifferent to whether it has current employees work more hours, hires more employees to work the same average workweek as current employees, hires part-time workers, or some combination of these strategies.

Fixed costs per worker, such as hiring and training costs, will cause employers to economize on the number of workers by having every employee work a large number of hours. A second type of fixed cost consists of those occurring throughout the period of employment that are not related (or not fully related) to hours of work. A tax on employment based on the number of employees instead of on wages or hours of labor is one example. Any payroll tax having an annual earnings limit, such as Social Security and unemployment insurance, falls in this category, as do similarly based contributions to private pension and welfare plans. Many fringe benefits are essentially independent of hours worked. For example, if an employer provides health insurance to all workers who work more than 30 hours a week, these costs will not increase when workers are scheduled for more hours.

A third form of fixed costs per worker involves what happens in the workplace itself. Workers need a certain amount of time to start and end each shift, no matter how long that shift may be. A nurse coming on duty must be briefed by the previous shift on the condition of each patient. A factory worker must retrieve tools from the toolroom, change into work clothes, and get to the work station. A salesperson must spend the requisite amount of time at the water cooler discussing last night's game with coworkers. Similarly, at the end of a shift, the next shift must be briefed, tools put away, and showers taken. Thus, the first and last hour on the job will be less productive than the intervening ones, and an employer can expect less total output from six 4-hour shifts a day than three 8-hour ones.

On the other hand, there are offsetting reasons why employers do not want their employees to work too many hours. The overtime pay for workers who exceed the limits imposed by the Fair Labor Standards Act (or required in many union agreements) provides an obvious incentive to limit the hours worked by each employee by hiring more workers.

Productivity may also decline as workers spend more hours on the job. Fatigue will eventually reduce workers' effectiveness. When and how rapidly this effect sets in will depend on the physical and mental demands of the job. A classic study of time and motion in the 1920s found that output per hour rose during the first hour on the job, fell slightly through most of the rest of the day, and fell drastically during the final hour of work. Among those workers who were allowed to take breaks from work, however, output jumped back up to its peak.[26] Among contemporary American workers, coffee breaks, lunch, and other breaks account for nearly four hours of weekly

---

[26]P. Sargant Florence, *The Economics of Fatigue and Unrest,* New York: Holt, (1924).

work time. The evidence suggests that, given the length of today's workday, breaks are sufficient to enable workers to maintain effort on the job and that further increases would not raise productivity during the rest of the workday.[27]

The factors discussed in this section can be combined into the formal analysis shown in Figure 5.5, which is drawn assuming that capital services are fixed.[28] The presence of start-up and fatigue effects on productivity per hour means that the **isolabor curves** L_0 and L_1, which show the combination of workers and hours per worker that produce the same effective labor input, will exhibit diminishing marginal rates of substitution between hours and workers and be convex to the origin. This is analogous to the production isoquants between capital and labor discussed in Chapter 4.

The shape of the **isocost of labor curves** C_0 and C_1 is somewhat more complex. Fixed costs per worker for hiring and fringe benefits mean that they will also be convex to the origin. The existence of overtime premiums mean that they will have a kink at the point where the premium kicks in (H^* in Figure 5.5). The isocost curves become steeper at this point because each additional hour per worker requires the sacrifice of more workers to hold costs constant. As with the trade-off between labor and capital in Figure 4.6, only one optimal combination of workers and hours per worker is possible for each output level, shown as the tangency points in Figure 5.5. Connecting these points gives an expansion path showing how this combination will change as output changes. As we have drawn Figure 5.5, the employer's optimal combination of workers and hours implies some overtime. It is easy to see, however, why the length of workweeks is likely to be concentrated around H^* hours (40 in the U.S.). Given the kink in the isocost curves at this point, a wide range of isolabor curves will achieve a pseudo-tangency at this point.[29]

Businesses do respond to changes in the relative costs of workers and hours by substituting in the expected direction. Studies in the U.S. of differences among industries and among individual companies in 28 cities showed substitution between part- and full-time workers when the relative costs of employing them change. A very careful study of labor costs in Germany over a 30-year period indicated that a reduction in variable relative to fixed payroll

---

[27]Frank Stafford and Greg Duncan, "The Use of Time and Technology by Households in the United States," *Research in Labor Economics* 3: 335–375 (1980); Daniel Hamermesh, "Shirking or Productive Schmoozing," *Industrial and Labor Relations Review* 43: 121S–133S (1990).

[28]This discussion is based on Robert Hart, *The Economics of Non-Wage Labour Costs,* London: George Allen and Unwin, (1984).

[29]We use the term *pseudo-tangency* since the slope of the isocost curve is actually undefined at this point. If an isolabor curve just touches the isocost curve at this point, however, it remains the lowest cost at which that effective level of labor input can be purchased.

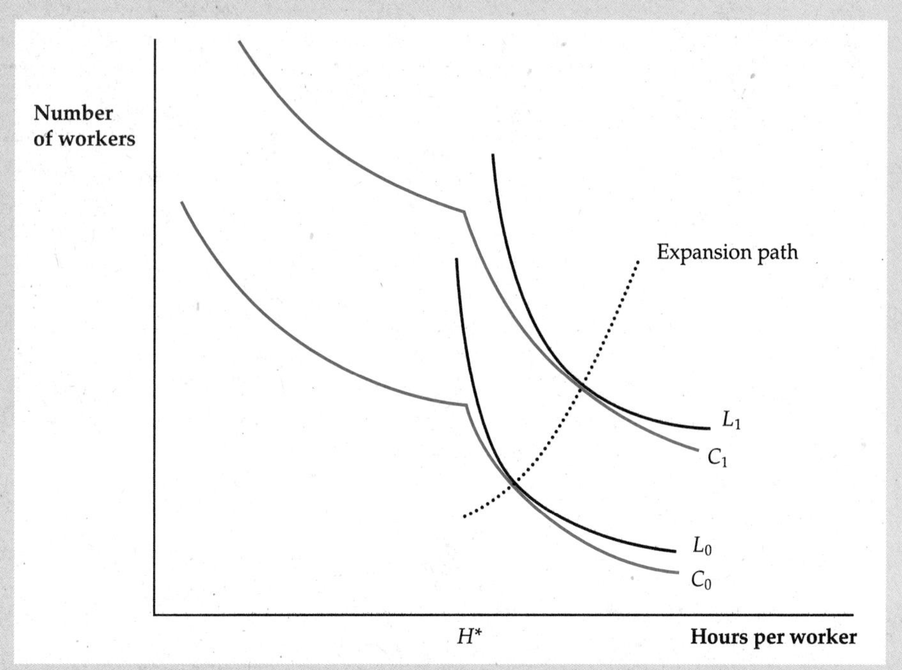

FIGURE 5.5 THE TRADE-OFF BETWEEN WORKERS AND HOURS PER WORKER

Fixed costs per worker create a convex isocost of labor curve with a kink at H^*, the number of hours above which an overtime premium must be paid. Start-up costs and fatigue mean that hours and workers are not perfect substitutes, creating convex isolabor curves. The optimal combination of workers and hours to produce any level of output occurs where these two curves are tangent.

taxes that lowered the relative cost of hours per worker compared to number of workers caused firms to increase hours per worker.[30]

Between World War II and the early 1980s, the use of overtime in U.S. manufacturing, the only sector for which good data are available, rose by 1 percent per year.[31] Overtime peaked at 3.8 hours per week per production

[30]Robert Hart and Seiichi Kawasaki, "Payroll Taxes and Factor Demand," *Research in Labor Economics* 9: 257–285 (1988); Ronald Ehrenberg, Pamela Rosenberg, and Jeanne Li, "Part-time Employment in the United States," in Robert Hart (ed.). *Employment, Unemployment and Labor Utilization*, London: Unwin Hyman, (1988); Mark Montgomery, "On the Determinants of Employer Demand for Part-time Workers," *Review of Economics and Statistics* 70: 112–117 (1988).

[31]Ronald Ehrenberg and Paul Schumann, *Longer Hours or More Jobs?* Ithica, N.Y.: New York State School of Industrial and Labor Relations, (1982), p. 11.

POLICY ISSUE

MANDATED HEALTH INSURANCE

Consider what happens to the choice between workers and hours per worker if costs per worker rise while cost of additional hours remain unchanged. This situation is exactly what would happen if a firm that currently does not provide health insurance were required to start providing it. Figure 5.6 presents this analysis. The isocost curve after the mandate (C_0') is flatter than before the law (C_0) since each additional worker hired requires that hours for existing workers be reduced by a greater amount if costs are to be held constant. C_0' also represents a higher level of costs than C_0. If the firm wished to continue producing at the same output level, it would substitute hours for workers along isolabor curve L_0, moving from point P to point Q. Since labor is now more expensive overall, however, the firm will both substitute capital for labor and reduce total output as we saw in Chapter 4. This adjustment will cause the effective amount of labor demanded to shift, toward the origin, perhaps to L_1, and the workers-hours combination to shift to point R. Both effects will reduce the number of workers the firm employs.

So far, this discussion has assumed that the wage is fixed, as it is for minimum wage workers, so that markets cannot adjust to changes in fixed costs created by the insurance by reducing wages. Other workers, if they value the insurance, may be willing to reduce wages somewhat to offset the cost. These savings can never be enough, however, for the costs of labor not to increase. The reason is simple. If the workers valued the insurance enough that their wages could be reduced sufficiently to cover its cost, then as we will see in Chapter 10, the employer would already have offered the insurance and paid the lower wages. The fact that the insurance was not provided prior to the mandate indicates that its value to workers is less than its cost to employers. Thus, the analysis presented here should apply to all workers. Indeed, estimates are that the health insurance mandate proposed by President Clinton in 1994 would have reduced employment by between 300,000 and 800,000 jobs even with subsidies to many employers and by more than 2 million jobs if there were no subsidies.[32]

worker in 1973. Even in the trough of the very severe 1982 recession, average overtime hours in manufacturing stood at 2.3 hours, compared to only 2 hours in the less severe 1958 recession. Since 1982 no trend has been observable. One possible explanation for this increase and subsequent leveling off is that, relative to premiums for overtime work which have generally been constant, per-worker costs of employment rose as a percent of compensation until the early 1980s, and then stayed constant thereafter.

[32]Alan Krueger, "Observations on Employment-Based Government Mandates, With Particular Reference to Health Insurance," Princeton University Industrial Relations Section Working Paper No. 323 (1994); June O'Neill and David O'Neill, *The Employment and Distribution Effects of Mandated Benefits*, Washington, D.C.: American Enterprise Institute (1994).

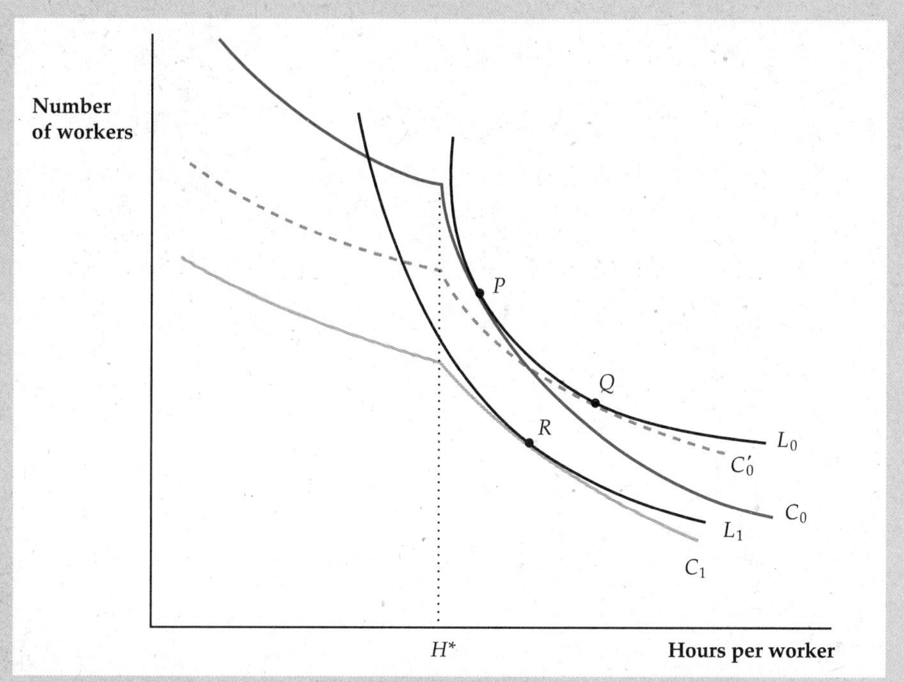

FIGURE 5.6 EFFECT OF A MANDATED EMPLOYEE BENEFIT
A mandated benefit will increase fixed costs per worker, flattening and increasing the isocost curve from C_0 to C_0'. This causes the firm to reduce the number of workers and increase hours per worker for any level of output, moving from *P* to *Q*. Since the mandated benefit increases overall labor costs, it will also create a substitution effect towards capital and a scale effect from reduced sales. These will cause the firm to move from *Q* to *R* and further reduce employment.

SUMMARY

The demand for labor is negatively related to the wage rate a business must pay regardless of whether the firm is a perfect competitor in its product market. Similarly, businesses that do not maximize profits but instead minimize costs or even function as cooperatives, have a negative elasticity of demand for labor. Businesses that are monopsonists in the market for a particular type of labor or in a geographical labor market, will react by reducing employment when demand for their product drops, just like other companies. Their demand is, however, less elastic than similar firms that are not monopsonists.

POLICY ISSUE

PROTECTING PART-TIME WORKERS

Part-time workers often lack the protection governments offer full-time workers against layoffs. In addition they generally have fewer employee benefits. Among workers in establishment with more than 100 employees in 1993, part-time workers were less than one-third as likely to receive medical insurance through their employers as full-time workers. Only 24 percent of part-time employees had such coverage, as opposed to 82 percent of full-time employees. Moreover, part-time workers were only half as likely as full-time workers to receive pension benefits beyond Social Security contributions (40 percent versus 78 percent).[33] Governments have responded to these differences. The European Community has adopted a resolution requesting member nations to extend equal protection to part-time workers. Canada requires prorated pensions for part-time employees who work more than 20 hours per week. The state of Massachusetts requires employer-provided health insurance for employees who work as few as 17 hours per week. What is the effect of these laws?

These policies raise the cost of part-time workers, leading employers to reduce their demand for part-timers by substituting both full-time workers and capital services. Direct evidence on the effect of requiring employers in Britain to offer job security only to full-time workers shows that businesses switched toward using more part-time workers.[34] Applying the same stringent restrictions to part-time workers would result in a shift back toward the use of more full-time workers, because it would raise the fixed costs of workers relative to hours per worker.

These laws also raise the cost of labor exactly like the employment-security legislation discussed earlier. As such, they reduce total labor input through both substitution and scale effects. Protection is provided for those part-time employees who are able to find or keep jobs. Their health and pension benefits improve. It happens, however, at the cost of reducing the number of jobs for part-timers and reducing the total number of employee-hours demanded.

Turnover costs incurred when a firm adds new employees or gets rid of experienced workers induce employers to change employment slowly when demand for their product changes. Often it pays businesses to alter hours per employee before resorting to changes in employment. Varying the intensity of work demanded of their employees may be the first response to changes in product demand. Turnover costs are higher among skilled workers. This explains why their employment is relatively stable over the business cycle. Turnover costs also explain why labor productivity falls during recessions. Employment protection policies increase turnover costs and induce businesses to smooth employment fluctuations still further.

---

[33]United States Department of Labor, Bureau of Labor Statistics, *News* 94–477, Washington, D.C., (September 1994).

[34]R. Disney and E. M. Szyszczak, "Protective Legislation and Part-Time Employment in Britain," *British Journal of Industrial Relations* 22: 78–100 (1984).

Some nonwage labor costs raise the price of an additional worker, while others raise the price of an additional hour. The relative importance of these two types of costs determines the firm's choice of workers and hours per worker. Changes in these nonwage costs determine changes in the prevalence of overtime hours. Policies altering these costs also affect other outcomes, including employers' demand for part-time workers. Like employment-protection policies, any change that raises nonwage costs has the additional effect of reducing the total demand for employee-hours, as employers substitute away from labor and toward other factors of production.

QUESTIONS AND PROBLEMS

5.1 Given the following information, complete the table as shown and determine the approximate number of workers to be hired by the firm in equilibrium.

Workers	Total Product	Marginal Product	Selling Price per Unit	Marginal Revenue Product	Wage	Total Labor Cost	Marginal Labor Cost
0	0	—	—	—	—	—	—
1	10		$10.00	$100.00	$5.00	$5.00	
2	19		9.50		5.50		
3	27		9.00		6.50		
4	34		8.50		7.75		
5	40		8.00		9.50		
6	45		7.50		11.50		
7	49		7.00		14.00		

5.2 Explain the following outcomes in the market for professional athletes:

a. The highest-earning baseball players make almost 20 times as much as the highest-earning rodeo professionals.

b. The average pay among the 20 highest-paid baseball players is typically almost twice the average among the 20 highest-paid football players. (Hint: Football owners share television revenues to a greater extent than do baseball owners.)

c. Thirteen of the 20 highest-paid football players in 1990 were quarterbacks; none was a lineman.

d. The top three earners in professional sports in 1990 were boxers Buster Douglas, Mike Tyson, and Evander Holyfield.

5.3 During the 1980s the federal government aided states in adopting programs that encouraged employers to share work during recessions by paying unemployment benefits to workers who were on reduced hours but still worked part time. Nearly a dozen states did so. Analyze the impact of this subsidy on the firm's choice of workers and hours per worker, and on total employee-hours demanded under the assumption that businesses pay the taxes that finance this program.

5.4 Many proponents of tax reform in the United States would like to impose payroll taxes on employer-paid employee benefits. (These benefits are taxed elsewhere, for example, in Australia since the mid-1980s.) Essentially, employers would pay Social Security taxes on health and pension benefits they set aside for their workers, just as they now do on wages. Assume that all employers provide the same health and pension coverage to each of their workers. What would be the effect of this proposal on total employee-hours, employee-hours by skill category, total employment, and hours per worker?

5.5 Suppose the U.S. Congress increased the premium required for overtime work from 50 percent to 100 percent. What would be the impact of this law on employment levels, average hours worked, and the earnings of the average worker under each of the following scenarios? You should illustrate your answers with appropriate graphs.

a. Workers and firms are free to contract for both wages and hours worked.
b. Firms set wages, but workers are free to pick how many hours they want to work at that wage.
c. Wages are set by law (as they are for minimum wage workers), but firms are free to decide how many hours they will offer each worker.

5.6 Part-time employment has grown as a share of total employment in most countries in recent years. Discuss as many factors as you can that might explain such growth. You should consider both demand- and supply-side causes.

5.7 Several bills have been introduced into Congress recently that would require employers to finance health benefits for all employees, including part-time workers. What effect would this legislation have on.

a. total employment,
b. hours per worker,
c. total hours worked,
d. relative demand for skilled versus less-skilled workers?

5.8 We have seen that a perfectly discriminating monopsonist will demand labor in the same manner as a competitive firm and, therefore, achieve economic efficiency. How might a firm structure its compensation package so as to pay workers their individual supply prices. How feasible do you think such policies would be? What forces, if any, might cause them to break down?

5.9 Consider a worker-managed firm that has as its goal maximizing a "utility" function $U = U(w, L)$, where w = wage and L = employment.

a. Derive the short-run (K fixed) labor demand for this firm assuming that its technology exhibits constant returns to scale. Illustrate how you would do this using a graph.

b. Compare this graph to that of a profit-maximizing firm. Which firm pays the higher wage? Which hires more workers?
c. How would your answer change if the firm's objective were to maximize the wage rate?

5.10 Consider a firm that faces a temporary reduction in demand for its product. It can respond to this situation in three ways: (1) reduce the number of hours demanded from each worker, (2) reduce the number of workers employed, or (3) leave employment and hours unchanged but reduce the productivity of each employee-hour. Discuss under what circumstances you would expect to see each of these responses.

KEY WORDS

deregulation of industry
employee buyout
isocost of labor curve
isolabor curve
labor hoarding
labor-managed firm
marginal labor cost (*MLC*)
marginal revenue product (*MRP*)
market power
monopsonist
negative externality
nondiscriminating monopsony
nonwage labor costs
perfectly discriminating monopsonist
rate of return
supply price
turnover costs
wage bill

Part Three

External Labor Markets

In the past two sections we analyzed factors determining the supply of and demand for labor services. Now we turn to the interaction of these forces. While the analysis of many markets can be confined to forces that determine supply and demand, with little attention being paid to the mechanics of the market itself, this is not true of even highly competititve labor markets. Labor services, unlike goods, are embodied in people, a fact that has important consequences for the nature of labor markets.

Chapter 6 will discuss the interaction of supply and demand to determine equilibrium wages and employment levels. It will also analyze the consequences of the fact that investment in human capital generally takes much longer than investment in plant and equipment. Finally, there will be a discussion of the search mechanisms by which workers and employers are matched.

Chapters 7 and 8 focus on the outcomes of this matching process. Chapter 7 examines mobility of workers between locations, occupations, and firms. Chapter 8 discusses one of the politically important outcomes of the labor market, the existence, distribution, and persistence of unemployed workers (unemployment) and capital (job vacancies).

SUPPLY AND DEMAND TOGETHER: THE SEARCH PROCESS

THE MAJOR QUESTIONS

- ▲ How will changes in the determinants of supply affect the wage rate and employment in the market?
- ▲ How will changes in the determinants of demand affect these two central outcomes?
- ▲ How do workers obtain information about jobs that leads them to accept particular jobs?
- ▲ What determines when workers decide to stop searching for a job and accept an offer of employment?
- ▲ How do employers find workers to hire?
- ▲ How do firms decide which workers from a group of applicants receive offers of employment?
- ▲ How does the search process by workers and firms explain characteristics of equilibrium in labor markets that differ from those in conventional product markets?

SUPPLY AND DEMAND FOR LABOR: A BRIEF REVIEW

So far we have seen the general shapes of supply and demand curves in the labor market. We know that for the economy as a whole the supply of labor is relatively inelastic and does not respond much to changes in wage rates. The same is not true for the supply of labor to sectors, regions, or firms. As the unit of analysis becomes smaller and smaller, an increasing ability to attract workers from other employers means that the supply of labor becomes more elastic. For many individual firms it is reasonable to assume that the supply of labor is perfectly elastic at the market wage. The longer the time period under analysis, the more elastic the supply of labor will be since more and more workers have the time required to acquire skills or make other adjustments.

We also know that the demand for labor will be downward-sloping for all types of employers including profit-seeking firms, not-for-profit organizations, worker cooperatives, and government units.[1] Elasticity of demand will depend on many factors including: the elasticity of product demand, the ease of technological substitution, the elasticity of supply of substitute inputs into production, and the share of labor in total costs. Once again elasticities are larger in the long run as firms have more opportunity to adjust methods of production.

HOW SUPPLY AND DEMAND DETERMINE WAGES AND EMPLOYMENT

What we need to know is how labor supply and demand interact in the market in response to the changes that continually buffet it. How are wage rates and employment affected by the wide range of changes that occur naturally in the labor market or are imposed on it by government policy? Even where supply and demand do not determine an equilibrium in a market characterized by a shortage or a surplus, *shifts* in supply or demand will change observed wages and employment in predictable directions. As discussed in Chapter 1, this process of contrasting equilibria before and after something has changed is known as comparative static analysis. In comparative static analyses we do not ask *how* the economy moved from the old equilibrium to the new equilibrium, merely how these equilibria differ with respect to price and quantity. These questions regarding the timing and path of the adjustment between the equilibria are known as **dynamic analysis.**

Figure 6.1 shows how the labor market might adjust to an increase in the demand for some type of labor. Suppose that this is the labor market for television camera operators before and after the advent of the Cable News Network (CNN). Before CNN, the market was in equilibrium at point *A*, with wage w_0 and employment level E_0. When the new network came on the air, more camera operators were demanded at each wage. Thus, the short-run labor demand curve shifted to the right. Initially, there would be some supply response. Perhaps some older camera operators postponed their retirement because of the higher wages now available. Other operators might have worked longer hours, either because the substitution effect was greater than the income effect, or because they expected the higher wages to be temporary. These adjustments mean that in the short run, the new equilibrium will

[1]At least under reasonable assumptions about the behavior of organizations that do not maximize profits.

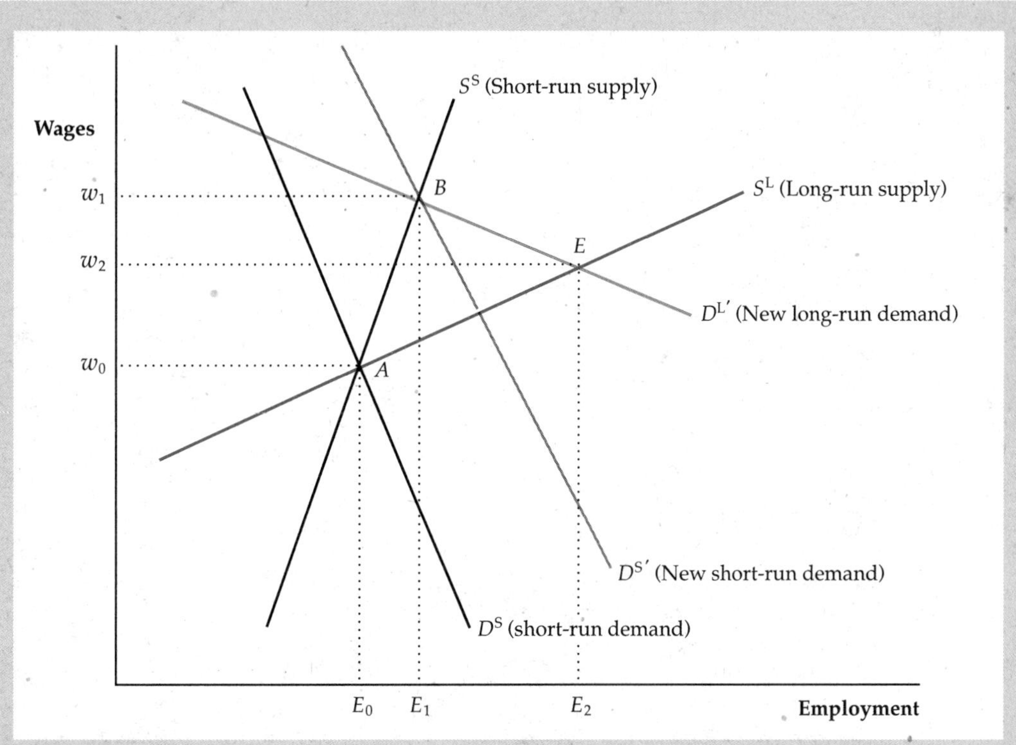

FIGURE 6.1 LABOR MARKET ADJUSTMENT TO A CHANGE IN DEMAND
An increase in labor demand causes a movement from *A* to *B* along the short-run labor supply curve. In the long run both demand and supply are more elastic, and the new equilibrium is at point *C* with a greater increase in employment and a smaller increase in wages than in the short run.

be at point *B*, with wage w_1 and employment level E_1. Wages have increased considerably while employment has only risen a little.

In the long run, both the supply and demand relationships become more elastic. Young people who see the high wages available to camera operators will learn the profession. Some camera operators may move to the U.S. from other countries. On the demand side, broadcast companies faced with high wages for camera operators will search for ways to use fewer of them. Pool arrangements allowing one camera to provide video to several networks will be signed. Perhaps a "robot camera" controlled by the director will be invented. Gradually the wage will fall and employment will increase even more until a new long-run equilibrium is reached at point *C*, with wage w_2 and employment of E_2. Although we have discussed the short and long run and know something of the path wages and employment take over time, this analysis has still not been fully dynamic because we do not know the speed at which these adjustments will occur.

EQUILIBRIUM WITH LINEAR DEMAND AND SUPPLY CURVES

Labor demand and supply curves shown in Figure 6.1 are *linear* and can be written as

$$E_d = a + bw$$

and

$$E_s = c + dw$$

where b and d show how labor demand and supply respond to changes in wages and, since the demand curve slopes down, $b < 0$. The amount of labor demanded and supplied when wages are zero are shown by a and c. We presume that $a > 0$ (i.e., firms would like to employ at least one worker if workers were free), and c could be positive or negative. If c is negative (labor supply at zero wages would be less than zero or to the left of the origin), then no workers would enter the profession unless they were paid a positive wage. On the other hand, if c is positive, some workers would be available to employers even if the wage were zero. For example, as the existence of community theater demonstrates, some people are willing to work as actors even if they do not get paid.

Equilibrium in this market requires finding a wage where the quantity supplied equals the quantity demanded. Setting demand equal to supply, we have

$$a + bw = c + dw.$$

Solving this expression for w gives

$$w^* = \frac{a - c}{d - b}$$

where $b < 0$. This expression for w^* can be substituted into either the demand or the supply equation to solve for the equilibrium level of employment:

$$E^* = \frac{ad - bc}{d - b}.$$

While linear demand and supply curves look simple at first glance, they are often difficult to work with because their elasticity is different at each point on the curve. To see this point, recall the formula for an elasticity of either demand or supply:

$$\epsilon = \frac{w}{E}\frac{\Delta E}{\Delta w}.$$

Along a straight-line demand or supply curve the slope of the curve ($\Delta E/\Delta w$) is constant (and equal to b or d in our equations), but the ratio of wages to employment (w/E) will be different at each point. Therefore, elasticities will be constantly changing and will depend on where the curves are evaluated.

EQUILIBRIUM WITH CONSTANT ELASTICITY DEMAND AND SUPPLY CURVES

To avoid the problems created when elasticities are constantly changing, economists frequently use demand and supply curves that have a constant elasticity at each point. One simple form of such demand and supply curves is

$$E_d = Aw^{\epsilon_d}$$

and

$$E_s = Bw^{\epsilon_s}$$

where $\varepsilon_d < 0$ and $\varepsilon_s > 0$ are the elasticities of demand and supply, respectively. Figure 6.2 shows a demand and supply curve with this form. These are not unreasonable shapes for the labor market. The slope of the demand curve is consistent with the marginal rates of technical substitution we saw in Chapter 4. As employment falls (due to rising wages), it gets harder and harder to replace the few remaining workers no matter what happens to wages. Similarly, the shape of the supply curve is consistent with the typical pattern of income and substitution effects we saw in Chapter 2, with income effects becoming increasingly important at higher wages.

These demand and supply curves have the convenient property of being linear if we rewrite them by taking the natural logarithm of each side, giving

$$\ln E_d = \ln A + \epsilon_d \ln w$$

and

$$\ln E_s = \ln B + \epsilon_s \ln w.$$

Once again, the equilibrium wage and employment level can be found by equating demand and supply:

$$\ln A + \epsilon_d \ln w = \ln B + \epsilon_s \ln w,$$

which, after rearranging terms and solving for w, gives

$$\ln w^* = \frac{\ln A - \ln B}{\epsilon_s - \epsilon_d}.$$

Substituting this equation into either the demand or the supply curve yields the equilibrium level of employment

$$\ln E^* = \frac{\ln A\epsilon_s - \ln B\epsilon_d}{\epsilon_s - \epsilon_d}.$$

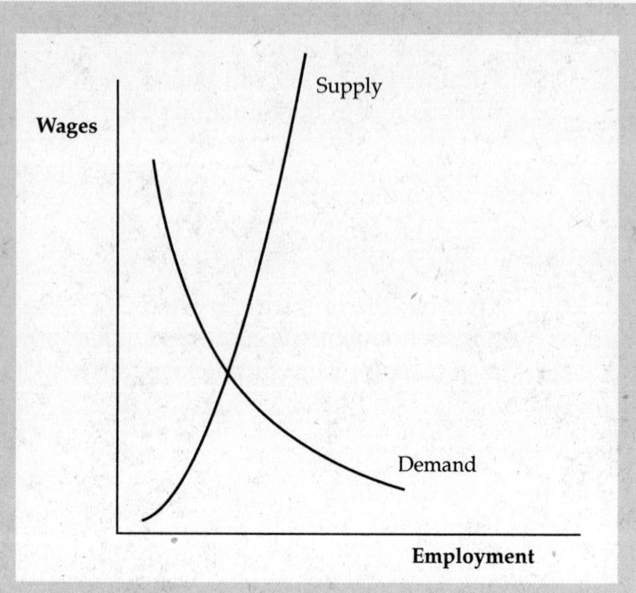

FIGURE 6.2 CONSTANT ELASTICITY DEMAND AND SUPPLY CURVES

A supply curve with constant elasticity exhibits an increasing income effect at higher wages but is not backward-bending. A demand curve with constant elasticity exhibits a diminishing marginal rate of substitution of labor for capital as more capital is used in production.

LONG-RUN IMPACT—AN EXAMPLE

The virtue of using the forms of the supply and demand curves discussed above can be seen when we want to analyze the impact of various changes on the labor market. For example, suppose we wanted to see what happens if the supply of labor falls by a given percent. This proposition is equivalent to multiplying the supply equation by one minus this percentage. (For example, if supply were 40 percent less at every wage, we would multiply B in the supply equation by 0.6.) Call this multiplier m and rewrite the supply equation as

$$E_{s'} = mBw^{\epsilon_s},$$

Linearized in logs this is

$$\ln E_s = \ln m + \ln B + \epsilon_s \ln w,$$

which gives the new equilibrium wage

$$\ln w^{*n} = \frac{\ln A - \ln m - \ln B}{\epsilon_s - \epsilon_d}$$

The change in the log of the wage is

$$\ln w^{*n} - \ln w^{*o} = \frac{-\ln m}{\epsilon_s - \epsilon_d}$$

Taking the anti-logs of each side gives

$$\frac{w^{*n}}{w^{*o}} = e^{(-\ln m/(\epsilon_s - \epsilon_d))}$$

Now use the approximation $e^y \approx (1 + y)$ if y is small to get

$$\frac{w^{*n}}{w^{*o}} = 1 + \frac{-\ln m}{\epsilon_s - \epsilon_d},$$

which, rearranging terms and substituting (w^{*o}/w^{*o}) for 1, gives a formula for the percentage change in wages:

$$\frac{w^{*n} - w^{*o}}{w^{*o}} = \frac{-\ln m}{\epsilon_s - \epsilon_d}.$$

Here is a specific example. One study has found the elasticity of labor supplied to U.S. manufacturing was 5.5 while the elasticity of demand for this sector was –0.55.[2] Thus, higher wages easily attract workers to manufacturing from other sectors, but firms find it relatively difficult to substitute other factors for labor in production. Suppose that the supply curve for labor to manufacturing fell by a massive 50 percent. Substituting these figures into our equation for the percentage change in wages gives

$$\frac{w^{*n} - w^{*o}}{w^{*o}} = \frac{-\ln(.5)}{5.5 - (-.55)} - \frac{-(-.693)}{5.85} = .118 = 11.8\%.$$

Thus, even though the supply of labor fell by 50 percent, the large elasticity along the new supply curve in response to increased wages means that actual wages only rose by about 12 percent.

An analogous equation exists for the change in employment. All that is needed, as can be seen by examining the formula for equilibrium employment in the previous section, is to multiply the log of the coefficient indicating the magnitude of the change in the demand or supply curve by the elasticity from the *other* equation. In our example of a 50 percent decrease in supply, –(ln (.5)) would be multiplied by the elasticity from the demand equation (–.55). Since –(ln(.5)) equals .693, the percentage decrease in employment is

---

[2]Richard Freeman, "Employment and Wage Adjustment Models in U.S. Manufacturing, 1950–1976," *Economic Forum* 11: 1–27 (1980).

$$\frac{E^*_n - E^*_o}{E^*_o} = \frac{(.693)(-.55)}{5.85} = \frac{-.381}{5.85} = -.0651 = -6.5\%.$$

The major effect of the decrease in supply is to raise the wage rate. Employment would fall more if the demand elasticity were greater and, for a given drop in supply, if the supply elasticity were lower.

In many cases we do not have estimates of supply and demand elasticities for an industry or occupation. Instead, the puzzle is to explain how changes in supply and demand interact to create changing wage and employment patterns over time. Figure 6.3 graphs the salaries of college professors relative to wages in the private sector. We graph an index that sets this ratio equal to 100 in 1959.[3] During the 1960s college professor's salaries rose slightly relative to wages of all nongovernment workers in the U.S. economy. Their relative salaries fell precipitously in the 1970s, dropping by nearly 20 percent when compared to economy-wide pay. From 1979, professors' pay rose again so that by 1990 it was higher relative to all workers' salaries than at any time since 1959. What explains the sharp downward trend and its subsequent reversal?

A complete approach would take the data on professors' salaries plus the number of professors, their fields, their ranks, and so on, and analyze them using multivariate regression analysis of a supply-demand framework like the equations shown above. We would look for factors that shifted the demand and supply curves so that we could identify the elasticities. Although we will not do a full analysis here, we can speculate on what might shift these curves. Good examples of demand curve determinants are measures such as college enrollment per capita, gifts to colleges, and real spending per student on higher education. Good examples of supply curve determinants are the number of students obtaining graduate degrees (since they form the pool of potential college professors) and salaries in other professions that PhDs could choose.

Just looking at some of these measures explains a lot about the causes of the trends in Figure 6.3. Although enrollment per capita doubled in the 1960s, it also rose during the 1970s, from 4.2 percent of the population to 5.3 percent, and then stayed roughly constant in the 1980s. This factor, therefore, does not fit the movement in professors' salaries. Real spending on higher education more than tripled during the 1960s, but it still increased by 30 percent in the 1970s and rose at the same rate per year through 1986. While these factors might explain the relative increase in salaries in the 1960s, they cannot explain the drop in the 1970s or the rise in the 1980s.

The best simple explanation goes back to our discussion of the rate of return to college education, which was high in the late 1960s, fell sharply in the 1970s, and rose substantially in the 1980s. The rate of return to college education is strongly positively correlated with the ratio of professors'

[3]These data are based on information from *AAUP Bulletin,* (Summer 1972), Figure II; *Academe,* (March–April 1991) Table I, and from *Economic Report of the President,* Table B–44.

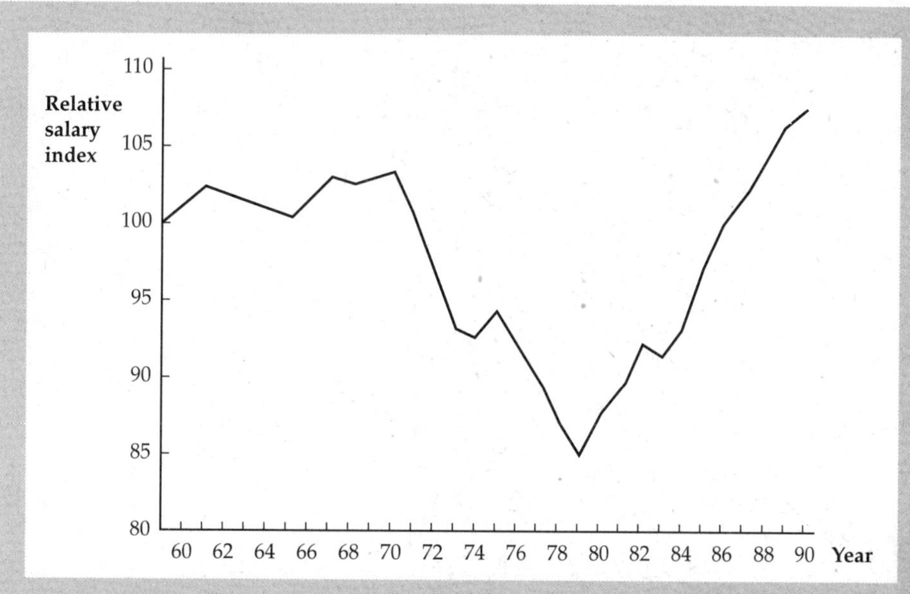

FIGURE 6.3 RELATIVE SALARIES OF PROFESSORS: 1959–1990
Professors' salaries fell when the relative incomes of college graduates were low in the 1970s, but rose in the 1980s when returns to education in other professions increased, thereby also increasing the opportunity cost of being a professor.

salaries to average wages. When it rose, alternatives for college students became more attractive and shifted the supply curve in this market to the left. Thus, wages of professors had to increase in order to attract students to go on to graduate school.

ADJUSTMENT LAGS AND CYCLES IN OCCUPATIONAL WAGE RATES

Changes between equilibria in labor markets do not occur instantaneously. As we saw in the discussion of supply and demand determinants in Chapters 2 and 5, both may respond to any new set of conditions with a lag. The evidence suggests that lags in demand are far shorter than those in supply. It is fairly easy to add workers to an existing plant. Even if a new plant must be built or new machines acquired, this can usually be accomplished within a year or two.

Workers are likely to perceive changed conditions more slowly. In many occupations years of training are required before a fully qualified work force is available. (Recall the difference between the short- and long-run supply curves in Figure 3.9.) When a change in some underlying condition shifts the demand or supply schedule, the difference in the time it takes them to adjust affects how employment and wages change in moving from the initial to the

POLICY ISSUE

WHO REALLY PAYS FOR YOUR SOCIAL SECURITY AND UNEMPLOYMENT INSURANCE?

In the United States, as in many developed countries, **payroll taxes** are often imposed on employment. Examples include the taxes used to finance Social Security, unemployment insurance, and workers' compensation. Congress frequently spends a great deal of time debating whether to impose these taxes on firms or on workers. Does this debate have any meaning or is it simply political posturing?

Figure 6.4 analyzes the impact of a payroll tax imposed to finance a government program. In Figure 6.4(a) we assume that *all* of the tax is imposed on firms. In other words, the law says that whatever wage they pay their employees, the firm must also pay a certain amount in taxes. Figure 6.4(b) assumes that *all* of the tax is imposed on the workers. They must pay a given amount in taxes to the government. Congress (and governments in other countries) seems to think that the first option will be better for workers, because it allows them to keep all of their wages, thus raising their income. Simple economic analysis using Figure 6.4 shows the fallacy of this reasoning. Such a conclusion relies on a hidden and erroneous assumption that wages are the same before and after the tax is imposed.

Examine first Figure 6.4(a). Suppose that the tax is a constant amount t for each hour worked. The effect of this tax is to increase the cost to the employer at any wage rate by an amount equal to t. It shifts the demand curve to the left and reduces demand. At every wage w on the **effective demand curve** in Figure 6.4(a), the quantity of employee-hours the firm demands is equal to what the firm would have demanded without the tax at wage $w + t$. The equilibrium without the tax is at point A with employment E_0 and wage w_0. The equilibrium with the tax is at point B with employment E_1 and wage w_E (where the subscript E indicates the wage received by the employee.) The labor cost to the firm is this wage *plus* the tax or w_F where $w_F = w_E + t$, however. The total amount of tax paid, the rectangle $w_E w_F CB$, is divided into a part born by the employer, $w_0 w_F CD$, and a part that falls on the employee, $w_E w_0 DB$. Of course, if the industry is competitive, profits before and after the tax must be zero, and the true division is between the portion of the tax born by the worker and the portion born by the consumer through higher prices.

In Figure 6.4(b) the tax is nominally paid by the employee. This situation results in a lower take-home wage and shifts the supply curve so that the number of employee-hours supplied at any wage is equal to what would have been supplied at a wage of $w - t$ without the tax. The equilibrium shifts from point A with employment E_0 and wage w_0 to point C with employment E_1 and wage w_F. Although each hour costs the firm w_F, the employee only gets to take home a wage of $w_E = w_F - t$.

The conclusion is striking and important. When a payroll tax is imposed, the effect of this tax on employment, labor costs to the firm, and take-home wages to the employee *does not depend on who is assessed the tax.* What does determine how much tax is paid by workers and how much by firms or consumers are the elasticities of the labor supply and demand curves. In Figure 6.5 we assume that the tax is nominally paid by the employer as in Figure 6.4(a). Figure 6.5(a) shows that when the supply of labor is very elastic while the demand for labor is inelastic, almost all of the tax falls on firms and consumers. On the other hand, as seen in Figure 6.5(b), when the supply of labor is inelastic and the demand for labor is elastic, most of the tax is paid by the worker. The same result would have been found had Congress nominally applied the tax to the worker.

If the supply elasticities for adult males listed in Chapter 2 characterize the economy as a whole, Figure 6.5(b) is a good description of the economy. With a nearly vertical supply curve, workers bear most of the burden of a payroll tax increase in the form of a lower wage rate than would otherwise exist. If the elasticities characterizing married women with young children are more typical, the situation depicted in Figure 6.5(a) is relevant. Employers must bear much of the burden in the form of higher labor costs per worker.

Substantial effort has been expended to estimate what actually happens to wage rates when payroll taxes are increased. Evidence from Sweden and the United Kingdom, both of which experienced rapid increases in payroll taxes in the 1970s, indicates that within a year after a payroll tax increase about half of the rise in labor costs had already been offset by lower wages. Evidence on the U.S. experience since World War II suggests a similar result.[4] Whatever the empirical evidence, the conclusion is clear: No matter who the government tries to make pay the tax, the actual **tax incidence** will be determined by the market through the interaction of elasticities of labor supply and demand.

final equilibrium. Lags in supply are especially important in markets such as highly skilled professions, where new entrants must commit themselves to long periods of training that will yield returns years later when market conditions may have changed drastically. As an example, take the market for lawyers. The decision to attend law school is made during a college student's senior year or before, but the new lawyer does not enter the job market until three years later.

Insights into the behavior of markets with lags can be derived from a very basic model. To keep things simple, assume that workers always believe that future wages will equal current wages. This assumption means that the supply of workers in any period depends on the wages of workers t years earlier, where t is the length of time needed to train for the occupation. (In this example, t would be the three years it takes to complete law school.) Again for simplicity, assume that there are no lags in demand and, therefore, that current demand for labor depends on current wages.

This market is depicted in Figure 6.6. Suppose the labor market is initially in equilibrium at point A with employment E_0 and wage w_0. What would happen if a new law were passed creating more grounds over which people could sue each other? This would increase the demand for lawyers at every wage, shifting the demand curve to the right. In the short run, the number of lawyers is fixed at E_0. Thus, the market would clear at point B on the demand

[4]Charles Beach and Frederick Balfour, "Towards Estimation of Payroll Tax Incidence" *Economica* 50: 35–48 (1983); Bertil Holmlund, "Payroll Taxes and Wage Inflation: The Swedish Experience," *Scandinavian Journal of Economics* 85: 1–15 (1983); Richard Dye, "Payroll Tax Effects on Wage Growth," *Eastern Economic Journal* 11: 89–100 (1985). OECD, *Employment Outlook* (various issues), discusses the incidence of the payroll tax in many developed countries, other studies are summarized in Table 5.1 of Daniel Hamermesh, *Labor Demand* Princeton, N.J.: Princeton University Press, (1993).

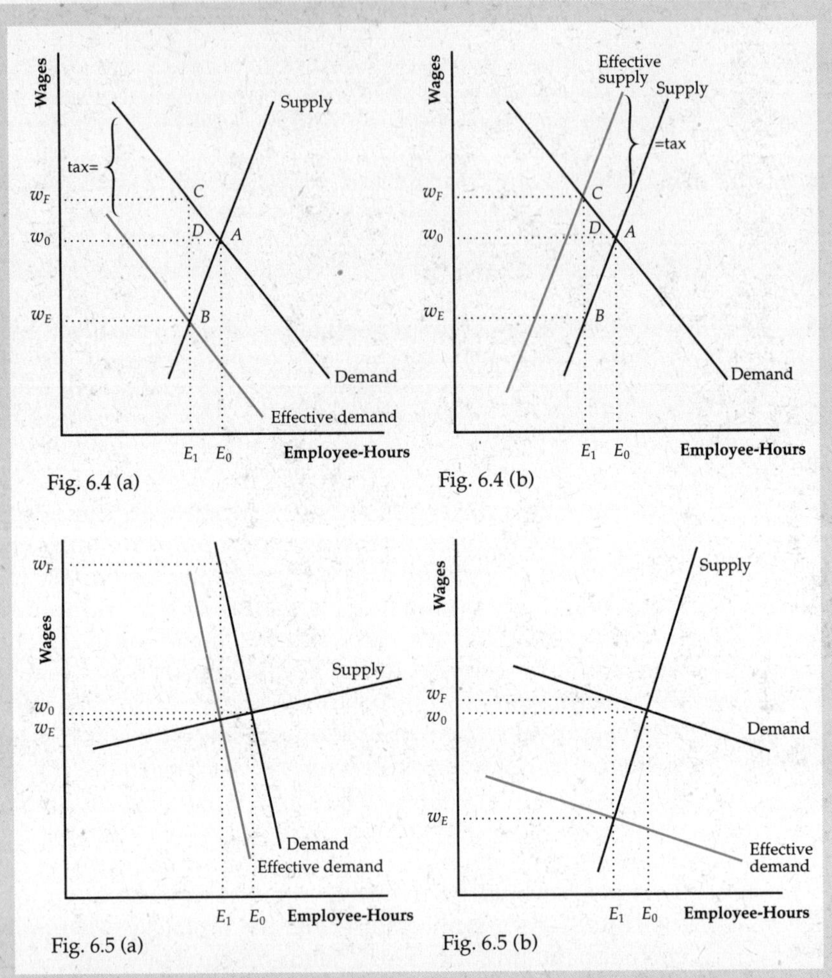

FIGURE 6.4 THE INCIDENCE OF PAYROLL TAXES

A payroll tax imposed on employers, as in Figure 6.4(a) reduces the demand for labor at every wage rate, shifting the demand curve down by the amount of the tax. Employment falls from E_0 to E_1 and wages fall from w_0 to w_E. If the tax is imposed on the worker, the labor supply curve shifts up as in Figure 6.4 (b). Employment again falls from E_0 to E_1. Wages rise from w_0 to w_F, but after taxes they again equal w_E. The actual incidence of the tax is not affected by on whom it is imposed.

FIGURE 6.5 DETERMINANTS OF THE INCIDENCE OF PAYROLL TAXES

With an elastic supply of labor but an inelastic demand, most of the burden of the tax falls on firms and consumers as in Figure 6.5 (a). When the situation is reversed with demand elastic and supply inelastic, the burden of the tax falls on workers as in Figure 6.5 (b).

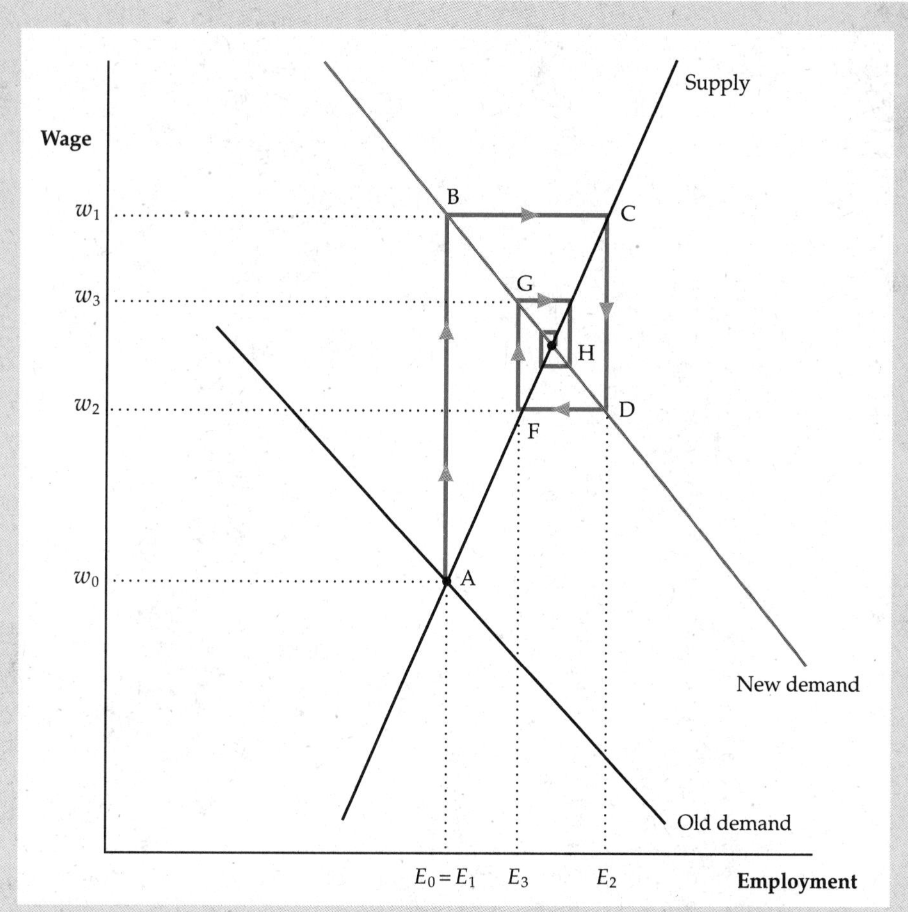

FIGURE 6.6 A MARKET WITH LAGS IN SUPPLY

If potential workers judge future wages on the basis of current wages, a shift in demand may create cycles in wages and employment around the new equilibrium level at *H*. The path of wage and employment dynamics (*A*→*B*→*C*→*D*→*E*→*F*→*G*→*H*) creates a pattern resembling a cobweb.

curve, and the wage would be w_1. Students, who expect this wage to be the same in the future, would want to supply E_2 workers at point *C* on the supply curve. When these E_2 lawyers come on the market, the only way they can find work is at point *D* with wage w_2. Believing that this wage will persist, students plan to supply E_3 lawyers in the next period, but when this period arrives the wage will rise to w_3 on the demand curve.

The spiral line with arrows in Figure 6.6 shows the path of wages and employment over time in this market. This **cobweb model** (so-called because the lines connecting points *A, B, C, D,* and *F* resemble a spider web) is a way to describe many professional occupations where there is a lag between the decision to train and the time when the formal training is completed. As Figure 6.6 is drawn, if there is no further shift in the demand or supply curves, wages and employment will converge to the new equilibrium at point *H*. They will cycle, going up and then down several times, but with a smaller swing each time, until the equilibrium is reached.

This does not have to happen. Figure 6.6 is drawn with the supply curve steeper than the demand curve, an assumption that need not hold. Suppose, instead, that supply was more elastic than demand for this occupation. In this case, the swings would be larger and larger in each period, and wages and employment would "explode" away from, rather than converge toward, the new equilibrium. Try to draw such a supply and demand curve, and see if you can trace out the path of wages and employment over time.

Cobwebs can arise in occupations where there is a long training period and where supply decisions are based on current market conditions rather than on good forecasts of future changes in returns to that training. We saw in Chapter 3 that higher wages induce people to enter occupations (i.e., they affect the supply of labor to the occupation). Unusually large growth in the number of entrants to an occupation reduces wages because the short-run supply curve shifts to the right. Data from the 1950s through the 1970s show that an extra 10 percent increase in the crop of new lawyers depressed starting salaries by 4 percent within a year. During the same period a 10-percent increase in the number of new physicists caused a 2-percent drop in the average salary.[5] The lagged responses mean that starting salaries in these markets fluctuate in cycles of lengths roughly equal to the time it takes to acquire the formal training specific to the occupation.

The importance of information about salaries and job opportunities is underlined by the cobweb phenomenon. If college students' expectations about future wages were **rational** (based on an accurate model that could predict future wages), fewer would choose to enter an occupation such as the law in response to a current high starting salary. They would realize that today's high salary indicates that salaries will be relatively lower when they graduate. Since cobwebs in salaries exist, students' wage expectations must not be fully rational. Studies have found that even professionals forecast future salaries badly.[6] Nonetheless, for some occupations including economists, lawyers, and teachers, evidence exists that potential entrants forecast well enough to take into account more than just the current salary in choos-

---

[5]Richard Freeman, *The Overeducated American*, N.Y.: Academic Press, (1976), p. 126, Richard Freeman, "Supply and Salary Adjustments to the Changing Science Manpower Market: Physics, 1948–1973," *American Economic Review* 65: 27–39 (1975).

[6]Jonathan Leonard, "Wage Expectations in the Labor Market: Survey Evidence on Rationality," *Review of Economics and Statistics* 64: 157–161 (1982).

ing occupations. This behavior keeps salary fluctuations below what they would be if potential entrants to the occupation were unaware of salary cycles and looked only at current starting salaries.[7]

SEARCH IN THE LABOR MARKET

So far we have treated labor markets as if the eventual equilibrium between supply and demand involved a single wage and employment level. In other words, in the market for a particular type of labor, all workers wanting employment were employed at a single market-clearing wage. In reality, this **law of one wage** is a poor characterization of labor markets. Apparently identical workers earn vastly different wages, and unemployment exists where not all workers who want to work at the available wages have a job. In order to explain these phenomena, economists have developed models of **search** in the labor market.

Search takes place in labor markets for two main reasons. First, even within one occupation many important differences exist among both workers and jobs. For example, within the narrowly defined occupation of order-processing clerks in high-technology industry in California in 1982, the average wage ranged from $4.30 to $11.80 per hour.[8] These differences may reflect more than just wages. Differences between jobs with the same title are often complex, multidimensional, and difficult to quantify. The fixed costs of employment discussed in Chapter 5 ensure that, in most cases, a person holds a job for a substantial period of time. A hiring transaction is a large one for both parties, more like buying a car than a loaf of bread, and for the worker a transaction that is not frequently repeated. When engaging in such large, nonrecurring transactions (rather than small, frequent ones) it makes sense to devote time and energy to searching if the available jobs have any differences in wages or characteristics.

CHANNELS OF JOB SEARCH

We begin our discussion of labor market search by examining the **channels of employment information** by which workers and firms learn about each other. It helps to classify search mechanisms along two dimensions:

---

[7] Dennis Hoffman and Stuart Low, "Rationality and the Decision to Invest in Economics," *Journal of Human Resources* 18: 480–496 (1983); Aloysius Siow, "Occupational Choice under Uncertainty," *Econometrica* 52: 631–646 (1984); Gary Zarkin, "Occupational Choice: An Application to the Market for Public School Teachers," *Quarterly Journal of Economics* 100: 409–446 (1985); Mark Berger, "Predicted Future Earnings and Choice of College Major," *Industrial and Labor Relations Review* 41: 418–429 (1988).

[8] Jonathan Leonard, "Carrots and Sticks: Pay, Supervision and Turnover," *Journal of Labor Economics* 5: S136–S152 (1987).

formal/informal and extensive/intensive. **Formal search** mechanisms are organized and structured. They frequently make use of **labor market intermediaries**. Examples of formal search methods include employment agencies, the public employment service, union hiring halls, and college placement offices. **Informal search** channels are more random and haphazard. They include referrals from present employees and *gate hiring,* where applicants responded to notices of vacancies posted on employers' premises, such as signs in restaurant windows saying, "dishwasher wanted." The most informal method of all is the walk-in, where the application is not solicited in any way.

Search processes also range from extensive to intensive. **Extensive search** involves making a lot of contacts but without devoting much time and energy to finding out about each possibility. You might, for example, decide to mail a résumé to every firm in your field in a city where you would like to live. **Intensive search**, on the other hand, involves relatively few contacts but a great deal of attention devoted to each one. You might spend time finding out the products, histories, and needs of a few companies and tailor a specific application letter to each firm. You might even try to find out if anyone you knew had a friend in the firm to whom they could recommend you.

There is no single "best" way to search for a job. Most workers use a variety of methods, and most firms find employees from several sources. The relative success of various methods will depend on the type of job and worker involved. Table 6.1 shows the methods used by unemployed job seekers in 1994. Job search methods are almost identical in Canada, with 65 percent of

TABLE 6.1 METHODS USED TO SEARCH FOR JOBS, UNEMPLOYED PERSONS BY AGE, 1994 (PERCENT USING THE METHOD)[a]

	Age							
	16–19	20–24	25–34	35–44	45–54	55–64	65+	Total
	Informal Search Method							
Friends or relatives	13.2	16.9	20.2	21.4	23.5	20.6	20.6	19.0
Gate applications	68.2	69.2	68.7	68.8	69.0	67.7	62.8	68.6
	Formal Search Method							
Public employment agency	10.3	21.2	22.6	25.0	24.4	30.5	13.5	20.6
Private agency	2.4	6.1	7.8	8.1	9.4	6.9	4.1	6.7
Placed or answered ads	13.4	20.9	24.0	25.7	25.8	23.8	22.2	22.1
Average number of methods used[b]	1.6	1.8	1.9	2.0	2.0	1.8	1.6	1.9

[a]Because many workers used more than one search method in a month, the sums of each column exceed 100 percent.

[b]Also includes mail applications, and other.

Source: *Employment and Earnings,* (January 1995), Table 33, p. 204.

unemployed searchers applying directly to firms; about 50 percent using the public employment service; 40 percent reading ads; and considerably smaller numbers relying on unions, friends and relatives, and private employment agencies.[9] Surprisingly, walk-ins are by far the most common form of search used in both the U.S. and Canada. Younger workers, who often have the fewest skills, rely especially heavily on unsolicited applications.

Among formal sources, private employment agencies are of greatest importance in white-collar markets. With the growth of white-collar employment, it is not surprising that private agencies have also expanded very rapidly. Between 1963 and 1982 the number of agencies tripled, and employment in the agencies quintupled.[10] A conspicuous characteristic of private agencies is their willingness to make substantial expenditures on advertising to attract applicants. Furthermore, in private agencies the payment of counselors on a commission basis gives the staff a strong incentive to make placements, although it sometimes encourages unethical practices such as attempting to recruit previously placed workers. As Table 6.1 indicates, however, few of the unemployed rely on these agencies. Those who do are most likely to be more mature workers who have the skills the agencies specialize in providing. Thus, the agencies primarily serve employed workers who are searching for a new job while employed.

Newspaper advertisements placed by employers reach a wide audience at relatively low cost. Table 6.1 shows they produce a large flow of applicants, none of whom has been screened. They are used, therefore, mostly in markets where labor is scarce, by large employers with personnel departments that can carry out screening, and for jobs where very little skill or screening is necessary. Some amount of preselection can be achieved by careful choice of newspapers. For example, specialty newspapers such as the *National Business Employment Weekly* have arisen to meet the needs of employers and workers searching in narrow occupations in a national market. All auditions for professional actors are advertised in one weekly newspaper, *Backstage,* and there is even a bimonthly publication that only lists job vacancies for PhD economists.

Among formal sources, the public employment service (state employment agency) would appear to have two great advantages. It charges no fees to either the employer or the employee, and it generally has the largest pool of information about unemployed workers and job vacancies. These advantages might be expected to give it a more central role than it actually plays. In neither the U.S. nor Western Europe is the public employment service a major source of job placements, probably because these agencies are asked simultaneously to fulfill two different and irreconcilable missions. On the one hand,

[9] Lars Osberg, "Fishing in Different Pools: Job-Search Strategies and Job-finding Success in Canada in the Early 1980s," *Journal of Labor Economics* 11: 348–386 (1993).

[10] Clive Bull, Oscar Ornati, and Piero Tedeschi, "Search, Hiring Strategies, and Labor Market Intermediaries," *Journal of Labor Economics* 5: S1–S17 (1987).

TABLE 6.2 AVERAGE WEEKLY JOB-SEARCH ACTIVITIES OF UNEMPLOYED PERSONS BY SEX, AGE, AND MARITAL STATUS, 1980

	Married Men	Married Women	Single Women	Youth
Employers contacted	2.6	1.9	2.2	2.0
Employers visited	1.8	1.3	1.5	1.5
Jobs applied for	1.4	1.2	1.4	1.4
Hours searching	14.4	9.3	10.8	9.2

Source: Michael Keeley and Philip Robins, "Government Programs, Job Search Requirements, and the Duration of Unemployment," *Journal of Labor Economics* 3: 347 (1985).

they are supposed to be labor market intermediaries, whose goal is to provide the best match between firms and workers. On the other hand, they are seen as social service agencies who should serve the unemployed and those who cannot otherwise find jobs. In recent years public assistance programs have increasingly required recipients to register with the public employment service in order to be eligible for benefits. This practice has led employers to suspect that public employment service counselors (who are paid fixed salaries rather than commissions for making successful matches) "deal from the bottom of the deck," sending the least attractive applicants who need the job the most, rather than the most attractive applicants who would be likely to find a job anyway. Knowing this fact, good workers are likely to avoid the public employment service so they will not be stigmatized as badly needing a job.

Not every contact with a potential employer yields a job offer. In two studies, one of young unemployed workers and another of unemployed workers of all ages, offers were received from about one-sixth of the employers contacted. Different channels of job search had sharply different chances of generating an offer. Relying on friends and relatives yielded the most offers per contact, while the state employment agency yielded the fewest. Contacts through friends and relatives were also most likely to result in the worker accepting a job, perhaps because friends and relatives are likely to have reliable information about both the job seeker and the opening that allows him or her to make especially good matches. They are also likely to provide inexpensive training and monitoring once a worker is hired. Evidence shows that workers recommended by current employees receive higher starting wages and last longer with firms than those hired by other means. Thus, this channel of information is apparently especially valuable, but as data in Table 6.1 show, these contacts are less readily available to youth than to older workers.[11]

[11] Harry Holzer, "Search Method Use by Unemployed Youth," *Journal of Labor Economics* 6: 1–20 (1988); David Blau and Philip Robins, "Job Search Outcomes for the Employed and Unemployed," *Journal of Political Economy* 98: 637–655 (1990); Curtis Simon and John Warner, "Matchmaker, Matchmaker: The Effect of Old Boy Networks on Job Match Quality, Earnings, and Tenure," *Journal of Labor Economics* 10: 306–329 (1992).

POLICY ISSUE

THE DANGERS OF APPEARING TO NEED A JOB

Evidence that a reputation for trying to place the workers most in need of a job rather than the most qualified applicants could hurt the effectiveness of the public employment service comes from an experiment conducted in the early 1980s in Dayton, Ohio. A sample of low-skilled unemployed workers was randomly divided into three groups. One group was provided with a voucher informing employers that if the worker were hired the government would provide the employer a tax credit of 50 percent of the worker's salary for the first year on the job (up to a maximum of $3000) and 25 percent of the second year's salary (up to $1500). The second group was given vouchers providing a cash payment to the employer of these amounts independent of the employer's tax liabilities. The third and final group was a **control group** that was given no subsidy at all.

It was expected that the vouchers, by lowering the cost of hiring workers in the first two groups, would increase their chances of finding a job. In fact, after six months, slightly less than 13 percent of these workers had found a job, compared to over 15 percent of the control group. Not only did the experiment fail to increase workers' chances of employment, it appeared to reduce them![12]

Why were firms more willing to hire the control group even though their net wages were up to 50 percent higher? Since the workers were randomly assigned to the three groups, there was on average no difference in their qualifications. Instead, by signalling that they were eligible for an employment subsidy, workers in the experimental groups apparently informed employers of their low quality and reduced their probability of getting a job. This finding is an excellent example of what is known as the **law of unintended consequences**. Often, programs designed with what appear to be the best intentions end up delivering perverse results unless all the incentives are analyzed very carefully.

Overall, unemployed workers contact substantial numbers of employers in their efforts to find work and spend a lot of time in the process. The data in Table 6.2 show that the typical unemployed married man contacts between two and three employers per week, and spends nearly 15 hours per week while searching. The number of contacts and the time spent in searching are less for single women, and less still among married women and youth.

SEARCH BY EMPLOYED WORKERS

Not all the workers who look for jobs are unemployed. Overall, in the U.S. about 20 percent of new hires come directly from other jobs, with the rest divided equally between those hired from the unemployed and those previously out of the labor force. In the United Kingdom as many about 40 percent of new hires come directly from other jobs. The figure for the rest of

[12]Gary Burtless, "Are Targeted Wage Subsidies Harmful? Evidence from a Wage Voucher Experiment," *Industrial and Labor Relations Review* 39: 105–114 (1985).

Europe is much lower, ranging from 7 percent in France to 17 percent in Germany.[13] Workers who are dissatisfied with their jobs for any reason may look for other positions while retaining their present ones. In the U.S. roughly one-third of the adult men who are searching are employed, as are one-fifth of adult women, but only 10 percent of youth. Ten percent of employed Americans report they have searched for other work during the previous year. Among young people (17 to 24) this figure rises to 19 percent for men and 16 percent for women. In the U.K in 1984 between 5 and 6 percent of employed workers were actively engaged in job search. Persons who want to work more hours per week than their current job allows are nearly twice as likely to search while employed. Those whose current job pays less than the wages of other workers with the same objective characteristics also search more. Obviously, since investments in specific human capital are less at the beginning of a worker's tenure with a firm, on-the-job search decreases the longer a worker has been with a firm.[14]

The cost of a search is reduced if people retain their jobs, since the major cost of searching while employed is the loss of leisure time rather than the loss of income. Of course, since employed workers already have a job, the potential benefits from searching are also lower. Table 6.3 presents a comparison of job search by a representative sample of employed and unemployed searchers. The data show that there is little difference in search effort by employment status *among those employed workers who choose to search*. The reduced costs and benefits appear to cancel each other out.

Is it better to search while employed or unemployed? The best way to compare the productivity of searching is to examine the success of these approaches. The second line of Table 6.3 shows clearly that those who search while employed obtain more offers per employer contacted. Moreover, as the third line shows, this large flow of offers allows the employed searcher to be more choosy about which one to accept. The same is not true among the few young workers who search while employed. They do no better than their unemployed counterparts. On the other hand, for workers of all ages a spell of unemployment between jobs is associated with greater wage gains in the subsequent job. It is not clear whether this result occurs because these work-

---

[13]Olivier Blanchard and Peter Diamond, "The Beveridge Curve," *Brookings Papers on Economic Activity*, 1–76 (1989); Richard Jackman, Richard Layard, and Christopher Pissarides, "On Vacancies," *Oxford Bulletin of Economics and Statistics* 51: 377–394 (1989); Michael Burda and C. Wyplosz, "Gross Worker and Job Flows in Europe," *European Economic Review* 38: 1287–1315 (1994); P. Gregg and J. Wadsworth, "Opportunity Knocks? Job Separations, Employment Inflows and Claimant Status in Britain," Centre for Economic Performance, London School of Economics Discussion Paper (1994); Christopher Pissarides, "Search Unemployment With On-the-Job Search," *Review of Economic Studies* 61: 457–475 (1994).

[14]Blau and Robins, "Job Search;" Matthew Black, "An Empirical Test of the Theory of On-the-Job Search," *Journal of Human Resources* 16: 132 (1981); Donald Parsons, "The Job Search Behavior of Employed Youth," *Review of Economics and Statistics* 73: 597–604 (1991); Christopher Pissarides and J. Wadsworth, "On-the-Job Search: Some Empirical Evidence for Britain," *European Economic Review* 38: 385–401 (1994).

TABLE 6.3 JOB SEARCH EFFORT AND SUCCESS, 1980

	Employed	Unemployed
Contact rate/week	2.18	2.11
Offers/contact	.24	.17
Acceptances/offer	.55	.67

Source: Blau and Robins, "Job Search;" Table 3.

ers have to be compensated for the time they spent unemployed, or because they are not a representative group and left particularly unattractive jobs, or because they are more effective searchers.[15]

A MODEL OF THE SEARCH PROCESS

Economists have developed several different models of how workers go about searching for a job.[16] All of them begin with the same fundamental insight:

> There are costs and benefits to search and it only pays to continue searching if the benefits you expect to receive from the additional time and resources devoted to search are greater than the costs.

There are both direct and opportunity costs involved in search. Direct costs include such items as bus or plane fares, gasoline, postage, telephone charges, fees for counselors who help write résumés, and the expense of newspaper ads placed by a worker.

There are two forms of opportunity costs involved with job search. The first is the value of the time the worker devotes to the search. As anyone who has recently looked for a job knows, the time involved in seeking out openings, making contacts, revising résumés, and attending interviews can be substantial. If the worker were not looking for a job she could be doing other things with this time—going to the movies, reading a book, jogging in the park. In any case, an opportunity cost a of job search is the utility she would have received from how she would otherwise have spent her leisure time. If she is searching for a new job while employed, one of the things she might have done with this time is to work more hours on her current job. In this case, the opportunity cost is the income she forgoes by searching rather than working.

---

[15]Lawrence Kahn and Stuart Low, "The Relative Effects of Employed and Unemployed Job Search," *Review of Economics and Statistics* 64: 234–241 (1982); Harry Holzer, "Job Search by Employed and Unemployed Youth," *Industrial and Labor Relations Review* 40: 601–611 (1987); John Antel, "The Wage Effects of Voluntary Labor Mobility With and Without Intervening Unemployment," *Industrial and Labor Relations Review* 44: 299–305 (1991).

[16]For early discussions of search, see George Stigler, "Information in the Labor Market," *Journal of Political Economy* 70: 94–105 (1962); John J. McCall, "Economics of Information and Job Search," *Quarterly Journal of Economics* 84: 113–126 (1970).

This observation leads to the second, more subtle opportunity cost of job search. Suppose an unemployed worker begins looking for a job. At some point he may be offered a job, but decides not to take it since he believes that if he looks a bit longer he can find a better opportunity. Now the opportunity cost of his continuing to search becomes the income he forfeits by not starting work immediately on the job he has been offered. The same is true of an employed worker who finds a better job than she currently has, but decides to hold out for an even better offer.

It should be clear from this discussion that, for most people in most situations, the largest component of search costs are the opportunity costs. Public policies designed to reduce the direct costs of search are likely to have little effect since these costs are typically low to begin with. On the other hand, public policies that reduce the opportunity costs of search are likely to have a major impact on the amount of search workers conduct. The most obvious example of a public policy that reduces the opportunity costs of search is unemployment insurance. By replacing some of a worker's income while he searches, this insurance significantly reduces the cost of not accepting the best job found to date.

Economists modelling the job search process have used several different assumptions about how the labor market works.[17] In this discussion we will act as if jobs differ only in the wages they offer. In reality, of course, they also differ in a number of other ways. We will return to these differences in Chapter 10. If we wanted to incorporate them here, all we would have to do is substitute the term *utility* for *wages* and recognize that a worker's utility is determined by her income and the other conditions on her job. Among the various issues about the market that must be addressed when modelling workers' job searches are the following.

1. What jobs are available? In other words, what is the distribution of wages among the available jobs? Each time a worker is offered a job, it can be regarded as one draw from this distribution of possibilities, just as when a card player takes a card, he is drawing from the distribution of cards in the deck. His chances of drawing an ace are higher the more aces there are in the deck.
2. Does the worker know the distribution of available wages when he starts searching or must he learn it as he goes along? You can imagine graduating from UCLA with a good idea of the wages paid engineers in California if your fraternity keeps records of what last year's brothers were offered. On the other hand, you can also imagine landing at L.A. International Airport as a personal trainer fresh off the beaches of Australia with no idea of the going rate for your talents in America.

[17] See Dale Mortensen, "Job Search and Labor Market Analysis," in Orley Ashenfelter and Richard Layard (eds.). *Handbook of Labor Economics,* Amsterdam: North Holland (1986) and Theresa Devine and Nicholas Kiefer, *Empirical Labor Economics: The Search Approach,* New York: Oxford University Press (1990).

3. What happens to a job offer once a worker receives it? If she does not accept it on the spot, is the opportunity given to someone else, or is the offer subject to **recall?** That is, can the worker return and accept any previous offer no matter how long ago it was made? Or is reality somewhere in between? If you return to accept an offer made some time ago, it may or may not still be available, with the probability decreasing the longer ago it was made.
4. What are the worker's alternatives? Is it easier or harder to search while employed? Having to go to work makes it harder to make contacts looking for a new job. On the other hand, being employed is a good signal that you are a reliable worker and may improve your chances of being offered a job. Another aspect is the income available if a worker turns down a job to continue the search. In particular, if unemployment benefits eventually run out, job seekers can be expected to search harder and be more likely to accept a job near this expiration date.

Evidence of the importance of unemployment benefit duration for job search behavior can be seen by comparing workers covered under different regimes or examining behavior when benefit periods change. In the U.S., the average length of unemployment was 18 weeks in the mid-1980s, while in Germany it was 46 weeks. Much of this disparity is apparently due to differences in the length of eligibility for unemployment benefits, which under normal conditions last for 26 weeks in the U.S. but a full year or more in Germany. By the late 1980s, Germany had increased the maximum length of benefits to 32 months for some workers. Unemployment rates and the average length of time unemployed workers in the covered groups spent looking for a job increased when this change occurred.[18]

In an extreme case, income limits can mean that the rule that a worker should continue to search if the benefit of doing so exceeds the cost might not predict behavior. For example, suppose that you *knew* with certainty that if you kept looking for three more months you would find a job that paid double the best offer you had to date, but that if you accepted a job now you would not be able to get this better job later. From a cost/benefit framework, it probably makes sense to hold out for the better job. But suppose you had no money left, no unemployment insurance, and three small children to feed. If you could borrow the money to live for the next three months, you would certainly do so and pay back the loan from your higher future income. Unemployed workers are not, however, particularly good credit risks, and if you are **capital market constrained** (meaning no one will lend you money) you might have to accept the best job you can find now even if the benefits from more search are clearly greater than the costs.

---

[18]Richard Layard, Stephen Nickell, and Richard Jackman, *Unemployment: Macroeconomic Performance and the Labour Market,* New York: Oxford University Press (1991); Jennifer Hunt, "The Effect of Unemployment Compensation on Unemployment Duration in Germany," *Journal of Labor Economics* 13: 88–120 (1995).

Of course, none of the characterizations of the search process outlined above is the "right" one, but rather, each describes a different part of the overall labor market. The search process of a teenager looking for a short-term, low-wage job during summer vacation will be very different from that of a college graduate looking to start a long-term career.

THE SIMPLEST MODEL OF JOB SEARCH

To understand job search better let us see how the world looks if we make some of the assumptions outlined above. The easiest world to understand is one in which

1. the worker knows exactly what jobs are potentially available;
2. once a job is discovered, it is always available;
3. the worker faces no capital market constraint, so she can continue to search as long as it is worthwhile; and
4. the worker can make only one job contact per period.

Figure 6.7 represents the distribution of wages for all the jobs that a particular worker with particular skills might be offered.[19] (It would look different for another worker.) These jobs are such that if the worker applied, she would receive an offer and be employed. The curve $f(W)$ is a *probability distribution* of wage offers. The area under the curve must sum to 1 (that is, it must contain all the available jobs). As drawn, there are some very good jobs that the worker might find, but there are also some very bad ones and a larger number of average jobs.

The highest possible wage that this worker could ever hope to get is shown as W_{max}. Obviously, if the worker knew which employer was offering that job she would simply go there, apply for the job, and work happily ever after. Unfortunately she doesn't know who is offering this job. All she can do is search.

A person who searches randomly simply makes contact (using no particular search strategy) with potential employers and sees what, if any, job is available. If p is the percent of employers who have job openings for which the worker is qualified, then the *expected* wage from the first job contact will be $p(W_{mean})$, where W_{mean} is the mean or average wage among those available to the worker. If $p(W_{mean})$ is greater than the costs of the first contact, the potential worker will make this contact. If it is not, the worker will stay out of the labor force (or on a current job).

Now suppose the worker has received an offer of a job at wage W_1. Should she accept this offer or continue looking? Once again she must com-

[19] To be precise, the wages in this figure are actually the present value of the incomes the worker would earn for the total period she worked on the job. We will, therefore, distinguish them from wages in each period by using a capital W.

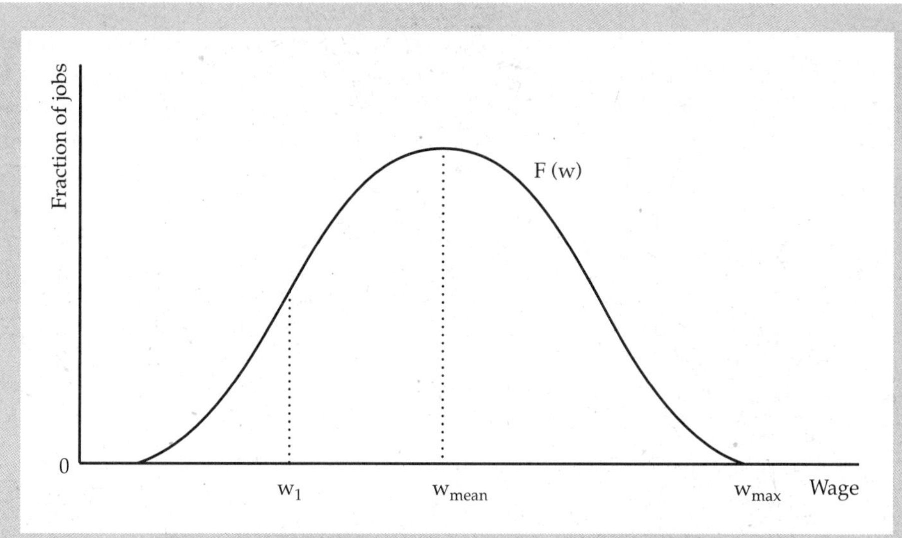

FIGURE 6.7 A DISTRIBUTION OF POTENTIAL WAGES
At any time a given worker may be offered many different wages on different jobs. The attempt to find a better wage motivates search and job turnover.

pare the costs and benefits of looking for another period. The costs now include the fact that she will not be earning the wage she has already found if she continues to look. (We assume potential damage to her reputation prevents her from taking the first job and quitting a month later if she finds a better one.)

What are the benefits of continuing to look? With recall, the first job will still be there if she wants it. Therefore, she will only accept the second job if it offers a wage higher than the first one. The expected benefit from another period of search is given by the formula

$$E(B_2) = p(1 - F(W_1))\,(E(W) \mid W > W_1) - w_1.$$

Although this formula may look complicated, it is easier if we break it down into four parts:

1. P (the fraction of employers with job openings for which this worker is qualified) is the probability that the contact will yield an offer.
2. $(1 - F(W_1))$ is the probability that, if the contact yields an offer, the wage will be greater than W_1. $F(W_1)$ represents the fraction of jobs with wages less than W_1. If 30 percent of jobs have wages less than W_1, then the only ones relevant here are the 70 percent with greater wages, so $(1 - F(W_1))$ would equal $(1 - .3)$ or $.7$.
3. $(E(W) \mid W > W_1)$ is just the expected (mean) wage *conditional* on only looking at the wages greater than W_1. Obviously, since we excluded all

the low wage jobs (with $W < W_1$), this conditional mean will be greater than W_{mean}, the mean wage for the entire distribution.

4. Since the worker already had a job offer of W_1, the benefits from this period of search are only the expected *increase* in her salary, so we subtract w_1 where we use lowercase w to remind us that this is only the earnings in one period, not the present value of lifetime earnings represented by uppercase W.

The issue of whether to search for subsequent periods can be analyzed in exactly the same way, only instead of W_1, all the expressions will have the highest wage found in *any* previous period. One subtle but important point is that after the first period, identical workers will not have the same costs and expected benefits from future search. Consider two workers who each face the same distribution $f(W)$ of potential jobs. By pure luck the outcomes of their first periods will differ. Some may not find a job at all, while wages will differ for those who do.

Of course, rational workers will not engage in random job search. Instead, they will first look at employers they think are especially likely to offer high-paying jobs. They will also start looking where costs of search are lowest, perhaps at employers near their home or where they already know people. The rule followed by such a rational searcher will be

> In each period look for a job at the remaining employer where the expected benefit less the cost is the greatest.

We have seen several reasons why the cost of additional search can be expected to rise and the expected benefit fall as the length of time the worker has been searching increases. Costs will rise because workers look at the least costly alternatives first; the longer they have been searching the higher will be the best wage they have already found (and, therefore, the greater will be the opportunity cost of further search); and, finally, the longer they search the more likely they are to have exhausted their unemployment benefits or savings. Similarly, the expected benefits from search will fall because workers will look at the most promising firms first; as the best wage they have already found increases over time, the possibilities of doing even better in future decrease; and, finally, the longer they search the shorter will be the remaining work life over which they can earn higher wages.

This pattern is depicted in Figure 6.8 by an increasing marginal cost of each additional contact, shown along the curve MC_0 and a decreasing marginal benefit of search curve, MB_0. Consider people who have contacted N_0 employers. Should they contact yet another one, or should they take the best offer so far? With only N_0 employers contacted, the benefits of investigating another opportunity exceed the costs of this extra contact by an amount AB. They should search out another opportunity. If they have already contacted N^* employers, however, they would be wise to take the best offer found to date. Although an additional contact may yield a very fine offer, the chances are slim. By failing to take the best offer already found, they are forgoing the certainty of a fairly high wage and also spending more time and money look-

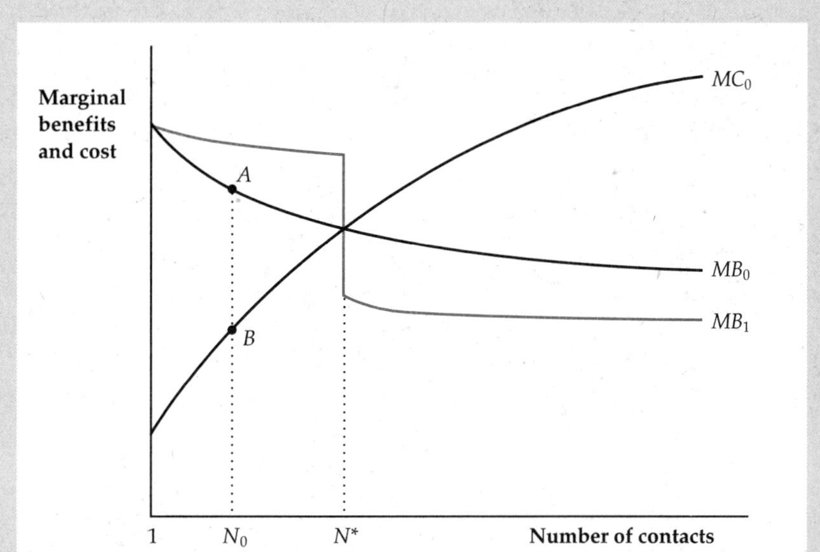

FIGURE 6.8 THE COSTS AND BENEFITS OF SEARCH
The marginal cost of searching will increase as low-cost prospects have been investigated and income constraints become more binding. Meanwhile, the benefits from additional search will fall as the best opportunities have already been investigated and as the quality of the best job already found increases, leaving less room for improvement. After N^* it will not pay to search any longer, and the worker will accept a job.

ing for work. In the example in Figure 6.8 it does not pay to search over more than N^* employers. Going beyond N^* contacts produces $MB_0 < MC_0$. While the worker will, on average, gain from another contact, the expected gain is less than the certain expenses of searching and the certain loss of wages.

The marginal benefit and cost curves in Figure 6.8 are smooth, reflecting the average opportunities of a large group of workers during their searches. For any individual worker, however, the marginal benefit curve is not likely to be smooth. As discussed above, each contact may or may not yield an offer. The marginal benefit curve may decline slowly during those periods when no offers are forthcoming, but on any given contact a worker may receive an excellent offer. At this point the marginal benefit to another contact falls sharply. The pattern for a worker who initially receives no (or very poor) offers but then receives an excellent offer on contact N^*, is shown by MB_1 in Figure 6.8. The marginal benefit curve has now fallen so far that it drops below the marginal cost, and the worker takes the job offered. This case is more realistic than that depicted by the smooth marginal benefit and cost curves. It still shows, however, that additional search reduces the marginal benefit from even more search.

The marginal benefits to search vary among labor markets, at different times, and for different people depending on their circumstances. The demographic differences in search intensity seen in Table 6.2 are consistent with this view. Among those groups of workers seeking jobs that are expected to last longer (especially married men) search is more intense, suggesting that for them MB_0 is higher. The costs of search will also vary with the density of the labor market. In a larger labor market where many employers are in close proximity MC_0 is lower, reflecting the fact that it takes less additional time and money to investigate another opportunity. In such markets, workers can be expected to engage in more search before they accept a job. Indeed, unemployed workers who reside in metropolitan areas in the U.S. contact significantly more employers during a month of unemployment than otherwise identical unemployed workers who do not live in urban areas.[20]

MORE COMPLEX MODELS OF JOB SEARCH

What happens if we change the assumptions used to derive the simple model of job search described above? The answer is: "Not much." For example, if a worker does not know the distribution of available jobs, each contact produces some information about what jobs are available. This information has value and increases the marginal benefit from search. As we have already discussed, borrowing constraints increase the marginal costs of search, especially as they come closer to binding (i.e., when the worker's savings begin to run out). If a worker can make more than one contact per period, then decisions have to be made about both how long and how hard to search, but the principle remains of continuing to search as long as the marginal benefit from increased time or increased intensity exceeds the marginal cost.

When job offers may be filled by others if a worker does not accept them immediately, an additional level of uncertainty is introduced. Imagine the extreme case, where if a worker does not accept a job the moment it is offered, it is gone forever. Seeing the labor market this way naturally leads to an alternative way of describing the search process. When the worker receives a job offer he compares it to a minimum acceptable offer called his **asking wage** or **acceptance wage**.[21] If the offered wage is greater than this asking wage, he takes the job. If not, he turns it down and keeps searching.

Cost/benefit comparisons still underlie this asking-wage analysis. In making each decision about whether to accept a job, the worker is comparing the costs with the benefits of continuing to search. In the extreme case, the bene-

[20] Robert Chirinko, "An Empirical Investigation of the Returns to Search," *American Economic Review* 72: 498–501 (1982).

[21] In the context of job search models this minimum acceptable wage is frequently called the *reservation wage*. We have chosen to use the somewhat less common term, *asking wage,* in order not to create confusion with the related, but somewhat different meaning of reservation wage as used in Chapter 1.

POLICY ISSUE

PAYING THE UNEMPLOYED TO TAKE JOBS

Unemployment insurance (UI) is paid in the U.S. to qualified job losers. In 1993 these transfer payments amounted to more than $35 billion. One of the conditions for receiving them is an active search for work. Recipients must demonstrate to local officials that they have contacted employers. These requirements should increase the amount of search undertaken by beneficiaries, resulting in quicker reemployment.

On the other hand, unemployment insurance provides a means of support that reduces incentives to look for work. Recipients know that they will receive as much as 50 percent of their previous earnings after taxes. This situation reduces the marginal benefit of contacting employers. With a reduced benefit from searching, the amount of search undertaken will decline.

Since UI payments have conflicting effects on the recipients' search behavior, the net effect must be determined by examining how unemployed workers actually react. The answer seems quite clear. Workers who receive UI payments search less intensely than similar unemployed workers. One study found that the average worker receiving UI searched 1.6 fewer hours per week than unemployed workers who did not receive payments. Among people who received UI, those whose benefits represented a greater fraction of their prior wages searched less. Another analysis suggests that this effect is strongest for married men, with UI benefits having essentially no impact on the search time of women. Analysis of the same data showed that UI recipients use more methods of looking for work, but contact fewer employers per time period. This finding probably results from the requirement that people receiving benefits must use the state employment agency to seek work.[22]

The net effect of the unemployment insurance program is to diminish weekly search efforts by unemployed workers. Partly in recognition of this problem, a number of European countries and several U.S. states have experimented with attempts to "cash out" UI benefits. If somebody receiving benefits gets a job early during a spell of unemployment (in Illinois, within the first 11 weeks), they receive a bonus (in Illinois, $500). In terms of our analysis, MB_0 is raised for the first 11 weeks by the payout of UI benefits conditional on taking a job. This incentive should increase search effort and the likelihood of finding a job in the first period.

Is the bonus effective in getting people to search more? Research has concentrated on whether people eligible for the bonus spend less time unemployed compared to a control group of otherwise identical people not eligible for the bonus. Studies of the bonus in Illinois and New Jersey suggest that it reduced the average time of receiving UI benefits by about one week (about 5 percent).[23]

---

[22]John Barron and Wesley Mellow, "Search Effort in the Labor Market," *Journal of Human Resources* 14: 389–404 (1979); Frederick Tannery, "Search Effort and Unemployment Insurance Reconsidered," *Journal of Human Resources* 18: 432–440 (1983); Michael Keeley and Philip Robins, "Government Programs, Job Search Requirements, and the Duration of Unemployment," *Journal of Labor Economics* 3: 337–362 (1985); and Blau and Robins, "Job Search."

[23]Stephen Woodbury and Robert Spiegelman, "Bonuses to Workers and Employers to Reduce Unemployment: Randomized Trials in Illinois," *American Economic Review* 77: 513–530 (1987); Patricia Anderson, Walter Corson, and Paul Decker, "The New Jersey Unemployment Insurance Reemployment Demonstration Project Follow-Up Report," U.S. Department of Labor, Unemployment Insurance Occasional Paper 91–1 (1991); Patricia Anderson, "Time-varying Effects of Recall Expectation, a Reemployment Bonus, and Job Counseling on Unemployment Durations," *Journal of Labor Economics* 10: 99–115 (1992).

fits will generally be lower than if jobs remained open, since the next contact might result in a job offer at a lower wage than the current offer, which will no longer be available. The costs will generally be lower also, since the opportunity cost of continued search is simply the current offered wage, rather than the *best* offer received to date.

In setting the asking wage, the worker is also making a cost/benefit calculation. Picking a high asking wage has a benefit. When a job is accepted, earnings will be higher for the rest of the working life, but it also has a cost. The higher the asking wage, the longer it will take to receive an offer that exceeds this wage.

Typically, asking wages are revised downward during search to be more consistent with offers received. Most workers begin their search with overly optimistic views about what might be available for them. (In technical terms, they believe the distribution of wages shown in Figure 6.7 lies to the right of where it actually is.) Strong evidence suggests that workers base their initial asking wages on previous wages, which include returns on both general and specific training, rather than only on their general training attractive to other employers. As they contact more employers, searchers acquire more realistic information about their alternatives, and their asking wage drops. This effect is magnified by financial pressures as savings are exhausted. Generally, the fall in asking wages is relatively rapid at the beginning of the search process, but becomes more gradual as workers learn the relevant range of job offers. After that, they are unwilling to cut their asking wages as rapidly, perhaps because their search effort has convinced them that their revised asking wage is within the range of offers they are likely to receive. This pattern changes again when a worker's savings or unemployment benefits are about to run out. Then workers feel intense pressure to find a job and cut their asking wages rapidly. A decline in the asking wage has been noted among people searching for work in studies of the U.S. and the U.K.[24]

The asking wage schedule differs among workers. Higher unemployment benefits shift the asking-wage schedule upward. Evidence for the U.S. and the Netherlands shows that they reduce job searchers' incentives to lower their asking wages to levels consistent with finding work quickly. Married men's asking wages fall more rapidly than those of otherwise identical single men, because family responsibilities require them to become reemployed more quickly. People who have had more stable employment,

---

[24]Nicholas Kiefer and George Neumann, "An Empirical Job-Search Model, with a Test of the Constant Reservation-Wage Hypothesis," *Journal of Political Economy* 87: 89–108 (1979); Steven Sandell, "Job Search by Unemployed Women: Determinants of the Asking Wage," *Industrial and Labor Relations Review* 32: 368–378 (1980); William Barnes, "Job Search Models, the Duration of Unemployment, and the Asking Wage: Some Empirical Evidence," *Journal of Human Resources* 10: 230–240 (1975); Stephen Jones, "The Relationship between Unemployment Spells and Reservation Wages as a Test of Search Theory," *Quarterly Journal of Economics* 103: 741–767 (1988).

and who presumably seek such employment again, have asking wages that fall less rapidly.[25]

Search by more than one worker can create economic inefficiencies. Problems of **economic rivalry** exist when several agents strive to achieve a common goal with all the benefits going to the first one to reach it. Each searcher will pick an intensity based on his own costs and benefits. An externality results because each worker ignores the costs imposed on other job applicants when increases in his search intensity reduce their probability of finding an attractive job. Programs such as unemployment insurance that reduce workers' search intensity can, in such cases, improve overall economic welfare.

SEARCH BY EMPLOYERS

Employers with vacancies to fill also engage in search. Although the process is also based on cost/benefit analyses, it appears that the strategy followed by employers is somewhat different than that followed by employees. When a firm has or anticipates having an opening, it typically attempts to generate a large pool of applicants at one time. One study has found that 76 percent of all vacancies are filled by applicants who contacted a firm within *two weeks* of a vacancy being posted. On average, however, it took nearly three months to hire one of these applicants for the open job.[26] This finding suggests that employers prefer a strategy designed to reveal the entire distribution of available applicants at once, to a **sequential learning** strategy of evaluating one applicant at a time.

Once the pool of applicants is known, employers devote far more resources to evaluation and selection than they did to generating the initial pool. This difference in strategies makes sense if there is more uncertainty among employers about the quality of applicants than there is among workers about the quality of jobs. Only if none of the applicants meets the firm's minimum **hiring standard** will the firm reopen the search and attempt to generate more applicants. Indeed, the study cited above found that the number of applicants for vacant jobs falls rapidly after the first weeks the job is available but then *increases* if the job has not been filled within three months.

Employers who offer low wages have to search longer and often have to use more expensive channels of recruiting, such as paying employment agencies for referrals, than employers who offer high wages. High-wage employers can choose among the many good applicants who present themselves as

[25] Dirk Gorter, "The Relation between Unemployment Benefit, the Reservation Wage and Search Duration," *Oxford Bulletin of Economics and Statistics* 55: 199–214 (1993); Kiefer and Neumann, op. cit.; John Warner, J. Carl Poindexter, and Robert Fearn, "Employer-Employee Interaction and the Duration of Unemployment," *Quarterly Journal of Economics* 94: 211–234 (1980).

[26] Jan van Ours and Geert Ridder, "Vacancies and the Recruitment of New Employees," *Journal of Labor Economics* 10: 138–155 (1992).

soon as it is known that they have vacancies. For example, a study of various-sized employers found that larger firms attract more applicants per vacant position, possibly because they also pay higher wages.[27] Thus, high wage costs are to some extent offset by lower costs of recruitment, screening, and training. But there is no reason to expect the offset to be complete, particularly where the high-wage employers are required by collective bargaining agreements to pay more than they would choose to pay in the absence of unions.

Employers who have trouble attracting applicants will eventually have to lower their hiring standards. Among otherwise identical employers, those with smaller flows of applicants have been found to spend fewer resources per applicant in screening. In economic booms, when very few high-quality workers are likely to be unemployed, such firms take longer to fill each vacancy, perhaps because they need time to bring their hiring standards into line with the characteristics of available workers.[28] Implicitly, employers react to the difficulty of hiring by lowering the asking quality for positions they are trying to fill.

EQUILIBRIUM IN THE LABOR MARKET

When underlying demand or supply forces change, search by employers and by both employed and unemployed workers brings about a new equilibrium in a competitive labor market. Search is the process that leads wages in competitive markets to change.

We have presented some simple models of the search process. In reality the process is far more complex and can best be described as one of matching employers offering a position with multiple dimensions to workers whose characteristics and tastes for various aspects of jobs differ. This matching takes place under conditions where workers are partly ignorant of the full range of offered wages, and employers lack perfect knowledge of their appli-

---

[27] John Barron, Dan Black, and Mark Loewenstein, "Employer Size: The Implications for Search, Training, Capital Investment, Starting Wages and Wage Growth," *Journal of Labor Economics* 5: 76–89 (1987). The hypothesis that employers can substitute search costs for wages was first advanced by George Stigler in "Information in the Labor Market," *Journal of Political Economy* 70: S94–S105 (1962). Other results that tend to confirm the hypothesis are in Albert Rees and George P. Shultz, *Workers and Wages in an Urban Labor Market,* Chicago: University of Chicago Press, (1970), pp. 207–210.

[28] John Barron and John Bishop, "Extensive Search, Intensive Search and Hiring Costs: New Evidence on Employer Hiring Activity," *Economic Inquiry* 23: 363–382 (1985); Jan van Ours and Geert Ridder, "Cyclical Variation in Vacancy Durations and Vacancy Flows: An Empirical Analysis," *European Economic Review* 35: 1143–1155 (1991).

cants' reservation wages. This mutual ignorance is one of the reasons for the wide range of wages observed for workers in the same occupation within a single geographic labor market.[29] Nevertheless, the basic process is always one of workers and firms searching and making decisions by comparing costs and benefits. The wage and the quality of workers are important determinants of the search and matching process. A narrow range of wages and hiring standards reflects either less dispersed distributions of job and worker quality or a greater amount of information on the part of employers and workers.

Consider the response to an outward shift in employers' labor-demand schedules caused by an increase in product demand. Employers find that the wages they are offering are not sufficient to attract enough acceptable applicants to both replace employees leaving the firm and to expand employment by the amount dictated by increased product demand. Finding an insufficient flow of new workers, employers will raise the wage offer somewhat to attract workers of the desired quality. Simultaneously, they may reduce their hiring standards. Both actions increase the flow of acceptable workers to the firm. Eventually part of the additional demand for labor is met, and part is choked off by the higher wage that employers must now pay. An increase in total employment is produced by workers drawn into the labor market and by the fact that, with higher wages, workers spend less time searching. The system is back in equilibrium, with higher wages, more workers employed, and a higher asking wage of those workers engaged in job search reflecting the now higher distribution of wages being paid.

The process works similarly if some event changes the supply of labor to a particular market. Assume that the supply decreases because of an increase in wages in occupations that workers regard as alternatives. We offered this explanation for the increase in professors' salaries during the 1980s shown in Figure 6.3. Employers will find that too few of their wage offers are being accepted to maintain a work force of the desired quality. Just as when the demand for labor rises, employers will reduce the hiring standards, offer higher wages to increase the acceptance of jobs by workers who are searching, and so forth. The new equilibrium will be established with a higher distribution of wage rates offered in the market and a higher level of asking wages by those workers who search in this market. Because the amount of labor demanded has dropped due to the increase in wages, employers will search for fewer workers.[30]

---

[29] Solomon Polachek and Bong Joon Yoon, "A Two-Tiered Earnings Frontier Estimation of Employer and Employee Information in the Labor Market," *Review of Economics and Statistics* 69: 296–302 (1987).

[30] Dale Mortensen, "Job Search, the Duration of Unemployment and the Phillips Curve," *American Economic Review* 60: 847–862 (1970) describes this process.

SUMMARY

After market conditions change, competitive labor markets move toward equilibrium through a process of workers and employers revising the wages they seek or offer. The long-run impact on wages is smaller the larger the elasticities of demand and supply in a particular labor market. The long-run effect on employment of demand shifts increases with the elasticity of supply. The long-run impact of supply shifts is greater when demand elasticity is larger. Substantial lags resulting from a slow rate of supply adjustment may cause short-run employment and wage changes to cycle around the eventual impacts of the altered market conditions.

Labor market adjustments take place because workers search for new jobs and employers search for new workers. Both employed and unemployed workers engage in substantial amounts of search activity. The information upon which their search is based comes from a variety of formal and informal sources. Formal sources, such as advertisements and private employment agencies, are more important in markets for white-collar workers. Informal sources, such as referrals by other employees, are relied upon more in markets for blue-collar labor.

Search behavior is based on comparing the costs and benefits of accepting the best job (or worker) currently available with those from continued search. Search entails frequent revision of wages that are offered and sought, even when market conditions are not changing. Workers who have been unemployed for a while will lower their asking wages, while employers with unfilled vacancies will raise their wage offers or reduce hiring standards. When the labor market is tighter, employers raise their offered wages or lower their hiring standards. Workers are induced to take jobs earlier than they would otherwise. When labor markets are loose, employers, finding that their job offers are being accepted more readily, offer wages below what they had planned or raise their hiring standards. Any change in demand or supply conditions will change the search behavior of both workers and employers.

QUESTIONS AND PROBLEMS

6.1 The government decides that there are too few economists in the U.S. and undertakes to train an additional 6,000 economists. Currently there are 30,000 economists in the country, earning on average $50,000 per year. Assume that, if nothing else changes, an increase in the wage rate of 1 percent reduces employers' demands for economists by 0.75 percent; a similar increase in the wage rate increases the number of people willing to become economists by 1.25 percent. Help your professor by analyzing the impact of the government program on his or her current earnings. Help the government by calculating the net effect on the number of economists employed of this attempt to increase supply by 6,000.

6.2 Suppose the market for court reporters is characterized by

$$L_d = 50{,}000 - w$$

and

$$L_s = w_{-1}$$

where "–1" denotes the previous year. Assuming the wage in 1992 was $30,000, fill in the table below:

Year	Number Employed	Wage
1993		
1994		
1995		

Is there an equilibrium wage in this example? Will it ever be reached? What should a smart potential court reporter do given the strange nature of this market?

6.3 A standard justification for government intervention in a market is that individuals and firms are unable to take into account all the benefits or costs of their actions. With this in mind, discuss reasons why taxpayers should subsidize the placement of workers through the employment service.

6.4 Suppose you are given the following information on the number of possible contacts with employers that an unemployed worker may make in a week. How many contacts should the worker make and why?

Contacts	Benefit from Another Contact	Cost of Making Another Contact
1	$15	$3
2	12	7
3	10	10
4	9	12
5	8	13
6	7	14

6.5 One study of the market for state and local government employees found that the supply elasticity to this market was $\varepsilon_s = 2.0$, whereas the elasticity of demand in the market was $\varepsilon_d = -0.53$.[31] Suppose that new programs increased the demand for government workers by 10 percent. What would be the impact on wages and employment in the state and local government sector?

6.6 Suppose the U.S. government was debating between two policies that advocates claimed would help the labor-market position of low-income workers. The first policy would increase the minimum wage by 25 percent. The second would offer a refundable earned-income tax credit equal to 25 percent of the earnings of workers who earned the minimum wage. Assume that all workers are covered by the minimum wage and that the tax credit could be financed by a national sales tax of 1 percent. Unemployed workers receive benefits equal to $100 a week. Analyze the impact of each policy on the employment and earnings of low-wage workers, as well as income inequality and the incomes and well-being of Americans in general.

6.7 All wages in Travail Valley fall between $6.00 and $12.00 an hour. The fraction of current job openings that pay each wage rate is shown below.

Wage	Fraction of Jobs
$6.00	10%
$7.00	20%
$8.00	20%
$9.00	20%
$10.00	15%
$11.00	10%
$12.00	5%

a. Suppose that each month yields exactly one job offer. What is the probability that one month of search will yield each possible wage rate? How long should a worker plan on searching to expect to find a wage of at least $6.00? How about $7.00 and so on?

b. If search costs $2000 a month, what is the expected cost to a worker of holding out for a job that pays each wage between $6.00 and $12.00?

c. Suppose that a job, once found, will last exactly three years and involve 2000 hours of work each year. As a worker, you must decide what wage will be high enough to induce you to stop

[31]Orley Ashenfelter "Demand and Supply Functions for State and Local Government Employment" in Orley Ashenfelter and Wallace Oates (eds.). *Essays in Labor Market Analysis* New York: Wiley, (1977), pp. 7–9.

searching and accept the offered job. Suppose you have found a job offering $8.00 an hour. Should you accept this job or look for another month? Show your calculations. How about if you had found a job paying $10.00?

6.8 What is likely to happen to the acceptance wage and the duration of job search when each of the following happens? Why?

a. Unemployment insurance payments increase.
b. The economy enters a recession so that it takes longer to generate each job offer.
c. The introduction of new industries reduces searchers' certainty about the characteristics of the jobs available.
d. Legislation is passed that increases the costs of layoffs, and, therefore, the average length of each employment spell increases.

6.9 Suppose that in a local labor market the labor demand and supply curves are:

$$Q^s(t) = 100\,w(t)$$

$$Q^d(t) = 800 - 100\,w(t).$$

a. What are the equilibrium wage rate and level of employment in this market?
b. Assuming the size of the labor force remains unchanged from its equilibrium level, what will the unemployment rate be if a minimum wage of $6.00 an hour is imposed on this market.
c. Describe the dynamics that would occur in this market if the initial labor supply curve were, instead

$$Q^s(t) = 100\,w(t-1)$$

and this curve then experiences an exogenous shift to

$$Q^s(t) = 150\,w(t-1).$$

6.10 Discuss the effects that each of the following is likely to have on the probability that an employed worker will engage in search for another job:

a. the local unemployment rate;
b. the worker's age;
c. the worker's education level;
d. the worker's tenure in her current job;
e. the growth in demand for the product of the firm where the worker is currently employed; and
f. the population (and employment) density of the area where the worker lives.

KEY WORDS

asking wage or acceptance wage
capital market constraint
channel of employment information
cobweb model
control group
dynamic analysis
economic rivalry
effective demand curve
extensive search
formal search
hiring standard
informal search
intensive search
labor market intermediaries
law of one wage
law of unintended consequences
payroll taxes
rational expectations
recall
search
sequential learning
tax incidence

7

MIGRATION AND TURNOVER

THE MAJOR QUESTIONS

- ▲ What characteristics make it more or less likely that workers will change locations or jobs?
- ▲ How do economic effects, in particular differences in wages and unemployment rates, affect mobility?
- ▲ What are the impacts of mobility on those who move and on places or business to which they move?
- ▲ Is mobility or its impact significantly affected by public policies?

GENERAL ISSUES

Migration between geographical areas and mobility between jobs are the primary manifestations of the search process. Although many considerations motivating the discussion of search underlie the analysis of mobility, there are issues specific to mobility that we did not cover in Chapter 6. The importance of migration, one major type of mobility, can be seen in Table 7.1, which lists the percentage of population that changed region of residence in each of two years in six developed countries. Even though differences in region size mean that the rates of migration are not strictly comparable between countries, two facts stand out. First, these annual percentages are quite large even though they exclude the substantial mobility that takes place within regions. (For example, in the U.S. migration within the New England states would not be counted in this table.) Second, they show a clear trend toward declining interregional migration. The importance of the second major form of migration, movement between countries, is indicated by Table 7.2 which shows the percentage of the population that is foreign-born for a number of countries.

The analysis of workers' decisions about changing jobs and/or locations is formally similar to the analysis of investment in schooling in Chapter 3.

TABLE 7.1 INTERNAL MIGRATION RATE (PERCENT CHANGING REGION) 1970, 1987

	1970	1987
United States	3.6	2.8
Australia	1.7	1.6
Canada	1.9	1.5
Germany	1.8	1.1
Italy	1.1	0.5
Japan	4.1	2.6

Source: OECD, *Employment Outlook*, (1990), Table 3.3.

TABLE 7.2 PERCENTAGE OF POPULATION FOREIGN BORN (1987 AND 1991)

	1987	1991
United States	6.2	7.9
Canada	16.1	15.6
Germany	6.9	7.3
United Kingdom	3.2	3.1
Sweden	4.8	5.7
Switzerland	14.9	17.1
Netherlands	4.0	4.8

Source: OECD, *Employment Outlook*, (1994), Table 4.10.

Consider a worker whose possible streams of future earnings are shown in Figure 7.1. He will earn a stream indicated by the profile E_0 if he remains where he is. If he moves to his best alternative job or location, his earnings will follow the profile E_1. For simplicity, we have defined earnings to include, in addition to labor income, the nonmonetary value of any other characteristics of the locations or firms. These differences might be things like climate or working conditions. If the worker moves, he will incur out-of-pocket costs equal to C. These costs must be compensated for through higher earnings over the worker's remaining work life. Earnings may be higher from the time of mobility (profile E_1^*), or they may be initially lower (profile E_1). These lower initial earnings may arise if the worker forfeits a large amount of specific human capital as a part of the move.

As in analyzing investment in education, we must discount the costs and returns back to the present. The out-of-pocket costs of moving (transportation, costs of job search, and others) must also be included in the cost/benefit calculation. In algebraic terms, the worker's decision involves comparing

$$Z_0 = \sum_{t=A}^{R_0} \frac{E_0}{(1+r)^{t-A}}$$

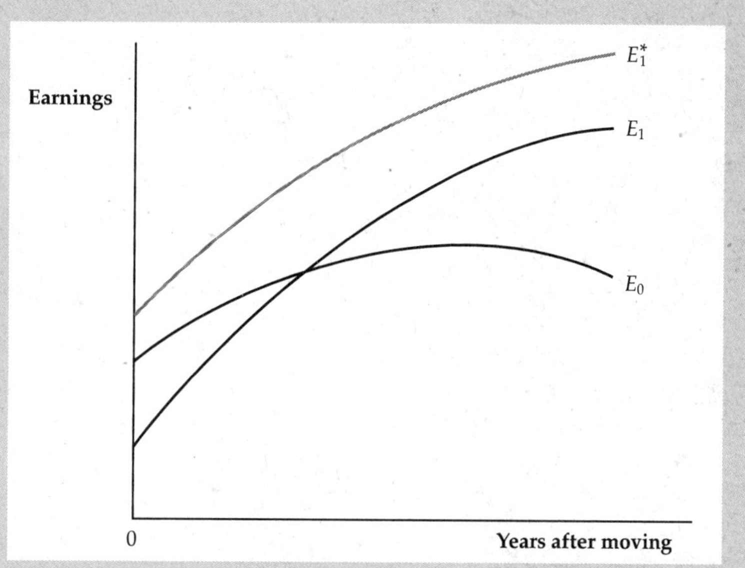

FIGURE 7.1 THE INDIVIDUAL'S MOBILITY CHOICE
Workers incur costs of changing employers or locations in order to receive benefits in terms of the higher earnings profiles E_1 or E_1^* as compared to E_0.

to

$$Z_1 = \sum_{t=A}^{R_1} \frac{E_1}{(1+r)^{t-A}}$$

where A = worker's current age
r = rate of discount
t = a particular year
C = out-of-pocket costs of mobility
R_i = worker's expected age of retirement in each job.

Actually, at any time a large number of potential moves are possible for any worker. Implicitly, he should make the above comparison for all possible moves and take the option where the difference is greatest. In practice, workers may only compare a few of the most likely options, using a **rule of thumb** to exclude the rest. The economic rule for examining possible moves is

> Move if the expected present value of earnings in the new job minus the costs of moving exceeds the present value of earnings in the current job. If this relationship is true for more than one potential move, take the option where the difference is greatest.

MIGRATION

It is immediately apparent that economic motives are important in migration decisions when there are large disparities in income levels. The tremendous flow of immigrants to the U.S. from southern and eastern Europe before World War I is a conspicuous example, as are the flows from Puerto Rico to the mainland U.S.; from Appalachia and the rural South to factories along the Great Lakes; from the West Indies, Pakistan, and India to the U.K. after World War II; and most recently from Mexico, the Caribbean, and Asia to the U.S. Little migration occurred in the opposite direction. Few Britons migrated to South Asia in the 1940s, and few Americans are migrating to Mexico or Asia now. Many of these immigration flows would have been larger or continued longer had they not been restricted through rigid control by the receiving countries. The flows after World War II also illustrate the role of costs. In many cases a prewar trickle became a large postwar flood when air transport became available at fares far below those of passenger ships.

INDIVIDUAL MIGRATION DECISIONS

Let us consider in more detail the predictions about the patterns and economic effects of migration that stem from the simple general theory of mobility presented above. In doing so we need to distinguish between **gross migration rates** (the percentage of a population that moves at all) and **net migration rates** (the difference between the percentage inflow and outflow from an area, country, or region). The data in Tables 7.1 through 7.3 measuring gross migration rates are important in understanding *who* is likely to migrate. Net migration rates are useful in describing the impact of migration on a labor market.

The theory in the previous section shows that the likelihood of migration will be greater among young workers. For them $Z_1 - Z_0$ may be large enough to overcome the costs of migrating because they have more working years to enjoy higher earnings in the new location. This prediction is borne out by the

TABLE 7.3 GROSS MIGRATION RATES BETWEEN U.S. COUNTIES, BY AGE AND EDUCATION 1991–1992 (IN PERCENT)

	Education (Years of Schooling)					
Age	0–8	9–11	12	13–15	16	17+
25–29	5.2	8.6	9.0	10.9	14.0	20.0
30–34	3.3	7.1	7.1	8.3	9.2	11.8
35–44	4.7	5.4	4.9	5.4	6.4	6.3
45–64	2.8	3.2	3.1	4.5	3.7	4.9

Source: Computed from *Current Population Reports* P–20, No. 473, Table 4.

data in Table 7.3. At each level of education, migration rates drop off sharply from a peak early in the work life. The probability of migrating is more than twice as high among young adults as it is among people 45 to 64.

The decline in migration rates with age is not due solely to differences in earnings streams resulting from a longer time horizon. With the same earnings difference, older workers are less likely to migrate. This finding points to the role of **psychic costs** in mobility. More than just money is involved in workers' calculations of migration costs. They also include the effects of leaving family, friends, and familiar surroundings for a strange and potentially hostile environment. The psychic costs of breaking these ties increase rapidly with age, so that the purely monetary return to migration increasingly overstates workers' perceived rates of return as they age.[1]

The higher migration rates of more educated workers shown in Table 7.3 reflect the fact that this labor market is national in scope. There are many fewer jobs in any one area for highly specialized workers (and many fewer such workers). In addition, differences in salaries between jobs are likely to be larger for more educated workers whose jobs are less standardized. Thus, it is worthwhile to search widely for these jobs.

How does the discussion in this section help to explain the decline in interregional mobility shown in Table 7.1? With better communication and improved less expensive transportation, migration rates should have risen over time, not fallen. During this period the average age of the population was rising, however, in some cases by as much as three years. This changing age structure is consistent with the observed downward trend in migration.

Greater income differentials, the distance between E_1 and E_0 in Figure 7.1, increase the amount of migration. For example, in the United Kingdom in 1984 each 1 percent wage increase in a particular region reduced the probability of out-migration by 4 percent. Similarly, regions of Sweden with wages 10 percent above national average attract a 5 percent greater influx of immigrants from other Scandinavian countries.[2]

THE ROLE OF UNCERTAINTY

The discussion of Figure 7.1 implies that workers know with certainty what the paths E_0 and E_1 look like. Clearly, they do not, or a $1 increase in expected income from their destination job would have the same positive effect on migration as a $1 decrease in income from their current job. Any migration, however, is fraught with *uncertainty about economic alternatives.* Workers

---

[1]Solomon Polachek and Francis Horvath, "A Life Cycle Approach to Migration," *Research in Labor Economics* 1: 103–149 (1977).

[2]Christopher Pissarides and Jonathan Wadsworth, "Unemployment and the Inter-Regional Mobility of Labour," *Economic Journal* 99: 739–755 (1989); Per Lundborg, "An Interpretation of the Effects of Age on Migration: Nordic Immigrants' Choice of Settlement in Sweden," *Southern Economic Journal* 58 (1991).

will attach substantially greater uncertainty to income prospects in other areas than to those in their current homes, and this uncertainty modifies their present value calculations of the costs and benefits of migration. If workers are **risk averse,** they will modify their calculation to require higher expected earnings after the move to compensate for greater uncertainty about earnings in their new location.

The degree of uncertainty is enhanced by the possibility of *unemployment in the potential destination.* As we should expect, the unemployment rate of migrants is not only higher than that of nonmigrants, but varies more with changes in business conditions. A small reduction in demand resulting in only a slight increase in unemployment among established workers might cause a large reduction in new hires. The amount of new hiring in an area is a far better predictor of migration than the unemployment rate. Where population is denser (so more job openings can be easily searched) in-migration rates are greater. Workers migrate to places where jobs are available, that is, where there are high **vacancy rates.** The number of unemployed workers competing for these jobs does not seem to have a very large deterrent effect. The sensitivity of rates of migration to the amount of hiring in potential destination areas can be quite startling. For example, interregional migration rates of manual workers in the United Kingdom were only half as high in the recession of 1984 as in the better times of 1977.[3]

Variations in expected income and changes in unemployment and hiring rates, which affect the probability of obtaining these incomes, alter the streams of returns presented in Figure 7.1. Uncertainty about income or unemployment in migrants' potential destinations gives any variations in these factors a far greater impact on the likelihood of migration than is produced by variations in them at home. Migration to 20th-century America has been much more a "pull" than a "push," meaning that conditions in destination areas appear to play a greater role than those in source locations. Uncertainty also influences why the migration rates shown in Table 7.3 rise with education. More educated people have better information about alternative job opportunities, lessening their uncertainty about moving.

Psychic costs and uncertainty about entering a new area can be reduced by migrants' own behavior. The most obvious way is for migrants to congregate in particular neighborhoods in the destination cities and to establish stores, bars, clubs, and churches that reflect their special tastes. Some neighborhoods in Queens in New York City are largely Dominican, Haitian, or Korean, and there are sections of Melbourne, Australia, that are heavily Greek, Italian, or Turkish. The presence of ethnic neighborhoods is especially important among less-skilled and older immigrants, for whom assimilation

---

[3]Gary Fields, "Place-to-Place Migration: Some New Evidence," *Review of Economics and Statistics* 61: 21–32 (1979); Lundborg, "An Interpratation;" Pissarides and Wadsworth, "Unemployment and."

into a strange environment may be harder than for younger, more educated workers.[4]

In effect, having contacts in a destination lowers the costs of moving there and may also increase the returns by helping migrants search effectively in the job market, thus setting up a process of **chain migration** where many workers from one source end up in the same destination. In the late 19th and early 20th centuries, it was not uncommon to find many workers from the same village in Eastern Europe working in a single factory in the U.S. When large numbers of workers moved from Appalachia to Michigan to work in the auto industry, bus companies kept track of which towns sent workers to which factories so they could add buses to appropriate routes back to the South when particular factories shut down for retooling.

THE EFFECT OF DISTANCE

Despite efforts to replicate home institutions in the destination area, many migrants return home, disappointed with life in their new location. For example, while 4.5 million people immigrated to the United States in the 1970s, 1.6 million people, many of them recent immigrants, emigrated from it. Since the U.S. stopped requiring annual alien registration in the early 1980s, it is no longer possible to calculate how many previous immigrants leave the U.S. each year. There is, however, no evidence that this ratio has decreased in recent years. The very possibility that migration will end in a reverse move lowers the expected return to migration, since it reduces the expected stream of benefits from moving ($Z_1 - Z_0$). For those who remain in the new area, the costs of transportation are more than just for the first trip, since the cost of later visits home for illness or death in the family or for holidays must also be counted.

The psychic costs of migrating long distances help explain why the power of income differentials diminishes sharply with increases in the distance between origin and destination. One study in 1960 found that it took an additional difference of nearly \$5 between the present values of earnings streams Z_1 and Z_0 to offset the deterrent effect of each extra mile of distance between regions. A more recent study found that, when other factors are equal, doubling the distance reduced the probability by 50 percent that someone from another Nordic country would choose to migrate to various regions in Sweden.[5] These strong deterrent effects imply that much more than just the

[4]Ann Bartel and Marianne Koch, "Internal Migration of U.S. Immigrants," in John Abowd and Richard Freeman (eds.). *Immigration, Trade and the Labor Market,* Chicago: University of Chicago Press, (1991).

[5]Larry Sjaastad, "Income and Migration in the United States," (PhD Diss., University of Chicago, 1961); John Vanderkamp "Migration Flows, Their Determinants and the Effects of Return Migration," *Journal of Political Economy* 79: 1012–1031 (1971); Lundborg, "An Interpratation."

money cost of moving and financing return visits causes the reduction in migration as distance increases.

The remarkably large deterrent effect of distance may be due to workers' lack of information about more distant labor markets. People may have a good idea about conditions in nearby labor markets because they have contact with residents and access to news media from the region. More distant labor markets, even within the same country, may be largely unknown. The importance of information is evident from a study in Canada showing that the deterrent effect of distance was less between 1971 and 1981 than it had been between 1956 and 1970.[6] Improved communications and increased education were probably responsible for this change.

SIMULTANEOUS MIGRATION IN BOTH DIRECTIONS

So far we have not considered anything beyond the average characteristics in the home and potential destination locations. Even if two areas have the same average wage, it will still pay for some people to move between them.[7] Gross migration may be large even if net migration is zero. Random changes in individual opportunities mean that workers are continually moving even if there is no average difference between locations. Consider what happens when the New York Knicks trade a guard to the Chicago Bulls for a center. Net migration is zero even though a worker moved in each direction.

Systematic movement between areas with the same average characteristics can also occur. Figure 7.2 shows the hypothetical distribution of workers by wage rate in two countries with the same average wage. Wages in Country *B* are much more unevenly distributed than those in Country *A*, where a large percentage of the work force is clustered around the mean. Assume that high-wage workers will be at the same place in the wage distribution in each country. High-wage workers who migrate from *A* to *B* can expect to improve their wage, since above-average workers in *B* do very well. Indeed, anyone with above-average wages in *A* who expects to wind up at the same place in the wage distribution will be better off migrating to *B*.

The opposite is true for low-wage workers. Country *A* provides a lot of security for low-wage people. Most have wages that are close to the average. They would not wish to migrate to *B*, where many workers earn wages far below the average. On the other hand, low-wage workers in Country *B* have a large incentive to migrate to *A*. Assuming they wind up in the same relative position in the labor market, they will obtain higher wages by doing so. In short, if people's relative wages in the two countries are correlated positively, and both countries have the same average wage, gross migration of high-

[6]R. Paul Shaw, "Fiscal versus Traditional Market Variables in Canadian Migration," *Journal of Political Economy* 94: 648–666 (1986).

[7]This discussion is due to George Borjas, "Self-Selection and the Earnings of Immigrants," *American Economic Review* 77: 531–553 (1987).

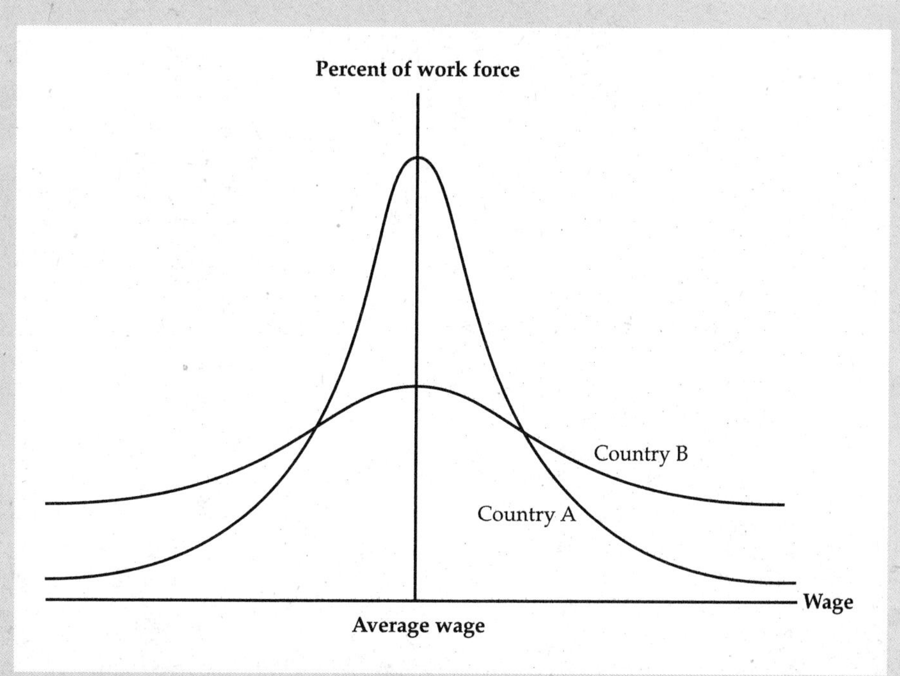

FIGURE 7.2 MIGRATION AND THE DISTRIBUTION OF WAGES
Given the same mean wage in two areas, workers with above-average productivity will want to move to the area with the less-equal distribution, while workers with below-average productivity will want to relocate to the area with the more-equal distribution.

wage workers will be from the country with more-equal wage rates to that with less-equal wages. Low-wage workers will migrate from the less-equal to the more-equal country. That this kind of calculation affects behavior is shown by the fact that in the 1980s young workers with more education (more likelihood of being a high-wage worker) were more likely to emigrate from states where wages were relatively equal.[8]

The implication is clear. Countries that adopt policies to equalize the wage distribution will create selectivity among both in- and out-migrants that causes the average quality of the worker to decline. The very productive will

[8]George Borjas, Stephen Bronars, and Stephen Trejo, "Self-Selection and Internal Migration in the United States," *Journal of Urban Economics* 32:159–185 (1992).

move to countries where they can earn greater returns on their talent (or where lower taxes enable them to keep more of what they earn). The less productive will be attracted to countries where redistribution polices increase their incomes. This effect is perhaps easiest to see where there are no legal barriers to migration, such as between the U.S. and Puerto Rico. Migrants from Puerto Rico (where the supply of skilled workers is very low and there is a great deal of income inequality) come disproportionally from among less-educated workers. For example, men who migrated from Puerto Rico to the U.S. before 1975 had nearly 1.5 fewer years of schooling than those who stayed behind.[9]

It is clear that economic motives are important in migration decisions where gross disparities exist in income levels or distributions. Yet it would be incorrect to give the impression that only economic forces govern internal and international migration. Many international migrants are refugees from war or from political, religious, or racial persecution, as the influx of Southeast Asians into the U.S. and Australia in the mid- to late-1970s illustrates. Sometimes refugees blaze a path that is followed by others whose motives are more clearly economic. Many voluntary migrants move for non-wage reasons. For example, migration by American retirees to Florida and Arizona, or by British retirees to the coast of Spain, is not motivated by differences in wages or unemployment between home and destination. For these migrants, the return to migration is primarily due to the differences in climate and costs of living, but the cost/benefit calculation remains the same.

FAMILY MIGRATION DECISIONS

This discussion has treated migration as though it were a single person's decision about the economic advantages resulting from a move, including any psychic costs and uncertainty. This approach is narrow to the extent that it ignores joint decision making by a husband and wife.[10] Migration decisions are largely made in an attempt to maximize a couple's joint economic well-being. Like the labor supply decisions we discussed in Chapters 1 and 2, joint decision making is likely to become increasingly important as married women's commitment to the labor market increases.

The conditions determining a typical family's decision are shown in Figure 7.3. The husband's net gain from migration, $G^h = Z_1^h - Z_0^h$, is shown on the horizontal axis. The wife's net gain, $G^w = Z_1^w - Z_0^w$, which equals the difference between her discounted earnings in the new location and the old less her costs of moving, is shown on the vertical axis. If the wife's earnings are

[9]Fernando Ramos, "Outmigration and Return Migration of Puerto Ricans," in George Borjas and Richard Freemen (eds.). *Immigration and the Work Force,* Chicago: University of Chicago Press, (1992).

[10]This analysis is based on Jacob Mincer, "Family Migration Decisions," *Journal of Political Economy* 86: 749–774 (1978).

POLICY ISSUE

1992 AND INTERNATIONAL MIGRATION IN EUROPE

After December 1992 all barriers to internal migration within the European Union (EU) ceased to exist. What are the potential impacts of this truly revolutionary change on the labor market in Europe? To some extent, comparison with what was going on before 1992 will underestimate the impact of the change, since substantial relaxation of barriers already existed. In 1988 net migration rates ranged from −1.6 percent of population in Ireland (Eire) to +0.8 percent in Germany. Not all but most of this migration was within the EU.[11]

The direction of the change is clear. It will increase gross migration and should also increase net migration, as citizens of low-wage and/or high-unemployment member countries move elsewhere within Europe. We cannot predict the size of the impact, but considering the evidence on migration we have seen so far, a major impact would be surprising. First, the deterrent effects of distance and unfamiliar languages have not been removed. Second, coupled with the easier movement of labor is the substantially easier movement of capital investment within the EU. If capital can move and create jobs in low-wage areas, there is less incentive for labor to move. The fact that cross-border mobility within the EU is likely to be relatively low is evident from the fact that, in 1991, even though it was already fairly easy to move within the EU, in every member country except Luxembourg and Belgium fewer than 3 percent of all workers were from another EU country. It was true, however, that the lowest number of foreign workers (0.2 percent of the labor force or less) was found in Spain, Portugal, and Greece, the lowest-wage EU members, while the highest (2.8 percent) was found in France and Germany. In sum, 1992 was a milestone for Europe in many ways, but it is not going to produce sudden massive flows of international migration within the EU.

below her husband's, the maximum net gain in her lifetime earnings, $0W$, is less than her husband's, which has a maximum of $0H$. The family's decision rule for migration is

> Migrate if $G^h + G^w > 0$, in other words, if the move raises the present value of the family's net income. If this is true for more than one potential move, take the option that has the largest value.

In Figure 7.3, any combination of G^h and G^w to the right of the 45-degree line indicates a positive sum of the net gains, but because the wife's maximum gain is limited to $0W$, and the husband's to $0H$, only those points below the horizontal line AB and to the left of the vertical line BC are possible. Thus, the only sums of net gains that are both positive and possible are shown by the shaded triangle ABC.

Migration will be economically beneficial to both spouses' economic prospects only for net gains in the rectangle $0WBH$. In the cases indicated by

[11]European Community Statistical Office, *Demographic Statistics,* (1990), Table A-3.

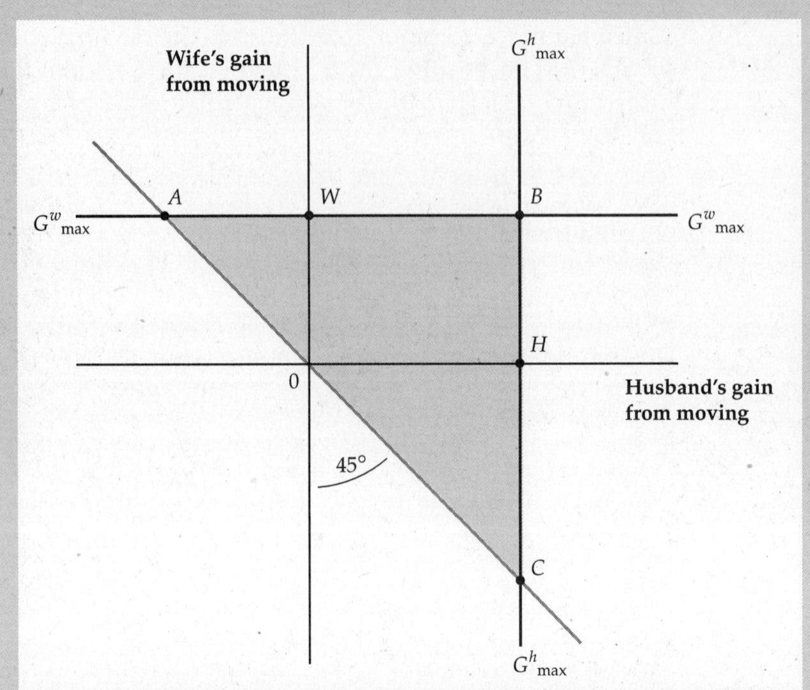

FIGURE 7.3 FAMILY MIGRATION DECISIONS
Only in area $0WBH$ are both the husband and wife better off following a move. In the triangles $0AW$ and $0CH$ one spouse sacrifices because the gain to the other spouse is large enough to make the family better off.

the triangle $0AW$, the family will move with $G^h < 0$ and $G^w > 0$. Here men are **tied migrants**. In a larger number of cases, shown by the larger triangle $0HC$, the family will move with $G^h > 0$ and $G^w < 0$. Because in most cases men's wages are higher and their attachment to the labor force stronger than those of their spouses, a family's voluntary decision to migrate will often raise the family's income but reduce the wife's labor market opportunities. In these cases, wives are tied migrants.

This is exactly what occurs. Among American families who moved between 1967 and 1971, the earnings of husbands increased substantially on average, while earnings of the wives who moved with them fell. Similarly, among Canadian families who moved between 1965 and 1971 the wife's earnings were sharply reduced by the move. Among Swedish couples in 1971 the same phenomenon was observed, with the greatest losses suffered by the most highly educated women.[12] Points in the triangle $0HC$ appear to be somewhat more common than those in the rectangle $0WBH$.

As women become more attached to the labor market and their wage rates move closer to those of men, more cases of migration will occur in which the husband is the tied migrant. This outcome can be seen by considering the effects of an upward shift in the line AB in Figure 7.3, indicating a greater net gain to the wife from migration. The triangle $0AW$ becomes larger, whereas $0HC$ is unchanged.

More important, there will be many more cases in which migration does not take place. The area to the left of the 45-degree line increases more in response to a rise in the wife's wage than does the area in the triangle ABC. Greater investment by either spouse in on-the-job training that is at least partly specific makes migration less attractive for the entire family. These phenomena help explain the trend toward less migration shown in Table 7.1, where, in all six countries, women's labor force participation has increased since 1970. Moreover, women's wage rates in most of these countries have also risen compared to men's, reflecting women's increased job experience. Both changes raise the line AB in Figure 7.3, leading to a drop in family gross migration rates.

When discussing labor supply in Chapter 1, we saw that families might make decisions in a more complex way than simply maximizing their joint income. Perhaps they engage in bargaining over what to do. In this case, they will unambiguously move if the outcome is in the rectangle $0WBH$ where both spouses are better off. In the triangles $0AW$ and $0CH$ the spouse who gains from the move may have to compensate the losing spouse, perhaps by increasing the intra-family transfer of income or by offering to do more of the household chores.

With more marriages ending in divorce, migration rates will change in a complex way. The greater possibility of divorce may induce both marriage partners, but especially women who have traditionally spent more of their time at home, to invest in skills that make them productive in the labor market. This investment in itself, however, increases tied migration because it increases the size of the triangles $0AW$ and $0HC$ relative to the rectangle $0WBH$. This effect, in turn, may increase unhappiness within the marriage and increase the possibility of divorce.

[12] Steven Sandell, "Women and the Economics of Family Migration," *Review of Economics and Statistics* 59: 406–414 (1977); E. Kenneth Grant and John Vanderkamp, "The Effects of Migration on Income: A Micro Study," *Canadian Journal of Economics* 13: 381–406 (1980); Bertil Holmlund, *Labor Mobility*, Stockholm, Sweden: Industrial Institute for Economic and Social Research, (1984).

POLICY ISSUE

MIGRANTS AND WELFARE PROGRAMS

In the U.S. welfare—largely Aid to Families with Dependent Children (AFDC)—was mandated by the federal government but individual states set the benefit levels, leading to wide differences among states in the generosity of benefits. Until it was ruled unconstitutional in 1969, people moving into most states could not receive welfare until they had lived there for some period of time. Recently, California and several other states have attempted to limit benefits for people moving into the state to what they would have received in their former states. Would more federal control, and presumably more uniform benefits, affect flows of population? Do people migrate between states in part to collect welfare and unemployment benefits? Compared to most of the countries from which immigrants to the U.S. come, welfare benefits in the U.S. are very high. Do people migrate to the U.S. in the hopes of collecting these generous benefits? To the extent that welfare and unemployment benefits affect migration patterns, they reduce the incentive for workers to respond to differences in employment opportunities by supplying their labor services where they command the highest pay.

Evidence regarding the role of welfare programs in migration is mixed. Immigrants to the U.S. in the 1960s and 1970s were unlikely to collect welfare (AFDC) benefits in the first few years. If they did, the amount was usually small. As their stay in the U.S. lengthened, the chance of having received benefits rose. More recently, immigrants have made greater use of the welfare system. In 1970 only 5.5 percent of immigrant households who had been in the U.S for five years or less were on welfare. By 1990 this figure had risen to 8 percent. Among those who had been in the U.S. from five to ten years, 6.5 percent were on welfare in 1970, compared to almost 11 percent in 1990. Overall, in 1990, although only 8 percent of household heads in the U.S. were foreign-born, these households accounted for 10 percent of households receiving public assistance and 13 percent of the cash benefits being paid.

Does this mean that families are moving to the United States because of generous welfare benefits? The answer is "probably not." Much of the increase can be explained by the fact that families that come to the U.S. as refugees have a much higher rate of welfare participation. In 1990 nonrefugee immigrant households had a welfare participation rate of less than 8 percent (less than 1 percentage point higher than native-born households). Among refugees, however, the participation rate reached as high as 16 percent. Among specific groups, such as those from Cambodia and Laos, the participation rate was as high as 50 percent. This finding is not surprising. Unlike most migrants, refugees from political persecution do not make a decision to leave their home countries because of higher expected earnings elsewhere. Instead, they flee an intolerable situation and end up in whatever country will take them. It would be amazing if their human capital were well-suited to their eventual destination.[13]

---

[13] George Borjas, "Immigration and Welfare," in Ronald Ehrenberg (ed). *Research in Labor Economics, Vol 15.* Greenwich, Conn.: JAI Press, (1995).

Looking at interstate migration, differences in welfare benefits do have a small effect on flows of migration. Among U.S. states in the 1970s and early 1980s, while very few households that were eligible for AFDC moved, those that did were more likely to go to states offering high AFDC benefits. In Canada during 1956 to 1981, when unemployment insurance benefits were higher, there was a slight reduction in the probability of leaving one's home province.[14]

To some extent the economic forces affecting migration include welfare and unemployment benefits, but the evidence indicates that these effects are small, in part, because state governments base their AFDC payments on those in other states, reducing incentives for welfare recipients to migrate in search of higher benefits.

EFFECTS ON THE MIGRANT

Having made a decision to migrate, workers in the new location must use the human capital they accumulated in their original location, a difficult process. Migrants cannot be sure of doing as well in the destination area as otherwise similar nonmigrants. While we assumed in our discussion of Figure 7.2 that the worker who moved between Countries *A* and *B* would obtain the same relative position in the distribution of wages, this correlation will not be perfect. Employers may give preference to local workers whose references are easily checked and who are less likely to quit because of homesickness or family emergencies that call them back.

Even after an initial period of unemployment has ended, migrants may be more exposed to the possibility of future unemployment than nonmigrants. They may also have to accept lower wages than nonmigrants because they do not yet have some of the specialized skills that produce higher average earnings in the new area. Some of the things they learned in school or on the job at the old location may yield little payoff in the new country or area. (Knowing who to bribe for an export license in Moscow will be of little value in Brooklyn.) These skills are **location-specific human capital** that are only of value in the location where the investment was made. It is not surprising that the rate of return to schooling among foreign-born Americans is only 80 percent of that for natives. Similarly, the rate of return to on-the-job training

---

[14]Edward Gramlich and Deborah Laren, "Migration and Income Redistribution Possibilities," *Journal of Human Resources* 19: 489–511 (1984); Shaw, "Fiscal versus"; Rebecca Blank, "The Effects of Welfare and Wage Levels on the Location Decisions of Female-Headed Households," *Journal of Urban Economics* 24: 186–211 (1988); James Walker, "Migration Among Low-Income Households: Helping the Witch Doctor Reach Consensus," University of Wisconsin-Madison Institute for Research on Poverty Working Paper No. 1031 (1994).

received before migration is less than half that of the training migrants subsequently acquired in the U.S.[15]

Offsetting these factors is migrants' willingness to take risks, as demonstrated by their decision to try a new and unknown labor market. This behavior suggests that migrants will, on average, be different from other workers in characteristics such as drive or motivation that are hard to measure but may be very important for labor market success. Thus, the gains from migration may be greater for them than they would have been for the typical nonmigrant. Because of the monetary and psychic costs involved, migration on average selects workers who are inherently more likely to succeed in the new labor market. The validity of this view is demonstrated by evidence that, among new immigrants in 1979, those who were less likely to have been forced to migrate were able to earn higher wages in their first year in the United States.[16]

Traditionally, these advantages eventually helped migrants overcome their somewhat inappropriate training and lack of familiarity with the new environment. Typical immigrants may even have earned more than otherwise identical natives. Immigrants who arrived in the U.S. during the 1960s earned more than natives with similar experience by about 1980. Data from Canada for 1971 and 1981 suggest that on average immigrants "caught up" to natives' wages about 20 years after arriving in Canada. The same was true for Australia in the 1970s and early 1980s, but only among less-skilled immigrants. Highly educated immigrants did not catch up to natives.[17]

More recent cohorts do not exhibit this convergence to native wages, in part, because they start out at a much worse disadvantage. In 1970, immigrants who had been in the U.S. for five years or less earned 17 percent less than native workers. By 1990 recent immigrants earned 32 percent less. While immigrants' earnings grew over time, earnings of those who had arrived in the U.S. in recent years showed little evidence of more rapid growth than those of native workers. Thus, they will never catch up. Similarly, immigrants who arrived in Canada during the 1960s earned about 5 percent less than native workers. By the 1980s this figure had risen to

---

[15] Barry Chiswick, "The Effect of Americanization on the Earnings of Foreign-born Men," *Journal of Political Economy* 86: 897–921 (1978); James Stewart and Thomas Hyclak, "An Analysis of the Earnings Profiles of Immigrants," *Review of Economics and Statistics* 66: 292–295 (1984).

[16] Borjas, Bronars, Trejo, "Self-Selection."

[17] David Bloom and Morley Gunderson, "An Analysis of the Earnings of Canadian Immigrants," in Abowd and Freeman, *Immigration, Trade;* John Beggs and Bruce Chapman, "Male Immigrant Wage and Unemployment Experience in Australia," in *Immigration, Trade;* George Borjas, "Assimilation and Changes in Cohort Quality Revisited: What Happened to Immigrant Earnings in the 1980s?" *Journal of Labor Economics* 13: 201–245 (1995).

TABLE 7.4 LEGAL IMMIGRATION TO THE UNITED STATES, BY ORIGIN AND AGE, 1820–1992 (THOUSANDS PER YEAR)

Source Area	Year							
	1820–1992	1931–1940	1941–1950	1951–1960	1961–1970	1971–1980	1981–1990	1991–1992
Europe, Canada, and Oceania	248	46	81	173	156	99	87	160
Mexico	22	2	7	30	46	65	165	580
Other Western Hemisphere	26	3	12	32	85	117	181	271
Asia	31	2	4	15	43	159	282	358
Africa	1	0	1	1	3	8	19	32
Total	328	53	104	251	333	448	734	1401

Source: U.S. Department of Justice, Immigration and Naturalization Service, *Statistical Yearbook of the Immigration and Naturalization Service, 1992*, Washington, D.C.: U.S. GPO (1995).

almost 35 percent, and predictions are that it would take 137 years for their earnings to match those of natives.[18]

What caused this striking change in the economic progress of immigrants to the U.S. and Canada? Partly, the cause has been the changing nature of the immigrants themselves. As Table 7.4 shows, during the 1970s and especially since 1980, the flow of immigrants shifted from Europe, Canada, Australia, and New Zealand to Latin America and Asia. Immigrants from Europe, Canada, and Oceania (Australia and New Zealand) fell from 87 percent of all immigrants in the 1930s to 69 percent in the 1950s, 47 percent in the 1960s, 22 percent in the 1970, and only 12 percent in the 1980s. Meanwhile, the share of immigrants from Latin America rose from 10 percent before World War II to 47 percent today. (The figures for 1991 to 1992 are heavily influenced by naturalizations of illegal immigrants that took place in 1991. In 1992 the faction of immigrants from each source closely resembled that of the 1980s.) Similarly, immigrants from Asia increased from 4 percent to 38 percent of all immigrants. For many of these later groups, language is much more of a problem in the labor market.

[18]Borjas, "Assimilation and Changes;" David Bloom, Gilles Grenier, and Morley Gunderson, "The Changing Labor Market Position of Canadian Immigrants," *Canadian Journal of Economics*, forthcoming.

Several studies have demonstrated that fluency in the English language plays an important role in the eventual economic success of immigrants to the U.S.[19] In addition, the prior training and experience of immigrants is likely to be more useful the closer the economic system and industry structure of their home country are to those of the U.S. One would expect an immigrant from a developed, capitalist country to have human capital that could be easily used in the U.S. The same is not true of a peasant from a communist country.

One factor contributing to this trend is the relative decline in demand for low-skilled workers in the U.S., although the best estimate is that these relative wage changes can account for less than one-fifth of the decline in immigrants' relative earnings.[20] A much more important factor is probably the relative decline in the skills of immigrants themselves. In 1970 about 40 percent of native workers and 48 percent of immigrants had not completed high school. By 1990, this figure had fallen to fewer than 15 percent of native workers, as compared to 37 percent of immigrants and about 40 percent of immigrants who had arrived since 1970.[21]

Why did the composition of immigrants to the U.S. shift so much? In large part it is because immigrants who arrived in recent years are much less likely to have moved for economic reasons. In 1965, the Immigration and Nationality Act was amended to place a much higher priority on having a family member in the U.S. as a reason to receive a visa. The fraction of immigrants who came to the U.S. for family rather than economic reasons has increased continually since then. Moreover, a much higher fraction of immigrants in the 1970s and 1980s were refugees, who obviously migrate for noneconomic reasons, than was true in the 1950s and 1960s. Large numbers of refugees were accepted after the end of the Vietnam War. In addition, in the late 1980s a special program was created to admit refugees fleeing religious persecution in the Soviet Union. All of these refugees could be expected to progress less rapidly in the labor market than those who came for economic reasons. The same shifts can be seen in Canada, where in the 1960s three-quarters of immigrants were admitted because of their skills and one-

---

[19]Walter McManus, "Labor Market Costs of Language Disparity: An Interpretation of Hispanic Earnings Differences," *American Economic Review* 75: 818–827 (1985); Barry Chiswick, "Speaking, Reading and Earnings Among Low-Skilled Immigrants," *Journal of Labor Economics* 9: 149–170 (1991); Barry Chiswick and Paul Miller, "Language in the Immigrant Labor Market," in Barry Chiswick (ed.). *Immigration, Language and Ethnicity: Canada and the United States,* Washington, D.C.: American Enterprise Institute, (1992).

[20]George Borjas, "The Economics of Immigration," *Journal of Economic Literature* 32: 1667–1717 (1994).

[21]Borjas, "The Economics of Immigration."

quarter for family reunification or refugee reasons. By the 1980s, these proportions were reversed.

EFFECTS ON THE RECEIVING LABOR MARKET

Migration affects labor markets as well as individual migrants. The potential size of these impacts can be substantial. During the early 1980s legal net migration added about 0.2 percent per year to the U.S. population. This addition represented as much as one-fourth of the net annual population increase. The late 1980s and early 1990s saw a significant jump in the number of legal immigrants to around 0.5 percent of the U.S. population each year. This phenomenon was temporary, due to a number of special programs that did not last more than a few years.

No one knows how many illegal immigrants live in the U.S. Almost 3 million illegal aliens applied for amnesty under the provisions of the 1986 **Immigration Reform and Control Act (IRCA).** This figure is about half the number of legal immigrants admitted to the U.S. during the previous ten years. Estimates of the number of illegal permanent residents in the United States during the mid-1980s ranged up to 12 million, with a good estimate of the number of illegal Mexican immigrants alone being 1.8 million (0.7 percent of the U.S. population).[22] Given that return migration is substantially larger among illegal immigrants and that many were not eligible for amnesty under IRCA, the suggestion is that illegal immigration may be as large as legal immigration each year.

As data in Table 7.4 show, the number of immigrants in recent years is much greater than it was from 1950 to 1970, but compared to the entire span of U.S. history, immigration today is relatively small. The average population in the U.S. between 1820 and 1922 was less than half of what it was in the 1980s. Comparing the first and last columns of the table shows that, relative to the size of the population, today's immigration flows are not above historical averages. Indeed, in the peak immigration years of 1901 to 1910, the U.S. added over 1 percent a year to its population through immigration.

In other countries where migration rates are even greater, the impact of net migration can be even larger. For example, in Australia during the late 1980s net migration exceeded the change in population stemming from natural increases. The data for Ireland discussed in the Policy Issue on

---

[22]George Borjas, Richard Freeman and Kevin Lang, "Undocumented Mexican-born Workers in the United States: How Many, How Permanent?" in Abowd and Freeman (eds.). *Immigration, Trade.* The uncertainty about the number of illegal migrants since the passage of IRCA in 1986 is shown in the *Wall Street Journal,* (June 3, 1991), p. A6.

POLICY ISSUE

CONTROLLING U.S. BORDERS

The large number of illegal immigrants to the U.S. has led to frequent calls for policies designed to prevent this flow. The 1986 immigration law imposed fines on employers who knowingly hired illegal workers (and required employers to check documents designed to establish the legality of those they hired). There is little evidence that these **employer sanctions** had any effect. Surveys of villagers in Mexico report no difference after the law in immigrants' behavior or in the number of people from the villages living in the U.S. The number of people apprehended by the U.S. Border Patrol while attempting to enter the U.S. illegally did fall from 1.8 million in 1986 to about 1 million a year. This number is still very large and recent evidence shows that it is rising again. There is also evidence that the major effect of increased enforcement of immigration laws is that illegal immigrants simply stayed longer on each visit to the U.S. in order to lower their risk of apprehension and did not make temporary trips home for holidays and family reasons.[23]

Recent proposals for decreasing the flow of illegal immigrants have been far more drastic. One group in the Southwest wants to fortify the entire Mexican border with barbed wire and electric fences. In 1994 California voters overwhelmingly passed a law denying illegal immigrants the right to have their children educated in public school or receive other than emergency medical treatment in public health-care facilities. Some have called for amending the U.S. Constitution to provide that only children of legal residents born in the U.S. are American citizens, as opposed to the current rule that confers citizenship on anyone born in the country, even if their parents are here illegally (or came as tourists). Finally, since the evidence is that illegal immigrants can easily purchase forged documents that will allow them to pass employers' checks under IRCA, many experts support a national computerized registry of all legal residents and an official national identity card or internal passport, as is used in many European countries.

Any of these changes would involve a drastic modification of one or more aspects of American life. The issue for public debate is whether Americans feel that the problems caused by illegal immigration are serious enough to warrant such responses. After all, prior to the 1920s there was no such thing as an illegal immigrant, and the only persons denied entry to the U.S. were criminals, the insane, and those who were ill. Of course, decreased travel costs and lower psychic costs due to more readily available telephone connections as well as greater familiarity with the U.S. through television and movies have drastically altered cost/benefit calculation since the 1920s.

---

[23]Katharine Donato, Jorge Durand, and Douglas Messey, "Stemming the Tide: Assessing the Deterrent Effect of the Immigration Reform and Control Act," *Demography* 29: 139–157 (1992); Sherrie Kossoudji, "Playing Cat and Mouse at the U.S.-Mexican Border," *Demography*, 29: 158–180 (1992).

European Integration show that negative net migration might also be important enough to affect the labor market.[24]

Depending largely on what they bring with them to their new country, migrants affect the labor market they enter in several ways. If arriving immigrants exactly mirrored the current population in their human and physical capital, they would increase the supply of all inputs and the demand for outputs proportionately. Thus, the primary effect would be through generating economies or diseconomies of scale. If immigrants have more physical capital than the average native, the result will be to increase the rate of return to labor, especially skilled labor that is complementary with capital. This effect can be seen in the recent wave of immigration from Hong Kong to western Canada in anticipation of this British colony's return to China.

In the U.S. and other countries that were major net recipients of immigrants during the 1970s and 1980s, the average migrant was probably less skilled than the average native, especially if we measure skill by years of schooling, as our previous analysis of human capital suggests is reasonable. If immigrants are largely unskilled workers, the net effect will be to increase the rate of return to capital (and the skilled labor that is a complement to capital), and reduce the earnings of unskilled workers. This impact will be partly offset, however, by a scale effect from any increase in demand generated by lower prices or the purchases of immigrants themselves. Of course, many of the negative effects occur only if the unskilled migrants find jobs that low-skilled natives would otherwise have taken. If the migrants, especially illegal ones, take jobs that would have gone unfilled, perhaps because those jobs pay wages below the minimum wage, no substitution effect occurs. The only impact in that case is a scale effect that increases the well-being of all workers. The final impact will be on consumers. If immigration lowers labor costs, it will also lower costs of production and prices.

The impact of net international migration on the wages of native workers is an empirical issue. Not surprisingly, economists have devoted a great deal of attention to measuring it. Much of the evidence implies that net flows of the magnitude into the United States since the 1960s have had little, if any, negative impact on the wages or unemployment rates of native workers. If there has been any effect, it has been on wages of the most recent prior group

---

[24] Commonwealth of Australia, Bureau of Immigration Research, *Australia's Population Trends and Prospects, 1990*, Canberra, (1991).

of immigrants.[25] These studies typically attempt to measure the impact of immigrants by comparing wages and unemployment rates of native workers in cities where there have been a lot of immigrants with those in cities that have received few immigrants.

Macroeconomic studies suggest a much larger impact of immigration on natives. Given reasonable elasticities of demand, one study suggested that up to a third of the 10 percent decline in the relative wages of high school dropouts in the period from 1980 to 1988 could be attributed to the large number of unskilled immigrants during that period.[26]

One way of reconciling these findings is to see how native workers respond to the arrival of immigrants. If a large number of immigrants arrive in a particular city, they would be expected to increase unemployment rates and depress wages in that city, thereby making it less attractive to natives who would either move away or at least not move to this city. Thus, any impact of immigrants would be national and could not be seen by examining differences between cities. Indeed, there is good evidence that this is just how native migrants respond to immigrant arrivals.[27]

Taken altogether, the evidence suggests that the impact of immigration on labor-market outcomes of natives has been relatively small. Even this conclusion overstates the detrimental impact immigration has on the economic returns to native workers. Although the human capital acquired before migration is not entirely applicable to the new country, it does raise migrants' productivity above what it would be without the investment. Taxpayers in the new country paid nothing to finance immigrants' premigration investments in human capital, yet immigrants pay higher taxes. Migration therefore gives taxpayers in the receiving country, both employers

---

[25] C. R. Winegarden and Lay Boon Khor, "Undocumented Immigration and Unemployment of U.S. Youth and Minority Workers," *Review of Economics and Statistics* 73: 105–112 (1991); Glenn Withers and David Pope, "Immigration and Unemployment," *Economic Record* 61: 554–563 (1985); Robert LaLonde and Robert Topel, "Labor Market Adjustments to Increased Immigration," in Abowd and Freeman (eds.). *Immigration, Trade*; Kristin Butcher and David Card, "Immigration and Wages: Evidence from the 1980s," American Economic Association, *Proceedings* 81: 292–296 (1991); George Borjas, "Immigrants, Minorities and Labor Market Competition," *Industrial and Labor Relations Review* 40: 382–392 (1987); Frank Bean, Lindsay Lowell, and Lowell Taylor, "Undocumented Mexican Immigrants and the Earnings of Other Workers in the United States," *Demography* 25: 35–52 (1988).

[26] George Borjas, Richard Freeman and Lawrence Katz, "On the Labor Market Effects of Immigration and Trade," in Borjas and Freeman (eds.) *Immigration, and.*

[27] Randall Filer, "The Effect of Immigrant Arrivals on Migratory Patterns of Native Workers," in Borjas and Freeman (eds.) *Immigration, and*; Michael White and Lori Hunter, "The Migratory Response of Native-Born Workers to the Presence of Immigrants in the Labor Market," Brown University, PSTC Working Paper No. 93–08 (1993); William Frey, "The New White Flight," *American Demographics* 16 4: 40–48 (1994).

and workers, a windfall of human capital for which they have not paid but from which they reap returns.

EFFECTS ON THE SENDING COUNTRY

The situation is different in countries that are net exporters of labor. Most countries regard the outflow of unskilled labor tolerantly while attempting to restrict its inflow. Attitudes are just the reverse toward international flows of highly skilled labor such as scientists, engineers, and physicians. The concern of the countries of origin is expressed in the common term **brain drain**. Professional workers who change countries usually get higher incomes and frequently better working facilities and opportunities for advancement. But the home country, which seldom views the permanent emigrants as part of the group whose welfare it seeks to maximize, is concerned that it has invested in their education and does not share in the returns.

The potential for immigration flows to reduce human capital stocks in the sending countries can be quite substantial. Nearly one-third of legal immigrants to the United States during the 1980s were professionals or managers. This flow represented a large loss of prior investment in human capital that had been partly financed by citizens of other countries whose workers emigrated. A major effect of this brain drain is to raise the wages of skilled workers in the sending countries since the supply of skills is reduced and competition for their labor increases. The wages of unskilled workers in the sending countries might also rise, since skilled and unskilled workers are substitutes.

Estimates of emigration's impact on the source country must also take into account the effect of **remittances** to emigrants' families. These flows of funds can contribute substantially to the incomes of those left behind and the overall welfare of the sending country. One careful study of emigration from El Salvador during the 1980s indicates that the large outflow of labor (estimated to have totalled between 10 and 15 percent of the population) consisted disproportionally of more educated workers. These workers sent home average remittances that *exceeded* what they would have earned had they remained in El Salvador. The net effects of emigration were to lower the labor force participation rate of those remaining in El Salvador due to the income effects created by the remittances, to increase wages (especially for urban males), and to lower unemployment rates by as much as 50 percent.[28]

---

[28] Mats Lundahn, "International Migration, Remittances and Real Incomes: Effects of the Source Country," *Scandinavian Journal of Economics* 87: 647–657 (1987); Panos Hatzipanayotru, "International Migration and Remittances in a Two-Country Temporary Equilibrium Model," *Journal of Economic Studies* 18: 49–62 (1991); and Edward Funkhouser, "Mass Emigration, Remittances, and Economic Adjustment: The Case of El Salvador in the 1980s," in Borjas and Freeman (eds.) *Immigration, and.*

DOES MIGRATION EQUALIZE LABOR MARKET OUTCOMES?

The direction of net migration accords with the predictions of economic theory. People move toward places where they obtain higher earnings, and away from locations where their earnings are low. Economic theory also predicts that where there is freedom of migration and capital movement the migration of labor, together with the reverse migration of capital, will bring the incomes and unemployment rates of different areas into equality. Restrictions on international migration may explain why this equalization has not yet occurred across countries. Other reasons must be found if it has not occurred among regions in the U.S.

Partially, the theory deals with a system in equilibrium that is disturbed by a single shock, but many disequilibria are not caused by single events. In the case of a one-time disturbance, positive net migration in the direction of the area with higher income will eventually close the income gap. Continuing disequilibria caused when the working-age population steadily grows more rapidly than employment opportunities in a given area can only be alleviated by a rate of migration larger than the difference between the two growth rates. Despite heavy out-migration, some areas can, therefore, have continuing surpluses of unskilled labor. Like the Red Queen in *Through the Looking Glass*, they must run very fast just to stay in the same place. The examples of Ireland or certain parts of Appalachia illustrate this point.

Despite an incomplete equalization of earnings across areas and continually arising shocks to equilibrium, migration clearly has eliminated many differences in wages. In 1950 the median income of full-time year-round male workers in the South was 79 percent of the median for the entire U.S. By 1987, it was 97 percent. In the 1950s and 1960s migration away from the South clearly produced the effect predicted by theory. Indeed, the effect was so strong that during the 1980s net interregional migration was toward the South. That wages are not exactly equal across regions is due partly to differences in amenities such as climate or living costs (discussed further in Chapter 10), and partly to the continuing shocks that prevent any economic system from ever coming into equilibrium.

Over the past 40 years in the U.S., a change in demand for the output produced in a particular state economy that reduced employment by one worker will result in an increase in unemployment of 0.3 workers and a decline in labor force participation of 0.05 workers in the first year. The remaining reduction of 0.65 workers is dissipated through an increase in net out-migration. By five to seven years after a shock to labor demand, the entire response came from changes in net out-migration, and both unemployment and labor force participation rates had returned to their initial level. On the other hand, the apparent time required for wages to approach their initial level is at least twice as long, and employment not only never recovers, it never increases above the post-shock level. The failure of employment levels to rebound indicates that mobility of workers is much more important than mobility of capital in reestablishing equilibrium. The behavior of wages is explained by the fact that a decline in employment reduces housing prices, so that wages do not have to reach their initial level for real incomes to be equal again.[29]

POLICY ISSUE

DID CASTRO BOMB MIAMI?

Obviously Fidel Castro did not bomb Miami with airplanes, but during a four-month period in 1980, 125,000 people were sent from Cuba to Miami on chartered boats. Of this number roughly half settled permanently in the Miami area, producing an approximately 7 percent increase in the size of the labor force. If ever there was a natural experiment in the effects of immigration on a labor market, the Mariel boatlift was surely it. Small changes in immigration patterns may not affect a labor market, but this change was large enough that, if immigration affects wage and employment outcomes among natives, the impact should have been visible in Miami in the early 1980s.

To examine this issue one cannot just look at wages and unemployment in Miami before and after the boatlift. The entire U.S. economy entered its longest and deepest recession since the 1930s just when the boatlift occurred, but no one would claim the boatlift caused the recession. Measuring the impact of the boatlift requires comparing the differences between wage rates and unemployment in Miami and the U.S. as a whole before and after the boatlift. When this comparison is made, the answer is clear. After the boatlift natives' wages and unemployment in Miami did not differ in any significant way from those elsewhere in the country. How could this be? Once again, the answer apparently lies in the movement of native workers. Following the 1980 boatlift, Miami's rate of population growth fell dramatically. Indeed, by 1986 despite the large influx of immigrants into Miami, the city's population was no larger than it was projected to be before the boatlift began.[30]

---

[29]Olivier Blanchard and Lawrence Katz, "Regional Evolutions," *Brookings Papers on Economic Activity, 1,* 1–75 (1992). See also Susan Houseman and Katherine Abraham, "Regional Labor Market Responses to Demand Shocks: A Comparison of the United States and West Germany," unpublished paper, University of Maryland (1990); Robert Barro and Xavier Sala-i-Martin, "Convergence across States and Regions," *Brookings Papers on Economic Activity, 1,* 107–158 (1991).

[30]David Card, "The Impact of the Mariel Boatlift on the Miami Labor Market," *Industrial and Labor Relations Review* 43: 245–257 (1990).

JOB TURNOVER

PATTERNS OF JOB TURNOVER

Although migration is an important force in affecting wage and employment determination among labor markets, it represents only a small part of the labor mobility in an economy. This effect is shown very clearly from data in Table 7.5 for a random sample of household heads in the United States between 1968 and 1982. This table shows the average number of different kinds of moves made during this period. Within each level of educational attainment, the number of job changes dwarfed the number of moves across county or state lines. Clearly, if the number of job changes is from two to four times the number of moves across county lines, most job turnover does not involve migration. This is especially true since some migration occurs without a change in job when employees are transferred between locations in a large corporation.

Although the U.S. has a more mobile work force than many other developed economies, job turnover in other countries is not small. Data for Sweden show that job changing during the mid-1980s occurred at more than half the rates shown in Table 7.5. As in the U.S., the large majority of job changes did not involve migration.[31]

Workers sometimes change jobs with or without changing locations because they must. They have been dismissed for misconduct or poor performance, or have been made superfluous by technological change or shifts in demand. These workers represent **discharges** or **involuntary mobility**. Although common usage often refers to people who have been dismissed as being "laid-off," the term **layoff** actually has a distinct and different meaning. Technically, a person who is on layoff is temporarily not working at a job to which they will return. An example might be when auto workers are not required in the plant while it is being retooled to produce a different model. Of course, being on layoff may motivate workers to look for other, more stable jobs and lead to their eventually quitting their current employers.

Workers who choose to change jobs typically are dissatisfied with their present ones or expect to do better elsewhere. Moves by these workers represent **quits**, or **voluntary mobility**. In this section we discuss the determinants of voluntary mobility. Discharges are discussed in Chapter 9, since they are especially closely tied to the determinants of wages and incentives in internal labor markets.

Does the term *quit* really mean anything? After all, a smart employer can get most workers to quit simply by withholding wage increases long enough.

---

[31]Anders Björklund and Bertil Holmlund, "Job Mobility and Subsequent Wages in Sweden," in Jouke van Dijk, Hendrik Folmer, Henry Herzog, and Alan Schlottmann (eds.). *Migration and Labor Market Adjustment*, Boston: Kluwer, (1989).

TABLE 7.5 GEOGRAPHIC MOBILITY AND JOB TURNOVER, HOUSEHOLD HEADS, 1968–1982 (NUMBER OF MOVES)

	Education (Years)		
Migration	*12*	*16*	*17+*
County	.36	.61	.63
State	.23	.29	.47
Job Turnover			
Job	1.46	1.05	1.06
Occupation	2.44	1.42	1.14
Industry	1.15	.96	.67

Source: Axel Börsch-Supan, "Education and its Double-Edged Impact on Mobility," *Economics of Education Review* 9 (1990), Table 3.

Are quits, therefore, really layoffs in disguise? The issue is the relationship between productivity and wages in the current and alternative firms. As long as a firm can pay workers the value of their marginal product, they will be happy to keep these workers on the payroll. This does not guarantee that the workers' marginal products in their current firms are as high as they would be with another employer. Thus, workers may want to change employers even if their current employer does not want to see them go (perhaps due to the firm having made investments in the workers' training). The distinction between voluntary turnover and layoffs rests on who initiates the job turnover.[32]

Why is there so much voluntary mobility? If all labor markets were initially in equilibrium, voluntary mobility would occur only when a change caused the relative attractiveness of jobs to change. Productivity in the current firm may fall, leading to a discharge if wages are not flexible downward. If wages are flexible downward or productivity in another firm rises, workers may quit. These changes induce a one-time flow of labor toward jobs that have become more attractive.

Labor flows may also be longer-lasting. Compensation in many jobs is always above that needed to attract recruits, creating a steady excess supply of applicants currently employed at less-attractive jobs. Such situations can result from high wages set through collective bargaining. They can also exist in order to enhance productivity in the high-wage firms. We will return to why this might be so in Chapter 9. In such cases voluntary mobility will occur whenever there are openings in the high-wage jobs, but relative wages may never be equalized.

[32] This discussion is based on Kenneth McLaughlin, "A Theory of Quits and Layoffs with Efficient Turnover," *Journal of Political Economy* 99: 1–29 (1991).

Voluntary mobility may also be a way for workers to acquire information about the labor market. In essence, voluntary mobility can be part of workers' search. Workers may not be able to get all the information they require about an employer unless they actually try out a job for a while. This behavior can create "**job shopping**," where workers find out which employers and occupations are most suitable to their skills, interests, and habits through trial and error.[33] This process is likely to be especially important for young workers and for those whose lack of education reduces their access to other sources of information about various jobs, particularly since such workers are not likely to lose much investment in specific human capital if they change jobs. By the 10th year after entering the labor market, the average young white male has held 7 different jobs and only 1 worker in 20 has not changed jobs. Wage gains from changing jobs account for about one-third of the total increase in wages during the first 10 years in the labor market.[34]

We saw in the previous section that educated workers are *more likely* to migrate. The data in the top half of Table 7.5 confirm this. Job turnover drops off sharply, however, with additional education, as reading across the rows in the bottom half of Table 7.5 demonstrates. How can these two findings be reconciled? Less-educated workers do engage in more job shopping and have less-specific human capital to inhibit their moving. On the other hand, labor markets for unskilled workers are primarily local in nature. A janitor who wants to try being a parking-lot attendant does not have to move to another city to do so. Firms are also more likely to transfer well-educated workers to different locations.

Data for the United States and the United Kingdom shown in Table 7.6 also demonstrate that younger workers are more likely to quit. Although there are problems making cross-country comparisons using these data, the higher quit rates in the U.S. may reflect the same greater mobility compared to Europe that we saw in the migration rates in Table 7.1. Reading across the rows in the table shows that job mobility falls off very rapidly as workers age (except among workers in the United States who are new to their jobs). This pattern, too, may be a result of job shopping. Once workers have sampled a few different jobs, they have a much better idea of where their talents and interests lie and, therefore, a much lower need to try further alternatives. Alternatively, the pattern of declining quits with age may reflect increased investments in specific human capital or greater psychic costs as workers age. In addition, the lower remaining length of working life reduces the gains from any given difference in wages.

Firm-specific training (the fixed costs that make trained workers more valuable than others to their present employer discussed in Chapter 3)

---

[33] William Johnson, "A Theory of Job Shopping," *Quarterly Journal of Economics* 92: 261–278 (1978), develops this idea.

[34] Robert Topel and Michael Ward, "Job Mobility and the Careers of Young Men," *Quarterly Journal of Economics* 62: 439–479 (1992).

TABLE 7.6 ANNUAL RATES OF JOB LEAVING, BY AGE AND TENURE, UNITED STATES, 1981, AND UNITED KINGDOM, 1979 (PERCENT PER YEAR)

		Age			
Years of Tenure	Country	25–29	30–39	40–49	50–59
0–1	United States	54	52	50	52
	United Kingdom	19	17	9	2
1–5	United States	24	18	15	12
	United Kingdom	10	10	7	1
5–10	United States	—	9	5	2
	United Kingdom	—	10	7	6
10–15	United States	—	—	7	5
	United Kingdom	—	11	9	8

Source: OECD, *Employment Outlook*, (1984), Table 34.

automatically creates a deterrent to voluntary mobility. As long as workers share part of the returns to such training in the form of higher compensation than they could obtain elsewhere, their incentives to quit the firm are reduced. Employers, seeking to reduce turnover costs, thus have an incentive to force workers to pay for at least part of their specific training, providing a return by paying higher wages or benefits after training than they otherwise would. Where specific on-the-job training is more extensive, we will observe less voluntary mobility among firms.

The discussion in Chapter 3 demonstrated that a good proxy for a worker's firm-specific training is his job tenure (the amount of time spent with an employer). The evidence in Table 7.6 shows that mobility is reduced by tenure with the current employer, independent of the age of the worker. Reading down the columns for each country, the rate of job leaving generally decreases as job tenure increases. The same phenomenon has been observed in data for many countries. Especially interesting is evidence on turnover from the U.S. and Japan. Turnover rates in Japan are much lower, mainly because wages rise more rapidly with tenure. In Japanese-owned plants in the U.S., however, turnover rates are the same as those in Japan.[35] Since the relationship between job tenure and wages in Japanese-owned U.S. plants is also the same as in Japan (but different from other U.S. plants), this finding

[35] Jacob Mincer and Yoshio Higuchi, "Wage Structures and Labor Turnover in the United States and Japan," *Journal of the Japanese and International Economies* 2: 97–133 (1988).

suggests that economic factors are more important than cultural differences in determining job mobility.

It is the fact that job tenure with an employer raises wages that makes workers less likely to quit the longer they have been on a job. If wages are held constant, a worker with longer tenure is *more* likely to quit his job. Consider Figure 7.4. Max begins his job at time t_0 and sees his wages increase along tenure profile P_0. Maxine, who is in all respects an identical worker to Max, searches longer and finds a better job, perhaps because she had lower costs of search. She begins work at time t_1 and sees her wages grow along tenure profile P_1. Both profiles increase rapidly at first but more slowly later on due to the declining investment in human capital we discussed in Chapter 3. Now compare Max and Maxine when each is earning a wage of w^*. This will occur at time t_2 for Maxine and t_3 for Max. Clearly Max has more tenure on the job $(t_3 - t_0)$ than Maxine $(t_2 - t_1)$, yet there will be far more alternative jobs that would tempt Max away from his current job (with a wage profile growing along P_0) than could attract Maxine away from profile P_1. Thus,

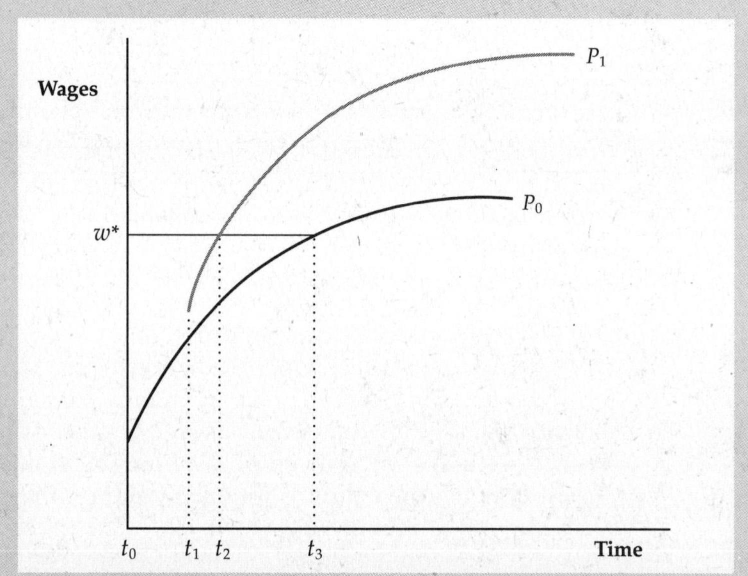

FIGURE 7.4 EFFECT OF TENURE ON QUITS HOLDING WAGES CONSTANT

At a given wage w^*, a worker with long tenure on a job (t_3 on profile P_0) will face worse future prospects on that job than a worker with shorter tenure ($(t_2 - t_1)$ on profile P_1). Thus, if wages are held constant, workers with greater tenure are more likely to quit for another job.

workers who have already found a high-wage job are less likely to improve their lot by moving to another job.

The evidence strongly supports this analysis. Among young men, the annual probability that they will change jobs falls to about half its initial level over the first 12 years of working. If wages are held constant, however, their probability of quitting triples. Workers are also less likely to quit when they expect their wages with their current firm to increase over time. Among otherwise identical workers, those in firms in which the top wage on the job is greater are less likely to quit.[36]

Demographic factors may also produce differences in voluntary mobility, even after economic determinants are taken into account. There is little difference between the likelihood of black and white workers quitting a job. Indeed, allowing for black-white differences in wages, educational attainment, and other measures of skill, blacks are less likely to quit a job than are otherwise identical whites. This finding may reflect the fact that historically for blacks working at any given wage, there were fewer higher-wage jobs available for which they could search than were available to whites working at that wage.

Women are more likely to quit their jobs than men. This difference may reflect differences in the opportunities they face. When their lower wages and shorter labor market experience are accounted for, studies in the U.S. and the U.K. show that there is less difference between men and women in the probability of quitting a job. In addition, the probability that women will quit their jobs has declined rapidly in recent cohorts, although it is still not as low as for men. Accounting for differences in experience and pay, married women are less likely to quit than single women, and those with newborn children are more likely to quit than other women.[37] If women are more likely to quit jobs to leave the labor force rather than to take another job, differences in experience will already reflect this higher propensity to quit.

Women who expect to leave the labor force for fertility-related reasons will have a smaller incentive to change employers since they will not have an

---

[36] Topel and Ward, "Job Mobility;" Mark Meitzen, "Differences in Male and Female Job-quitting Behavior," *Journal of Labor Economics* 4: 151–167 (1986).

[37] Francine Blau and Lawrence Kahn, "Race and Sex Differences in Quits by Young Workers," *Industrial and Labor Relations Review* 34: 563–577 (1981); Andrew Weiss, "Determinants of Quit Behavior," *Journal of Labor Economics* 2: 371–387 (1984); W. Kip Viscusi, "Sex Differences in Worker Quitting," *Review of Economics and Statistics* 62: 388–398 (1980); John Shorey, "An Analysis of Sex Differences in Quits," *Oxford Economic Papers* 35: 213–227 (1983); Loren Solnick, "Marital Status, Children and Female Quitting," Industrial Relations Research Association, *Proceedings*, 41: 549–556 (1988); Audrey Light and Manuelita Ureta, "Panel Estimates of Male and Female Job Turnover Behavior: Can Female Nonquitters Be Identified?" *Journal of Labor Economics* 10: 156–181 (1992).

extended period in which to reap any higher earnings on a better job. This may explain why among men in the first three years on the job, those with greater tenure are less likely to quit, while among women, the opposite is true.[38]

Workers who change jobs within a labor market can change occupation, industry, employer, or any combination of these. Young workers are less likely to quit new jobs if they have worked in the same occupation in their previous job, because they can bring their occupation-specific training with them. Many potential moves would involve losing this training. As in so many other aspects of labor market behavior, the role of education is especially important. Occupational mobility decreases with education, suggesting that education and occupation-specific investment are positively related (as the discussion in Chapter 3 implied).[39]

As Table 7.5 showed, occupational mobility is more frequent than mobility between employers. There are common patterns of occupational mobility that do not require changing employers but instead involve either a promotion with a firm or a gradual change of duties and responsibilities, with the worker combining the activities of both occupations in changing proportions. Professors become department administrators but still teach and do research, although in reduced amounts. If they are promoted to deans or college presidents, they have switched to academic administration, a different occupation from college teaching, and are unlikely to be teaching or doing research any more. Senior vice-presidents for research of huge, technologically oriented companies such as IBM and AT&T start out as full-time scientists. At some point, they gradually switch into partial and then into full-time administration of other scientists' research.[40] If you look at the career of the president of a major automobile company, you might see a person who at various times worked in the occupations of design engineer, marketing manager, and vice-president for European operations before reaching his current occupation.

The data in Tables 7.5 and 7.6 reflect the number of moves by individual workers over some period of time. An alternative, employer-based way of reflecting the same phenomenon is to measure the number of jobs vacated during a particular time period. Voluntary mobility is high by this measure as well. The first column of Table 7.7 shows data for the entire Canadian economy and for major industries in 1986. In most sectors quit rates averaged from 0.5 to 1 percent per month. That up to 1 percent or more of jobs

---

[38] Meitzen, "Differences in Male."

[39] Brian McCall, "Occupational Matching: A Test of Sorts," *Journal of Political Economy* 98: 45–69 (1990); Nachum Sicherman and Oded Galor, "A Theory of Career Mobility," *Journal of Political Economy* 98: 169–192 (1990).

[40] Jeff Biddle and Karen Roberts, "Private Sector Scientists and Engineers and the Transition to Management," *Journal of Human Resources* 29: 82–107 (1994).

TABLE 7.7 QUIT RATES BY MAJOR INDUSTRY, CANADA

Industry	Percent per Year, 1986	Percentage Change, 1981–1982 Recession
Total	7.7	−42
Construction	6.1	−49
Manufacturing	8.0	−53
Distributive services	6.6	−49
Business services	8.2	−37
Consumer services	12.3	−31
Public services	2.8	−39

Source: Garnett Picot and John Baldwin, "Patterns of Quits and Layoff in the Canadian Economy," *Canadian Economic Observer*, (October 1990).

are vacated each month is quite typical of developed economies, as similar data for Sweden, Japan, and the United States show.[41]

The very substantial variation in quit rates across occupations seen in Table 7.7 is due to differences in the amount of firm-specific training and the other determinants of voluntary mobility that we have already discussed. The very high turnover in consumer services in Canada is a result of low wages paid in this sector combined with the small amounts of training required. The low voluntary mobility in public services reflects the relatively high average level of pay and benefits in this sector. The low turnover in construction, despite a lack of firm-specific investment, is another good illustration of the effect of high wages.

Table 7.7 shows that in all industries the quit rate dropped during the severe 1981–1982 recession. This drop is a reflection of reduced job opportunities during the recession. Workers respond very strongly to a decline in job opportunities. Over a several-decade period in the U.S., each 1 percent increase in real GNP raised the quit rate in manufacturing by 9 percent. A study of the U.K. between 1971 and 1983 showed that higher unemployment also sharply reduced quitting. The effect was mainly through a reduction in the number of people who quit to search for jobs while unemployed. This behavior is just what the theory of job search predicts, since when unemployment is high the benefits of search are reduced.[42]

---

[41] Holmlund, *Labor Mobility*, Table 2.1. For the United States no data on quit rates by industry were collected after 1981, but the monthly quit rate in manufacturing over the post World War II period before then averaged nearly 2 percent. (Thomas Kniesner and Arthur Goldsmith, "A Survey of Alternative Models of the Aggregate U.S. Labor Market," *Journal of Economic Literature* 25: 1241–1280 (1987)).

[42] Kniesner and Goldsmith, "A Survey;" Barry McCormick, "Quit Rates over Time in a Job-Rationed Labour Market: The British Manufacturing Sector, 1971–1983," *Economica* 55: 81–94 (1988).

Table 7.1 documented a downward trend in geographic mobility in many developed economies. Information is not available on a wide enough range of economies to draw conclusions about trends in voluntary mobility. There did appear to be a downward trend, however, in the quit rate in manufacturing in the U.S. over the period from 1950 to 1980. Accounting for changes in unemployment and the demographic mix of the labor force, the quit rate declined by over 10 percent during this period.[43] This decline may be a reflection of an increase in the fixed costs of employment, including firm-specific training. It is particularly striking since improved transportation and wider availability of information about other regions should have resulted in greater mobility, other things being equal.

THE BENEFITS FROM VOLUNTARY MOBILITY

Since mobility is largely for economic reasons, we should expect workers' economic situations to improve following changes in jobs or locations. This is clearly what happens. Estimates of the wage gain from changing jobs range from a little over 2 percent in Sweden to as much as 9 percent in Canada, with the U.S. lying somewhere in the middle.[44] Young workers who quit their jobs have both higher wages and more rapid wage growth on their new jobs than they would have had if they stayed with their old employers. This pattern does not mean, however, that all young workers would be better off quitting. Young workers who choose to remain in their jobs also appear to do better than they would have if they quit. Workers have sorted themselves into two groups, movers and stayers, based on what is advantageous to them. Both quitting and staying reflect rational calculation by employees in evaluating their own personal returns from mobility.

There are interesting differences by age in the gains to voluntary mobility. Studies of older workers in both the United States and Sweden show that they do not reap as large a wage increase from changing jobs as younger workers. Older workers have more specific human capital to lose in a job

---

[43] James Ragan, "Investigating the Decline in Manufacturing Quit Rates," *Journal of Human Resources* 19: 53–71 (1984).

[44] George Borjas and Sherwin Rosen, "Income Prospects and Job Mobility of Younger Men," *Research in Labor Economics* 3: 159–181 (1980); Jacob Mincer, "Wage Changes in Job Changes," *Research in Labor Economics* 8: 171–197 (1986); Björklund and Holmlund "Job Mobility;" Michael Abbott and Charles Beach, "Wage Changes and Job Changes of Canadian Women: Evidence From the 1986–87 Labour Market Activity Survey," *Journal of Human Resources* 29: 429–460; Michael Abbott, Charles Beach, and Stephan Kaliski, "Wage Changes and Job Changes of Canadian Men: Empirical Evidence," in Louis Christofides (ed.). *Aspects of Labour Market Behaviour: Essays in Honour of John Vanderkamp*, Toronto: University of Toronto Press, (1995).

POLICY ISSUE

HEALTH INSURANCE AND JOB MOBILITY

Employers frequently use fringe benefits (such as **vested pension** plans for which workers are ineligible until they have been employed for a minimum period) to help bind workers to their current firm and reduce the loss of the firm's investments in human capital caused by mobility. Other fringe benefit plans may reduce turnover for unintended reasons. In the United States about 75 percent of married men have health insurance through their employer. If they change employers they may face waiting periods or exclusions for preexisting conditions that limit their access to coverage on their new employer's plan (if this employer even offers health insurance). This situation might cause workers who are afraid of losing health insurance coverage to remain with their current employer even if their productivity were higher elsewhere. That this **job lock** does not result from firms' desire to retain specific human capital is clear, however, from the fact that it is created by the health coverage provisions of *other* firms rather than by those of the worker's current employer. In addition, it differentially affects workers who are in poor health, not the employees a firm is most likely to want to retain.

Interesting insights into the possible strength of job lock from health insurance coverage can be obtained by comparing the mobility of workers who would not lose insurance if they changed jobs with those who would. For example, barriers to mobility from insurance should not exist for men who have insurance from another source such as their wife's employer, the Veterans' Administration (due to prior military service), or their union. Making these comparisons, one study has estimated that fear of losing health insurance lowers mobility among men who have no coverage other than their employer's plan by about 25 percent. Two other studies that used similar techniques but different data sources, however, did not find any evidence of reduced mobility due to fears of losing health insurance.[45]

Partially in response to this possible effect, the U.S. has adopted a rule (known as COBRA for the Comprehensive Omnibus Budget Reconciliation Act of 1985 that contained this provision) that any employee who leaves an employer must be able to purchase up to 18 months of health insurance from their employer's group plan at a price no more than 102 percent of what their employer paid for their coverage.

[45]Brigitte Madrian, "Employment-Based Health Insurance and Job Mobility: Is There Evidence of Job-Lock?" *Quarterly Journal of Economics* 109: 27–54 (1994); Douglas Holtz-Eakin, "Health Insurance-Provision and Labor Market Efficiency in the United States and Germany," in Rebecca Blank and Richard Freeman (eds.). *Social Protection Versus Economic Flexibility: Is There a Trade-Off?*, Chicago: University of Chicago Press (1994); John Penrod, "Employer-Provided Health Insurance and Job Mobility; A Test of "Job-Lock," Princeton University Industrial Relations Section, Photocopy (1993).

change. We have already seen that this factor will make them less likely to quit their employers. When they do quit, the forfeiture of the returns from this capital means that any given new job will lead to a lower wage gain for them. In addition, since older workers have already had a long time to search for a good match between their talents and the needs of an employer, it is likely that the difference between their productivity on their current job and the best they could find elsewhere is relatively small. Since there are smaller gains from mobility for older workers, only those with the lowest costs of moving will be observed changing employers.

Is there too much or too little mobility in the economy? There is an obvious economic interest in reallocating workers where their productivity is the greatest, which is what happens when a worker quits one job for higher wages elsewhere. The problem is that, if firms are afraid of losing investments in human capital when workers quit, they will be less likely to invest in it. This is a classic case of the economic phenomenon known as an **externality**. The decisions of one person (the worker) impose a cost (the lost investment) on another person (the employer). If this externality exists, firms will invest too little in developing the human capital of their workers.

As always, the answer is to make the decision maker take these costs into account, which can be done in one of two ways. The worker could be made to pay for all types of human capital investment, or other costs could be imposed if the worker quits a firm. Firms that stand to lose investments in specific human capital go to great lengths in order to reduce the amount of worker mobility. There are several ways that costs could be imposed on workers who opt to change jobs. Some involve the structure of pay and will be discussed in Chapter 9. Others use fringe benefit programs and will be discussed in Chapter 10.

SUMMARY

The mobility of workers among labor markets and jobs is a manifestation of a job search process that benefits both workers who move and, in many cases, the economy as a whole. Workers considering moving compare the costs, in terms of forgone income, out-of-pocket costs, and psychic costs involved in moving, to the benefits of higher utilities in new locations or jobs. Larger wage differentials induce more migration, as do larger differences in unemployment rates. Variations in available jobs in areas to which people might migrate have especially large effects on rates of migration. Higher wages on workers' current jobs make them less likely to change jobs. Because workers consider the entire stream of future gains from mobility, older workers are much less likely to change jobs, especially when the change might require a geographical move.

Insofar as mobility leads workers away from employers or areas where wages are depressed and unemployment is high, it also benefits the workers who remain behind by raising their wages. This effect is less pronounced if

POLICY ISSUE

HOUSING AND JOB TURNOVER

Achieving the social benefits that arise from voluntary mobility involving migration requires that workers be able to move. In an economy with severe shortages of housing, or where access to housing is controlled by the government, the optimal rate of labor mobility may not be reached because workers cannot find housing where job opportunities exist. This phenomenon has been a particular problem in the transition economies of Eastern Europe where economic opportunities created by emerging capitalism are often not in the regions where communist authorities built housing. This disparity has created large variations in regional unemployment rates. In 1993, for example, Czech workers who wanted to move from Bruntal, where there were 25 unemployed workers for every vacant job, to Prague, where there were 7 vacant jobs for every unemployed worker, were prevented from doing so by the impossibility of finding a vacant apartment in Prague.[46]

Even in unregulated labor markets housing and job mobility are tied together. For example, black workers at one company in the late 1970s were more likely to quit than white workers with the same demographic characteristics. Once racial differences in the length of the worker's commute to work were accounted for, however, black workers quit their jobs at a slower rate. Usually if workers own their own homes, they are much less likely to change jobs. In both the U.K. and the U.S., it is especially true if workers live in a location where housing prices have fallen and the proceeds from the sale of their homes may not be enough to cover their outstanding mortgage balances.[47]

There is an exception to the generalization that home owners are less likely to change locations for employment reasons. In both the U.K. and the U.S. there are typically long waiting lists for public housing. People in New York City who have waited up to ten years for a subsidized apartment with a rent considerably below the market rate will be reluctant to move to another city where job prospects may be better, but where they will have to go to the bottom of the waiting list for another apartment at a below-market rent.[48] Thus, public policies designed to help in one problem area (access to housing) may exacerbate unemployment problems by inhibiting the mobility necessary to take advantage of labor market opportunities.

---

[46]Michaela Erbenová, "Regional Unemployment Differentials and Labour Mobility: A Case Study of the Czech Republic," Prague: CERGE-EI Discussion Paper (1995).

[47]Jeffrey Zax, "Quits and Race," *Journal of Human Resources* 24: 469–493 (1989); Thomas Boehm, Henry Herzog, and Alan Schlottmann, "Intra-Urban Mobility, Migration and Tenure Choice," *Review of Economics and Statistics* 73: 59–68 (1991); Andrew Henley, Richard Disney, and Alan Carruth, "Job Tenure and Asset Holding," *The Economic Journal* 104: 338–349 (1994); Sewin Chan, "Revealed Preference from the Choice of Mortgage Contracts: How Mobility Can Be Inferred from Discount Points," Columbia University Department of Economics, Photocopy (1994).

[48]P. Minford, M. Peel, and P. Ashton, *The Housing Morass*, London: Institute for Economic Affairs (1987).

the labor of migrants is a complementary factor of production with that of the workers who remain. Workers in whom society has made substantial investments in human capital may leave those remaining in their initial location worse off as a result of their migration unless they send home substantial remittances. In areas with positive net migration, the workers already there may be hurt if competition from new workers outweighs increases in overall demand and additional capital brought by migrants. Other workers, whose labor is complementary with that of the migrants, will be helped by their entrance into the new labor market. The evidence shows that these effects on the wages of native workers have generally been quite small in developed countries. All residents of the receiving location benefit from importing human capital that was financed elsewhere. Whether there is too much or too little migration and job turnover is not clear. The effects of both are too complex to allow an answer to this question.

QUESTIONS AND PROBLEMS

7.1 Joseph Peregrine, age 35, is considering moving his family to a new location where he can earn $22,000 per year until retirement at age 65 once he finds a job, which will take him a year. His new employer will pay all the costs of the move. He currently earns $20,000 per year. If his discount rate is 5 percent, should he move the family? If his wife has been working and foresees that her earnings will be $1,000 per year lower in the new location, should the family move?

7.2 Nowheresville's leading employer leaves town, and the community suddenly becomes a depressed area. Discuss the short- and long-term impacts of this event on migration patterns, wage rates, and employment of the residents, distinguishing among them by age and sex.

7.3 Al Jones and Bob Smith are in the first period of a three-period career with Cadwallader's Packing Company. Their expected wages with Cadwallader's in each period are shown in the second and third columns of the table.

Period	With Cadwallader's		With Bean's	With Abel's
	Jones	Smith	Jones or Smith	Jones or Smith
1	$10	$10	—	—
2	10	15	$10	$15
3	10	20	10	20

The fourth column shows the wage each might get by quitting Cadwallader's after one period and taking a job with Bean's, a competitor; the fifth column shows the result if Jones or Smith takes a job with Abel's, another competitor, for periods 2 and 3.

a. Assuming there are no out-of-pocket costs of job mobility ($C = 0$), what will be Jones's and Smith's wages during the second and third periods of their careers? Will either of them quit Cadwallader's and, if so, which one?

b. What will be the change in wages between period 1 and period 2, and period 1 and period 3, for each worker? What do those wage changes say about the gains to moving compared to the gains from staying with an employer?

7.4 People in the United States suddenly lose their wanderlust and decide that they will stay on each job they take for at least one year. Discuss the impact of this change in tastes on: the wage-tenure relationship within a typical firm, wage gains between jobs, and the average real wage rate. How will the effects differ in their impacts on men and women? How will they differ in their impacts by age group?

7.5 One of your classmates has asserted that households in which both spouses work are more likely to migrate than those in which only one is employed because in two-worker households there is twice as much chance that someone will find a more attractive job elsewhere. Do you agree or disagree? Explain your reasoning.

7.6 Consider two proposed revisions of U.S. immigration policy. The first allows anyone who is disease-free and does not have a criminal record to enter the U.S. (the policy in the 19th and early 20th centuries). The second restricts immigration to the same number of people as now, but determines who gets to come by auctioning visas to the highest bidders. What would be the impact of each of these policies on

a. wages of skilled workers;
b. wages of unskilled workers;
c. interest rates;
d. the balance of trade;
e. inflation rates;
f. the U.S. budget deficit?

7.7 What will be the impact of mobility between regions on

a. the total output produced by the two regions;
b. the share of total income going to workers (as opposed to owners of capital) in the two regions; and
c. the average wage rate in the two regions?

7.8 Suppose you overheard the following statement in a bar near your campus: "My labor economics professor is crazy! She claimed that mobility of labor between regions will lead to wages being equal everywhere. I'm from the southern U.S., and I know workers where I live have earned less than those in New England for 130 years. This mobility theory must be all wrong!" Evaluate this claim.

7.9 Many claim that there is no real distinction between quits and layoffs in economic data. After all, if an employer wants to discharge a worker, he can simply make things so unpleasant on the job that the worker will decide to leave. In what sense (if any) do you find the distinction between a quit and a layoff to be economically meaningful? Should it matter for unemployment policy how large a fraction of the unemployed left their jobs in each of these ways?

7.10 Consider mobility between countries, regions, employers, and occupations. Are there likely to be differences in the factors determining the probability that a given worker will experience each type of mobility? If so, what are these differences? In particular, what factors will be relatively more important as determinants of each type?

KEY WORDS

brain drain
chain migration
discharge
employer sanctions
externality
gross migration rate
Immigration Control and Reform Act of 1986 (IRCA)
involuntary mobility
job lock
job shopping
layoff
location-specific human capital
net migration rate
psychic costs
quits
remittances
risk averse
rule of thumb
tied migrants
vacancy rate
vested pension
voluntary mobility

VACANCIES AND UNEMPLOYMENT

THE MAJOR QUESTIONS

- ▲ What jobs become vacant and how long do they stay vacant?
- ▲ Can we categorize unemployment in a way that helps us to think about its causes?
- ▲ How is our understanding of unemployment aided by distinguishing between how many people become unemployed and the length of time each person stays unemployed?
- ▲ How does unemployment differ by demographic group, by industry, and by geographic region?

JOB VACANCIES

Job vacancies are open positions that employers seek to fill. They occur when workers quit or are discharged for cause, when product demand rises, or when changes in relative input prices cause firms to want to substitute labor for other inputs. In many cases employers will promote or reassign workers already in the firm. (These internal labor markets within firms will be discussed in Chapter 9.) Thus, the posted vacancy may be for an entirely different position as the firm seeks to replace a transferred or promoted worker. Eventually, however, the employer must hire from outside the firm, and a formal vacancy will occur.

In attempting to fill the vacancy, wages may have to be increased to attract the desired applicants. This rise in wages typically will choke off some of the demand for labor that generated the vacancy in the first place.

Most vacancies are for low-skilled work, in part because firms consciously fill higher level positions by promoting from within. In addition, if hiring is to replace workers who have left voluntarily, the very strong negative correlation between quit rates and wage levels seen in Chapter 7 ensures that newly announced job openings will be disproportionately for low-skilled positions.

Openings for low-skilled workers do not, however, constitute as large a fraction of the stock of vacancies at a given time as they do of the flow of new vacancies that become available in a given interval. This is because jobs for low-skilled workers are filled more rapidly than jobs requiring greater skill. The **duration of vacancies**—how long a vacancy remains unfilled—increases with the level of skill required for the job. For example, in the Netherlands between 1980 and 1988 the average duration of vacancies filled by university graduates was over twice as long as those filled by workers with the lowest educational qualifications.[1] In part, this situation occurs because the pool of job applicants consists mainly of low-skilled people, enabling employers to fill low-skilled jobs faster. In part, the greater fixed costs of hiring and of specific training needed for skilled workers give employers an incentive to search more carefully for them.

Obtaining information on the structure and number of job vacancies in the U.S. is very difficult. Most employers do not list vacancies with state employment agencies. A monthly survey comparable to the CPS that provides employer data on job vacancies does not exist, although such data were collected for manufacturing firms from 1969 to 1973. Results from one study that attempted to measure vacancies in the U.S. are presented in the first two rows of Table 8.1. These vacancy data seem to imply that there are usually more unemployed workers than vacant jobs. This finding is supported by manufacturing data from 1969 to 1973, as well as by data from a study of 28 U.S. labor markets that found vacancy rates (V) to be only one-fourth the unemployment rate (U), even in a year when unemployment was not unusually high.[2]

These figures are likely to be seriously misleading, however. Many vacancies undoubtedly go unreported, often because employers fill jobs without formally advertising them. This situation suggests that, if the measured number of unemployed workers per vacancy approaches 1.0, there are probably more actual vacancies than unemployed workers. A low vacancy rate implies that the average duration of vacancies will be short. For instance, during the boom year of 1968 in the U.S., the best estimate is that the average vacancy stayed open only two weeks.[3]

Many European countries require employers to register vacant jobs with the government, which in theory should enable vacancies to be counted more precisely. In practice, however, it appears that registered vacancies in these countries are less than 30 percent of the jobs available at any time. Thus, comparisons of the number of job seekers per vacancy and the unemploy-

---

[1]Jan van Ours and Geert Ridder, "Cyclical Variation in Vacancy Durations and Vacancy Flows," *European Economic Review* 35: 1143–1155 (1991).

[2]Harry Holzer, "Structural/Frictional and Demand-Deficient Unemployment in Local Labor Markets," *Industrial Relations* 31: 307–328 (1992).

[3]Katharine Abraham, "Structural/Frictional Versus Deficient Demand Unemployment: Some New Evidence," *American Economic Review* 73: 708–724 (1983).

TABLE 8.1 VACANCIES AND UNEMPLOYMENT, SELECTED COUNTRIES, 1968–1994

	1968	1973	1978	1982	1989	1994
United States						
Unemployed per vacancy	1.3	3.7	7.0	—	—	—
Unemployment rate (%)	4.0	5.5	7.0	9.7	5.3	6.1
West Germany						
Unemployed per vacancy	1.0	0.3	5.2	11.3	8.1	10.5
Unemployment rate (%)	1.4	0.8	4.5	6.7	7.9	9.3
Sweden[a]						
Unemployed per vacancy	1.4	2.8	2.7	7.0	1.9	25.1
Unemployment rate (%)	2.0	2.5	2.2	3.1	2.1	7.7
United Kingdom						
Unemployed per vacancy	2.8	2.7	8.5	25.1	8.3	17.9
Unemployment rate (%)	2.5	3.0	5.8	11.8	6.3	9.4

[a]Data are for 1969 and 1988 instead of 1968 and 1989.

Sources: Katharine Abraham, "Structural/Frictional versus Deficient Demand Unemployment: Some New Evidence," *American Economic Review* 73 (1983), Table 4; Per-Anders Edin and Bertil Holmlund, "Unemployment, Vacancies and Labour Market Progammes: Swedish Evidence," in Fiorella Padoi Schioppa (ed.). *Mismatch and Labour Mobility*, Cambridge: Cambridge University Press, (1991); and OECD, Main Economic Indicators, various issues.

ment rate in the United Kingdom and Sweden shown in Table 8.1 also seem to suggest that, as in the United States, the number of vacant jobs does not approach the number of unemployed workers. The experience in West Germany is somewhat different. During much of the 1960s and early 1970s there were probably more vacancies than unemployed workers in Germany. When the underreporting of vacancies is taken into account, this finding may be true for the other countries shown as well.

TYPES OF UNEMPLOYMENT

Unlike vacancies, there are huge quantities of data and other information on unemployment and unemployed workers, partly because more countries have regular surveys of workers than of firms. In addition, since workers without jobs are more attention-getting than job openings, it is not surprising that economists have paid more attention to issues involving unemployment than to those dealing with vacancies. This imbalance is unfortunate since unemployment and vacancies are closely linked, and it is hard to understand one without the other.

Economists typically divide unemployment into four conceptual types. The first is **seasonal unemployment** and consists of workers who are without jobs because it is difficult or impossible for them to perform their work at certain times of the year. Examples might be ski instructors in the summer, concrete workers in the winter when the temperature is below freezing, or fishermen who can only work when government regulations declare certain species to be in season. In general, seasonal unemployment is not regarded as an economic problem. Workers know it exists when they choose the occupation, and must, therefore, make enough while employed to compensate for the season they spend unemployed. Most unemployment data for the U.S. is **seasonally adjusted** to remove any seasonal effects from the recorded unemployment rate.

The other three types of unemployment are linked to the analysis of vacancy rates. Consider the data for 28 labor markets graphed in Figure 8.1.[4] Each point in the figure shows the combination of recorded vacancy and unemployment rates that prevailed in a particular local labor market in 1980. Also drawn is the negatively sloped regression curve that relates these two rates most simply. This curve is known as a **Beveridge curve.** The existence of such a relationship between unemployment and vacancy rates has been documented in almost every developed country.[5]

The general form of the Beveridge curve is shown in Figure 8.2. For any given structure of the labor market, vacancies and unemployment are negatively related along a curve like the one marked *AA,* just as they were in Figure 8.1. Increases in aggregate demand result in movements to the left along the curve representing a given market structure, while decreases in aggregate demand produce movements to the right. These changes along the curve that result from changes in aggregate demand are discussed in Chapter 16. Here we consider how the curve might shift over time, and how to use it to distinguish among different types of unemployment.

All positions at which the number of unemployed workers is equal to the number of vacancies lie on the 45-degree line from the origin. This line gives a basis for distinguishing between types of unemployment. To the right of this ray is **demand-deficient unemployment,** meaning that the number of unemployed workers exceeds the number of vacancies. To the left, there is

---

[4]Holzer, "Structural/Frictional."

[5]Abraham, "Structural/Frictional Versus"; Richard Jackman, Richard Layard, and Christopher Pissarides, "On Vacancies," *Oxford Bulletin of Economics and Statistics* 51: 377–394 (1989); Wolfgang Franz, "Hysteresis Effects and the NAIRU: A Theoretical and Empirical Analysis for the Federal Republic of Germany," in Richard Layard and Lars Calmfors (eds.). *The Fight Against Unemployment,* Cambridge, Mass.: MIT Press, (1987); Morley Gunderson and Noah Meltz, "Labour Market Rigidities and Unemployment in Canada," in Morley Gunderson, Noah Meltz, and Sylvia Ostry (eds.). *Unemployment: International Perspectives,* Toronto: University of Toronto Press (1987); Barry Hughes, "International Migration and the Australian Beveridge Curve," Office of the Treasurer, Canberra, Australia, Photocopy (August 1986); J. F. Jacques and F. Langot, "La Dynamique de la Courbe de Beveridge," in Pierre Henin (ed.). *La Persistance du Chomage,* Paris: *Economica* (1993); Eli Berman, "Help Wanted, Job Needed: Estimates of a Matching Function from Employment Service Data," Department of Economics, Maurice Falk Institute Discussion Paper No. 94.01 (1994).

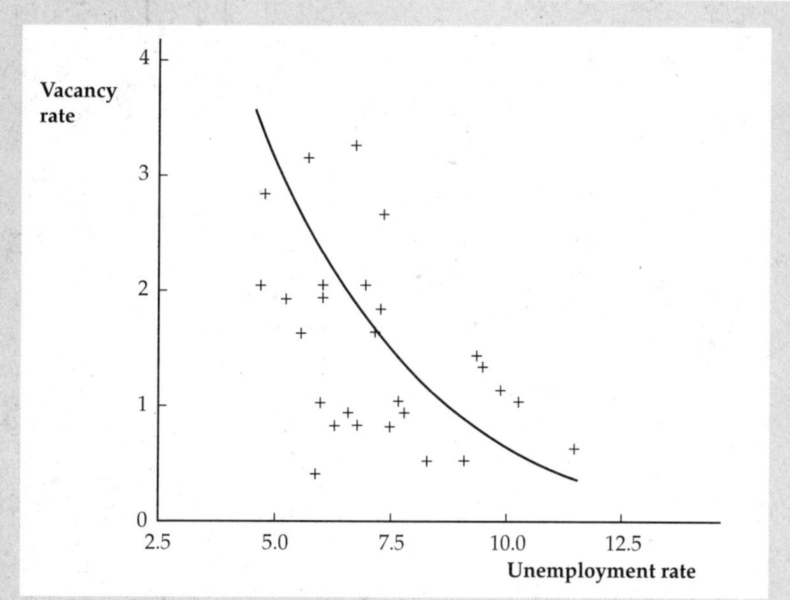

FIGURE 8.1 VACANCY AND UNEMPLOYMENT RATES, 1980
Downward sloping Beveridge curve shows that high unemployment rates are associated with low vacancy rates across U.S. local labor markets.

excess demand for labor. On or to the left of the 45-degree line on curve *AA*, all unemployment is either **structural unemployment** or **frictional unemployment.**

Structural and frictional unemployment can be distinguished by the relationship between the requirements of the vacant jobs and the unemployed workers available to fill them. We use the term *frictional unemployment* to refer to situations where the workers and jobs are appropriate for each other, and the unemployment is simply the result of the natural search process discussed in the previous two chapters. *Structural unemployment* refers to a situation where there is a fundamental mismatch between the available jobs and unemployed workers with respect to skills or residence. Thus, the fact that there are vacant jobs for computer programmers in San Jose may be small consolation to an unemployed steelworker in Pennsylvania. In reality, as we have seen in our discussions of training and mobility, characteristics of neither jobs nor workers are immutable. Over time workers will retrain or relocate and employers will alter hiring standards. Thus, it is frequently useful to refer to structural-frictional unemployment as a combined category.

In none of the labor markets shown in Figure 8.1 does the vacancy rate exceed the unemployment rate. If vacancies were accurately reported, this relationship would imply that each market contained an element of

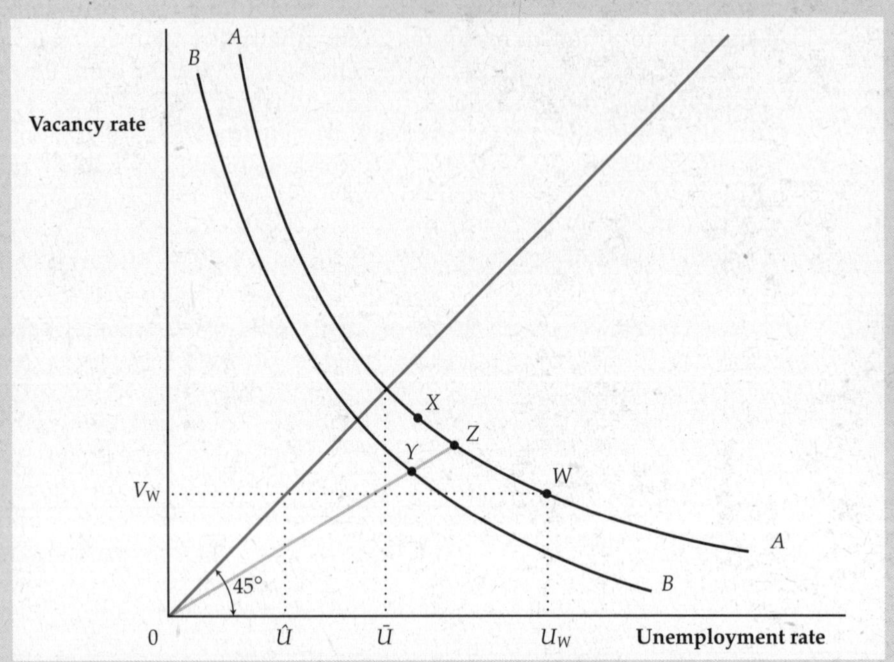

FIGURE 8.2 THE RELATIONSHIP BETWEEN UNEMPLOYMENT AND JOB VACANCIES

If vacancies are accurately measured, combinations to the right of the 45-degree line show the presence of demand deficient unemployment. Beveridge curves farther away from the origin (such as *A*) result from labor market institutions that produce higher structural-frictional unemployment at any given macroeconomic condition.

demand-deficient unemployment. If, however, we adjusted the data for this underreporting and rescaled the vertical axis in Figure 8.1, we might find that many of the labor markets would be to the left of the 45-degree line.

Our main interest in this chapter is the extent and composition of structural-frictional unemployment. Ideally, we would like to examine unemployment outside the context of the business cycle, at times when demand-deficient unemployment is stable at an optimal level (perhaps even zero). Note, however, that there are still many possible levels of *U* and *V* along the 45-degree line that are consistent with demand-deficient unemployment being zero. The Beveridge curve can lie farther away from or closer to the origin. For any overall economic situation, there are fewer vacancies and less unemployment along Beveridge curve *BB* in Figure 8.2 than there are along *AA*.

Policymakers often care about what the unemployment rate is on the 45-degree line on the Beveridge curve that characterizes the economy at a given point in time. Alternatively, this statement means determining the unemployment rate when demand-deficient unemployment is zero, an easy task if vacancy rates were measured well. An increase in demand-deficient unemployment is indicated by a movement such as from *X* to *Z*, with vacancies decreasing and unemployment increasing. Greater structural-frictional unemployment is indicated by a movement such as from *Y* to *Z*, where both unemployment and vacancies increase by an equal proportion. In general this shift would be regarded as a movement from a more to a less attractive Beveridge curve unless the greater number of unemployed workers and vacancies enabled better quality matches to be made. There is strong evidence that Beveridge curves in many countries, especially those in Europe, have shifted to a less favorable position during the past two decades.[6]

Figure 8.2 can be used to explore ways that a given total amount of unemployment can be broken down into demand-deficient and structural-frictional unemployment. Suppose that the labor market is at point *W* on curve *AA*, with an unemployment rate of U_W, and a vacancy rate of V_W. Defining demand-deficient unemployment as zero when the vacancy rate equals the unemployment rate, the rate of demand-deficient unemployment might appear to be $U_W - V_W$. This relationship would put the boundary between the two components at $\hat{U}$, with the distance $0\hat{U}$ equal to the structural-frictional component, and the distance $\hat{U}U_W$ equalling demand-deficient unemployment. It is clear from the diagram, however, that the distance U_W overstates the number of jobs that would need to be created to reduce demand-deficient unemployment to zero. If demand is increased with no change in the structure of the labor market, the economy will move leftward along *AA*, and equality between unemployment and vacancies will be reached at the unemployment rate $\bar{U}$, along the 45-degree line. At this point the structural-frictional component $0\bar{U}$ is larger than $0\hat{U}$. Since the increased demand for labor has not consisted entirely of demand for people with the skills and in the locations represented by the unemployed, the number of unfilled vacancies has risen.

A great deal of interest exists in knowing when there is zero demand-deficient unemployment, in part because of its connection to macroeconomic policy design. Whether a government pursues a stimulatory macro policy should depend on whether it believes the policy will accelerate short-run inflationary pressures. The civilian unemployment rate in the United States in 1994 was 6.1 percent. Many economists would agree that this rate almost entirely reflected structural-frictional unemployment and that on average during 1994 there was little, if any, demand-deficient unemployment. As we will see in Chapter 16, however, a stimulatory macro policy may be inflationary, even when there is no demand-deficient unemployment, if it increases demand in those areas where there are substantial structural vacancies.

---

[6]Richard Layard, S. Nickell, and Richard Jackman, *Unemployment, Macroeconomic Performance and the Labour Market,* Oxford: Oxford University Press (1991).

UNEMPLOYMENT DYNAMICS

UNEMPLOYMENT FLOWS

We can begin to understand some of the determinants of $\bar{U}$ in Figure 8.2 by considering the movements into or out of unemployment that comprise **unemployment flows.** As in Chapter 1, let L be the labor force, E be employment and U be unemployment. If the economy is in equilibrium, the number of people leaving unemployment each month must equal the number entering unemployment each month. Therefore, with a stable labor force participation rate:

$$nU = sE$$

where n = the fraction of unemployed leaving unemployment, and
s = the fraction of employed who become unemployed.

Since $L = E + U$, we can rewrite this equation as

$$nU = s[L - U].$$

This equation can be solved for U to give:

$$U = L \times \frac{s}{s+n}$$

or

$$URATE = 100 \times \frac{s}{s+n}$$

where

$$URATE = \text{the unemployment rate}$$

and we multiply by 100 to express it as a percentage.[7]

Table 8.2 shows the flows s and n for several countries in 1992. The rate of inflow is very much smaller than the rate of outflow. In other words, an unemployed worker is much more likely to find a job each month than an employed worker is to lose one. Also shown in the table are unemployment rates for each country. In some of the countries there clearly was demand-deficient unemployment in 1992. In others, including the United States, Sweden, and Japan, however, demand-deficient unemployment was relatively low.

It is interesting to compare unemployment flows in these three countries. The striking difference is the far higher rates of both inflow into and outflow from unemployment in the U.S. than in the other two countries. The U.S. economy is characterized by people entering jobs at a much higher rate than

---

[7]This exposition is based on Robert Barro, *Macroeconomics*, New York: Wiley (1990).

TABLE 8.2 FLOWS INTO AND OUT OF UNEMPLOYMENT, 1992, SELECTED COUNTRIES (AS PERCENT OF SOURCE GROUP)

Country	Inflow (s)	Outflow (n)	Standardized Unemployment Rate
United States	2.8	32	7.3
Australia	1.5	10	10.7
Canada	3.3	23	11.2
France	0.5	4	10.4
Japan	0.5	21	2.2
Spain	1.2	4	18.1
Sweden	1.1	17	4.8
United Kingdom	1.3	10	10.0

Sources: OECD, *Employment Outlook* (1994), and *OECD Jobs Study: Facts, Analysis, Strategies* (1994), adjusted to let the labor force be the basis for s.

in other countries, as shown by the high rate of outflow n. Thus, although workers are much more likely to become unemployed in the U.S., once unemployed they find jobs much more quickly than workers elsewhere.

The dynamic analysis of equilibrium unemployment allows us to pinpoint the effects of factors that raise or reduce structural-frictional unemployment. Factors that increase s increase equilibrium unemployment; factors that increase n reduce equilibrium unemployment. In terms of some of the institutions we discussed in Chapter 6, improvements in the employment service or other agencies that help match unemployed workers to vacant jobs more efficiently would raise n. Such improvements would shift the Beveridge curve in Figure 8.2 inward. Higher unemployment benefits would reduce time spent searching for jobs and increase the acceptance wage, thus reducing n and shifting the Beveridge curve outward. Greater industrial diversity in a labor market means that when demand drops in one industry, vacant jobs may be available for workers in other industries so that they need not experience any unemployment. This reduces s and thus reduces structural-frictional unemployment.[8]

DURATION VERSUS INCIDENCE

Looking at unemployment flows is a useful way to study unemployment, especially if we are interested in tracing the effects of institutions and policies on movements into and out of unemployment. It is less useful if we are interested in examining the **burden of unemployment** on the unemployed as measured by their loss in well-being.

[8]Curtis Simon, "Frictional Unemployment and the Role of Industrial Diversity," *Quarterly Journal of Economics* 103: 715–728 (1988).

POLICY ISSUE

CHANGING STRUCTURAL-FRICTIONAL UNEMPLOYMENT

Most economists believe that the amount of structural-frictional unemployment in the U.S. rose slowly from the late 1950s through the late 1960s, then rose sharply to a peak in the early 1980s, and stayed roughly constant or fell slightly from the mid-1980s.[9] The total increase during this nearly 40-year period has been between 1.5 and 2 percentage points. What caused this increase in structural-frictional unemployment that shifted the Beveridge curve out? Will it reverse itself in the future?

One source of the increase is clear. The demographic mix of the labor force during the period shifted away from groups that always exhibit low rates of unemployment. In 1957, males aged 25 to 54 accounted for 46 percent of the U.S. civilian labor force, while in 1982 they represented only 37 percent. As we saw in Chapter 1, this relative decline was due to the rapid increase in the labor force participation of adult females, combined with increased potential teenaged labor force resulting from the baby boom. If the structure of the labor force in 1979 had been the same as it was in 1957, the unemployment rate in 1979 would have been only 5.0 percent instead of the actual 5.8 percent. Changes in demography thus account for 0.8 percentage point of the 2.0 percentage point increase in structural-frictional unemployment.

Also contributing to this higher unemployment was the expansion in the number of firms and workers covered by unemployment insurance between 1960 and the late 1970s. One estimate suggests that this increased coverage accounted for half a percentage point of additional unemployment. On the other hand, the growth of other transfer programs reduced unemployment. In Chapter 1 we showed how the growth of disability insurance induced workers to leave the labor force. Because of the progressiveness of the disability insurance benefit structures, the workers who left were likely to have been low-paid and low-skilled and, therefore, to have had an above-average rate of unemployment. The expansion of disability insurance and Social Security retirement benefits reduced the labor force by encouraging older workers with the highest chance of being unemployed to leave. This effect is hard to measure, but it could easily have offset the impact of the expanded unemployment insurance program. On net, the growth of transfer programs probably had little if any effect on the structural-frictional unemployment rate.[10]

The remaining part of the increase in structural-frictional unemployment might be accounted for by shifts in industrial structure and by changes in mobility across sectors. These shifts generated an increase in *s* over an extended period of time. One estimate attributes 0.5 percentage points of the remaining higher structural-frictional unemployment in 1979 as compared to 1957 to the effects of shocks to energy prices. During the 1970s

---

[9]Robert Gordon, *Macroeconomics,* Boston: Little Brown (1990).

[10]Daniel Hamermesh, "Transfers, Taxes and the NAIRU," in Laurence Meyer (ed.). *The Supply-Side Effects of Economic Policy,* Boston: Kluwer-Nijhoff (1981).

workers' propensity to change industries also decreased, making the effects of any sectoral shocks more severe.[11]

With the aging of the baby-boom generation, the demographic mix of the labor force is shifting back toward groups with low unemployment. By 1994 the fraction of the labor force who were men aged 25 to 54 had increased 1.7 percentage points to 38.7 percent. The impact of energy problems on structural-frictional unemployment also lessened during the 1980s, so that *s* dropped. For a variety of reasons, including less generous benefits, unemployment insurance has added less to unemployment since the early 1980s, causing *n* to increase.[12]

All of these changes will lead structural-frictional unemployment to fall in the 1990s. At least a part of these improvements will be offset, however, by increases in structural unemployment resulting from the global reallocation of industries brought about by movements toward freer trade.

Consider the following possibilities. The unemployment rate in 1994 was 6.1 percent. It would have been at that level if 6.1 percent of the labor force were unemployed for the entire year. If, for example, workers began their spell of unemployment on January 1, the average **duration of unemployment** would be 52 weeks at year's end, and the **incidence of unemployment** (the fraction of workers experiencing any unemployment) would be 6.1 percent. Alternatively, the unemployment rate could have been 6.1 percent if every labor force participant experienced a spell of unemployment of 3.2 weeks (6.1 percent times 52 weeks) in length during 1994, but the incidence of unemployment would have been 100 percent.

In the United States, the average duration of spells of unemployment reported in the CPS during 1994 was 4.3 months. It is important to realize that this is *not* the average length of spells of unemployment. It represents the answer to the question "how long have you been unemployed?" asked of the *currently unemployed*. By definition, people who are currently unemployed have not yet completed their spells of unemployment. Spells currently in progress must be longer than they have been to date by the time they are completed. On the other hand, by surveying people on a particular date, those experiencing a long spell are more likely to be asked the question

---

[11]David Lilien, "Sectoral Shifts and Cyclical Unemployment," *Journal of Political Economy* 90: 777–793 (1982); Katharine Abraham and Lawrence Katz, "Cyclical Unemployment: Sectoral Shifts or Aggregate Disturbances?" *Journal of Political Economy* 94: 507–522 (1986); Kevin Murphy and Robert Topel, "The Evolution of Unemployment in the United States: 1968–1985," in Stanley Fischer (ed.). *NBER Macroeconomics Annual 1987*, Cambridge, Mass.: MIT Press (1987). The 0.5 percent point figure is calculated as the change in the difference between the structural-frictional unemployment measure in Lilien, "Sectoral Shifts," p. 790, which includes this effect, and Gordon, *Macroeconomics*, which does not.

[12]Rebecca Blank and David Card, "Recent Trends in Insured and Uninsured Employment: Is There an Explanation," *Quarterly Journal of Economics* 106: 1557–1589 (1991).

than those experiencing a short spell.[13] Thus, the relationship between average length of spells of unemployment in progress on a given date may be more or less than the average length of all spells of unemployment in an economy.

Assuming we have a measure of the average length of **completed spells of unemployment** and ignoring movements into and out of the labor force, we can write the unemployment rate as

$$URATE = 100 \times SPELLS \times \frac{DUR}{52},$$

where $SPELLS$ = number of spells per worker in the civilian labor force,
and DUR = average duration of spells, in weeks.

Suppose spells in progress have the same length as completed spells of unemployment. Then in this formula, the 1994 average duration of 18.8 weeks and national unemployment rate of 6.1 percent combine to give an incidence of unemployment of about 17 percent.

Because the pattern of flows into and out of unemployment differs between the U.S. and most other industrialized nations, the average duration of unemployment spells differs greatly. Most countries do not publish data on the average duration of unemployment, but data are available on the percent of the labor force who have been out of work for a long time. Table 8.3 presents the fraction of the unemployed who have been out of work for 6 months or more and 12 months or more as well as the overall unemployment rate for 3 recent years.

The most striking difference among the countries listed is the incidence of long-term unemployment. Very long-term unemployment is about the same in Canada, Sweden, and Japan as it is in the U.S. In European Union countries such as Germany, France, and the U.K., however, many unemployed workers have been unemployed for at least a year. It is particularly informative to compare Germany and the U.S., since as a rule these two countries have had about the same overall unemployment rate in recent years. In 1989, for example, with identical unemployment rates, half the unemployed in Germany had been unemployed for at least a year as opposed to less than 6 percent in the U.S. This remarkably large difference reflects the very low rate of outflow from unemployment in Germany and high rate in the U.S. that were shown in Table 8.2. It also implies that in Germany the burden of unemployment is spread much more unequally across the labor force.

---

[13]To see this, suppose, for example, that there were two types of unemployed, those who were out of work for 52 weeks each spell and those whose spells lasted only 1 week. Further, suppose that there were 52 times as many of the second type, one of whom became unemployed every week of the year. Now suppose that in the final week of the unemployment spell of the long-term unemployed person you asked the length to date of those with spells currently in progress. The answer would be 26.5 weeks (52 weeks plus 1 week divided by 2). The average length of all spells during the year, however, would have been slightly less than 2 weeks (52 weeks plus 52 times 1 week divided by 53).

TABLE 8.3 UNEMPLOYMENT RATES AND LONG-TERM UNEMPLOYMENT, 1983–1993

	1983			*1989*			*1993*		
Country	Rate	% > 6 Months	% > Year	Rate	% > 6 Months	% > Year	Rate	% > 6 Months	% > Year
United States	9.5	23.9	13.3	5.4	9.9	5.7	7.2	20.4	11.7
Australia	9.9	52.7	27.5	6.1	40.6	23.1	10.8	57.1	36.5
Canada	11.8	28.8	9.9	7.5	20.8	6.8	11.1	31.4	14.4
France	8.3	67.0	42.2	9.4	63.7	43.9	11.6	58.2	34.2
Germany	7.7	64.8	39.3	5.6	66.7	49.0	5.8	55.4	33.5[a]
Japan	2.6	31.5	12.9	2.3	37.3	18.7	2.5	34.4	17.2
Sweden	3.5	24.9	10.3	1.4	18.2	6.3	8.2	32.0	10.9
United Kingdom	12.4	68.0	47.0	7.2	52.7	40.8	10.3	57.3	35.4[a]

[a]1992 data.

Source: *OECD Employment Outlook*, (1994), Tables K and P.

There is a second major difference between patterns shown for various countries in Table 8.3. In the U.S., it is evident that long-term unemployment responds to the business cycle. There was much more long-term unemployment in 1993, when the U.S. was emerging from a recession, than there was in 1989 at the peak of a boom. This responsiveness to the business cycle is much less pronounced in Western Europe, where long-term unemployment seems to be more structural in nature and does not respond much to overall economic conditions.

Of course, there is a converse side to the figures presented above. If the average spell of unemployment is much shorter in the U.S. than in Germany, then for the overall unemployment rate to be the same in both countries, either many more Americans experience unemployment each year or the same persons must have several spells of unemployment. For example, a college student who is in the labor force during the summer may work with a temporary help agency and experience several one-week spells of unemployment that summer. Each spell would be very short, but the overall burden on the student could be substantial. If workers experience **multiple spells** of unemployment, the burden of unemployment on any unemployed worker may be greater than the average spell length, since the total number of weeks out of work in a year would be greater than the average spell length.

There is some evidence that the average duration of unemployment in the U.S. is not as short as it once was. The increase in structural-frictional unemployment noted in the Policy Issue Box is almost entirely an increase in the average duration of unemployment. There has been no major trend in incidence between the late 1960s and the mid-1990s. The increase in duration may have been due to workers searching longer. Search theory would predict such an increase for two reasons, the first being the dispersion of wages increased during this period. As we saw in Chapter 6, a greater dispersion of

POLICY ISSUE

EURO-SCLEROSIS

In 1994 several countries including Austria, Sweden, Finland and Norway voted on whether to join the European Union (EU). Many of the emerging market economies of Central and Eastern Europe have indicated their desire to join the EU as soon as possible. While there are many advantages to membership in the EU, the unemployment experience of its members is not one of them.

Table 8.4 shows the average unemployment rate for several periods in the U.S., Japan, EU member countries (weighted by population), and non-EU European countries. The trend is striking. Both periods from 1969 to 1973 and 1986 to 1992 contained relatively mild recession years (1970 and 1991). A slight increase occurred in the overall unemployment rate in the U.S., in line with the demographic and other shifts discussed earlier. There were larger increases in the rest of the industrial world, including very large ones among EU members. This contrast is especially stark if one compares Denmark, an EU member, with Sweden, a very similar country that was not then an EU member. Denmark's average unemployment rate of 0.95 percent between 1969 and 1973 rose steeply to an average of 9.72 percent between 1986 and 1992. Meanwhile, Sweden's average unemployment rate of 2.22 percent in 1969 to 1973 rose only slightly to 2.37 percent in 1986 to 1992.

It is not at all clear what has caused this relative shift.[14] Several possible reasons *not* appearing to play a major role are the following: changes in labor force productivity; differences in government expenditures as a share of GDP; union militancy; the fraction of lost income replaced by unemployment benefits; and legislation regarding labor standards, such as employee representation and other working conditions. One apparent explanation lies in an increasing mismatch between workers' skills and labor market demands coupled with rigidities that prevent wages from adjusting to these shifts. Factors that appear to play a role in this rigidity include minimum wages, differences in the length of eligibility for unemployment benefits, firing costs, and a significant reduction in rates of profitability and capital investment in EU countries relative to the rest of the developed world. The importance of unemployment benefits in creating long-term unemployment is further illustrated by comparing countries within the EU such as Spain and Portugal. Portugal, although an EU member since 1986, has had a much less generous unemployment system than Spain or other EU members with respect to who is eligible for unemployment benefits. For example, to receive unemployment benefits a worker must have been employed for six months out of the past four years in Spain but one-and-a-half out of the past two years in Portugal. This apparently goes a long way in explaining why Spanish unemployment rates are almost four times Portuguese ones even though in almost every other way the economies of the two countries are very similar. A second contributing factor might be the difference between the countries in the EU and the other countries in the table is the **marginal tax wedge** on labor, where the marginal tax wedge is defined as the sum of employees' and employers' Social Security contributions, personal income taxes, and consumption taxes. For 1992, this wedge for the average production worker was 63 percent in the EU, 40 percent in the rest of Europe, 39 percent in the U.S., and only 22

[14]The discussion that follows is based on Charles Bean, "European Unemployment: A Survey," *Journal of Economic Literature* 32: 573–619 (1994), and *OECD Employment Outlook*, (1994), Chapter 4, "Labour Standards and Economic Integration."

percent in Japan. Finally, there is evidence that increases in severance pay requirements if workers are discharged may have made employers less willing to hire new employees in Europe, thereby reducing the employment-to-population ratio and increasing unemployment. The best estimate is that moving from no severance pay requirement to 3 months of required severance pay for workers with 10 or more years of tenure reduces employment-to-population ratios by 1.15 percent (1.3 million jobs in the U.S.) and increases unemployment rates by 12.5 percent. Changes in severance pay requirements appear to have been particularly important in explaining increases in unemployment in Italy and France in recent decades.[15]

Whatever the causes, it is clear that the persistence of unemployment in EU countries is much greater than in other, similarly developed economies. Thus, shocks to demand that produce temporary increases in unemployment elsewhere appear to permanently increase the equilibrium level of unemployment in the EU. Potential members may want to consider whether there is something inherent in the structure and operation of the EU that causes this phenomenon before rushing to join.

TABLE 8.4 UNEMPLOYMENT RATES FOR VARIOUS REGIONS, 1969–1992

	1969–1973	1974–1979	1980–1985	1986–1992	Percent Increase Between 1969–1973 and 1986–1992
United States	4.86	6.68	8.00	6.13	26.1
Japan	1.22	1.93	2.42	2.40	96.7
Non-EU Europe[a]	1.50	2.09	3.12	3.40	126.7
European Union[b]	2.96	4.95	9.57	9.91	234.8

[a]Includes Austria, Finland, Norway, Sweden, and Switzerland.

[b]Includes Belgium, Denmark, France, West Germany, Ireland, Italy, Netherlands, Spain, and United Kingdom.

Source: Calculated from Bean, "European Unemployment," Table 1.

[15]C. Bean, R. Layard, and S. Nickell, "The Rise in Unemployment: A Multi-Country Study," *Economica* 53: S1–S22 (1986); Michael Burda, "Wait Unemployment in Europe," *Economic Policy* 7: 393–416 (1988); Bean, "European Unemployment;" F. Padoa-Schioppa (ed.). *Mismatch and Labour Mobility*, Cambridge: Cambridge University Press (1990); Edward Lazear, "Job Security and Unemployment," in Yoram Weiss and Gideon Fishelson (eds.). *Advances in the Theory and Measurement of Unemployment*, New York: St. Martin's Press (1990); OECD, *OECD Jobs Study* (1994); Olivier Blanchard and Juan F. Jimeno, "Structural Unemployment: Spain versus Portugal," *American Economic Review* 85: 212–218 (1995); Henri Sneessens and Fatemeh Shadman-Mehta, "Real Wages, Skill Mismatch, and Unemployment Persistence, France 1962–89," *Annales d'economie et de statistique* 37/38 (1995) in press.

wages increases the payoff to more search, and therefore increases the period spent unemployed while searching. Second, the growth of two-earner households has meant that the economic cushion of many unemployed workers has increased, thus raising their asking wages.[16]

It may be that the very fact of being unemployed itself harms a worker's chances of obtaining a job. Is unemployment a **stigma** in the labor market? For unemployment to be a stigma it must be the case that the longer a worker is unemployed, the more difficult it becomes to leave unemployment. In terms of the dynamics of unemployment, a stigma implies that n drops as the duration of unemployment increases. This phenomenon is known as **state-dependence,** since the value of the parameter under consideration (n) depends on the how long the worker has been in the state of being unemployed. One reason why state-dependence might exist is if, in response to a large number of applicants generated by a vacancy, employers used the time since a worker's last job as a screening device for either deciding which applicants would be placed on a short list for further interviewing or in ranking those on the short list for hiring. There is some evidence that this is how employers behave.[17]

Data on the rate of outflow from unemployment of men in 12 U.S. states from 1978 to 1983 are shown in Figure 8.3.[18] There are two obvious trends in this data. The probability of an unemployed worker finding a job in any week falls rapidly during the first two months of unemployment and then is roughly constant until he has been unemployed for about six months. This is the point at which unemployment benefits typically expire in the U.S., causing the costs of remaining unemployed to rise dramatically and leading many workers to accept a job.

The drop in the probability of leaving unemployment (called the **hazard rate** for exiting unemployment) in the first few weeks may not represent a stigma. This period is very short for workers to be stigmatized by being unemployed. It is likely, instead, to reflect **heterogeneity** or differences in workers. Those workers with unusually good prospects will find jobs relatively quickly, leaving only those with poorer prospects to remain unemployed for two months or longer. Thus, the higher exit rate for those who have been unemployed a short time reflects the average of some workers with a very good chance of finding a job and other workers with worse prospects. As spell lengths increase, the fraction of workers with high probabilities of finding a job remaining in the sample decreases, and the average exit rate for those remaining also decreases.

---

[16]Murphy and Topel, "The Evolution;" Jonathan Leonard and Michael Horrigan, "The Unemployment Experience of the Workforce," *Research in Labor Economics* 11: 201–222 (1990).

[17]Elazar Berkovitch, "A Stigma Theory of Unemployment Duration," in Weiss and Fishelson (eds.). *Advances in the Theory*; Olivier Blanchard and Peter Diamond, "Ranking, Unemployment Duration and Wages," *Review of Economic Studies* 61: 417–434 (1994).

[18]These weekly data on n are from Bruce Meyer, "Unemployment Insurance and Unemployment Spells," *Econometrica* 58: 757–782 (1990).

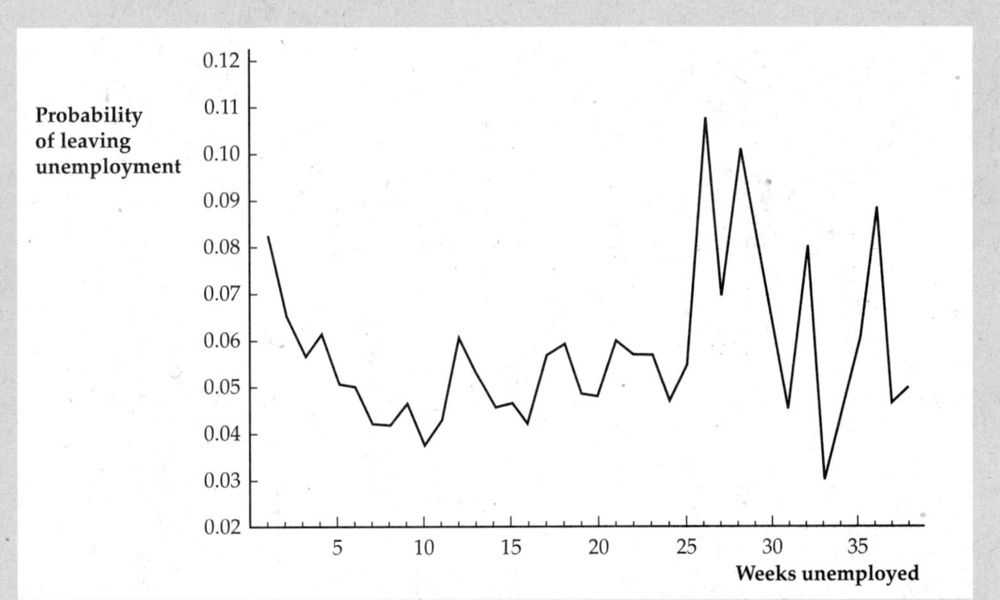

FIGURE 8.3 RATE OF LEAVING UNEMPLOYMENT BY WEEK, 1978–1983
The probability of leaving unemployment falls during the first few weeks of a spell, then remains relatively constant until benefits are exhausted, after which it rises sharply.

That this pattern would exist, even if n did not decline for any individual worker, is supported from findings from a sample of unemployed Swedish workers followed between 1965 and 1980. Similarly, in Spain, where the fraction of long-term unemployed is very high, being unemployed longer did not reduce a worker's chances of leaving unemployment. For the average unemployed worker, there is little evidence that leaving unemployment is any more difficult in the 40th week, for example, than it was in the 10th week. For some demographic groups or occupations, however, being unemployed longer may be more of a stigma. Studies of young British workers, for example, have shown that it is more difficult to leave unemployment the longer the person has been out of work.[19]

---

[19]Per-Anders Edin, "Unemployment Duration and Competing Risks: Evidence from Sweden," *Scandinavian Journal of Economics* 91: 639–653 (1989); Alfonso Alba-Ramirez and Richard Freeman, "Jobfinding and Wages When Long-run Unemployment is Really Long: The Case of Spain," National Bureau of Economic Research, Working Paper No. 3409, (August 1990); Lisa Lynch, "State Dependency in Youth Unemployment: A Lost Generation?" *Journal of Econometrics* 28: 71–84 (1985).

POLICY ISSUE

WORK SHARING AND THE INCIDENCE OF UNEMPLOYMENT

A number of European countries have introduced **work-sharing** programs designed to spread the burden of unemployment among more workers. Where these programs provide very generous compensation for partial unemployment (**short-time employment**), evidence exists that they result in greater variation in hours of work and lower variation in employment over the business cycle than would otherwise have been the case. With prodding from the federal government, some states have introduced such programs on an experimental basis in the U.S.[20]

There is good reason for policymakers to be concerned about whether a nation's unemployment rate arises from many short spells or from fewer long ones. Most workers can survive a short period of unemployment with little difficulty. Some lost income will be replaced by unemployment insurance benefits, and living standards can be maintained by drawing down savings or by borrowing. The longer unemployment persists, however, the more serious its consequences become. Eligibility for unemployment insurance benefits is eventually exhausted, savings are used up, and further credit is unavailable. In very long spells of unemployment, work skills can deteriorate from disuse. Work-sharing programs can be rationalized as a way of making the average worker better off.

Consider an economy consisting of many identical workers, each of whom supplies labor to the market along curve S in Figure 8.4.[21] The horizontal axis shows the number of hours per year that each worker is willing to supply at a given wage. The wage at which each marginal hour of labor is supplied is the value of an extra hour of leisure. At a market wage of w^m the typical worker wishes to supply 2000 hours per year. The difference between w^m and the supply curve at each point shows the surplus the worker gains from working that hour, in other words, the difference between the wage she receives and the value of the leisure hour she must give up.

Assume that demand is high enough to provide employment for all but 2000 of the total hours supplied to the economy. Those 2000 hours of unemployment could all be borne by one worker, who would be unemployed the entire year. Ignoring search costs, which we assume are the same during each hour of unemployment, the monetary loss to that worker is the lost wage income, $0w^mCF$. The true loss is only w^rw^mC, however, since the worker would have derived value equal to $0w^rCF$ from the leisure she could have consumed were she not working.

---

[20]Kenneth Burdett and Randall Wright, "Unemployment Insurance and Short-Time Compensation: The Effects on Layoffs, Hours per Worker, and Wages," *Journal of Political Economy* 97: 1479–1496 (1989); Susan Houseman and Katherine Abraham, "Labor Adjustment under Different Institutional Structures: A Case Study of Germany and the United States," in Fredrick Buttler et. al. (eds.). *Institutional Frameworks and Labor Market Performance* New York: Routledge (1995); Marc Van Audenrode, "Short-Time Compensation, Job Security, and Employment Contracts: Evidence from Selected OECD Countries," *Journal of Political Economy* 102: 76–102 (1994).

[21]This argument and figure expand upon Michael Hurd, "A Compensation Measure of the Cost of Unemployment to the Unemployed," *Quarterly Journal of Economics* 95: 225–244 (1980).

Now suppose that the burden of the 2000 hours of unemployment was split equally between two workers. Each would work 1000 hours per year and be unemployed for 1000 hours (consume 1000 hours of leisure). The lost wage income for each is shown by the rectangle *GDCF*. The total wage loss for the two workers together is the same as the wage loss if one person bore the entire burden of unemployment. The true loss per worker, however, is the triangle *EDC*. The total loss is, therefore, twice this area. This is less than $w^r w^m C$, the loss experienced by the one worker who bore the entire burden of 2000 hours of unemployment. The reason is that the first few hours spent out of work yield a lot of enjoyment as leisure and do not entail substantial financial adjustments. For this reason work sharing is an attractive way to reduce the burden of long-term unemployment. This same effect is accomplished by the high incidence but short relative duration of unemployment in the U.S. Given that long-term unemployment is much more widespread in most of Europe, it is not surprising that formal job-sharing policies have received more attention there. Of course, if work-sharing programs reduce the incentive of workers to leave declining industries, they will make it more difficult for the economy to respond to structural shifts and could increase the overall unemployment rate.

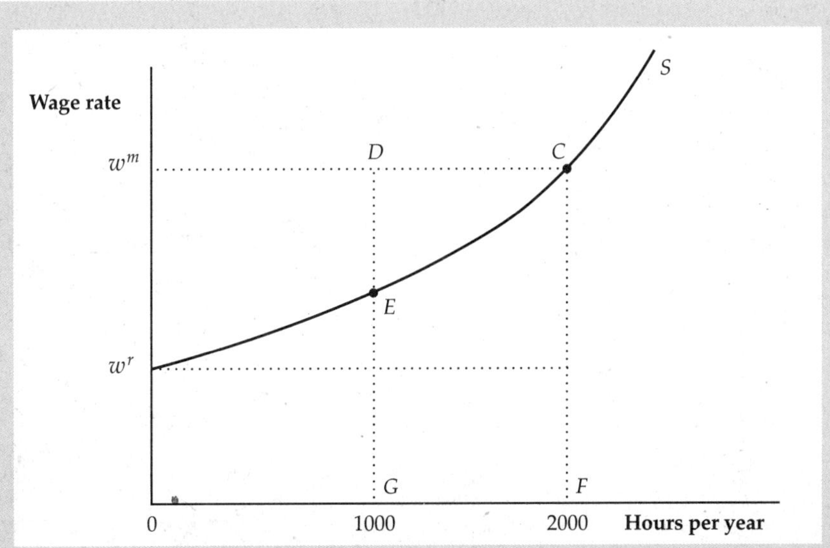

FIGURE 8.4 THE BURDEN OF UNEMPLOYMENT

Because of declining marginal utility of leisure (and money), the total loss to society from a given amount of unemployment will be less if that unemployment is shared among more than one worker.

THE STRUCTURE OF UNEMPLOYMENT

Differences in unemployment rates, incidence and duration among demographic groups, and geographic areas are pronounced. This **structure of unemployment** varies over time, in ways that we will discuss in Chapter 16. It also has common characteristics at all times within the U.S. as well as in many other countries.

AGE, GENDER, AND RACIAL/ETHNIC DIFFERENCES IN UNEMPLOYMENT

Differences in unemployment rates by demographic group are caused by several factors considered in previous chapters. Data on unemployment rates by age, sex, and race/ethnicity for 1994 are shown in Table 8.5. Since there was little, if any, demand-deficient unemployment that year, differences in this table reflect almost entirely differences in structural-frictional unemployment.

As can be seen from the bottom row of Table 8.5, unemployment rates of men and women are about equal. Until quite recently, this has not been the case. Historically, women's unemployment rates have been much higher than men's, with a difference in structural-frictional unemployment rates of about two percentage points in 1968. Why has this difference disappeared? One explanation is the tremendous growth in female labor force participation over the past 30 years. Because of their increased labor force attachment, women now have fewer spells of unemployment resulting from transitions into the labor force. There has also been a relative increase in the rate at which women leave unemployment and find jobs (a relative increase in n) that may account for about half of the convergence in men's and women's unemployment rates.[22] Another part of this convergence results from a shift in labor demand toward industries and occupations that have historically relied on female workers.

The very high rates of unemployment among teenagers in the U.S. shown in Table 8.5 are consistent with both fixed costs of employment, which imply lower unemployment where the investment in the employee is greater, and job shopping, which predicts more search at the beginning of a worker's career. Even with no overall demand-deficient unemployment, structural shifts will result in declining employment in some industries or firms. Young workers, having little specific training and usually employed in relatively unskilled jobs, will be among the first dismissed if demand decreases.

Many teenagers also move in and out of the labor force frequently. Often they are in school most of the year and must search for a new job each time they enter the labor force. Young workers in school are often "target savers" who work only long enough to accumulate the cash needed for a specific

---

[22]Janet Johnson, "Sex Differentials in Unemployment Rates: A Case for No Concern," *Journal of Political Economy* 91: 293–303 (1983); Larry DeBoer and Michael Seeborg, "The Unemployment Rates of Men and Women: A Transition Probability Analysis," *Industrial and Labor Relations Review* 42: 404–414 (1989).

TABLE 8.5 UNEMPLOYMENT RATES BY AGE, SEX, RACE, AND ETHNICITY, 1994

	Males			*Females*		
Age	White	Black	Hispanic	White	Black	Hispanic
16–17	16.5	39.3	33.3	16.6	32.9	29.7
18–19	14.7	36.5	22.5	11.8	32.5	18.1
20–24	8.8	19.4	10.8	7.4	19.6	13.5
25–54	4.3	9.1	7.7	4.4	8.7	9.3
55 and over	4.0	6.4	8.0	5.2	4.8	6.6
All ages, 16 and over	5.4	12.0	9.4	5.2	11.0	10.7

Source: *Employment and Earnings,* (January 1995), pp. 165–167.

expense, such as tuition or a car, and then drop out of the labor force until they perceive another spending need.

The startlingly high unemployment rate among youth raises an important question. If teenagers experience unemployment, will they also be afflicted by higher unemployment rates throughout their working lives because of this unfortunate experience? Or does teenage unemployment merely interrupt the accumulation of human capital, so that the only long-term effect is a slightly lower wage rate later in life? In other words, does unemployment create a permanent **"scarring"** that harms workers' subsequent labor market outcomes? The scarring problem is conceptually different from the stigma of unemployment. A *stigma* refers to an increase in the difficulty of obtaining work as unemployment duration increases. *Scarring* refers to what happens after the spell of unemployment has ended.

Evidence for the U.S. indicates that the number of weeks a youth is employed in a particular year is not greatly affected by his or her unemployment in previous years. There is also little evidence of scarring, as seen in either lower wages or higher unemployment five years later, among older workers who are displaced from their jobs. Thus, scarring does not seem to be a problem in the U.S. There is some evidence that it may be more important in other countries. It may, for example, play a significant role in the much longer duration of unemployment in Western Europe.[23]

[23]David Ellwood, "Teenage Unemployment: Permanent Scars or Temporary Blemishes?" in Richard Freeman and David Wise (eds.). *The Youth Labor Market Problem: Its Nature, Causes and Consequences,* Chicago: University of Chicago Press (1982); Christopher Ruhm, "Are Workers Permanently Scarred by Job Displacements?" *American Economic Review* 81: 319–324 (1991); Niels Henning Bjørn, "Persistent Effects of Early Unemployment: The Case of Apprentices," Aarhus School of Business, Photocopy (1991); Gebhard Flaig, Georg Licht, and Viktor Steiner, "Testing for State Dependence Effects in a Dynamic Model of Male Unemployment Behaviour," in Henning Bunzel, Peter Jensen, Niels Westergard-Nielsen (eds.). *Panel Data and Labour Market Dynamics,* Amsterdam: North-Holland (1993), pp. 189–214.

TABLE 8.6 Unemployment Rates by Age, Selected Industrialized Countries, 1993

Country	Total	Teenagers[a]	20–24	25+
United States	6.7	19.0	10.5	5.8
Australia	10.8	23.0	16.1	8.5
Canada	11.1	19.9	16.4	10.0
France	11.6	26.5	24.4	9.8
Italy[b]	10.5	40.8	29.8	7.6
Japan	2.5	7.1	4.7	2.0
Spain	22.4	50.3	40.5	19.3
Sweden	8.2	19.2	18.1	8.1
United Kingdom	10.3	19.2	16.4	8.7

[a]Ages 16–19 in United States, United Kingdom, Sweden, and Spain; 14–19 in Italy; 15–19 elsewhere.

[b]1992 data.

Source: OECD, Employment Outlook, (1994), Tables 1.13, K, and O.

Unemployment among youth is higher than among adults in every developed country. Table 8.6 shows the age structure of unemployment in 1993 for several nations, using adjusted unemployment data that are comparable across countries. Although unemployment rates decline with age in all the countries listed, the decrease between teens and young adults is much greater in the U.S. than in any other country except Japan. The ratio of the teen unemployment rate to the adult rate was higher to begin with in the U.S., however, than in most of the other countries listed.

The importance of labor market policy in affecting these demographic differences should not be underestimated. Part of the relatively high teen unemployment rate in the U.S. could be due to the effect of the minimum wage. The importance of labor market policy in affecting the unemployment rate of youth is also apparent in Sweden, where the unemployment rate of males aged 16 to 19 rose rapidly relative to the adult rate during the 1960s and 1970s when government policies made it much more difficult to lay off workers.[24] These changes increased fixed employment costs, which reduced employers' willingness to hire new workers.

In 1994 the unemployment rate for married men in the U.S. was 3.7 percent, well below the rate of 6.1 percent for all men. This figure is the flip side of the higher labor force participation rate of married men discussed in Chapter 1. The chain of causation may be complex. Marriage itself may make

[24]Linda Leighton and Siv Gustafsson, "Differential Patterns of Unemployment in Sweden," in Ronald Ehrenberg (ed.). *Research in Labor Economics,* Vol. 6. Greenwich Conn.: JAI Press (1984), pp. 251–285.

a man search more intensely, or it may cause him to behave better on the job, reducing his likelihood of being discharged. A married man is also less likely to quit a job than a single man. Alternatively, whatever causes men to remain bachelors or makes their marriages unstable could also make it harder for them to find and hold jobs. Finally, women may simply be more attracted to men with jobs.

As Table 8.5 shows, for both sexes the ratio of black to white unemployment in 1994 was well above two. This ratio has been above two since the mid-1950s, although it was lower before then. Numerous government programs, both those designed to render discrimination clearly illegal and those that attempted to directly lower black unemployment rates, have failed to reduce the ratio of black to white unemployment.

Especially remarkable are the very high relative unemployment rates for black youth. Again, the changes are striking. In 1954, there were *no* differences in unemployment rates between black and white teenagers. Both were around 14 percent. By 1994, the white rate had remained essentially unchanged at 15.1 percent while the black rate had risen to 35.2 percent. That more than one-third of black teenagers in the labor force were unemployed *at a time of when there was little demand-deficient unemployment in aggregate* should disturb any observer.

There are a number of reasons why this may have occurred. Expansion in minimum-wage coverage may have hurt teenagers with the least skill the most. Much of the employment among young blacks in 1954 was in agriculture in the South, an industry that has declined to insignificance in the intervening 40 years. Changes in family structure have also been especially pronounced among black households. In 1970, 59 percent of black children lived in a household with both parents. By 1993 this had fallen to 36 percent, with 64 percent living in single-parent homes. Although the fraction of white children without a male role model in the home had risen from 8 percent to 17 percent, it was still far less than among blacks.

The data for Hispanics in Table 8.5 must be interpreted carefully, since they include some people who are classified as whites and others who are classified as blacks. In addition, Hispanic unemployment rates mask vast differences by group. Figures for Cuban Americans are close to the overall white unemployment rate while those for Puerto Ricans and Mexican Americans are as high or higher than for blacks.

Unemployment rates of Hispanic youth are higher overall than those of whites. Even as Hispanics accumulate experience, their unemployment rates remain substantially above those of all whites. Nonetheless, Hispanic unemployment rates are generally below those of blacks except for older age groups. Older Hispanics are very likely to have migrated to the U.S. from Mexico with relatively little education. Over time the unemployment rates of Hispanics have been rising relative to whites and coming more and more to resemble those of blacks.

The differences in unemployment rates among groups are substantial. It remains to be seen, however, if they are due to group membership itself or differences among groups in other characteristics. That is, do they reflect differences in unemployment rates between otherwise identical blacks and whites, and

Hispanics and non-Hispanic whites, or do they result from differences in such aspects of human capital as skills, motivation, knowledge of English, and so on?

We want to adjust the black or Hispanic unemployment rate to ask, "What would the unemployment rate of this group be if they had the same characteristics as whites?" As we will see in Chapter 14 when we discuss wage discrimination, answering this question is extremely difficult. The reason is that researchers can never be sure if the characteristics they can *measure* and assume are related to productivity really capture all the relevant differences between groups. For example, it is one thing to adjust unemployment rates to assume that blacks and whites had, on average, the same number of years of education. But what if those years of education were largely in one-room, rural Southern schools or gun-infested urban ghettos for blacks and well-equipped tranquil suburbs for whites? It is almost impossible to believe that researchers have captured every relevant difference in human capital or motivation.

When the available proxies for productivity are used to adjust black unemployment rates, an unexplained difference remains. Even within occupations, after controlling for differences in experience, years of education, and the amount of formal on-the-job training, black unemployment rates exceed those of comparable whites. These differences could reflect discrimination in the hiring or discharge process. They could also result from the indirect effects of other types of labor market or nonlabor market discrimination, or they could be caused by unobserved differences in workers' characteristics and behavior.

When comparing Hispanics and non-Hispanic whites, however, no unexplained difference in unemployment rates remains once differences in the groups' schooling, experience, and English-language ability are taken into account.[25] Thus, while we must remain agnostic on whether differences in unemployment rates between blacks and whites could be the result of discrimination, it appears safe to conclude that this is not a factor in Hispanic and other white differentials.

Are demographic differences in unemployment rates due to differences in s or in n? Clearly both matter, and the answer will vary depending on the demographic groups one wishes to compare. As a generalization, differences among groups in the rate of inflow, s, typically contribute much more to differences in unemployment rates than differences in the rate of outflow from unemployment, n.[26] The major causes of demographic differences in unemployment rates are the differences in people's chances of becoming unemployed and not in finding a job once employed.

---

[25]John Abowd and Mark Killingsworth, "Do Minority/White Unemployment Differences Really Exist?" *Journal of Business and Economic Statistics* 2: 64–72 (1984); Leslie Stratton, "Racial Differences in Men's Unemployment," *Industrial and Labor Relations Review* 46: 451–463 (1993).

[26]Thomas Coleman, "Unemployment Behavior: Evidence from the CPS Work Experience Survey," *Journal of Human Resources* 24: 1–38 (1989).

TABLE 8.7 AVERAGE DURATION OF UNEMPLOYMENT TO TIME OF INTERVIEW (IN WEEKS) BY SEX, AGE, RACE, ETHNICITY, AND MARITAL STATUS, 1994

Status	Male	Female	Total
All workers, 16 and over	9.8	8.5	9.2
By Age			
16–19	6.2	5.1	5.7
20–24	7.8	7.4	7.7
25–34	10.4	8.9	9.7
35–44	12.1	9.6	10.7
45–54	14.4	11.3	13.0
55–64	14.1	11.6	13.1
65 and over	12.2	8.6	10.1
By Race			
Whites, 16 and over	9.3	7.8	8.6
Blacks, 16 and over	11.8	10.2	11.0
Hispanics, 16 and over	9.9	9.0	9.5
By Marital Status			
Married, spouse present	11.5	8.5	—
Single (never married)	8.4	7.8	—
Other	11.9	9.6	—

Source: *Employment and Earnings,* (January 1995), p. 202.

Another way of asking this question is, "Are demographic differences in unemployment rates due to differences in incidence or duration?" Demographic differences in duration are shown in Table 8.7. Average duration is higher among males than females. Since unemployment rates are about the same for the sexes, this means the incidence of unemployment among males is lower than among females. An unemployed male typically does not drop out of the labor force after being unemployed for some time. This is a more reasonable option for some unemployed females with better opportunities at home. These women will cease to be counted as unemployed. In addition, as we saw in Chapter 6, men's longer expected job tenure once they are employed makes it optimal for them to search longer for an especially good job.

The duration of unemployment generally rises with age. Since Table 8.5 showed that unemployment rates generally fall with age, this means the incidence of unemployment decreases very sharply as workers age. Both patterns reflect the long-term employment relationships (discussed in Chapter 9) that older workers have established with their employers, and the inclination of younger workers to intersperse job shopping with periods out of the labor force to attend school full-time or enjoy protracted leisure.

The long duration of unemployment among married men, despite their relatively intensive job search, seems mysterious. We noted earlier that married men search more than otherwise identical single men do, so that the duration of married men's spells of unemployment should be shorter, not longer. The mystery is solved if we realize that the *average* married man differs from the *average* single man in another important way: he is older. The difference between men classified by marital status mainly reflects the rise in unemployment duration as men age.

The duration of unemployment is somewhat higher among blacks than among whites, although not by an amount sufficient to account for the much higher black unemployment rate. This implies that the incidence of unemployment is also higher among black workers. Interestingly, the data in the third column of Table 8.7 show that Hispanics have a lower average duration of unemployment than whites in general. This result holds for all three of the largest Hispanic groups—Mexican Americans, Cuban Americans, and Puerto Ricans.[27] The higher unemployment rates for Hispanics shown in Table 8.5 are mostly due to a much greater incidence of unemployment.

Examining data on the duration and incidence of unemployment also sheds light on the high rate of black teenage unemployment. One study has found that black teens were three times as likely as white teens to move from employment to unemployment, and only one-third as likely to move from unemployment to a job. They were no more likely than white teens, however, to drop out of the labor force if unemployed. The problem is both that s is higher among black teens than among whites, and n is lower. Black teens, therefore, had much longer spells of unemployment than whites—80 percent longer for males and 60 percent longer for females.[28]

The theory of job search also explains other differences among workers in the duration of unemployment. We saw in Chapter 6 how unemployment insurance benefits can lengthen the duration of unemployment by making job seekers less willing to take less-desirable jobs. Indeed, each 10 percent increase in unemployment benefits in the United States appears to increase the average duration of spells of unemployment by about 2 percent, and also to increase the number of recipients with multiple spells of unemployment. This finding should not be too disturbing. One of the purposes of unemployment insurance is to make possible a longer and more thorough search for work. (As we saw in Chapter 6, however, the receipt of unemployment benefits reduces the intensity of search efforts, although it may increase total search effort by lengthening the time spent unemployed.) Liberalization of benefits clearly has the effect of raising the unemployment rate. Reducing the

---

[27]Gregory DeFreitas, "Ethnic Differentials in Unemployment Among Hispanic Americans," in George Borjas and Marta Tienda (eds.). *Hispanics in the U.S. Economy,* New York: Academic Press (1985).

[28]Kim Clark and Lawrence Summers, "The Dynamics of Youth Unemployment," in Freeman and Wise. *The Youth Labor Market,* p. 217.

net benefit, as was done in the U.S. in 1979 when benefits became taxable, reduces the duration of spells of unemployment.[29]

DIFFERENCES BY OCCUPATION AND EDUCATION

Data on unemployment rates by major occupation are shown in Table 8.8. They are substantially lower in the occupations that require high levels of skill and education. Table 8.9 shows how different aspects of unemployment varied with educational level in the U.S. between 1976 and 1981. It is clear that the stability of employment increases as workers become more educated. This fact reflects higher fixed costs leading to a much lower rate of inflow into unemployment among more skilled workers. When skilled workers do become unemployed they flow out of unemployment and into new jobs slightly more rapidly, perhaps because other employers are willing to offer slightly less-skilled jobs to them. There is also evidence that rates of job loss, while higher overall for less-educated men, also vary more over the business cycle so that in periods of expansion there may be little difference across educational groups.[30]

GEOGRAPHIC DIFFERENCES IN UNEMPLOYMENT

In addition to demographic and occupational differences in unemployment there are important differences in unemployment rates by geographical area. Table 8.10 lists unemployment rates in two years for several states. In each year, essentially all the unemployment in the aggregate economy can be viewed as structural or frictional. Some concentrations of unemployment are long-lived, reflecting the decline of localized industries or the large-scale displacement of labor by technological change. West Virginia, in which unemployment rose after World War II because of the decline in coal mining, still exhibited the above-average unemployment that it had throughout this period as late as 1994. Persistent unemployment above the national average may also reflect a labor force whose skill and demographic mix is weighted more heavily toward groups that exhibit high unemployment rates. New Mexico, with a large Hispanic population, is one such example.

Unusually high regional unemployment rates should eventually be eliminated by the workings of the market. Workers will tend to move away from (or avoid moving to) areas with high unemployment. In some depressed communities the combination of unemployed labor and vacant factories will attract new industry. Changes in the regional flows of consumer and government

---

[29]Alan Gustman, "Analyzing the Relation of Unemployment Insurance to Unemployment," *Research in Labor Economics* 5: 69–114 (1982); James Cox and Ronald Oaxaca, "Unemployment Insurance and Job Search," *Research in Labor Economics* 11: 223–240 (1990); Gary Solon, "Work Incentive Effects of Taxing Unemployment Benefits," *Econometrica* 53: 295–306 (1985).

[30]Henry Farber, "The Incidence and Costs of Job Loss," *Brookings Papers on Economic Activity* Microeconomics 1: 73–119 (1993).

POLICY ISSUE

THE BLACK YOUTH UNEMPLOYMENT PROBLEM

A major purpose of such programs as subsidized summer jobs has been to reduce the very high unemployment rates shown for black youth in Table 8.5. These policies cannot be designed well, however, if we do not know the causes of the problem they aim to solve.

As we saw in Chapter 4, only a small part of this high unemployment rate is due to the unwillingness of employers to hire young blacks at jobs where the minimum wage must be paid. Another possibility is that the structure of labor demand means that there are few jobs for teenagers in or near the often-segregated neighborhoods where many black youth reside. The evidence on this possibility is mixed, but taken together it implies that the need for black youth to travel long distances to where jobs are located accounts for at most only a small part of the problem. In one study of Chicago, labor market outcomes for black youth were almost identical on the West Side where unskilled jobs were plentiful (it was the location of the national warehouse of Sears Roebuck at the time) and on the South Side where they were almost nonexistent.[31]

Other explanations stem from considerations of job search behavior and workers' experience early in their job tenure. Black youth have higher asking wages compared to their skills or the wages on their previous jobs than white youth. The discussion in Chapter 6 showed how a high asking wage will lead workers to search longer. Also, black youth are less likely to be successful users of the informal methods of job search that their white counterparts employ to generate most of their job offers. Both of these differences lower the rate at which black youth leave unemployment. Once black youth obtain low-level jobs, their experience is also worse than that of whites. They are much more subject to discharge than whites, in part because of a higher rate of absenteeism.[32] As a result, their rate of inflow to unemployment is increased.

This evidence implies that black youth unemployment rates will be reduced only by efforts along several dimensions. One interesting finding from a number of studies is that unemployment rates are much lower (and other labor market outcomes better) for young blacks who attend church regularly. It is interesting to speculate whether these differences are due solely to differences in the characteristics of those who attend church and those

---

[31] David Ellwood, "The Spatial Mismatch Hypothesis: Are There Teenage Jobs Missing in the Ghetto?" in Richard Freeman and Harry Holzer (eds.). *The Black Youth Employment Crisis*, Chicago: University of Chicago Press (1986); Keith Ihlanfeldt and David Sjoquist, "Job Accessibility and Racial Differences in Youth Employment Rates," *American Economic Review* 80: 267–276 (1990).

[32] Harry Holzer, "Reservation Wages and Their Labor Market Effects for Black and White Male Youth," *Journal of Human Resources* 21: 157–177 (1986); Harry Holzer, "Informal Job Search and Black Youth Unemployment," *American Economic Review* 77: 446–452 (1987); Peter Jackson and Edward Montgomery, "Layoffs, Discharges and Youth Unemployment," in Freeman and Holzer, *The Black Youth Employment*. For an overview of this problem, see Albert Rees, "An Essay on Youth Joblessness," *Journal of Economic Literature* 24: 613–628 (1986).

who do not, or whether the congregation plays a role in providing information about workers and jobs that promotes successful hiring.[33]

Given the available evidence, labor market programs should probably involve much more counseling and provision of information about the labor market, and much more guidance from experienced workers who have been successful in obtaining and holding jobs.

TABLE 8.8 UNEMPLOYMENT RATES BY OCCUPATION GROUP, 1994

Occupation Group	Percent
White-collar workers	
Managerial and professional workers	2.6
Technical, sales, and support workers	5.0
Blue-collar workers	
Precision production, craft, and repair workers	7.9
Operators, fabricators, and laborers	9.9
Service workers	
Private household	6.5
Protective services	4.7
Other services	8.1
Farming, forestry, and fishing	8.2

Source: *Employment and Earnings*, (January 1995), p. 197.

spending can stimulate demand in a local economy that previously contained many unemployed workers. Such an outcome is especially likely when the educational attainment of local workers grows sharply, with the increasingly skilled work force attracting capital investment.

Although the overall picture conveyed by the data in Table 8.10 is one of flux, unemployment persists among some states and regions in the United States. The correlation across states between the relative employment rate over periods as long as three to four decades is as high as 0.80. Thus, although a large part of interstate unemployment differences is eliminated over time, differences in industry structure, and especially the degree of diversity in employment opportunities in various areas create considerable persistence over time. Low unemployment regions tend to be those with a

[33] See several papers in Richard Freeman and Harry Holzer (eds.). *The Black Youth*, especially Richard Freeman, "Who Escapes? The Relation of Church-Going and Other Background Factors to the Socio-Economic Performance of Black Male Youths from Inner-City Poverty Tracts." See also, Anne Case and Lawrence Katz, "The Company You Keep: The Effects of Family and Neighborhood on Disadvantaged Youths," NBER Working Paper No. 3705 (1991).

TABLE 8.9 UNEMPLOYMENT DYNAMICS FOR DIFFERENT LEVELS OF EDUCATION, 1976–1981

	Less Than High School	High School Graduate	Some College	College Graduate
Unemployment rate	7.0	4.1	3.3	1.9
Annual incidence of unemployment	9.5	6.4	4.7	3.5
Probability of separation[a]	17.9	13.4	12.8	10.5
Probability of unemployment given separation	53.2	48.6	37.8	33.2
Duration of unemployment of job separators (weeks)	13.8	12.1	11.6	11.0

[a]A separation occurs whenever an employment spell is terminated, whether by the employee (a quit) or the employer (a discharge).

Source: Jacob Mincer, *Studies in Human Capital*, Brookfield, Vt.: Elgar, (1993), p. 214.

TABLE 8.10 UNEMPLOYMENT RATES IN SELECTED STATES, 1968 AND 1994

State	1968	1994
California	4.5	8.6
Colorado	3.0	4.2
Illinois	3.0	5.7
Massachusetts	4.1	6.0
Michigan	4.3	5.9
New Mexico	5.1	6.3
New York	3.5	6.9
South Carolina	4.3	6.3
Texas	2.7	5.4
Utah	5.2	3.7
West Virginia	6.4	6.9
United States (total)	3.6	6.2

Sources: *Manpower Report of the President,* (1971), Table D–4; *Employment and Earnings,* (May 1995), pp. 164–168.

high share of agriculture in employment, modest levels of unionization, and relatively low levels of government spending on income support programs.[34]

The international comparisons of unemployment flows shown in Table 8.2 suggest that the U.S. may not be typical in its degree of variability of unemployment across regions. Comparing unemployment rates by region in the mid-1980s to rates for regions in various years from 1960 to 1975, in the U.S. and Germany changes in regional rankings by unemployment rates were substantially more common than in Australia, Canada, Italy, Sweden, and the United Kingdom.[35] In many countries some geographical differences in unemployment are often very persistent, arising in part from workers' desires to be in pleasant areas offering high wages and generous transfer programs, and in part from strong ties of family and location.

As we saw in Table 7.1, interregional migration in the U.S. is larger than in most other countries. This fact, combined with the greater variation over the business cycle and greater flows into and out of unemployment seen in this chapter, presents a picture of the U.S. labor market as much more fluid than elsewhere. This flexibility provides a greater ability to adapt to the constant changes in a dynamic modern economy.

SUMMARY

When product demand rises or workers quit, vacancies are created. These are often filled from outside, either by hiring workers away from other employers or by hiring from the pool of unemployed workers and new labor force entrants. In each economy at any point in time there is a level of structural and frictional unemployment that will be produced by labor market institutions and behavior.

Unemployment rates rise when the rate of outflow of unemployed workers to jobs decreases. They also rise when more workers enter unemployment, either from employment or from outside the labor market. Unemployment rates increase when either more people experience unemployment or when people's spells of unemployment lengthen. Even though unemployment rates in the United States are not usually lower than in other industrialized countries, people leave unemployment at a more rapid rate in the U.S., and the average duration of unemployment is shorter.

---

[34]Stephen Marston, "Two Views of the Geographic Distribution of Unemployment," *Quarterly Journal of Economics* 100: 57–80 (1985); Kevin J. Murphy and Robert Topel, "The Evolution of;" George Neumann and Robert Topel, "Employment Risk, Diversification, and Unemployment," *Quarterly Journal of Economics* 106: 1341–1365 (1991); Richard Vedder and Lowell Gallaway, *Out of Work: Unemployment and Government in Twentieth-Century America,* New York: Holmes & Meier (1993).

[35]OECD, *Employment Outlook,* (1989), Table 3.4.

Unemployment rates are higher among minorities than among whites, and higher among youth than among adults. Unemployment rates of women in the United States are now no different than those of men. Women and youth have shorter spells of unemployment than adult men, although the incidence of unemployment among women and youth is greater than among adult males. Unemployment rates are higher among workers in occupations requiring fewer skills and less education. While there is some persistence in the pattern of unemployment across states and regions, especially in the United States much of the geographical difference in unemployment that exists at a point in time is eliminated by the migration of workers and firms.

QUESTIONS AND PROBLEMS

8.1 a. What policies and institutional changes might occur in the United States to make s fall to the lowest rate shown in Table 8.2? If this happened, what would the unemployment rate in the U.S. have been?

b. What policies and institutional changes might occur in other countries to cause their n to rise to equal that of the U.S.? If those changes occurred, what would the unemployment rates in the other countries listed in Table 8.2 have been?

8.2 In 1986 the average unemployment rate was 7 percent.

a. What would the duration of unemployment have been if the incidence of unemployment were the same for everyone?

b. Since the mean duration of unemployment was actually 15 weeks, what percentage of the labor force actually would have experienced unemployment if there had been no movements into or out of the labor force, and if nobody experienced multiple spells of unemployment?

8.3 There are two groups in the labor force, the Blues (B) and the Grays (G). The Grays believe that they are discriminated against in the labor market because their unemployment rate is 6 percent ($URATE_G = 6$), while the unemployment rate of the Blues is only 4 percent ($URATE_B = 4$). The Blues believe there is no discrimination, because they are much more highly educated than the Grays. The average Blue has 14 years of schooling, the average Gray only 12 years.

An economist has determined that the only thing that affects unemployment rates is education. She finds that each extra year of education is associated with an unemployment rate that is 0.5 percentage point lower. Who is right, the Blues or the Grays?

8.4 Within each pair, which of the two is bigger, and why?

a. unemployment duration, men versus women;

b. unemployment duration, youth versus adult men;

c. unemployment incidence, youth versus adult men;
d. unemployment rate, youth versus women; and
e. unemployment rate, men versus women.

8.5 Imagine that you are the minister of labor in the government of Bulgaria. As your country develops a market economy you must design a set of laws and institutions to govern the labor market. You have seen that there are significant differences in the structure of the labor markets in the U.S. and the EU. Discuss these differences as well as the advantages and disadvantages of each. Which would seem particularly important to you if you wanted to keep unemployment as low as possible in Bulgaria?

8.6 There is no question that youth unemployment is typically higher than unemployment for other groups. What factors might cause unemployment rates for those under 24 to be higher than for others? Which of these factors might be regarded as normal functioning of the labor market, and which suggest pathologies that call for governmental intervention?

8.7 Suppose that the wage in a labor market fell. What impact would you expect this to have on unemployment in that labor market? Would the impact be different for frictional and structural unemployment? Why or why not?

8.8 One of the main characteristics of the transition from communism in Eastern Europe was an increase in unemployment. Suppose that you are given the following pieces of data for several countries:

	Inflow Rate	Outflow Rate	Mean Duration
Czech Republic	0.6	25.8	10
Hungary	0.5	7.0	27
Poland	0.7	4.0	40
Slovakia	1.0	9.8	25

a. For each country, calculate both the unemployment rate and the incidence of unemployment.
b. What would you expect the Beveridge curve to look like for these countries?

8.9 Given what you know about the various types of unemployment, suppose that Congress is considering several reforms to the unemployment insurance system. The first of these would increase how long a worker could receive unemployment benefits. The second would increase the replacement rate. The third would remove the upper limit on benefit so that workers would have the same percentage of their salary replaced no matter what they had earned prior to becoming unemployed. The fourth would provide partial benefits to those who work fewer hours than they desire. The fifth, and final, reform would make workers eligable for unemployment insurance benefits after a brief waiting period no matter how they became unemployed, including quitting their job or entering the labor force. Explain the impact of each of these changes on the:

a. mean duration of unemployment;
b. inflow rate (s);
c. outflow rate (n);
d. intensity of search; and
e. incidence of unemployment.

What do your answers above tell you about the impact of these changes on the overall unemployment rate?

8.10 As we have seen, the U.S. economy is characterized by relatively low unemployment rates with this unemployment being composed of frequent spells of short duration. Western Europe on the other hand is characterized by high unemployment rates and extremely long duration, but fewer spells. Given these facts and what you know about the causes of unemployment in each region, how would you expect the unemployment pattern to differ between the U.S. and Europe for

a. workers with different levels of education (especially those with little schooling);
b. recent immigrants;
c. young workers;
d. women; and
e. workers over age 55.

KEY WORDS

Beveridge curve
burden of unemployment
completed spells of unemployment
demand-deficient unemployment
duration of vacancies
duration of unemployment
frictional unemployment
hazard rate
heterogeneity
incidence of unemployment
job vacancies
marginal tax wedge
multiple spells of unemployment
scarring
seasonal unemployment
seasonally adjusted data
short-time employment
state-dependence
stigma
structural unemployment
structure of unemployment
unemployment flows
work sharing

Part Four

Internal Labor Markets

The previous section documented the massive amount of mobility and search behavior that occurs in industrialized economies. We saw how important these factors are in bringing markets into equilibrium and how they can explain the existence of structural-frictional unemployment. Labor markets consist of much more than the matching of workers and firms, however. Once employed, workers form long-term attatchments to their employers or their locations. This behavior leads to the study of internal labor markets.

Internal labor markets consist of all the ways in which employment relationships are structured to create and maintain incentives for workers to produce when there are investments in specific human capital that would be lost if the employment relationships were severed. These incentives are discussed in detail in Chapter 9. Research on these questions forms the newest and fastest-growing area in labor economics. For this reason, more than in any other chapter in this text, much of the discussion in this chapter is preliminary and definitive answers must be left for further research.

A second aspect of internal labor markets is how various characteristics of jobs are "priced." We know that different jobs are more or less attractive to workers because of their location or working conditions. It is natural to expect that more attractive jobs will be able to attract workers at lower wages than less attractive ones. The implicit market for job charcteristics and nonwage compensation (fringe benefits) is the focus of Chapter 10.

9

EFFORT, WAGES, AND JOB STRUCTURE

THE MAJOR QUESTIONS

- ▲ How can employers create and maintain incentives for workers to produce in a situation where either firms and/or workers have previously invested in specific training?
- ▲ How do different mechanisms for paying workers such as piece rates, bonuses, commissions, time rates, and fixed salaries affect effort?
- ▲ How are jobs structured to take into account long-term relationships between workers and employers?
- ▲ How do employers choose whom to promote to fill vacancies at higher levels in the business?
- ▲ What does the existence of an internal labor market imply about the relationship between age and earnings beyond the role of firm-specific training discussed in Chapter 3?
- ▲ How do long-term relationships generate unemployment? What is the role of maintaining workers' incentives to provide effort in this process?

THE IMPORTANCE OF LIFETIME JOBS

As we saw in Chapter 8, mobility among firms and across geographic areas is concentrated among the young. As workers age, their chances of leaving a job decrease, so that many workers in their 30s will hold their current jobs for the rest of their working lives. The data in Table 9.1 bear out this observation. In this study both women and men held an average of 10 jobs over their lives, but 9 of these jobs were held before age 45, and 7 were held before age 30. While overall mobility is very high, most workers appear eventually to form a steady long-term relationship with a single employer. Although the term is obviously a bit of an exaggeration, calling the relationship between many adult workers and their employer a **lifetime job** or a **career job** is instructive.

TABLE 9.1 JOB-HOLDING PATTERNS BY AGE, UNITED STATES, 1978

		Cumulative Number of Jobs Held	
Age Group	New Jobs per Year	Women	Men
16–17	0.39	0.7	0.8
18–19	0.53	1.8	1.9
20–24	0.42	3.8	4.1
25–29	0.30	5.2	5.8
30–34	0.24	6.4	7.0
35–39	0.19	7.4	7.9
40–44	0.16	8.3	8.7
45–49	0.12	9.0	9.3
50–54	0.09	9.4	9.8
55–59	0.07	9.8	10.2
60–64	0.05	10.0	10.5
65–69	0.03	10.2	10.7
70+	0.01	10.2	10.8

Source: Robert Hall, "The Importance of Lifetime Jobs in the U.S. Economy," *American Economic Review* 72: 716–724 (1982), Tables 3 and 6.

The patterns of mobility implied by the data in Table 9.1 are not new. Table 9.2 shows that the extent of long-term jobs among male workers has been relatively stable since the interruptions caused by World War II. Workers employed in 1981 were slightly more likely to be working for the same firm 10 years later than people employed in 1973. Among men approaching retirement age, over one-third have been on the same job for more than 20 years and about 60 percent have been on the same job for more than 10 years. Within the overall stability, long-term jobs seem to have become more prevalent among the highly educated but declined among the less educated. Women's median job durations have been increasing in recent years paralleling their greater labor force attachment, although their job durations are still significantly lower than for men at every age.[1]

Lifetime jobs seem to be more important now than in the late 19th century. This pattern is not restricted to the United States. Similar patterns of long-duration jobs exist in other industrialized countries. Indeed, average job tenure in the U.S. is lower than in most developed economies. In 1991, the

[1]Francis Diebold, David Neumark, and Daniel Polsky, "Job Stability in the United States," NBER Working Paper No. 4859 (1994); Kenneth Swinnerton and Howard Wail, "Is Job Stability Declining in the U.S. Economy?" *Industrial and Labor Relations Review* 48: 293–304 (1995); Henry Farber, "Are Lifetime Jobs Disappearing? Job Duration in the United States: 1973–1993," Princeton University Industrial Relations Section Working Paper No. 341 (1995).

TABLE 9.2 JOB DURATION FOR MALES IN THE U.S., 1951–1993

	Age Category			
Year	25–34	35–44	45–54	55–64
1951—Median duration	2.8	4.5	7.6	9.3
1963—Median duration	3.5	7.6	11.4	14.7
1968—Median duration	2.8	6.9	10.2	14.8
1973—Median duration	3.1	6.5	11.3	14.4
% > 10 yrs.	8	36	54	60
% > 20 yrs.	NA	6	28	39
1978—Median duration	2.8	6.8	11.1	14.6
% > 10 yrs.	8	36	53	60
% > 20 yrs.	NA	6	29	40
1983—Median duration	3.3	7.3	12.7	16.4
% > 10 yrs.	7	36	56	64
% > 20 yrs.	NA	4	28	40
1987—Median duration	3.2	7.1	11.8	15.1
% > 10 yrs.	8	35	52	59
% > 20 yrs.	NA	4	26	37
1993—Median duration	3.5	6.9	11.7	14.0
% > 10 yrs.	8	34	52	57
% > 20 yrs.	NA	4	27	36

Source: Henry Farber, "Are Lifetime Jobs Disappearing? Job Duration in the United States: 1973–1993," Princeton University Industrial Relations Section Working Paper No. 341 (1995).

average U.S. worker had been on his or her current job a little less than seven years, compared with over ten years in France, Germany, and Japan. In Japan the average worker has held fewer than half as many jobs at each age as his or her American counterpart.[2]

EFFORT, PRODUCTIVITY, AND PAY

As we saw in Chapter 2, workers' efforts on the job can vary greatly, thus providing management with a great deal of scope to influence output by providing incentives that affect effort. If labor is cheap, the costs of a leisurely work

---

[2]Susan Carter and Elizabeth Savoca, "Labor Mobility and Lengthy Jobs in Nineteenth Century America," *Journal of Economics History* 50: 1–16 (1990); OECD, *Employment Outlook*, 1993; Masanori Hashimoto and John Raisian, "Employment Tenure and Earnings Profiles in Japan and the United States," *American Economic Review* 75: 721–735 (1985). The operation of internal labor markets was first pointed out by John Dunlop, "The Task of Contemporary Wage Theory" in George Taylor and Frank Pierson (eds.). *New Concepts in Wage Determination*, New York: McGraw-Hill, (1957), and developed further by Peter Doeringer and Michael Piore, *Internal Labor Markets and Manpower Analysis*, Lexington, Mass.: Heath (1971).

pace are not great. If labor is expensive, employers will take greater care to see that it is not wasted, but the extent to which effort provided by workers can be controlled by supervision is limited. It is affected by custom and the actions of unions. Attempts to force a pace of work that workers regard as unreasonable, even though it may have been achieved elsewhere, can lead to resistance of various forms, including failure to carry out the work properly. This behavior occurs in nonunion as well as union establishments.

The ability of supervision to regulate effort is also severely restricted by difficulties in observing and **monitoring** such a tenuous concept as effort. The difficulty in monitoring effort has led to employment contracts designed to create incentives to induce self-monitoring on the part of employees. In general, these provisions are referred to as **implicit contracts** since they are not written down and cannot be enforced in a court of law as they could be if they were **explicit contracts**.

Because implicit contracts cannot be enforced by legal means, they must be designed to be self-enforcing. The structure of the employment relationship must provide incentives for both workers and firms to live up to their bargains. We call agreements where it is in the best interest of each party to honor the agreement **incentive compatible**. When an agreement is incentive compatible, it is not necessary to worry about whether or not it can be enforced in court since no one will violate it.

It is easy to see why implicit contracts play an important role in determining effort in the labor market. Imagine trying to enforce an explicit contract that said the worker "promises to work as hard as he can." How could a judge and jury ever hope to determine whether any level of output was the best a worker could do? Thus, employers must seek to establish labor market institutions that give workers an incentive to work hard without any outside sanction.[3]

METHODS OF PAY: PIECE RATES

In previous chapters we have typically assumed that workers are paid an hourly wage for each hour they work. The reality is much more complicated. Workers may be paid according to one or more of three basic compensation schemes:

1. an hourly wage independent of output, known as a **time rate**;
2. according to output, called a **piece rate**; or
3. an unvarying **salary** or a **flat rate**.

[3]Two excellent and easy-to-understand summaries of the ideas behind implicit contracts are H. Lorne Carmichael, "Self-Enforcing Contracts, Shirking, and Life Cycle Incentives," *Journal of Economic Perspectives* 3: 65–83 (1989), and Edward Lazear, "Labor Economics and the Psychology of Organizations," *Journal of Economic Perspectives* 5: 89–110 (1991).

TABLE 9.3 METHOD OF PAY, SELECTED MANUFACTURING INDUSTRIES, UNITED STATES (PERCENT OF ESTABLISHMENTS)

	Method		
Industry	Time	Merit	Piece
Cotton textiles	65	9	26
Wool textiles	61	17	22
Textile dyeing and finishing	73	20	7
Shirts	3	23	74
Plastics	43	52	5
Paints	58	42	0
Industrial chemicals	79	20	1
Household furniture	18	63	19
Steel	54	42	4
Nonferrous foundries	38	47	15

Source: Charles Brown, "Firms' Choice of Method of Pay," *Industrial and Labor Relations Review*, 43: S165-S182 (1990), Table 2.

Many pay schemes provide for a combination of these methods. Thus, waiters may be paid both an hourly wage and receive tips, a form of piece rate. The design of their pay scheme can greatly influence workers' choices regarding effort supply.

Table 9.3 shows the extent of piece rates, time rates, and merit pay (a combination of time and piece rates where workers are rated at intervals and assigned hourly rates based on output) in selected manufacturing industries in the U.S. Piece rates are clearly not common, but neither are strict time rates pervasive in these industries. In other industries both merit pay and piece rates, often in the form of commissions to sales workers, are more common. What determines where these different methods are used, and how do they affect effort and, therefore, output?

Where the pace of work is under the control of the individual worker, as in sewing garments (see the data on shirtmaking in Table 9.3) or picking fruits and vegetables, individual piece rates are common. Where cooperation among workers is important, various kinds of group incentives covering departments, establishments, or whole enterprises may be used. We would also expect to see piece rates where it is easy to measure what workers produce. Indeed, that is exactly what occurs. Analyses based on the data in Table 9.3 show that piece rates are less common in larger companies. Evidence that employers are aware of how piece rates can be used to conserve on the costs of supervising workers goes as far back as the late 1800s when employers made greater use of piece rates in jobs filled by inexperienced female workers who had recently entered the labor market and might otherwise have required substantial supervision.[4]

Comparisons of earnings of workers on piece rates and time rates suggest that piece-rate payment mechanisms elicit more output. Some estimates indicate that piece-rate workers receive between 7 and 15 percent higher pay than otherwise identical workers in the same occupation and industry who are paid time rates. Another study showed that their output per hour is about 15 percent higher. Some limited evidence, however, shows that workers whose pay depends on supervisors' ratings do not make more than otherwise identical workers paid flat time rates.[5]

It is possible, however, that these differences do not result from greater effort by workers paid piece rates, but rather because more able or more energetic workers choose jobs in plants that offer piece-rate pay. Consider Figure 9.1. Suppose that each worker's effort is *fixed* according to his or her ability, so that piece rates cannot produce any true effect on effort. Under a piece-rate mechanism, workers' pay equals the value of what they produce. Under a time-rate scheme, in a competitive product market the average pay must equal average output (less the cost of capital services). Otherwise, the firm would be losing money or making abnormal profits.

Costs of administering a piece-rate system (such as counting and logging the output of individual workers) mean that the employer cannot afford to pay a worker on piece rates anything until those costs, $0M$, are covered. This is essentially a charge on workers who wish to be paid piece rates. From that point on, wages rise steadily with worker's output (ability), along the line *MAP* in Figure 9.1. Alternatively, there is a fixed time-rate payment, w_r, that lets the firm paying time rates break even. With this time rate, any worker who is capable of producing only Q_0 or less will seek to work in the time-rate firm, while the more able workers who can produce more than Q_0 will earn higher wages by opting for the piece-rate company. The better workers will receive piece-rate pay, even though piece rates do not cause them to produce more. The only effect of piece rates in this example is to induce workers to sort themselves by method of payment.[6]

Even though more able workers are more likely to choose firms that pay piece rates, it is still possible to measure how changes in piece rates affect workers. One possibility is to see what happens when piece rates are intro-

---

[4]Claudia Goldin, "Monitoring Costs and Occupational Segregation by Sex," *Journal of Labor Economics* 4: 1–27 (1986); Charles Brown, "Firms' Choice of Method of Pay," *Industrial and Labor Relations Review* 43: S165–S182 (1990).

[5]John Pencavel, "Work Effort, On-the-Job Screening, and Alternative Methods of Remuneration," *Research in Labor Economics* 1: 225–258 (1977); Eric Seiler, "Piece Rate vs. Time Rate: The Effect of Incentives on Earnings," *Review of Economics and Statistics* 66: 363–376 (1984); Charles Brown, "Wage Levels and Method of Pay," *Rand Journal of Economics* 23: 366–375 (1992).

[6]Edward Lazear, "Salaries and Piece Rates," *Journal of Business* 59: 405–431 (1986).

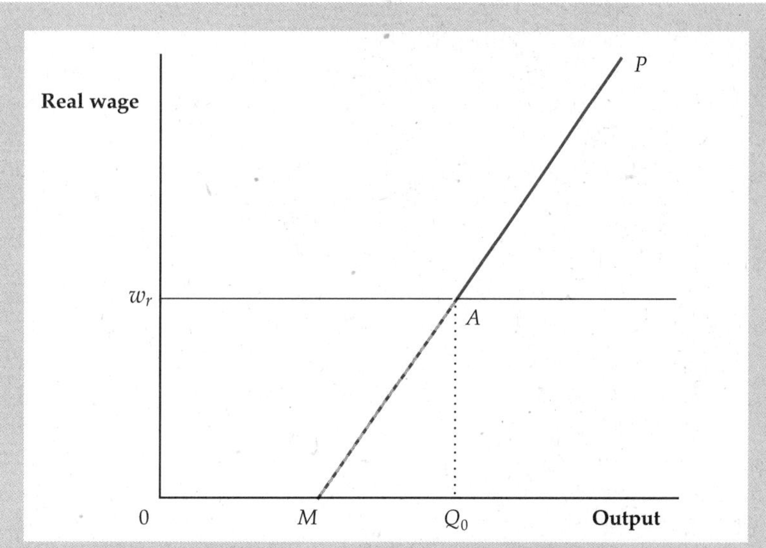

FIGURE 9.1 METHOD OF PAY AND WORKERS' SELF-SORTING

Piece-rate pay schemes will be more attractive to more productive workers (with quality greater than Q_0), thereby causing the average earnings of workers paid piece rates to exceed those of workers paid time rates even if piece rates do not affect productivity.

duced into or changed in a single firm with a fixed work force. In a study of one very large "firm," the United States Navy, where recruiters are paid piece rates based on how many enlistees they enroll, a study examined output when piece rates were increased. Recruiters responded to higher payoffs per enlistee by signing up more young men and women for the navy.[7] This is strong evidence for the effect of piece rates on effort.

Figure 9.1 suggests that the dispersion of earnings among piece-rate workers will be greater than among time-rate employees, because piece rates allow earnings to reflect variations in workers' effort and ability to a greater extent. In Figure 9.1, the pay of time-rate workers is constant at $0w_r$. Among piece-rate workers it varies along *AP*. In fact, within a narrowly defined industry the distribution of total earnings is much wider among workers who receive incentive pay than among those paid by the hour. Similarly, among otherwise identical workers whose pay is based on commissions, which are a

[7]Beth Asch, "Do Incentives Matter? The Case of Navy Recruiters?" *Industrial and Labor Relations Review* 43: S89–S106 (1990).

form of piece rate, earnings are more dispersed than among those who received time-rate pay.[8]

Even this greater dispersion, however, may be less than would arise if each worker were free to respond to incentives on a purely individual basis. Incentive pay is frequently provided to work groups rather than individuals. Data from one American electronics company show that for the same group of workers an individual piece-rate system resulted in higher average earnings and greater dispersion of earnings than when they were switched to group piece-rate pay.

An individual's supply of effort is often regulated by informal norms within the work group in both union and nonunion situations.[9] This regulation arises from a desire to prevent less-capable workers from being shown up as inadequate or lazy and to prevent the employer from making the achievements of the particularly able into a standard for all. The implicit control often takes the form of a quota or **bogey** of work that no one is expected to exceed. Those who do may be ostracized or even threatened with physical harm. If technical change makes a job easier, traditional work quotas can become unreasonably low. In such circumstances employers often attempt to renegotiate the effort bargain by offering other advantages in return for a more reasonable work pace.

Employers must be careful about offering piece rates where it is difficult to monitor the quality of output. In addition, piece rates can have perverse incentives when employees themselves can determine the demand for their product. In one study of doctors in the Czech Republic, when the compensation scheme was changed from salaries (which were on the low end of the average for all workers) to piece rates based on the number of procedures performed, the number of procedures increased by 20 percent in a single year.[10]

METHODS OF PAY: SALARIES

Many workers (about 11 percent of employees in one group of firms surveyed in 1993) are paid a flat salary that is independent of how many hours they

---

[8]Seiler, "Piece Rate," and John Barron and Mark Lowenstein, "On Imperfect Evaluation and Earning Differentials," *Economic Inquiry* 24: 595–614 (1986).

[9]Andrew Weiss, "Incentives and Worker Behavior: Some Evidence," in Haig Nalbantian (ed.). *Incentives, Cooperation and Risk Sharing*, Totowa, N.J.: Rowman & Littlefield (1987). The classic study of informal restrictions is Stanley Mathewson, *Restriction of Output Among Unorganized Workers*, New York: Viking (1931).

[10]Randall K. Filer, Jaromír Veprek, Olga Výborná, Zdeněk Papeš, and Pavel Veprek, "Health Care Reform in the Czech Republic," in Jan Svejnar (ed.). *The Socio-economic Impact of the Transition in the Czech Republic*, New York: Academic Press (1995).

work. While this payment scheme would appear to be the exact opposite of incentive pay, flat rates also turn out to play a role in promoting worker effort. Workers are likely to be paid a salary rather than a time rate in jobs where

1. the employee maintains a good deal of control over the pace of work;
2. the output over any short period of time is difficult to observe and measure, or it is hard to ascertain the individual employee's contribution to that output; and
3. the time that it will take to complete a task is uncertain and hard to predict.

In jobs of this type, a worker's output is only loosely related to the number of hours she spends at the workplace.[11]

Salaries can increase labor productivity in such jobs by providing an incentive for investment in efficiency-improving human capital. Any acquisition of skills that enables a worker to produce the same output in less time will provide that worker with more leisure without reducing pay. Similarly, greater effort should enable the worker to complete assigned tasks in less time, again increasing leisure without reducing pay. The first of these incentives suggests that wage profiles should be steeper for salaried workers than for otherwise identical time-rate workers, while the second implies that they should be higher, on average, for salaried workers. Both of these predictions have been borne out in a study of a large sample of workers in the U.S. In addition, as would be predicted, salaried workers are far more likely to participate in employer-sponsored training programs that could increase their productivity.[12]

BONUSES, PROFIT SHARING, AND EFFORT

Bonuses are extra payments offered as lump sums to workers based on assessments of their output. They represent an additional way for employers to link pay to performance. Such payments are most common in the United States among managerial employees, although they have spread to some production workers, including, for example, many auto workers. Bonuses are

[11]Robert Goldfarb, "The Employer's Choice of Paying Wages or Salaries," *Proceedings of the Fortieth Annual Meetings*, Madison, Wisc.: Industrial Relations Research Association, (1994) pp. 241–247; Eugene F. Fama, "Time, Salary and Incentive Payoffs in Labor Contracts," *Journal of Labor Economics* 9: 5–44 (1991).

[12]Sheldon Haber, "Participation in Industrial Training Programs," *Small Business Economics* 3: 39–48 (1991); Sheldon Haber and Robert Goldfarb, "Does Salaried Status Affect Human Capital Accumulation?" *Industrial and Labor Relations Review* 48: 322–337 (1995).

TABLE 9.4 FREQUENCY AND LEVEL OF BONUS PAYMENTS, NEWLY HIRED EXECUTIVES, 1987

1987 Cash Compensation	Percent with Bonus	Bonus as Precent of Base Salary[a]
$50,000–$70,000	39	11
$70,000–$90,000	68	15
$90,000–$110,000	76	18
$110,000–$130,000	82	28
$130,000–$160,000	86	33
$160,000–$250,000	93	43
Over $250,000	99	79

[a]For those with bonuses.

Source: Calculated from "Worldwide Executive Mobility," *Harvard Business Review* 66:(4) 105–123 (1988), Table 10.

included in compensation packages for executives in 94 percent of manufacturing firms. As can be seen in Table 9.4, they are more common and form a larger portion of compensation among higher-paid executives. One reason for the widespread use of bonuses is that they are apparently much more effective in reducing turnover among managerial personnel than are differences in wages.[13]

Executive bonuses in Japan appear to be nearly as common as, and structured similarly to, those in the U.S. In both countries the compensation of top executives is positively related to both stock performance and current cash flow. In Japan and Korea bonuses or **profit sharing** (regular nonwage payments based on the performance of the division or enterprise) extend much deeper and are widespread even among production workers. Profit-sharing bonuses typically average over one month's wage in Korean manufacturing and about three months' wages in Japan. Six percent of a random sample of German workers participated in profit sharing in 1984, as did 43 percent of British workers. In a different survey from the same year, 17 percent of all European Union workers received some form of bonus or profit sharing linked to the performance of the company in which they worked, with 11 percent receiving a bonus of less than one month's pay and 6 percent receiving more than one month's pay. Profit sharing has also been attracting increasing attention in the U.S., with between 10 and 20 percent of unionized

[13]Arthur Blakemore, Stuart Low, and Michael Ormiston, "Employment Bonuses and Labor Turnover," *Journal of Labor Economics* 5: S124–S135 (1987).

workers, but probably a smaller percentage of nonunion workers, receiving at least part of their pay based on group profits.[14]

If profit sharing generates long-term increases in productivity, we should expect it to become universal as firms adopting it drive out those that fail to do so. Since workers will earn more and employers will obtain higher profits through their workers' increased efforts, firms that adopt profit sharing should grow. That the Japanese and Korean economies have grown rapidly since the mid-1970s might seem to suggest that their profit sharing increases productivity, but it would be extremely hasty to jump to such a conclusion. There are numerous other differences between these and other economies that could generate the same effect, and the relative importance of pay schemes has not yet been established.

Empirical research to demonstrate the influence of profit sharing on productivity is very difficult. In part, it is hard to determine causality. Are firms that adopt profit sharing more profitable, or are more profitable firms more likely to share profits? We have already seen that more productive people will sort themselves into firms that base pay on productivity even if the pay scheme itself does not affect their productivity. After attempting to take these problems into account, a variety of studies have found that companies with profit sharing have higher labor productivity than firms that seem otherwise the same. These productivity differences range from a few percent in the United Kingdom to as much as 30 percent in Germany. It appears that profit sharing can increase effort and productivity but that the attitudes of management and workers have major effects on how successful it is.[15]

EFFICIENCY WAGES

One key question is whether paying higher wages will, in itself, cause workers to provide greater effort. Where real wages are very low, a wage increase may elicit a greater supply of effort simply because better-paid workers have a more

[14]Takatoshi Ito and Kyoungsik Kang, "Bonuses, Overtime and Employment: Korea vs. Japan," *Journal of the Japanese and International Economies* 3: 424–450 (1989); Robert Hart and Olaf Hübler, "Are Profit Shares and Wages Substitute or Complementary Forms of Compensation?" *Kyklos* 44: 221–231 (1991); David Blanchflower and Andrew Oswald, "Profit-Related Pay: Prose Discovered?" *Economic Journal* 98: 720–730 (1988); Linda Bell and David Neumark, "Lump-Sums, Profit-Sharing and Labor Costs in the Union Sector of the United States Economy," *Economic Journal* 103: 602–619 (1993); Steven Kaplan, "Top Executive Rewards and Firm Performance: A Comparison of Japan and the United States," *Journal of Political Economy* 102: 510–546 (1994).

[15]John Cable and Nicholas Wilson, "Profit-Sharing and Productivity: An Analysis of U.K. Engineering Firms," *Economic Journal* 99: 366–375 (1989); John Cable and Nicholas Wilson, "Profit-Sharing and Productivity: Some Further Evidence," *Economic Journal* 100: 550–555 (1990); Sushil Wadhwani and Martin Wall, "The Effects of Profit-Sharing on Employment, Wages, Stock Returns and Productivity," *Economic Journal* 100: 1–17 (1990).

adequate diet and better medical care, and will, therefore, be able to work harder for essentially biological reasons. Such a situation means that productivity (which we have measured as *VMP*) will not be independent of wages. It is reasonable to believe that this effect, which economists call **efficiency wages,** will operate in low-wage economies where workers' health is poor.

Most research supports the assertion that better nutrition improves productivity in developing countries. One especially detailed study showed that improved nutrition, which presumably is purchased with higher wages, resulted in higher output by ditch diggers in Kenya. Another demonstrated the role of higher wages in improving productivity among farmers in West Africa, and yet another showed that long-term nutritional gains, reflected in greater body weight, augmented the productivity of Indian farm laborers.[16]

This evidence suggests it is worth thinking about how the interaction of wages and effort affects other labor markets. Is it also true that higher wages elicit greater effort in developed economies? Figure 9.2 shows how the demand for labor would be derived for a firm whose workers' efficiency is influenced by their wage rates. Instead of a single *VMP* curve, there is a family of such curves. A different curve exists for each wage, with higher wages creating greater productivity and, therefore, corresponding to generally higher *VMP* schedules. The demand curve *D* connects the points at which each wage crosses its own *VMP* schedule, at points such as *A*, *B*, and *C*. The demand curve is steeper than any of the *VMP* curves where it crosses them. Under conditions where productivity increases with the level of wages, the elasticity of demand for labor is lower than when effort is independent of the wage rate. Part of the cost of higher wages is offset by the increase in productivity. Thus, the scale and substitution elasticities are reduced by the efficiency effects of higher wages.

The wages chosen for illustration in Figure 9.2 differ by constant amounts. The corresponding increments in product have been drawn so that they are always smaller than the increments in wages.[17] Indeed, if the worker's productivity responds to higher wages, a smart employer should increase wages only if the increase adds more to productivity than to costs. The rule for optimizing efficiency wages is:

---

[16]R. M. Brooks, M. C. Latham, and D. W. T. Crompton, "The Relation of Nutrition and Health to Worker Productivity in Kenya," *East African Medical Journal* 56: 413–422 (1979); John Strauss, "Does Better Nutrition Raise Farm Productivity?" *Journal of Political Economy* 94: 297–320 (1986); Anil Deolalikar, "Nutrition and Labor Productivity in Agriculture: Estimates for Rural South India," *Review of Economics and Statistics* 70: 406–413 (1988).

[17]This condition is violated in Harvey Leibenstein, "The Theory of Underemployment in Backward Economies," *Journal of Political Economy* 65: 91–103 (1957), one of the earliest and most complete discussions of the economy of high wages. The theory of efficiency wages is discussed by George Akerlof and Janet Yellen, *Efficiency Wage Models of the Labor Market*, Cambridge: Cambridge University Press (1986); Andrew Weiss, *Efficiency Wages*, Princeton, N.J.: Princeton University Press (1990).

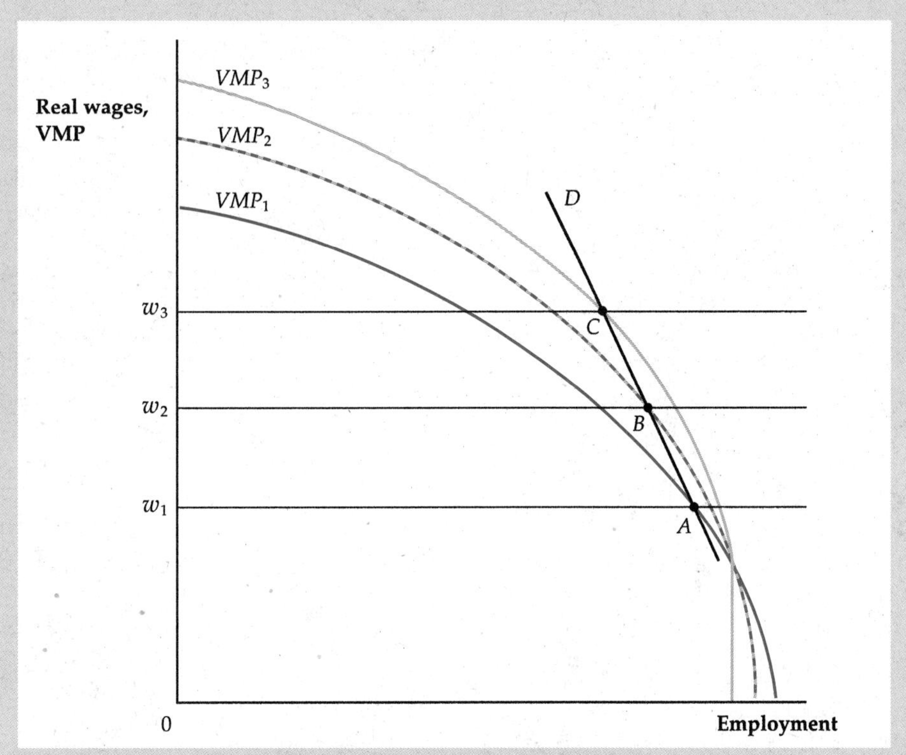

FIGURE 9.2 THE LABOR MARKET WITH EFFICIENCY WAGES
Higher wages that make a job more attractive may increase a worker's value of marginal product, making the demand curve *D* less elastic.

> Raise wages until the marginal increase in the VMP is equal to the marginal increase in the wage rate.

This decision rule assumes that workers are not perfectly efficient machines for converting higher wages into added product. At some point the incremental effort must be less than the incremental wage. Otherwise, firms would pay infinitely high wage rates.

The marginal product curves in Figure 9.2 also converge as employment increases. Eventually they even cross because when higher wages induce greater effort, all other factors being fixed, fewer workers will be required to reach the level where total product is maximized and *VMP* equals zero. If we assume, for example, that ten poorly paid workers working for a week could cultivate a field so thoroughly that further cultivation would not increase its output, the same outcome might be reached in a week by eight well-paid workers.

In analyzing efficiency wages, it is important to distinguish between changes in *absolute* and *relative* wages. The examples of greater nutrition increasing output in developing countries are related to absolute wages. The fact that one farmer's field hands could produce more when they were better fed did not depend on the wages paid on neighboring farms. If every farmer increased wages at the same time, all would see their output rise.

Most of the arguments for why wages might have an impact on output in developed economies refer to relative wages. Workers may express their satisfaction with wage increases by expanding their effort, and by reducing their propensity to leave the firm and impose costs of turnover on their employers. As seen in Chapter 7, higher wages lead to less turnover. This increases the payout period on investments in firm-specific human capital, leading to greater investment and raising workers' productivity.

Higher relative wages will enable firms to pick and choose among a larger pool of better applicants. In addition, when a firm is paying wages that exceed those available on other jobs for which workers might be hired, the fear of being discharged and having to settle for lower wages elsewhere provides a powerful disciplinary threat. Thus, higher wages paid to apparently identical workers have been found to be related to a lower probability of discharge for disciplinary reasons.[18]

A classic incident used to suggest the existence of efficiency wages is the introduction of the $5.00 daily wage at the Ford Motor Company in 1914 when the going wage elsewhere was about $2.50 a day. This raised productivity and reduced turnover. Absenteeism among existing workers fell from about 10 percent a day to less than 0.5 percent. Much of the impact, however, came from the ability of the firm to hire better workers. Police used water hoses to quell riots by job-seekers, and Henry Ford himself was so besieged by job applicants that he took to leaving his office through the window.[19]

Of course, it is impossible for *every* firm to pay higher relative wages. What remains very much an open question is whether an increase in the general level of wages that did not shift relative wages would have any impact on productivity in a modern economy.

The discussion has examined efficiency wages through workers' behavior. An alternative explanation that can allow for an effect of economy-wide wage increases is **shock theory**. Any organization operates with some slack or inefficiency which can be reduced if the organization is seriously threatened. This shock will produce a higher marginal productivity schedule for labor in response to a sudden wage increase, since attention will be given to eliminating inefficiency. In effect, the argument is that it costs management

---

[18]Peter Capelli and Keith Chauvin, "An Interplant Test of the Efficiency Wage Hypothesis," *Quarterly Journal of Economics* 106: 769–787 (1991).

[19]Daniel Raff and Lawrence Summers, "Did Henry Ford Pay Efficiency Wages?" *Journal of Labor Economics* 5: S57–S86 (1987); Peter Collier and David Horowitz, *The Fords: An American Epic*, New York: Summit Books (1987).

resources to utilize labor efficiently. When labor is cheap it does not pay to devote as much to its supervision and control as when labor is expensive.

It is important to note that one cannot confirm shock theory merely by observing that a wage increase causes firms to use more or newer machinery per unit of labor. Such changes are exactly what the marginal productivity theory of demand predicts will happen as capital is subtituted for labor along an isoquant. Shock theory requires that the isoquant for any given output level shift inward (requiring less capital and/or labor) because of innovations in technique or organization induced by the increase in wage rates.

JOB HIERARCHIES AND PAY

In many firms there are patterns of progression from job to job. In industries such as steel and refining, long chains of progression, called **job ladders**, lead to highly skilled jobs. Training for each job takes place by working at a job lower down the ladder. Firms with job ladders often hire from the external labor market at the lowest job level, called the **port of entry**. This is just one of the many ways that firm-specific training can create the pattern of long-term attachment to a single employer seen in Table 9.1.

The wedge between the internal and external labor markets creates a need for **internal wage structures** relating rates of pay among jobs. Employers need to structure pay to

1. motivate workers to be productive;
2. encourage workers to leave the firm when their productivity falls far short of their wage; and
3. provide a way to determine who should move up the job ladder.

Each of these needs contributes to the features commonly found in firms' internal labor markets.

With insulation from the external labor market, the setting of specific wage rates for individual jobs becomes subject to a great deal of managerial discretion. It is not merely a matter of comparing *VMP* at one point in time to the cost of labor in the external market. To cope with this difficulty, employers, especially larger ones, have devised a variety of methods that make the wage scale rise with seniority, yet allow what seems like an objective determination of relative rates of pay. Instead of setting wage rates individually for each job in plants that have long job ladders, employers set wages for **key jobs**, typically those for which some comparable external market exists. Wages in **job clusters** around the key job are set using evaluations made by experts or agreed on in collective bargaining.

Although job ladders may exist in some firms, examination of hiring and promotion patterns within specific firms indicates that movements from job to job within firms follow complex patterns that differ greatly across individual workers. In addition, while it is usually easy to classify jobs within a firm into a well-structured hierarchy, hiring from the external labor market typically occurs at all levels and the characteristics and performance of those hired from outside the firm are similar to those promoted from within.[20]

SENIORITY AND WAGES AGAIN

There are strong theoretical reasons why it may be in both workers' and employers' best interests for wages to be low early in the career but to rise as workers acquire more seniority. The issue is how to create incentives so that workers put forth the effort they are supposed to under the terms of their contract. Suppose that monitoring is imperfect or costly, so that if workers **shirk** or do not fulfill all the duties of their job, there is only a probability that they will get caught. If they are caught they will be discharged, but for this threat to be effective there must be some penalty attached to being fired. If workers are paid the value of their marginal product in each period in every firm, then there is little real penalty to being discharged. The dismissed worker will simply accept another job at a different firm paying the value of his or her marginal product. Thus, discharge does not provide an incentive to work hard (avoid shirking), and the *VMP* curve in Figure 9.3 will be along VMP_1.

One way to provide workers with an incentive not to shirk is to make them pay a penalty if they are fired. They might be required to post a **bond** when they were hired, saying that if they were detected shirking they would be discharged, and the employer would get to keep the bond. In fact, many workers would find it difficult to raise the cash to actually post such a bond. An approximately equivalent result can be accomplished, however, by paying young workers less than the value of their marginal product. Suppose that wages are set equal to w_0 for workers with zero tenure but increase along line w_0w the longer the worker remains with the firm.

Since workers now have an incentive to avoid being detected shirking, their effort on the job will rise, and the *VMP* curve will increase to VMP_2. Unless the firm paid workers a wage equal on average to VMP_2 over their lifetimes, it would be making unusually large profits. New firms would enter the industry, competing these profits away. If workers leave the firm after T years, the w_0w line must be located so that the present values of triangles w_0AB and BCD are equal. Up to point B (tenure of t_B) workers are earning less than the value of their marginal product, VMP_2. Beyond t_B years of service, they earn more than VMP_2 by an amount that exactly offsets

[20]James Rosenbaum, *Career Mobility in a Corporate Hierarchy*, New York: Academic Press (1984); Edward Lazear, "The Job as a Concept," in William Burns (ed.). *Performance Measurement, Evaluation and Incentives*, Boston: Harvard Business School Press (1992); George Baker, Michael Gibbs, and Bengt Holmstrom, "The Internal Economics of the Firm: Evidence From Personnel Data," *Quarterly Journal of Economics* 109: 881–919 (1994).

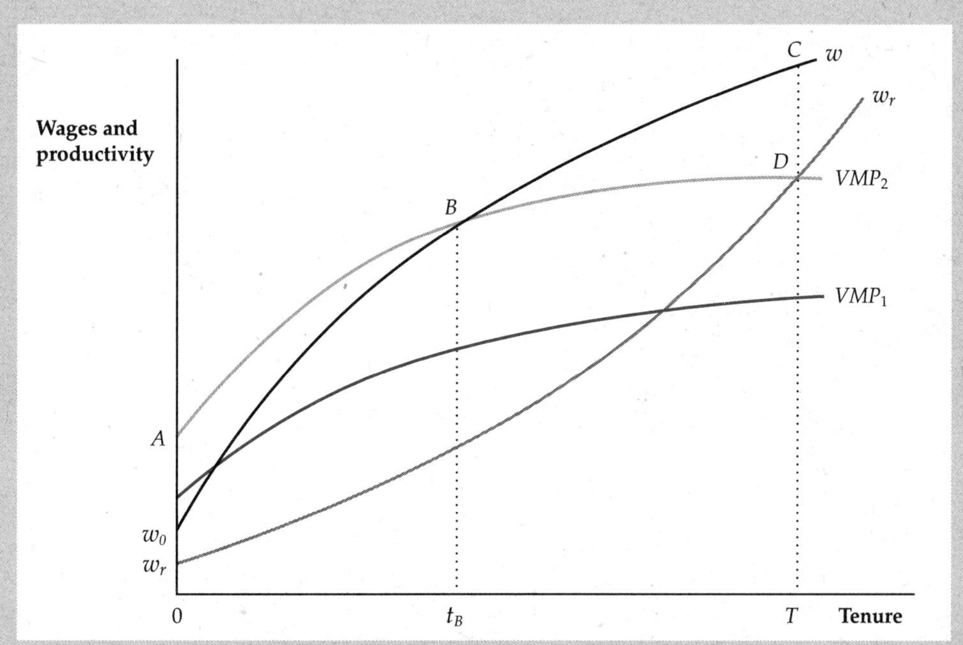

FIGURE 9.3 WAGE GROWTH, PRODUCTIVITY, AND RETIREMENT
Making workers post a bond by accepting wages less than the value of the marginal product early in their careers may increase their productivity by providing an incentive not to shirk job duties. Since wages will exceed *VMP* late in the career, however, some mechanism must be found to induce workers to retire at the optimal age (where *VMP* falls below their reservation wage).

the underpayments they posted as their bond in earlier years. Over their working lives employees earn a total of $T \times VMP_2$. Their lifetime earnings are higher than they would be in the absence of this payment scheme that induces them to produce more. The area under w_0w up to T equals the area under VMP_2, which exceeds that under VMP_1. In this example the workers obtain all of the increased profits generated by their extra effort.[21]

Why would firms honor this contract? After all, if they found some excuse to fire workers after t_B they would not have to return the bond the

[21]This diagram is based on Edward Lazear, "Agency, Earnings Profiles, Productivity and Hours Restrictions," *American Economic Review* 71: 606–620 (1981). Note that for this contract to entirely eliminate the problem of shirking, the gain to workers from shirking must be very small at the beginning of the contract (when the deferred wages are low). That this may not always be the case is shown in George Akerlof and Lawrence Katz, "Do Deferred Wages Eliminate the Need for Involuntary as a Worker Discipline Device?" in Weiss and Fishelson (eds.). *Advances in the Theory.*

worker posted with the firm. This situation suggests that some of the extra output generated by the pay scheme should be given to the firm. Then the firm would have an incentive to honor its contracts since, if it failed to do so, the **reputation effect** would prevent it from hiring workers under such a contract in the future. The need to ensure that the firm keeps its part of these bargains may also explain the existence of severance pay and why the particular workers laid-off in a demand slump are usually heavily controlled by exogenous factors such as seniority.

Examples of labor contracts of the type we have just discussed, which are clearly designed to provide workers with an incentive to behave in the firm's interest, go as far back as the 17th century. At this time competition between Britain and France for the control of Canada was intense. The Hudson's Bay Company was the exclusive agent of the British Crown in much of Upper Canada (now Ontario), where it bought furs from independent trappers. Worried that its agents might sell secret information about the best trapping areas to rival French traders, the company withheld 25 percent of its North American workers' pay until they had returned to England and could no longer profitably disclose company secrets.

Current evidence that upward-sloping wage profiles are created by the need to motivate workers is provided by a study of fast-food outlets. In company-owned stores, where the possibility for direct supervision by the owner is weak, the wage/tenure profile is steeper than in outlets franchised to an independent owner who is present in the store to observe the workers. Other confirmation of such models comes from the fact that jobs involving repetitive, easy-to-monitor tasks are less likely to offer either delayed payments such as pensions or higher wages for older workers.[22]

We have now seen three different reasons why wages might be expected to be higher the longer a worker has been with a given firm. Chapter 3 discussed the role of increases in the stock of firm-specific investment as workers' tenure with the firm rises. Chapter 6 showed that workers with poor quality matches will leave firms, thus ensuring that only especially well-suited (and, therefore, higher paid) workers will remain to accumulate long tenures. Now we have demonstrated that a positive relationship between wages and tenure is an efficient mechanism to induce workers to produce more, thus raising lifetime compensation and increasing the competitiveness of firms. Empirical evidence suggests that all three of these explanations play a role in the observed pattern of wages.[23]

Intriguingly, one recent study that was able to obtain wage and output data for a sample of 933 Israeli firms found that earnings and productivity

[22]Robert Hutchens, "A Test of Lazear's Theory of Delayed Payment Contracts," *Journal of Labor Economics* 5: S153–S170 (1987); Alan Krueger, "Ownership, Agency and Wages: An Examination of Franchising in the Fast-Food Industry," *Quarterly Journal of Economics* 106: 75–102 (1991).

[23]Robert Hutchens, "Seniority, Wages and Productivity: A Turbulent Decade," *Journal of Economic Perspectives* 3: 49–64 (1989).

profiles sloped upward at almost exactly the same rate. It found that middle-aged workers earned 20 percent more than young workers and were 22 percent more productive. Older workers earned 36 percent more and were 34 percent more productive than young workers. If confirmed by other studies, these findings suggest that the human capital and matching explanations play a larger role in determining the connection between wages and seniority than the incentive story.[24]

TOURNAMENTS AND EXECUTIVE PAY

Increases in earnings with seniority characterize the compensation of executives in the same way that job ladders do among industrial workers. The reasons are much the same: executives must also be motivated to perform. In the case of executive salaries, however, the differences are more exaggerated. A company's chief executive may earn twice or more as much as each vice president. In the United States in 1992, for example, the top executive in the typical large manufacturing corporation earned $775,000, while the second highest-paid executive earned "only" $469,000 (and the fifth highest only $287,000).[25] It is unlikely that the president's productivity is twice that of any other executive. Instead, the tremendous return to attaining the top job is like winning the first prize in a **tournament**. By working harder, everyone improves his or her chances of winning the prize—the promotion to a big salary. In effect each promotion in a job hierarchy is a round in the overall tournament.

Promotion tournaments have an obvious appeal as a motivation device. Unlike many other pay schemes, they do not require employers to be able to observe the actual output of every worker. Only relative output matters. In addition, using tournaments as incentives does not require that employers' estimates of productivity be totally accurate. In fact, as long as the imprecision in these estimates is not too great, uncertainty about productivity makes the system work *better*. For an employee to be motivated by a tournament, he must perceive that he has a chance to win and that this chance will increase if he works harder. If employers could tell each worker's output perfectly, the only way a worker could win would be by being the most productive. With some uncertainty, he might win just by being close enough, a more achievable outcome for all workers.

Each worker evaluates how much effort to provide (how hard to compete in the tournament) by comparing the costs of expending this effort with the expected benefit, defined as the return from winning multiplied by the change in the probability of winning created by putting forth the effort. A number of

---

[24]Judith Hellerstein and David Neumark, "Are Earnings Profiles Steeper than Productivity Profiles?" *Journal of Human Resources* 30: 89–112 (1995).

[25]Conference Board, *Top Executive Compensation: 1993 Edition*, New York: The Conference Board (1993).

POLICY ISSUE

ABOLISHING MANDATORY RETIREMENT

Increasing wages with seniority to induce increased output makes remaining in the firm an increasingly attractive option for workers. As a general rule, it is optimal for workers to retire when the output they would produce by working another year (their *VMP*) is less than the marginal disutility they would experience by working that year. In Figure 9.3, workers whose disutility or reservation wage is indicated by the line $w_r w_r$ should optimally retire after T years of service. Indeed, this strategy is how the firm and worker would pick a value of T to use in adjusting the wage profile to be sure that w_0AB was equal to BCD. At this point in their careers, however, the wage they are being paid far exceeds their *VMP* (or the disutility of working another year). Thus, even though it is socially optimal to retire at tenure T, it will be privately optimal to continue to work.

If workers continued to work past T in Figure 9.3, the part of their *VMP* they left with the employer by accepting low wages early in their career would no longer be sufficient to "pay for" the excess wages they would receive after t_B. Thus, employers must find some way to persuade these workers to retire at T. Traditionally, this was done by adopting a **mandatory retirement** age beyond which workers were no longer permitted to work.[26] Estimates of the number of older males who were employed in firms that imposed retirement ranged from one-third to one-half.[27]

Since 1986, age discrimination laws in the U.S. have made mandatory retirement policies illegal for all but a few occupations (such as airline pilots and police). If there were no alternative way to induce retirement at the optimal age, the effect of these laws would be to eliminate the possibility of using upward-sloping wage profiles to provide an incentive for reduced shirking. Compensation would be reduced to VMP_1 in Figure 9.3.

Fortunately, the design of pension plans can play a similar role. These plans have developed structures that provide powerful incentives for workers to retire at certain ages. A detailed examination of the provisions of ten pension plans showed that the discounted value of future benefits reached a peak in all but one of them at or before age 62. The declines in the discounted value are quite rapid after age 62 in some plans. Access to a pension means that, even though $w - w_r$ is large, the gains to taking retirement rather than postponing it are so great that the firm can induce its workers to leave. There is evidence that pensions fulfill this purpose and provide strong incentives to retire at certain ages by reducing the value of workers' pensions should they continue to work past the optimal age.[28]

---

[26] Edward Lazear, "Why Is There Mandatory Retirement?" *Journal of Political Economy* 87: 1261–1284 (1979).

[27] Duane Leigh, "Why Is There Mandatory Retirement? An Empirical Reexamination," *Journal of Human Resources* 19: 512–531 (1984).

[28] Olivia Mitchell and Gary Fields, "The Economics of Retirement Behavior," *Journal of Labor Economics* 2: 84–105 (1984); Alan Gustman and Thomas Steinmeier, "An Analysis of Pension Benefit Formulas, Pension Wealth and Incentives from Pensions," in Ronald Ehrenberg (ed.). *Research in Labor Economics*, Vol. 10, Greenwich, Conn.: JAI Press (1989); Richard Ippolito, "Toward Explaining Earlier Retirement After 1970," *Industrial and Labor Relations Review* 43: 556–569 (1990); Robin Lumsdaine, James Stock, and David Wise, "Pension Plan Provisions and Retirement: Men and Women, Medicare and Models," NBER Working Paper No. 4201 (1992); Alan Gustman, Olivia Mitchell, and Thomas Steinmeier, "The Role of Pensions in the Labor Market," *Industrial and Labor Relations Review* 47: 417–438 (1994).

factors influence how large a prize will be required to induce optimal effort. When the field of competitors is relatively homogeneous, the prize must be larger since a given effort expenditure is less certain of achieving success. The shorter the remaining work life, the greater the prize must be. A long horizon (many rounds in a tournament, many levels on the job ladder) gives people substantial incentive to work hard even though the immediate prize may be small, since winning this round earns the right for them to compete in future rounds. But in the final round (in the competition among vice-presidents) there is no future. Only the immediate payoff is left, so the pay structure must be especially steep to induce people to put forth the appropriate effort. Similarly, the more competitors there are for each "winning" slot, the greater the winner's payoff must be in order for it to appear worthwhile to compete.[29]

There is one important drawback to using tournaments as a motivation device that may limit both their prevalence and the size of the prize that can be awarded. Employers must be alert to the possibility of **sabotage**. If winning the tournament depends only on relative performance, it does not matter if a worker improves her own performance or reduces that of her competitors.

Two approaches have been taken to examine whether the theory of tournaments explains internal wage structures, and thus whether pay and effort are related in the way the theory implies. The first is to examine either actual tournaments, such as sporting events, that offer prizes based on the ranking of players or to construct experimental tournaments. Although far removed from most labor markets, evidence from these tournaments can show whether people facing possible prizes respond as the theory predicts. Increasing the payoff to performing better (equivalent to making the compensation-performance profile steeper) has been found to induce greater effort in the final round of four-round professional golf tournaments in both Europe and the United States. Students who participated in laboratory experiments that constructed tournaments also acted in accordance with the theory's predictions.[30]

---

[29]Edward Lazear and Sherwin Rosen, "Rank-Order Tournaments as Optimum Labor Contracts," *Journal of Political Economy* 89: 841–864 (1981) and Sherwin Rosen, "Prizes and Incentives in Elimination Tournaments," *American Economic Review* 76: 701–715 (1986), develop these ideas.

[30]The sporting events are reported in Ronald Ehrenberg and Michael Bognanno, "The Incentive Effects of Tournaments Revisited: Evidence from the European PGA Tour," *Industrial and Labor Relations Review* 43: 74S–88S (1990) and Ronald Ehrenberg and Michael Bognanno, "Do Tournaments Have Incentive Effects?" *Journal of Political Economy* 98: 1307–1324 (1990). The experiments are discussed in Clive Bull, Andrew Schotter, and Keith Weigelt, "Tournaments and Piece Rates: An Experimental Study," *Journal of Political Economy* 95: 1–32 (1987) and Robert Drago and John Heywood, "Tournaments, Piece Rates and the Shape of the Payoff Function," *Journal of Political Economy* 97: 992–998 (1989).

The alternative approach is to examine how closely the actual structure of executive or other pay conforms to this view of internal wage structures. This approach imposes a difficult test, since many more noneconomic incentives may be operating than in sports or lab experiments. Nonetheless, tournaments are one of the only ways to rationally explain the high relative pay of top corporate executives. Internal wage structures become steeper within corporations the higher up the management ladder one goes. This pattern is consistent both with the need to offer higher prizes as the "field" becomes more homogeneous and as the horizon becomes shorter. Compensation increases for promotion to top executive jobs are greater if the person is promoted from among a larger pool of competitors. In addition, among chief executives of large U.S. corporations, payment for current performance is more important the closer the executive is to mandatory retirement, just as the theory predicts.[31]

UP-OR-OUT CONTRACTS

One extreme form of a tournament is found in many industries that employ **up-or-out contracts**. Under such contracts, workers must either be promoted by a certain time or fired. One common example of such a contract is used by universities with their faculty. If a professor is not awarded tenure (typically within six years), he must be discharged. Up-or-out contracts are also common in many professional practices such as law firms, where young lawyers are either offered a partnership by a fixed date or are asked to leave the firm.

The rationale for contracts of this type has to do with incentives to keep firms honest in situations where workers and firms are tied by investments in specific human capital. Workers must choose how much to invest in specific human capital. The level of this investment is not observable by firms, but productivity is observed. If the firm and worker were to sign a contract specifying that the worker would be retained by the firm and paid a wage equal to productivity, the firm would have an incentive to cheat and claim that the worker had a low level of productivity, thereby paying a low wage. With investment in specific human capital, even this low wage might be more than the worker could earn elsewhere. Thus, the worker cannot keep the firm honest by threatening to quit. Since the firm will not pay the worker the full

---

[31] Robert Gibbons and Kevin J. Murphy, "Optimum Incentive Contracts in the Presence of Career Concerns," University of Rochester, Photocopy, (1990); Jonathan Leonard, "Executive Pay and Firm Performance," *Industrial and Labor Relations Review* 43: 13S–29S (1990); Brian Main, Charles O'Reilly III, and James Wade, "Top Executive Pay: Tournament or Teamwork?" *Journal of Labor Economics* 11: 606–628 (1993).

POLICY ISSUE

LIMITING PAY OF TOP EXECUTIVES

The Corporate Pay Responsibility Act, proposed in 1991, claimed to be an attempt to give shareholders more control over the salaries of top executives of U.S. corporations. The proposed act was a response to the fact that in 1990, the compensation of chief executives of the top 10 U.S. corporations ranged from $1.3 million to $5.4 million, while in a random selection of much smaller corporations from Fortune 500 companies, salaries ranged from $0.5 million to $4.7 million.[32] While this proposal had substantial emotional appeal, is there a justification for government interference in private salary decisions, other than the average person's dismay at seeing someone else receive such a huge salary?

The discussion of tournaments shows that these huge prizes can be an incentive enabling firms to elicit effort from all of their executives and to choose the best executives for higher-level jobs. Thus, limiting the salaries of top executives could result in less productivity from the entire managerial work force in the firm. If, on the other hand, there is no relationship between executive pay and company performance, no harm would come from limiting the pay for top executives (thus reducing the prizes in the tournaments).

A substantial body of research has shown that rates of return on capital and rates of increase in stock prices are greater when the pay of chief executives of U.S. corporations is higher.[33] Whether the relationship is strong enough to justify the actual salaries is debatable. This research and the analysis of tournaments suggest, however, that if it had been enacted, the proposed limits on executive compensation could have reduced corporate performance by limiting corporations' ability to motivate their executives.

value of any return on investment, however, the incentive to invest is too low, and an inefficiently small level of investment will take place.

Now suppose that the firm is not offered the choice of paying different wages to workers with high and low productivities. Instead, they must either retain workers and pay them the high productivity wage or discharge them. In this case the firm cannot obtain any advantage by misrepresenting the productivity of workers since they lose the services of any workers they claim have low productivity.[34]

---

[32] S. 1198, introduced by Senator Carl Levin of Michigan. The data on compensation are from *Business Week*, May 6, 1991.

[33] Sherwin Rosen, "Contracts and the Market for Executives," in Lars Werin (ed.). *Contracts: Determinants, Properties and Implications*, London: Blackwell (1992).

[34] C. Kahn and G. Huberman, "Two-sided Uncertainty and 'Up-or-Out' Contracts," *Journal of Labor Economics* 6: 423–444 (1988); Michael Waldman, "Up-or-Out Contracts: A Signaling Perspective," *Journal of Labor Economics* 8: 230–250 (1990).

THE INTERNAL LABOR MARKET, LAYOFFS, AND UNEMPLOYMENT

Chapter 8 showed that most developed economies exhibit some structural-frictional unemployment at all times. In addition to the search behavior in external labor markets discussed earlier, this unemployment arises as a result of the workings of internal labor markets.

Table 9.5 shows that job losers constituted a large percentage of unemployed workers even when, as in 1994, there was little demand-deficient unemployment. This pattern is especially true among adult men, who are most likely to be in lifetime jobs. One of the reasons is that **temporary layoffs** (short-term separations with a very high probability of recall) account for a substantial fraction of people who are unemployed because they lost their jobs. Among all three demographic groups on which data are presented in Table 9.5, layoffs account for about one-fourth of job losers. Nearly one-third of those placed on temporary layoffs are recalled to work within one month of when they became unemployed. This fact is a major reason for the relatively short duration of unemployment in the United States compared to other countries we saw in Chapter 8.[35]

Workers with greater prior tenure with a firm are far more likely to be recalled to a firm when placed on temporary layoff. One study found that those with 12 or more years of tenure were between three and six times more likely to be recalled from layoff. This behavior is consistent with either firms wishing to retain the benefits of investments in specific human capital or their need to honor implicit contracts where workers have posted significant bonds. Interestingly, the relationship between tenure and recall from layoff was much less strong in slack labor markets as measured by relative growth within the worker's industry and geographic region. This relationship was unchanged when the rate of technological change was taken into account, suggesting that the underlying cause was a greater propensity for employers to break implicit contracts when times were bad rather than a lower value of specific human capital in such times.[36]

As with quit rates, there are interesting demographic differences in the chance a worker will be laid off, with blacks more likely to be laid off than whites. Even accounting for differences in total experience, tenure, education, occupation, and industry, the average black male worker is at least 5 percent more likely to be laid off than an otherwise identical white male. Comparing black and white females, the difference is at least 15 percent.

[35]Martin Feldstein, "The Importance of Temporary Layoffs: An Empirical Analysis," *Brookings Papers on Economic Activity*, 733 (1975); Lawrence Katz, "Layoffs, Recall and the Duration of Unemployment," National Bureau of Economic Research, Working Paper No. 1825, (January 1986).

[36]Todd Idson and Robert Valletta, "The Effects of Sectoral Decline on the Employment Relationship," Columbia University Department of Economics Working Paper No. 654 (1993).

TABLE 9.5 PERCENTAGE DISTRIBUTIONS OF UNEMPLOYED JOB LOSERS, 1994

	Total	Men 20+	Women 20+	Teens
On layoff	25.6	25.3	24.7	37.1
Other job losers	74.4	74.7	75.3	62.9
Total	100.0	100.0	100.0	100.0
Job losers as a percent of all unemployed	47.7	63.3	43.7	14.0

Source: *Employment and Earnings,* (January 1995), p. 199.

Since these differentials exist even after accounting for differences in tenure, they do not result from blacks' more recent access to many jobs. Whether they result from discrimination or unmeasured productivity-related characteristics is an open question. White women, on the other hand, are at most half as likely to be laid off as white men with the same tenure and experience and in the same occupation and industry. Black women are also less prone to layoff than black men.[37]

In addition to those permanently or temporarily laid off due to demand shifts, job losers also include people who have been discharged from their jobs for various reasons. Employers almost always have the right to discharge or fire workers for cause, such as stealing, fighting, or refusing legal orders. In Europe and Japan other discharges are extremely rare. In the U.S. in most union and many nonunion plants, discharges without cause are allowed only during the first few months of employment. In other plants, however, **employment-at-will** prevails and employers can fire a worker whenever they wish, but, even when employers have this freedom, discharges account for less than one-tenth of job separations. Employers do not like to fire people unless necessary. Thus, being discharged is a signal to other potential employers that the worker has problems. It is not surprising that having been discharged reduces an employee's subsequent earnings by between 10 and 15 percent compared to workers with an otherwise apparently identical work history and demographic characteristics.[38]

Table 8.2 showed a low rate of structural-frictional unemployment in Japan. One reason for this difference from the U.S. might be the well-developed internal labor markets in Japan that lead to the much longer average duration of jobs that we noted earlier in this chapter. Despite the rigidity of wages offered by Japanese firms, especially the larger firms in which wage

---

[37]Francine Blau and Lawrence Kahn, "Causes and Consequences of Layoffs," *Economic Inquiry* 19: 270–296 (1981).

[38]Donald Parsons, "Reputational Bonding of Job Performance: The Wage Consequences of Being Fired," Ohio State University, Photocopy (1990).

progressions and structured job ladders are most prevalent, Japanese firms make very few temporary layoffs. One reason for this striking difference between two otherwise fairly similar countries are the bonuses paid to broad groups of workers, not just to managers as in the United States. Their magnitude provides substantial scope for reducing labor costs when product demand falls. The greatest year-to-year variation in bonuses is in industries where product demand is most variable. Bonuses in all firms fluctuate sharply with fluctuations in employment. In addition, basic wages also appear to fluctuate more with respect to profits in Japan than in the U.S.

Another reason is that Japanese firms make greater use of subcontracting than many American firms. Often these subcontractors are small, family businesses, so when demand falls the major firm is able to preserve employment by shifting work away from subcontractors to its core workers. The subcontractors do not lay off workers, they simply demand fewer hours from each worker.[39]

SHIRKING AND UNEMPLOYMENT

An important explanation for the existence of some unemployment relies on internal labor markets and the prevention of shirking. As we have seen, effort is related to wages, with high wages providing incentives to work hard in order to avoid being discharged. Consider the labor market depicted in Figure 9.4. For simplicity, we assume that the long-run supply of labor is completely inelastic at S^L, so that the labor force is constant at L. We also assume that all employers pay the same wage so that, no employer can motivate employees by paying a higher *relative* wage. The key question is: "How much will employers have to pay so that workers do not shirk their responsibilities?" If very few workers are employed, even a low wage will get employees to work hard. The alternative, if one is caught shirking, is losing one's job and having to look for another. With unemployment very high, the shirking worker who is discharged is likely to be unemployed for a long time. As employment increases and unemployment drops, employers must pay higher wages to motivate their workers. The loss to workers if they are caught shirking is smaller, since the lower unemployment rate means they will find it easier to get a new job if they are fired.[40]

---

[39] Masanori Hashimoto, "Bonus Payments, On-the-Job Training, and Lifetime Employment in Japan," *Journal of Political Economy* 87: 1086–1104 (1979); Richard Freeman and Martin Weitzman, "Bonuses and Employment in Japan," *Journal of the Japanese and International Economies* 1: 168–194 (1987); Robert Evans, Jr. "Japan's Labor Market: Continuity and Change," *Keio Business Journal* 25: 85–94 (1989); Kazutoshi Koshiro, "Bonus Payments and Wage Flexibility in Japan," in Kazutoshi Koshiro, *Employment Security and Labor Market Flexibility: An International Perspective*, Detroit, Mich.: Wayne State University Press (1992).

[40] This discussion is based on Carl Shapiro and Joseph Stiglitz, "Equilibrium Unemployment as a Worker Discipline Device," *American Economic Review* 74: 433–444 (1984) and Edmund Phelps, "Consumer Demand and Equilibrium Unemployment in a Working Model of the Consumer-Market Incentive-Wage Economy," *Quarterly Journal of Economics* 107: 1003–1032 (1992).

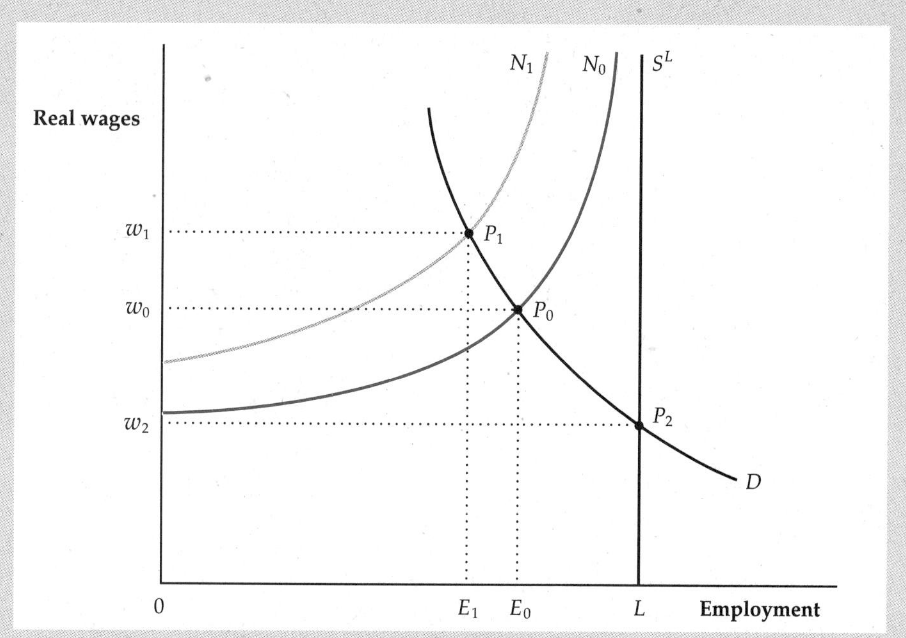

FIGURE 9.4 SHIRKING AND UNEMPLOYMENT
When unemployment rates are low, the penalty from losing a job is smaller, so efficiency-wage premiums must be larger if they are to discourage shirking. Higher unemployment benefits will make losing a job less of a threat and shift the no-shirking condition, raising wages and unemployment rates.

The curve N_0 graphs this upward-sloping **no-shirking condition**. It is like a supply curve in that it shows the wage rate necessary to elicit a given amount of effort. It does not, however, represent variation in the number of workers with wages like an ordinary supply curve, since we have assumed that the labor force is fixed at L. The crucial thing about N_0 is that it becomes vertical as it approaches S^L. The reason is that, as the amount of unemployment is reduced to nearly zero, employers have no convincing threat to workers who shirk. If workers are discharged, the absence of unemployment means they can find another job instantly. Employers would have to pay an infinite wage to induce workers not to shirk.

The demand curve D in Figure 9.4 is the standard demand curve derived in Chapter 4. If wages were at w_2, where the long-run supply curve intersects the demand curve, there would be no unemployment. Employers would find themselves with unmotivated workers and reduced output and could try to raise wages to induce their employees to produce. Assuming that the costs of these higher wages are less than those imposed by the shirking, point P_2 cannot be an equilibrium. Only at P_0, the intersection of the demand curve with the no-shirking condition, is the wage high enough that workers have no incentive to shirk. This equilibrium yields a wage of w_0 and employment of E_0. In equilibrium there is unemployment in an amount of $L - E_0$. The combination of employers' desires to maintain efficiency and their inability to monitor workers perfectly leads them to set wages in such a way that unemployment arises.

In Chapter 6 we saw how unemployment insurance might lengthen search and increase search unemployment. Is this also true if the unemployment is generated through the action of internal labor markets and employers' efforts to discourage shirking by paying higher wages? If the government raises unemployment benefits, the potential losses to workers who shirk are less. If they are discharged, they will receive a higher income while unemployed than before the increase in benefits. To induce them not to shirk, the employer must pay a higher wage. This means the no-shirking condition shifts up, to N_1. Equilibrium employment drops to E_1, and unemployment rises to $L - E_1$.

There is both microeconomic and macroeconomic evidence that supports this analysis. One study of the U.S. automobile industry found that fewer workers are dismissed for cause where the difference between the wage paid to auto workers and the average wage in the locality is greater. Presumably, faced with a larger drop in earnings if they are dismissed, fewer workers engage in shirking, so fewer are discharged. Evidence for French firms shows that the rate of dismissals of workers with a particular skill is lower where employers spend more on training, and presumably, supervising employees.[41]

At the macroeconomic level, there is strong evidence that, once the overall attractiveness of a region is taken into account, there is a negative relationship between current wages in a geographic area or industry and the current level of unemployment in that local labor market. An elasticity of wages with respect to local unemployment of about –0.1 has been found for a wide range of countries including the U.S., the U.K., Canada, South Korea, Austria, Italy, Holland, Switzerland, Norway, Germany, Ireland, Australia, India, Japan, and the Côte d'Ivoire.[42]

EFFICIENCY WAGES AND DIFFERENCES IN WAGES ACROSS INDUSTRIES

Table 9.6 presents relative earnings in various industries for several countries. Wage differentials among industries seem to be very persistent across countries. The pattern is even more impressive if one delves deeper than looking at the figures in the table allows. Across 14 developed and developing

---

[41] Peter Cappelli and Keith Chauvin, "An Interplant Test of the Efficiency Wage Hypothesis," *Quarterly Journal of Economics* 106: 769–788 (1991); G. Ballot, D. Gaumont, and J. Lanfranchi, "A Model of Shirking and Dismissals with a Test Based on a Panel of Industrial Firms," ERMES Working Paper, Université de Paris II (1990).

[42] David Blanchflower and Andrew Oswald, *The Wage Curve*, Cambridge, Mass.: MIT Press (1995) summarizes the literature in this area.

TABLE 9.6 INDEXES OF INDUSTRY AVERAGE WAGE, 1993, SELECTED COUNTRIES (TOTAL NONAGRICULTURE = 100)

Country	Manufacturing	Mining and Quarrying	Construction	Transport, Storage, and Communications	Clothing Manufacturing	Iron and Steel Manufacturing
United States	108	135	133	—	65	129
Australia	102	158	102	106	79	106
Canada	113	162	127	121	64	140
Germany	99	102	100	—	69	104
Hungary	78	114	71	86	56[a]	96[a]
Japan	94	109	113	112	48	105
South Korea	91	101	118	89	82[a]	146[a]
United Kingdom	102	126	103	105	68	120

[a]1992.

Source: International Labor Organization, *Yearbook of Labour Statistics*, (1994), Tables 16–20.

countries in 1982, the correlations of wages in narrowly defined manufacturing industries were mostly above +0.5.[43] No doubt part of the high correlation is due to differences in required skills that are the same no matter where the industry is located. An additional part is due to consistent differences in the desirability of the jobs found in these industries discussed in Chapter 10. These factors cannot, however, account fully for the industry wage differences since there are consistent excess supplies of labor to the high wage industries.

A part of the answer lies in the fact that the relative strength of unions across industries discussed in Chapter 13 is similar in different countries. All these factors taken together, however, cannot explain the pattern of earnings differences across industries. The second column of Table 9.7 shows industry wage rates relative to an average wage index of 100 after adjusting for a large variety of economic and demographic characteristics. One problem with these adjustments is that workers in different industries may differ in ways that cannot be captured by the variables available to researchers. The third column in Table 9.7 reports the results of a very clever method of getting around this problem. While the unmeasured characteristics of miners may differ from those of bankers, those of a given worker do not change when she switches from mining to banking. The third column reports the results from panel data for several years during which many workers changed the industry in which they were employed. This study, therefore, standardizes for the

[43]Alan Krueger and Lawrence Summers, "Reflections on the Inter-industry Wage Structure," in Kevin Lang and Jonathan Leonard (eds.). *Unemployment and the Structure of Labor Markets*, London: Basil Blackwell (1987). See also Bertil Holmlund and Johnny Zetterberg, "Insider Effects in Wage Determination," *European Economic Review* 35: 1009–1034 (1991).

TABLE 9.7 ADJUSTED INDUSTRY WAGE DIFFERENCES, UNITED STATES (AVERAGE = 100)[a]

	Current Population Surveys 1974–1980	
Industry	Cross-Section Method	Panel-Data Method
Mining	117	107
Construction	119	107
Manufacturing	107	103
Transportation and public utilities	112	102
Wholesale and retail trade	88	96
Finance, insurance, and real estate	104	103
Services	92	96

[a]Both methods account for differences in occupation, location, experience, education, union status, marital status, race, and sex. The panel-data method also controls for unobserved individual characteristics.

Source: Computed from Alan Krueger and Lawrence Summers, "Efficiency Wages and the Interindustry Wage Structure," *Econometrica* 56 (1988), Tables IV and V.

same factors as in the cross-section estimates in column two plus any **unobserved characteristics** of workers by examining what happens when workers switch industries. Other studies that examine only workers who left firms for reasons beyond their control (thereby eliminating any problems of selectivity in who left the firm) or that used a variety of test scores as measures of differences in workers' ability also find that differences in wages across industries cannot be explained by differences in the workers found in these industries.[44]

The data in the table make it very clear that even accounting for a huge variety of determinants of wages does *not* completely explain differences in wage rates among industries. Those differences are reduced, especially when panel-data methods of adjustment are used, but substantial adjusted wage differences still remain. What else is missing from the puzzle?

One of the best possible explanations for interindustry differences is that industries with larger workplaces and bigger firms pay higher wages. There is no doubt that there are **size differentials**. In one recent study of manufacturing plants, otherwise comparable nonproduction workers earned 32 percent more if they worked in a plant with more than 2500 other workers than

---

[44]Robert Gibbons and Lawrence Katz, "Does Unmeasured Ability Explain Inter-Industry Wage Differences?" *Review of Economic Studies* 59: 515–535 (1992); McKinley Blackburn and David Neumark, "Unobserved Ability, Efficiency Wages and Interindustry Wage Differentials," *Quarterly Journal of Economics* 107: 1421–1436 (1992).

TABLE 9.8 WAGE RATES BY PLANT SIZE, SELECTED MANUFACTURING OCCUPATIONS

Industry and Occupation	Size of Establishment and Wage Rate			
All manufacturing (July 1993)	50–499	500–999	1000–2499	2500+
Tool and die makers	$15.35	$15.94	$17.49	$20.63
Maintenance electricians	$13.75	$15.70	$16.71	$19.50
Material handling laborers	$7.93	$9.24	$12.90	$15.54
Buyers and contracting specialists, Level I (weekly)	$470	$515	$558	$604
Personnel specialists Level II (weekly)	$540	$602	$653	$724
Drafters, Level II (weekly)	$442	$457	$490	$519
Secretaries, Level III (weekly)	$502	$522	$525	$559
Motor vehicle parts (August 1989)	<250	250–499	500+	
Metal finishers	$7.95	$8.98	$10.70	
Class A hand welders	$9.94	$11.15	$12.60	
Textiles (August 1990)		100–499	500+	
Cloth doffers		$6.69	$6.96	
Drawing frame operators		$7.30	$7.54	
Men's and boy's shirts (September 1990)	20–249	250+		
Assemblers	$5.51	$6.65		
Collar Pointers	$5.53	$5.92		

Sources: Bureau of Labor Statistics, *Bulletin*, Nos. 2384, 2386, 2405, and 2458.

they would have earned in a plant with fewer than 250 workers.[45] The top part of Table 9.8 illustrates this for wage rates in several occupations in manufacturing. The bottom part of Table 9.8 shows that same results hold even in very detailed occupations within narrowly defined industries. In each industry, for the vast majority of jobs, wages are higher in larger firms or establishments, although the relationship appears stronger for production jobs than for clerical and managerial ones.

The implications of Table 9.8 are borne out by detailed analyses of many different sets of data for a variety of countries. In cross-section data for the U.S. from various years in the 1970s and 1980s, each doubling of the size of the establishment or of the firm increased wages by between 1 and 4 percent, depending on the data analyzed. The same size/wage relationship exists in other countries, including Japan, Korea, and Germany. In Germany and Italy, for example, companies with more than 2000 employees paid workers with the same demographic characteristics and human capital 15 and 14 percent

[45] Timothy Dunne and James Schmitz, Jr., "Wages, Employment Structure and Employer Size-Wage Premia: Their Relationship to Advanced-Technology Use at U.S. Manufacturing Establishments," *Economica* 62: 89–107 (1995).

more, respectively, than those with fewer than 20 employees. In the U.K. workers in plants with more than 500 workers earned 18 percent more than those in plants with fewer than 100 workers after controlling for human capital, industry, and occupation. In France the difference between plants with over 5000 workers and those with less than 20 was 16 percent. Wages are higher, other things being equal, in large plants independent of the size of the company. They are also higher in larger companies independent of the size of the plant.[46]

Being able to attribute interindustry wage differentials to differences in the sizes of plants and businesses tells what is happening. It does not, however, explain why big firms and plants pay higher wages. Unpleasant working conditions in bigger plants and companies are *not* an explanation. Workers find larger workplaces more pleasant, other things being equal, and quit rates have been shown to decrease with firm size in the United States and in other countries.[47]

These differences in quit rates are very important to understand the relationship between size and wages. Although lower quit rates might exist because workers have invested more in specific human capital (see Chapter 3), the differentials continue to exist when measures of specific human capital, such as experience, are taken into account.[48] Thus, the lower quit rate implies that workers find jobs in larger establishments more attractive than elsewhere. This finding suggests that employers must be paying more than they have to to attract labor.

Why would they do this? Once again, the answer lies in efficiency wages. It seems reasonable to assume that it is harder to monitor workers to deter misbehavior in larger plants. As the probability of detection goes down, the penalty if detected must go up to provide the same incentive to work diligent-

---

[46] Charles Brown and James Medoff, "Employer Size and the Payment of Factors," *Journal of Political Economy* 97: 1027–1059 (1989); Walter Oi, "Employment Relations in Dual Labor Markets," *Journal of Labor Economics* 8: S124–S149 (1990); Knut Gerlach and Elke Maria Schmidt, "Firm Size and Wages," *Labour* 4: 27–50 (1990); Carlo Dell'Aringa, "Collective Bargaining and Wage Determination in Italian Manufacturing," University of Rome, Unpublished Paper, (1991); Timothy Dunne and Mark Roberts, "Plant, Firm, and Industry Wage Variation," Pennsylvania State University, Photocopy (1990); J. Lhértier, "Les Déterminants du Salaire," *Économie et Statistique* No. 257 (1992); B. Main and B. Reilly, "The Employer Size-Wage Gap: Evidence for Britain," *Economica* 60: 125–142 (1993); Wesley Mellow, "Employer Size and Wages," *Review of Economics and Statistics* 64: 495–501 (1982).

[47] Lucia Dunn, "Work Disutility and Compensating Differentials: Estimation of Factors in the Link between Wages and Firm Size," *Review of Economics and Statistics* 68: 67–73 (1986); Walter Oi, "Heterogeneous Firms and the Organization of Production," *Economic Inquiry* 21: 147–171 (1983).

[48] Alphonse Holtzman and Todd Idson, "Employer Size and On-the-Job Training Decisions," *Southern Economic Journal* 58: 339–355 (1991); Kenneth Troske, "Evidence on the Employer Size-Wage Premia From Worker-Establishment Matched Data," U.S. Department of Commerce, Bureau of the Census Center for Economic Studies, Photocopy (1993).

ly. This means that the size of the efficiency wage premium must be greater in larger plants. Size premia are smaller for nonproduction workers where monitoring concerns may be lower. More importantly, they are related to the amount and complexity of the capital workers use. This relationship is not surprising since costs will be greater when shirking by the worker also causes a large amount of expensive capital to be underutilized. Size premia are smaller in unionized plants, perhaps because union work rules render monitoring issues less important. Even though they pay higher wages, the efficiency impact seems to be large enough that profits in larger companies are not greatly reduced by the higher pay they offer.[49]

Further support for the existence of efficiency wages comes from the fact that the size of industry wage premiums is positively related to the fraction of autonomous jobs where workers control their own hours and work pace. This relationship holds even after controlling for workplace size, firm size, and capital labor ratio, and presumably reflects a greater difficulty monitoring workers who control their own workpace. There is evidence, however, that firms in high-wage industries (where firms are larger) employ workers who are of better quality in ways that are unobservable to empirical researchers. Thus, workers who change industries do not receive any apparent increase in their wages when they move to an industry with higher average wages. This casts doubt on the efficiency-wage explanation and suggests that the reason for higher wages in larger firms may have to do with economies of scale in hiring that enable firms that are in the labor market more often to identify better quality workers.[50]

SELF-EMPLOYMENT

Self-employment is the ultimate internal labor market in that the individual is both manager and worker. Although reported self-employment income also includes the return to any capital the worker has invested (which, in the case of some self-employed workers such as doctors, can be substantial), most of

---

[49]Walter Oi, "The Fixed Employment Costs of Specialized Labor," in Jack Triplett (ed.). *The Measurement of Labor Costs*, Chicago: University of Chicago Press (1983); Latty Katz and Larry Summers, "Industry Rents: Evidence and Implications," *Brookings Papers: Microeconomics*, (1989), pp. 209–290; Walter Oi, "Employment Relations in Dual Labor Markets," *Journal of Labor Economics* 8: S124–S149 (1990); Kevin Lang, "Persistent Wage Dispersion and Involuntary Unemployment," *Quarterly Journal of Economics* 106: 181–202 (1991); Dunne and Schmitz "Wages, Employer"; Troske, "Evidence on the Employer."

[50]Kevin Murphy and Robert Topel. "Efficiency Wages Reconsidered: Theory and Evidence," in Yoram Weiss and Gideon Fishelson (eds.). *Advances in the Theory and Measurement of Unemployment*, New York: St. Martin's Press (1990); Mahmood Arai, "An Empirical Analysis of Wage Dispersion and Efficiency Wages," *Scandinavian Journal of Economics* 96: 31–50 (1994).

TABLE 9.9 NONFARM SELF-EMPLOYMENT, SELECTED COUNTRIES, 1969, 1993 (PERCENTAGE OF TOTAL EMPLOYMENT)

Country	1969	1993
United States	7.0	8.2
Australia	9.3	14.3
Germany	8.3	8.3
Japan	14.6	12.3
Spain	16.1	17.1
United Kingdom	6.5	11.2

Sources: OECD, *Employment Outlook*, (1985), Table 13; International Labour Organization, *Year Book of Labor Statistics*, (1994), Table 2.

these earnings represent labor income. Not only must those who are self-employed monitor any employees they may have, they must also create incentives for themselves to produce.

Self-employment does not comprise a large part of the labor market in developed economies. In the data in Table 9.9 the range is from one-twelfth to one-sixth of total employment. The highest levels are found in Greece and Italy where about one-fourth of nonfarm workers are self-employed. There are no uniform trends in the percentage of self-employed workers across developed economies. Within each country, however, there are distinct trends. For example, in the United States the fraction fell from World War II until the late 1960s, then rose steadily for the next 25 years.[51]

Why do workers choose self-employment? To some extent opting for self-employment is opting to avoid supervision and to monitor oneself. People who choose self-employment are inherently different from those who become employees, in ways that suggest a greater ability to cope with the lack of supervision. For example, self-employed workers report spending less than half as much time on coffee, lunch, and other breaks as conventional employees. On the other hand, entering self-employment may be largely a decision regarding occupational choice, independent of any monitoring considerations. In this light, it should depend on the factors we discussed in Chapter 3. Evidence for the United States since World War II suggests that economic factors including the possibility of using self-employment to avoid taxation, the difference between self-employment earnings and wages and salaries for a demographic group, and overall business conditions are important determinants of this choice. In particular, self-employment rises during recessions when regular jobs may be harder to find and laid-off executives may enter self-employed "consulting." Finally, evidence across 21 countries in 1990

[51] David Blau, "A Time-Series Analysis of Self-Employment in the United States," *Journal of Political Economy* 95: 445–467 (1987).

indicated a very strong positive relationship between the extent of self-employment and the degree of employee-protection regulation, such as restrictions on discharges and severance pay requirements in the labor market. When regular employment is severely regulated, firms will be less willing to hire workers and will rely on using self-employed contractors to avoid the regulations.[52]

Self-employment is a much larger fraction of employment in many developing economies where many workers are self-employed peasant farmers who must make decisions about the consumption of the staple good they grow, as well as how much to work on their own or other farmers' land, and how much hired labor to employ. This set of decisions sounds extraordinarily complex, as choices about labor demand seem inextricably linked to those about labor supply. If, however, the peasant farmer and hired laborer are close substitutes in production and earn the same wage rate if they seek work elsewhere, the decisions are easier. In this case decisions about labor demand and those about consumption and labor supply can be treated separately, and the analyses of Chapters 1 through 5 are valid for the peasant farmer.[53]

This analysis is presented in Figure 9.5, which combines a labor demand graph from Chapter 4 with a labor supply graph from Chapter 2. In order to do this, we have reversed the direction of the horizontal axis on the labor supply graph so that hours of work increase to the right. This means that the slopes of the indifference curves and budget line might appear reversed. The curve *TP* shows the total output at each input of hours by the peasant and any hired workers, just like the *TP* curve in Figure 4.2. The wage rate for both peasants and farm workers is initially w_0. At this wage rate the peasant will want to supply H_0^S total hours of labor, since the highest indifference curve he can attain is I_0. At such a high wage rate, however, it does not pay for him to produce more than he could using H_0 hours of labor. He therefore chooses to produce at point *B*, where the slope of the line w_0w_0, which is the wage rate, equals the slope of the *TP* curve, which is the marginal product of labor. With this low production, he works only H_0 hours on his own land and works $H_0^S - H_0$ in the market. His labor and that of any hired workers is too valuable in the market and relatively too unproductive on his own land for him to hire

[52] Blau, "A Time Series"; Daniel Hamermesh, "Shirking or Productive Schmoozing: Wages and the Allocation of Time at Work," *Industrial and Labor Relations Review* 43: S121–S133 (1990); Peter Dolton and G. H. Makepeace, "Self Employment among Graduates," *Bulletin of Economic Research* 42: 35–53 (1990); Theresa Devine, "The Recent Rise in U.S. Self-Employment," Department of Economics, Pennsylvania State University, Photocopy (1992); Robert Fairlie and Bruce Meyer, "The Ethnic and Racial Character of Self-Employment," NBER Working Paper No. 4791 (1994); *OECD Jobs Study: Evidence and Explanations—Part II: The Adjustment Potential of the Labor Market* (1994).

[53] See the discussions in Mark Rosenzweig, "Labor Markets in Low-Income Countries," in Hollis Chenery and T. N. Srinivasan (eds.). *Handbook of Development Economics*, Amsterdam: North-Holland (1988); and Inderjit Singh, Lyn Squire and John Strauss (eds.). *Agricultural Household Models: Extensions, Applications and Policy*, Baltimore: Johns Hopkins Press (1986).

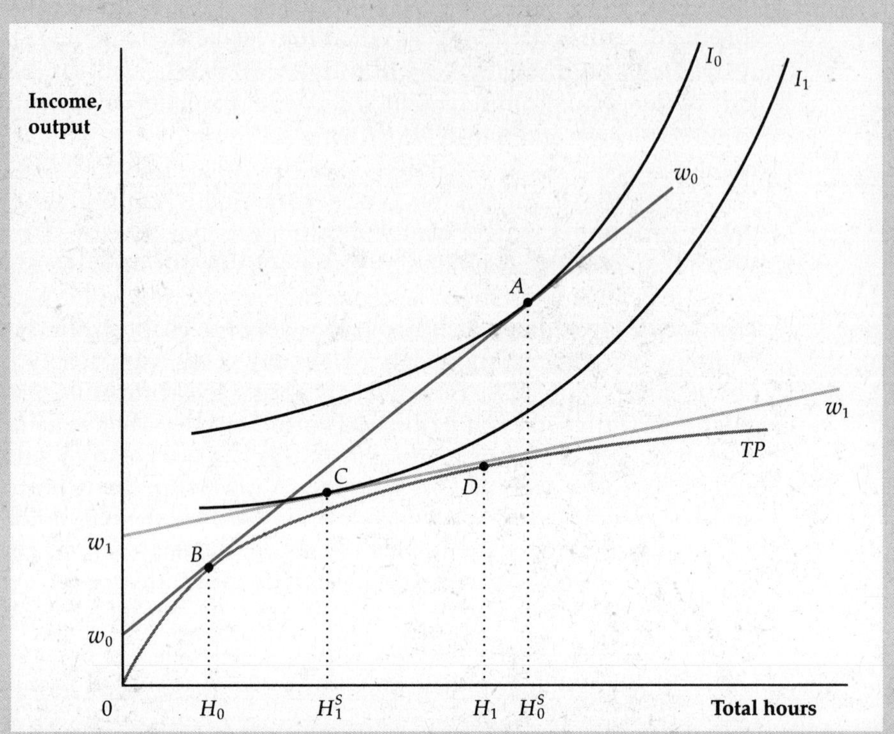

FIGURE 9.5 EMPLOYMENT DECISIONS OF THE SELF-EMPLOYED MANAGER/WORKER

Self-employed owner/operators who can both hire workers and work in the outside labor market themselves will make independent production and consumption decisions. At low wages (w_1) they will use more labor in production and hire workers. At high wages (w_0) they will work more hours themselves (including time spent in the external labor market) but employ less labor in their business.

workers or even to spend all his time working his own land. By combining self-employment with market work he simultaneously satisfies the utility-maximizing conditions of Chapter 2 and the profit-maximizing conditions of Chapter 4.

With the lower wage shown by the slope of w_1w_1 the situation changes. The peasant can earn less in the market, so as the figure is drawn his supply of hours is reduced to H_1^S. He achieves maximum satisfaction at point C on the lower indifference curve I_1. With labor this cheap, however, he wishes to increase his production to point D, where H_1 hours are used on the land. Thus, he employs $H_1 - H_1^S$ hours of hired labor. In short, when the wage rate falls, he hires more workers and increases production, just like the typical profit-maximizing employer. When the wage rate falls, he supplies less effort to his own and other production for the market, just like the typical worker who is not on a backward-bending part of his labor supply curve such as that shown for high wage rates in Figure 2.2.

Whether peasant farmers behave the way Figure 9.5 predicts is an open question. We know that many small landholders throughout the world also supply some labor to the formal market. A study of Indian agriculture, however, indicates that the basic assumption that the labor of peasants and hired workers are easily substituted is incorrect, while an examination of Indonesian farmers suggests it is reasonable.[54] Even if the assumption is not perfect, however, the analysis has the great advantage of providing a framework for thinking about how self-employed peasant farmers should behave in the labor market, and for demonstrating that the analysis of labor supply and demand in this text can be helpful even in this unusual context. A similar analysis has been shown to be useful in analyzing the behavior of physicians in the U.S., farm owners in Canada, and dairy farmers in Utah.[55] The implications of the separation property can also be useful in analyzing decisions of small independent contractors in such diverse industries as construction and software writing.

SUMMARY

In contrast to the high mobility of young workers, many older workers remain with the same employer for decades. This close attachment can lead to the development of long lines of promotion and substantial investments in firm-specific human capital, and, therefore, to the creation of internal labor markets. Within these markets, optimizing wage structures are created to induce workers to produce more and to allow for the promotion of more productive workers into positions of greater responsibility. Pensions arise as a way of inducing workers to retire in situations where their pay exceeds their productivity.

---

[54] Anil Deolalikar and Wim Vijverberg, "A Test of Heterogeneity of Family and Hired Labor in Asian Agriculture," *Oxford Bulletin of Economics and Statistics* 49: 291–305 (1987); Dwayne Benjamin, "Household Composition, Labor Markets and Labor Demand," *Econometrica* 60: 287–322 (1992).

[55] Douglas Brown and Harvey Lapan, "The Supply of Physicians Input Services," *Economic Inquiry* 17: 269–279 (1979); Ramon Lopez, "Estimating Labor Supply and Production Decisions of Self-Employed Farm Producers," *European Economic Review* 28: 61–82 (1984); James Thornton, "Estimating the Behavior of Self-Employed Business Proprietors: An Application to Dairy Farmers," *Southern Economic Journal* 60: 579–595 (1994).

Policy Issue

PAYING UNEMPLOYED WORKERS TO BECOME SELF-EMPLOYED

During the 1980s France and the United Kingdom gave unemployed workers a chance to use their unemployment pay to set up small businesses. A similar proposal was introduced in the United States in 1987 that would have allowed a limited number of states to experiment with paying workers their unemployment benefits in a lump sum for use in starting their own businesses.[56] Part of the motivation for this proposal was the belief that it would overcome difficulties people have in borrowing to set up a business and would lead unemployed workers to become employers who create jobs.

The American proposal died in committee. Though an innovative idea, it is doubtful how successful it could have been. It is unlikely that many unemployed workers would risk their benefits, which they often need just to maintain a minimum living standard. If they did risk them, the evidence in Chapter 4 that many new businesses are very short-lived means that many of those who took advantage of the proposal would be worse off than before. Indeed, businesses created under these programs in France and the U.K. failed at an even higher rate than other new businesses. The successful businesses were those where, although the owner had been receiving unemployment benefits, he or she had substantial human capital.[57] If this experience carried over to the U.S., workers who set up the new businesses would be unable to maintain living standards and purchasing power as envisioned by the legislation that created unemployment insurance in the United States. That so many new businesses are created in the U.S. and other countries each year suggests that there is little need for yet more stimuli to induce workers who are suited to self-employment to strike out on their own, or to tempt those who are not suited to risk their security.

Different mechanisms for paying workers affect effort differently. Piece-rate payments allow earnings to reflect effort more accurately than is possible with time rates. Bonuses, including profit sharing, are another way employees are induced to work harder. They form a large part of compensation in some economies. Fixed salaries may give incentives to produce output faster and more efficiently in certain circumstances. Even the self-employed must decide how much to produce and whether to produce on their own or to hire coworkers.

The existence of internal labor markets provides a reason for the existence of unemployment levels that are inversely related to wage rates in a

[56] HR 530, January 8, 1987. For an analysis of the structure of the European programs, see Nigel Meager, "Self-Employment Schemes for the Unemployed in the European Community: The Emergence of a New Institution and Its Evaluation," in Günther Schmid (ed.). *Labor Market Institutions in Europe*, Armonk N.Y.: M. E. Sharpe (1994).

[57] Marc Bendick and Mary Lou Egan, "Transfer Payment Diversion for Small Business Development," *Industrial and Labor Relations Review* 40: 528–542 (1987).

labor market. This pattern occurs because of the increased need to maintain incentives for workers to supply effort in situations when alternative jobs are readily available.

QUESTIONS AND PROBLEMS

9.1 List all the jobs you have held (different employers for whom you have worked) since you entered the labor force. How does your list compare to the information provided in Table 8.1? Which of these jobs involved employment at ports of entry to job ladders?

9.2 Gungho Electronics, a profit-maximizing firm, faces *VMP* schedules that depend on the wage rate it pays:

Number of Workers	*VMP* when Wage = \$13	*VMP* when Wage = \$17
1	\$18	\$20
2	16	18
3	14	16
4	12	14
5	10	12

a. If the wage is \$13, how many workers will Gungho employ? If the wage is \$17, how many? How does your answer to this second question differ from what it would be in a plant where the first *VMP* schedule applies no matter what the wage is, and why?

b. Remember that the sum of the *VMPs* up to each employment level equals the total revenue produced by that level of employment. If Gungho can set *both* its wage rate and employment levels, what would it choose for each of these? If the final column above were for a wage of \$14.50 instead of \$17, what would your answer be? Why does the answer differ when this assumption is changed?

9.3 You are the employer in a large firm. You offer workers a wage determined according to:

$$Wage = \$5.00 + .10 \times Years\ with\ the\ Firm.$$

All workers enter the firm at age 25. Each worker produces output valued at \$7.00 during each hour at work.

a. Can your firm survive without inducing workers to retire at some age? If yes, explain why; if no, at what age would you want them to retire, and why?

b. Assume you do wish to induce the workers to retire. Assume also that workers value their leisure at \$6 per hour, and that all workers in the firm put in 2000 hours per year. Construct a pension scheme that will suffice to get workers to retire voluntarily at the age you want them to leave.

9.4 You are selecting from among your junior executives someone to fill the position of vice-president. How do you structure incentives to get them all to produce, even though only one will be promoted? How do you avoid the possibility that one executive, not the most able or in the long run most efficient, can fool you into promoting him by working unusually hard during the period while you are evaluating the executives for promotion?

9.5 Under some conditions, workers' wages may increase either more or less rapidly than their productivity. What models give rise to each of these patterns? What do these models enable you to predict about which type(s) of workers can expect to see their wages rise more or less rapidly than their productivity?

9.6 There are several occasions when it might be efficient and optimal from both employers' and employees' points of view for wages to diverge from the value of an employee's marginal product. Discuss two of these occasions and explain how the breaking of the equality between wages and value of marginal product will improve the functioning of the labor market.

9.7 Analyze the effect of changing the form of compensation in a firm from a wage system to one of piece-work where workers are paid on the basis of their units of output. What incentives would this establish, and how would worker behavior be altered? Now, suppose that instead of a simple piece-work system, the scheme worked as follows: each worker will be allowed to set an individual "target" output. There will then be a two-tier piece rate, with one rate for units below the target and a second, higher rate for units above the target. In order to encourage workers to set high targets for themselves, both of these rates will depend on the target the worker chooses. A higher target will result in both rates being greater than they would have been had the worker chosen a lower target. What incentives for labor supply and other worker behavior will this scheme establish?

9.8 Human capital, job search, and implicit contract theories all suggest that wages should be positively associated with job tenure. What is the causal mechanism in each case? How would you attempt to distinguish among these empirically? Are they each consistent with the additional observation that wage/tenure profiles are typically flatter in unionized firms? Why or why not?

9.9 The share of employment in service firms grows while that in manufacturing declines as countries grow richer and technology advances over time. What would this shift lead you to predict will happen to the prevalence of various forms of compensation (i.e., piece rates, time rates, salaries, bonuses, etc.)? Why do you predict the changes you envision?

9.10 One possible disadvantage of pay schemes based on performance is the difficulty of determining individual pay when output requires cooperation among many workers. In what types of employment is this likely to be the greatest problem? How might you design a pay system that provides maximum work incentive in such cases? Does your design conform to what you observe about compensation in actual establishments?

KEY WORDS

bogey
bond
bonuses
career job
efficiency wages
employment-at-will
explicit contract
flat rate
implicit contract
incentive compatible contract
internal wage structure
job cluster
job ladder
key job
lifetime job
mandatory retirement
monitoring
no-shirking condition
piece rate
port of entry
profit sharing
reputation effect
sabotage
salary
shirk
shock theory
size differential
temporary layoffs
time rate
tournament
unobserved characteristics
up-or-out contract

10

JOB AMENITIES AND EMPLOYEE BENEFITS

THE MAJOR QUESTIONS

- ▲ How does the danger inherent in jobs in a particular industry affect wages?
- ▲ How does the variability of employment and the risk of unemployment affect wages?
- ▲ What other characteristics of jobs have an impact on wages?
- ▲ How do the characteristics of a job's location affect the pay a worker receives?
- ▲ How do the nature of technology and the tastes of workers interact to generate the wage differentials we observe in the market?
- ▲ What forms of compensation are workers provided in addition to their wages?
- ▲ What fraction of compensation takes the form of benefits in addition to wages, and how does this differ across different types of workers?
- ▲ What are the reasons that workers and firms may opt for compensation in benefits rather than wages?

THE MARKET FOR NONWAGE ASPECTS OF JOBS

In the first three sections of this book we have acted as if wages were the only form of compensation workers received. The fact that apparently identical workers are observed to receive different wages was explained as a result of unobserved differences in human capital (Chapter 3), randomness in the search process (Chapter 6), and internal labor markets operated by firms (Chapter 9). We now turn to two other reasons for this observation: the fact that jobs themselves differ in their characteristics and the fact that wages form only a part of compensation for most workers. Desirable job characteristics and nonwage compensation are similar in that workers purchase each by accepting lower wages than they otherwise might have earned.

Think of the maximum possible monetary income that a worker could receive if he took the job with the worst working conditions and no fringe benefits as his potential **full income**. The worker could purchase a more desirable job by giving up some of this potential income. This reduction in pay in return for an attractive job characteristic is known as a **compensating differential.**

If jobs with attractive working conditions did not pay lower wages than other jobs available to workers with a given set of talents, they would be flooded with applicants. This insight is not new. Adam Smith wrote in 1776:

> The whole of the advantages and disadvantages of the different employments of labor and stock must, in the same neighborhood, be either perfectly equal or continually tending to equality. If in the same neighborhood there was any employment evidently either more or less advantageous than the rest, so many people would crowd into it in one case, and so many would desert it in the other, that its advantages would soon return to the level of other employments.[1]

Consider the market for labor in jobs characterized by a specific **disamenity,** some aspect of the job that most workers would find unpleasant. The disamenity could be anything, including risk of injury, dirtiness of the work, temperature at the workplace, or risk of unemployment. Indifference curve I_1 in Figure 10.1 shows the combinations of pay and level of the disamenity that leave one particular worker (call him Max) feeling equally well-off.[2] Indifference curve I_1 slopes upward since the disamenity is a bad rather than a good thing, and therefore, Max requires more pay to compensate for more of the disamenity. It slopes up at an increasing rate because the more of the disamenity Max bears, the higher the pay he will require to offset ever greater amounts. Indifference curve I_1' describes another set of combinations of pay and disamenity, all of which keep Max equally well-off, but at a higher level of utility than along I_1. Max prefers I_1' to I_1 since he receives more pay at each level of the disamenity.

Max is only one of many workers. Maxine's tastes for pay and the disamenity are described by indifference curves like I_2. In some sense Maxine is less bothered by the disamenity than Max. Suppose they both were on a job with disamenity level D_4. Maxine could be compensated for a small increase in the disamenity from D_4 with a much smaller pay increase than would be required to keep Max equally satisfied. (Looking at both workers' tastes at the level of disamenity D_4 at point A, I_2 is flatter than I_1.) Similarly, Maximilian,

---

[1]Adam Smith, *The Wealth of Nations*, New York: Random House (1937), Book 1, Chapter 10. See also the discussion in Albert Rees, "Compensating Wage Differentials," in Andrew Skinner and Thomas Wilson (eds.). *Essays on Adam Smith*, Oxford: Clarendon Press (1975).

[2]This method of analysis originated in Sherwin Rosen, "Hedonic Prices and Implicit Markets," *Journal of Political Economy* 82: 34–55 (1974).

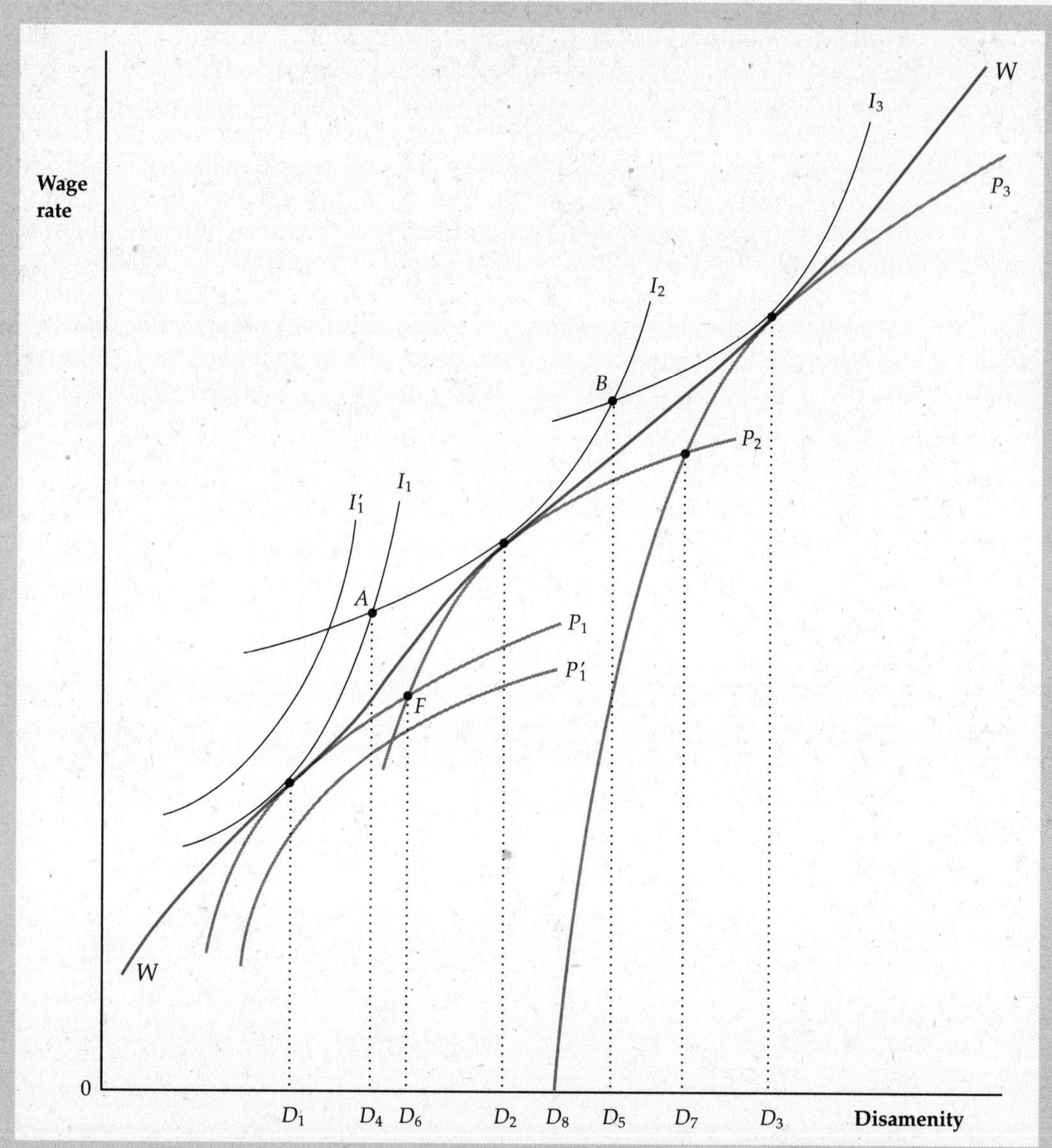

FIGURE 10.1 THE MARKET FOR A DISAMENITY
Workers and employers will be sorted so that those with the least dislike for a disamenity will be employed by the firm that finds it most difficult to remove that disamenity. The market-clearing relationship between wages and the level of the disamenity is less curved than either any worker's indifference curve or any firm's isoprofit curve.

with indifference curves like I_3, is even more willing to accept small increases in the disamenity. Moving right from D_5 at point *B*, he can be kept equally happy with a smaller increase in pay than is required by Maxine at that point. Note that we have drawn only one indifference curve each for Maxine and Maximillian. There are, in fact, infinitely many such curves for each worker, with movements to the northwest in Figure 10.1 denoting higher utility.

Just as workers have different tastes for the disamenity and different degrees of willingness to trade pay for it, employers have different abilities to offer combinations of pay and the disamenity. Available technology dictates that some jobs will be less agreeable than others along certain dimensions. Steel manufacturing, for example, is necessarily hotter and dirtier than retailing. In every case, however, employers of workers in a particular occupation can vary the disamenity by devoting resources to its removal. Even a steel mill can be air-conditioned, although at a very high cost.

The profits of Employer 1 in Figure 10.1 are the same at all points along the isoprofit curve P_1. The curve P_1 slopes up because if a greater level of the disamenity is tolerated, the employer must spend less on its removal and can offer workers greater pay instead. Assuming that employers do the least costly things to reduce the disamenity first, as less and less of it remains, removal of each additional bit will cost more and more. To keep profits the same, the employer must therefore cut pay more for each unit of disamenity removed when less of the disamenity remains. P_1 thus becomes steeper as one moves to the left in Figure 10.1. P_1' shows another of Employer 1's isoprofit curves. Profits are higher on P_1' because less pay is offered at any given level of the disamenity.

Other employers have different abilities to remove the disamenity. It is harder to air-condition a steel mill than a store. Those like Employer 2 can remove the disamenity only at higher cost. At point *F*, their profits, as shown by the isoprofit curve P_2, can only be maintained by a sharper cut in pay than that made by Employer 1 as the disamenity is reduced below D_6. Employer 3 finds it even harder to remove the disamenity. Indeed, as the isoprofit curve P_3 is drawn, even at a wage rate of zero the employer could not reduce the amount of the disamenity below D_8.

What does equilibrium in this labor market look like? People like Max, who are very bothered by the disamenity, will seek jobs where they must endure relatively little of it. They will work for an employer like Employer 1, who finds it fairly easy to operate a workplace with low levels of the disamenity and will "consume" D_1 of the disamenity. Maxine and Maximilian will be employed in firms that are less able to reduce the amount of the disamenity, consuming levels D_2 and D_3 respectively. Workers with the least dislike for the disamenity will be matched by the market with employers who have the greatest difficulty in removing the disamenity. The market will be observed offering a greater monetary reward to those otherwise identical workers whose workplace eliminates less of the disamenity. In Figure 10.1 the market trade-off between pay and the disamenity is shown by the line *WW*. Its slope is positive because even those workers who are least bothered by the disamenity must be paid more to get them to work in firms that have difficulty removing it.

The position of *WW* is determined by the workings of the product market. If *WW* were higher, firms would be paying such high wages at each level of the disamenity that they would lose money. The wage rate would have to fall to give firms a competitive rate of profit. On the other hand, if the wages were so low at each disamenity that excess profits were being made, new companies would enter the market and bid up the wage until only competitive profits were being earned.

The trade-off *WW* is much flatter than would be required if all workers were like Max. Very large pay premiums would have to be offered by firms like Employer 3 in order to induce these workers to accept jobs that involve large amounts of the disamenity. Other things being equal, the greater the workers' distaste for a disamenity, the greater the pay premium associated with it, and the smaller the amount of the disamenity present in the workplace. If all employers were like Employer 1 and could remove the disamenity at little cost, we would observe relatively little of the disamenity in the market.

This discussion may seem to contradict reality. After all, the dirtiest, most dangerous jobs are not associated with the highest pay. Professors and lawyers usually earn more than sanitation and construction workers. These gross pay differentials, however, do not standardize for factors such as the ability and amount of formal training. Professors and lawyers incur much greater costs of schooling than sanitation and construction workers. The theory of compensating differentials only states that pay premiums for disamenities will exist in the long run among people who are *otherwise identical* along such dimensions as training, education, and other characteristics.

RISKS AND HAZARDS ON THE JOB

The first disamenities we examine are hazards on the job. Work is dangerous. In the United States in 1992, over 6000 workers were killed on the job, and about 3 million cases of work-related injury or illness forced workers to miss time from work. The distribution of work-related injury and illness is by no means uniform among industries. For example, 23 percent of workers in meat packing were severely enough injured on the job to miss time from work during 1992, as were 18 percent of workers in shipbuilding. At the opposite extreme, only 0.5 percent of workers in legal services and 0.7 percent of workers in accounting, auditing, and bookkeeping were injured. Construction and mining are much more dangerous than finance and services. This tremendous diversity of experience suggests that there should be substantial differences in pay to compensate for the large differences in risks from work.

TRENDS, DURATION, AND INCIDENCE OF DEATHS AND INJURIES ON THE JOB

Table 10.1 shows trends in deaths on the job in four countries since the mid-1960s. Data for the U.S. for selected years since 1973 are shown in the

TABLE 10.1 TRENDS IN WORKPLACE FATALITIES, 1965–1992, SELECTED COUNTRIES (DEATHS PER 100,000 WORKERS)

	1965	1975	1985	Early 1990s
France	19.9	15.9	7.9	7.4
Germany	19.2	13.5	10.0	7.0
Italy	22.0	20.4	12.6	11.2
United Kingdom	4.6	2.9	1.9	1.2

Sources: OECD, *Employment Outlook,* (1989), Table 4.1; ILO *Year Book of Labour Statistics,* (1994), Table 30.

TABLE 10.2 WORKPLACE FATALITIES AND INCIDENCE, DURATION, AND LOST WORKDAYS DUE TO OCCUPATIONAL ILLNESS OR INJURY, SELECTED YEARS, 1973–1993

	1973	1975	1979	1982	1988	1993
Fatalities per 100,000 workers	—	9.4	8.6	7.4	5.0	5.2
			Injuries and Illnesses			
Incidence per 100 workers	3.4	3.3	4.3	3.5	4.0	3.8
Duration (days)	15.7	17.0	15.7	16.8	19.0	—
Workdays per 100 workers	53.3	56.1	67.7	58.7	76.1	—

Sources: *Occupational Injuries and Illnesses in the United States by Industry* (1984), Text Tables 1 and 4; (1988), Text Tables 1 and 7; Guy Toscano and Janica Windau, "The Changing Character of Fatal Work Injuries," *Monthly Labor Review* (Oct. 1994); *Survey of Occupational Injuries and Illnesses in the United States by Industry* (1994), Table 1.

first row of Table 10.2. The data are not comparable across the five countries, since definitions differ, but do not change much within a country over time. The data show a sharp downward trend in the rate of workplace fatalities among all five nations. In large part this decrease reflects the shift we have seen in all countries away from agriculture, mining, and manufacturing (three relatively dangerous industries) to service industries (which tend to be relatively safe). For example, each $465 million of output in agriculture is estimated to involve one occupational death as opposed to the $5925 million of sales required to generate one death in finance, insurance, and real estate.[3]

[3]W. Kip Viscusi and Richard J. Zeckhauser, "The Fatality and Injury Costs of Expenditures," *Journal of Risk and Uncertainty* 7: 19–41 (1994).

TABLE 10.3 OCCUPATIONAL DEATHS PER 100,000 WORKERS

Industry	1978	1993
Mining	43.8	26.0
Construction	30.5	13.7
Manufacturing	5.9	3.9
Transportation and public utilities	18.7	12.9
Finance insurance & real estate	5.4	1.5
Services	3.0	2.4

Sources: "Work-Related Deaths for 1978," U.S. Department of Labor, *News 79–787;* and Guy Toscano and Janica Windau, "The Changing Character of Fatal Work Injuries," *Monthly Labor Review* (October 1994).

As Table 10.3 shows, however, improvements in safety have occurred within individual occupations. Thus, a part of the overall decline may reflect a willingness of workers to sacrifice a greater amount of pay to purchase occupational safety. Wealthier workers seek out safer workplaces. As workers become increasingly affluent, they can be expected to take part of the wage gains generated by their increased productivity in the form of improvements in workplace safety. Evidence for a sample of workers in the U.S. in 1977 bears this out. Workers with higher nonlabor income were found in safer workplaces even after controlling for their education, experience, and demographic characteristics. Similarly, workers whose qualities make them more productive with the same investment in human capital give up some of the extra income they might earn by sorting themselves into jobs with a lower risk of being killed at work.[4]

As with unemployment, we can break the time lost to workplace illnesses and injuries into duration and incidence components. The number of workdays lost per 100 workers can be written as:

$$\textit{Workdays lost} = \textit{injured workers} \times \textit{average duration of injury}.$$

As the data in the bottom part of Table 10.2 show, while only 3.8 percent of American workers are injured on the job each year, the average duration of loss is quite substantial. Moreover, unlike the rate of workplace fatalities, the incidence and duration of workplace injuries have risen slightly since 1973 (the earliest period for which comparable data were collected). This apparent rise may not, however, represent a real increase in the number of injuries workers suffer on the job. In part, they may be the result of rising incomes. Workers with greater income may be more willing to report an injury and

[4]Jeff Biddle and Gary Zarkin, "Worker Preferences and Market Compensation for Job Risk," *Review of Economics and Statistics* 70: 660–667 (1988); John Garen, "Compensating Wage Differentials and the Endogeneity of Job Riskiness," *Review of Economics and Statistics* 70: 9–16 (1988).

take time off from work. Those with few savings may have to continue working in pain to meet their expenses. In addition, changes in insurance coverage and the legal environment may have made injured workers more likely to report their injuries.

PAY DIFFERENCES DUE TO DANGEROUS OR UNPLEASANT WORK

Substantial differences clearly exist among industries in rates of work-related deaths and injuries. This fact does not necessarily mean, however, that pay will be greater in industries with higher rates. If enough workers do not mind what others view as a disamenity, there will be no premium attached to jobs with that characteristic. Although very few workers welcome the possibility of being killed or maimed on the job, attitudes toward these risks vary substantially. Perhaps there are enough workers who are not too bothered by dangerous jobs that the premiums paid need not be very large.

Substantial effort has been devoted to measuring the extra compensation provided for the risk of being killed on the job. The typical study measures the wages w of a large number of workers, the characteristics X that these workers bring to the job (including human capital and demographic characteristics), and the number of injuries or deaths in various occupations among a fixed-sized group of workers (say, 100,000). These factors yield a statistical equation:

$$w = F(X) + bP$$

where F = a function showing the effect of each component of X on wages, and

b = the impact on wages of additional death or injury among the group of workers.

The estimate of b is the estimated compensating differential for the risk of death or injury P.

The evidence is now overwhelming that workers who face a higher probability of death on the job receive higher pay than otherwise identical workers. Among 24 American studies, the size of this compensating differential for the risk of death varies from as little as \$700 (1994 dollars) to as much as \$18,000 of extra pay per year for each one-thousandth increase in the probability of being killed. The average across all the studies was about \$5,600 in extra pay for each one-tenth percentage point increase in the probability of being killed on the job. With 5 deaths per 100,000 workers, a one one-thousandth increase in the probability of death is a 20 percent increase. Comparable studies of the United Kingdom, Australia, Canada, and Japan all show compensating differentials within this range.[5]

---

[5]Kip Viscusi, "The Value of Risks to Life and Health," *Journal of Economic Literature* 31: 1912–1946 (1993); W. S. Siebert and X. Wei, "Compensating Wage Differentials for Workplace Accidents: Evidence for Union and Nonunion Workers in the U.K.," *Journal of Risk and Uncertainty* 9: 61–76 (1994).

POLICY ISSUE

DISABLED BY STRESS?

Begun in seven states in 1911, the **workers' compensation** system is the oldest social insurance program in the U.S. Employers are required to compensate injured workers according to schedules that are set by laws that have been enacted in each state. The system was supposed to provide speedy and certain payment to workers who were injured on the job in return for eliminating costly and burdensome legal disputes over liability.

In recent years, however, claims under this system have grown very rapidly. During the 1980s, payments under this system grew by almost 10 percent a year during a period when prices overall were rising at about 4.3 percent a year. In addition, since the system is governed by state laws, costs vary dramatically in different states. California, with about 11.5 percent of U.S. workers accounts for over 17 percent of workers' compensation payments. New York, on the other hand, contains 6.7 percent of the nation's workers but accounts for only 4.7 percent of workers' compensation payments. One furniture manufacturer reported paying $400,000 in 1992 for workers' compensation insurance for its 110 workers in a California plant but only $8,000 for 110 workers doing the same job in North Carolina. What accounts for these large differences?

A major factor is the state law's treatment of stress. As originally designed, the workers' compensation system was supposed to deal with easily defined injuries such as severed fingers or broken legs. In recent years a growing fraction of claims have been for vague and hard-to-document disabilities such as work-related stress. While certain traumatic events such as witnessing a coworker being shot to death in a robbery might lead to legitimate work-related stress, many of the claims that have inflated costs in recent years seem much more tenuous. For example, several California policemen reported themselves disabled and claimed workers' compensation benefits because they saw the famous videotape of the Rodney King beating on television. In California it became almost routine for workers to claim to be disabled by stress if they were fired or laid-off from their jobs. When a garment plant shut down in 1991, 26 workers immediately claimed to be unable to work because of the stress of losing their job. All 26 were represented by the same attorney and had medical evaluations consisting of a check-list filled in on a word processor by the same clinic. One clinic charged almost $15,000 to declare 5 discharged kitchen workers unable to work for at least three months due to emotional stress even though 4 of the 5 already had other jobs. Egged on by some lawyers and doctors, stress-related claims in California jumped by 700 percent during the 1980s.

Other states were much less generous with respect to workers' claims for emotional disability caused by stress on the job. The furniture company cited above had only two claims in its North Carolina plant, where stress-related claims are not recognized. It had 60 claims in California, almost all of which were from employees who claimed to be disabled because they were discharged or their hours were reduced. In response to this escalating burden, in 1993 California amended its law to require employees to establish that at least 51 percent of the stress that caused their disability happened on their job, up from the previous standard that forced employers to pay if as little as 10 percent of the employee's stress was job-related. Estimates are that this reform alone will save employers in California $1.5 billion (about 15 percent of workers' compensation costs). To the extent that California's experience is reflected in the national statistics, either because many other states followed a similar pattern or because California itself constitutes such a large fraction of the nation, the escalation of disability claims proportedly caused by stress in recent years will have distorted apparent trends in workplace disabilities.[6]

---

[6] *Los Angeles Times*, August 23, 1992, p. D1 and December 27, 1992, p. C7; *Wall Street Journal*, July 19, 1993, p. A2.

Even within the narrowly defined occupation of police officer, police in otherwise identical cities where the risk of death on the job was one-thousandth higher received nearly $1300 (1994 dollars) of extra pay per year.[7] The evidence is clear that there is a significant compensating wage differential for the risk of death on the job.

Pay premiums for the risk of injury on the job are likely to be smaller and more difficult to discern than the compensating differentials for the risk of death on the job. There is increasing evidence, however, that workers' aversion to risk requires employers to pay more to those who are more likely to suffer injuries. Among 14 studies that investigated this issue, the estimated lifetime pay premium for each expected injury on the job ranged from $15,000 to $100,000 (1994 dollars). One study of 6 manufacturing industries between 1947 and 1973 found pay premiums of between 0.2 and 2.0 percent associated with each 10 percent increase in the accident rate. Workers in U.S. industries where the risk of injury was 10 percent above average received wages in 1969 that were 1 percent above average. In another study of American workers in 1977, working in an industry where the risk was 10 percent above average raised earnings by 0.5 percent. The size of the compensating differential for risk of injury appears to be larger for unionized employers.[8]

This compensating wage differential is paid mainly for increases in the expected duration of the workplace injury. An increase in the incidence of injuries that raises the expected workdays lost by 1 percent produces a much smaller compensating differential than an increase in duration that has the same effect on lost work time. The reason is similar to why, as we saw in Chapter 8, programs to reduce the average duration of spells of unemployment by work sharing might be justified. The loss of utility from being out of work for one week each year is less than the loss from being out of work for ten weeks every tenth year.[9] As a whole, the evidence is clear that the market compensates workers for the possibility of being injured on the job by forcing employers whose workplaces are dangerous to offer compensation above that offered in safer workplaces.

Return to Figure 10.1 and assume that the disamenity being measured is workplace danger. Data on the characteristics of workers in different jobs and the pay premiums they receive allow us to infer what kinds of workers

---

[7] Stuart Low and Lee McPheters, "Wage Differentials and Risk of Death: An Empirical Analysis," *Economic Inquiry* 21: 271–280 (1982).

[8] Hal Sider, "Work-Related Accidents and the Production Process," *Journal of Human Resources* 20: 47–63 (1985); Biddle and Zarkin, "Worker Preferences;" David Fairris, "Compensating Payments and Hazardous Work in Union and Nonunion Settings," *Journal of Labor Research* 13: 205–221 (1992); Viscusi, "The Value of."

[9] Daniel Hamermesh and John Wolfe, "Compensating Wage Differentials and the Duration of Wage Loss," *Journal of Labor Economics* 8: S175–S197 (1990); W. Kip Viscusi and Charles O'Connor, "Adaptive Responses to Chemical Labeling," *American Economic Review* 74: 942–956 (1984).

correspond to the individuals whose indifference curves are described by I_1, I_2, or I_3. Married males receive greater pay premiums for risks of fatality or injury on the job than unmarried males, and nonwhites receive higher premiums for risks than whites.[10] Whether this effect is because married men and nonwhites are more risk-averse (i.e., place a higher value on safety relative to income) than others, or because they are more likely to locate in jobs that are less safe and, therefore, provide above-average risk premiums, is unclear.

In addition to the risk of death or injury, other aspects of work such as noise, stress, heat or cold, requirements of physical strength, lack of freedom to set one's own hours may fall into the category of disamenities. One study for the U.S. has found higher pay in jobs that require workers to put forth more effort and assume more responsibility and lower pay in jobs that offer physically pleasant workplaces, more intellectual challenge, more interpersonal contact, and convenient hours. Another study for Sweden found higher wages in jobs that were mentally demanding, hectic, noisy, and smokey.[11] Once people have entered an occupation that requires substantial training, the effect is even clearer. Wages for PhDs in the United States in the late 1980s were between 10 and 20 percent higher in industry than in colleges and universities, presumably because working in an academic setting provided more freedom to schedule work and choose topics of study. Similarly, lawyers who choose public-interest law earn less than other lawyers, a reflection in part of their willingness to give up some earnings to do "good works."[12]

THE ROLE OF TASTES

Differences in people's tastes and preferences may make it difficult to find compensating differentials for many job characteristics. A disamenity for some people may be an amenity for others. Thus, whether a characteristic raises or lowers wages will depend on how many people view the characteristic favorably versus how many jobs provide it. Consider Figure 10.2, which shows the market for a particular job characteristic. Suppose this characteristic involves running as a part of the job. Some people are joggers who would presumably be willing to pay in the form of reduced wages for the

---

[10] Greg Duncan, "Earnings Functions and Nonpecuniary Benefits," *Journal of Human Resources* 11: 462–483 (1976); Richard Thaler and Sherwin Rosen, "The Value of Saving a Life: Evidence from the Labor Market," in Nestor Terleckyj (ed.). *Household Production and Consumption*, New York: Columbia University Press (1975).

[11] Greg Duncan and Bertil Holmlund, "Was Adam Smith Right After All? Another Test of the Theory of Compensating Wage Differentials," *Journal of Labor Economics* 3: 366–379 (1983); Randall Filer, "The Search for Compensating Differentials: Is There a Pot of Gold After All?" Charles University, CERGE-EI Working Paper No. 41 (1993).

[12] Charles Brown, "Equalizing Differences in the Labor Market," *Quarterly Journal of Economics* 94: 113–134 (1980); John Goddeeris, "Compensating Differentials and Self-Selection: An Application to Lawyers," *Journal of Political Economy* 96: 411–428 (1988); Albert Rees, "The Salaries of Ph.D.'s in Academe and Elsewhere," *Journal of Economic Perspectives* 7: 151–158 (1993).

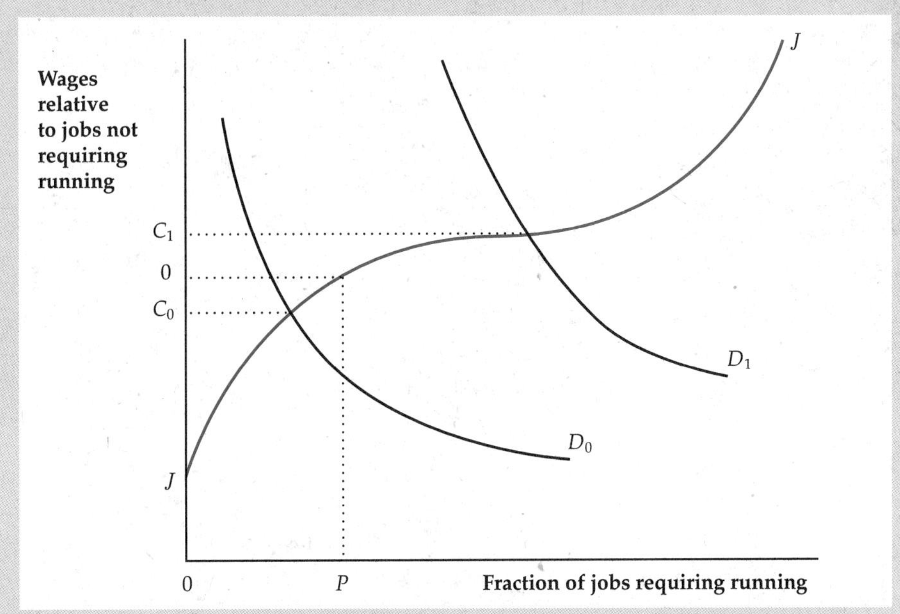

FIGURE 10.2 WORKER TASTES AND THE SIGN OF COMPENSATING DIFFERENTIALS

When some workers regard a characteristic positively while others view it negatively, the sign of the compensating differential will be negative or positive depending on the relative size of these two groups and the demand of firms for jobs with that characteristic.

opportunity to combine their daily run with work. Others are couch potatoes who would have to be bribed with higher wages if they were required to run on the job. The curve *JJ* shows the attitude of workers toward jogging. *P* percent of workers regard jogging as a desirable characteristic of jobs and would be willing to take a job with the opportunity to run at a lower wage than an otherwise equivalent job that denied them this opportunity. The amount of the discount they would accept varies depending on how strongly they value running opportunities.

The remaining workers require a premium for being required to run on the job, with the amount of the premium increasing as workers with a greater distaste for running are required to fill jobs requiring this characteristic. Whether the compensating differential for running on the job is positive or negative depends on the demands of firms. For some jobs, running increases productivity and firms will pay more to have workers run. For others it may have no impact one way or the other, but firms will structure jobs to allow workers to run if by doing so they can get labor less expensively. Finally, in some jobs running interferes with productivity and firms will allow workers to jog only if they work for significantly lower wages. In Figure

10.2, if the demand curve for workers who run on the job is D_0, then the compensating differential will be negative, while if there is more demand for runners as on demand curve D_1, the marginal worker will dislike this aspect of a job and the compensating differential will be positive.

Many characteristics of jobs, such as responsibility and interaction with other people may be regarded positively by some workers but negatively by others. One person's stressful job may be another's challenging opportunity. The problem with this analysis is that it makes any empirical test of the theory of compensating differentials very difficult. No matter what result is found, it is possible to say that the result makes sense given some structure of workers' preferences. This is why the theory is usually tested by studying job characteristics like the risk of death where it is easy to imagine that all workers view the characteristic as a disamenity

WORKPLACE STANDARDS—OCCUPATIONAL SAFETY AND HEALTH

The economic analysis of occupational safety can help us to understand the effects of workplace standards such as those set by the Occupational Safety and Health Administration, the agency responsible for enforcement of the

POLICY ISSUE

HOW MUCH IS A LIFE WORTH?

Courts are frequently called on to assess damages when someone is killed or injured. Government agencies considering adopting a regulation that might save lives need to evaluate whether these benefits justify the costs the regulation will impose in terms of higher prices or lower wages. Economists are often asked to provide expertise in these situations, the question being "Just how much is a life worth?"

Two distinct approaches have been developed to answer this question. The more common uses human-capital theory to determine the present value of the lost earnings the person would have received. An alternative **hedonic approach** bases the measurement on lost enjoyment of life by the injured party. This is done by estimating the compensating differential that workers and consumers require to undertake a more dangerous job or activity.

The two approaches give sharply different results. The human-capital method places the present value of the average worker's earnings at about $500,000. Among studies of compensating differentials, the medium estimates implicitly value a life at $2 to $5 million. How should the expert decide which to use?

The answer to this question depends on the purpose for which the estimate is required. In wrongful death cases, courts are typically asked to compensate survivors for their losses. The dead themselves are not a party to the case. Thus, an estimate based on the earnings of the deceased minus the amount that would have been spent to support them may provide a reasonable estimate of the loss to the survivors.

The compensating differential approach makes much more sense in a regulatory context. It accounts for the enjoyment people derive out of life, over and above the value of their production. Surely the benefits of saving a life ought to include the enjoyment the person would have felt, not just what she produces.

Occupational Safety and Health Act (OSHA) of 1970. These standards typically consist of limits on the maximum amounts of a disamenity that is allowed in the workplace. Among the more well-known examples are standards on noise levels and on the amount of cotton dust in the air in textile plants.[13]

The effect of this legislation on workers' well-being in a competitive labor market can be seen from Figure 10.3. Without the regulation, these workers would choose a combination of job characteristics and income that provides them with a wage rate of w^* and an amount of the disamenity D^*. Given their productivity and the structure of firms' costs, I_1 is the highest indifference level workers can attain. Suppose a standard is imposed requiring firms to operate with no more than D_1 of the disamenity. If the firm is earning competitive profits, the only way to pay for this reduction in disamenity is to reduce wages along the *WW* line. If they are forced to accept a job with no more than D_1 of the disamenity, the best the workers can do is earn wage w_1 and be on indifference curve I_1', a lower utility than they could have achieved in the absence of the standard. The difference $w^* - w_2$ represents the reduction in pay workers would be willing to accept in order to obtain a reduction in the disamenity from D^* to D_1 while remaining on indifference curve I_1. The distance $w_2 - w_1$ represents a loss to workers, who are forced to take a larger cut in pay than they would be willing to offer for the reduction in the disamenity from D^* to D_1.

This argument assumes that the labor market is described by competition among both workers and employers. Competition may exist for workers at the margin who are deciding which occupation or industry to enter. Having made this choice, however, workers may have built up specific human capital that locks them into the industry. Unexpected changes in the amount of disamenities will not be reflected in the wages of more senior workers. The fact that compensating differentials for the risk of injury on the job are larger for workers in their first several years with a company provides some evidence for this effect.[14] Expected changes, on the other hand, must be incorporated into the lifetime earnings profile so that earnings in the occupation reflect the disamenities of working in it, although with long-term employment relationships the timing of the compensating differentials might not be the same as the differences in job characteristics.

Insufficient or inaccurate information about the nature of risks can be a long-run cause of a market failure that creates an inappropriate compensating differential for unsafe work. The evidence presented earlier only shows that workers receive compensation for workplace risks. Whether these premiums

---

[13] A discussion of standard setting under OSHA and its problems is contained in W. Kip Viscusi, *Risk by Choice: Regulating Health and Safety in the Workplace*, Cambridge, Mass.: Harvard University Press (1983).

[14] Shulamit Kahn, "Occupational Safety and Worker Preferences: Is There a Marginal Worker?" *Review of Economics and Statistics* 69: 262–268 (1987).

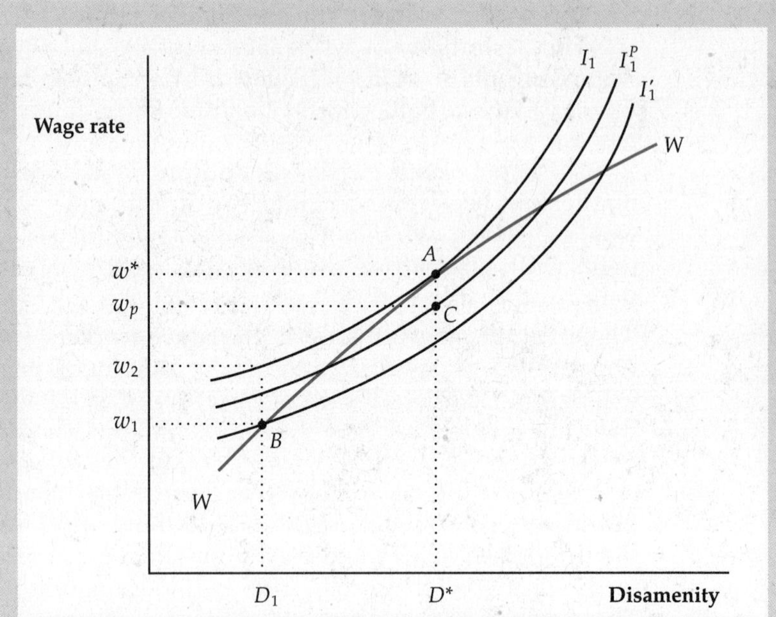

FIGURE 10.3 THE IMPACT OF A WORKPLACE STANDARD IN A COMPETITIVE MARKET

If a maximum level of a disamenity that is less than a worker would have chosen is imposed by the government, the result will be to lower the worker's wages and utility. When penalties are small enough, this reduction in wages and utility will take place with no change in the level of the disamenity.

are enough to reflect all the safety and health risks of the job cannot be determined. Workers may have more accurate information on frequent and observable events such as work injuries. Information is probably less accurate on the extent to which chemicals, dust, or asbestos in the workplace are carcinogens that can produce an above-average cancer rate 30 years or more after initial exposure. What matters is whether workers over- or underestimate the extent of the risk they face. Evidence shows that the typical individual is likely to significantly overestimate the probability of rare, but very bad, events such as airplane crashes or workplace deaths.[15] This bias means that the market-determined compensating differential will be larger than would be required if workers correctly perceived the risk they faced. It also suggests that workers will sort themselves such that the most informed

[15] Baruch Fischoff et al., *Acceptable Risk*, Cambridge: Cambridge University Press (1981); John Geweke, *Decision Making Under Risk and Uncertainty*. Norwell, Mass.: Kluwer (1992); Eric Johnson, et al., "Framing Probability Distortion and Insurance Decisions," *Journal of Risk and Uncertainty* 7: 35–51 (1993).

workers will be found in the most dangerous jobs.

The desirability of workplace standards aside, whether they can induce improvements in workplace health and safety depends on the size and frequency of the penalties for violations. Return to Figure 10.3 and suppose that the value of the fine for violating the standard would only be large enough to reduce wages from w^* to w_p. In this case, a firm that adhered to the standard would be at a competitive disadvantage compared to a firm that offered workers a wage of w_p and disamenity level D^*, since point C on indifference curve I_1^p is clearly preferred to point B on I_1'. Thus, the optimal choice for this firm is simply to pay the fine and reduce wages enough to cover the penalty. The effect of the regulation is to reduce workers' incomes and increase government revenue without altering the amount of the disamenity.

Based on the available evidence, it is very difficult to show that a fear of inspections and subsequent penalties induces employers to abide by standards. The evidence is not even clear that the inspections themselves actually affect workplace safety. There is some evidence, however, that the certainty of being penalized by OSHA if a violation is found has a bigger effect in improving safety than does the size of the penalty applied.[16]

RISKY EMPLOYMENT AND INCOME

In addition to the probability of death or injury, another type of job-related risk is the risk that earnings might vary over time. Most people are risk-averse and would prefer a constant income to the same average income with greater variability. Otherwise equivalent jobs where the earnings over one's working life are more uncertain should be less attractive to potential entrants. Similarly, occupations where hours of work are more variable (because full-time work is punctuated by spells of unemployment) should also be less attractive. Imagine a worker confronted by the choice between two jobs, each offering the same wage rate and average hours worked. In one, however, the number of hours worked is constant in each period, while in the other, although the expected number of hours worked is the same, there is a great deal of period-to-period variation. Most workers would prefer the job with fixed hours to the riskier job, even though each yields the same expected income and leisure. This preference can be demonstrated for typical workers using the same analysis that led to our conclusions about labor force participation and the choice of hours of work in Chapters 1 and 2.

---

[16]John Ruser and Robert Smith, "Reestimating OSHA's Effects," *Journal of Human Resources* 26: 212–236 (1991); John Scholz and Wayne Gray "OSHA Enforcement and Workplace Injuries: A Behavioral Approach to Risk Assessment," *Journal of Risk and Uncertainty* 3: 283–305 (1990); Wayne Gray and Carol Jones, "Are OSHA Health Inspections Effective? A Longitudinal Study in the Manufacturing Sector," *Review of Economics and Statistics* 73: 504–508 (1991).

POLICY ISSUE

BETTER EXPERIENCE RATING FOR WORKERS COMPENSATION

Table 10.4 shows the incidence in 1988 of occupational injuries per 100 workers among firms of different sizes. In the U.S. there is a very pronounced inverse U-shaped relation between employer size and the frequency of work-related injuries. The same relationship exists even within manufacturing, as column 2 of Table 10.4 shows. What causes this unusual phenomenon?

While some large companies self-insure their liabilities under workers' compensation laws by paying benefits directly, many businesses cover the risk by paying premiums to insurance companies. To some extent these premiums are experience rated so that employers with greater claims against them pay higher premiums. Employers who have generated more frequent and severe accidents in the past pay higher insurance rates now. The structure of the insurance premiums, however, makes this relationship very weak among firms that have fewer than 500 employees, since each small firm is not likely to have had enough experience with injuries to enable insurers to set an appropriately experience-rated premium.[17]

Experience rating helps to explain the lower injury rates observed in larger firms. Large employers have an incentive to operate safely, since if they do they will pay lower insurance premiums. This behavior is especially true among the very large firms that generally self-insure, because they pay the entire cost of their workers' compensation. The low injury rates in very small firms are not explicable in terms of the structure of the workers' compensation system, since insurance premiums for small employers are not fully experience rated. Perhaps the more intimate nature of the small workplace induces employees to be more careful, or perhaps small firms with their lower capital intensity provide fewer opportunities for injury because there are fewer repetitive tasks that induce boredom and carelessness.

The differences in experience rating by firm size suggest not only that there is an incentive for larger firms to reduce injuries, but that this incentive affects firms' behavior. As individual states adopted workers' compensation laws between 1900 and 1940—making employers liable for accidents—injury rates were reduced below what they were in states without the laws. Employees of self-insured firms in one state (Minnesota) returned to work faster after injuries than other workers with the same characteristics, presumably because their employers had more incentive to reduce costs by getting them back on the job more quickly.

Both across states and over time, higher workers' compensation benefits increase the number of workdays lost to injury claims, although this effect is smaller in more experience-rated establishments. When the Canadian province of Ontario shifted from flat rating to experience rating for firms in the forestry and construction industries in 1984, deaths from workplace accidents fell by almost half in forestry and by one-quarter in construction. Consistent with these observations is evidence from the late 1970s that the provision of workers' compensation benefits reduces compensating wage differentials for both the

---

[17]Louise Russell, "Safety Incentives in Workmen's Compensation Insurance," *Journal of Human Resources* 9: 361–375 (1974).

risk of industrial fatality and the risk of injuries (by making workers more willing of bear risks). In the case of injuries, workers' compensation reduces compensating wage differentials by half.[18]

Together with the evidence on the relationship between firm size and the extent of experience rating of insurance premiums, these findings strongly support the view that increasing the degree of experience rating in workers' compensation would be a good way to reduce injury rates. If compensating differentials are insufficient because the market for safety is imperfect, a properly structured workers' compensation system can improve workers' well-being. More experience rating may be a better way to reduce injuries than legislating safety standards for the workplace.

In the absence of any restrictions on the hours they can work, the workers shown in Figure 10.4 would choose to work H^* hours. Point P where indifference curve I_1 is tangent to budget line AB is the best they can do. Assume they are now faced with the possibility of being able to obtain only H_1 hours during half the weeks of the year. To be as well-off in those weeks as they are in the weeks they can work H^* hours, they would have to be at point R. Since we are assuming that the average number of hours over the year is the same as it would be if they could always work H^* hours, during the other half of

TABLE 10.4 OCCUPATIONAL INJURY INCIDENCE PER 100 FULL-TIME WORKERS, BY SIZE OF EMPLOYER, 1993

Number of Employees	Private Sector (1)	Manufacturing (2)
1–19	4.3	7.0
20–49	7.8	11.1
50–99	9.8	12.9
100–249	10.5	12.1
250–499	9.3	10.4
500–999	8.5	8.9
1000–2499	8.1	9.1
2500+	8.1	9.9

Source: *Survey of Occupational Injuries and Illnesses in the United States by Industry*, (1994), Table 1.

[18]James Chelius, *Workplace Safety and Health: The Role of Workers' Compensation*, Washington, D.C.: American Enterprise Institute (1977), pp. 75–80; Stuart Dorsey and Norman Walzer, "Workers' Compensation: Job Hazards and Wages," *Industrial and Labor Relations Review* 36: 642–654 (1983); W. Kip Viscusi and Michael Moore, "Workers' Compensation: Wage Effects, Benefit Inadequacies and the Value of Health Losses," *Review of Economics and Statistics* 69: 249–261 (1987); Alan Krueger, "Workers' Compensation Insurance and the Duration of Workplace Injuries," National Bureau of Economic Research, Working Paper No. 3253, (February 1990); John Ruser, "Workers' Compensation and Occupational Injuries and Illnesses," *Journal of Labor Economics* 9: 325–350 (1991); Christopher Bruce and Frank Atkins, "Efficiency Effects of Premium-setting Regimes under Workers' Compensation: Canada and the United States," *Journal of Labor Economics* 11: S38–S69 (1993).

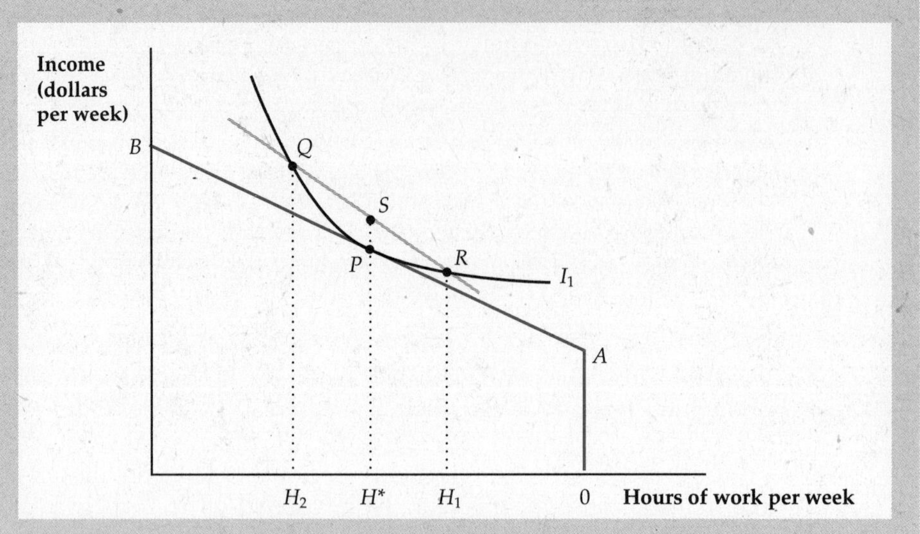

FIGURE 10.4 UNCERTAINTY ABOUT HOURS OF WORK

When hours of work vary between H_1 and H_2, average wages will have to be higher to leave workers with the same level of utility on indifference curve I_1 as would be achieved with stable hours of H^*.

the year they would have to be able to work H_2 hours per week. During these weeks, to be as well-off as they were at point P the workers must be at point Q. If the worker spent half the year at point R and half the year at point Q, the average income over the year would be at the midpoint of the line that connects them, or point S. If the worker could earn this income with certainty every week, however, she could clearly be on a higher indifference curve than I_1. Since expected hours are the same if she works H^* each week, or works H_2 and H_1 each half the time, average earnings must be higher when the variation in hours is greater if the worker is to remain on indifference curve I_1.

This discussion shows that the typical worker views the risk of unemployment as something to be compensated for by higher pay. As with any other disamenity, workers' distastes will differ, so that workers will be arrayed according to their distastes as in Figures 10.1 or 10.2. Because of the pay premium required, employers will have an incentive to avoid variations in hours of work. Avoiding them is costly, however. Employers would have to maintain their work force in a time of slack product demand, or refrain from using overtime during cyclical booms. This situation makes employers' isoprofit curves in the market for the disamenity of risky employment look like those in figure 10.1. Taken together, employers' and employees' behavior will produce an increasing pay premium for greater risks of unemployment in the job. The premium will be another reflection of the implicit contracts between workers and their employers that we discussed in Chapter 9.

This analysis suggests that real wage rates should be higher in occupations or industries where the unemployment rate is higher, just the opposite of what we saw in Chapter 9. The reconciliation of these two theoretical relationships lies in the time period under study. The migration that equilibrates utilities between local labor markets is a costly process that takes time to occur. In long-run equilibrium, unless there are other location amenities that differ between areas, those with higher average unemployment rates will have to offer higher average wages as a compensating differential. At any point in time, however, if the unemployment rate in a local labor market increases, employers can pay a lower wage while still motivating workers not to shirk, as we discussed in Chapter 9.[19]

One study of a national sample of workers found that in the long run each 1 percent increase in unemployment in the state where the worker resides was associated with a 0.2 percent higher real wage rate. Differences in unemployment rates among industries also induce compensating wage differentials.[20] During the 1970s real wage rates were higher in industries where unemployment is more variable over time due to greater cyclical fluctuation in unemployment rates. Similarly, there was also a positive compensating wage differential in occupations where wage rates were more variable over time.[21]

The compensating wage differential for more variable employment or wages will be reduced if there are other mechanisms that compensate workers for the risk of unemployment. Higher unemployment insurance (UI) benefits reduce the pay premium associated with the risk of unemployment on a nearly one-for-one basis. This offsetting effect suggests that, as with pay premiums for the risks of work-related injuries or fatalities, the labor market could provide the compensation that government programs offer. As in the case of workers' compensation, the provision of such programs reduces the compensation offered by the market. In the U.S. in 1986, the average reduction in wages due to the presence of unemployment insurance is just about exactly the cost of providing UI benefits, suggesting that a private insurance market could have provided the benefits. In addition, the compensating differential for unemployment risk was negative and significant, a reversal in

[19] David Blanchflower and Andrew Oswald, "International Wage Curves," in Lawrence Katz and Richard Freeman (eds.). *Differences and Changes in Wage Structure*, Chicago: University of Chicago Press (1995).

[20] Robert Hall, "Why Is the Unemployment Rate So High at Full Employment?" *Brookings Papers on Economic Activity* 1: 369–402 (1970); James Adams, "Permanent Differences in Unemployment and Permanent Wage Differentials," *Quarterly Journal of Economics* 100: 29–56 (1985); Elizabeth Li, "Compensating Differentials for Cyclical and Noncyclical Unemployment," *Journal of Labor Economics* 4: 277–300 (1986).

[21] John Abowd and Orley Ashenfelter, "Anticipated Unemployment, Temporary Layoffs and Compensating Wage Differentials," in Sherwin Rosen (ed.). *Studies in Labor Markets*, Chicago: University of Chicago Press (1981); James Brown and Harvey Rosen, "Taxation, Wage Variation and Job Choice," *Journal of Labor Economics* 5: 430–451 (1987).

sign from the situation in the 1970s. This suggests that increases in the generosity of the UI system in the early 1980s made risky jobs with insured unemployment more attractive than otherwise similar jobs where work is certain. When workers obtain protection from uncertainty about wages, they are also willing to accept lower average wages. In union contracts negotiated between 1967 and 1982 workers who received automatic wage increases if prices increased accepted wages that were 2 percent lower than those in otherwise identical bargaining situations where no such protection was obtained.[22] Coupled with evidence on the effect of unemployment on wage differentials, these results underscore the conclusion that most workers are averse to bearing risks that involve their incomes and must be compensated in order to do so.

LOCATIONAL AMENITIES

In Chapter 7 we showed how interregional migration tends to eliminate pay differences across regions among workers with the same skills. In the United States this process has resulted in a substantial narrowing of the divergence of real wages between the North and South. The difference has not, however, entirely disappeared. In other countries wages also differ persistently among regions. Wages are consistently lower in Canada's Atlantic provinces, for example. After adjusting for differences in workers' demographic characteristics and human capital, remaining wage differentials might reflect a persistent disequilibrium in the labor market. Alternatively, they might show that at the margin workers prefer the **locational amenities** (the enjoyable location-specific characteristics) of working in these lower-wage areas.

We can distinguish between these two possibilities using the same analysis as we applied to compensating differentials for risks and hazards on the job. The disamenity on the horizontal axis in Figure 10.1 could be a characteristic such as extremes of temperature, lack of sunshine, or heavy precipitation. Employers will be forced to offer pay premiums if the jobs they wish to fill are located in areas where the disamenity is substantial. The market for the locational disamenity will be characterized by the same heavy *WW* line in Figure 10.1 that characterizes the market for any disamenity.

The importance of pay premiums for locational disamenities is illustrated especially well by the market for professors. This market is at least nationwide, and one in which employers have little choice about location. A Nobel Prize–winning Harvard physicist was approached about a job by a large public university in a small city in the Southwest. When asked about living in a

[22] Abowd and Ashenfelter, "Anticipated Unemployment;" Adams, "Permanent Differences;" Wallace Hendricks and Lawrence Kahn, "Wage Indexation and Compensating Wage Differentials," *Review of Economics and Statistics* 68: 484–492 (1986); David Anderson, "Compensating Wage Differentials and the Optimal Provision of Unemployment Insurance," *Southern Economic Journal* 60: 644–656 (1993).

hot climate away from the urban amenities of Boston, he answered that the heat appeared to be less of a problem the more he heard about the salary he would be offered. One Big Ten university pays substantially less in most fields than other universities but has continued to attract some of the leading scholars in many disciplines. Its administrators argue that salaries 10 percent lower than elsewhere are a price people must pay to enjoy its beautiful scenery and pleasant environment.

If businesses located in areas that workers would rather avoid must pay more, how can they compete with employers located elsewhere who have lower labor costs? If they are free to relocate their business, they will move to the area of lower labor costs. Employers in many industries are not free to relocate, however, or can do so only at the expense of higher costs for nonlabor inputs into production. Ohio taxpayers would probably look askance if the faculty voted to relocate Miami of Ohio to South Florida, and Appalachian coal cannot be mined by workers living in Arizona. Less directly, the total cost of producing steel may be lower if the plants are located between Chicago and Pittsburgh, even if labor costs are higher, because the costs of transporting the two major inputs into steelmaking, iron ore and anthracite coal, are minimized at this location. A location that suffers from what workers view as disamenities must be more productive in some other way. Otherwise, no firm would produce there. Production considerations must create employer isoprofit curves for locational disamenities of the shape that we saw in Figure 10.1.

Thus, whether locational characteristics in fact produce pay differences is essentially an empirical question. It depends on the ability of employers to relocate away from what is viewed as a disamenity by workers and on differences among workers in their distastes for the disamenity. Some evidence on the importance of locational disamenities as they affect pay premiums is shown in Table 10.5. The estimates are based on multivariate regressions using the 1980 Census of Population. The numbers presented in the table

TABLE 10.5 EFFECTS OF LOCATIONAL AMENITIES AND DISAMENITIES ON WAGE RATES, U.S. COUNTIES, 1980

(Dis) Amenity	Change	Percentage Change in Wage Rate
Sunshine	30%–80%	–6.8
Humidity	20%–90%	+6.8
Windspeed	5–15 miles per hour	+14.4
Violent crime	Average to 2x average	+5.8
Visibility	0–25 miles	–1.0
Superfund sites in county	0–4	+16.4

Source: Calculated from Glenn Blomquist, Mark Berger, and John Hoehn, "New Estimates of the Quality of Life in Urban Areas," *American Economic Review*, 78: 89–107 (1988), Table 1.

represent the compensating differential for altering the particular amenity or disamenity by an amount shown in the column labelled "Change." Lower wages in an area with more sunshine, and higher wages in windier and more humid climates show that workers are concerned about the weather. The costs of locating businesses interact with the preferences of the marginal worker to make sunshine an amenity on average, and to make a more blustery, wetter climate a disamenity.

The table also shows that, on average, workers are willing to pay for living and working in a less-polluted environment. There is a negative compensating wage differential for better visibility, and a large positive differential for being located in a county that contains more "Superfund" sites (locations identified as being especially badly polluted and targeted for clean-up). Doubling the rate of violent crime raises the average wage by nearly 6 percent, other things being equal.

The study underlying Table 10.5 shows that, at the margin, workers must be compensated for living where there is more crime and pollution and where there is less sunshine and a more unpleasant climate. Other studies also show that these factors are disamenities that generate positive compensating wage differentials. They stem in large part from dislike by the overwhelming majority of workers for disamenities that influence behavior on the supply side of the labor market. Permanent changes in the relative demand for labor across areas have only slight effects on the sizes of these differentials.[23]

The existence of these differentials means that, so long as the location of jobs continues to be affected by differences in nonlabor costs, there will be inter-area differences in pay among otherwise identical workers. These compensating differentials reflect an equilibrium between workers' tastes and employers' costs, and they will not, therefore, be eliminated by migration between areas.

PUBLIC-PRIVATE PAY DIFFERENCES

One industry that might consistently pay different wages to identical workers is the nonprofit and government sector. Employers there need not minimize economic costs, so the pay they offer to equally qualified workers in equally risky jobs may differ from that in the for-profit sector. Consider the data presented in Table 10.7, showing the ratio of earnings of full-time civilian government workers in the U.S. to the average for the entire economy. In 1994 federal government employees earned substantially more than workers in the private sector, although their relative advantage has fallen since the

[23] Jennifer Roback, "Wages, Rents and the Quality of Life," *Journal of Political Economy* 90: 1257–1278 (1982); Sherwin Rosen, "Wage-Based Indexes of Urban Quality of Life," in Peter Mieszkowski and Mahlon Straszheim (eds.). *Current Issues in Urban Economics*, Baltimore, M.D.: Johns Hopkins University Press (1979); Robert Topel, "Local Labor Markets," *Journal of Political Economy* 94: S111–S143 (1986).

POLICY ISSUE

NICE PLACES TO LIVE AND WORK

Local boosters in just about every city are fond of proclaiming what a pleasant place to live their town is. Often they cite evidence that their city is ranked high in surveys of people's attitudes about where they would prefer to live. These surveys are subjective responses and do not satisfy an economist's desire to obtain objective measures of how people compare different areas. Using the theory of compensating differentials and estimates of the impact of locational amenities, we can provide such objective measures and learn how people really rank different areas when they have to "put their money where their mouth is."

The study on which Table 10.5 is based, in addition to producing measures of compensating wage differentials for amenities and disamenities, also produced similar estimates of compensating differentials in housing prices, since people will pay more to live in less-polluted areas with better climates and less crime.[24] The authors combined the estimates of the compensating differentials in housing prices and wages to obtain the net effect of all the amenities on the quality of life in each area. An area that had little crime, nice weather, low pollution, and other amenities would have a high quality of life by this measure. The negative compensating differentials in wages and the higher housing prices that these characteristics produce showed how much people were willing to pay to obtain them. The authors thus produced a *market-based* measure of the **quality of life** indicating the value people attach to living in particular areas.

The top and bottom five, as well as selected other areas, from the roughly 250 counties studied are listed in Table 10.6, along with the value the market attaches to the package of amenities that the location provides. For example, the $5,914 for Pueblo, Colorado, shows that the marginal person values its characteristics enough to be willing to pay that much more per year to live and work there rather than in an average area. The –$3,339 for St. Louis shows that people must be compensated that much per year in higher wages and lower housing costs to live there instead of in the average area. The average earnings of full-time workers in 1994 were around $24,000, and housing costs for the average household were slightly less than $6,000. Given these averages, the differences between the most and least attractive areas are relatively large. These results suggest that people are willing to pay a lot to live in more desirable locations.

mid-1970s after having risen very sharply from the late 1950s through the early 1970s. State and local government workers, on the other hand, earned no more than workers in the private sector.

The ratios presented in Table 10.7 are gross wage differences, unadjusted for the many other differences that may distinguish both workers and jobs in the public and private sectors. The data in Table 10.8 account for differences in human capital (education and experience), some demographic characteristics, and location. After all these adjustments are made, a substantial wage differential remains for federal workers, suggesting that

[24]Glenn Blomquist, Mark Berger, and John Hoehn, "New Estimates of the Quality of Life in Urban Areas," *American Economic Review* 78: 89–107 (1988).

TABLE 10.6 RANKING OF QUALITY OF LIFE, CITIES, 1980

City	Value of Package of Amenities (1994 dollars)
Top 5	
Pueblo, Colorado	$5914
Norfolk, Virginia	3787
Denver, Colorado	3771
Macon, Georgia	2877
Reno, Nevada	2834
Selected Other Cities	
San Diego, California	1112
Los Angeles, California	757
San Francisco, California	295
Chicago, Illinois	–86
New Orleans, Louisiana	–134
New York City, New York	–471
Baltimore, Maryland	–550
Bottom 5	
Detroit, Michigan	–2279
Houston, Texas	–2524
Birmingham, Alabama	–2769
Milwaukee, Wisconsin	–3221
St. Louis, Missouri	–3339

Source: Bloomquist et al., "New Estimates."

TABLE 10.7 RATIO OF EARNINGS OF FULL-TIME PUBLIC EMPLOYEES TO ALL FULL-TIME EMPLOYEES' EARNINGS, 1956–1993

Year	Federal Civilian Workers	State and Local General Government
1956	1.19	0.92
1966	1.31	0.99
1976	1.40	1.00
1986	1.27	1.00
1990	1.26	1.04
1993	1.33	1.04

Sources: U.S. Department of Commerce, *Survey of Current Business,* selected issues.

an identical worker would receive more in the federal government than in the private sector. Federal workers apparently received a significant wage premium.

Although this is true for federal workers on average, other data suggest that among the top civil servants the wage premium may be zero or negative. Among elected or appointed federal officials the premium is clearly negative.

TABLE 10.8 RATIO OF ADJUSTED HOURLY WAGES, PUBLIC TO PRIVATE EMPLOYEES, 1973–1975 AND 1988[a]

Education	*12 years*		*16 years*	
Years of experience	5	25	5	25
Federal				
1973–1975	1.17	1.20	1.17	1.31
1988	1.20	1.18	1.04	1.15
State and local				
1973–1975	0.99	0.95	0.99	0.98
1988	1.07	1.02	0.88	0.84

[a]Adjusted for differences in race, sex, part-time, work and urban location.

Source: Calculated from Lawrence Katz and Alan Krueger, "Changes in the Structure of Wages in the Public and Private Sectors," *Research in Labor Economics* 12: 137–172 (1991).

These people appear to sacrifice income to take high-level public jobs. This "sacrifice" may be an investment if their wages after leaving government exceed what they would have earned had they not entered public service. It may also, at least in part, represent a compensating differential for the prestige of a top government job and the power to influence public policy.[25]

For college graduates the adjusted differences show the same decline in wages since the mid-1970s in the federal sector that is exhibited by the gross differences in Table 10.7. This pattern is not true among high school graduates, for whom wages in the federal government have consistently exceeded those in the private sector by about 20 percent. Remembering the evidence in Chapter 3 on the very sharp increase in the returns to college education between the early 1970s and the late 1980s, it is easy to explain this pattern. Average federal pay scales for more educated workers have gone up less rapidly than private pay.

The same pattern is seen if the wage differential is analyzed for workers with different occupations. The premium paid senior managers and professionals in the federal government after standardizing for education, age, marital status, race, and part-time employment fell from 20 percent in 1979 to 3 percent in 1989. During the same period, the premium paid to clerical workers remained unchanged at 11 percent while that paid to manual workers increased from 9 percent to 24 percent.[26]

---

[25]Arnold Weber and George Burman, "Compensation and Federal Executive Service, Survey and Analysis," in *Staff Report to the Commission on Executive, Legislative and Judicial Salaries*, Washington D.C.: U.S. Government Printing Office (1977).

[26]Rebecca Blank, "Public Sector Growth and Labor Market Flexibility: The United States vs. The United Kingdom," in Rebecca Blank (ed.). *Social Protection versus Economic Efficiency: Is There a Tradeoff?* Chicago: University of Chicago Press (1994).

None of the factors already shown to produce compensating wage differentials can account for the differences in Table 10.8. Federal workers indicate that their jobs are less repetitive, offer better working conditions, and require less physical strength than the average private-sector job. Moreover, federal workers are more likely to work year-round than private-sector workers. Thus both hazards in the workplace and risks of unemployment are lower for the average federal worker. The existence of compensating differentials for these risks suggests that the true wage differential is actually higher than indicated in Table 10.8. In addition, employee benefits are a greater percentage of payroll in the federal sector, raising the difference in compensation even more. Accounting for unmeasured differences in productivity by using longitudinal data on workers who switch sectors also shows that federal employees are paid more than otherwise identical private-sector workers. In short, all adjustments suggest there is a substantial difference in pay for equal work between otherwise identical federal and private workers.[27]

If pay for equally desirable jobs differs, we would expect there to be long queues of workers seeking federal jobs and lower quit rates from federal than private-sector jobs. This is exactly what we find. Applications for each federal job exceed those for jobs in the private sector by 20 percent, while the quit rate from federal jobs is much lower (although this difference is to some extent because the federal pension system creates substantial incentives to remain on job).[28]

In state and local governments the situation is quite different. These workers typically do not receive higher wage rates than private-sector employees. Adjusting for differences in the workers' and jobs' characteristics, as in the bottom part of Table 10.8, there is a slight advantage in pay among less-educated state and local government employees, and a substantial disadvantage among college graduates. As with federal employees, relative pay has worsened for college graduates and has stayed the same or improved among high school graduates when compared to the private sector. In 1989 managers earned 15 percent less in state and local governments than otherwise identical workers earned in the private sector while manual workers earned 15 percent more than in the private sector. Again, as with federal workers, the true pay differential may be more favorable to state employees than is indicated by Table 10.8, since their working conditions are less onerous and their benefit packages better than those of private workers. Among local government employees considered separately, however, jobs appear somewhat

---

[27] Alan Krueger, "Are Public Sector Workers Really Overpaid? Evidence from Longitudinal Data and Queues," in Richard Freeman and Casey Ichniowski (eds.). *When Public Sector Workers Unionize,* Chicago: University of Chicago Press (1988).

[28] Kathleen Classen Utgoff, "Compensation Levels and Quit Rates in the Public Sector," *Journal of Human Resources* 18: 394–406 (1983); Richard Ippolito, "Why Federal Workers Don't Quit," *Journal of Human Resources* 22: 281–299 (1987); and Krueger, "Are Public Sector."

riskier and more subject to undesirable working conditions than the average private-sector job.[29]

In sum, there is an overall advantage to working for the government in the United States, but this advantage varies by level of government. Federal workers receive more than otherwise identical private workers, while state and local government employees' pay differs little from that of their private-sector counterparts. This difference between levels of government may be due to market limitations on the power of state and local governments to pay higher than necessary wages that do not exist for the federal government. Government wages have to be financed through current or future taxes. If local and, to a lesser extent, state governments pay more than they must to attract labor, their citizens will leave for areas that do not pay excessive wages and can, therefore, charge lower taxes for the same level of government services. This situation creates substantial incentives for local officials to minimize labor costs. Movement between localities within a state is quite easy and may not even require a change in job. Movement among states is somewhat more difficult but still fairly common. On the other hand, emigration from the United States to avoid taxes is very rare, so the federal government can finance excessive wages with higher taxes without fear of driving away the citizens who pay these taxes. In the long run the political process may serve to limit taxes at the federal level, although the evidence in Table 10.8 suggests that, so far, this limit has proven ineffective.

Evidence for the United Kingdom indicates that government workers earn about 10 percent more than comparable workers in the private sector, although senior managers and professionals appear to earn less than they would make in private jobs. In the Netherlands, on the other hand, once differences in worker characteristics are taken into account, government workers overall earn less than those in the private sector, with the difference being greatest for those in more complex jobs.[30]

EMPLOYEE BENEFITS

Compensation consists of two components: money wages, and **employee benefits,** often called **fringe benefits,** although today they are more than just a fringe. Throughout this book employee benefits have been neglected.

---

[29]Joseph Quinn, "Wage Differentials Among Older Workers in the Public and Private Sectors," *Journal of Human Resources* 14: 41–62 (1979); Blank, "Public Sector;" James Poterba and Kim Rueben, "The Distribution of Public Sector Wage Premia: New Evidence Using Quantile Regression Methods," NBER Working Paper No. 4734 (1994).

[30]Blank, "Public Sector;" Hans van Ophem, "A Modified Switching Regression Model for Earnings Differentials Between the Public and Private Sectors in the Netherlands," *Review of Economics and Statistics* 75: 215–224 (1993).

Our discussion of pay has dealt almost entirely with money earnings, in part, because most available data does not contain measures of fringe benefits. We now turn to the division of compensation between current money earnings and employee benefits. Many items that are often called fringe benefits are excluded from our discussion. Paid leave, such as vacations, holidays, and sick leave were appropriately considered in Chapter 2 as reductions in hours of work. This implies that the proper definition of money earnings is earnings per hour at work rather than the more common "earnings per hour paid for."

Employee benefits are any compensation that is not paid currently in money given directly to individual employees, but is, instead, paid by employers on behalf of employees, either individually or collectively. This concept does not include nonmonetary benefits of a job that involve no explicit cost to employers, nor does it include costs incurred in the reduction of disamenities, such as the choice of a more expensive but safer technology. Some employee benefits are required by law. In the United States, the three most important are unemployment insurance, Social Security (Old Age, Survivors, Disability, and Health Insurance), and workers' compensation insurance. Others are provided by agreement between employers and workers, either individually or through collective bargaining.

BENEFITS: GROWTH AND VARIETY

Compensation-in-kind has long been common in some occupations. Even in Colonial America parsonages were provided to ministers, and farmhands or domestic servants were given room and board. Today payment-in-kind usually takes the form of discounts (possibly as much as 100 percent) on an employer's products. Airline employees receive cheap or free flights, some college teachers receive reduced tuition for their children, auto salespeople have access to demonstration models at reduced prices, and telephone company employees receive large discounts on long-distance telephone service.

With the growth of industrialization, these traditional forms of payment-in-kind have become a less important part of compensation. In industrial societies compensation has increasingly been paid in cash, a tendency that reached its peak in the United States during the 1920s. Since then there has been rapid growth of newer forms of noncurrent or nonmonetary compensation, as can be seen in Table 10.9. These national income account data reflect all of what we call employee benefits except employer expenditures on such amenities as subsidized lunchrooms or recreation facilities. The table shows a very rapid increase in benefits as a share of total compensation, especially between 1960 and the late 1970s. This pattern leads us to ask why nonwage compensation has increased over the years, sometimes very rapidly.

The growth in employee benefits has been concentrated in the provision of protection against the risks of sickness, death, and unemployment, and in the provision for retirement. As Table 10.10 shows for one sample of firms, expenses for life insurance and health insurance and provision for retirement (both legally required and privately chosen) are almost 25 percent of total

TABLE 10.9 EMPLOYEE BENEFITS, TOTAL AND AS A PERCENTAGE OF TOTAL COMPENSATION, SELECTED YEARS, 1929–1993[a]

Year	Supplements to Wages and Salaries (in Billions)	Supplements as a Percentage of Compensation
1929	$0.7	1.3%
1939	2.2	4.6
1949	7.3	5.1
1959	21.4	7.6
1969	60.1	10.4
1979	239.5	16.1
1989	505.8	16.4
1993	725.9	18.1

[a]Supplements include employer contributions to social insurance and employer payments for private health, welfare, pension, and insurance plans. Compensation adds these to wages and salaries.

Source: Council of Economic Advisors, *Economic Report of the President*, (1995), Table B–25.

TABLE 10.10 EMPLOYEE BENEFITS BY TYPE, 1993 (PERCENTAGE OF PAYROLL)[a]

	All Companies	Manufacturing	Nonmanufacturing
Legally required payments	8.7	9.1	8.5
Old-age, survivors, disability, and health insurance	6.9	6.8	6.9
Unemployment compensation	0.6	0.8	0.6
Workers' compensation	1.2	1.5	1.0
Not legally required	19.2	17.6	19.7
Pensions	5.9	3.9	6.6
Life and health insurance and death benefits	11.1	11.7	10.8
Other agreed-upon payments[b]	2.2	2.0	2.3

[a]Data are based on a survey of 1057 firms of all sizes and cover employer's share of benefits only. Payment for time not worked, profit sharing plans, and bonuses are included in the original table and are excluded here.

[b]Includes separation pay, meals furnished, discounts on goods purchased, disability insurance, and miscellaneous payments.

Source: Adapted from Chamber of Commerce of the U.S., *Employee Benefits*, (1994), Washington, Table 4.a.

payroll costs. In this survey of over 1000 firms of all sizes, 98 percent of firms offered medical insurance, 88 percent offered employer-paid life insurance, and 82 percent offered a pension plan. Similarly large fractions of compensation are devoted to these purposes in other industrialized countries, although in many they are provided by governments and financed by taxes on payrolls and earnings.

MARKET EFFECTS ON BENEFITS

The great advantage of current cash compensation is that it maximizes workers' freedom to spend their income how and when they like and to make only those provisions for contingencies and risks they desire. In contrast, other forms of compensation determine part of workers' consumption pattern for them. At worst, the consumption imposed on workers may be worthless. For example, group life insurance may have little value to single workers without dependents while family medical coverage will not matter to the resolute bachelor. The corporate gymnasium does not benefit those who do not exercise, nor do single college professors benefit from free tuition for family members. Employees whose families are generally healthy benefit relatively little from any health insurance they receive.

In general, a worker will prefer a dollar of after-tax earnings to a dollar of employee benefits tied to the provision of a particular commodity or service. Consider workers like those whose behavior is depicted in Figure 10.5. They receive after-tax compensation of 0*C*. They can always opt to spend some of these earnings on such things as health insurance, life insurance, or retirement annuities. Their tastes between dollars spent on an employee benefit and dollars received as disposable income are shown by their indifference curves. These have the usual shape (see Chapter 1), because increasing amounts of the employee benefit yield successively less additional satisfaction. With a private budget line of *CD*, they would choose to buy an amount 0*A* of the employee benefit, since point *P* on indifference curve I_1 is the highest indifference level they can attain.

Assume now that the employer offers benefits in the amount 0*B* and reduces the wage sufficiently to pay for these benefits. If the employer faces the same cost for the benefit as the worker, the budget line will remain *CD*. Only by sheer accident will the employer pick the exact amount of the benefit that the worker would have chosen (i.e., 0*B* will be equal to 0*A*). If workers have different preferences, then by definition, a common benefit package offered to all cannot be optimal for all. Thus, the utility of the worker shown is reduced by his forced nonoptimal consumption of the benefit, and I_0 lies below I_1.

Why, then, are employee benefits so common? One answer lies in the fact that the cost of a benefit is not the same when it is purchased by an employer as it would be if purchased by the worker. There are two reasons why benefits cost less when they are provided by employers. There are substantial *economies of scale* in purchasing such services as insurance. Because of sav-

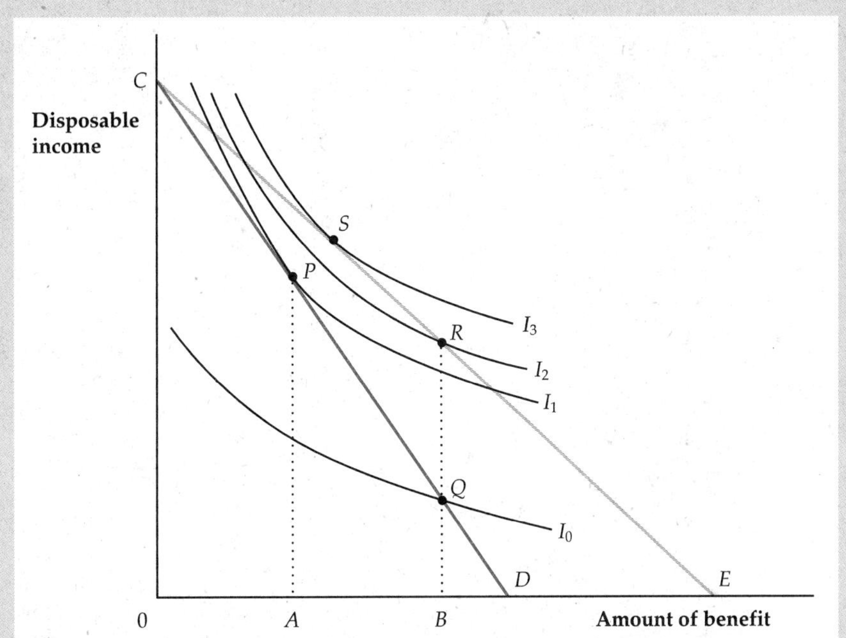

FIGURE 10.5 EMPLOYEE BENEFITS AND UTILITY
Forcing consumption of a specific bundle of benefits and income is likely to lower a worker's utility. Tax-free treatment of fringe benefits can make consumption of a fixed bundle more attractive, although the worker would achieve an even higher level of utility if he were able to pick his fringe benefits under a cafeteria plan.

ings in administrative costs, insurance carriers may issue group policies at much lower cost than individual ones. In general, however, individual employees cannot opt out of the group. Insurers quite rightly fear the problem of **adverse selection**, in which the biggest potential users of the insurance remain covered while people unlikely to use it avoid coverage. Economies of scale also help to explain the growth of pension plans covering several employers, since these also reduce administrative costs.[31]

A second reason why employer-provided benefits cost less than individually purchased ones is that most benefits provided by an employer either escape income taxation entirely or are taxed on more favorable terms than cash wages. The personal income tax on employer contributions to pensions is deferred until the pension is received. By that time the interest on the contributions has accumulated free of tax. The worker may also be in a lower tax

[31]Olivia Mitchell and Emily Andrews, "Scale Economies in Private Multi-Employer Pension Systems," *Industrial and Labor Relations Review* 34: 522–530 (1981).

bracket after retirement. Employer-paid health insurance premiums are not taxed, nor are most premiums paid by an employer for workers' life insurance. The relevant consideration for the worker is how much a dollar of compensation taken as benefits will buy compared to a dollar taken as wages. Suppose wages are taxed at a **marginal tax rate** (the tax paid on the last dollar of earnings) of t, where $0 < t < 1$. The price of a dollar's worth of benefits compared to a dollar's worth of goods bought using taxable earnings is $[1 - t]/1$, or $1 - t$. For example, if a worker is taxed at $t = 1/3$ and wishes to buy $1000 worth of health care out of his earnings, it will cost him $1500 of before-tax earnings. The same $1000 of health care would require giving up only $1000 of before-tax earnings if the care were paid for through employer-provided health insurance.

Thus, if the benefit in Figure 10.5 were purchased by the employer, the budget line would be *CE* rather than *CD*. Even constraining the level of the benefit to 0*B*, not the level the worker would freely choose, can leave the worker better off on indifference curve I_2 than he would be if he picked the optimal level of the benefit but had to purchase it privately at point *P* on indifference curve I_1.

Of course, the employee could be even better off if he were allowed to pick the level of benefit he wanted but purchase this benefit at the employer's cost along budget line *CE*. In this case, he would pick point *S* on indifference curve I_3. In recent years many employers have approximated this option by implementing **cafeteria benefit plans.** Under these plans an employee is given a budget for employee benefits and allowed to choose among a wide variety of benefits that exhaust the budget. If some of the options contained in the cafeteria plan are things that the employee would spend money on over and above what is provided by the benefit package, such as child care or savings for retirement, the effect of these plans is to allow the worker to pick any point on budget line *CE* in Figure 10.5 and, therefore, the plan will increase workers' utility over a fixed benefit plan at no additional cost to the employer. It is not surprising that cafeteria plans are becoming more common. In just four years between 1990 and 1993, the fraction of firms that allowed workers some degree of choice over the composition of their benefit package increased from 41 percent to 53 percent.[32]

Tax considerations go a long way in explaining both the growth of employee benefits through time and their positive correlation with the level of earnings. Personal taxes have grown greatly in importance since the 1920s and are progressive with respect to wage and salary income. Personal tax rates rose steadily from the 1940s through the early 1980s and then remained relatively constant during the 1980s. This pattern is consistent with the pattern of changes in the share of benefits in total compensation shown in Table 10.9. For example, earnings as a fraction of compensation of office employees in large manufacturing establishments fell from 0.92 to 0.88

[32] U.S. Chamber of Commerce, *Employee Benefits* (1994).

between 1966 and 1974. The rise in the marginal income tax rates that faced workers during this period, coupled with changes in their pretax incomes, accounted for two-thirds of this drop. Among manufacturing workers who have the same total compensation, but different tax rates because of nonlabor income or their spouse's earnings, those facing higher tax rates are more likely to work for employers who spend more for pension and health insurance benefits (and, therefore, less on wages). In addition, employee benefits are more extensive and employees pay less for them in states where high state tax rates increase the cost advantage of employer-provided benefits.[33]

The growth of employee benefits has also been partly due to the *income elasticity of demand for benefits*. As with the demand for amenities, higher wages produce an income effect on the demand for benefits. The income elasticity of demand for benefits appears to be greater than one. When incomes are low, workers are more interested in cash income with which they can buy food and shelter than in saving for retirement or purchasing insurance against a catastrophe that probably will not happen.[34] Given the rapid growth of real incomes in the United States between the 1940s and the late 1970s, an income elasticity greater than one is a major cause of the growth of the share of benefits in total compensation shown in the last column of Table 10.9. The fact that real incomes rose much less rapidly in the 1980s also contributed to the slowdown in the increase in the share of compensation devoted to employee benefits during that decade.

There are reasons why employers will never find it optimal to offer employees complete freedom of choice over the composition of benefit packages. As we saw in the previous chapter, certain employee benefits may be necessary for the design of optimal incentive-compatible contracts. Employers may need to require workers to consume pensions in excess of what the workers would pick in order to provide sufficient incentives for retirement to enable the productivity-improving benefits of upward-sloping wage profiles.

In addition, employers may use the design of employee benefits as a **screening device** to determine the composition of their work forces. Suppose, for example, an employer knows that married workers are more stable and put forth more effort on the job. While it is likely to be impractical (or even illegal) to advertise that only married people need apply for a job or to pay a salary that discriminates on the basis of marital status, nothing prevents the employer from offering family medical insurance as an employee

---

[33]Stephen Woodbury and Wei-Jang Huang, *The Tax Treatment of Fringe Benefits*, Kalamazoo, Mich.: The W. E. Upjohn Institute (1991); William Alpert, "Manufacturing Workers' Private Wage Supplements," *Applied Economics* 15: 363–378 (1983); Robert Barro and Chaipat Sahasakul, "Average Marginal Tax Rates from Social Security and the Individual Income Tax," *Journal of Business* 59: 555–566 (1986); William Gentry and Eric Peress, "Taxes and Fringe Benefits Offered by Employers," NBER Working Paper No. 4764 (1994).

[34]Stephen Woodbury, "Substitution Between Wage and Nonwage Benefits," *American Economic Review* 73: 166–182 (1983).

POLICY ISSUE

DOES THE IRS REDUCE WORKPLACE DIVERSITY?

For many years the U.S. Internal Revenue Service (IRS) has required employers to offer benefits on a nondiscriminatory basis to all employees if those benefits are to qualify for exclusion from income taxation. For example, a company cannot offer substantial tax-exempt benefits to its top executives if it fails to offer the same benefits to other workers. How does this affect the labor market?

Because any single employer cannot offer unusually large benefits to only those employees who want them and smaller benefits (but higher wages) to others, workers have an increased incentive to sort themselves to different employers according to their tastes for benefits. Similarly, because they must choose an inflexible package of benefits, employers have greater incentives to attract a more homogeneous group of workers. By banning discrimination by type of compensation, the government encourages the market to produce greater segmentation of workers. The role of fringe benefits in encouraging this kind of sorting is apparent in cross-section data for the 1980s and in time series covering the years 1955 to 1979.[35]

benefit. Since such insurance is worth far more to a married worker than a single one, it will serve to make the job relatively more attractive to the married workers the employer wants to attract. Similarly, pension plans may attract workers who are more future oriented while life insurance plans can be used to attract those who are more risk averse, and company gyms will make a firm more attractive to physically fit workers. By careful design of its fringe benefit package, an employer can exert a great deal of influence over the characteristics of its work force. Evidence that workers sort themselves according to the fringe benefits employers offer comes from surveys where workers without health and pension benefits reported they would be willing to give up $6,400 in earnings to receive such benefits while those who had them reported their pay would have to be increased by almost $11,000 to persuade them to give up their benefits.[36]

SUMMARY

Higher pay is offered to compensate for characteristics of work that employees generally find distasteful. The extent of this compensation depends on the

[35]Frank Scott, Mark Berger, and Dan Black, "Effects of the Tax Treatment of Fringe Benefits on Labor Market Segmentation," *Industrial and Labor Relations Review* 42: 216–240 (1989).

[36]Craig Olson, "The Value of Health and Pension Benefits to Workers," *Proceeding of the Forty-Sixth Annual Meeting of the Industrial Relations Research Association*, (1994), pp. 37–47.

POLICY ISSUE

TAXING THE COMPANY CAR

In 1985 the IRS issued regulations that made explicit a requirement that workers' personal use of company cars must be taxed as ordinary income.[37] This move was unusual, as most nonmonetary benefits escape taxation, but it is one that the IRS would like to extend to other types of payments-in-kind. There is no doubt that this rule initially achieved its goals of increasing tax revenue and having a greater share of that revenue paid by higher income workers (among whom, as we have seen, benefit coverage is more generous). In the long run, however, could it actually affect the distribution of after-tax incomes?

The answer to this question depends on whether compensating wage differentials offset higher employee benefits, leaving after-tax compensation unchanged when a benefit becomes taxable. For example, taxing employee benefits may merely induce workers to demand higher wages in order to supply their labor to firms that previously offered unusually generous benefit packages. The evidence suggests this is what happens. Among otherwise identical workers in the private sector in 1969, earnings were roughly $1 lower for each $1 increase in employers' costs of pensions. Among otherwise similar police and firefighters in 1973, earnings were lower where cities offered more generous pension coverage. A study of the introduction of various state and federal mandates that required employers to include childbirth benefits in medical insurance packages found that there was almost a dollar-for-dollar reduction in the wages of women of childbearing age to compensate for the cost of these benefits but no change in the compensation of other workers.[38] This evidence implies that after-tax compensation increases by much less than $1 for each extra dollar of employer-paid employee benefits. It shows that taxing benefits will not narrow differences in incomes as much as its short-run effects alone would suggest. On the other hand, the tax revenue will increase by more than what would be generated solely from tax on the benefit since the additional wages will also be subject to the income tax.

extent of workers' distastes and on employers' cost of improving the offending characteristics compared to the cost of paying a higher wage. Workers receive higher pay for jobs that are unsafe or that offer worse prospects for stable employment and income.

The demand for amenities associated with work has a positive income elasticity, so workers with more skills spend some of their additional potential earnings for jobs that are safer and more stable. Unless one accounts for differences in skills, this effect leads to a negative association between workers'

---

[37]*New York Times,* January 3, 1985, p. IV. 2.

[38]Bradley Schiller and Randall Weiss, "Pensions and Wages: A Test for Equalizing Differences," *Review of Economics and Statistics* 62: 529–538 (1980); Ronald Ehrenberg, "Retirement System Characteristics and Compensating Wage Differentials," *Industrial and Labor Relations Review* 33: 470–483 (1980); Jonathan Gruber, "The Incidence of Mandated Maternity Benefits," *American Economic Review* 84: 622–641 (1994).

earnings and their likelihood of being in risky jobs. Accounting for these factors, otherwise identical workers receive higher earnings in jobs where the risk of earnings loss, through workplace death or injury or because of unemployment, is greater. The effects are especially large for the risk of death on the job. Workers also sacrifice wages to live and work in certain areas, behavior that produces interarea differences in the pay for identical jobs. The average federal worker is paid more than the comparable private employee, but the same is not generally true of state and local public employees.

Earnings differentials understate differences in total compensation, since higher skilled workers receive a greater part of their compensation in the form of employee benefits than do other workers. This situation is due to the nontaxation of employee benefits and to underlying preferences that make the demand for employee benefits income elastic. Both of these factors helped to induce rapid growth in employee benefits as a fraction of total compensation in the United States through the early 1980s, as well as the halt in this growth since that time.

QUESTIONS AND PROBLEMS

10.1 Suppose one-third of all workers demand an extra 50 percent above the standard wage rate of $10 per hour in order to work in dirty jobs, while two-thirds of the work force will work in dirty jobs at $10 per hour.

a. Assume employers' demand is independent of the relative wages that must be paid in clean and dirty jobs. How much extra will be paid for dirty work if one-half the jobs are dirty? How much if three-fourths of the jobs are dirty?

b. Now assume that the fraction of dirty jobs employers offer is equal to 1-*d*, where *d* is the fraction by which the wage on dirty jobs exceeds that on clean jobs. What will *d* be in equilibrium, and what fraction of the work force will work in dirty jobs? Will any workers earn more than their reservation wage? If so, what would you try to do as a smart employer?

10.2 As a judge in a wrongful death case you are confronted by sharply differing estimates of the loss suffered. The plaintiff's expert uses the hedonic approach and claims the loss is $3 million. The defendant's expert uses the human-capital approach and claims the loss is $500,000. List as many arguments as you can in favor of using each approach, and decide which method you think is more justified.

10.3 The average wage in the northern, auto-producing state of Michigan is about 15 percent above the national average. List the factors that might produce this difference, and indicate how much of an effect each accounts for. Are they large enough to produce the 15 percent wage differential?

10.4 The wage differences in Table 9.6 that are computed using cross-section data do not account for differences in plant or firm size or for differences in the extent of on-the-job risks. The differences calculated using panel data implicitly make that accounting. Compare the changes between columns 1 and 2 for each industry. Do the drops agree with your intuition about which industries have the greatest on-the-job risks and the largest workplaces? Do the increases occur where jobs are pleasant and workplaces are small? Do differences in risks or differences in the sizes of plants and firms seem to have bigger effects in producing the changes within the pairs of columns?

10.5 An employer bargains with its workers over two issues, an increase in wages and the full provision of health insurance, which currently costs employees $50 per month. The company makes the following two offers to the union: (a) a wage increase of $50 per month, or (b) complete payment of the cost of health insurance with no wage increase. Which choice would the workers prefer, and what circumstances will affect their choice?

10.6 Pension plans can be of two types: defined benefit plans that pay a pension according to a fixed formula based on income and years of work and defined contribution plans where an employer contributes a specific amount to an account for each worker each year and the size of the worker's pension depends on the performance of the investments made by his pension plan. Which of these types of plans would be better able to achieve the goals obtained by mandatory retirement policies before they were outlawed in the U.S.? Why would one type of pension be better in obtaining the desired outcome?

10.7 It is sometimes curious why employers provide workers with fringe benefits rather than simply paying them money and letting the workers choose what insurance and other fringes they want to purchase. What are the main attractions of fringe benefits from the point of view of workers? How about from the point of view of employers? What can you say about the types of jobs that are likely to provide the highest ratio of fringe benefits to salary and the reasons for differences among jobs in this ratio?

10.8 Suppose that as an employer you wanted to attract each of the following types of labor. How might you design a package of employee benefits to make the desired workers more likely to apply to your firm?

a. Workers who will have fewer health insurance claims, thereby lowering your insurance costs;
b. Workers less likely to sue you;
c. Workers less likely to change jobs;
d. Workers more likely to work weekends;
e. Workers who are better informed about current events?

10.9 Most government jurisdictions, including the U.S. federal government have laws that require pay in the public sector to be equal to pay for similar jobs in the private sector. Would you expect such a law to lead to a permanent excess supply of workers for government jobs? Why or why not?

10.10 We have seen, as a general rule, that competitive markets will give rise to compensating differentials for many, if not most, aspects of jobs that workers find unpleasant. For example, wages are higher in jobs where workers face greater safety hazards and greater risk of unemployment. Given this labor market mechanism, what reasons, if any, might there be for government programs designed to regulate these risks?

KEY WORDS

adverse selection
amenity
cafeteria benefit plan
compensating differential
compensation-in-kind
disamenity
employee benefits
fringe benefits
full income
hedonic approach
locational amenities
marginal tax rate
Occupational Safety and Health Act (OSHA) of 1970
quality of life
screening device
workers' compensation

Part Five

Unionized Labor Markets

So far our discussion of labor markets has considered the behavior of individual workers and employers, with only passing references to trade unions. Unions and collective bargaining, however, play a major role in the determination of wage levels and wage structures, as well as in many other aspects of employment relations. Between 15 and 25 percent of nonfarm employees in the United States have been members of unions or employee associations in recent years, but the effects of collective bargaining extend beyond its impacts on union members. In many other countries rates of unionization are much higher.

The discussion here focuses on the economic functions of trade unions. Because of the increasing importance of public-sector unions in the United States, we also discuss the political role of unions. That role is much more important outside the United States, especially in the most heavily unionized nations. We do not examine all aspects of union behavior, leaving many of them to the study of industrial relations. For example, even within the area of collective bargaining, such topics as grievance machineries and seniority are not considered.

Our study of unions is divided into three chapters. In Chapter 11 we examine the economic determinants of the level and growth or decline of trade unionism and discuss the possible employment and wage goals that a union might pursue. Chapter 12 analyzes the methods unions use in attempting to obtain their goals. The process of collective bargaining, including the strikes that occasionally result, can be studied fruitfully using economic analysis. In Chapter 13 we consider evidence of unions' ability to achieve their goals through their impact on wages, employment, and mobility, outcomes whose determination in competitive markets we studied in Chapters 6 to 10.

11

UNIONS: GROWTH AND GOALS

THE MAJOR QUESTIONS

- ▲ How do patterns of unionization differ among industries and occupations?
- ▲ What causes these differences?
- ▲ How and why does unionization differ across demographic groups?
- ▲ What have been the patterns of union growth or decline in the United States and elsewhere?
- ▲ How can the change in union membership be explained, and, especially, how have government policies affected union membership?
- ▲ What are unions' goals in dealing with employers?

WHY STUDY UNIONS?

Despite a waning influence in recent years, unions remain among the most important institutions in modern economies and continue to have a substantial impact on the labor market. The history of the 20th century in the U.S. and many other countries is fraught with violent conflicts between union members and their employers. Many men and women defined their identities as union members above all else. Many workers died asserting their right to bargain collectively.

Analyzing what the union movement has become today is important in understanding why it may no longer play the pivotal role it once did. To understand today's unions we must ask who joins them and why as well as the effectiveness of unions in representing the goals of their members when bargaining with employers. Moreover, much of the employment relationship between nonunion workers and their employers is based on patterns set in union negotiations. Thus, even workers who are not union members have an interest in understanding the behavior of unions since what unions and their members demand today is likely to become common for all workers tomorrow.

A BRIEF SUMMARY OF FEDERAL LAWS ON COLLECTIVE BARGAINING

Some working knowledge of the institutional framework defined by the major federal legislation governing **collective bargaining** (the joint determination of wages and working conditions by management and unions acting on behalf of their workers) is helpful in understanding the role of unions in the U.S. economy.[1] In chronological order these laws are:

Norris-LaGuardia Act, 1932. Outlaws hiring requirements (so-called yellow-dog contracts) in which employees pledged not to join unions and limits employers' use of antitrust laws to obtain court-ordered injunctions to restrict union activities.

National Labor Relations (Wagner) Act (NLRA), 1935. Establishes the **National Labor Relations Board (NLRB)** as the governing mechanism for labor relations in all firms engaged in interstate commerce. The NLRB orders **representation elections**, in which workers vote on whether to be represented by a union. These elections occur within a **bargaining unit** of workers that the NLRB defines as having a common interest for the purposes of an election and any possible contract that may subsequently be negotiated. The NLRB interprets the NLRA to determine what are **unfair labor practices** by employers during these elections and the lives of collective-bargaining contracts between unions and employers.

Taft-Hartley Act, 1947. Defines a set of unfair labor practices by unions and places restrictions on unions' ability to compel workers to become union members, including allowing states to prohibit **union shops** (establishments where the collective-bargaining contract requires workers to join the union once they are hired). The Taft-Hartley Act also requires workers' approval for strikes.

Landrum-Griffin Act, 1959. Regulates internal union politics and management in an attempt to increase members' control of union activities.

This federal legislation governs interstate commerce in the private sector. All states have laws governing private-sector labor relations in the few firms not subject to the NLRA. More importantly, federal legislation cannot cover state and local public-sector employment, so states have passed laws that regulate collective bargaining by state and local government employees. Many states have also created institutions that regulate public labor disputes in ways similar to the NLRB.

---

[1]The field of industrial relations is summarized in such texts as D. Quinn Mills, *Labor-Management Relations*, New York: McGraw-Hill (1994); Arthur Sloane and Fred Witney, *Labor Relations*, Englewood Cliffs, N.J.: Prentice-Hall (1991); and James Begin and Edwin Beale, *Practice of Collective Bargaining*, Homewood, Ill.: Richard D. Irwin (1989).

THE UNION STATUS OF JOBS

The position of unions in the U.S. economy can be examined profitably using tools as simple as supply and demand analysis. The quantity being examined is the percent of the jobs that are unionized. Although many things affect who becomes unionized, economic factors are central. We summarize them in Figure 11.1 by graphing the ratio of nonunion to union compensation (wages plus employee benefits) on the vertical axis. Because there are other reasons for desiring a union, including the ability to regulate arbitrary behavior on the part of employers or to influence undesirable working conditions, some workers will want to join a union even if the ratio of nonunion to union compensation is greater than one. On the other hand, the fact that unions charge their workers dues, may cause lost wages due to strikes, and impose constraints on the individual freedom of workers means that some workers will require nonunion wages to be considerably below union wages before they will agree to join. Indeed, members of some religious groups are prevented by their beliefs from joining any organization other than their church. Presumably, these workers would not join a union even if the ratio of nonunion to union wages approached zero. In sum, if unions are more successful in raising compensation, the number of union jobs demanded will be greater, as shown in Figure 11.1 by the demand curve *D*.

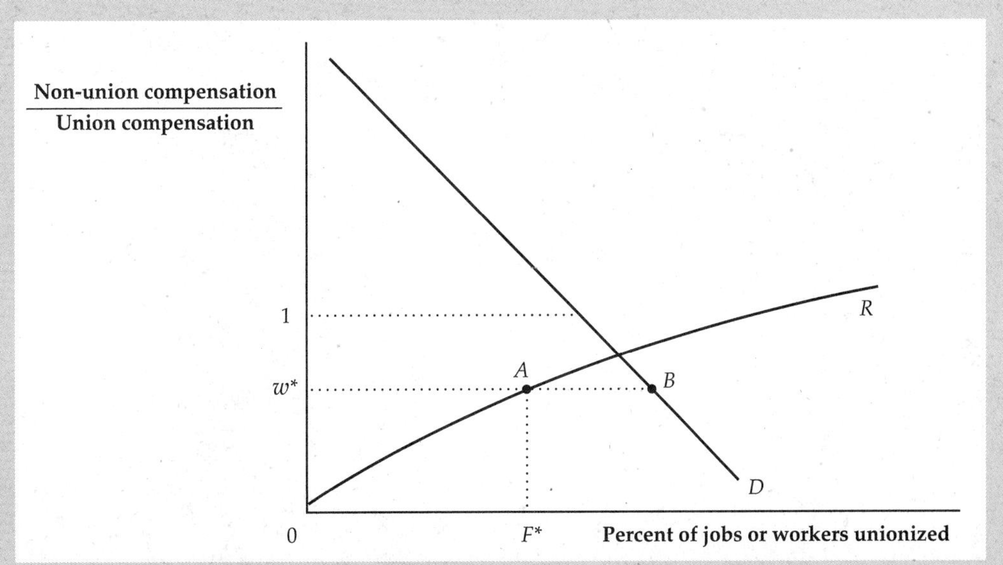

FIGURE 11.1 THE UNION STATUS OF JOBS
Workers' demand for unionization (*D*) and employers' incentive to resist unionization (*R*) both depend on the wages of union members relative to nonunion workers. The interaction of these factors determines the level of unionization in the economy.

The extent of union membership also depends on employers' resistance to becoming unionized. When nonunion compensation is especially low relative to union compensation, employers will be much less willing to become unionized. This situation is reflected in the upward-sloping employer-resistance curve *R* in Figure 11.1. As the figure is drawn, the demand and resistance curves intersect where the ratio of nonunion to union compensation is less than 1.0. The outcome provides union compensation above what is paid in comparable nonunion establishments. This outcome, which we discuss at length later in this chapter and in Chapter 13, is standard. Unions raise compensation.

If unions are successful in obtaining a higher wage, creating a lower nonunion–union compensation ratio such as w^*, the demand for union jobs would be high and employers would have a lot to lose by becoming unionized. A queue of *AB* workers would form for the scarce union jobs.[2] As in the case of the minimum wages (shown in Figure 4.12), these jobs must be rationed. Part of a union's function is to determine how unionized jobs are allocated to workers in the queue. Anything that reduces employers' resistance will increase the extent of unionism in an economy. Anything that increases the demand for union jobs will raise the extent of unionism only if the unions' advantage in compensation is simultaneously reduced. Otherwise, the queue will merely become longer.

WHO BECOMES UNIONIZED?

We first use this analysis to examine the industrial, occupational, and demographic incidence of unionism. Both employers and workers determine the position of their curves in Figure 11.1 through cost-benefit analysis. Each worker faces costs from joining a union in terms of dues, lost income from strikes, and reduction of individual freedom. In addition, since unions tend to impose standardized wages for large groups of employees, especially productive workers may also find that joining a union lowers their wages. Each worker must compare the costs that joining a union will impose with the benefits in terms of potentially higher wages and fringe benefits, better working conditions, or protection from layoff.

Employers face a similar cost-benefit comparison. Resisting a union involves costs. Consultants may be hired, strikes or other disruptions of production may occur, and the employer may have to pay higher wages or provide better working conditions to forestall workers' desire to unionize. On the

---

[2]Jacob Mincer, "The Economics of Wage Floors," in Ronald Ehrenberg (ed.). *Research in Labor Economics,* Vol. 6, Greenwich, Conn.: JAI Press (1984), pp. 311–333.

other hand, successful resistance has considerable benefits. Wages may be lower than they would be in the presence of a union. In addition, without the work rule restrictions imposed by the union, the employer has considerably more freedom to adapt staffing levels and job duties to changes in technology or product market conditions.

Because union representation in the U.S. is decided by majority vote in elections within bargaining units, there will always be some workers who would like to be represented by a union but are not because they are a minority within their bargaining unit. These workers may be motivated to seek employment elsewhere where they would be covered by a union. Conversely, there will be some workers who oppose unionization but find themselves in bargaining units where the majority of workers have voted for a union. Once again, in deciding whether to quit their jobs, these workers will have to compare the advantages of changing to another job where they can exercise their desire to not belong to a union with the costs from job search and loss of match-specific human capital. Since we generally observe only whether a worker is covered by a union contract, studying union membership decisions is a complicated process. We have to take into account that some nonunion workers would prefer to be a union member while some members would like not to have to belong to a union.[3]

CHARACTERISTICS OF FIRMS

One factor that clearly affects the probability a worker will belong to a union is the existence of **product market power** that gives a firm the ability to obtain profits exceeding the competitive return on capital. Individual employees will find it difficult to extract a share of these excess profits because they lack the bargaining power to pose a serious threat to the employer's position. Collectively, however, workers can hope to extract some of the firm's profits by threatening to withhold their labor (strike), thus imposing a cost on the firm greater than the share of profits they seek. Thus, we would expect to see a greater benefit to unionization, and, therefore, more workers desiring unionization in firms with market power.

If, on the other hand, a union increases wages in a firm without market power, the result is likely to be losses and eventual bankruptcy. Thus, the benefits from resisting unionization are quite high for competitive firms. Firms with excess profits, however, will not find their very existence threatened if they are forced to give some of these profits to workers, and may be less resistant to employees' demands for union.

The structure of labor demand can also affect the probability of unionization. Its effects can be inferred from our discussion of Marshall's laws in

---

[3]See John Abowd and Henry Farber, "Job Queues and the Union Status of Workers," *Industrial and Labor Relations Review* 35: 354–367 (1982).

Chapter 4. If the demand for labor is quite elastic, the employer can realistically threaten to reduce employment should the workers organize and seek to raise wage rates. On the other hand, workers can seek higher wages with less fear of losing their jobs if demand is less elastic. Thus, worker demand for unionization will be greater in firms with less elastic demand curves. Resisting the organizing attempts of blue-collar workers is harder for employers who are less able to substitute white-collar workers and capital for blue-collar workers. Finally, if labor accounts for a large share of total costs, the employer has a greater incentive to resist unionization.

Among manufacturing industries in the United States in 1972, the estimated elasticity of labor demand in nonunion establishments was –1.03 while that in union establishments was –0.81. A study of Canadian manufacturing between 1971 and 1981 showed even larger differences in estimates of the elasticity of substitution between capital and labor in nonunion compared to heavily unionized industries. Unionization is more likely in manufacturing establishments where blue-collar labor is substantially less substitutable for white-collar labor and capital.[4] Although part of these differences may be imposed by union work rules that reduce labor demand elasticities by limiting management flexibility, much stems from unions' greater success in organizing where flexibility is inherently less.

Firm size also affects whether workers are unionized. Organizing a workplace takes substantial effort by both the workers themselves and their potential union. Even after a representation election has been won and a contract negotiated, contract administration requires substantial resources. These costs must be covered through dues paid by union members. Since both activities are likely to be characterized by economies of scale, the dues (and, therefore, the costs of unionization to the workers) will be lower in larger establishments, increasing the demand for unionization in large firms or plants. From the firm's standpoint, larger plants are likely to be more bureaucratized even without unions. Thus, the rigidity imposed by union contracts may be less costly in these plants, and their operators will resist unionization less intensively. Indeed, in 1974 the average establishment in heavily unionized industries had five times as many employees as the typical establishment in other industries.[5]

Large plants typically develop in industries that require capital-intensive technology to achieve the lowest average cost. Where employers have invested large amounts in equipment, they will institute strict work rules to protect this equipment, and ensure that it yields a high return by being utilized con-

---

[4]Richard Freeman and James Medoff, "Substitution Between Production Labor and Other Inputs in Unionized and Non-unionized Manufacturing," *Review of Economics and Statistics* 64: 220–233 (1982); Dennis Maki and Lindsay Meredith, "A Note on Unionization and the Elasticity of Substitution," *Canadian Journal of Economics* 22: 792–801 (1987); Steven Allen, "Union Work Rules and Efficiency in the Building Trades," *Journal of Labor Economics* 4: 212–242 (1986).

[5]Daniel Mitchell, *Unions, Wages, and Inflation*, Washington, D.C.: Brookings Institution (1980), p. 84.

tinuously and efficiently. Greater capital intensity induces tight scheduling that increases workers' demands for unionism. A good example is the automobile industry before 1938.

In 1973 firms in heavily unionized industries employed 50 percent more capital per worker than firms in industries with below-average unionization. Workers who stated they worked with machines most of the time had a 24-percentage-point greater likelihood of being unionized than other workers with the same demographic characteristics. Part of this difference, however, reflects the *outcome* of the unionization process. Firms faced with unionized workers will substitute capital for labor.

Job characteristics affect the benefits workers obtain from unionization. Workers who stated they were not free to determine their work schedules were 20 percentage points more likely to be unionized than other workers. Workers in jobs requiring more physical effort were also more likely to be union members. Occupations in which tasks were more repetitive were also more heavily unionized. Unions were more likely to win representation elections between 1977 and 1980 where a firm's production was more capital intensive.[6] All of these facts point to the importance of the structure of technology in affecting whether an establishment becomes unionized.

The incidence of unionization across the private sector is quite consistent with these considerations. The left half of Table 11.1 shows the pattern by industry of **collective-bargaining coverage** (the percentage of workers whose wages and working conditions are governed by a union contract). The industries with below-average unionization, such as wholesale and retail trade, finance, and services, have relatively little product-market concentration. On the other hand, manufacturing, transportation, public utilities, and mining are characterized by firms with substantial product-market power and the use of capital-intensive methods of production. Only construction, a very competitive industry, does not have large firms in concentrated product markets. Since construction workers are often highly skilled, however, they face an inelastic demand for their labor. In addition, a federal law, the **Davis-Bacon Act**, as well as state laws in the vast majority of states, effectively requires that all construction financed with public funds must be performed by union workers, thereby artificially increasing the demand for union construction workers. Indeed, the fraction of construction workers who belong to unions is actually *less* than the share of public construction in total construction (27 percent in 1993).

---

[6]Mitchell, *Unions, Wages,* p. 84; Frank Stafford and Greg Duncan, "Do Union Members Receive Compensating Wage Differentials?" *American Economic Review* 70: 355–371 (1980); Solomon Polachek and Curtis Simon, "Monitoring and the Rate of Unionization," FIEF, Working Paper No. 43, January 1988, Stockholm, Sweden; Cheryl Maranto, "Corporate Characteristics and Union Organizing," *Industrial Relations* 27: 352–370 (1988).

TABLE 11.1 UNIONIZATION BY INDUSTRY AND OCCUPATION, PERCENT OF EMPLOYED, 1994

Industry	Members	Coverage	Occupation	Members	Coverage
Agriculture	2.1	2.8	*White-collar*		
Mining	15.7	17.1	Managerial and professional	14.4	17.3
Construction	18.8	19.9	Technical, sales, and support	10.3	12.1
Manufacturing	18.2	19.7	*Blue-collar*		
Transportation and public utilities	28.4	30.7	Precision production, craft and repair	23.9	25.6
Wholesale and retail trade	6.2	6.8	Operators, fabricators, and laborers	24.1	25.6
Finance, insurance, and real estate	2.3	3.1	*Service*		
Services	6.2	7.3	Protective	41.5	44.1
			Other services	9.7	10.9
Government	38.7	44.7			

Source: *Employment and Earnings*, (January 1995); p. 216

The same processes appears to operate in other countries. In Japan, Great Britain, and continental Europe, workers' decisions about joining unions appear to be influenced by the costs and benefits.[7]

THE INCIDENCE OF UNIONIZATION IN THE PUBLIC SECTOR

While government is not capital intensive, it is characterized by large establishments and few (often one) employers within a market. These facts alone, however, do not explain the huge difference in the extent of private versus public-sector unionization the United States. Today, among the ten major sectors of the U.S. economy only government is heavily unionized, making it worthwhile to examine the incidence of public-sector unionism more closely.

It is important to realize that the 44.7 percent rate of union coverage in 1994 shown in Table 11.1 does not prevail uniformly across the sector. Table 11.2 shows the incidence of collective-bargaining coverage by industry within

[7]Sarosh Kuruvilla, et al. "Union Participation in Japan: Do Western Theories Apply?" *Industrial and Labor Relations Review* 43: 374–389 (1990); Anthony Ferner and Richard Hyman, *Industrial Relations in the New Europe*, Oxford: Blackwell (1992); Bob Mason and Peter Bain, "The Determinants of Trade Union Membership in Britain: A Survey of the Literature," *Industrial and Labor Relations Review* 46: 332–351 (1993).

TABLE 11.2 PUBLIC-SECTOR COLLECTIVE-BARGAINING COVERAGE, 1988 AND 1994

Industry	Percent Covered 1988	1994
Elementary and secondary schools	53.7	56.6
Colleges and universities	18.3	25.1
Libraries	21.9	13.6
Executive and legislative offices	13.0	3.0
Justice and public safety	49.8	51.5
Administration of human resources, environmental, housing, economic programs, and public finance	34.5	30.7
National security and international affairs	24.3	21.0

Sources: 1988: Michael Curme, Barry Hirsch, and David Macpherson, "Union Membership and Contract Coverage in the United States, 1983–1988," *Industrial and Labor Relations Review* 44 (1990), Table 4; 1994: calculated from Current Population Survey, March 1994 Public Use File.

the public sector. Of particular note is the concentration of public-sector unionism in two functions, elementary and secondary education and protective services such as firefighting and police. This concentration is consistent with the argument that labor-demand elasticities affect unionization. These governmental functions have low demand elasticities for labor, so there is less possibility than in other governmental functions to reduce the use of unionized workers when they demand higher compensation. In addition, public outcry when schools are closed or police and fire protection is absent significantly increases the cost to public employers of resisting demands in these areas. On the other hand, if the local library or city administration is closed by a strike, most citizens feel relatively unaffected.

The comparative cost of resistance in the public versus the private sector (and, therefore, the potential benefits to workers from unionization) is one of the major reasons for the greater prevalence of unions in the public sector. When a private-sector firm is forced by a union to increase wages, the result is an immediate loss of sales and lower employment. When the government grants a wage increase it can simply force the "customer" to pay a higher price by voting a tax increase. The power of taxpayers to respond to this increase in the "price" of the government activity by moving to another locality is much less immediate or certain than the response by consumers to higher product prices.

The economic differences are compounded by political effects. Managers of private-sector firms are responsible to the firm's owners, whose interests are clearly to resist higher than competitive wages (taking into account any benefits from efficiency wages discussed in Chapter 9). Politicians, on the other hand, respond to voters' interests, especially the demands of organized special-interest groups. Many voters are also public-sector employees who will benefit directly if public-sector unions win higher wages. Still more are relatives of public-sector employees. Finally, private-sector union members may also have an interest in having more powerful public-sector unions since they affect the overall union wage rate in an area.

To a much greater extent than in the private-sector, government-employee unions rely on political leverage, including efforts to convince the public of the need to maintain funding for union activities and lobbying elected officials to prevent budget cuts, in order to achieve their goals. Perhaps most importantly, these unions devote substantial effort to electing people who are sympathetic to their aims and who are likely to liberalize, or at least not tighten, laws governing bargaining by public employees.

Before the 1960s the incidence of unionization in the public sector was much less than in the private sector. A wave of legislation in the 1960s legalizing collective bargaining for government employees in many states was followed by laws imposing on governments a duty to bargain and, frequently, to submit disputes to mandatory arbitration. There is good reason to believe that these laws are a major reason behind the increasing extent of public-employee unionization in the United States. During the early 1980s, states with more lenient laws on public-sector bargaining had more heavily unionized public employment. Although the passage of a more lenient collective-bargaining law in Illinois led to some resistance by local governments, it also sharply increased the incidence of unionization among Illinois teachers. When some states eased restrictions on police bargaining, unionization of police rose shortly afterward, while it did not increase much where stringent laws remained in place.[8]

CHARACTERISTICS OF WORKERS

As cost-benefit analysis predicts, workers with wages farthest below the average within a plant are most likely to vote for a union, as are workers in plants where wages are farthest below the average in the industry. Also, the greater the dispersion in wages within a plant, other things such as skill levels being equal, the more likely workers are to vote for a union. Unionization is one way that workers respond to what they perceive as management arbitrariness in the form of different compensation for workers with the same objective characteristics. On the other hand, when the skill mix in a workplace is the heterogeneous, workers are less likely to vote for a union, probably because a

[8]Richard Freeman and Robert Valletta, "The Effects of Public Sector Labor Laws on Labor Market Institutions and Outcomes;" Gregory Saltzman, "Public Sector Bargaining Laws Really Matter: Evidence from Ohio and Illinois;" and Casey Ichniowski, "Public Sector Union Growth and Bargaining Laws;" all in Richard Freeman and Casey Ichniowski (eds.). *When Public Sector Workers Unionize,* Chicago: University of Chicago Press (1988).

very diverse mix of workers will find it hard to accept the common contract that is the norm in unionized settings.[9]

Among white-collar workers, whose wages are on average greater than those of blue-collar workers and who tend to have greater autonomy on their jobs even in the absence of unionism, the incidence of unionization is relatively low. Unionization is highest among blue-collar workers largely because, as we have discussed, the characteristics of blue-collar jobs increase workers' desires for unionization. Tradition may also be important since there is no long history of attempts to unionize among lower-wage, white-collar workers. Of course, the absence of such attempts may be because white-collar workers' preferences have made them much more difficult to organize than similarly paid blue-collar workers.

If discrimination against blacks and Hispanics has resulted in their receiving lower wages than non-Hispanic white workers or being treated differently in other ways, then, to the extent that unions are perceived as a force for reducing discriminatory practices, these groups will be more likely to vote for union representation. Table 11.3 shows the extent of collective-bargaining coverage by demographic group in the United States in 1994. There is little difference between non-Hispanic whites and Hispanics in the incidence of unionism, but blacks are more likely than other groups to be covered by collective bargaining. In large part this difference is because blacks are disproportionately represented among public-sector workers, where we have already seen high rates of unionization.

Blacks are even more likely than whites to desire a union job (83 percent versus 58 percent in one study, 88 percent versus 67 percent in another). Yet, because blacks who seek such jobs are less likely than whites to obtain them, the racial difference in the fraction unionized is smaller. Thus, the time blacks spend in the queue for the desirable union jobs that employers and unions must ration (*AB* in Figure 11.1), is relatively long compared to whites. It could be that blacks are discriminated against by employers by being denied access from the queue to the available unionized jobs, or it could be that they bring fewer productive attributes to the labor market than other workers who also want the above-equilibrium union wages.

---

[9]The discussion in this section is based upon Henry Farber and Daniel Saks "Why Workers Want Unions: The Role of Relative Wages and Job Characteristics," *Journal of Political Economy* 88: 349–369 (1980); William Dickens, "The Effect of Company Campaigns on Certification Elections," *Industrial and Labor Relations Review* 36: 560–575 (1983); Henry Farber, "The Determination of the Union Status of Workers," *Econometrica* 51: 1417–1437 (1983); Duane Leigh, "The Determinants of Workers' Union Status: Evidence from the National Longitudinal Surveys," *Journal of Human Resources* 20: 555–566 (1985); and Rebecca Demsetz, "Voting Behavior in Union Representation Elections: The Influence of Skill Homogeneity and Skill Group Size," *Industrial and Labor Relations Review* 47: 99–113 (1993).

TABLE 11.3 COLLECTIVE BARGAINING COVERAGE BY SEX AND ETHNICITY, PERCENT OF EMPLOYED, 1994

	Men	Women
White	18.9	14.1
Black	25.9	20.8
Hispanic	15.9	14.2
Total	19.6	15.1

Source: *Employment and Earnings,* (January 1995), p. 214.

While female workers are more likely to vote for unionization when given the chance, they are less highly unionized than men. Table 11.3 shows that women were about three-fourths as likely as men to be covered by collective bargaining in 1994. Since workers with shorter expected tenure with an employer will receive lower total benefits from organizing a union or bearing the costs of a strike, there should be less organizing activity among women than among men. The same principle explains why unionization is much less common among jobs held by young workers, who have higher-than-average mobility as they engage in job shopping or intermittent labor force participation, and why older workers nearing retirement are less likely to vote for unionization. The increase in women's labor force attachment in recent years may explain why the gap in male and female union membership rates fell by 36 percent between 1973 and 1994.[10]

More educated workers have usually acquired skills that enable them to avoid the worst effects of management arbitrariness. Formal education teaches many skills, one of which may be an ability to "get by." Even after accounting for the differences in wages generated by differences in education, more educated workers may have other reasons not to desire unionization. They are likely to be in jobs with better working conditions. More importantly, since unions tend to equalize wages by raising those of less productive workers at the expense of more productive workers, the potential benefits to more educated (and, therefore, more productive) workers will be less. Thus, we observe that more educated workers vote less frequently for unionization when confronted with the opportunity.

The left side of Table 11.4 presents the extent of **union membership** (the fraction of workers who belong to unions) by years of education. The more

[10]Barry Hirsch and John Addison, *The Economic Analysis of Unions: New Approaches and Evidence,* Boston: Allen and Unwin (1986); William Evan and David Macpherson, "The Decline of Private-Sector Unionism and the Gender Wage Gap," *Journal of Human Resources* 28: 279–296 (1993).

TABLE 11.4 UNION MEMBERSHIP, BY EDUCATION AND SELECTED STATES, PERCENT OF EMPLOYED, 1994

Education		State	Private Sector	Public Sector
≤11 years	11.0	New York	17.9	72.6
12 years	17.4	Hawaii	19.3	59.4
13–15 years	15.0	Michigan	18.3	56.1
16 or more years	16.0	New Jersey	15.6	62.0
		Washington	16.1	45.5
		Virginia	5.4	14.6
		Texas	4.6	17.8
		Mississippi	5.3	11.7
		North Carolina	3.5	13.7
		South Carolina	2.4	11.8

Source: Barry Hirsch and David Macpherson, *Union Membership and Earnings Data Book 1994* Washington: BNA (1995).

educated are less likely to be union members than those with a high school education or less, although the fact that college graduates are slightly more heavily unionized than college dropouts reflects the high incidence of unionization among public schoolteachers. The extent of membership is less than the extent of collective-bargaining coverage by several percentage points. This situation occurs because under many contracts workers cannot be forced to join if they do not want to, but all members of a bargaining unit that has voted for a union must be covered by any contract the union negotiates. In some states, the workers who do not opt to join a union can still be forced to pay dues to the union under an **agency shop** provision.

The right-hand panel of Table 11.4 lists the incidence of union membership in the five most and least heavily unionized states in the continental U.S. There are sharp interregional differences in the incidence of unionism. Workers in the South and West are much less likely to be unionized, while unionization is highest in the Northeast and North Central regions. Other data show that Southern workers are less likely than other workers to demand union jobs (49 percent compared to 58 percent in one study, 60 percent versus 67 percent in another). Although these differences are too small to account for the much lower incidence of unionism in Southern states, the lack of interest combines with employers' greater resistance to produce a very low fraction of unionized workers. While the demand for unionism is lower in the South, queues for union jobs are longer there than elsewhere.

Data on the geographic incidence of unionism also point to some of the origins of public-sector unionism. Where private-sector unionization is more extensive, so is unionization in the public sector. Part of the reason is that laws making union organization easier (and reducing the ability of governments to resist union demands) were adopted where private-sector unions were strong and could bring political pressure for these laws. In addition, public employees' demand for union services is greater in those states where greater unionism in the private sector reflects a general desire for union coverage.

POLICY ISSUE

RIGHT-TO-WORK LAWS

Under Section 14(b) of the Taft-Hartley Act, individual states are free to adopt **right-to-work legislation** that prohibits union or agency shops.[11] As of 1994, 21 states had right-to-work laws on the books, nearly all of which had existed since the 1950s. Eleven of these states were in the South, five in the West, and five in the North Central region. All five of the least unionized states listed in Table 11.4 have right-to-work laws. Have these laws lowered the incidence of unionism? Or would unions' relative inability to organize Southern plants have occurred even if the Taft-Hartley Act had never allowed states to exercise this option?

States with right-to-work laws clearly have a lower incidence of unionism than other states. Even accounting for the demographic and industrial mix of a state's work force, states that had such laws in the 1970s had a 5-percentage-point lower incidence of union membership than other states in the same geographic region.[12] This difference could be either because these laws discouraged union membership, or because both low union membership and the laws reflect the strength of employers' opposition to, and workers' lack of interest in, unionization.

The coexistence of right-to-work laws and a low incidence of unionization reflects correlation rather than causation. While it is true that the passage of a right-to-work law slowed the flow of new members into unions, this reduction dissipated quickly. The difference in the fraction of workers unionized between states that later adopted right-to-work laws and other states was as great in 1939, before the laws were passed, as it was in the 1950s and 1960s. Queues for unionized jobs are no longer in right-to-work states than in similar states without such laws. Workers in right-to-work states simply have a lower demand for unionism than otherwise identical workers in the same region of the U.S.[13]

---

[11] Federal law prevents any contract from requiring a **closed shop** in which workers must be members of the union *before* they can be hired by a firm.

[12] Barry Hirsch, "The Determinants of Unionization: An Analysis of Interarea Differences, *Industrial and Labor Relations Review* 33: 147–161 (1980).

[13] David Ellwood and Glenn Fine, "The Impact of Right-to-Work Laws on Union Organizing," *Journal of Political Economy* 95: 250–273 (1987); Keith Lumsden and Craig Petersen "The Effect of Right-to-Work Laws on Unionization in the United States," *Journal of Political Economy* 83: 1237–1248 (1975); Henry Farber, "Right-to-Work Laws and the Extent of Unionization," *Journal of Labor Economics* 2: 319–352 (1984).

UNION GROWTH

Institutional economists have developed a variety of theories to explain the presence of trade unions in industrial economies.[14] The best known, the **job scarcity hypothesis,** views unions as a response by workers to fears that layoffs or insufficient work will result in some members of the group not being employed. This notion may lie behind many of the political efforts by unions. In the U.S., for example, trade-union support for higher overtime premiums and programs to share work (see Chapters 5 and 8) can be seen as attempts to stretch what is believed to be a limited supply of jobs. Similarly, unions' support of minimum wage legislation and restrictions on immigration can be regarded as an attempt to reallocate a limited job pool away from low-wage nonunion workers to more highly paid union members just as resistance to free trade can be viewed as an attempt to keep foreign workers from having access to a limited supply of jobs.

While this view provides some insights, the market approach presented earlier is much more successful in analyzing trends in unionization. The figures in Table 11.5 show that unionization in the U.S. increased rapidly shortly after the Wagner Act became effective. Although the data after 1975 are not entirely comparable with earlier years, they are sufficiently similar to allow the conclusion that unionization as a percentage of the labor force reached a peak from the mid-1940s to around 1960 and has declined drastically since then. In fact, the extent of the decline is understated by the use of economy-wide data. Private-sector unionization has fallen much more rapidly. Part of its decline has been offset by the explosion of unions in government.

Increases in unionization during the late 1930s largely resulted from the encouragement given by the Wagner Act and other New Deal programs, although high unemployment during the Depression also stimulated the demand for unionization. When unemployment is high, indicating that some workers have been forced to accept layoffs, the desire of those remaining to protect themselves against additional losses of employment, and their resentment at managers exercising discretion over employment, can lead them to seek unionization.

While unemployment will increase workers' demand for unionization, the slack labor demand that accompanies unemployment will also increase employers' resistance. In a slack product market, profit will be low, so there is little to give workers. In addition, a larger number of unemployed workers will make it easier to replace those who go on strike. The net effect is thus an empirical issue. Several studies of union growth suggest that there was a weak positive correlation between union growth and the unemployment rate, at least through 1970. In the United States between 1909 and 1960, each additional percentage point of unemployment resulted in an increase

[14] See Mark Perlman, *Labor Union Theories in America,* Evanston, Ill.: Row (1958).

TABLE 11.5 UNION MEMBERSHIP IN THE UNITED STATES, SELECTED YEARS 1930–1994

Year	Number (Thousands)	Percent of Nonagricultural Employment
1930	3,401	11.6
1935	3,584	13.2
1940	8,717	26.9
1945	14,322	35.5
1950	14,267	31.5
1955	16,802	33.2
1960	17,049	31.4
1965	17,299	28.4
1970	19,381	27.3
1975	19,611	25.5
1980	20,095	22.1
1985	16,996	18.0
1990	16,740	16.1
1994	16,714	15.7

Sources: *Handbook of Labor Statistics,* (1980), Table 165; for 1980 from Bureau of Labor Statistics, *Earnings and Other Characteristics of Organized Workers,* Bulletin No. 2105; for 1985 from *Employment and Earnings,* January 1986, p. 213; for 1990, January 1991, p. 228; for 1994, January 1995, p. 216.

in the growth rate of the unionized work force of 0.25 percent. Although most of this relationship reflects union growth during the Great Depression, the relationship also existed before and after the 1930s. In the United Kingdom between 1893 and 1970, each 1-percentage-point increase in unemployment raised the growth rate of the unionized work force by 0.05 percent. In Canada, each 1-percentage-point increase in unemployment raised the growth rate of the unionized work force by 0.5 percent between 1925 and 1966.[15]

The argument that cyclical increases in unemployment induce an expansion of unionism cannot be extended to the data shown in Table 11.5 for the post–World War II period. Indeed, since 1974 even when unemployment in the U.S. has been relatively high, unionization has declined very rapidly. The

[15] Orley Ashenfelter and John Pencavel, "American Trade Union Growth: 1900–1960," *Quarterly Journal of Economics* 83: 434–448 (1969); George Bain and Farouk Elsheikh, *Union Growth and the Business Cycle,* Oxford: Blackwell (1976); Michael Abbott, "An Econometric Model of Trade Union Membership Growth in Canada, 1925–1968," Working Paper No. 154, Princeton University Industrial Relations Section, (1982).

same pattern can be seen even more strongly in European data where the rapid increase in unemployment we observed in Chapter 8 has been combined with a decline in unionization in most countries. What explains this trend?

Insight into the answer to this question comes from representation elections. Since additional expenditures on organizing benefit current members through reduced competition from nonunion workers, one might think that unions would have increased their efforts to organize additional workers as their share of the American work force declined. Apparently, however, organizing efforts did not increase. The first column of Table 11.6 shows a steady downward trend in the fraction of nonunion workers who have taken part in representation elections (usually initiated by unions). Although unions garnered a decreasing percentage of votes and won fewer elections between 1955 and the early 1980s, this decline has ceased and may have been reversed since then. The decline has continued, however, in the number of workers who get as far as voting in elections.

Since in the U.S., elections are called when a significant fraction of the work force in a bargaining unit expresses a desire to be represented by a union, this decline may represent a lessening of workers' interest in unions. On the other hand, workers' interest is often stimulated by an organizing campaign conducted by a union. Judging by the fact that expenditures on organizing have not kept pace with GNP growth, unions are not trying to organize workers to the extent they once were. Between 1953 and 1974 union organizing expenditures per nonunion worker, a good measure of

TABLE 11.6 PARTICIPATION AND OUTCOMES OF REPRESENTATION ELECTIONS, UNITED STATES, 1955–1993

Fiscal Year	Total Votes as a Percentage of Nonunion Nonfarm Employment (1)	Percentage of Elections Won (2)	Percentage of Votes Cast for Unions (3)
1955	1.2	67.6	74.0
1960	1.1	58.6	64.1
1965	1.0	60.2	62.4
1970	1.0	52.4	57.7
1975	0.8	46.2	49.5
1980	0.6	43.9	43.8
1985	0.3	42.4	45.7
1988	0.2	46.3	48.0
1993	0.2	50.3	49.5

Source: Calculated from National Labor Relations Board, annual reports (monthly reports for 1993).

unions' efforts at expanding their coverage, barely stayed constant in real terms during a time when real wages and real GNP grew.[16] The issue is whether this decline is a *cause* of the lower number of elections or merely a rational response to the lower number of workers interested in union membership. One study has found that virtually *all* of the decline in union membership in the U.S. between 1977 and 1991 was the result of declining worker demand for union representation.[17]

There is further direct evidence that workers' demand for unionism has changed. In 1960 unions gained 34 times more workers through elections creating new bargaining units than they lost through **decertification elections** in which currently unionized workers vote on whether to become nonunion. By 1980 this ratio had fallen to 9 to 1, and by 1993 it stood at 6.9 to 1.

Even with a decline in organizing efforts, if currently unionized plants were expanding employment, the incidence of unionization would be expanding. In fact, during the 1980s the large majority of the decline in unionization was due to a relative decline in the size of unionized establishments.[18]

The analysis of Figure 11.1 can provide some insight into why unionization declined. Consider first the employers' resistance to unionization. Increasing foreign competition in the early 1980s reduced monopoly profits and raised the cost of higher union wages, thus increasing employers' resistance to new organization. It also caused already organized plants to lose sales and reduce employment. Employers' opposition to unionization was especially strong during the 1980s in companies that expected unions to raise wages the most and in industries where the relative cost of union labor was the highest. The altered political climate of the Reagan years no doubt also had some effect in increasing employers' resistance.[19]

On the demand side, the mix of workers in the labor force has shifted toward people who are less likely to want to belong to a union. Particularly important have been the increases in female, better-educated, and white-

---

[16] Paula Voos, "Union Organizing: Costs and Benefits," *Industrial and Labor Relations Review* 36: 576–591 (1983); Paula Voos, "Trends in Union Organizing Expenditures, 1953–1977," *Industrial and Labor Relations Review* 38: 52–63 (1984).

[17] Henry Farber and Alan Krueger, "Union Membership in the United States: The Decline Continues," in Bruce Kaufman and Morris Kleiner (eds.). *Employee Representation: Alternatives and Future Directions,* Madison, Wisc.: IRRA (1993).

[18] Stephen Bronars and Donald Deere, "Union Organizing Activity and Union Coverage, 1973–1988," Texas A&M University, Photocopy (November 1989).

[19] Richard Freeman and Morris Kleiner, "Employer Behavior in the Face of Union Organizing Drives," *Industrial and Labor Relations Review* 43: 351–365 (1990); Peter Linneman, Michael Wachter, and William Carter, "Evaluating the Evidence on Union Employment and Wages," *Industrial and Labor Relations Review* 44: 34–53 (1990); John Abowd and Henry Farber, "Product Market Organization, Union Organizing Activity and Employer Resistance," National Bureau of Economic Research, Working Paper No. 3353, (May 1990).

collar workers. Much of the decline in unionization between the mid-1950s and 1980 can be explained by changes in the demographic mix of the labor force and the structure of jobs by occupation and industry.[20]

Another explanation for the decline in demand for unionization is that nonunion workers have become more satisfied with their jobs and feel that unions have less to offer them. These feelings arise in part from the fact that government has increasingly provided the services once offered by unions. To the extent that the demand for unionization is, as institutional theories of union growth have claimed, in part a demand for job security and protection from management caprice, legislative protection is a substitute for union benefits. The passage of federal and state laws restricting employers' rights to dismiss workers reduced the incidence of unionization.[21] In addition, government regulation of such factors as workplace safety (through OSHA) and pension rights and safety (through the **Employment Retirement Income Security Act, ERISA**) has decreased the benefits that unions can provide potential members.

Although they may have started later and been somewhat less severe than in the U.S., there have been declines in union membership in most industrial economies. Table 11.7 shows the extent of union membership in several economies. Only in Canada and Sweden did membership not decline between 1980 and 1990. Indeed, in France and Spain the reduction in union membership was even greater than in the U.S. Careful studies of the reasons for the decline in union strength in the U.K. show that, like in the U.S., it did not result from unionized establishments becoming nonunion. Rather, nonunion establishments grew more rapidly than unionized ones and as markets became more competitive new plants opened during the 1980s were more likely to operate without a union.[22]

In every country, coverage under union contracts is greater than actual membership in unions. In the U.S. and Canada, this difference is relatively small. In 1990 when membership in the U.S. was 16 percent of wage and salary workers, coverage was 18 percent. The corresponding figures for Canada were 36 percent and 38 percent. In Japan, there are more union members (25 percent of wage and salary workers) than workers covered by

---

[20]William Dickens and Jonathan Leonard, "Accounting for the Decline in Union Membership, 1950–1980," *Industrial and Labor Relations Review* 38: 323–334 (1985); Richard Freeman and James Medoff, *What Do Unions Do?* New York: Basic Books (1984), Table 15-2.

[21]Henry Farber, "The Decline of Unionization in the United States," *Journal of Labor Economics* 8: S75–S105 (1990); George Neumann and Ellen Rissman, "Where Have All the Union Members Gone?" *Journal of Labor Economics* 2: 175–192 (1984).

[22]Phillip Beaumont and Richard Harris, "Union De-Recognition and Declining Union Density in Britain," *Industrial and Labor Relations Review* 48: 389–402 (1995); Richard Disney, Amanda Gosling, and Stephen Machin, "British Unions in Decline: Determinants of the 1980s Fall in Union Recognition," *Industrial and Labor Relations Review* 48: 403–419 (1995).

TABLE 11.7 UNION MEMBERSHIP, SELECTED COUNTRIES, 1970–1990 (PERCENT OF WAGE AND SALARY EARNERS)

Country	1970	1980	1990
United States	23	22	16
Australia	50	48	40
Canada	31	36	36
France	22	18	10
Germany	33	45	33
Italy	36	49	39
Japan	35	31	25
Spain	22	25	11
Sweden	67	80	83
United Kingdom	45	50	39

Source: OECD, *Employment Outlook* (1994), Table 5.7.

union contracts (23 percent). In Europe, however, the differences between membership and coverage can be quite large. In Germany, where only 32 percent of workers were union members in 1990, 90 percent were covered by the terms of union contracts. In France 10 percent were members, but 92 percent of workers were covered by union agreements.

What accounts for these enormous differences? In large part they result from a combination of negotiations in these countries being carried out by national or sector-wide employer associations and government policies that impose collective-bargaining outcomes on an entire industry or sector. These **extension mechanisms** result in the terms negotiated by a union also applying to firms where workers are not union members. In addition, there is no legal requirement in these countries that the majority of workers in a plant must agree to be represented by a union. If an employer association decides to negotiate with a union, then any agreement reached can be imposed on workers in a plant, even if most of those workers are not members of the union.

One result of the extension of union agreements to nonunion firms is that the incentive for workers to join unions is reduced. Why should they pay the costs of unionization, including dues and lost work time due to strikes, if the law will give them the benefits of any contract won by the union anyway? Thus, the difference between unionization rates and coverage rates is greatest where extension is most prevalent.[23]

[23] OECD, "Collective Bargaining: Levels and Coverage," *Employment Outlook* (1994).

POLICY ISSUE

HOW SHOULD WORKERS' EXPRESS THEIR DESIRES?

One of the most striking differences in Table 11.7 is between the U.S. and Canada, where unionization rates are over twice as high. Even after standardizing for discrepancies in industry structure, differences between these similar countries are substantial. This contrast has led labor unions attempting to reverse their decline in the U.S. to seek to modify American labor laws to resemble those in Canada.

A major change sought by unions involves the determination of when unions acquire the right to represent workers in a bargaining unit. In the U.S., if a sufficient number of workers sign a petition indicating that they wish to be represented by a union, the NLRB will hold a representation election by *secret ballot*. In Canada, if over 50 percent of the workers have signed the petition, no election is held on the grounds that the majority of workers have already made their preferences known. Not surprisingly, unions are more successful in organizing workers in Canada. In the U.S., the total number of votes for the union in a secret-ballot election typically is much lower than the number of workers who signed a petition in support of the union.

The reasons for this difference is clear. Between the time an election is called and when it is held the employer has an opportunity to present the negative side of joining a union to counter the union campaign that may have persuaded workers to sign petitions. In addition, there may have been subtle or overt pressure on workers from union organizers to sign the petition even though the worker did not really desire to be represented by a union. Thus, it is clear that adoption of the Canadian rule would increase union membership but at the expense of reducing the extent of democracy in the American workplace.[24]

UNION GOALS

Models of union goals can be divided into two groups depending on how they postulate the union interacts with firm management. The first group, called **right-to-manage models**, assumes that the union and firm negotiate to set the wage rate, but that the employer has control over the amount of labor used in production. The second group, known as **efficient bargaining models**, assumes that unions and the firm jointly determine both wage rates and employment levels. This control may be either explicit or indirect through various work rules written into the contract. Both approaches assume that the union has some monopoly power in the market for labor of the type used

[24]Joseph Rose and Gary Chaison, "New Measures of Union Organizing Effectiveness," *Industrial Relations* 29: 457–468 (1990); W. Craig Riddell, "Unionization in Canada and the United States: A Take of Two Countries," in David Card and Richard Freeman (eds.). *Small Differences That Matter: Labor Markets and Income Maintenance in Canada and the United States,* Chicago: University of Chicago Press (1993).

POLICY ISSUE

UNION BUSTING, MODERN STYLE

Union leaders argue that employers have become more adept in dealing with NLRB election procedures. Employers' resistance is increasingly served by an industry of specialists who offer consulting services designed to increase the probability that an employer will win a representation election. Unionists claim that the NLRB and the courts have become increasingly promanagement. One of the biggest irritants was the Supreme Court's 1984 *NLRB v. Bildisco & Bildisco* decision, in which the court held that a company could unilaterally cancel its contract with a union as part of its reorganization during bankruptcy. Do decisions like this affect organization efforts? More generally, how effective are employers' efforts to reduce the likelihood of unionization by using stronger antiunion tactics?

Otherwise identical workers are less likely to vote for union representation in elections in which employers engage in campaigns to remain union-free, including efforts by low-level supervisory personnel to discourage workers from supporting a union. The fraction of representation elections won by unions fell significantly during the years between 1965 and 1980 when an increase in unfair labor practices by employers may indicate more aggressive opposition. In part, increased employer resistance is a response to the increased cost of unionization as represented by decreases in w^* in Figure 11.1.[25] When the courts and the NLRB create a climate that is conducive to such resistance, however, the evidence indicates that it reduces unions' ability to organize additional workers.

by the firm and that the firm is not a perfect competitor in its product market. If it were, any attempt to raise wages or raise employment at the competitive wage would drive the firm out of business.

Although Samuel Gompers, long-time president of the American Federation of Labor (AFL), answered "More, more and then still more!" when asked what unions wanted, no union can consistently get more of everything it desires. The difficulty in analyzing the decisions facing a union's leadership is made clear if we consider the role of unions in attempting to affect both wages and the level of employment. A union's concern with employment levels is part of its broader concern with job scarcity and job security. The term *job security* includes the distribution of employment among members. In formal models, however, the focus is typically limited to the less inclusive goals of increasing total employment and expanding union membership.

---

[25]Freeman and Kleiner, "Employer Behavior"; Dickens, "The Effect of Company Campaigns"; Richard Freeman, "The Effect of the Union Wage Differential on Management Opposition and Union Organizing Success," American Economic Association, *Papers and Proceedings* 76: 92–96 (1986); and, with results that are somewhat less supportive, Robert Flanagan, "NLRA Litigation and Union Representation," *Stanford Law Review* 38: 957–989 (1986).

The starting point for discussing a firm's demand for labor in Chapters 4 and 5 was the model of the profit-maximizing firm. The concept of profit maximization provides a clear and effective way of summarizing the goals of a firm's management in negotiations with unions. Unfortunately, there is no such consensus on the goals unions bring to the bargaining table, making it much more difficult to construct a simple model of what a trade union seeks to maximize.

Far more than the firm, the union is both an economic and a political entity. Although ultimate power nominally rests with corporate stockholders and with union members, both corporate management and union leadership play critical roles in determining policy. In most unions, wage bargains must be taken to the membership for ratification, and decisions by the leadership are not always endorsed. As a tactic in negotiation with management, leaders may sometimes send agreements back for ratification, knowing that they are unacceptable. At other times they are genuinely surprised by the repudiation of a bargain that they firmly believed to be the best obtainable. In contrast, corporate management and directors have full authority to negotiate wages without consulting the stockholders. In the long run they may suffer if they make a bad bargain, but in the short run their decisions will not be challenged.

Furthermore, union leaders face greater risks than corporate directors when they seek reelection. In corporations the rule of one share, one vote makes it very expensive to challenge management by soliciting proxies. In contrast, the one-person, one-vote rule of unions, although it does not eliminate the advantages of incumbency, poses greater potential threats. Such major American unions as the American Federation of Teachers, the United Mine Workers, and the American Federation of State, County and Municipal Employees have defeated incumbent presidents.

The sharing of power in a union between leadership and membership creates difficulties in constructing a formal model of union behavior because there may be differences in aims or emphasis between them. Leaders are often better informed about conditions in the firm than their members. As we will see in the next chapter, union leaders may find it difficult to convince their members of what the firm can provide without threatening their own jobs. In addition, union leaders may have personal goals with respect to their influence in the labor movement or the national political scene that are not shared by the members. Thus, union leaders may not always be **perfect agents** of the preferences of the union members. It is often helpful to analyze labor negotiations as if they involved three parties—the firm, the union leadership, and the union membership—each with its own set of goals.

A second source of difficulty in analyzing union goals is that the gains won in collective bargaining with a particular firm do not go directly to the union but instead to individual union members employed by the firm. The difficulty of redistributing them later to other members, either within or outside the firm, reduces the control union leaders can exercise over the allocation of the gains that result from their efforts. This situation is in sharp contrast to the corporation, where profits may be reallocated to other uses before any distribution to stockholders.

UNION GOALS IN RIGHT-TO-MANAGE MODELS

Keeping these difficulties in mind, let us examine union goals in the context of models in which the employer determines the amount of labor to use in response to a negotiated wage rate. This means that the firm must always be on its demand curve for labor, shown as *DD* in Figure 11.2. The position of this demand curve is determined by the factors considered in Chapters 4 and 5. The curve labeled *MWB* is the marginal wage bill that corresponds to *DD*. It shows the addition to the total **wage bill** (employment times the wage rate) produced by changing employment by one worker along the demand curve. In Figure 11.2 the workers' best alternative wage (i.e., the wage the union member could obtain in the competitive labor market given his skills) is denoted w_S. The line labeled *S* is, therefore, the horizontal supply curve of labor to the firm showing the wage the firm would have to pay if it were nonunion.

The union can make a variety of choices that are consistent with outcomes along the demand curve. Each implies something different about the goals of the union. It should be clear from the outset that a goal of maximizing wages makes little sense. If the union obtained the highest wage it could

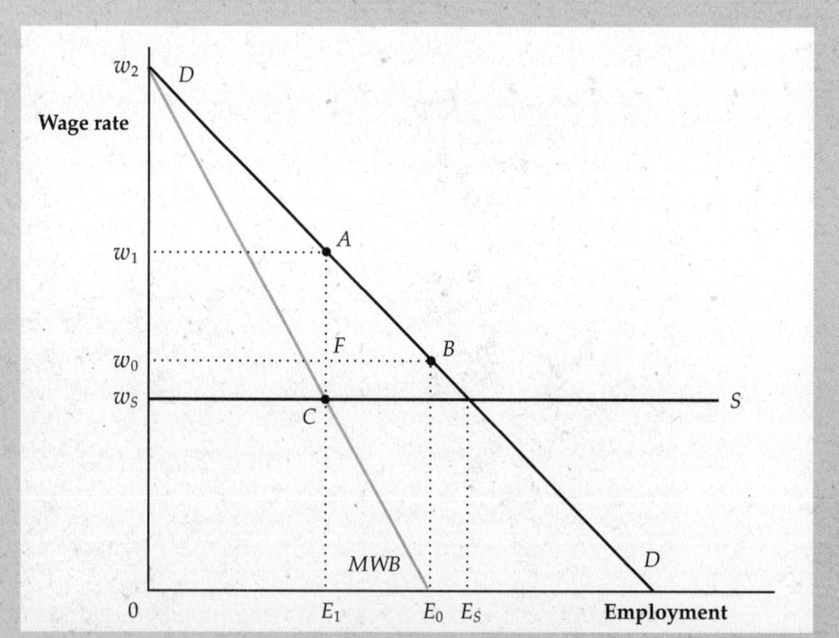

FIGURE 11.2 WAGE SETTING ON THE DEMAND CURVE
Alternative union goals might involve maximizing employment at point (w_s, E_s); the wage bill (at w_0, E_0); or the total compensation of the membership including wages in alternative employment (at w_1, E_1).

(slightly less than w_2), there would only be one worker employed at the firm. At the other extreme, if the unions sought to maximize membership, the wage would be w_S, and there would be no difference between a unionized and a nonunion firm.

Thus, unions are typically assumed to maximize some function that includes both wages and membership (employment) levels. One alternative that has been suggested frequently is to maximize the wage bill.[26] The wage bill is maximized where the *MWB* is zero and the elasticity of labor demand equals –1. If the wage were lowered slightly, the drop in the wage would be exactly offset by the effect of the slight increase in employment. The wage bill is shown in Figure 11.2 as the area of the rectangle under any point on the demand curve. Thus, at a wage of w_1, the wage bill would be $0w_1AE_1$. Given the demand curve *DD*, the largest such rectangle possible is $0w_0BE_0$, formed when wages are w_0, employment is E_0, and the *MWB* is zero.

Assuming that the union seeks to maximize the wage bill has problematic implications. For example, suppose the wage were at w_1, a high enough level that the demand for labor is elastic. In this case the union should come into labor negotiations demanding a reduction in wages. If wages were reduced to w_0, the gain in the wage bill ($E_1FBE_0 - w_0w_1AF$) would be positive. Never in recorded history, however, have we seen a union leader pounding the table to demand a wage cut, even though some employers must have operated on the elastic portion of their demand curve. An even greater problem with wage-bill maximization is that it rests on arbitrary assumptions about the supply price of labor, the nonunion wage w_S. It is entirely possible that the nonunion wage is such that wage bill would be maximized at a wage less than w_S. It is impossible to see why any union member or honest union leadership would want such a solution. Nor would employers want it, since they would be unable to recruit labor if workers could obtain nonunion jobs at the wage w_S, above what was being offered in the union job.

An alternative approach assumes that unions maximize **wage rents**. With this goal, the union would seek the highest total income for its members under the assumption that those who are not employed by the firm will receive the alternative wage w_S. This strategy is equivalent to maximizing the excess of earnings over w_S. Following the analog of the product-market monopolist, the union would seek to set the wage at w_1, where the marginal wage bill is equal to the supply price of labor. The employer, taking w_1 as given, will employ E_1 workers. The union is then maximizing the rent:

$$Rent = [w_1 - w_S]E_1$$

and obtains the greatest total earnings for its members.

The difficulty with either of these simple rules is that they fail to reconcile the conflicting interests of union members. Consider what would happen

[26] The wage-bill maximization hypothesis was first proposed by John Dunlop, *Wage Determination Under Trade Unions*, New York: Macmillan (1944).

if the wage were increased slightly above either w_0 or w_1. Most of the workers who were previously employed would still have their jobs. They would, however, be better off since they would be receiving higher wages. Only a few workers would be worse off because they had lost their jobs. If the union leader put the issue to a vote, as long as the workers knew which ones would be laid off if wages were increased, there would always be a majority vote for the higher wage.

The key issue is who would vote in the next union election. If the membership of the union were fixed at some high level (say E_S in Figure 11.2), and all the members voted in elections, there would be a limit on how high the wage would rise. This limit would be where just $E_S/2 + 1$ workers remained employed. If those who do not find a union job drop their membership, however (after all, why should they continue to pay dues?), then the result is much less stable, and there will be continued pressure for small increases in wages. These models of **insider dominated unions** suggest that wages will be higher and employment lower than if both current and potential members of the union were included in the determination of preferences.

The difficulties inherent in both of these demand models can also be illustrated by considering the case of an **industrial union** that represents all the workers in an industry and includes two distinct classes of members: a small group of craft workers and a large group of operatives. In the U.S., the United Auto Workers is a good example. The discussion in Chapter 4 shows that the demand for more-skilled workers is less elastic than that for less-skilled. The solution that maximizes rents would involve paying a higher wage to the craft workers for whom demand is less elastic, but if the union achieves large wage gains for its craft members and small or no gains for the more numerous operatives, it has no way to channel part of the extra wages of the craft workers to the operatives. Since transfers between union members are never observed, union leaders are forced to settle for a smaller total gain more evenly distributed. There is good evidence, both for specific crafts and for a random sample of craft workers, that this process causes craft members of industrial unions to sometimes fare badly.[27]

A more general formulation of union goals postulates a union objective function that combines wages and employment in a less rigid form than either the wage bill or the wage rent. Unions are assumed to maximize a collective **welfare function** that is determined by their political process and takes the form:

$$U = [w - w^*]^a[E - E^*]^{(1 - a)}$$

where w^* and E^* are an alternative wage rate and level of employment, and a is some number between zero and one that shows the importance the union

[27] Albert Rees and George Shultz, *Workers and Wages in an Urban Labor Market*, Chicago: University of Chicago Press (1970), Chapter 10; Jody Sindelar, "Intraunion Redistribution of Economic Rents," University of Chicago Graduate School of Business, Photocopy (1983); John Creedy and Ian McDonald, "Models of Trade Union Behaviour: A Synthesis," *Economic Record* 67: 346–359 (1991).

attaches to gains in wages compared to losses of employment. One study that examined wage (and thus employment) policies showed that several locals of the International Typographical Union value *both* higher wages and expanded employment, but that they are not willing to trade wages for employment in a way that maximizes either the wage rent or the wage bill. The same inference can be drawn from the behavior of unions in woodworking plants in British Columbia, Canada; coal miners in both the U.S. and the U.K.; and airline mechanics in the U.S. Although all these studies showed that both wages and employment levels were valued by unions, estimates of their relative importance differed considerably. The implied elasticity of substitution between these two goals varied from 0.18 and 2.10, with no consistent pattern between these extreme values.[28] Unions that set wages and allow employers to determine the amount of union labor to be used are aware that higher wages lead to fewer jobs for their members. Their wage policy cannot, however, be described as maximizing any simple sum such as rent or the wage bill.

Unions' ability to achieve higher wages with little loss of membership or employment depends critically on the elasticity of demand for union labor. With a lower elasticity, either the wage bill or rent maximizing wage (w_0 and w_1 in Figure 11.2) can be pushed higher. With the more complex goal of maximizing U, the union will still seek to decrease the elasticity in order to reduce the drop in employment when it raises wages. The elasticity can be kept low if the union can restrict the use of nonunion substitutes for products made with union labor. Thus, most unions are very concerned to organize all firms within an industry. In the 1980s, for example, the United Auto Workers made major efforts to organize workers employed by Japanese auto manufacturers that had built plants in the U.S. Even in automobile manufacturing this strategy has not always been successful—despite the relative ease of organizing when establishments operate on a large scale—and many of these plants continue to operate without a union.

When there are many small establishments, organizing becomes still more difficult. This effect is illustrated by the continuing tendency of small companies to relocate in order to avoid unionization. For the same reason, unions are major opponents of moves toward free trade that lower prices to consumers by reducing firms' product market power. Unions have even

---

[28] Henry Farber, "The United Mine Workers and the Demand for Coal: An Econometric Analysis of Union Behavior," Unpublished PhD Dissertation, Princeton University (1977); James Dertouzos and John Pencavel, "Wage and Employment Determination Under Trade Unionism: The International Typographical Union," *Journal of Political Economy* 89: 1162–1181 (1981); John Pencavel, "The Trade-off Between Wages and Employment in Trade Union Objectives," *Quarterly Journal of Economics* 99: 215–231 (1984); Alan Carruth and Andrew Oswald, "Miner's Wages in Post-War Britain: An Application of a Model of Trade Union Behaviour," *Economic Journal* 97: 431–445 (1985); David Card, "Efficient Contracts with Costly Adjustment: Short-run Employment Determination for Airline Mechanics," *American Economic Review* 76: 1045–1071 (1986); Felice Martinello, "Wage and Employment Determination in a Unionized Industry: The IWA and the British Columbia Wood Products Industry," *Journal of Labor Economics* 7: 303–330 (1989).

engaged in television advertising campaigns in an attempt to reduce the elasticity of substitution between union and nonunion products. Perhaps the most famous of these was the "Look for the Union Label" jingle of the International Ladies' Garment Workers Union.

Right-to-manage models of union behavior can be summarized by examining Figure 11.3. The union is assumed to maximize a collective utility function that values both wages and employment. U_0 and U_1 show two indifference curves derived from such a function. U_1 is preferred by the union to U_0 since there exists at least one point on it that provides both higher wages and more employment than any given point on U_0. Two of the firm's isoprofit curves are shown as P_0 and P_1. Since the demand curve, D, shows how much labor a profit-maximizing firm would employ at any wage rate, profits could be held constant if either more or fewer workers were employed only by pay-

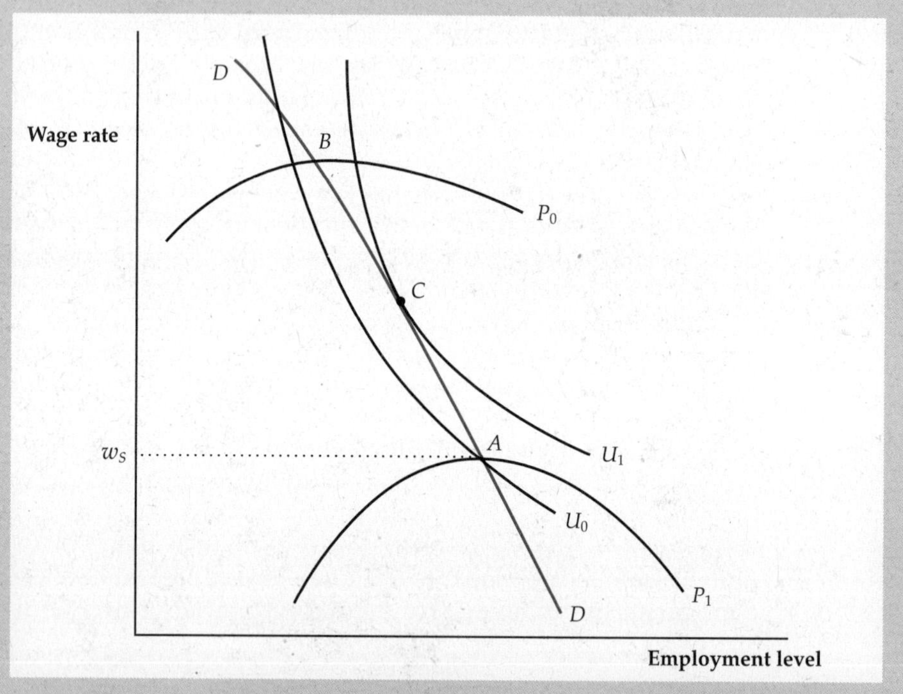

FIGURE 11.3 COLLECTIVE BARGAINING IN RIGHT-TO-MANAGE MODELS

A union that cares about both wages and employment levels will maximize its well-being at point *C* where one of its indifference curves is tangent to the firm's demand curve. The firm will maximize its profits at point *A*, the highest isoprofit curve it can achieve if it paid the market wage w_s. The outcome of bargaining between the union and the firm will be at a point between *A* and *C* that depends on the relative bargaining power of the two parties.

ing a lower wage rate. The competitive wage is w_S. Without a union the firm would pay this wage, employ E_S workers, and earn profits of P_1 at point *A*. In Figure 11.3 we assume that the firm has market power and that, therefore, P_1 is greater than zero. Isoprofit curve P_0 represents the combinations of wages and employment levels where the firm earns no economic profits. Thus, the only feasible outcomes lie along the demand curve segment between points *A* and *B*. At wages lower than point *A*, the firm could not attract any workers. At wages higher than point *B*, the firm would go out of business.

If the union were free to pick any wage it wanted, subject only to the condition that the firm would then determine the level of employment, it would pick wage w_1 and end up at point *C* on indifference curve U_1. Notice that as Figure 11.3 is drawn, the union's preferences result in an outcome that does *not* shift all of the firm's profit to the union. If the union and the firm bargain over the wage level, the final outcome will be at some intermediate point between point *A* and point *C*, the location of which depends on the relative strengths of the union and the firm in bargaining, a subject that we will discuss in the next chapter.

Figure 11.3 also makes clear why unions have little impact in competitive industries. In such an industry, isoprofit curve P_1 would represent zero profits. If wages were any higher than w_S, the firm would suffer losses and eventually close down. Thus, the best the union can do is to be on U_0 at the competitive wage and employment level. In this case, unions can offer relatively little to attract potential members.

EFFICIENT BARGAINING MODELS—SHARED CONTROL OVER EMPLOYMENT

So far we have assumed that the union formulates its demands for wages and other components of pay in the expectation that employers will then adjust employment in response to the agreed upon wage. This strategy amounts to assuming that the final outcome will lie on the demand curve for labor. It can easily be shown, however, that such an outcome is **Pareto inefficient**, meaning that one or both parties to the agreement can be made better off if the final outcome lies off the demand curve.

Consider Figure 11.5 (page 444), which repeats the analysis in Figure 11.3. Suppose that in a right-to-manage world the union and firm would have settled on wage w^* and that the employer, therefore, would have hired E^* workers. With this outcome, the employer would be on isoprofit curve P_0, while the union would be on indifference curve U_0. Clearly, any point in the shaded area (all of which involves lower wages but greater employment than at point *A*) would give the firm higher profits and the union higher welfare. Points between *A* and *B* that lie exactly on isoprofit curve P_0 would leave the firm equally well off but improve the union's welfare, while points along the union indifference curve U_0 would improve firm profits without reducing the welfare of the union members.

By analogous reasoning, it is easy to show that a change in wages and employment that improves Pareto efficiency can occur from any point that is

POLICY ISSUE

UNION GOALS AND ANTITRUST POLICY

Under the antitrust laws of the United States (in particular, the Clayton Act of 1914) unions are explicitly exempt from prosecution for being combinations in restraint of trade. Certain actions that a union takes jointly with employers, however, can constitute restraints of trade. In *United Mine Workers v. Pennington* in 1965 the Supreme Court ruled that the union was guilty of colluding with certain employers to raise wage rates in order to harm another group of employers.[29] How can a union help itself by colluding with some employers to raise wages throughout the industry? Why not just impose different wage increases on different firms?

The answer can be seen in Figure 11.4. LC_0 is the long-run average cost curve in the industry before the union imposes the wage increase. It shows the per-unit cost of producing at each output level in the long run after the firm has had time to adjust its capital and labor inputs to produce a particular amount of output as efficiently as possible. With the configuration of costs (including wages) that prevailed before the wage increase, the most efficient size of a firm in the industry (the lowest average cost) was at output level Q_0. Because larger firms used more capital-intensive methods of production, the increased wage represented a smaller rise in cost per unit of output for them than for small firms. Thus, after the union imposed wage increase, the long-run average cost curve rose to LC_1, and the efficient scale of operations increased from Q_0 to Q_1.

The union benefitted from this change in two ways. First, union workers employed in large firms received a wage increase. More importantly, competition from employees in small firms was reduced, because the smaller firms became relatively less profitable. Since the United Mine Workers, like other unions, had had difficulty in maintaining union organization in small companies, the wage gains benefitted employees in the larger firms by functioning as a substantial barrier to entry into the industry for new small companies that the union leadership felt would be difficult to organize and would compete with the larger, unionized firms.

not a tangency between a union indifference curve and a firm isoprofit curve. The locus of tangencies between these curves is called the **contract curve**. Any point along this curve between points *F* and *G* in Figure 11.5 will make both the union and the firm better off than they were at point *A*. Thus, we would expect the final wage and employment level to lie somewhere between points *F* and *G*, with the exact location depending on the relative strengths of the union and the firm.

An obvious test of whether right-to-manage models or the efficient bargaining models characterize relations between unions and firms is whether the resulting contracts lie along the labor demand curve (as they would in a

[29] The discussion is based upon Oliver Williamson, "Wage Rates as a Barrier to Entry: The Pennington Case in Perspective," *Quarterly Journal of Economics* 82: 85–116 (1968).

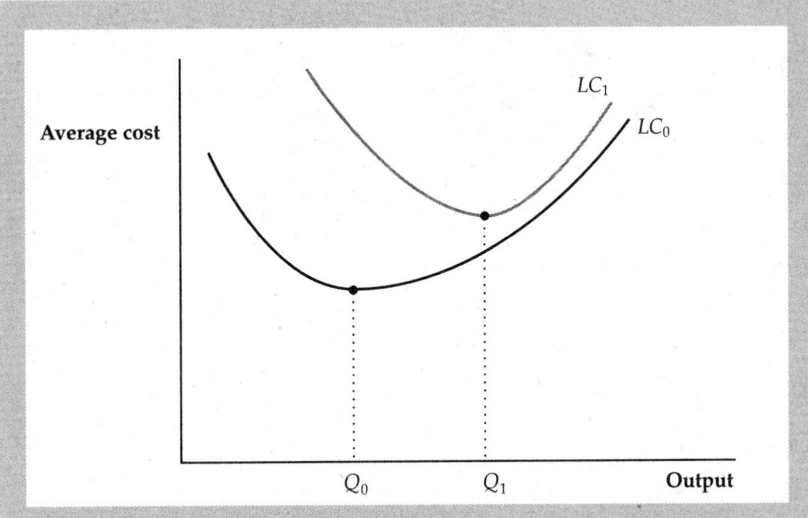

FIGURE 11.4 COST, CAPITAL INTENSITY, AND UNION WAGES
By raising labor costs more for small firms than large firms, a union can shift production toward large firms that are easier to organize.

right-to-manage world) or along a contract curve to the right of the labor demand curve (as in an efficient-bargaining world). The best statistical evidence to date suggests that union contracts are not efficient in the sense that we have defined efficiency. Several studies using data from the U.S., Canada, the U.K., and France find results consistent with unionized firms' operating along a conventional labor demand curve, perhaps augmented by efficiency wage considerations.[30]

The efficient-bargaining view of union goals seems more closely supported by data for **craft unions**, which represent workers with similar skills no matter in which industry they work. Newspapers employing members of the

[30]James Brown and Orley Ashenfelter, "Testing the Efficiency of Employment Contracts," *Journal of Political Economy* 94: S3–S39 (1986); David Card, "Unexpected Inflation, Real Wages and Employment Determination in Union Contracts," *American Economic Review* 80: 669–688 (1990); S. Machin, A. Manning, and C. Meghir, "Dynamic Models of Employment Based on Firm-Level Panel Data," University College London, Photocopy (1991); S. Nickell and S. Wadhwani, "Employment Determination in British Industry: Investigations Using Mocro Data," *Review of Economic Studies* 58: 955–970 (1991); Walter Wessels, "Do Unions Contract for Added Employment?" *Industrial and Labor Relations Review* 45: 181–193 (1991); J. Abowd and F. Kramarz, "A Test of Negotiation and Incentive Compensation Models Using Longitudinal French Enterprise Data," Insée, Paris, Photocopy (1992).

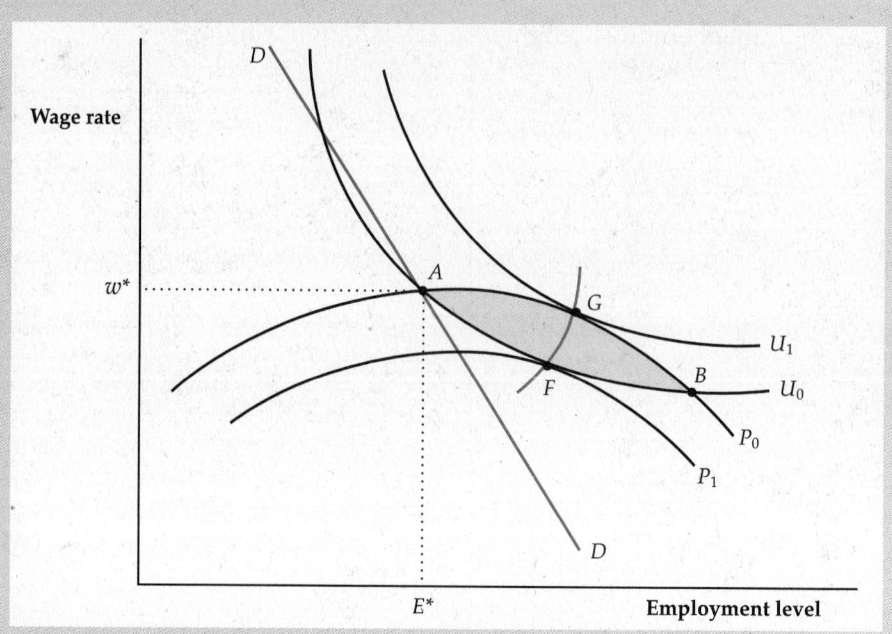

FIGURE 11.5 EFFICIENT COLLECTIVE BARGAINING MODELS
If unions care about both employment and wages, no matter what point a union and firm agree to on the firm's demand curve, there must be combinations involving lower wages and higher employment that make both the union and the firm better off. Efficient contracts lie along contract curve *FG*.

International Typographical Union between 1945 and 1973 did not move along a well-defined demand curve in response to wage changes imposed by the union. Instead, there was a range of wage and employment outcomes from which the union chose given its members' preferences and the other labor market conditions facing employers. Evidence for public-sector firms also indicates that employment levels matter, although it is difficult to determine whether this finding is due to union demands or the goals of the public officials themselves. Thus, employment in British coal mines before privatization was higher than would have been consistent with profit maximization and the negotiated wage. In the 1970s in school districts where teachers' unions had greater control over class size, teachers also received higher wages. Instead of higher wages forcing school districts to use fewer teachers, where the unions were more powerful, they obtained both higher wages and greater employment opportunities for their members than in other districts. One U.S. study found that public-sector unions increased employment among financial officials, wages among police, and both wages and employment among firefighters and sanitation workers.[31]

Since the concept of Pareto efficiency is a rather weak criterion, it is disturbing to think that unions and firms behave in a way that is not in their joint interest. After all, it is rather easy to specify both wages and employment levels in a labor contract. As we will see in the next section, even if exact employment levels are not specified in the contract, work rules can force an employer off its demand curve to the right.

A reconciliation may come from the earlier discussion suggesting unions may not care very much about employment levels.[32] Suppose a well-specified rule exists where each worker knows the order in which he would be laid-off if employment were reduced. Typically, this involves a **last-in, first-out rule** in which layoffs occur in inverse order of **seniority**. In this case, if E_M is the employment level at which the decisive voter (usually assumed to be the **median voter**) is sure of keeping her job, then the union's indifference curves will look like U_0 through U_2 in Figure 11.6. The efficient outcomes are still where the union indifference curves are tangent to the firm's isoprofit curves, but as can be seen in Figure 11.6, these efficient outcomes now lie along the firm's demand curve.

UNION EMPLOYMENT AND WAGE POLICIES IN PRACTICE

Despite the results discussed above, in many cases unions have clearly forced firms to employ more workers than if they were on their demand curves. Although collective bargaining rarely specifies levels of employment along with wages, contracts often include agreements over both wages and the intensity of work. Another approach is to bargain over wages and the labor-capital ratio, for example, by specifying the size of the crew on a train or an airplane. A final approach involves specific and detailed **jurisdiction** rules regarding which union must perform certain tasks. Bargaining over these topics can produce **restrictive work practices,** more commonly called **featherbedding,** through which unions try to create additional

[31] Thomas MaCurdy and John Pencavel, "Testing Between Competing Models of Wage and Employment Determination in Unionized Markets," *Journal of Political Economy* 94: S40–S87 (1986); Randall Eberts and Joe Stone, "On the Contract Curve: A Test of Alternative Models of Collective Bargaining," *Journal of Labor Economics* 4: 66–81 (1986); C. R. Bean and P. J. Turnbull, "Employment in the British Coal Industry: A Test of the Labour Demand Model," *Economic Journal* 98: 1092–1104 (1988); Robert Valletta, "Union Effects on Municipal Employment and Wages: A Longitudinal Approach," *Journal of Labour Economics* 11: 545–574 (1993).

[32] This discussion is based on Andrew Oswald, "Efficient Contracts Are On the Labor Demand Curve," *Labour Economics* 1: 85–113 (1993).

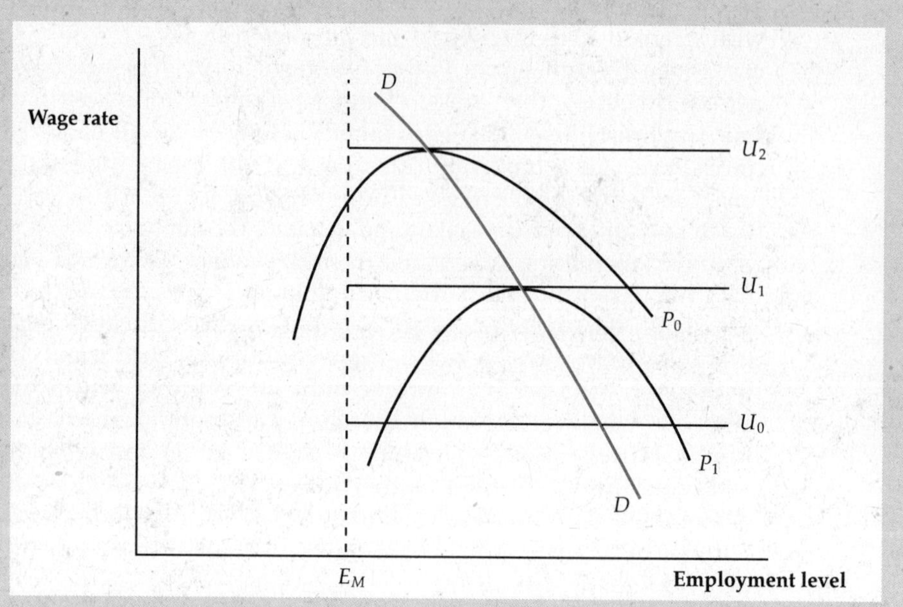

FIGURE 11.6 EFFICIENT COLLECTIVE BARGAINING WITH LAYOFF RULES

If union policies are determined by a democratic process and the median voter knows at what wage demand will be low enough that he will be laid off, union preferences will not give any positive weight to employment levels and the efficient contract will be on the firm's demand curve.

employment.[33] Such formal practices exist largely among craft unions, although informal equivalents occur at the plant level in some industrial unions.

Examples abound. The "bogus" rules of many International Typographical Union locals required the resetting of material printed by newspapers from papier-mâché matrices received from the advertisers. Many musicians' union locals have contract rules that require employing a minimum number of orchestra members for any show containing music. One Broadway producer reportedly became so incensed at this excess staffing, that when producing a show that needed only a four-piece combo, he soundproofed a room in the basement of the theater and required the extra musicians to play patriotic songs for two hours rather than simply sign in and depart for the nearest

---

[33]George Johnson, "Work Rules, Featherbedding, and Pareto-optimal Union-Management Bargaining," *Journal of Labor Economics* 8: S237–S259 (1990).

bar as they had traditionally done. Railroads in the U.S. continued to operate with firemen long after they had converted to diesel power. In one extreme case, even though bridge painters wear safety harnesses and typically hang nets below where they are working, the painters' union used to require that a union member be stationed in a boat below the job in case a painter fell into the water. Of course, since the operating engineers' contract required that only they could operate machinery on construction projects, the boat also had to contain an operating engineer to run the motor.

By specifying employment per task, a union neither determines the total amount of member employment nor specifies the ratio of member employment to all other inputs. Firms have the option of substituting away from the capital that requires the use of the minimum number of workers. At the industry level the union's employment requirement raises costs and prices and, therefore, lowers output. In the final analysis, the ability of unions to achieve efficient bargains, or even have much direct control over employment, is more limited than featherbedding practices would suggest.

If staffing requirements are set too high, total employment at a given union wage could be reduced below the level that employers as a group would offer in the absence of the requirement. When railroad unions increased the size of freight train crews, the ratio of capital to labor was increased by having more and larger cars per train.

Minimum sizes of orchestras for musicals, for example, will result in a reduction in both performances and the number of shows produced. There will also be a tendency to use larger theaters for musicals (a change in factor proportions), which will contribute to even fewer performances. For these reasons, requiring a specified number of musicians per performance will not guarantee an increase in total employment.

In many cases, featherbedding represents an attempt to push labor demand off the demand curve in response to a technological change that sharply reduces the demand for union labor in a particular craft while at the same time increasing the profitability of the firm. A struggle results between management, which seeks to reap the profits from the improvement, and the union, which wishes to maintain employment for its membership.

Attempts at featherbedding often find their initial impetus in the expansion of a competing industry. Television has reduced employment in the motion picture industry, just as the automobile and airplane have reduced employment in railroad passenger service. Unions in the declining industries have struggled to maintain employment by imposing restrictions on employers' attempts to economize on their labor inputs. These strategies may be successful in the short run, if they are backed by the threat of total shutdown during a strike. In the long run, however, they are usually unsuccessful. The reason is clear from the preceding discussion. In a declining industry, employers typically have no excess profits that the union can extract. In such cases, it is not a matter of pushing the employer to the right of the demand curve. Instead, the union must accommodate a demand curve for labor that is shifting leftward because of the decline in demand for the industry's product.

Among unions' concerns about their compensation policy, a crucial feature is the current money wage. As the models of implicit contracts in Chapter 9 imply, other things being equal, workers prefer wages that do not fluctuate. Unions are especially concerned with maintaining the current money wage and will pay for this with severe contractions in employment, even though they would not insist on increasing the money wage if the consequences for employment were not nearly as severe. In other words, the weight given to the membership size or employment in the face of wage cuts is much smaller than for wage increases. Union preferences about wage changes (like those of most workers) are asymmetric. This preference is understandable since the workers who would be laid-off if employment were reduced are current members of the union who are known by other members. On the other hand, those who would be hired if employment were to increase are unknown individuals who are probably not current union members.

Unions have on rare occasions engaged in **concessionary bargaining** and have agreed to wage reductions at the firm or establishment level when a threat exists that an establishment would shut down or relocate unless the union granted a wage reduction. Unions often resist such concessions since they fear that providing relief to one firm will induce other unionized employers to demand similar treatment. Moreover, the union cannot be sure that the employer will not close the plant even with the wage cut. Wage cuts appear to have only a small impact on the likelihood that a troubled firm will decide remain open. Union members and leaders are aware of this fact when management asks for concessions.[34]

Union members' real wages are often protected from price inflation by **escalator clauses** or **cost-of-living adjustments (COLAs)** in collective bargaining agreements lasting more than one year. Such clauses provide for periodic changes in money wages based on changes in the Consumer Price Index (CPI) during the life of the agreement. In the United States, the average contract containing a COLA protected workers from about 60 percent of the nominal inflation that occurred between the mid-1960s and the early 1980s. Similar rates of protection were observed in Canada.[35] Workers appear willing to bear some of the risk that inflation will erode their real wages in order to bargain for other things, and therefore they accept COLA adjustments of less than 100 percent. As seen in the policy issue, however, indexation need not be as high as 100 percent to fully compensate workers for the effects of inflation.

The wage demands of any one union are strongly influenced by comparisons with other groups of workers with whom there have been traditional

[34]Paul Gerhart, *Saving Plants and Jobs*, Kalamazoo, Mich.: W. E. Upjohn Institute (1987).

[35]Wallace Hendricks and Lawrence Kahn, *Wage Indexation in the United States*, Cambridge, Mass.: Ballinger (1985), Chapter 6; David Card, "Cost-Of-Living Escalators in Major Union Contracts," *Industrial and Labor Relations Review* 37: 34–48 (1983).

POLICY ISSUE

WHAT COULD SOCIAL SECURITY LEARN FROM UNION BEHAVIOR?

The fact that COLA clauses typically increase wages by less than two-thirds of the rate of increase in the CPI may not mean that they do not fully protect workers from increasing prices. To be fully protected, workers do not need to have the same consumption after inflationary price increases; they need to have the same utility. Often this requirement can be achieved by a wage increase that is less than the increase in the CPI. The key is that not all prices increase at the same rate. Consumers substitute away from goods with relatively large price increases and buy more of goods with lower rates of price increase.

Figure 11.7 shows a consumer's choice between two goods. To keep the figure simple, we assume that all the inflation consists of an increase in the price of Good 2. Before the price increase the consumer with indifference curves I_0 and I_1 faced budget line *AB* and determined her optimal consumption to be at point *M* on indifference curve I_0. Now suppose that the price of Good 2 increased, shifting her budget line to *AC*. A COLA of 100 percent would enable her to continue purchasing the bundle represented by point *M*. Thus, at the new prices, her wages would have to increase sufficiently to shift her budget line to *DE*. With this budget line, however, she would opt to increase her purchase of the now relatively less expensive Good 1 and shift her consumption to point *N* on indifference curve I_1. A COLA of 100 percent increases the worker's utility. She could be kept equally well-off after the inflationary price increase by a smaller shift in her budget line to *FG*, causing her to consume at point *O* and remain on indifference curve I_0.

The fact that unions settle for less than 100 percent indexation of wages has an important implication for Social Security policy. Social Security payments do not need to be increased by 100 percent of the increase in the CPI each year to leave seniors' utility unchanged. Since these payments are the largest single government expenditure, comprising about 22 percent of the federal budget, many people concerned about the size of the budget deficit have argued that the **overindexation** of Social Security benefits offers an area where budget outlays could be reduced without lowering the well-being of the retired. Proposals to make just such a change were discussed by Congress in late 1995. The behavior of trade unions faced with inflation implies that this is, indeed, a reasonable suggestion.

parities or differentials. The logic of such comparisons is often open to question since the appropriate comparison is a matter of dispute. Unions will try to make those most favorable to a wage increase, while management will make those least favorable. Once a particular comparison has been accepted as equitable, however, it becomes difficult to change even if underlying economic factors shift. One author has referred to these relationships as **orbits of coercive comparison**.[36]

Despite long-established pay comparisons, conventional wage relationships sometimes do change, even among unionized workers. Traditional

[36] Arthur Ross, *Trade Union Wage Policy*, Berkeley, Calif.: University of California Press (1948).

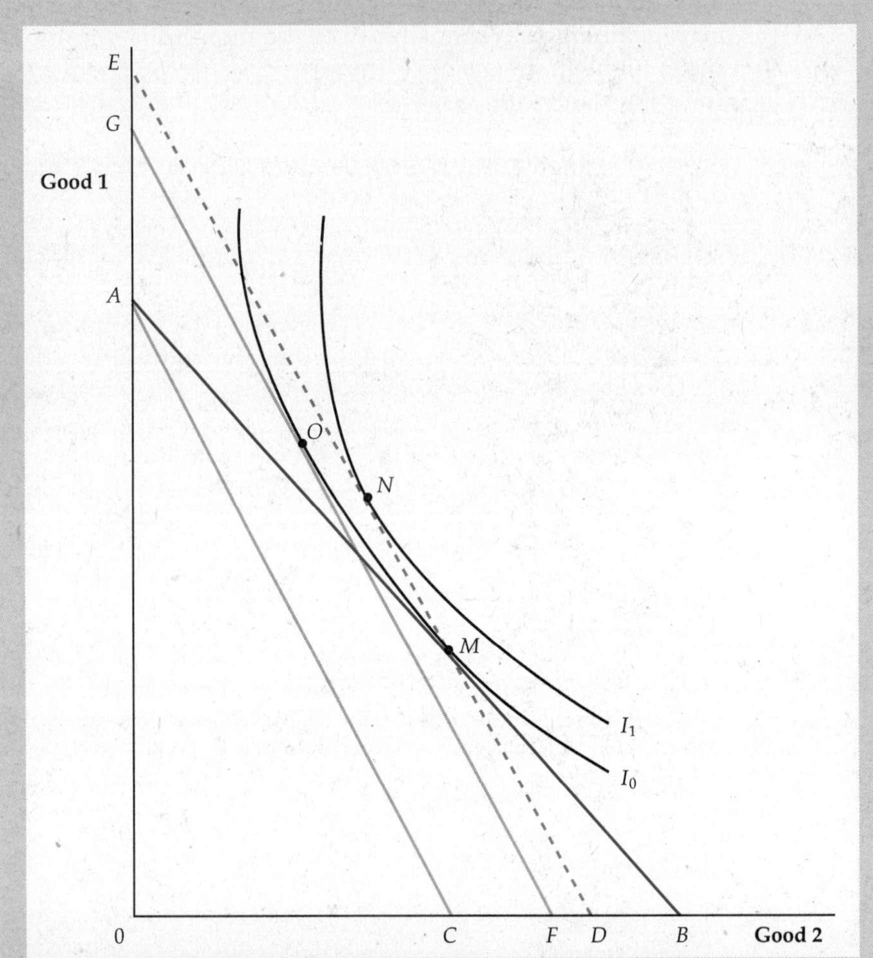

FIGURE 11.7 INDEXATION AND INFLATION
When inflation also involves changing relative prices, the budget line will change slope from *AB* to *AC*. Indexation that provides sufficient income for the consumer/worker to continue to purchase initial bundle *M* by shifting the budget line to *ED* will increase utility since the consumer will substitute toward the relatively less expensive good and consume at point *N*. A smaller increase in wages to budget line *GF* will leave utility unchanged after inflation.

differentials are often established in absolute terms (cents per hour) rather than in percentage terms, because less-skilled workers form the majority in most unions. A given increase in a firm's labor cost will provide larger raises to these workers if it is used to provide each worker the same absolute increase rather than the same percentage increase in wages. Eventually, however, the relative value of the differential is eroded by rises in the general level of money wages until it no longer is sufficient compensation for the extra training or responsibility of the more skilled group. In such cases the more highly paid group may exert pressure to widen the absolute differential. When this situation arises within one union, these efforts may take the form of attempts or threats to form a separate union. The special increases given to skilled craft workers in some general wage settlements in the automobile industry are cases in point.

Demands of a particular group of union workers to achieve parity with a more highly paid group doing comparable work often have special force because worker sentiment is mobilized around a concrete goal rather than simply a demand for "more." The force of such definitions of equity in forming union goals contrasts with the outcome of maximization models in which there is no room for concepts of equity. The successful drive of Canadian automobile workers for wage parity with the American employees of the same companies is an example of one such goal.

In the long run the attention that employers, the public, and other unions give to claims for relative wage increases is influenced strongly by labor market conditions. For example, the claim of unionized teachers that their pay is inadequate to compensate them for their long training was more convincing when there was a shortage of teachers in the 1960s than when there was a surplus in the late 1970s. It has become more convincing again now that the surplus has mostly disappeared.

SUMMARY

Less than one-sixth of American workers are members of trade unions, a sharp drop from a peak of one-third or more between 1945 and 1960. Workers' demand for union jobs depends on the relative costs and benefits of becoming union members. Employers' resistance to unionization depends on the relative costs and benefits of opposing union organizing efforts. The observed level of unionization reflects both workers' desires for union membership and their success in finding union jobs.

Higher unemployment increases the demand for unionization but also increases employers' resistance. Until the 1960s this situation led to union growth when unemployment rose. Unionized workers are more likely to be found in firms in concentrated industries that use a capital-intensive technology in large-scale operations. Nonwhites are more likely than whites to be union members, while women are less likely to be unionized than men.

Political factors, including the actions of governments, are very important determinants of union growth. They help to explain why unionization is far more extensive in the public than in the private sector in the United States, and why public-sector unionization is more widespread in some states than in others. Political factors are also a major reason for the large international differences in rates of unionization and for the growth of unions in some countries while they were simultaneously declining elsewhere. Public-sector unionization also exceeds private-sector levels because employers are not as constrained by market impacts when they increase wages.

Unions pursue a variety of goals, including higher compensation and levels of union membership. No single conception of their goal, such as maximizing the wage bill or achieving the greatest excess of earnings above nonunion workers, characterizes unions' actions very well. There is a good deal of doubt over whether unions and firms negotiate efficient contracts.

Employment goals often involve attempts to prevent employers from reducing the amount of union labor demanded in response to union-imposed wage increases. Featherbedding practices may represent unions' attempts to force employers off their demand curve. Wage goals frequently include protection from nominal wage cuts and inflation, and the maintenance of pay relative to some other group of workers.

QUESTIONS AND PROBLEMS

11.1 Your union must decide where to concentrate its efforts in organizing new workers next year. You could try to organize:

a. A group of Southern high school graduates who work in a service industry.
b. A group of skilled black workers, entry into whose profession is regulated by the government of a Northern state.
c. A group of young female part-time clerical workers.

Given that you face limits on your budget for organizing, and given your desire to have a successful organizing campaign, attach priorities to organizing these three groups and explain why you made the ranking you chose.

11.2 What effect might the following changes have on the growth of unions in the United States?

a. A drop in real wages.
b. An increase in the unemployment rate.
c. A repeal of right-to-work laws.
d. An increase in the inequality of earnings in the work force.

11.3 Suppose that we have the following data about Worldwide Wickets' (WW) wire-pulling plant, which sells wires for $5 per unit. Assume it does not need to worry about the cost of its capital equipment.

Number of Workers	Total Output
1	10
2	19
3	27
4	34
5	40
6	45

7	49
8	52
9	54
10	55

a. What wage will its union set to maximize the wage bill?
b. What wage will its union set to maximize the total rents earned by its members if they can earn $20 per hour in nonunion jobs?
c. What is the range of outcomes over which the union can bargain with WW about both wages and employment, subject to the restriction that the firm not lose money?

11.4 You are a union leader in a plant where your union has signed a contract specifying that no existing members can receive wage increases below inflation in the CPI, but that people hired after the starting date of the contract may. Compared to the situation under standard wage policy, what problems are you likely to face from new employees, senior employees, and management? Answer the question by keeping in mind union wage behavior under the contract range approach to analyzing union goals.

11.5 As Figure 11.3 is drawn, an all-powerful union would still leave some economic profits with the firm. What would this diagram look like in the situation where the union appropriated all of the profits?

11.6 One of the most striking patterns in recent years has been the reversal of the relative success of public- and private-sector unions. What accounts for the differences between these groups of unions in their ability to organize workers and why their historic pattern of relative strength appears to have been reversed in recent years?

11.7 Suppose the U.S. were to adopt a law that served to extend the terms of union contracts to nonunion workers in an industry such as exists in many European countries. What impact would such a law have on the extent of unionization in the U.S.? Is your answer consistent with the relative extent of unionization in economies that have such laws? Explain why or why not.

11.8 Unions in the U.S. typically fall into one of two types: craft or industrial. What type(s) of workers are most likely to form each type of union? How would you predict that unions of these two types would differ in the goals they set in bargaining with employers?

11.9 What do you expect the extent of union membership to be in the U.S. 10 years from now? What about 20 years from now? What factors do you think will give rise to the trends you predict? Do you anticipate the same change in unions' strength in Western Europe? Why or why not?

11.10 Unions in the U.S. have typically been ambivalent about the introduction of government regulations designed to improve working conditions in industry. Why might they feel this way? How, as a union leader, would you respond to a proposed regulation governing the length of time and conditions under which workers may use computer terminals on the job?

KEY WORDS

agency shop
bargaining unit
closed shop
collective bargaining
collective-bargaining coverage
concessionary bargaining
contract curve
cost-of-living adjustments (COLAS)
craft union
Davis-Bacon Act
decertification election
efficient bargaining models
Employment Retirement Income Security Act (ERISA)
escalator clause
extension mechanism
featherbedding
industrial union
insider dominated union
job scarcity hypothesis
jurisdiction
Landrum-Griffin Act of 1959
last-in, first-out rule
median voter
National Labor Relations (Wagner) Act (NLRA) of 1935
National Labor Relations Board (NLRB)
Norris-LaGuardia Act of 1932
orbits of coercive comparison
overindexation
Pareto efficient
perfect agents
product market power
representation elections
restrictive work practice
right-to-manage models
right-to-work legislation
seniority
Taft-Hartley Act of 1947
unfair labor practices
union membership
union shop
wage bill
wage rent maximization
welfare function

12

UNION METHODS: THE BARGAINING PROCESS

THE MAJOR QUESTIONS

- What economic factors affect bargaining over wages and employment levels?
- What determines the relative "bargaining power" of firms and unions?
- How does this balance of bargaining power affect the results of bargaining?
- What determines when a strike occurs?
- How frequent are strikes, and what are their economic impacts on strikers, employers, and the economy as a whole?
- How does the need of union leaders to be reelected affect the bargaining process?
- How does public policy affect the chance of a strike occurring?
- How does public policy, including government attempts to resolve disputes during bargaining, affect the outcome of strikes?

THE SOURCES OF BARGAINING POWER

The power of unions to wrest concessions from employers, including raising compensation above nonunion compensation or forcing employers to use additional union labor, is based almost entirely on the threat of a **strike** involving the concerted withdrawal of labor by all or some union members. Occasionally a **slowdown** or partial strike is used in place of a conventional strike. During a slowdown union members **work to rule** and reduce normal output by strict observance of all regulations, or they refuse to perform certain functions that are normally part of their job, even though they continue to perform others. The purpose of strikes and slowdowns is, of course, to impose costs on employers through lost output, profits, and customers if they do not accede to union demands. A full strike, as distinguished from a slowdown, also involves costs to the union because members do not receive wages. Unions on strike against an employer will attempt to increase the costs imposed on that firm by eliciting support from members of other unions to disrupt the firm's operation.

Alternative sources of union power such as political action, pressure on corporate boards of directors, boycotts, and control of labor supply tend to be much weaker and do not play a major role in determining wages and employment levels. A notable exception to this rule are government unions that win wage gains through influencing Congress, state legislatures, or city councils. Private unions have sometimes attempted to bargain for representation on corporate boards. Such representation was, for example, a part of the government bailout of the Chrysler Corporation in the late 1970s. Union representation on corporate governing boards is much more common in Europe. In Germany (and other countries that follow the German model), policies of **codetermination** require extensive, but minority, representation by workers on management boards. **Consumer boycotts** that attempt to impose costs on firms by denying them sales have generally been weak weapons for unions, although they were used with success by the United Farm Workers in the 1960s and 1970s in organizing California agriculture.

Probably the most powerful way a union can obtain control over wages and employment levels is by determining labor supply either through regulating all opportunities to learn a skill or by requiring that firms hire only workers who are already members of the union. Control of all training opportunities is very rare, if it exists at all. Even where unions have apprenticeship programs, many craft workers learn their skills in nonunion shops. Although closed shops requiring that only union members be hired are illegal, they exist de facto in some industries. Examples include longshoring, construction work, and many theatrical occupations. A common feature shared by these occupations is that workers are employed for short periods on a project-by-project basis. These unions have rigorous requirements for membership and undertake to assure employers regarding members' skills. In such industries, it is apparently less costly for employers to allow the union to control labor supply, with the resulting impact on wages, than it is to recruit and screen applicants themselves. In most cases, however, if unions prevent nonmembers from working for union employers, it is through an implicit threat to strike or impose costs by other means including violence if nonmembers are employed.

On the employer's side there are several possible sources of bargaining power. The strongest is the ability to replace strikers with other workers, called **strikebreakers**, (or, derogatorily, *scabs*) by the unions. This practice was common in the early part of the century but became less so from the 1930s through the 1970s. Slightly more employers have appeared willing to replace striking workers since about 1980. A more usual practice is to continue production operations, perhaps on a limited scale, by using managerial, supervisory, and clerical workers for production jobs. This method has been used by utility companies, petroleum refineries, and retail stores. In industries where sales take place from inventories, firms may be able to continue operation by producing extra output in anticipation of a strike, depleting inventories while the strike lasts, and then rebuilding them after the strike is settled. Where a company cannot carry on operations during a strike, its bargaining power depends largely on its financial resources that determine its ability to survive the losses imposed by the strike. The ultimate threat is that the strike will force the company to move its operations or even shut down permanently. This threat is especially convincing where the employer accounts for a large fraction of local employment, thus leaving few alternative jobs that strikers could obtain.

Just as with firms, different unions have differing abilities to withstand a strike. More skilled workers who have earned higher incomes will have greater savings that allow them to live for a longer period without work. In tight labor markets, striking workers may be able to find alternative temporary employment. A few states allow striking workers to receive unemployment or welfare benefits. Unions that cover workers in many different firms or industries may have a greater ability to sustain members who are on strike through subsidies from other members who are still working. This may explain why the United Automobile Workers, the United Steel Workers of America and the International Association of Machinists and Aerospace Workers, three already large unions, merged into one behemoth with close to two million members in 1995.

Taken together, this discussion implies that the balance of bargaining power varies widely in different bargaining situations. At one extreme, employers dealing with striking construction craft unions can have their jobs closed down for months, all the time continuing to pay enormous interest costs, while the strikers are working at good wages in some other nearby town. In such a case the fragmentation of bargaining units works to the advantage of the union. At the opposite extreme are local telephone companies or electric utilities where management and supervisory personnel can carry on the bulk of normal operations for months while strikers are out of work. Between these extremes lie the more usual cases in which strikes impose significant losses on both parties. This discussion suggests that we should define each side's **bargaining power** as its relative ability to impose costs on the other side.

Much of the focus of this chapter is on strikes, just as much of the focus of history books is on wars and their effects. Yet, like wars, strikes are quite rare. As with nuclear weapons, it is the *threat* of using them that gives both sides an incentive to reach a compromise. Thus, very few collective-bargaining situations lead to strikes. The overwhelming majority are settled peacefully. The first column of Table 12.1 shows the percentage of total work time

TABLE 12.1 INTERNATIONAL COMPARISON OF STRIKE ACTIVITY, 1993

	Percent of Total Work Time Lost[a]	Incidence (Percent of Total Employed)	Mean Duration (Days)
United States	0.014	0.15	21.4
Australia	0.04	6.4	1.3
Canada	0.02	0.73	7.8
France	0.01	0.02	13.9
Germany[b]	0.02	2.0	2.6
Italy[b]	0.05	14.7	0.9
Japan[b]	0.002	0.17	2.1
Mexico	0.09	0.36	58.1
Sweden	0.02	0.74	6.5
United Kingdom[b]	0.01	1.5	1.7

[a]Assumes 235 workdays per year.
[b]1992.
Source: Calculated from International Labour Organization, *Yearbook of Labour Statistics,* (1994), Tables 3 and 31. (Canada excludes strikes involving <500 workers; U.S. excludes <1,000 workers and <0.5 day; Japan excludes <0.5 day; and Australia excludes <10 days.)

lost to strikes and **lock-outs** (employers' closing a plant during a labor dispute in order to increase costs for workers) in 1993. In none of these developed economies was more than one-tenth of one percent of total available work time lost to strikes. In most, the loss was much less than one-twentieth of a percent of the economy-wide labor supply. Even the estimates in Table 12.1 overstate the true time lost since workers may be called on to work overtime to build up or replenish inventories before or after a strike.

THEORIES OF BARGAINING

THE BARGAINING PROBLEM

Economists have long been interested in formulating models of the bargaining process that takes place in union-management negotiations. This task has proven extremely difficult. The factors determining the outcome of collective-bargaining negotiations are so varied and complex that it is exceedingly hard to devise models that are both realistic and manageable.

The difficulty is that important differences exist between collective bargaining and the situations considered in more general bargaining models between two parties. For example, an important aspect of many general bargaining models is that the parties may permanently cease to deal with each other if the outcome is unsatisfactory to one of them. Much of general bargaining theory consists of determining the limits at which parties will break off negotiations altogether. Such a model is only partly relevant to collective bargaining, where the parties are generally forced to deal with each other permanently on some terms. Indeed, "bargaining in good faith" on certain issues is a requirement under the NLRA. Occasionally a small employer will go out of business rather than reach an agreement with a union. Occasionally a union may be broken by a strike, and the employer will operate with nonunion labor, as was the case with the U.S. air traffic controllers in 1981. But the vast majority of negotiations must result, either before or after a strike, in an agreement acceptable to both parties.

Much of general bargaining theory deals with the division between two parties of a fixed stock or a flow of constant size. Such models also are not usually applicable to collective bargaining. One of the most common reactions of employers or industries to wage settlements is to raise the price of the final product, which passes on some of the settlement cost to third parties. Employers may also adjust the level of employment as a result of a settlement. Thus, the terms of the settlement itself influence the size of the revenue flow to be shared. In the terminology of bargaining theory, union-management negotiations may not be a **zero-sum game**, but can instead be a **positive-sum game** or a **negative-sum game**.

Evidence on whether or not union-management bargaining is a zero-sum game is unfortunately fairly sparse. One study examining collective-bargaining agreements from a wide variety of American industries found that each unexpected increase in wages is offset by a loss to the firm's stockholders equal in present-value terms, suggesting workers and firms split a fixed pie (i.e., that this is a zero-sum game).[1]

Most bargaining theory also deals with cases where there are only two parties, whereas in collective bargaining there are almost always more than two. We noted in Chapter 11 that the goals or tactics of union leaders are not always acceptable to the members. Leaders may find themselves bargaining with the employer in one direction and with their own membership in the other. In addition, the public is often an interested party either because a strike might harm users of the product or service produced, or because a generous settlement would lead to price increases. Such effects can bring about government intervention in negotiations that often becomes another active force in determining the outcome.

The kind of bargaining model most easily expressed in precise terms deals with only one outcome. Bargaining between unions and firms, however, occurs simultaneously over wages, employment levels, working conditions, discharge rules, disciplinary procedures, and many other aspects of the employment relationship. Because of this multidimensionality, a concession

---

[1]John Abowd, "Collective Bargaining and the Division of the Value of the Enterprise," *American Economic Review* 79: 774–809 (1989).

in one area, such as working conditions, may be traded for a concession in another, such as wages.

Assuming that the outcome of bargaining in one period does not affect the outcome in the next also helps make a bargaining model manageable. This condition does not hold in collective bargaining. If a union had a long strike in the previous bargaining round, it will regard a strike in the current round as more costly, since its members will not want to go without wages repeatedly. On the other hand, the threat of a strike may not seem credible if strikes never occur. Evidence for the U.S. indicates that strikes are more likely to occur where the previous labor contract has been in force longer and where no strike has occurred in the two most recent rounds of negotiations.[2] A successful strike, by convincing the employer that the union is strong, can produce gains that last beyond one bargaining period. If an employer claims that sales prospects are poor in order to win low wages in one negotiation, the union will have an opportunity to observe whether the employer was telling the truth or not before the next time the contract is renegotiated. Collective bargaining is, therefore, what is known as a **supergame** where strategy and behavior in one bargaining round affect the other side's strategy and behavior in subsequent rounds.

Despite these formidable difficulties, many of the propositions of formal bargaining theory are applicable to union-management negotiations. The focus is once again on cost-benefit analysis. Each party to the bargain compares its probable gain from a strike with the costs it perceives. It is willing to strike (or accept a strike) rather than settle if the present value of the expected gain exceeds the expected cost. Since bargaining always involves an attempt by each party to conceal its true position from the other, however, and thus to create uncertainty, the expected gains and costs cannot be known in advance with any precision. Uncertainty about the potential impacts of alternative settlements is part of every bargaining situation.

Parties to negotiations often cite statistics on wages, profits, and so forth to reduce this uncertainty. For example, employers might present information showing how poor profits have been, and how high wages are when compared to wages in other companies. A union might present figures showing that its members are paid less than employees of other firms doing similar work. The purpose of these figures could be to convince employers that they will not be at a competitive disadvantage if they accept union demands. In most cases, however, their purpose is to show that the union is prepared to strike rather than accept a settlement it considers unfair. By increasing employers' estimates of the probability that it will strike, the union thus increases the amount employers will offer to avoid a strike.

---

[2]Martin Mauro, "Strikes as a Result of Imperfect Information," *Industrial and Labor Relations Review* 35: 522–538 (1982); David Card, "Longitudinal Analysis of Strike Activity," *Journal of Labor Economics* 6: 147–176 (1988); John Schnell and Cynthia Gramm, "Learning by Striking: Estimates of the Teetotaler Effect," *Journal of Labor Economics* 5: 221–241 (1987).

POLICY ISSUE

LANDRUM-GRIFFIN AND UNION MILITANCY

Among its provisions the Labor-Management Reporting and Disclosure Act (Landrum-Griffin Act) required that elections of union officers be held on a regular and not too infrequent schedule (at least every five years for national unions and every three years for local unions). By promoting "union democracy" this legislation may also have a significant impact on the behavior of negotiators and the likelihood of a strike. Union members, who are often not as well informed about the firm's condition as their leaders, may be more militant than the leadership. They may, therefore, press for more extreme negotiating positions than the leadership would have taken. By subjecting union officials to possible defeat at the next election, increased union democracy may encourage them to respond more readily to the members' wishes. This possibility can exaggerate the unusual characteristics of collective negotiations as a bargaining process involving more than two parties.

Greater union democracy appears to increase unions' militancy, as measured by indexes of strike activity. A multivariate regression that accounted for numerous other factors that might affect strike activity found significantly more strikes after 1959, when the Landrum-Griffin Act was passed, than before. The effect seemed to dissipate somewhat in the 1970s but was still present.[3] We may conclude from the evidence on the Landrum-Griffin Act that workers are more militant than their leaders, and their militancy has more impact when internal union politics are more democratic.

TO STRIKE OR NOT TO STRIKE?

The most well-known model of strikes, created by 1972 Nobel laureate Sir John Hicks, is depicted by the solid curves in Figure 12.1.[4] We compress all the issues over which bargaining occurs into the one measure, the wage w.[5] Looking at the course of bargaining as viewed from the start of the strike, curve EE shows the rate at which the employer will concede during the lifetime of the strike. The curve UU shows the union's pattern of concessions. This model predicts that the strike will last exactly S^* weeks until each side has conceded enough to bring the offers and demands into equality.

---

[3]Orley Ashenfelter and George Johnson, "Bargaining Theory, Trade Unions and Industrial Strike Activity," *American Economic Review* 59: 35–49 (1969); Bruce Kaufman, "The Determinants of Strikes in the United States, 1900–1977," *Industrial and Labor Relations Review* 35: 473–490 (1982).

[4]J. R. Hicks, *The Theory of Wages*, 2nd ed., London: Macmillan (1964), Chapter 7.

[5]This is not as unreasonable as it might first seem. As we saw in Chapter 10, workers will pay for many aspects of jobs with reduced wages. In the current analysis, we can simply add these payments back in to compensation and consider the wage in the discussion as "full wage" as defined in Chapter 10.

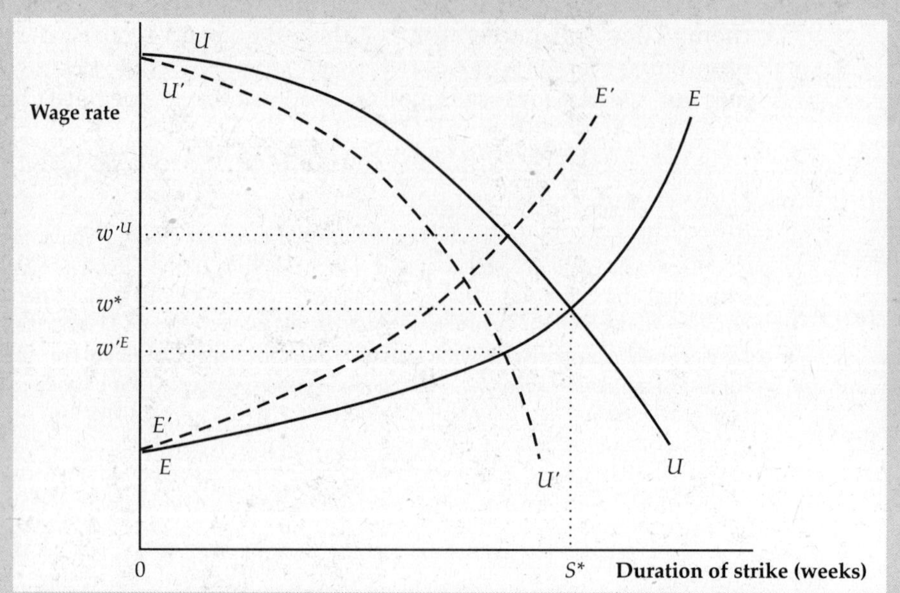

FIGURE 12.1 STRIKE DURATION AND WAGE OUTCOMES WITH AND WITHOUT FULL INFORMATION

When the union concedes along curve U while management increases its offer along E, a strike can be expected to last S^* weeks and result in wage w^*. This outcome is inefficient since the same wage without the strike would make both parties better off. One reason why the efficient outcome may not happen is if one or both sides misperceives the concession schedule of the other party.

The difficulty with this model is that a strike is irrational. If each side knows the other's rate of concession, both would be better off by agreeing to a settlement at w^* without bearing the costs of the strike. Thus, we must seek other reasons why strikes may be in the interest of one or both parties. Several have been proposed.

One reason why strikes may occur is that the two parties misperceive each other's concession schedules, resulting in their not expecting the same settlement or strike duration. Suppose that at the start of the strike the union expects management to concede along the dashed curve $E'E'$ in Figure 12.1 while management expects the union to concede along $U'U'$. The union expects to be able to obtain a settlement at w'^U after a strike shorter than S^*. The management expects to get a settlement at w'^E, also after a shorter strike.[6] The difference in the expected outcomes produces a difference

[6]This exposition is due to Barry Hirsch and John Addison, *The Economic Analysis of Unions*, London: George Allen and Unwin (1986), Chapter 4.

between the two parties' estimates of the probable costs of a strike to each of them. These misperceptions of the other party's costs and the size of the eventual settlement are what cause a strike to occur. Because they are rational, but based on misperceptions, models of this type have come to be known as **optimal accident models**.[7]

Such models predict that a strike is more probable the greater the uncertainty about the other side's resources and behavior, since the parties are more likely to differ in their perceptions of strike costs. Fewer strikes occur in the U.S. among unions and firms that have been bargaining together a long time, presumably because there is less uncertainty in such relationships. Strikes are also less common in industries where settlements typically follow patterns that reduce uncertainty. At U.S. companies in the mid-1970s strikes were more likely when profits were more variable, and hence more uncertain, but were not affected by the level of profits, just as the theory predicts. Both strike probability and duration are greater when the variance in the forecast error of a firm's future sales estimates is greater.[8]

A related set of **asymmetric information models** goes one step further and claims that instead of strikes being merely the result of misperception of the other side's position, they are *required* in order to force the other side to reveal information accurately.[9] These models assume that firms have private information regarding future sales and profit prospects. Unfortunately, firms have an incentive to claim that things look bad even when they do not in order to obtain concessions from the union. In such a world, the optimal response by the union is to make a wage claim that the firm can afford if profits actually will be good, but cannot grant if future profits will be low. Since the firm cannot meet this demand if profits truly will be poor, they will have to take a strike. On the other hand, if profits really will be high a strike will be very costly and the firm will opt to pay the demanded wages. Thus, the firm must accept a strike to provide proof to the union that conditions

---

[7] W. Stanley Siebert and John Addison, "Are Strikes Accidental?" *Economic Journal* 91: 389–404 (1981).

[8] Melvin Reder and George Neumann, "Conflict and Contract: The Case of Strikes," *Journal of Political Economy* 88: 867–886 (1980); Martin Mauro, "Strikes as a Result of Imperfect Information," *Industrial and Labor Relations Review* 35: 522–538 (1982); Joseph Tracy, "An Investigation Into the Determinants of U.S. Strike Activity," *American Economic Review* 76: 423–436 (1986); Joseph Tracy, "An Empirical Test of an Asymmetric Information Model of Strikes," *Journal of Labor Economics* 5: 149–173 (1987); Douglas Herrington, "The Effect of Private Information on Wage Settlements and Strike Activity," Princeton University Industrial Relations Section Working Paper No. 231 (1988); Robert Forsythe, John Kennan, and Barry Sopher, "An Experimental Analysis of Strikes in Bargaining Games with One-Sided Private Information," *American Economic Review* 81: 253–278 (1991).

[9] Beth Hayes, "Unions and Strikes With Asymmetric Information," *Journal of Labor Economics* 2: 57–83 (1984); Oliver Hart, "Bargaining and Strikes," *Quarterly Journal of Economics* 104: 25–43 (1989); John Leach, "Strikes as the Random Enforcement of Asymmetric Information Contracts," *Journal of Labor Economics* 10: 202–218 (1992).

are actually as bad as management has claimed, thereby persuading the union to accept a lower wage.

Since strikes reveal that the state of the world is bad in these models, they lead to a prediction that wages will be lower if a contract is agreed to following a strike than they would have been had agreement been reached without the strike. This prediction is confirmed. Data on bargaining in the U.S. during the 1970s and early 1980s and for Canada from 1964 to 1985 showed that wage increases were smaller where strikes, especially long strikes, occurred.[10]

A final reason why strikes may be rational focuses on the relationship between union leaders and their membership.[11] In these models the asymmetry of information is not between the union leaders and management, who are both fully informed, but between these two parties and the union membership. The membership is more radical in its demands than the firm can afford. The union leadership is faced with the dilemma of how to bring the membership into line with what it is possible to achieve. If they attempt to resolve this situation by persuasion, they will acquire a reputation for being "soft" and the stooges of management. If, on the other hand, they call a strike, they will appear militant to their members. Eventually, the members themselves will have suffered enough from the strike that they become willing to settle for the contract that their leaders knew all along was the best they could obtain. Although the strike imposes costs on both firm and workers, it is rational from the point of view of the union leaders because it preserves their reputation with their members at no cost to themselves.

During a strike two forces tend to bring the positions of the parties closer together. First, the daily costs of a strike to each party are almost certain to increase as the strike continues. Second, if negotiation goes on during the strike, it improves each party's knowledge of the other's true position, thus reducing uncertainty and inaccuracy of information. The combination of rising costs and improved information eventually leads to a settlement.

The costs to a union of a short strike may be very low if the members have previously been working steadily. They can draw on savings for living expenses during the strike and can buy some necessities on credit. Some members may be tired of work and have things they want to do around the house. For example, strikes are very common in the Appalachian coal fields when hunting season opens. As a strike goes on, savings are depleted, creditors become less willing to extend further credit, the union's fund for strike benefits is drawn down, and the most important projects around the home

[10] Sheena McConnell, "Strikes, Wages and Private Information," *American Economic Review* 79: 801–815 (1989); David Card, "Strikes and Wages: A Test of an Asymmetric Information Model," *Quarterly Journal of Economics* 105: 625–660 (1990).

[11] Ashenfelter and Johnson, "Bargaining Theory."

requiring free time have been completed. Thus, the costs of continuing the strike rise in each succeeding week.

The costs of short strikes to employers who produce a commodity rather than a service will be low if they or their customers can build up inventories in anticipation of a strike and draw them down during the strike. Since World War II higher inventories have been associated with longer strikes. Thus, strikes are more common in industries where it is easier to substitute pre- and poststrike production for strike-inhibited output. As the strike lengthens, however, inventories are depleted and sales stop. Customers turn to alternative sources of supply, with the danger that they will not return to their former supplier when the strike is over. Evidence that strikes impose costs on a firm's owners comes from stock prices. In a sample of strikes occurring between 1962 and 1982 the value of shareholders' equity in corporations fell on average 3 percent after a strike began, as compared to identical nonstruck firms during the same periods of time.[12]

Although the costs of a strike to both parties rise with time, there are many cases in which the costs rise faster for the union. This situation will be particularly true where the employer is a large corporation with great financial resources and where the strike involves all the members of a union rather than a small group who can be supported by those still working. The greater staying power of large corporations has led to the generalization that unions tend to win short strikes but management tends to win long ones, and to the recommendation that managements must occasionally accept long strikes to establish matters of principle.[13]

The discussion so far has been about the private and possibly temporary costs of strikes to firms and their employees. Public policy should be concerned not with the private costs, but with the **social cost of a strike** including the lost output resulting from it. This concern led to the inclusion in the Taft-Hartley Act of an 80-day so-called cooling-off period that can be declared by the president to give bargainers more time to reach agreement when a strike that might produce substantial social costs is imminent. Whether this interference in private-sector bargaining is justified depends on the potential size of the social costs that a strike would impose. Social costs are undoubtedly far less than the wages lost by strikers or output not sold by the firm. To the extent that customers find other suppliers, economy-wide production will be reduced by less than the struck firm's lost output. The buildup of inventories before a strike and the replenishing of inventory stocks

---

[12] Melvin Reder and George Neumann "Conflict and Contract;" Brian Becker and Craig Olson, "The Impact of Strikes on Shareholder Equity," *Industrial and Labor Relations Review* 39: 425–438 (1986).

[13] E. Robert Livernash, "The Relation of Power to the Structure and Process of Collective Bargaining," *Journal of Law and Economics* 6: 10–40 (1963).

afterward also reduce the net loss to society. The extra wages received during the inventory buildups before and after a strike and the wages received by employees of the struck firm's competitors both offset part of the lost earnings of the strikers.

Evidence from U.S. manufacturing from 1958 to 1977 showed no significant effect of strikes on output in 38 of 63 industries. In the others, strikes resulted in lost output equal to only 0.2 percent of annual production. Evidence for Canada from 1962 to 1982 showed only one industry where the loss resulting from strikes exceeded 1 percent of potential production. In part, this effect occurs because of the beneficial effects on nonstruck companies in an industry. In U.S. airlines through 1986, nonstruck carriers' profitability was enhanced when competitors were struck. In lumbering in British Columbia through 1984, strikes had only small and temporary effects on production and on prices that might reflect shortages. The evidence makes it clear that the social costs of strikes are not very great.[14]

THE BARGAINING PROCESS AND OUTCOMES

The actual process of bargaining is summarized in Figure 12.2, a diagrammatic representation of the parties' positions during a hypothetical wage negotiation. Wages are measured on the vertical axis, with the wage under the old contract denoted by w_0. Time is measured on the horizontal axis. Unlike Figure 12.1, in which the possibilities for wage outcomes and strike duration were viewed from the start of a strike, Figure 12.2 presents a stylized version of actual occurrences viewed as the process is happening. Negotiations are assumed to begin in week 0, six weeks before the expiration of the previous agreement. The union makes an initial wage demand, D_1. A week later management makes its first counteroffer, O_1.

The initial demands and offers are almost always farther apart than the serious positions of the parties and are intended to stake out the general area within which bargaining will take place. One reason why initial offers are more radical than the parties' true desires arises from the policies of the NLRB as interpreted in a court decision concerning the General Electric Company. For a long time the company followed a pattern of making a well-

[14] George Neumann and Melvin Reder, "Output and Strike Activity in U.S. Manufacturing: How Large Are the Losses?" *Industrial and Labor Relations Review* 37: 197–211 (1984); Dennis Maki, "The Effect of the Cost of Strikes on the Volume of Strike Activity," *Industrial and Labor Relations Review* 39: 552–563 (1986); Morley Gunderson and Angelo Melino, "Estimating Strike Effects in a General Model of Prices and Quantities," *Journal of Labor Economics* 5: 1–19 (1987); Richard DeFusco and Scott Fuess, "The Effects of Airline Strikes on Struck and Nonstruck Carriers," *Industrial and Labor Relations Review* 44: 324–333 (1991); Harry Paarsch, "Work Stoppages and the Theory of the Offset Factor," *Journal of Labor Economics* 8: 387–417 (1990).

POLICY ISSUE

FIRING SCABS

In 1938 the United States Supreme Court ruled (*NLRB v. Mackay Radio & Telegraph Co.*) that employers are allowed to hire permanent replacements for strikers if the company has not been found guilty of unfair labor practices. With the recent increase in the use of replacements in strikes, a major legislative goal of organized labor in the United States has been to require employers to reemploy strikers after a strike ends. Although such proposals were repeatedly defeated in Congress in the late 1980s and early 1990s, in 1995 President Clinton attempted to issued an executive order barring federal contracts to firms hiring permanent replacements for striking workers. This order was immediately challenged by majorities in both houses of Congress as well as in the courts although the first attempt to override it fell victim to a filibuster. It is clear that the issue of permanent replacements for striking workers will remain contentious for some time to come. In the late 1980s U.S. employers used permanent replacements in roughly one-sixth of the (very few) private-sector strikes that occurred.[15] What would be the impact of outlawing this practice on the probability of a strike occurring and on the outcomes of bargaining?

To answer these questions we should first consider when an employer will use replacements. If the strikers have substantial firm-specific skills, permanent replacements are less likely to be hired. Employers will not wish to lose the past investments in whose costs they shared. Even if workers' skills are general, lower unemployment rates among skilled workers means that employers will not have a ready supply of replacement workers. Permanent replacements are, therefore, most likely to be used in relatively unskilled work, at times when unemployment is high, and in those industries that require little specific training.

If replacing strikers were banned, the initial effect might be to increase uncertainty. We saw that any increase in uncertainty raises the probability that a strike will occur, so its passage would increase strike activity. In Québec, where similar legislation has been in effect since 1977, strikes have indeed lasted longer than elsewhere in Canada.[16]

Eventually bargainers would become accustomed to the law, and uncertainty over the other side's behavior would fall. By removing one possible action by management, the law might even reduce uncertainty in the long run. A number of studies have found a positive relationship between the use of replacement workers and the length of strikes. Of course, this association could have arisen either because using replacement workers lowered the cost of the strike to the employer or because only employers who rationally anticipated a long strike found it necessary to employ strikebreakers.[17]

---

[15]General Accounting Office, *Labor-Management Relations: Strikes and the Use of Permanent Strike Replacements*. January 1991.

[16]Morley Gunderson and Angelo Melino, "The Effects of Public Policy on Strike Duration," *Journal of Labor Economics* 8: 295–316 (1990).

[17]Cynthia Gramm, "Empirical Evidence on Political Arguments Relating to Replacement Worker Legislation," *Labor Law Journal* 42: 491–495 (1991); Craig Olson, "The Use of Strike Replacements in Labor Disputes: Evidence from the 1880s to the 1980s," University of Wisconsin-Madison, Photocopy (1991); David Card and Craig Olson, "Bargaining Power, Strike Durations and Wage Outcomes: An Analysis of Strikes in the 1880s," *Journal of Labor Economics* 13: 32–61 (1995); John Schnell and Cynthia Gramm, "The Empirical Relations Between Employers' Striker Replacement Strategies and Strike Duration," *Industrial and Labor Relations Review* 47: 189–206 (1994).

In any case, relative bargaining strengths would certainly be affected. With removal of the threat that their jobs may be permanently lost, the union's cost of striking is reduced. In terms of Figure 12.1 both *UU* and *EE* would shift upward. The outcome would be that the union would achieve more of its goals of higher compensation and employment protection. Although it need not produce any long-term effect on strikes, the legislation will permanently make the outcomes of bargaining more favorable to the union and less favorable to firms and consumers.

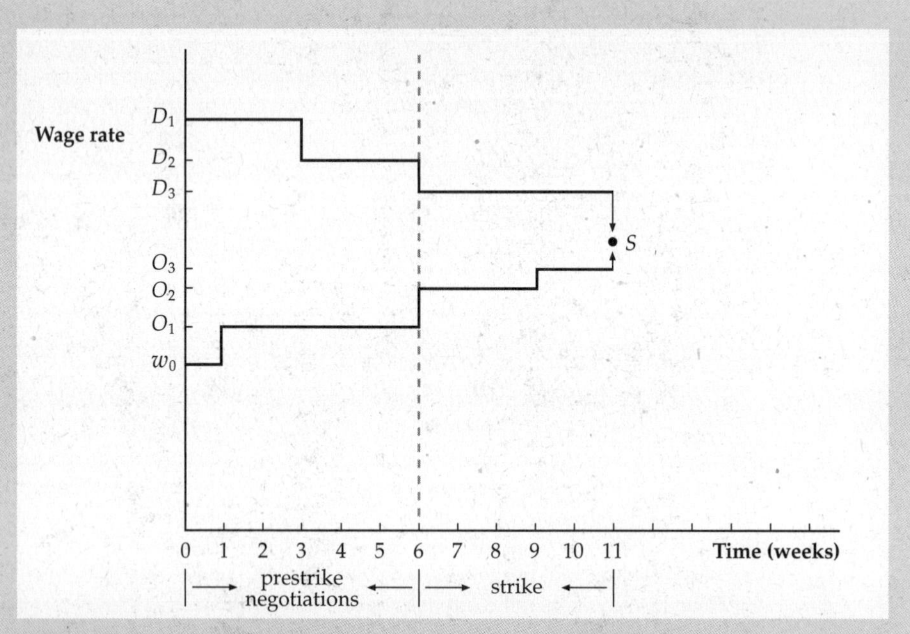

FIGURE 12.2 A DIAGRAMMATIC REPRESENTATION OF WAGE NEGOTIATIONS

Both sides tend to concede near the strike deadline and make major concessions right at the time of settlement.

publicized initial offer representing the most it felt it could afford and refusing to modify it during negotiations, a practice now called **Boulwarism** after the executive who was the company's chief negotiator. This conduct was held by a U.S. Court of Appeals to be a refusal to bargain in good faith, an unfair labor practice under the NLRA. Thus, both unions and management have an incentive to make wild initial demands so that they have room to offer concessions and appear to be bargaining in good faith.

In our hypothetical stylized example, the union reduces its demand to D_2 after two more weeks of negotiation. Nothing happens for three weeks until the night before the contract is due to expire and the strike is scheduled to begin. At that time each side changes its position as it recognizes that the other is serious about accepting a strike and not merely bluffing, and therefore realizes that maintaining its position raises the expected cost of a strike. Management raises its offer to O_2, hoping to avoid losing customers during a strike and attempting to induce the union to lower its wage demand still more. The union lowers its wage demand to D_3, the lowest wage settlement that the leadership believes its membership would accept in the absence of a strike.

Last-minute bargaining is typical of union-management negotiations. Strike votes are often taken, but previously "hard and fast" positions are abandoned immediately before the strike deadline. This type of behavior is quite rational. The party that is more successful in convincing the other side of its willingness to bear the costs of a strike will be more successful in inducing the other side to change its demand or offer. With the strike deadline near, each party, afraid that a strike may be more costly than the potential gains it might produce, abandons its steadfast position and changes its negotiating stance.[18]

Despite the last-minute flurry of bargaining in our example, the sides fail to reach an agreement and a strike begins at the contract expiration date. Actually, in many bargaining situations, the union decides to continue to work under the old contract's terms even after its expiration date. In one recent sample of over 5000 negotiations, no settlement was reached by the expiration of the previous contract 57 percent of the time, but a strike occurred in less than 20 percent of these cases or less than 12 percent of all negotiations. In the remaining negotiations, the union continued to work under the old contract until a settlement was reached, typically about a month after the expiration of the old contract.[19]

To return to our stylized example in Figure 12.2, three weeks after the start of the strike, management improves its offer to O_3. Although the union does not accept this offer, the remaining gap is now narrower. A final compromise is reached in the fifth week of the strike at wage S, somewhat above O_3.

Clearly the number and timing of these moves in the negotiation process varies greatly from one negotiation to another. The positions of the two parties need not converge continuously. For example, management might offer one wage before contract expiration on the condition that it be accepted without a strike. If this offer is not accepted and a strike occurs, the cost of the strike will reduce the firm's ability to pay higher wages and management

---

[18] John Cross, *The Economics of Bargaining*, New York: Basic Books (1969).

[19] Peter Crampton and Joseph Tracy, "Strikes and Holdouts in Wage Bargaining: Theory and Data," *American Economic Review* 82: 100–121 (1992).

might have to reduce its offer. A study of eight bargaining situations in 1966 and 1967 showed that management concedes gradually and steadily throughout the duration of a strike. The management's offer curve, w_0S in Figure 12.2, is much more like a diagonal line between those points than like the step function shown in the figure. The union's demands change little during most of the strike but fall sharply shortly before the strike is over. The line D_1S shown in Figure 12.2 appears to characterize the typical union's negotiating position quite well. The union's rate of concession in a sample of ten bargaining situations between 1954 and 1970 was more rapid when wage-price guidelines were in effect. It was less rapid in firms where the share of labor in the firms' total costs was highest.[20] This latter finding is consistent with the observation that the union has more power in such cases since it is more difficult for management to keep the plant operating.

The evidence is that unions tend to make more exaggerated initial claims than firms. In a study of public-sector negotiations, the average wage gain was 12 percent, but the average initial union demand was 23 percent, and the average initial management offer was 8 percent. A study of bargaining with the Tennessee Valley Authority found that the settlements averaged 6 percent, but initial union demands averaged 12 percent, and initial management offers averaged 3 percent.[21] Management cannot realistically offer a zero-wage increase or a wage cut except in times of severe financial distress when it is faced with the possibility of bankruptcy. This constraint usually puts a floor of zero on its initial offer. The union, on the other hand, has more potential room for bluffing by staking out an exorbitant demand as its initial position. Their tendency to engage in such behavior may be exacerbated if the union leadership feels obligated to bluff in order to retain members' support.

STRIKE ACTIVITY

The impact of strikes on labor force activity can be measured in exactly the same way that we analyzed unemployment in Chapter 8. The overall rate of time lost from work listed in the first column of Table 12.1 is affected both by the **incidence of strikes** (the percentage of workers who strike in a year) and the **duration of strikes** (the average length of a strike). The data provided in Table 12.1 are produced by the relationship:

---

[20] Yochanan Comay, Arie Melnik, and Abraham Subotnik, "Bargaining Yield Curves and Wage Settlements: An Empirical Analysis," *Journal of Political Economy* 82: 303–313 (1974); Henry Farber, "Bargaining Theory, Wage Outcomes, and the Occurrence of Strikes," *American Economic Review* 68: 262–271 (1978).

[21] Daniel Hamermesh, "Who 'Wins' in Wage Bargaining?" *Industrial and Labor Relations Review* 26: 1146–1149 (1973); Roger Bowlby and William Schriver, "Bluffing and the 'Split-the-Difference' Theory of Wage Bargaining," *Industrial and Labor Relations Review* 31: 161–171 (1978).

$$\text{Percent of time lost} = \frac{\text{strikers}}{\text{employment}} \times \frac{\text{strike duration}}{\text{days in work year}} \times 100$$

where the number of work days in a year, typically somewhat less than 240, depends on the number of holidays and vacation days for which the worker is eligible.

LEVELS, TRENDS, AND INTERNATIONAL COMPARISONS

As column 1 of Table 12.1 makes clear, strikes are not a frequent occurrence in collective bargaining. Only tiny fractions of work hours in the United States and elsewhere are lost to industrial disputes. Table 12.2 describes the recent history of strike activity in the U.S. Since 1981, data have been available only on strikes involving at least 1000 workers, so Table 12.2 does not indicate all time lost to strikes. When data were available on all strikes, those involving more than 1000 workers accounted for about two-thirds of total time lost. This fraction may have changed since 1981, but probably not by a great deal. Even in 1959, the year that the greatest fraction of work time was lost to strikes since 1948, only 0.5 percent of workdays were lost. Strikes in any particular year involve only a small fraction of employed workers, as seen in column 2 of Table 12.2. In each year since 1980, fewer than 5 percent of union members took part in a strike or were locked out by their employers. In addition, while some strikes last a very long time, most do not. The average duration is little more than a month.

TABLE 12.2 WORK STOPPAGES INVOLVING 1000 OR MORE WORKERS, SELECTED YEARS, 1948–1993

Year	Percent of Total Work Time Lost	Incidence (Percent of Total Employed)	Median Duration (Days)
1948	0.22	3.0	18.2
1955	0.16	3.9	10.3
1960	0.09	1.5	14.8
1970	0.29	3.2	21.4
1975	0.09	1.2	18.2
1980	0.09	0.8	26.2
1985	0.03	0.3	22.6
1988	0.02	0.1	36.9
1989	0.07	0.4	37.6
1990	0.02	0.2	32.1
1993	0.01	0.02	21.8

Sources: *Monthly Labor Review*, (June 1983), Table 37; (June 1986), Table 29; (June 1990), Table 30; (June 1991), Table 30; (June 1994), Table 30.

The most noticeable trend in the strike data in Table 12.2 is the sharp decline in incidence. This change more than offset the increase in the average duration of strikes, resulting in a decrease in the percentage of total work time lost. The decline in the extent of unionism (shown in Table 11.5) explains only a small part of the drop in strike activity. While the incidence of unionism is only half what it was at its peak, the incidence of strikes is less than *one-tenth* of its postwar high. Union-management relations have become increasingly peaceful in the postwar period, a trend that began in the 1960s but has accelerated since then.

Where relations are not peaceful, the extent of conflict has actually increased in recent years, as seen in the increasing average duration of strikes. The data on duration listed in the table do not tell the whole story, since the distribution of strike duration is highly skewed. Between 1968 and 1976, 13 percent of strikes in U.S. manufacturing lasted at least 100 days, but 23 percent lasted less than 10 days. Between 1970 and 1989 the mean duration of strikes was 43 days, as opposed to a median duration of 27 days.[22] The large fraction of the strikes that are very short impose little hardship on either party. They can be viewed more appropriately as extensions of the last-minute bargaining that precedes the strike deadline than as the kind of strike designed to impose real costs on the firm.

Table 12.1 shows a truly remarkable diversity in the incidence and duration of strikes among industrialized countries. In some countries such as Italy, a large fraction of the work force is involved in strikes each year. In Italy unionization is very widespread and the communist party has been relatively powerful. Italian strikes are often prescheduled, short-term expressions of general political unrest rather than attempts to influence collective-bargaining outcomes. Comparing the second and third columns of Table 12.1 where the incidence of strike activity is relatively high, as in Australia, Italy, and the United Kingdom, the average duration of strikes is typically relatively short. By contrast, although only a relatively small fraction of the work force is involved in strikes in the U.S., the percent of work time lost is relatively high. Although strikes are relatively uncommon in the U.S., they last a relatively long time when compared to Japan and most of Europe. In these countries strikes are more often demonstrations of political unity than serious attempts to impose costs on firms. In Japan, strikes have assumed the role of a ritual demonstration during the annual "Spring Wage Offensive" when most contracts are negotiated and may last only a few hours.

CYCLICAL AND INDUSTRIAL DIFFERENCES

The fraction of the work force involved in strikes is higher when unemployment is lower. This result generalizes to many industrialized countries,

[22] John Kennan, "The Duration of Contract Strikes in U.S. Manufacturing," *Journal of Econometrics* 28: 5–28 (1985); Crampton and Tracy, "Strikes and Holdouts."

including the United States, Canada, Australia, and the United Kingdom.[23] Cyclical variation in time lost to strikes is composed of two, partly offsetting, relationships. Strike duration increases when unemployment is higher, but the incidence of strikes is sufficiently less in bad times so that the overall impact of higher unemployment is to reduce total time lost.[24]

How can these facts be explained? Arguing that unions' bargaining power increases during economic booms can explain changes in the outcomes of bargaining, but cannot explain whether a strike occurs and how long it lasts. Asymmetric information models suggest that strikes occur when unions need to force management to prove its claim that profit prospects are poor. In times of overall recession, the union may be more likely to believe this claim even without a strike. In addition, workers' attitudes toward risk can explain why strikes are more common when unemployment is low. In bad times workers may be aware of how poor their alternative opportunities are. They will, therefore, concede to management quickly rather than bear the risk of being out of work. This behavior reduces the incidence of strikes in recessions. Should the unusual event of a strike occur during a recession, it indicates so much animosity and divergence between the parties' perceptions that it takes longer to resolve than the more common strikes during better times.

Cyclical indicators other than the aggregate unemployment rate are also correlated with strike activity. Increases in the unemployment rate in the labor market where a plant is located reduce the likelihood of a strike. This effect is to be expected, since when the local labor market is slack workers are especially aware that they have few alternative opportunities. If the product market in which the firm sells is loose, the likelihood of a strike increases.[25] The union (or its members) has less information about the firm's problems than management. Without this information union demands are much higher than management is willing to offer, leading to a greater chance of a strike occurring. In terms of Figure 12.1, curve $E'E'$ lies well above curve EE. $U'U'$ may lie somewhat closer to UU since firms seem to misperceive the unions' position less than vice versa.

---

[23]For the United States see Albert Rees, "Industrial Conflict and Business Fluctuations," *Journal of Political Economy* 60: 371–382 (1952); Ashenfelter and Johnson, "Bargaining Theory," and Kaufman, "The Determinants." The foreign studies are Morley Gunderson, John Kervin, and Frank Reid, "Logit Estimates of Strike Incidence from Canadian Contract Data," *Journal of Labor Economics* 4: 257–276 (1986); John Pencavel, "An Investigation into Industrial Strike Activity in Britain," *Economica* 37: 239–256 (1970), and Philip Bentley and Barry Hughes, "Cyclical Influence on Strike Activity: The Australian Record, 1952–1968," *Australian Economic Papers* 9: 149–170 (1970).

[24]Susan Vroman, "A Longitudinal Analysis of Strike Activity in U.S. Manufacturing, 1957–1984," *American Economic Review* 79: 816–826 (1989); Alan Harrison and Mark Stewart, "Cyclical Fluctuations in Strike Durations," *American Economic Review* 79: 827–841 (1989).

[25]Joseph Tracy, "An Investigation into the Determinants of Strike Activity," *American Economic Review* 76: 423–436 (1986); Sheena McConnell, "Cyclical Fluctuations in Strike Activity," *Industrial and Labor Relations Review* 44: 130–143 (1990).

The pressure placed by union members on their leadership may also reflect the members' satisfaction with gains they have made in prior negotiations. If real wages are rising rapidly (perhaps because of productivity increases), the leadership will feel less obliged to press for an even larger wage increase. This pattern explains the greater strike activity, other things being equal, in the U.S. and the U.K. when real wages were rising less rapidly. Strikes are positively correlated with changes in price levels, and much of the variation in strikes over time can be explained by variation in the rate of inflation. When prices are stable, members are not likely to pressure their leadership for large increases as strongly as they might if inflation has eroded the purchasing power of previous wage increases. Evidence shows that when workers expect greater real wage increases in the future, they are less likely to strike. The same results have been found for Canada.[26]

The effect of inflation on strike activity can also be understood by analyzing the effects of uncertainty on each side's offers during bargaining. Anything that reduces uncertainty reduces the likelihood of a strike, implying that anticipated inflation will not increase conflict but unanticipated inflation will. This is exactly what occurs. In the postwar U.S. only unanticipated inflation has made strikes more likely. Where workers were protected from unexpected inflation by COLAs, even unexpected inflation did not increase the probability of a strike.[27]

Periods of wage controls or guidelines, such as those in effect in the United States from 1962 to 1966 and 1971 to 1974, reduce the range of possible wage outcomes over which unions and management can bargain. This reduction lowers the potential for differences in perceptions of strike costs to the other party. With less to discuss, there is less on which to disagree. With the government suggesting an acceptable wage increase, the possibilities for bluffing are reduced. The evidence suggests that the wage guidelines of 1962 to 1966 reduced strike activity, as did the various programs of wage controls in effect between 1971 and 1974. Wage controls in effect in Canada during the 1970s had a similar impact.[28] Of course, wage controls create a number of serious distortions in the economy, a subject to which we will return in Chapter 16.

---

[26] Ashenfelter and Johnson, "Bargaining Theory;" Bruce Kaufman, "Bargaining Theory, Inflation and Cyclical Strike Activity in Manufacturing," *Industrial and Labor Relations Review* 34: 333–355 (1981); Pencavel, "An Investigation;" William Moore and Douglas Pearce, "A Comparative Analysis of Strike Models During Periods of Rapid Inflation," *Journal of Labor Research* 3: 39–53 (1982). The evidence for Canada is from Gunderson, "Logit Estimates."

[27] Susan Vroman, "A Longitudinal"; Wallace Hendricks and Lawrence Kahn, *Wage Indexation in the United States*, Cambridge, Mass.: Ballinger (1985), Chapter 8.

[28] Ashenfelter and Johnson, "Bargaining Theory;" David Lipsky and Henry Farber, "The Composition of Strike Activity in the Construction Industry," *Industrial and Labor Relations Review* 29: 388–404 (1976); Jean-Michel Cousineau and Robert Lacroix, "Imperfect Information and Strikes: An Analysis of Canadian Experience, 1967–1982," *Industrial and Labor Relations Review* 39: 377–387 (1986).

TABLE 12.3 PERCENTAGE OF WORK TIME LOST BY INDUSTRY, EARLY 1990S, SELECTED COUNTRIES

Industry	United States 1989–1993	Australia 1989–1993	Canada 1989–1993	France 1989–1993
Manufacturing	0.03	0.18	0.10	0.03
Mining	0.37	0.74	0.38	0.06
Construction	0.01	0.05	0.18	0.006
Transportation, storage, and communications	0.26	0.07	1.04	0.02
Trade, restaurants, and hotels	0.004	0.005	0.01	0.002
Community, social and personal service	0.003	0.06	0.07	0.002
Total	0.03	0.06	0.06	0.01

Sources: See Table 12.1 (also see exclusions).

Great diversity in strike behavior exists among industries, even after accounting for differences in the extent of unionization. As the data in Table 12.3 show, certain industries are consistently more strike-prone than others, even under broadly different systems of collective bargaining. The amount of time lost to strikes is greater in mining and transportation than in other industries, while government and services lose below-average percentages of total work time to strikes.

Where an industry is heavily unionized and, especially, where there are substantial investments in firm-specific skills, there is little chance that customers can find nonunion substitutes or that employers can readily substitute new employees for strikers. In other industries, such as services, finance, and wholesale and retail trade, nonunion substitutes are more readily available for union-provided services and products whose flow is interrupted by a strike. Also, new workers can be trained fairly quickly because there is little firm-specific investment.

The only exception to these generalizations is government, which in the U.S. is the most heavily unionized industry and yet exhibits little strike activity. There are several probable reasons for the comparative absence of strikes in the public sector. In many jurisdictions laws prohibit strikes by government workers and provide alternative mechanisms of dispute resolution. The public nature of government budgets prevents substantial asymmetry of information between the expectations of management and the union. Finally, as we saw in the previous chapter, a number of factors make government officials less likely to resist union demands than private-sector managers who have to answer to stockholders.

The data in Table 12.3 show that where unions' relative bargaining power is greater, work time lost to strikes is also greater. Why greater union power should induce more strikes, rather than simply resulting in employment, wage, and other outcomes more favorable to the union, is not clear. Perhaps unions with more power have already extracted more from firms in previous negotiations, thereby increasing the likelihood that any given demand now would force the firm into the region of negative profits where it has no option but to resist the union's demand.

THIRD-PARTY INTERVENTION IN NEGOTIATIONS

We have been assuming that strikes end because of rising costs to one or both of the parties. In some cases, however, the public or other third parties believe that the social costs are much greater than those paid by the parties involved in the labor dispute. This is particularly true when the output of the struck enterprise or industry is a service or a perishable product. A strike against automobile producers could go on for months without seriously inconveniencing people, who hold a large stock of usable cars. On the other hand, strikes of trash collectors have immediate effects on the public. There is no way of using inventories to buffer the impact. Extra collections this week in anticipation of a strike will do consumers no good when the strike actually occurs. When the actual or potential costs of a strike to third parties are very high, government or other neutral intervention in the dispute usually occurs. Three kinds of neutral intervention are common. In increasing order of forcefulness these are **mediation** (or conciliation), **fact-finding**, and **binding arbitration.**

The role of a mediator in a wage negotiation is to try to discover through private talks with each party a position that is acceptable to both but that they have been unwilling to reveal to each other. Essentially the mediator reduces bluffing and uncertainty in the negotiations by giving each side a better understanding of the other's position. Since we saw earlier that imperfect information about the other party's strike costs can produce strikes, mediation can reduce the chance of a strike occurring or shorten an ongoing strike. Another important function of a mediator is to help talks resume when they have broken off. Mediation in labor disputes is routinely provided by the federal government (through the **Federal Mediation and Conciliation Service**) and many state governments at no cost to the parties.

Bargainers who cannot reach a settlement through negotiation even with the aid of a mediator may resort to neutral fact-finding. A fact-finder's job is to issue a public report detailing the conditions surrounding the dispute and suggesting an appropriate settlement. This step is included in the laws of a number of states regulating collective negotiations for public employees. In general, the weaker party in a dispute may be anxious to have third-party intervention such as fact-finding in the hope that the recommendations will bolster its cause. The stronger party, on the other hand, may resist intervention as long as possible. Attitudes of the parties toward intervention may also

POLICY ISSUE

PAYING UNEMPLOYMENT BENEFITS TO STRIKERS

Nowhere in the U.S. does legislation allow strikers to automatically receive unemployment benefits immediately after a strike or work stoppage begins. In New York, however, strikers become eligible for benefits after a strike has lasted eight weeks. In several other states, workers can obtain benefits after having held short-term interim jobs. The payment of benefits incenses employers, who view themselves as subsidizing their bargaining opponent (because their payroll taxes finance these benefits). Union leaders, on the other hand, argue that after eight weeks the issue should be viewed as the lack of job availability for workers who desire employment, so strikers should be treated like other unemployed workers. They also argue that workers should receive immediate payments if the work stoppage results from an employer locking workers out.

The interesting economic question is what effect do these benefit payments during work stoppages have on the likelihood of a dispute being settled, and hence on the frequency and average duration of strikes? Taking the example of the New York law, once the ninth week of a strike begins, the costs of continuing it are reduced and the willingness of the union membership to accept a settlement should decrease. The provision of unemployment benefits changes relative bargaining power in the union's favor. Whether it prolongs strikes depends on whether the bargainers perceive this change correctly. If they do, it will make the settlement more favorable to the union, but the likelihood of settling may be unaffected. If not, the law will retard the rate at which an agreement is reached.

Comparing strike duration between New York and the rest of the U.S., one study found that strikes in New York that had already lasted eight weeks had a much lower probability of being settled each week thereafter than strikes elsewhere. This finding implies that the payment of benefits increased the length of long-duration strikes. On the other hand, fewer strikes in New York than elsewhere lasted eight weeks or more. On average, no more days were lost to strikes in New York than in the rest of the U.S., although the social cost of strikes was probably higher because the proportion of long-duration strikes was greater. In states where the state employment agency rules whether strikers or employees of related firms that lose business during strikes can collect benefits, a more generous system of benefits produces more strikes.[29]

Where both parties know what unemployment benefits will be paid, there may be little impact on time lost to strikes. Information about the laws is symmetric and widely available, so this result is not surprising. Where there is uncertainty about whether benefits will be available, as in states that provide benefits to strikers or workers affected by strikes on an ad hoc basis, strikes are more likely. This effect is presumably the result of greater uncertainty about the relative strength of the bargaining parties.

---

[29]John Kennan, "The Effect of Unemployment Insurance Payments on Strike Duration," in National Commission on Unemployment Compensation, *Unemployment Compensation: Studies and Research*, Washington, D.C.: NCUC, (1981); Robert Hutchens, David Lipsky, and Robert Stern, *Strikers and Subsidies*, Kalamazoo, Mich.: The W. E. Upjohn Institute (1989).

depend on how the fact-finder is chosen. Unions are more likely to favor fact-finding if a mayor or governor who is elected with union support is to choose the fact-finder than if the fact-finder is to be truly impartial. Both parties may sometimes be willing to accept fact-finders' awards because they do not have to take responsibility for them. The union leader, for example, can tell members that a fact-finder's award is too small but that a strike against accepting the award would not be successful.

Even when fact-finders' recommendations are not accepted, they often form a basis for awards made under binding arbitration, in which the parties agree in advance that the arbitrator's decision will be adopted.[30] Unions and firms rarely agree to this procedure because it involves giving up their freedom of action. In some public-sector bargaining situations where the social cost of a strike is high (such as police and fire protection), however, binding arbitration is required by law to resolve disputes.

In the private sector, the most famous example of binding arbitration came in a series of contracts negotiated between the United Steel Workers and major steel companies in the late 1960s and early 1970s. Relations between firms and the union had become so rancorous that almost every contract negotiation ended in a strike. During each strike sales were lost to foreign competitors, imposing costs on both the union and the firm. In order to increase their incentives to settle, both parties signed an **Experimental Negotiating Agreement (ENA),** which provided that if no agreement were reached by the end of the contract, both parties were required to accept binding arbitration to determine the terms of the next contract. The result was to increase the costs of not reaching a settlement for both sides, since both the union and firm were afraid of giving up control to an arbitrator. Subsequent negotiations were, therefore, settled without a strike or resort to the arbitration process.

The effects of third-party procedures on outcomes such as wage increases and the incidence of strikes are unclear. The problem in all third-party procedures, but especially in arbitration, is to maintain the incentives for both sides to make concessions during negotiations, rather than to remain intransigent and hope the arbitrator will split the difference between them. The arbitrator must rely on the informational signals conveyed by the negotiators, and therefore, is someone who may be bluffed into allowing a settlement more favorable to one party in the dispute. This is also possible, of course, in fact-finding. Regular recourse to emergency fact-finding boards in wage disputes under the Railway Labor Act has resulted in the parties making few concessions in negotiations, and the process of collective bargaining almost being destroyed. This "narcotic effect" of third-party intervention has also been noted in negotiations by police and firefighters' unions. Its exis-

---

[30] Daniel Gallagher and M. D. Chaubey, "Impasse Behavior and Tri-Offer Arbitration in Iowa," *Industrial Relations* 21: 129–148 (1982).

tence suggests that when arbitration is possible, bargaining demands are less likely to reflect the underlying profit and utility-maximizing positions of the parties. This view is supported by evidence from Canada showing that wage settlements were less responsive to labor market conditions in negotiations that involved third-party procedures.[31]

Final-offer arbitration (FOA) is one way of restoring incentives for negotiators to make concessions.[32] This ingenious scheme requires the arbitrator to choose one or the other of the two sides' final positions. In effect, the incentive is now for each side to compete to be a bit more reasonable than their opponent. By preventing the arbitrator from splitting the difference between final offers, this scheme induces negotiators to reduce bluffing and reach agreement more quickly, and more often, on their own. FOA has been used in state statutes governing dispute settlement, particularly in negotiations involving police and fire protection and in professional sports.

In a sample of salary awards to baseball players, FOA led to a significantly higher variance of salaries than negotiated settlements, while in a sample of teachers in British Columbia conventional arbitration produced a lower variance of wages than negotiated settlements. This effect is exactly what would be expected, since FOA awards must take one or the other value at the time of impasse while conventional arbitrators tend to "split-the-difference."[33]

The questions of interest are whether this scheme consistently favors one side or the other, and whether it reduces conflict and results in quicker settlements. The answer to the first question is that it depends on the situation. Consider the data in Table 12.4 describing initial offers by both sides, the results of conventional arbitration in similar cases, and the results of FOA. In New Jersey in 1978 to 1980 the employer won only one-third of FOA awards. Union demands were much closer to conventional arbitration awards in similar cases, and their reasonableness appealed to FOA arbitrators. Compared to their behavior under conventional arbitration in which the arbitrator can pick any settlement, FOA induced greater moderation by unions than by

---

[31] Thomas Kochan and Jean Baderschneider, "Dependence on Impasse Procedures: Police and Firefighters in New York State," *Industrial and Labor Relations Review* 31: 431–439 (1978); Richard Butler and Ronald Ehrenberg, "Estimating the Narcotic Effect of Public Sector Impasse Procedures," *Industrial and Labor Relations Review* 35: 3–20 (1981); Douglas Auld, Louis Christofides, Robert Swidinsky, and David Wilton, "The Effect of Settlement Stage on Negotiated Wage Settlements in Canada," *Industrial and Labor Relations Review* 34: 234–244 (1981).

[32] Carl Stevens, "Is Compulsory Arbitration Compatible with Bargaining?" *Industrial Relations* 5: 38–52 (1966).

[33] Paul Burgess and Daniel Marburger, "Do Negotiated and Arbitrated Salaries Differ Under Final Offer Arbitration?" *Industrial and Labor Relations Review* 46: 548–559 (1993); Janet Currie, "Arbitrator Behavior and the Variances of Arbitrated and Negotiated Wage Settlements," *Journal of Labor Economics* 12: 29–40 (1994).

TABLE 12.4 CONVENTIONAL AND FINAL-OFFER ARBITRATION, NEW JERSEY AND IOWA

	New Jersey 1978–1980	Iowa 1976–1983
Union offer	7.99	7.54
Conventional arbitration award	7.80	5.96
Employer offer	5.74	4.89
Employer wins (percent of cases)	31.30	65.50

Source: Orley Ashenfelter, "Arbitrator Behavior," American Economic Association, *Proceedings* 77: 342–346 (1987).

management. In the second column of Table 12.4 the same information is provided for Iowa, where union offers far exceeded conventional arbitration awards, which were in turn much closer to managements' final offers. As a result, arbitrators sided with management's final offer two-thirds of the time. Taken together, the results in Table 12.4 imply that the side that is most reasonable wins under FOA.

On the second question, substantial evidence demonstrates that the existence of FOA leads to more negotiated settlements than conventional arbitration.[34] This finding is consistent with the evidence in Table 12.4. An awareness that the more moderate party is favored by arbitrators leads to more moderate behavior during bargaining and a greater chance that arbitration will not have to be invoked.

GOVERNMENT AS A SOURCE OF UNION POWER

The discussion so far has ignored the effects government can have on the bargaining power of the negotiating parties. We saw in Chapter 11 how political attitudes have affected the growth of unionization. Presumably they can also affect union power and the outcome of the bargaining process. In this section we first examine how different types of legislation regulating collective bargaining in the public sector affect outcomes. We then discuss ways in which private-sector unions try to obtain government interference to enhance their bargaining power.

[34]Henry Farber and Max Bazerman, "Divergent Expectations as a Cause of Disagreement in Bargaining: Evidence from a Comparison of Arbitration Schemes," *Quarterly Journal of Economics* 104: 99–120 (1989).

Until the 1960s, bargaining in government employment in the U.S. was rather different from bargaining in the private sector, because government employees were often not permitted to organize and were never legally permitted to strike. The main bargaining power of government employees was exerted through political processes by lobbying and efforts on behalf of candidates favorable to their positions. This is still the general situation for the federal government, although there have been a few strikes and slowdowns on the part of postal employees and air traffic controllers. In many states and localities, however, workers may now unionize. Strikes are increasingly common despite being illegal in all but a few states.

The rarity of strikes in public employment in North America makes it difficult to draw very many firm conclusions about how different kinds of legislation affect the outcomes of bargaining and whether a strike occurs. Comparing jurisdictions that outlaw strikes but require bargaining and those that have no legislation regulating public-sector unionism, there were no differences in wage settlements in the 1970s and 1980s. The absence of legislation (essentially a prohibition on formal bargaining) may, however, have led to more strikes, a situation that was not true during the same period in Canada, where provincial differences in regulatory legislation had no effect on the likelihood of strikes.[35]

Unions in the private sector are also heavily and increasingly involved in pressuring government. Until the 1920s the American trade union movement practiced a philosophy of **voluntarism**, shunning aid from government in the belief that on balance legislation would be detrimental to their interests. It was felt that benefits should be available only to unionized workers who won them through negotiations rather than provided to all workers by government policy. With the increased role of the government in the U.S. economy, this philosophy has long since been abandoned, and unions engage in lobbying and support of political candidates through contributions of money and volunteer time by union members. In the U.S. biennium of 1991 to 1992, union political action committees donated more than $41 million to political candidates, not including the donations made by individual members. Although a large amount, this was only about two-thirds of what corporations provided. Unions' more important contribution was the volunteer efforts of their members, who are 25 percent more likely than nonunion workers to have actively worked in an election campaign.[36] Candidates judged to support prounion

---

[35] Janet Currie and Sheena McConnell, "Collective Bargaining in the Public Sector: The Effect of Legal Structure on Dispute Costs and Wages," *American Economic Review* 81: 693–718 (1991).

[36] John Delaney and Susan Schwochau, "Employee Representation Through the Political Process," in Bruce Kaufman and Morris Kleiner (eds.). *Employee Representation: Alternatives and Future Directions*, Madison, Wisc.: Industrial Relations Research Association (1993).

POLICY ISSUE

STRIKES IN THE PUBLIC SECTOR

Although many states now allow public-sector workers to unionize, prohibition of strikes by public-sector workers is still common. The reasoning behind this prohibition has to do with the balance of bargaining power. In the private sector the union's ultimate weapon, the strike, is balanced by the firm's ultimate threat, to either relocate production or shut down entirely. The public-sector employer does not have this option. The city of Philadelphia cannot credibly threaten to abandon police protection if the police union demands wages that are too high. Neither can the Philadelphia school board threaten to relocate education to Mississippi where wages are lower. Since the public sector does not have its ultimate weapon of stopping production, allowing the union to retain the ability to strike could create an unfair imbalance of power.

Despite their illegality, strikes have become increasingly common among public-sector workers. Why has this happened and what might be done to prevent their occurrence? It is obvious that the fines and jail terms provided by the current law are ineffective. The reason lies in the structure of American government. A strike by public-sector employees creates severe disruption of life. Indeed, this is why such strikes are typically illegal. A mayor or governor facing a strike is under intense pressure from citizens to settle and reopen the schools or resume police protection or garbage collection rapidly. Given this pressure they have little ability to resist union demands.

Under the American principle of separation of powers, courts can enforce laws only if the executive branch (the mayor or governor as represented by the local prosecutor's office) brings a lawsuit. When a public-sector union goes on strike, it typically adds immunity from prosecution for the strike to its other demands. The public official who is under pressure to settle the strike has the power to grant this request and order that the violation of the law not be prosecuted. Without prosecution, there is no way that the law can be enforced, and it becomes impotent.

For this reason, a number of experts have called for amending state labor laws governing public-sector labor relations. These amendments might take one of two forms. They could give private citizens legal standing to sue unions and their leaders for damages caused by illegal strikes. Thus, the victim of a mugging or rape during a police strike could sue the union for her pain and suffering. Another option would be to give the court itself the ability to appoint special prosecutors to enforce the law, as is done in the federal government when conflicts of interest might prevent high officials from prosecuting themselves.

positions are helped in the hope that they will, if elected, oppose legislation that the union opposes and be more amenable to prounion legislation. Union political activity often consists of efforts to push legislation restricting competition from low-wage, nonunion labor or from imports. Research shows that donations by unions do influence votes in Congress on legislation of interest to the AFL-CIO, independent of representatives' other characteristics. At the state level, more heavily unionized states are more likely to have a state minimum wage law that requires wages in excess of the federal law.[37]

As we saw in the previous chapter, the increasing role of government may be one reason for the decline in union membership in recent decades. Thus, there may have been a good deal of wisdom in the policy of the early leaders of the American trade union movement. Outside the U.S., the link between unions and the political process is much more formal. While American unions have always had a policy of voting to "reward labor's friends and punish its enemies" regardless of party, unions in other countries often form permanent attachments to specific political parties. Thus, it is frequently impossible to distinguish between the British trade-union movement and the Labor party. In Italy there are three major national union federations, one linked with the former Communist Party, one with the Socialist Party, and one with the Catholic church (and the Christian Democratic Party). In France there are five national union federations, some associated with political parties and some resolutely not. Germany, on the other hand, has only one national federation that maintains political neutrality.

SUMMARY

Union-management bargaining is best understood as a continuing relationship involving at least the two immediate parties. In many situations, our understanding can be improved by also considering the conflicting goals of union leaders and union members, as well as the interests of the government. The greater the union's ability to inflict damage on a firm by reducing profits, the greater its power. The easier it is for management to operate during a strike or reduce the alternative income of union members, the greater will be the likelihood management can achieve its goals during bargaining. Although the relative strengths of the parties determine the level of compensation compared to similar nonunion situations, they do not determine the path of negotiations nor whether disputes will be settled peacefully. Resolution depends on each side's reactions to the other's demands, and, in general, on the ability of each to discern correctly what the other side is really seeking when it makes its demands.

Despite the attention focused on strikes, they are extremely rare in industrialized countries. In the U.S., fewer than 5 percent of unionized workers go out on strike each year, and less than 0.1 percent of available work time in

[37] Gregory Saltzman, "Congressional Voting on Labor Issues: The Role of PACs," *Industrial and Labor Relations Review* 40: 163–179 (1987); Allen Wilhite and John Theilmann, "Labor PAC Contributions and Labor Legislation: A Simultaneous Logit Approach," *Public Choice* 53: 267–276 (1987); James Cox and Ronald Oaxaca, "The Political Economy of Minimum Wage Legislation," *Economic Inquiry* 20: 533–555 (1982).

the economy is lost to strikes. In other industrialized economies strikes account for similarly small percentages of potential work time. The cost of strikes to society is far less than the loss in wages or output in the struck firm, both because other companies can pick up the slack, and because the struck company's output often adjusts before and after a strike.

A variety of laws seek to reduce the number of strikes in the private sector. Other laws regulate public-sector bargaining, including requirements for third-party procedures such as mediation and various types of compulsory arbitration. Still other policies, including wage controls and unemployment benefits, affect the outcomes of bargaining and whether strikes occur. A general conclusion is that these policies reduce the likelihood of a strike if they reduce one side's uncertainty about the other's position. They change the outcomes of collective negotiations when they change the relative bargaining strength of the parties.

QUESTIONS AND PROBLEMS

12.1 Would strikes be more likely where a collective-bargaining agreement is in place between a weak union and a strong management whose workers were just recently unionized, or where workers have been unionized for a long time and are dealing with a weaker management?

12.2 Wild 'n' Wooly Beverages (WWB) bargains with the United American Whiskymakers (UAW) over wages. WWB offers a $10 per hour raise initially, while the UAW asks for $20. WWB values the gains from bargaining as $10 - w$, while the UAW values the gains as $w^{.5}$, where w is the wage increase in excess of $10 obtained by the union (w is between 0 and $10). Does their bargaining produce the standard split-the-difference solution in terms of their valuations of the gains? Does it produce the solution that $w = \$5$? If yes, why; if no, why not?

12.3 Fill in the table below for the remaining data on strike activity in the U.S. *involving at least six workers.*

Year	Work Time Lost (Percent)	Strike Incidence (Percent)	Strike Duration (Days)
1948	0.30	4.7	
1960	0.14	2.4	
1969	0.24	3.5	
1979	0.15	1.9	

12.4 If you were a mediator involved in the negotiations depicted in Figure 12.2, what steps would you undertake to help the parties reach an earlier settlement? How can you minimize your impact on the outcome that the parties reach on their own?

12.5 Using what you have learned about union members, their interests and behaviors, and the relative strength of unions, please discuss what types of industries are most likely to have a strike during their collective bargaining relationship.

12.6 It can be said that many of the problems that call for the creation of incentive compatible implicit contracts in the world of individual workers and firms are mitigated, if not eliminated, when there are trade unions. What are these problems? Contrast the implicit contracts and unionization mechanisms for dealing with them.

12.7 Discuss the roles that "neutrals" play in modern American labor relations. (Hint: the major types of neutrals are arbitrators, mediators, and fact-finders.) When do we see each employed? In what type of situations are neutrals most likely to be used to set the terms of contracts? In general, how do unions and management feel about the use of neutrals? Why do they feel as they do?

12.8 Suppose that you are asked to advise the government of Malaysia, which is considering a law to ban all strikes by unionized workers. Instead they want to substitute a program of binding arbitration for all disputes including wages, benefits, staffing levels, and other conditions of employment such as exists for public-sector workers in some U.S. states. What would be the advantages and disadvantages of adopting such a policy for all workers, including those in the private sector? In light of these advantages and disadvantages, what would you advise the government of Malaysia? Would your answer be any different if you were advising a higher-income country such as Switzerland?

12.9 The word "international," in many union names typically means only that they have members in the U.S. and Canada. In light of increasing globalization of the economy, how will the fact that each trade union organizes workers within a single country influence the relative bargaining power of unions and firms? How will this fact affect the likelihood that a strike will occur in any given negotiation?

12.10 Although the outcome of any labor negotiation can be regarded as a result of the relative bargaining power of the union and the firm, at a more fundamental level relative bargaining power is heavily influenced by the "rules of the game" as set out in the applicable laws. Discuss as many ways as you can in which the federal and state governments in the U.S. have established laws and administrative rules that influence the relative strength of unions and firms.

KEY WORDS

- asymmetric information model
- bargaining power
- binding arbitration
- Boulwarism
- codetermination
- consumer boycott
- duration of strikes
- Experimental Negotiating Agreement (ENA)
- fact-finding
- Federal Mediation and Conciliation Service
- final-offer arbitration (FOA)
- incidence of strikes
- lock-out
- mediation
- negative-sum game
- optimal accident model
- positive-sum game
- slowdown
- social cost of a strike
- strike
- strikebreakers
- supergame
- voluntarism
- work to rule
- zero-sum game

13

UNIONS' IMPACTS ON LABOR MARKETS

THE MAJOR QUESTIONS

- How successful are unions in increasing the wages of their members?
- How has their success varied over time?
- How does the impact of unions on wages differ among sectors of the economy?
- Do unions have a greater impact on wages or on other types of compensation such as fringe benefits?
- How do unions affect the wages of nonunion workers?
- How do union-imposed changes in relative wages affect employment, mobility, and labor productivity?
- How do unions affect businesses' profitability and economic performance?

THE UNION/NONUNION WAGE DIFFERENTIAL

Table 13.1 shows the average earnings of full-time union and nonunion workers classified by industry or occupation. The last column shows the **wage gap** or the **union/nonunion wage differential** (M). This figure is the unadjusted effect of unions on relative wages. M is the percentage difference between the wages of union workers w_u and nonunion workers w_n and can be written as

$$M = 100 \times \frac{w_u - w_n}{w_n}.$$

Overall, as the bottom line of Table 13.1 shows, unionized workers have higher weekly earnings than nonunionized workers. This finding, however, does not enable us to conclude that unions raise the wages of their members.

TABLE 13.1 MEDIAN WEEKLY FULL-TIME EARNINGS, WAGE AND SALARY WORKERS, 1994

Occupation or Industry	Union Members	Nonmembers	M
Occupation			
Managerial and professional	$729	$672	8
Technical, sales, and support	518	407	27
Precision production, craft, and repair	672	458	47
Operators, fabricators, and laborers	514	327	57
Protective services	650	398	63
Other services	369	256	44
Industry			
Mining	664	634	5
Construction	696	425	64
Manufacturing	533	464	15
Transportation and public utilities	665	531	25
Wholesale and retail trade	453	352	29
Finance, insurance, and real estate	471	483	–3
Services	485	420	15
Government	623	493	26
Total	592	432	37

Source: *Employment and Earnings,* (January 1995), pp. 215, 217.

Ideally, we would like to measure the **wage gain** or the union/nonunion wage differential resulting from suddenly imposing unions on some workers in an economy where no unions previously existed, and then measuring what happened to the wages of the workers who were unionized. Unfortunately, we are not able to perform this experiment. Generally, what researchers are able to measure is the percentage difference between the wage rates of two apparently identical union and nonunion workers, which we will call M^* or the **adjusted wage gap**. The process of measuring the adjusted gap attempts to account for as many differences as possible between union and nonunion workers, other than union status, that might affect their wage rates. This procedure is based on multivariate regressions that include measures describing the demographic characteristics and the human capital embodied in workers.[1] While this measure is more illustrative than the unadjusted wage gaps shown in Table 13.1, it must be interpreted very carefully since, as we will see below,

[1]The distinction between wage gains and gaps is analyzed by H. Gregg Lewis, in *Union Relative Wage Effects: A Survey,* Chicago: University of Chicago Press (1986), Chapter 2.

it differs in a number of important ways from the answer to the question we really wanted to ask.

BASIC TECHNIQUES FOR MEASURING UNION WAGE GAPS

Several approaches to estimating M^* have been developed. The **intercity method** examines workers' wages within an occupation in different cities across which the extent of unionization in the occupation differs. Such studies account for other differences between cities that might affect the general wage level. The **aggregate method** examines the average wage rates of union and nonunion plants within an industry or compares wages in heavily unionized industries to those in less-unionized industries.

Similar studies based on occupations rather than industries also account for other factors affecting wage differences among industries or occupations. Often this analysis examines two industries or occupations having approximately the same wages before one becomes heavily unionized. The difference in wages after unionization provides an estimate of M^*.

The third approach uses data on the characteristics of large numbers of individuals to estimate an equation that includes whether they are union members or are covered by collective bargaining. This approach has largely replaced other methods in recent years as large samples of data on individuals have become available and decreasing computer costs have made analyzing such samples feasible. These studies hold constant workers' demographic characteristics, human capital, and other measures in a multivariate regression to isolate the effect of union membership or collective-bargaining coverage on wages.[2]

Among these three approaches to measuring adjusted wage gaps, regressions using individual data are likely to be the most reliable. Researchers are better able to control for individual differences using measures such as education and experience than to capture differences between cities or occupations that might affect wages.

A wide range of estimates of M^* has been obtained using these three approaches.[3] Obviously the estimates differ depending on such factors as the industries or occupations being analyzed, the year wages are measured, and the demographic characteristics of workers who form the samples used in the third approach. Nevertheless, for the U.S. the estimates of M^* using data covering a broad range of workers (mostly utilizing the aggregate and individual regression methods) cluster between 10 and 30 percent, with most studies in the lower half of this range. We can tentatively infer from these

---

[2]The intercity and aggregate approaches are developed in H. Gregg Lewis, *Unions and Relative Wages in the United States,* Chicago: University of Chicago Press (1963). The method of adjusted differences underlies much of the work summarized in Lewis, *Union Relative Wage Effects.*

[3]Lewis, *Union Relative Wage Effects.*

methods that the typical union in the U.S. raises wages by somewhat less than 20 percent. It is quite clear that $M^* < M$. The unadjusted wage gap shown in Table 13.1 (37 percent) overstates the true difference in wage rates between apparently identical union and nonunion workers. By inference, the characteristics of union workers such as their human capital and other wage-enhancing characteristics would raise their wages above those of the average nonunion worker even in the absence of unionism. Estimates of M^* have been made for countries other than the U.S. Table 13.2 shows one set of estimates generated in exactly the same way by using regression analysis of individual data from the mid-1980s for the U.S. and five other countries. The diversity among the estimates shows that, not surprisingly, the vastly different structures and extent of unionization among these countries generate very different impacts on wages. Unions in the U.S., where the incidence of collective bargaining is low, produce fairly large effects on relative wages compared to unions in many other countries. Whether this finding is because extension mechanisms reduce estimates of M^* more in other countries, or because the true wage gains are greater in the U.S. than elsewhere is not discernible. For example, German law extends some union wage gains to nonunion firms within an industry, effectively legislating a small M^*. These differences may also occur because unions in continental Europe are more interested than their U.S. counterparts in political goals, meaning that less energy is devoted to increasing members' wages above those of nonmembers in comparable workplaces.

Table 13.2 gives just one set of estimates of M^*. As with any attempt to infer the magnitudes of an economic effect, many more estimates are required before we have a good sense of the size of the effect. Fortunately, a large group of other studies for the United Kingdom also suggest that M^* is around 10 percent. Another study of Germany found essentially no adjusted wage gap. Many estimates of M^* for Canada using individual data cluster around 20 percent. Despite the much higher incidence of collective bargain-

TABLE 13.2 ADJUSTED UNION WAGE GAPS (IN PERCENT), SELECTED COUNTRIES, 1985–87

Country	M^*
United States	22
Australia	8
Austria	7
Germany	8
Switzerland	4
United Kingdom	10

Source: David Blanchflower and Richard Freeman, "Going Different Ways: Unionism in the U.S. and Other O.E.C.D. Countries," *Industrial Relations* 31: 56–79 (1992).

ing in Canada than in the U.S., the impact of unions on relative wages appears similar. Estimates of the adjusted wage gap for Australia are between 7 and 18 percent.[4]

DIFFERENCES BETWEEN THE WAGE GAP AND THE WAGE GAIN

All the measures of M or M^* discussed so far have been measures of the wage gap between union and nonunion workers calculated as

$$100 \times [w_u - w_n] / w_n.$$

This calculation does not show the impact of unions on their members. As we discussed earlier, what we really want to know is the wage gain M′ which, if the wage prevailing in the absence of unions would be w_0, is calculated as

$$100 \times [w_u - w_0] / w_0.$$

There are several reasons why measures of M^* are likely to be biased estimates of M′.

THREAT AND SUBSTITUTION EFFECTS

Even if we were able to account for all the differences between union and nonunion workers and jobs, the adjusted wage gap would not measure the wage gain. A number of factors could cause the adjusted wage gap to *underestimate the wage gain*. Some nonunion employers may raise their wages because union workers have won wage increases. By raising wages these employers hope to reduce the probability that a union will organize their employees. In some cases employers may even pay their workers the full union rate if this strategy will keep them nonunion. Avoiding the union gives them greater flexibility in personnel policies and the ability to operate while union plants are on strike. Workers in the nonunion plant also benefit from the absence of strikes, as well as saving the cost of union dues, although they lose any services the union provides in areas such as processing grievances

[4]For the U.K., Mark Stewart, "Relative Earnings and Individual Union Membership in the United Kingdom," *Economica* 50: 111–126 (1983); Anup Shah, "Job Attributes and the Size of the Union/Non-Union Wage Differential," *Economica* (51): 437–446 (1984); F. Green, "The Trade Union Wage Gap in Britain," *Economics Letters* 27: 183–187 (1988); David Blanchflower and Andrew Oswald, "The Wage Curve," *Scandinavian Journal of Economics* 92: 215–235 (1990); Mark Stewart, "Union Wage Differentials in the Face of Changes in the Economic and Legal Environment," *Economica* 58: 155–172 (1991). For Germany, Jan Svejnar, "Relative Wage Effects of Unions, Dictatorship and Codetermination: Econometric Evidence from Germany," *Review of Economics and Statistics* 63: 188–197 (1981). For Canada, Chris Robinson, "The Joint Determination of Union Status and Union Wage Effects: Some Tests of Alternative Models," *Journal of Political Economy* 97: 639–667 (1989), and the studies discussed therein. For Australia, Robert Kornfeld, "The Effects of Union Membership on Wages and Employee Benefits: The Case of Australia," *Industrial and Labor Relations Review* 47: 114–128 (1993).

and establishing and enforcing seniority rights. The positive effect of unions on the earnings of nonunion workers is called the **threat effect** because it results from the threat of attempts to organize the nonunion employer. Such direct threats are not the only way union wage gains can raise the wages paid by nonunion employers. In a tight labor market, nonunion employers may be forced to raise wages in response to increases in the union rate in order to recruit high-quality workers.

If we attempt to estimate the impact of collective bargaining by comparing wages in union and nonunion establishments in the same industry and locality, the threat effect will lead us to underestimate the wage gain. We may even find it to be zero. For example, in the U.S., the stronger the police union is in a geographic area, the closer are the wages of nonunion police to those of unionized police.[5] We must, therefore, make wider comparisons, perhaps across cities, which lead to a greater need to correct for differences between comparison groups of employees. Even this device does not remove threat effects entirely, since employers in one city can feel threatened by the growth of unions in another.

The fact that, as we saw in our discussion of skilled and unskilled workers in Chapter 4, union and nonunion workers are likely to be substitutes may also cause increases in the union wage to increase the wage of nonunion workers. If a union raises the wages of its members, it increases the price of products produced by firms that employ them. Consumers will substitute toward products produced by nonunion workers, increasing the demand for these workers and, all else equal, increasing their wages. Similarly, within a firm, if some workers are unionized while others are not, raising the wages of the union members may cause the firm to alter production technologies in order to use more nonunion labor.

There is a final problem with a number of studies that cause them to underestimate the impact of unions. Most data contain information about wages rather than total compensation. Unionized firms may provide a greater fraction of compensation as fringe benefits for several reasons. First, unions raise workers' incomes and most fringe benefits are luxury goods, as we saw in Chapter 10. A second reason is that employee benefits permit product differentiation by union leaders. The leader who first negotiates a new form of benefit, such as prepaid legal insurance for workers, is a popular innovator. The equivalent gain in cash wages would seem routine and in some cases insignificant. Finally, union workplaces tend to have more homogeneous workers than nonunion workplaces. The inefficiency that arises because fringe benefits force all workers in the covered group to have the same consumption will be smaller if the workers are similar to each other in their ages and backgrounds.

---

[5]Casey Ichniowski, Richard Freeman, and Harrison Lauer, "Collective Bargaining Laws, Threat Effects and the Determinants of Police Compensation," *Journal of Labor Economics* 7: 191–209 (1989).

Union workers are more likely to receive more major employee benefits than nonunion workers with the same characteristics working in the same industry. Moreover, when compared to nonunion workers who obtain the same types of benefits, those received by unionized workers are more generous. These considerations imply that the growth of unionization from the 1920s through the 1950s was partly responsible for the increased fraction of compensation accounted for by supplements, and that the deceleration of their growth since the 1970s may be related to the decline of unionization in the United States.[6]

Accounting for employee benefits shows that unions have a somewhat greater influence on pay than we suggested in Chapter 12. The **adjusted benefit gap,** analogous to the adjusted wage gap, is at least 20 percent. If the adjusted wage gap for otherwise identical workers is 10 to 15 percent, the adjusted total compensation gap may be 12 to 17 percent.[7]

QUALITY AND SPILLOVER EFFECTS

Other biases might cause the adjusted wage gap to *overestimate the wage gain*. When unions impose higher-than-equilibrium wages on employers, there will be a queue for these jobs. Employers respond to the higher wages they are forced to pay by selecting the best qualified workers from the queue. This behavior would pose no problem in estimating the adjusted wage gap if researchers could know everything employers know about workers. Unfortunately, much of the difference in quality cannot be measured, and worker characteristics that are easily measured and available to economists are generally very crude. While we may know how many years of school or years of work experience a worker has, these figures do not tell us the quality of his education, what he studied in school, or how much training he actually received on the job. Other factors that make some workers more attractive to employers are almost impossible to measure, including personal traits such as native intelligence, willingness to work, and punctuality. All these factors may be apparent to the employer or can be learned by checking references, but none can be observed by economists from the statistical data used to adjust M. Thus, nonunion workers who appear to have the same observable characteristics as union workers are likely to be less productive in ways that cannot be observed by researchers.

If, on average, unionized workers are likely to be of higher quality, their jobs are typically worse than those filled by otherwise identical nonunion workers. As we saw in Chapter 11, workers are more likely to vote to organize a union when their jobs involve undesirable working conditions. Thus, part

---

[6]Richard Freeman, "The Effect of Unionism on Fringe Benefits," *Industrial and Labor Relations Review* 34: 489–509 (1981)

[7]Lewis, *Union Relative Wage Effects.*

of what appears to be a union wage premium may simply represent compensating differentials for poor working conditions that would have raised nonunion workers' wages had they been employed in these jobs.

For the economy as a whole, a higher union wage may actually reduce the nonunion wage, also causing the estimated adjusted wage gap to overestimate the wage gain to unionization. The analysis is similar to that of the minimum wage in Figure 4.12 of Chapter 4. Just as imposing an effective minimum wage lowers employment in the covered sector, raising wages in union firms (or in nonunion firms that raise wages due to the threat effect) also reduces employment. As in Figure 4.12 (b), the supply of labor to the rest of the economy increases by an amount equal to or somewhat less than the reduction in employment in the unionized sector. Increased competition with workers who are already working or seeking jobs in the nonunion sector drives real wage rates down in the part of the nonunion sector where threat effects are weak.[8] This **spillover effect** suggests that the union/nonunion wage gap overestimates the actual wage gain.

In sum, threat and substitution effects lead us to understate the wage gain, but spillovers and the unmeasured characteristics of workers and jobs lead us to overstate it. Which of these two impacts is greatest is not discernible a priori. All we can know is that these potential biases exist and, therefore, that estimates of M^* should account for them as much as possible. We will see below how researchers have attempted to remove the biases. By the very nature of the problem, however, no estimate of M^* will measure the union wage gain precisely, since none can account for all the potential biases.

Whether the wage gap over or underestimates the wage gain depends on the situation being analyzed. When workers in closely related firms or industries are compared, the threat effect may predominate and the gap will underestimate the gain. When the comparison is more diffuse, such as when all workers in the economy are being compared, spillover and quality effects are likely to be more important, causing the adjusted wage gap to overestimate the wage gain. The best we can do is try to obtain an accurate measure of the percentage difference between union and nonunion wages, but this measure will still be different from the real question of interest: What is the percentage difference between union wages and what competitive wages would be if unions did not exist?

ATTEMPTS TO IMPROVE ESTIMATES OF THE WAGE GAP

Several strategies have been used in an attempt to remove the biases discussed in the previous section and bring measures of the adjusted wage gap closer to the underlying, but unmeasured, wage gain. None of the techniques

---

[8]Some evidence of a spillover effect is in Lawrence Kahn, "The Effect of Unions on the Earnings of Nonunion Workers," *Industrial and Labor Relations Review* 31: 205–216 (1978).

used is able to deal with all of the problems outlined above, and each has problems of its own. Taken together, however, they strongly indicate that the net effect of the biases means that the wage gap significantly overstates unions' true impact on wages.

ADJUSTING FOR JOB CHARACTERISTICS

A limited number of data sets contain information on job characteristics in addition to the usual measures of individual characteristics used to derive an adjusted wage gap. Several studies have examined what happens to estimates of M^* when these variables are included. As might be expected, M^* falls significantly. In one sample of male workers from 1975 and 1976, estimates of M^* without controlling for job characteristics were 13.9 percent. When the fact that union members were more likely to be in jobs paying positive compensating differentials was taken into account, however, the adjusted wage gap fell to 6.4 percent. In a different sample of male blue-collar workers from 1972 and 1973, the adjusted wage gap fell from 20.4 percent to 6.4 percent when job characteristics were held constant.[9]

ADJUSTING FOR UNOBSERVED DIFFERENCES IN WORKERS

One way of addressing the problem of workers' productivity differences is to standardize for the determinants of who joins unions. The vast differences among demographic groups, industries, and occupations noted in Chapter 11 in the incidence of unionism are factors that can be measured and thus accounted for in estimating M^*. Unfortunately, union and nonunion workers will also differ in unmeasured ways. Because employers choose the best people from the queue of those seeking union jobs, accounting for the positive correlation of union status and worker quality is important in removing any upward bias in M^*. One way involves using a complex statistical techniques called **sample selection corrections** on cross-section data. When these corrections were applied to a sample of middle-aged men in 1969 and 1971, estimates of M^* fell by one-third.[10]

As with estimates of compensating differentials and government pay premia discussed in previous chapters, the recent development of longitudinal data sets providing information on the same individuals for several years enables the use of a more complex method in attempting to control for

---

[9]Greg Duncan and Frank Stafford, "Do Union Members Receive Compensating Wage Differentials?" *American Economic Review* 70: 355–371 (1980). No more recent figures are presented because there have been no recent surveys of representative samples of workers that included good measures of working conditions.

[10]Gregory Duncan and Duane Leigh, "Wage Determination in the Union and Nonunion Sectors: A Sample Selectivity Approach," *Industrial and Labor Relations Review* 34: 24–34 (1980).

unmeasured individual differences between union and nonunion workers.[11] Since people move in and out of union jobs over the years, the data can be used to examine how workers' wages change when they enter union employment from nonunion jobs, or vice versa. Assuming underlying characteristics such as motivation, intelligence, and work effort do not change when workers change union status, longitudinal data on those who leave or join unions might allow us to account for the upward biases in M^* that result from unmeasured differences in characteristics among workers.

Table 13.3 shows several estimates of adjusted wage gaps using cross-section data and longitudinal techniques on those members of the samples who change union status. These estimates account for measurable changes in factors, such as occupation or industry, that accompany a change in union status. Estimates of the adjusted wage gap in column 4 produced by examining wage changes when a worker changes union status are significantly lower than those in column 3 from conventional cross-section regressions that do not standardize for unmeasured characteristics. Evidence from most of the other numerous studies on this issue also shows that accounting for unobserved differences in workers' characteristics lowers the estimate of M^*. Similar results have been found for other countries, such as Australia, where estimates of the adjusted wage gap fall from slightly over 12 percent in cross-section data to about 8 percent using longitudinal data.[12] It is clear that unionized firms compensate for imposed wage increases by hiring workers with more desirable unobserved traits. In part, however, changes in wages when workers change union status also reflect differences in working conditions between union and nonunion jobs. Thus, workers who switched from nonunion to union status between 1969 and 1971 reported a reduction in their ability to control their work environment and hours of work.[13]

There are, unfortunately, a number of problems with using longitudinal data in attempting to eliminate unmeasured personal and job characteristics. Some recorded moves from union to nonunion jobs or vice versa may actually result from errors in the data. Workers may not know if they are union members or, more likely, if their workplace is covered by collective bargain-

---

[11]The most widely used of these sets of data are: (1) The Panel Study of Income Dynamics, with annual information on 5000 families, beginning in 1968 and continuing annually to this day, collected by the Survey Research Center of the University of Michigan; and (2) The National Longitudinal Surveys. These consist of four separate samples (of young men, young women, middle-aged women, and older men), beginning in 1966 and concluding in the late 1970s or early 1980s, and a sample of youth 14 to 24 in 1979 that continues to this day, collected by the Center for Human Resource Research of Ohio State University.

[12]Lewis, *Union Relative Wage Effects*, Table 5.10; Robert Kornfeld, "The Effects of Union Membership on Wages and Employee Benefits: The Case of Australia," *Industrial and Labor Relations Review* 47: 114–128 (1993).

[13]Duncan and Stafford, "Do Union Members."

TABLE 13.3 ADJUSTED UNION-WAGE GAPS (IN PERCENT)

		Method of Estimating M*	
Group	Years Observed	Cross-Sectional	Longitudinal[a]
All workers	1974–1975, 1979	21	9
All workers	1970–1979	26	19
Men 14–24 in 1966	1971–1978	32	13
Male Household Heads	1976–1980	18	5–8

[a]This column is the average of comparisons between those who joined unions and those who did not, and between those who left unions and those who did not.

Sources: Rows 1 to 3—Calculated from Richard Freeman and James Medoff, *What Do Unions Do?* New York: Basic Books (1984), Tables 3–1 and 3–2; Row 4—George Jakubson, "Estimation and Testing of the Union Wag Effect Using Panel Data," *Review of Economic Studies* 58: 971–991 (1991).

ing. In one sample, employers and employees disagreed about 3.5 percent of the time about whether the worker was covered by a union agreement.[14]

Measurement errors create only slight problems in conventional cross-section estimates, but when using longitudinal data, they may cause more serious problems. If the measurement error is systematic, meaning that the worker always misreports his union status, the problem is trivial. It is serious if the reported errors are random and not constant over time. In this case, a large fraction of the people who look like they are changing union status will not actually have done so. Since people who are reported to change status in error presumably do not see their wages change just because they filled out a survey incorrectly, they will enter the analyses with zero wage change. Thus, the wage change observed for workers who report their status changing will be a weighted average of the actual change and zero, with the weights being the fraction that actually changed status and the fraction that only apparently changed because of reporting errors. Obviously, this weighted average will be less than the true effect, with the amount of the bias being a function of the fraction of reported status changes due to errors. Assuming that *all* differences between employees' and employers' reports of union status are measurement error (they might reflect differences in definition of what is really a union), and that *none* of this measurement error is consistent across years, as much as half of the apparent reduction in estimates of the impact of unions when longitudinal techniques are used might be due to measurement errors.

[14]Since this sample was from the Current Population Survey, part of the problem may be that the CPS asks one adult in the household for information about all members of the household. Thus, it may be that while workers know whether they are covered by a union contract, their spouses do not.

In reality, the extent of this problem is probably much less, so the basic conclusion holds that unmeasured differences in jobs and workers account for a significant portion of the apparent return to being a union member.[15]

Another problem with longitudinal estimates of unions' impact derived from workers who switch union status arises because such workers are not likely to be representative of all union or nonunion workers. As our discussion of search behavior in Chapters 6 and 7 implies, workers who switch from union to nonunion jobs are likely to be those who had particularly low wages in their union jobs and/or who found a particularly attractive nonunion job. The reverse is true for those who switch from nonunion to union jobs. These findings suggest that moves from union to nonunion status will *understate* the effect of unions while moves from nonunion to union status will *overstate* their impact. For example, the study reported in the last row of Table 13.3 that found an overall union impact of between 5 and 8 percent, estimated an impact of about 11 percent when examining those who joined unions, but only 3 percent when looking at those who moved from union to nonunion jobs. In an economy where union membership is declining over time, more workers are likely to be leaving than joining unions, and the estimated effect from workers who switch status may not be an accurate measure of unions' impact for those who remain in a union in both periods. The best we can say is that the joiners and leavers produce an upper and lower bound on the true impact. In any case, where they are available, both of these estimates are typically significantly lower than the cross-section estimates.[16]

ADJUSTING FOR THREAT, SPILLOVER, AND SUBSTITUTION EFFECTS

It is impossible to disentangle these effects, some of which should cause the adjusted wage gap M^* to overestimate the wage gain M' and others to underestimate it. We can obtain an indication of their combined effect, however, by examining the impact of the percent unionized in an industry on the wages of nonunion workers in that industry. If the threat and/or substitution effects dominate, this impact should be positive. If the spillover effect is more important, the impact of unions on wages of nonunion members should be negative. In each case, we are assuming that more diffuse effects on workers in other industries are much smaller and can be ignored.

One recent study that examined differences across industries and over time in the percentage of union workers found that each 10-percentage-point increase in the fraction of an industry's nonmanagerial workers belonging to a union lowered the wages of nonunion workers in that industry by about 3 percent of the average wage of all nonunion workers. Thus, the net impact

---

[15]Richard Freeman, "Longitudinal Analyses of the Effects of Trade Unions," *Journal of Labor Economics* 2: 1–26 (1984).

[16]George Jakubson, "Estimation and Testing of the Union Wage Effect Using Panel Data," *Review of Economic Studies* 58: 971–991 (1991).

of unions on the wages of nonunion workers appears to be significantly negative, although some earlier studies using only cross-section data have found essentially no impact.[17]

In sum, adjustments for the biases created by unmeasured worker and job characteristics, and threat, spillover, and substitution effects all indicate that the wage gain M' is significantly lower than estimates of the adjusted wage gap M^* in the American economy. Given a current unadjusted wage gap of 37 percent and an adjusted wage gap of around 16 percent, the true impact of unions on the wages of their members is probably between 8 and 12 percent.

THE ROLE OF THE EXTENT OF UNIONIZATION

Estimates of the adjusted wage gap will vary across industries and occupations according to the fraction of workers who belong to unions. The adjusted wage gap (and the underlying wage gain) is related to the fraction of workers in the occupation or industry who are organized. When this number is very small, unions generally have little effect. Since wages are usually an important element in costs, attempts to raise wages paid by the few union employers much above the level paid by their competitors puts union employers at a severe disadvantage in selling their product. This situation both strengthens their resistance to union pressure and encourages the union to moderate its demands. In such cases the union has relatively little bargaining power. At the opposite end of the scale, the union approaches its maximum effect on relative earnings well before it reaches 100 percent organization. The threat effect is likely to become more important to nonunion firms if there are only a few such firms remaining. Thus, unions should have the largest impact on relative wages in the middle range of the extent of unionization.

In the mid-1970s, at a time when the overall adjusted wage gap was around 20 percent, manufacturing and production workers in U.S. industries that were completely unionized received wages only 15 percent above wages paid to similar union workers in industries that were almost entirely nonunion. In 1979 wages of otherwise identical unionized Canadian workers in fully unionized industries were 13 percent above the wages of their counterparts in industries with almost no unionized workers.[18]

---

[17]Richard Freeman and James Medoff, "The Effects of Unions on the Earnings of Nonunion Workers," *Review of Economics and Statistics* 63: 561–572 (1980); William Dickens and Lawrence Katz, "Inter-Industry Wage Differences and Industry Characteristics," in Kevin Lang and Jonathan Leonard (eds.). *Unemployment and the Structure of Labor Markets,* New York: Basil Blackwell (1987); David Neumark and Michael Wachter, "Union Threat Effects and Nonunion Industry Wage Differentials," *Industrial and Labor Relations Review* 48: 20-38 (1995).

[18]Sherwin Rosen, "Trade Union Power, Threat Effects, and the Extent of Organization," *Review of Economic Studies* 36: 185–196 (1969); Freeman and Medoff, "The Impact of the Percentage;" Chris Robinson and Nigel Tomes, "Union Wage Differentials in the Public and Private Sectors," *Journal of Labor Economics* 2: 106–127 (1984).

CHANGES IN UNION WAGE EFFECTS OVER TIME

The effects of unions on earnings are not uniform over time, in part due to the interaction between **long-term union contracts** and the business cycle. Collective bargaining both raises wages and makes them more rigid by fixing them for definite periods. The duration of the typical American collective agreement is from one to three years, with three years being the most common length. Many agreements of more than one year provide for annual reopenings for wage adjustments, or predetermined wage increases during the life of the agreement (**deferred pay increases**). As we saw in Chapter 11, other agreements provide for increases based on movements in the Consumer Price Index (COLAs).

The existence of long-term contracts has different consequences at different phases of the business cycle. During the early phases of a recession, collective-bargaining agreements can keep union wages growing rapidly while wages elsewhere are stagnant. In booms and periods of rapid inflation the rigidity of union wages (especially those not protected by COLAs) becomes a disadvantage. Nonunion employers may raise wages more frequently than union employers in tight labor markets, thus both reducing the measured wage gap and the length of the queue for union jobs. In general the size of the union wage gap tends to increase in recessions and decrease in expansions.

Table 13.4 presents estimates of the adjusted wage gap and unemployment rate for five-year periods since 1920. The estimates for 1920 to 1954 are based on time-series data that show variations in the relative wage rates between two broad groups of industries, one highly unionized for much of the period and the other always substantially nonunion. For 1955 through 1974 the estimates use the aggregate method of comparing relative wages to the rates of unionization by industry. Since 1974 they are from regressions using cross-section data on individuals. The U.S. Department of Labor collected survey data for the years 1889 to 1890 to study the relative cost and efficiency of U.S. and European workers. Studies using this data find an adjusted union relative wage gap of 15 to 20 percent in Great Britain and between 20 percent (for unskilled workers) and 29 percent (for skilled workers) in the U.S.[19]

The table shows a dramatic increase in the size of the adjusted union wage gap during the Depression of the 1930s. No doubt this effect stemmed from downward wage rigidity in union contracts, coupled with a drop in prices that contributed to lower nominal nonunion wages. The table also shows a sharp decline in the union wage gap during World War II and the immediate postwar period. This decline may reflect the combined effects of government wage and price controls during the war and unanticipated infla-

---

[19]P. Dillon and Ira Gang, "Earnings Effects of Labor Organizations in 1890," *Industrial and Labor Relations Review* 40: 516–527 (1987); T. Hatton, G. Boyer, and R. Bailey, "The Union Wage Effect in Late Nineteenth Century Britain," *Economica* 61: 435–456 (1994).

TABLE 13.4 ESTIMATES OF THE EFFECT OF UNIONS ON RELATIVE WAGES, 1920–1994

Period	M*	Unemployment Rate
1920–1924	17	7.3[a]
1925–1929	26	5.0
1930–1934	46	16.4
1935–1939	22	16.8
1940–1944	6	6.5
1945–1949	2	3.9
1950–1954	12	4.0
1955–1959	17	5.0
1960–1964	17	5.7
1965–1969	11	3.8
1970–1974	14	5.4
1975–1979	18	7.0
1980–1984	16	8.3
1985–1989	17	6.2
1990–1994	17	6.5

[a]1922 to 1924 only.

Sources: *M**: 1920–1974, George Johnson, "Unionism in a Macroeconomic Context," Unpublished Paper, University of Michigan, (1983); 1975–1993, Barry Hirsch and David Macpherson, *Union Membership and Earnings Data Book 1994*, Washington, D.C.: Bureau of National Affairs (1994). Unemployment Rate: Before 1940, from Robert Coen, "Labor Force and Unemployment in the 1920s and 1930s," *Review of Economics and Statistics* 55 (1973), Table 2; and 1940–1990, Current Population Survey data.

tion after it ended. After 1950, the estimated effect of unions grew, reaching 17 percent between 1955 to 1964. During the accelerating inflation of the late 1960s and early 1970s it fell. Apparently unions underestimated the rate of inflation when negotiating long-term contracts.

From the mid-1970s through the mid-1980s unemployment remained relatively high, even during the cyclical recovery of the late 1970s. Union members' expectations caught up with the higher inflation rates, and greater use of indexed contracts protected many union members against unexpected inflation. These factors all caused the wage gap to rise. It is remarkable that the long expansion and low inflation of the Reagan years did not produce the reduction in M^* that typically accompanies lower unemployment. Except for the period around 1970, the effect of unions on relative wages has remained essentially stable at between 15 and 20 percent since 1950 no matter what the macroeconomic conditions.

Why did the union wage effect stay unchanged during the mid-to-late 1980s in the face of low unemployment and stronger foreign competition? Apparently unions changed the relative weights given to wages and employment levels in formulating their goals. The effects of unions' choices between wage and employment goals can be seen by comparing M^* since 1965 with the extent of union membership shown in Table 11.5. As the union sector has shrunk, M^* has not responded. The shrinkage has been most rapid in those times (such as the mid-to-late 1980s) when M^* has been highest. Apparently unions are willing to accept lower employment levels due to the decreased competitiveness of unionized firms in order to maintain the historic union wage premium over nonunion workers. As we have seen, the rate of return to education increased during this period, meaning that real wage increases were smaller than usual for highly paid, but not highly educated, union workers in manufacturing or service-sector jobs. Perhaps an attempt to preserve these workers' relative earnings explains the high weight unions have apparently placed on wages in the recent past.

Even in the absence of macroeconomic fluctuations, adjusted wage gaps vary according to the state of particular labor markets. Estimates of M^* were lower in industries where imports accounted for a greater share of output during the 1970s, and fell where imports grew most rapidly. The same responsiveness to imports did not occur during the 1980s. One study estimated M^* for teachers in 1974 as 7 percent, but found it to be 23 percent in 1977.[20] This change is consistent with the evidence in Table 13.4 and with the sharp deterioration in the market for teachers that accompanied reduced school enrollment in the U.S. in the late 1970s. Thus, studies of specific industries confirm the implications from aggregate data that unions have increasingly sacrificed their employment goal to their wage objectives, especially when the demand schedule for unionized labor shifts leftward.

WAGE GAPS BY TYPE OF UNION, SKILL LEVEL, AND INDUSTRY

So far, we have examined the average effects of unions on the relative earnings of their members. There is considerable dispersion around this average beyond what is produced by differences in the extent of unionization or the business cycle. Craft unions, for example, should have different effects from industrial ones. The skill level of unionized employees and the structure of the product market create differential impacts. The more political nature of public-sector unionism is likely to generate different effects on wages than are found in the private sector.

THE EFFECT OF UNION STRUCTURE

It is often thought that unions representing workers in a single craft have greater effects on relative earnings than more broadly based industrial

---

[20]William Baugh and Joe Stone, "Teachers, Unions, and Wages in the 1970s: Unionism Now Pays," *Industrial and Labor Relations Review* 35: 368–376 (1982); David Macpherson and James Stewart, "The Effect of International Competition on Union and Nonunion Wages," *Industrial and Labor Relations Review* 43: 435–446 (1990).

unions.[21] The bases of this expectation are Marshall's laws of derived demand discussed in Chapter 4. The less elastic the demand for the labor of its members, the higher will be a union's wage goals since an inelastic demand means a smaller percentage reduction in employment for a given percentage increase in wages. In the short run, at least, there are not likely to be many good substitutes in production for skilled craft workers. These unions thus have more to fear from substitution in consumption than from substitution in production. In this case, as we saw in Chapter 4, it is desirable to be "unimportant." If the wages of members of one craft are a small part of total cost, even a large wage increase will add only a small percentage to the total cost of a unit of output. A price increase that reflected this increase would cause only a small reduction in quantity demanded and, hence, in employment.

For example, assume that carpenters' wages make up only 10 percent of the cost of a house and that no substitution in production is possible. Thus, the isoquant is like that in Figure 4.8(a). A wage increase of 20 percent for carpenters would add only 2 percent to the cost of a house, and would probably have little effect on the number of houses built. If, however, the wages of carpenters were half the cost of a house, a 20 percent wage increase would add 10 percent to costs, and would cause a larger reduction in construction.

This analysis only applies when one craft bargains independently of others, as in the airline industry. On the other hand, where all crafts bargain together or where one craft sets a pattern that typically spreads to the rest, what matters is the importance of the craft group as a whole. Where this group is fairly small relative to total costs, as in newspaper publishing, the situation remains favorable to the unions. Where the wages of all crafts are a large part of total costs, as in residential construction, even a small craft no longer gains from being unimportant.

THE EFFECT OF SKILL AND DEMOGRAPHIC DIFFERENCES

Table 13.1 shows that in 1994 the unadjusted wage gap, M, was higher among operatives and laborers than among more skilled craft workers. Dozens of studies estimating adjusted wage gaps for workers with different skill levels have found the same result. Unions have, on average, less of an effect in raising craft workers' wages than those of other blue-collar workers. The largest values for M^* are found among laborers, where unions' impacts are several percentage points higher than for operatives or craft workers.[22]

The explanation for the inverse relation between the union wage effect and skills lies in the leveling effect of union wage policies. Industrial unions frequently seek the largest percentage wage increases for the least-skilled

---

[21]See, for example, Milton Friedman in David Wright (ed.). *The Impact of the Union,* New York: Harcourt Brace Jovanovich (1951) p. 208.

[22]The discussion in this subsection is based on Lewis, *Union Relative Wage Effects,* Tables 7.6, 7.7, 7.10, and 7.12.

workers, which is why unions often demand equal absolute increases for every worker in the bargaining unit. This **equalization hypothesis** explains many of the observed differences in adjusted wage gaps. Unions also seek to eliminate wage differentials between firms, creating greater increases in low-wage firms where workers are likely to have lower average skill levels. Construction, where skilled workers bargain independently from unskilled workers, is the only major industry in the U.S. where skilled workers have achieved as large a wage gap as unskilled workers. As we saw in Chapter 11, this leveling process across skill levels is likely to be the result of the greater voting power of unskilled workers in most industrial unions.

When comparing blue-collar and white-collar workers, the relatively small extent of organization of white-collar workers seen in Table 11.1, along with the discussion in this chapter, suggests that wage gaps will be higher among blue-collar workers. With a smaller fraction of white-collar workers organized, their ability to set wages above the competitive level for workers with comparable skills is likely to be limited. The evidence strongly supports this conclusion with every one of more than 30 studies finding that wage gaps are higher among blue-collar workers. The differences in M^* between white- and blue-collar workers range between 5 and 35 percentage points, with the best estimate being 15 percentage points. If 12 percent were the overall average M^* in the U.S. economy, it could be around 20 percent for blue-collar workers, but probably closer to 5 percent for white-collar workers. There is evidence that the equalization effects of union policies are even stronger in other industrial countries than in the U.S.[23]

The equalizing effects of union wage policies are also evident when we examine wage gaps for workers with different levels of education. A variety of estimates suggests that each extra year of schooling reduces M^* by 1 to 3 percentage points. Comparing a high school graduate to a college graduate, the adjusted wage gap among college graduates might be between 5 and 10 percent, while that for the high school graduate might be over 15 percent.

The leveling effect of unions is especially pronounced when we consider how M^* differs by age or labor market experience. If unions reduce the variance in wages, the adjusted wage gap will be highest for young workers (and any workers beyond the peak of their age-earnings profile). The data on M by age group in Table 13.5 demonstrate this effect for men. M falls sharply as men reach their late 20s, levels out through most of the work life, and may rise for older workers.[24] This evidence shows that the age-earnings profile among unionized workers is both higher and flatter than that of nonunion workers. The pattern in Table 13.5 is confirmed when adjusted wage gaps are

---

[23]Francine Blau and Lawrence Kahn, "International Differences in Male Wage Inequality: Institutions Versus Market Forces," NBER Working Paper No. 4678 (1994).

[24]Unionized workers typically have more generous pension benefits and less-attractive jobs than nonunion workers. Thus, they typically retire at a much younger age. The sharp jump in the wage gap for workers over the age of 65 is likely to be caused by unusual circumstances.

TABLE 13.5 UNADJUSTED WAGE GAPS (M) FOR FULL-TIME WORKERS BY AGE, RACE, AND SEX, 1994

	Men	Women
Age		
16–24	30	29
25–34	24	25
35–44	9	36
45–54	4	38
55–64	4	35
65+	50	42
Race		
White	25	41
Black	46	40
Hispanic	60	39

Source: Calculated from *Employment and Earnings*, (January, 1995), p. 215.

examined. Among male workers in the United States M^* is greater at age 18 than later in life. It reaches a minimum some time between ages 35 and 50, and then begins to rise.[25]

The data for women in Table 13.5 tell a somewhat different story. Unions do not equalize wages across age groups among women. The equalization hypothesis does, however, explain why M is higher for women than for men in most age groups. Since, as we will see in Chapter 14, average earnings of women are below those of men, unions' equalization of wages means that M will be higher among women. The difference in the pattern of M by age for men and women has two causes. The gap between women's and men's earnings grows within each cohort as it ages due to the fact that the cumulative difference in experience grows over time. In addition, the labor market behavior of current cohorts of young women is much closer to that of men than was true for their predecessors. Thus, it is not surprising that unions' equalizing effects have a greater impact for middle-aged women.

The data on regional differences in unionization in Table 11.4 clearly demonstrate that Southern states are much less heavily unionized than the rest of the U.S. Given the positive relationship between M^* and the percent unionized, this suggests that the adjusted wage gap should be lower in the South than elsewhere. The fact that the overall wage level is lower in the

[25]John Bound and George Johnson, "Wages in the United States During the 1980s and Beyond," in Marvin Kosters (ed.). *Workers and Their Wages*, Washington D.C.: American Enterprise Institute (1991).

South, however, suggests that unions' equalization efforts will cause M^* to be higher in low-wage areas, as unions try to take labor out of competition by equalizing wages across labor markets. The evidence shows that the equalization hypothesis produces the bigger effect, making M^* higher in the South than elsewhere. Although unionization is sparse in the South, unionized workers there do far better than nonunion Southern workers.

At first glance it might appear that the equalization hypothesis could also explain why unadjusted union/nonunion wage differentials are greater for black men than for white men, as seen in the bottom half of Table 13.5. However, in the early 1990's the union/nonunion wage gap adjusted for workers' characteristics was slightly *smaller* for blacks than for whites.[26] This suggests that the large apparent impact seen in Table 13.5 results primarily from a greater differential in quality between union and nonunion workers among black men than among white men.

THE EFFECT OF INDUSTRY STRUCTURE AND PUBLIC- VERSUS PRIVATE-SECTOR UNIONS

In Chapter 11 we showed that unions cannot raise wages and/or employment above nonunion levels and expect a firm to survive unless either the firm has product-market power or the union is able to increase productivity. Unions should, therefore, do better in concentrated product markets. If we look at manufacturing, seemingly the strongest unions are in highly concentrated industries such as basic steel and automobiles. On the other hand, outside manufacturing there are many strong unions in unconcentrated industries such as construction, trucking, and bituminous coal mining.

The view that unions gain more in noncompetitive industries is motivated by an assumption that they can succeed in capturing monopoly profits. This view considers them to have **countervailing power** that offsets the market power of the employer. On the other hand, unions in an unconcentrated industry may have **original power**. If the entire industry is unionized, by raising costs the union can raise product prices to the level where a firm with product-market power would have set them in the first place, as we saw in the Pennington Coal case discussed in the Policy Issue in Chapter 11. Instead of merely capturing monopoly profits from the employer, the unions create the profits from which they achieve wage gains by their own strength. In addition, monopolists might be willing to spend some of their profits to avoid unionization or to weaken a union that has organized their workers. This strategy would reduce union power and lead to a smaller wage gap in concentrated industries.

The evidence on how M^* varies with the extent of product-market concentration is mixed. Some studies find that M^* is no higher as markets become more concentrated while others find the opposite result. One recent careful study for Canada found that the elasticity of pay with respect to

---

[26]Hirsch and Macpherson, *Union Membership.*

POLICY ISSUE

APPLYING ANTITRUST LAWS TO UNIONS

During debate on the Taft-Hartley Act of 1947, the Senate came within one vote of passing the Ball Amendment, which would have restricted unions from bargaining on behalf of workers in plants in different metropolitan areas. Effectively, it would have meant the demise of national unions in the U.S. Since then bills have been repeatedly introduced into Congress to apply antitrust laws to union attempts to bargain collectively for workers in different labor markets. While these bills have not come nearly so close to passage, it is interesting to speculate on how this provision would have affected union bargaining power as measured by adjusted wage gaps.[27]

Most national unions of craft workers in the U.S. consist of very strong local unions that bargain with employer groups in one locality. In construction this bargaining structure results from the product market being effectively limited to the metropolitan area. Outlawing national unions would probably not have much effect on the relative bargaining strengths of workers and employers who are organized this way. Thus, the union wage gap of craft workers would probably not be affected severely by such a change. Neither would the premium achieved by unionized government workers, since bargaining in this sector is inherently local.

Industrial unions by definition cover workers of all skill levels in as much of an industry as possible. In many cases the bargaining structure is national, with much of the determination of wages and benefits taking place nationwide. Legislation such as the Ball Amendment would disrupt such bargaining completely. With easy substitution of output from plants where local unions are relatively weak, the power of relatively strong local unions would be reduced. Since industrial unions in manufacturing consist disproportionately of lower-paid operatives, such legislation would probably reduce the adjusted wage gap among operatives and widen the differential between skilled and unskilled workers. The equalization of wage rates shown by the evidence on wage gaps by skill level would be reduced.

lagged employer profits (which, presumably, were created by market power) was 0.006.[28] We will return to this issue when we discuss the impact of unions on productivity and profits below.

As we have seen, unions in principle have more power in dealing with government employers than with private-sector ones. If unions anywhere should have large effects on wages it should be in the government sector. The

---

[27]A recent bill was H. 78, 99th Congress, introduced by Philip Crane of Illinois. The discussion of the Ball Amendment was by H. Gregg Lewis, "The Labor-Monopoly Problem: A Positive Program," *Journal of Political Economy* 59: 277–287 (1951).

[28]Many of the studies referred to in this section are discussed in Lewis, *Union Relative Wage Effects*, pp. 153–155. See also Barry Hirsch and Robert Connolly, "Do Unions Capture Monopoly Profits?" *Industrial and Labor Relations Review* 41: 118–136 (1987), and Louis Christofides and Andrew Oswald, "Real Wage Determination and Rent-Sharing in Collective Bargaining Agreements," *Quarterly Journal of Economics* 107: 985–1002 (1992).

fact that unions are expanding only in the public sector may give them more power there.

Arguments that wage effects should be larger in government employment ignore other differences between the public and private sectors. Perhaps large wage gaps are causing unionization levels to decline in the private sector. The services performed by government differ from those located in the private sector. Thus, the underlying derived demand elasticities that largely determine the success of unions in raising wages will differ between the two sectors. To the extent that fewer occupation-specific skills are required in the public sector, the bargaining power of public-sector unions will be reduced by the potential competition of nonunion employees and the threat of contracting work out to the private sector. As discussed in Chapter 12, the federal government and most U.S. states (as well as other countries such as Canada) have laws that restrict the ability of unionized workers to strike, thereby reducing the power that withholding their labor would give them as a means of achieving their wage and employment goals. Finally, the differences in age, sex, race, and skill composition between government and private-sector workers may mean that the public-employee unions have welfare functions weighting employment more highly than those of private-sector unions. For these reasons the adjusted relative wage gap may be lower in the public sector.

One study that adjusted for differences in worker quality found that M^* in the U.S. public sector was only 3 percent, as compared to 14 percent in the private sector. For Canada, estimates on data for 1981 found M^* to be 5 and 12 percent in the two sectors.[29] In part this difference is explained by the fact that unions have a greater impact on fringe benefits in the public than in the private sector. Thus, differences in the impact on total compensation are smaller. On balance, the best estimates of the public-sector wage gap indicate that it is between 3 and 7 percentage points smaller than in the private sector.[30]

This difference may exist partly because, as we saw in Chapter 10, wages of nonunion workers are significantly higher in the government sector to begin with. This differential is larger for precisely the unskilled and minority workers for whom the union typically raises wages the most. In addition, as we will see below, public-sector union workers are much better protected

---

[29] Joseph Gyourko and Joseph Tracy, "An Analysis of Public- and Private-Sector Wages Allowing for Endogeneous Choices of Both Government and Union Status," *Journal of Labor Economics* 6: 229–253 (1988); Michael Abbott and Thanasis Stengos, "Alternative Estimates of Union-Nonunion and Public-Private Wage Differentials in Ontario, 1981," Queen's Papers in Industrial Relations, 1987–4 (1987).

[30] H. Gregg Lewis, "Union/Nonunion Wage Gaps in the Public Sector," *Journal of Labor Economics* 8: S260–S328 (1990).

from changes in employment levels than those in the private sector. This finding indicates that there are differences in the welfare functions of public and private unions.

EFFECTS ON EMPLOYMENT AND TURNOVER

Union-imposed wage increases will result in employment reductions in the union sector as long as there is a downward-sloping demand curve for union labor. These **gross employment effects** are reductions in employment in the unionized firm or industry. They will exceed the **net employment effect,** economy-wide change in employment that results when unionization changes in one sector. The net effect is smaller because many workers who do not find jobs in the union sector find work in the nonunion sector, although probably at a lower competitive wage. The net effect will still be negative and total employment reduced as long as the labor supply curve slopes upward. Some workers who are forced into the nonunion sector will find that the wage available to them is less than their reservation wage and drop out of the labor force.

The discussion in Chapter 11 of featherbedding as an expression of unions' employment goals may complicate this simple analysis. After all, if unions negotiate employment off firms' demand curves, perhaps higher wages can be accompanied by higher employment in unionized firms. This effect can happen if unions either generate greater productivity or opt to spend the profits they extract from firms with market power on both higher wages and greater employment.

Compared with the hundreds of studies that underlie our discussion of unions' effects on wages, there are relatively few estimates of the effects of unions on employment. In the United Kingdom between 1980 and 1984, unionized firms grew 3 percent per year more slowly than nonunion firms in the same industry that faced the same change in product demand. Similarly, employment in unionized manufacturing plants in California grew by approximately 4 percentage points a year less than in nonunion plants. Over the long period between 1920 and 1980 relative hours worked were lower where unionization was higher. A U.S. study using the CPS for 1983 estimated that going from the least (8 percent) to the most heavily unionized labor market (39 percent) reduced employment by about 2 percent. The major effects were on the employment of women and youth. No effects on employment of prime-age males could be found. This result is consistent with the distinction between gross and net employment effects, the greater wage effect of unions for youth and women, and with the evidence in Chapter 2 that labor supply is quite inelastic for prime-age men. Prime-age men who do not obtain union jobs stay in the labor market in other, lower-paid, nonunion employment. Youth, and (decreasingly) prime-age women may drop out of the labor force if they cannot obtain the higher pay that union employment offers. This behavior creates a significant negative effect of unions on their employment.[31]

While net employment effects are typically small, gross employment effects may be large. They depend only on labor-demand elasticities which, as shown in Chapter 4, can be quite substantial for individual firms and even for entire sectors of the economy. In the bituminous coal industry, the adjusted wage gap widened rapidly after World War II, reaching as much as 35 percent by the late 1950s. Estimates show that this large wage gap reduced employment through substitution toward capital along production isoquants to roughly 80 percent of what it would have been otherwise. Falling product demand caused by higher prices reduced employment even further.[32] Clearly union members and their leaders must weigh the consequences for employment against the benefits that wage increases produce for those members who retain their jobs.

How does unionism affect job mobility? Among a large sample of American workers observed between 1968 and 1974, union members' probability of quitting (voluntary turnover) was only 6 percent per year, substantially less than the 9 percent probability of nonunion workers. Among a sample of young Australian workers in 1985 and 1986, quit rates were 20 and 26 percent for union and nonunion workers. Part of this difference was due to the higher wages received by union members, but part results from unionism itself. Even accounting for differences in wages and demographic characteristics, union workers had a substantially lower likelihood of quitting a job in any given year. Another way of looking at this phenomenon is to examine job tenure. Adjusting for differences in wages, schooling, and demographic characteristics between the two groups, union workers in the American sample had been on the job for a year longer than their nonunion counterparts. Among the young Australian workers, union members had been with their employers almost twice as long as otherwise identical nonunion workers.[33]

The difference in quit rates between union and nonunion workers cannot be explained by the union wage effect alone, since it is still present when wages are held constant. This could be explained if unionized firms offered

---

[31] John Pencavel and Catherine Hartsog, "A Reconsideration of the Effects of Unionism on Relative Wages and Employment in the United States: 1920–1980," *Journal of Labor Economics* 2: 193–232 (1984); David Blanchflower, Neil Millward, and Andrew Oswald, "Unionism and Employment Behaviour," *Economic Journal* 101: 815–834 (1991); Jonathan Leonard, "Unions and Employment Growth," *Industrial Relations* 31: 80–94 (1992); Edward Montgomery, "Employment and Unemployment Effects of Unions," *Journal of Labor Economics* 7: 170–190 (1989).

[32] H. Gregg Lewis, "Relative Employment Effects of Unionism," Industrial Relations Research Association, *Proceedings* 16: 104–115 (1963).

[33] Richard Freeman, "The Exit-Voice Tradeoff in the Labor Market: Unionism, Job Tenure, Quits, and Separations," *Quarterly Journal of Economics* 94: 643–674 (1980); Paul Miller and Charles Mulvey, "Australian Evidence on the Exit/Voice Model of the Labor Market," *Industrial and Labor Relations Review* 45: 44–57 (1991).

more specific training than nonunion firms in the same industry so that only part of the benefits that induce workers not to quit are reflected in current wages. Unfortunately, at least for the total amount of on-the-job training, the opposite is true. Unionized firms offer workers less training than nonunion firms in the same industry. Another possibility would be if unionized workers were inherently more satisfied with their jobs, in ways that wages and other easily measured outcomes only partially reflect. The opposite is the case here as well, however, with unionized workers expressing more dissatisfaction with their jobs than nonunion workers who have the same wage, education, and job tenure.[34]

Another reason why union members with the same wage and working conditions may be less likely to quit than nonunion workers is if unionized employers select more stable workers from the queue. Since it would reduce hiring and training costs, this selection mechanism could be a profit-maximizing response by the employer to a union-imposed relative wage increase. It is part of the same response that makes it so difficult to find a satisfactory estimate of the adjusted wage gap. Unfortunately, this provides only a partial explanation of the difference in quit rates between union and nonunion workers. One study found that young workers who had the same quit rates as other young workers before they took union jobs had lower quit rates after joining the union, even after adjusting for the wage gap between the two groups.[35]

Just as they reduce voluntary turnover, it is well established that unions increase layoffs. Layoffs (including temporary periods without work) are only characteristic of private-sector union workers. In the public sector, the opposite is true. When a government's fiscal situation deteriorates, union workers are much less likely to be laid-off than nonunion workers. This sharp distinction between the behavior of the two types of unions is consistent with their impacts on wages and with the discussion of union goals in Chapter 11. Private-sector unions produce larger adjusted wage gaps at the cost of higher layoff rates and presumably larger losses in employment. Public-sector unions do not increase their members' wages as much, but they do more to reduce layoffs and protect employment. Public-sector unions appear to value employment relatively more than private-sector unions, perhaps because their less-skilled membership is more risk averse.[36]

---

[34] John Barron, Scott Fuess, and Mark Loewenstein, "Further Analysis of the Effect of Unions on Training," *Journal of Political Economy* 95: 632–640 (1987); Joni Hersch and Joe Stone, "Is Union Job Dissatisfaction Real?" *Journal of Human Resources* 25: 736–751 (1990).

[35] Henry Farber, "Unionism, Labor Turnover, and Wages of Young Men," in Ronald Ehrenberg (ed.). *Research in Labor Economics,* Vol. 3: 33–53 (1980).

[36] Steven Allen, "Unions and Job Security in the Public Sector," in Richard Freeman and Casey Ichniowski (eds.). *When Public Sector Workers Unionize,* Chicago: University of Chicago Press (1988).

EFFECTS ON PRODUCTIVITY, INVESTMENT, AND PROFITABILITY

How can unionized firms survive competition from nonunion firms that do not have to pay the higher union wages? If a firm is earning economic profits, it can continue to sell at the same price as it would if it were nonunion, implicitly maximizing the sum of firm profits and **union rents** (which are a function of any increases in wages and employment negotiated by the union).

Unionized firms that do not have economic profits to share can pay union members higher wages and remain in business only if unionization increases labor productivity. Let us define **unit labor costs** (the wage bill per unit of output) as:

$$ULC = w \times \frac{L}{Y},$$

where L/Y = the inverse of labor productivity or of the average product of labor, AP_L.

The only way a unionized firm can hold costs constant and compete when it must pay a wage M^* percent greater than the nonunion wage is if labor productivity is also M^* percent greater. In that case, w will be M^* percent higher, L/Y will be M^* percent lower, and unit labor costs will be the same in the unionized firm as in nonunion firms.

If the greater productivity of union workers is inherent in the workers themselves, then the only things captured here are unmeasured quality differences, not the effect of unions. The point of interest is whether unionization itself could increase the productivity of a given group of workers. This idea is the opposite of what is often assumed.

While rigid union work rules and featherbedding practices should limit managerial freedom and *reduce* productivity, there are several mechanisms by which unions might induce an increase in productivity. As we saw in Chapter 4, an increase in wages will induce a substitution away from labor, which itself will make up for part of the higher wage paid to unionized workers. Management may also for a time be shocked into operating more efficiently. Shock theory is most plausible when applied to the unionization of a previously nonunion enterprise. In most cases unionization will produce both a substantial wage increase and a simultaneous challenge to managements' methods and unlimited authority. These changes could well inspire the firm to reexamine procedures with some care. Cost savings might enable the firm to mitigate the price increase that would otherwise occur because of the wage increase. This productivity increase, however, is likely to be small. If it were possible to increase productivity by changing the way the firm operates in response to a wage increase, it would also have been possible to do so even without the wage increase. The fact that this change did not happen indicates that, at least at the lower wage, the gains were not worth the effort. It is also hard to imagine repeated waves of successful innovation in response to annual wage increases negotiated with an established union.

Unions might also increase productivity because they reduce turnover, thus reducing the costs of hiring and training replacement workers, and leading to increased investments in specific human capital. Why might turnover be lower in unionized firms? As our discussion of efficiency wages in Chapter 9 suggests, workers who have more to lose if they are discharged have an incentive to shirk less. Once again, however, this offset can only be partial. If higher wages increased productivity through an efficiency wage process, nothing prevents a nonunion firm from paying these wages.

Thus, we must seek a way that unionization could increase workers' productivity simply *because* they are unionized. A number of studies (frequently by economists at Harvard University) have suggested that unions can provide workers with a **collective voice** that offers them a means of expressing their dissatisfaction with the workplace and makes them feel more attached to the employer, increasing both morale and effort.[37] Given that company-dominated employee associations are illegal in the U.S., this mechanism is not readily available to nonunion firms, although the idea of unions improving morale is somewhat inconsistent with the observation that absenteeism is 30 percent higher among union workers.[38]

Whether the net effect of unions on worker productivity is positive, let alone sufficiently large to compensate for the higher wages paid to otherwise similar union employees, is an open question. The first, relatively crude study of this issue used data for manufacturing industries in 1972 and a method like the aggregate approach to measuring adjusted wage gaps. It found an **adjusted productivity gap** of 22 percent favoring unionized firms. This finding is about the same size as the adjusted wage gaps estimated using this approach and suggests that productivity rises by enough to offset the higher union wages. More recent economy-wide studies for the U.S. have not confirmed this result. They have found that unions *decrease* productivity by a small amount.[39] In Germany unions appear to have no impact on productivity, perhaps because the German industrial relations system of works councils

---

[37] Albert Hirschman, *Exit, Voice and Loyalty,* Cambridge, Mass.: Harvard University Press (1973); Richard Freeman and James Medoff, *What Do Unions Do?* New York: Basic Books (1984).

[38] Steven Allen, "Trade Unions, Absenteeism, and Exit-Voice," *Industrial and Labor Relations Review* 37: 331–345 (1984).

[39] Charles Brown and James Medoff, "Trade Unions in the Production Process," *Journal of Political Economy* 86: 355–378 (1978); Kim Clark, "Unionization and Firm Performance: The Impact on Profits, Growth and Productivity," *American Economic Review* 74: 839–919 (1984); Brian Bemmels, "How Unions Affect Productivity in Manufacturing Plants," *Industrial and Labor Relations Review* 40: 241–253 (1987); C. Lovell, A. Knox, Robert Sickles, and Ronald Warren Jr., "The Effect of Unionization on Labor Productivity: Some Additional Evidence," *Journal of Labor Research* 9: 55–63 (1988); John Addison and Barry Hirsch, "Union Effects on Productivity, Profits and Growth: Has the Long Run Arrived?" *Journal of Labor Economics* 7: 72–105 (1989); Barry Hirsch, "Innovative Activity, Productivity Growth, and Firm Performance: Are Labor Unions a Spur or a Deterrent?" in Albert Link and V. Kerry Smith (eds.). *Advances in Applied Microeconomics,* Vol. 5, Greenwich, Conn.: JAI Press (1990).

provides similar environments in nonunion firms, although research into the effects of these councils also fails to show a positive impact on productivity. In Japan, on the other hand, productivity in unionized firms is about 15 percent lower than in comparable nonunion firms.[40]

Studies of specific industries suggest mixed effects of unions on productivity. A detailed examination of the cement industry using both cross-section and time-series data on the physical output of cement found 6 to 8 percent greater output per worker in unionized plants. An examination of coal mines in West Virginia in the 1920s, when unionization was occurring, showed that it reduced productivity at small mines but had no effect at larger ones. Unionized sawmills in the western U.S. were between 12 percent and 21 percent less productive than nonunion mills in 1986. Unionized workers constructing office buildings, on the other hand, appeared to be 30 percent more productive than their nonunion counterparts.[41]

There are a number of reasons why studies of the effect of unions on productivity may be biased upward. Suppose that unions have no overall effect on productivity but that there is a variance across firms, with productivity being increased in some and reduced in others. If a number of competitive firms were organized, those where productivity was reduced would have negative profits and would eventually close down. Thus, the surviving firms that are available for researchers to study are only those where productivity increased. One recent study has shown, however, that unions do not have an impact on the failure rate of firms. Given overall small impacts on productivity, this result implies that union wage increases come only at firms that have economic profits.[42]

A more fundamental problem comes from the measure of productivity used in studies such as the first example that found a large positive impact of unionization. Productivity is often defined as *value-added per worker*. There

---

[40] Claus Schnabel, "Trade Unions and Productivity: The German Evidence," *British Journal of Industrial Relations* 29: 15–24 (1991); Giorgio Brunello, "The Effect of Unions on Firm Performance in Japanese Manufacturing," *Industrial and Labor Relations Review* 45: 471–487 (1992); John Addison, Kornelius Kraft, and Joachim Wagner, "German Works Councils and Firm Performance," in Bruce Kaufman and Morris Kleiner (eds.). *Employee Representation: Alternatives and Future Directions* Madison, Wisc.: Industrial Relations Research Association (1993).

[41] Kim Clark, "Unionization and Productivity: Micro-Econometric Evidence," *Quarterly Journal of Economics* 95: 613–640 (1980); Steven Allen, "Unionization and Productivity in Office Building and School Construction," *Industrial and Labor Relations Review* 39: 187–201 (1986); William Boal, "Unionism and Productivity in West Virginia Coal Mining," *Industrial and Labor Relations Review* 43: 390–405 (1990); Merwin Mitchell and Joe Stone, "Union Effects on Productivity: Evidence from Western U.S. Sawmills," *Industrial and Labor Relations Review* 46: 135–145 (1992).

[42] Morgan Reynolds, "Trade Unions in the Production Process Reconsidered," *Journal of Political Economy* 94: 443–447 (1986); Richard Freeman and Morris Kleiner, "Do Unions Make Enterprises Insolvent?" NBER Working Paper No. 4797 (1994).

are two problems with this measure. Value-added confounds the impact of increases in output and increases in prices. Thus, in studies using this measure, if higher union wages lead to higher prices, productivity will apparently increase even if there is no impact on output. In addition, unions may have an effect on the capital/labor ratio that results in unionized firms using *less* capital per worker than otherwise identical firms, even though unions raise wages and should, in a conventional world, cause firms to substitute capital for labor. If unionized firms invested in new capital, their unions might capture some of the returns to this investment in the form of higher wages. This response would reduce the rate of return on investments and cause firms to invest less at the margin. In addition, unions tend to resist technological change in plants, thereby increasing the cost of installing new capital. For example, when Fleet Street newspapers in London installed new presses in the 1970s, in order to obtain agreement from their unions to this technological advance they were forced to make pension and redundancy payments that exceeded the cost of the presses themselves.[43] Several studies for both the U.S. and the U.K. have found that unionized firms invest less in new capital and use more labor-intensive production processes. A similar result can be inferred from the fact that unions in Japan reduce the ratio of profits to sales by almost twice as much as they reduce the rate of return on equity.[44]

Taken together, the evidence for specific industries and the more general evidence for entire economies make it very clear that, even where unions have a positive effect on productivity, it is much smaller than their effect on wages. Unions in the U.S. and elsewhere clearly raise unit labor costs. They probably also lower productivity.

If unions raise wages more than productivity, the implication is that they should reduce profits. Several studies show that unionized establishments earned lower rates of return on investment than nonunion establishments making the same product line. In one random sample unionized firms in the 1970s were only 85 to 90 percent as profitable as nonunion firms of the same size in the same industry. Other studies have found that the rate of return on equity in unionized firms was between 2 and 3 percentage points lower in both the U.S. and the U.K. Given typical rates of return, this finding suggests that unions reduce profits by 25 percent or more. Unions reduced the rate of

---

[43] P. A. Grout, "Investment and Wages in the Absence of Binding Contracts: A Nash Bargaining Approach," *Econometrica* 52: 449–460 (1984); Rick van der Ploeg, "Trade Unions, Investment, and Employment: A Non-Cooperative Approach," *European Economic Review* 31: 1465–1492 (1987); Kevin Denny and Stephen Nickell, "Unions and Investment in British Industry," *Economic Journal* 102: 874–887 (1992).

[44] Kim Clark, "Unionization and Productivity;" Randall Eberts, "Union Effects on Teacher Productivity," *Industrial and Labor Relations Review* 37: 346–358 (1984); John Abowd, "The Effects of Potential Unionization on Industrial Investment," Cornell University Department of Economics, Photocopy (1990); Barry Hirsch, "Firm Investment Behavior and Collective Bargaining Strategy," *Industrial Relations* 31: 95–121 (1992); Denny and Nickell, "Unions and Investment;" Brunello, "The Effect of Unions."

return on equity in Japan by 20 to 25 percent and the ratio of profits to sales by approximately 40 percent.[45]

Several studies show that, other factors held constant, the value of stock shares in a firm whose workers vote to unionize declines in response to the vote. Implicitly the market is signalling that unionization will reduce the firm's profitability. Similarly, when unions raise wages, the value of a firm's common stock falls dollar-for-dollar, implying that union wage increases directly reduce firm profits. Another study found that unionization reduced profits only in concentrated industries. In competitive industries, where there are no excess profits to be made, a firm that becomes unionized either increases productivity by as much as wages increase, and thus survives, or fails to do so and disappears from the industry. Among manufacturing firms in Great Britain between 1973 and 1982, those that paid above-equilibrium wages because of union contracts experienced declining market shares, while nonunion firms that paid equally high wages (presumably for efficiency-wage reasons discussed in Chapter 9) saw an increase in their market share.[46]

These results imply that unionized establishments will gradually account for a smaller share of output in industries where both union and nonunion establishments compete. The more profitable nonunion establishments will attract customers by selling more cheaply. In the aggregate, they suggest that the only way the union sector can maintain its share of output is by continual organization of new firms to replace workers lost in the declining unionized firms that have difficulty competing. The fact that this increase in organizing behavior has not happened in the United States in the past 30 years is shown by the discussion of union growth in Chapter 11 and by the data in Table 11.5.

UNIONS AND RESOURCE ALLOCATION

Because unions change relative wages and employment, they also affect the allocation of labor across sectors of the economy. Figure 13.1 shows the various components of this reallocation's impact on national income. This figure allows us to measure the **welfare effect of unions** (how they affect economy-wide well-being or total output). We assume that the economy is divided

---

[45] Clark, "Unionization and Firm Performance;" Brian Becker and Craig Olson, "Unionization and Shareholder Interests," *Industrial and Labor Relations Review* 42: 246–261 (1989); Stephen Bronars and Donald Deere, "Union Representation Elections and Firm Profitability," *Industrial Relations* 29: 15–37 (1990); Barry Hirsch, "Union Coverage and Profitability among U.S. Firms," *Review of Economics and Statistics* 73: 69–77 (1991); J. R. Cable and S. J. Machin, "The Relationship Between Union Wage and Profitability Effects," *Economics Letters* 37: 315–321 (1991); Brunello, "The Effect of Unions."

[46] Richard Ruback and Martin Zimmerman, "Unionization and Profitability: Evidence from the Capital Market," *Journal of Political Economy* 92: 1134–1157 (1984); John Abowd, "The Effect of Wage Bargains on the Stock Market Value of the Firm," *American Economic Review* 79: 774–800 (1989); Thomas Karier, "Unions and Monopoly Profits," *Review of Economics and Statistics* 67: 34–42 (1985); Jozef Konings and Patrick Walsh, "Evidence of Efficiency Wage Payments in UK Firm Level Panel Data," *Economic Journal* 104: 542–555 (1993).

POLICY ISSUE

DEREGULATION AND UNION IMPACTS

Evidence that higher union wages come at the expense of monopoly profits comes from natural experiments where these profits are suddenly and drastically eliminated. Prior to 1980, the U.S. Interstate Commerce Commission (ICC) severely restricted entry into the for-hire intercity and interstate cartage industry. Operators were required to have a route certificate to haul goods between any two points. The number of certificates issued for any route was strictly limited. The Motor Carrier Act of 1980 effectively eliminated these entry restrictions.

The effect of the route certificates was to establish a government-created monopoly for the firms that possessed them. Prices, even though regulated, were higher than they would have been without the artificial monopoly. Prices fell and traffic shifted back to the for-hire sector from firm-operated in-house trucking following deregulation. The union wage premium fell from 50 percent before deregulation to 30 percent or less afterward. While 30 percent still sounds like a lot, the evidence is that after deregulation almost the entire union wage premium represented unmeasured quality differences between union and nonunion drivers. When these differences are taken into account by using longitudinal data, the union wage premium in trucking following deregulation was only about 5 percent. Since union firms shrank significantly after deregulation and presumably kept only their best drivers, it is likely that quality differences were smaller before deregulation. This conjecture implies that the quality-adjusted union premium was *at least* 25 percent prior to deregulation (50 percent—30 percent—5 percent), and that deregulation removed over 80 percent of unions' excess wages by reducing the monopoly power of trucking firms.[47]

into two sectors, u and n, both originally nonunion. The demand for labor in these sectors is represented by the lines D_u and D_n. We assume for simplicity that the supply curves to each sector, S_u and S_n, are such that the wage is initially w_0 in both sectors. Employment is, therefore, initially E_{0u} and E_{0n}.

Sector u is subsequently organized by unions that negotiate a wage of w_u. We assume that employers determine the number of workers to be hired, so that the union is demand-constrained. Employment in the union sector falls to E_u, as employers and consumers substitute against union labor and union-made products. If we assume that workers who have lost their jobs prefer working at the nonunion wage to remaining unemployed while waiting for a union job, the supply of labor to the nonunion sector increases to S'_N. Wages in that sector, still determined competitively, fall to w_n.

There are two aspects to the loss in total output. The first is the obvious economy-wide reduction in employment. While $E_{0u} - E_u$ workers are displaced from the union sector, employment in the nonunion sector only

[47]Nancy Rose, "Labor Rent Sharing and Regulation: Evidence from the Trucking Industry," *Journal of Political Economy* 95: 1146–1178 (1987); Barry Hirsch, "Trucking Deregulation and Labor Earnings: Is the Union Premium a Compensating Differential?" *Journal of Labor Economics* 11: 279–301 (1993).

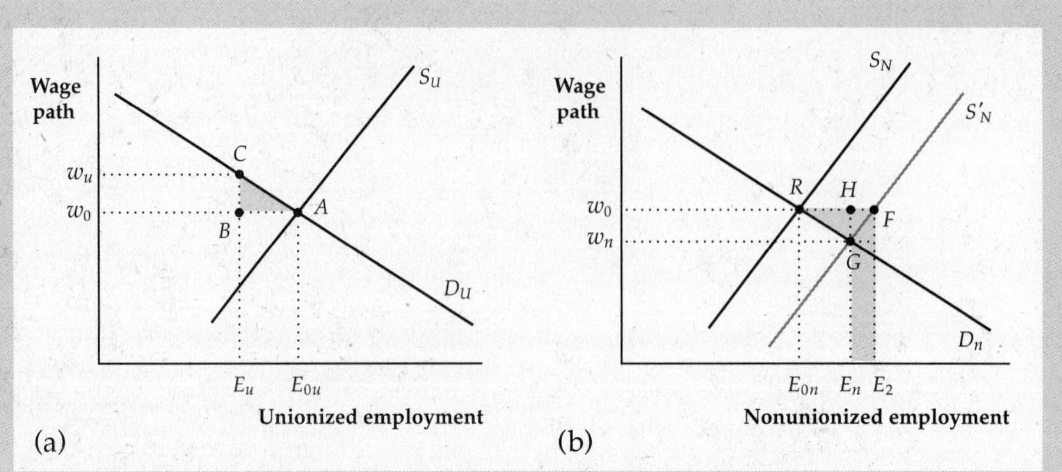

FIGURE 13.1 UNION EFFECTS OF RESOURCE ALLOCATION

Union-imposed wage increases result in two types of deadweight loss in the economy. Workers are reallocated to jobs where their productivity is lower—triangles *ABC* in Figure 13.1 (a) and *GHR* in Figure 13.1 (b). In addition, some workers drop out of the labor force, resulting in lost output of E_nHFE_2 in Figure 13.1 (b).

increases by $E_n - E_{0n}$. $E_2 - E_n$ workers find that the lower nonunion wage falls short of their reservation wage, and leave the labor force. This result is the net employment effect discussed earlier in this chapter.

The second source of loss would occur even if the supply of labor to the market were completely inelastic so that there would be no net employment effect. It arises because workers who have moved from the union to the nonunion sector are employed where their productivity is lower than before. Remember that the demand curve shows the *VMP* of each additional worker employed in a sector. Thus, the area under each demand schedule up to the level of employment in a sector is the value of the sector's total product. The decrease in output in the union sector is the trapezoid E_uCAE_{0u}, while the increase in output in the nonunion sector is the trapezoid $E_{0n}RGE_n$. Since the initial wage in both sectors was w_0, and since $E_{0u} - E_u = E_2 - E_{0n}$, the difference between the two trapezoids consists of the sum of the shaded areas in the two figures. The rectangle E_nHFE_2 represents the lost output resulting from the economy-wide fall in employment. The sum of the two triangles *ABC* and *GHR* represents the output loss due to the reallocation of labor from a more productive use in the union sector to a less-productive use in the nonunion sector. Even if there were no net employment effect, the economy would lose output of *ABC* + *GHR*. If the demand schedule is flatter in the nonunion sector, as the evidence on union and nonunion demand elasticities summarized in Chapter 11 indicates, the shift of labor from the union sector reduces *VMP* only slightly in the nonunion sector. In an extreme case, if demand in the nonunion sector were perfectly elastic so that D_n was flat around employment of E_{0n}, the only loss in output would be the triangle *ABC*.

Assuming that the true adjusted wage gap was 15 percent and ignoring any output losses resulting from net employment losses, one estimate placed the output loss in 1957 when the U.S. economy was much more heavily unionized (see Table 11.5), at only 0.14 percent of GNP. Another estimate based on slightly different methods found the effect to be 0.33 percent for the 1950s, again assuming that the adjusted wage gap was 15 percent. The most recent study accounts for a wide range of possibilities of employer and consumer substitution. Even assuming that $M^* = 25$ percent, it found that the lost output due to inefficient use of labor was only 0.2 percent of GNP in 1971.[48] Given the immense size of the U.S. economy, even a loss as small as 0.2 percent due to allocative inefficiencies caused by unions would amount to about 13 billion dollars in 1994. The losses resulting from restrictive work practices or from lost investment in machinery and industry- and firm-specific human capital when workers are displaced from the unionized sector are likely to be substantially larger.

SUMMARY

It is impossible to measure the true effect of unions on the wages of unionized workers because we cannot observe what their wages would be in the absence of unions anywhere in the economy. Estimates of the difference today between the average union worker's wage and that of the average nonunion worker with the same observable characteristics lie mostly between 15 and 20 percent in the United States and Canada. Once differences in unmeasured characteristics of workers and jobs are accounted for, the estimated wage difference is considerably smaller. Spillover effects appear to be larger than threat effects for the economy as a whole, although not for some specific industries. These factors further reduce the true impact of unions on wages. Union effects on wages are larger in the U.S. than in many other developed countries, where the goals of unions are probably as much political as economic.

Unions in the U.S. generally attempt to equalize wages within firms and industries, meaning that they produce larger wage effects for workers whose wages would otherwise be lower because of their skills, experience, region of residence, or possible discrimination. The wage effect of unions in the U.S. has historically risen in recessions and fallen in booms. It showed a steady

[48] Albert Rees, "The Effects of Unions on Resource Allocation," *Journal of Law and Economics* 6: 69–78 (1963); Harry Johnson and Peter Mieszkowski, "The Effects of Unionization on the Distribution of Income: A General Equilibrium Approach," *Quarterly Journal of Economics* 84: 539–561 (1970); and Robert DeFina, "Unions, Relative Wages and Economic Efficiency," *Journal of Labor Economics* 1: 408–429 (1983).

upward trend from the late 1960s through the early 1980s and has been essentially constant since then despite changes in business conditions.

Because labor demand schedules slope downward, higher union wages induce employers to decrease their use of labor. Although this gross employment effect can be fairly substantial, the net employment effect is smaller since the relative inelasticity of labor supply leads most workers who would have obtained union jobs to find work at lower wages in the nonunion sector. Unions in the United States and elsewhere probably reduce productivity and certainly do not increase it as much as they increase wages. This situation means that unions reduce the profitability of businesses they organize. This reduction reduces the competitiveness of these firms and is partly responsible for the downward trend in unionization.

The gross employment effects imply that unions shift workers to industries where they will be less productive, resulting in some loss of efficiency in the economy as a whole. While it sounds large in absolute terms, when measured as a percentage of GNP this loss is very small.

QUESTIONS AND PROBLEMS

13.1 You are asked by your employer to evaluate the effects on the firm's revenue and costs if production workers in the plant join a union. What information would you request from your employer to make the desired calculations? What information from this and previous chapters would you bring to bear on the issue? Do an illustrative calculation that is responsive to your employer's request.

13.2 Use the following data for 1994 to calculate the unadjusted wage gap M:

Occupation	Union Member	Nonunion
Technicians	$789	$549
Sales workers	408	466
Clerical workers	504	366

List some factors that would cause M^* to deviate from M, being specific in discussing each of the occupations for which data are presented.

13.3 The craft workers in a plant become unionized; other production workers in the plant remain nonunion. Compared to a case where the whole plant is unionized, how much of a wage gap over nonunion craft workers elsewhere will the new union be able to impose? What might the differences be in the productivity gap between craft workers in this plant and nonunion craft workers elsewhere, as compared to what it would be if all workers in the plant were unionized?

13.4 Assume that the elasticity of labor demand is –0.5 in both sectors of Figure 13.1. Assume also that in each sector the supply of labor to the sector has an elasticity of 2.0, but that the elasticity of supply to the entire economy is zero. If sector u accounts for 20 percent of employment initially, what is the impact of its becoming unionized with an adjusted wage gap M^* of 25 percent? Describe the effects on employment in the sector, employment economy-wide, and the size of the lost output, $ABC + GHR$.

13.5 There are approximately 120,000,000 workers in the U.S. Assume that if unions did not exists, each of these workers would earn $25,000. Suppose a union is successful in organizing 20 percent of these workers and obtaining a 10 percent wage increase for their members if the members remain employed. Using these facts and assuming that the elasticity of labor demand is –1.0, calculate:

a. the number of union and nonunion workers in the economy under the assumptions that (i) all workers who are not employed in the union sector are employed in the nonunion sector, and (ii) union members who do not obtain union jobs remain unemployed;
b. the average wage in the union and nonunion sectors under each assumption;
c. assuming that GDP consists entirely of employee compensation, the change in GDP resulting from unionization under each assumption.

Recalculate your answers to (a) through (c) under the assumption that the elasticity of labor demand is –0.5.

13.6 We have seen that unions typically raise the wages of their members by as much as 20 percent over those of statistically comparable nonmembers. What does this fact imply for the aggregate impact of unions on national output?

13.7 Adjusted wage gaps in other countries (such as those shown in Table 13.2) are typically smaller than those for the U.S. and Canada. Why might this be the case? Can you say anything about what the adjusted wage gain is likely to be in these countries relative to that in the U.S.?

13.8 Consider the following pairs of firms or industries. How would you expect a union's impact on productivity to differ between the firms in each pair? Explain your reasoning.

a. Fast food restaurants versus aircraft manufacturers
b. Baseball teams versus coal mines
c. Universities versus cruise ships.

13.9 What does the evidence about M* presented in this chapter tell you about the possible goals of unions discussed in Chapter 11? What additional evidence, if any, would you like to be able to reach a conclusion regarding the relative weight that different unions place on employment and wages in their welfare functions?

13.10 Unadjusted wage differentials are greater for black men than for white men while differentials adjusted for worker characteristics are smaller for black men. This implies that quality differences between union and nonunion workers are greater for blacks. Is this evidence that unions discriminate against black applicants for membership? What other possible explanations are there for the observed pattern? How might you distinguish between them empirically?

KEY WORDS

adjusted benefit gap
adjusted productivity gap
adjusted wage gap
aggregate method
collective voice
countervailing power
deferred pay increases
equalization hypothesis
gross employment effect
intercity method
long-term union contracts
measurement errors
net employment effect
original power
sample selection corrections
spillover effect
threat effect
union/nonunion wage differential
union rents
unit labor costs
wage gain
wage gap
welfare effect of unions

Part Six

Aggregate Outcomes in the Labor Market

In this section we study aggregate outcomes in the labor market. In large part these outcomes simply reflect a "summing up" of the individual decisions we have discussed in the previous sections. It is interesting, however, to see how the decisions made by millions of individual workers and employers determine the overall outcomes that form the focus of much political debate.

In Chapter 14 we discuss pay differences between identifiable groups in the economy such as men and women or workers of different races. We examine the role that discrimination might play in these differences, as well as alternative, nondiscriminatory explanations that might cause group differences in labor market outcomes. Group differences have received much attention from economists and policy makers. We hope to indicate what we now know, what we do not yet know, and what we may never know about the origins of group differences.

Individual decisions that determine incomes also combine to produce a distribution of earnings and a degree of inequality in incomes within the work force. In Chapter 15 we integrate information on the determinants of pay differences to infer how they integrate information on the distribution of earnings, and how they cause it to vary over time. We present additional theories to explain this distribution, and we study the determinants of labor's share of income (the total amount of compensation workers receive out of a particular level of output).

The final chapter of the book brings together a variety of facts and methods to analyze cyclical behavior in the labor market. The major focus is on unemployment and wage changes. Although we examined other forms of unemployment in Chapter 8, demand-deficient unemployment was defferred to this chapter.

Until the 1930s most economists believed that the labor market determined the pattern of relative wages and the general level of real wages. Nominal (or money) wages and the prices were thought to depend entirely on the changes in the quantity of money and its velocity of circulation, rather than on anything that happened in either labor or product markets. In other words, the economy could be divided into two separate sectors, monetary and real, with labor markets forming part of the real sector. All relative prices and the quantities of all real outputs and inputs(and, hence, all real incomes) would be determined in the real sector. The monetary sector would merely determine the nominal units in which prices were stated.

Although this view is not as common as it once was, no alternative has proven able to explain the behavior of wages over the business cycle in a way that wins the approval of most economists. Instead, a variety of views exist each of which is internally consistent, but none of which both explains all the phenomena meriting consideration and has been subjected to careful empirical study. This intellectual disarray characterizes the field of macroeconomic theory in general. Its importance for labor economics is that much of the behavior that macroeconomic theory seeks to describe stems from analyses of the labor market. Thus, throughout Chapter 16 we use the microeconomic theory developed in earlier chapters to attempt to explain the macroeconomic characteristics.

14

EFFECTS OF RACE AND GENDER ON EARNINGS

THE MAJOR QUESTIONS

- ▲ How large are earnings differences between men and women and between members of different racial groups in the U.S.?
- ▲ How do these differences compare with those found for similar groups in other countries?
- ▲ What do theoretical models tell us about the potential of discriminatory behavior to produce various outcomes observed in the labor market?
- ▲ What other factors might explain group differences in labor market outcomes?
- ▲ How have group differences changed over time?
- ▲ How effective have various public policies been in altering differences in labor market outcomes among various groups?
- ▲ Are there other possible policies, and what impacts might they have?

THE EXTENT OF GROUP DIFFERENCES

Nearly the only aspects of the study of racial or gender differences in the labor market where broad consensus exists among economists are that:

1. There are differences between members of various groups in average earnings and the distribution of workers across occupations, and;
2. These differences are reduced, but not eliminated, when observable differences in personal characteristics are taken into account.

TABLE 14.1 MEAN EARNINGS BY WORK STATUS, RACE, ETHNICITY, AND SEX, 1992

	All-Workers		*Full-Time Year-Round Workers*	
	Male	Female	Male	Female
White	$28,245	$15,279	$38,533	$25,727
Black	17,340	12,767	26,921	22,031
Hispanic	18,066	11,746	24,967	20,335
All persons	27,049	14,999	37,469	25,337

Source: Bureau of the Census, *Current Population Reports*, P–60, No. 184, Table 26.

It is worthwhile to begin by examining the size of earnings differentials by race, sex, and ethnicity in the U.S. Table 14.1 presents measures of annual earnings in 1992 for all persons who worked and for those who worked full-time and at least 50 weeks. Earnings in the latter group begin the process of adjusting for differences between workers by eliminating the impacts of unemployment and part-week or part-year work. They do not, however, eliminate all group differences in hours worked, including the probability and extent of overtime. Among steady workers, men earn substantially more than women within each racial or ethnic group. This difference is even more pronounced among all workers, because women more frequently work part-time. White males earn more than Hispanic males, who earn about the same as black males. (Remember from Chapter 1 that Hispanics, according to the official classifications by the U.S. Census Bureau, can be of any race.)

Among women, differences in earnings by race and ethnicity are much smaller. It is important to note that the earnings differences shown in Table 14.1 are gross differentials that are not adjusted for disparities in the amount of skill embodied in workers belonging to various groups or other differences that might exist between the groups.

Our discussion is generally based on comparisons of earnings among various groups in the labor market. Although the appropriate comparison is of total compensation for different groups, data on compensation are not as readily available as data on earnings or wages. In any case, the picture conveyed by earnings comparisons is unlikely to be badly biased. We saw in Chapter 10 that employee benefits, even though increasing in importance, are less than one-fourth of hourly earnings. Some evidence suggests that otherwise identical women receive slightly higher employee benefits relative to their earnings than do men. No comprehensive evidence is available for racial and ethnic groups on this criterion.[1]

The data in Table 14.2 on the distribution of workers by occupation and ethnicity show a smaller representation of blacks and Hispanics at higher levels on the occupational scale. Blacks are underrepresented among white-collar

[1]B. F. Kiker and Sherrie Rhine, "Fringe Benefits and the Earnings Equation," *Journal of Human Resources* 22: 126–137 (1987).

TABLE 14.2 PERCENTAGE DISTRIBUTIONS OF EMPLOYED PERSONS BY OCCUPATION GROUP, 1994

Occupation Group	White	Black	Hispanic[a]
Executive, administrative, and managerial	13.9	8.6	7.5
Professional specialty	14.7	10.1	6.6
Technicians and related support	3.1	2.9	1.9
Sales	12.6	8.2	9.4
Clerical	14.9	17.2	13.2
Total white-collar	59.2	47.0	38.6
Precision production, craft, and repair	11.4	8.1	13.0
Operators, fabricators, and laborers	13.7	20.8	22.9
Total blue-collar	25.1	28.9	35.9
Private household workers	0.6	1.1	2.1
Protective service	1.7	3.2	1.5
Other services	10.3	18.3	16.1
Total services	12.6	22.6	19.7
Farming, forestry, and fishing	3.1	1.5	5.8
Total	100.0	100.0	100.0
Number of workers (millions)	105.2	12.8	10.8

[a]Hispanics may be of any race.

Source: *Employment and Earnings*, (January 1995), p. 181.

workers, craft workers, and farmers, and they are overrepresented everywhere else. Hispanics are very much underrepresented in white-collar occupations and overrepresented elsewhere.

Differences in occupational distributions between employed males and females are shown in Table 14.3. These differences are as substantial as those by race and ethnicity. Women are overrepresented in white-collar and service occupations but underrepresented in blue-collar occupations, especially craft jobs. Within white-collar occupations, they are heavily overrepresented in clerical work and have somewhat fewer managerial and administrative jobs. A more detailed breakdown of occupations would show further differences. Although there is a somewhat higher proportion of women than men among professional and technical workers, some professional groups, such as lawyers, medical doctors, the clergy, and accountants, are heavily male, while others, such as elementary schoolteachers, nurses, and librarians are heavily female.

Differential labor market outcomes are not unique to the U.S. and female/male earnings ratios have been calculated for many countries. In every case women earn less than men. There are issues of potential discrimination against members of racial or ethnic groups elsewhere as well. In

TABLE 14.3 PERCENTAGE DISTRIBUTIONS OF EMPLOYED PERSONS BY OCCUPATION, GROUP, AND SEX, 1994

Occupation Group	Males	Females
Executive, administrative, and managerial	14.0	12.4
Professional specialty	12.5	16.3
Technicians and related support	2.8	3.6
Sales	11.4	12.8
Clerical	5.9	26.0
Total white-collar	46.6	71.1
Precision production, craft, and repair	18.4	2.2
Operators, fabricators, and laborers	20.4	7.7
Total blue-collar	38.8	9.9
Private household workers	0.0	1.4
Protective service	2.8	0.7
Other services	7.4	15.7
Total services	10.2	17.8
Farming, forestry, and fishing	4.4	1.2
Total	100.0	100.0

Source: Employment and Earnings, (January 1995), p. 174.

Canada these issues may focus on anglophone versus francophone, although there are also increasing black/white issues. Germany faces possible discrimination against Turkish immigrants, while in France it is Algerians who may be its victims. In much of Central Europe there may be discrimination against Romanies (Gypsies). In Malaysia, it is the minority Chinese who have been accused of discriminating against the majority Malay community.

In the United States, as in many other countries, different treatment of persons distinguished by race, religion, sex, or ethnicity begins at birth. Fewer resources may be devoted to the care of infants from different groups. Preschool children may receive amounts of early education that differ depending upon their race, ethnicity, or sex. The quality of schools to which children have access may differ. All of these differences may result from discrimination, but they are not **labor market discrimination** by which we mean differences that arise solely out of labor market experiences.

THEORIES OF DISCRIMINATION

The term **discrimination** literally means to distinguish. When we refer to a person of discriminating taste, we generally mean someone who can judge the quality of various things. Thus, to be able to discriminate between vintages of wine is a desirable. The term *discrimination* takes on a negative connotation in the labor market, however, where we use it to refer to treating identical workers differently.

In studying labor market discrimination, it helps to distinguish between **prejudice, differential treatment,** and **differential outcomes.** The term *prejudice* suggests a subjective dislike of a person or group. Prejudice can, but need not, lead someone to treat identical workers from different groups differently—true discrimination. Where discrimination arises from ignorance that leads employers to underestimate the productivity of workers against whom they discriminate or from an inability to determine their productivity, changes may be easier to achieve through improved information than when the discrimination arises from irrational attitudes and beliefs. As we shall see below, however, markets frequently constrain the actions of prejudiced individuals by making it difficult for individuals to exercise their prejudices. Even if some individuals do discriminate against members of certain groups, it is an open question whether the overall impact of this differential treatment will give rise to different outcomes.

Possible forms of discrimination include refusing to employ women or minorities in jobs for which they are qualified, employing them only at lower wages, or insisting on higher qualifications when they are employed at the same wage as other workers. In industrialized countries it is extremely rare for minorities to be paid lower wage rates than whites, or women than men, if they are working in the same job in the same workplace. This pattern was true even in 19th century America when there were no laws on this issue, although within-firm gender differences remained codified in Australian law until recent decades.[2] More probable forms of discrimination involve demanding higher qualifications for members of minority groups for doing the same work, or excluding members of minority groups from the better-paid jobs. When different employers in a market offer different wages for the same occupation, as is almost always the case, minorities tend to be overrepresented in the work forces of the employers who pay the lowest wage.[3]

There are four possible sources of discrimination in labor markets. Employers might treat workers from different groups differently because:

1. they themselves are prejudiced;
2. they believe that their employees are;
3. they believe that their customers are, or
4. government gives them incentives to discriminate.

Employers' testimony about the source of discrimination is not always reliable, since they may be tempted to deny their own prejudice by blaming others. It is important to understand, however, when employers' actions reflect their own attitudes and when they result from a market in which competition forces unprejudiced employers to take into account the attitudes of others.

---

[2]Myra Strober and Laura Best, "The Female/Male Salary Differential in Public Schools: Some Lessons from San Francisco, 1879," *Economic Inquiry* 17: 218–236 (1979).

[3]Albert Rees and George Shultz, *Workers and Wages in an Urban Labor Market,* Chicago: University of Chicago Press (1970), pp. 161–166.

A satisfactory theory of discrimination must explain the striking failure of group differences to be eliminated by the market. After all, if two groups of workers are equally productive but one is paid less, employers can make higher profits by employing workers in the second group. Employers who hire the disadvantaged group should be able to sell for less and drive the discriminators out of the product market, eventually resulting in the disappearance of the discriminatory wage differentials and patterns of employment by occupation. Thus, either the racial, sex, and ethnic differences in Tables 14.1, 14.2, and 14.3 must arise from causes other than labor market discrimination, or there must be some more complex pattern of behavior in the market.

DISCRIMINATION BY EMPLOYERS

The competitive theory of discrimination in employment has been given precise form by Gary Becker.[4] Each employer is viewed as having a **taste for discrimination,** measured by the wage the employer would offer a woman or minority worker relative to an equally qualified male or majority worker. For expository ease, we will often refer to discrimination against minority workers. This term should be understood to refer to any group against which there is potential discrimination. Typically these are members of racial minorities, but in the theoretical section this term may also be understood to include women, who form a majority of the population even if a minority of the labor force. Discrimination may also be directed toward less-obvious "minority" groups. There is evidence, for example, that even after adjusting for observable productivity, earnings are less for short, fat, ugly, or even bald people. In one recent study, men with "below-average looks" (only 12 percent of the population) earned 16 percent less than other men. For women with below-average looks, the earnings penalty was 12 percent. Obese women and short men also faced earnings penalties of over 10 percent when compared to otherwise similar workers. Greater physical attractiveness has been shown to generate higher starting salaries for both male and female MBAs and is associated with more rapid wage growth for women (but not men) from this group.[5]

If employers can hire a majority worker at the wage w, employer i's **discrimination coefficient** is

$$d_i = \frac{w}{w_m} - 1$$

---

[4]Gary Becker, *The Economics of Discrimination*, 2nd. ed., Chicago: University of Chicago Press (1971).

[5]Irene Frieze, Josephine Olson, and June Russel, "Attractiveness and Income for Men and Women in Management," *Journal of Applied Social Psychology* 21: 1039–1057 (1991); Daniel Hamermesh and Jeff Biddle, "Beauty in the Labor Market," *American Economic Review* 84: 1174–1194 (1994).

where

w_m = wage the employer is willing to offer the woman or minority person.

This equation is equivalent to saying that the employer demands greater output from minority workers than majority workers if they are to be offered the same wage. Their output must exceed the majority worker's output by the percentage d_i. Employers who absolutely refuse to hire a woman or a minority person at any wage, however low, have an infinitely large d_i. If d_i is negative, the employer is willing to pay more to an otherwise identical minority or female worker, and thus discriminates in favor of those workers. Obviously, employers' tastes for discrimination are hard to measure, but the concept embodied in the d_i is extremely useful in identifying the factors that lead to differential labor market outcomes by race, sex, and ethnicity.

Employers' discrimination coefficients are likely to reflect a wide range of attitudes, from the bigot who would not hire a minority even if the wage were zero, to the guilt ridden (or reverse bigot) who would prefer hiring the woman or minority person, other things being equal. We can array employers (weighted by the fraction of total jobs they have to offer) according to their d_i, their taste for discrimination, as shown in Figure 14.1. The total area under the curve that ranks employment opportunities by the employers' attitudes

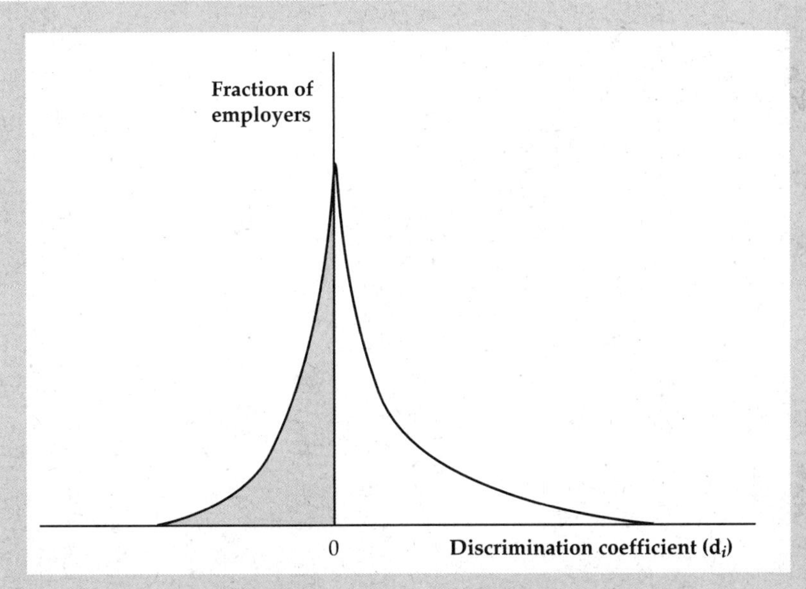

FIGURE 14.1 EMPLOYER'S TASTES FOR DISCRIMINATION
Employers with negative discrimination coefficients prefer hiring minority workers while those with positive coefficients will only hire such workers at lower pay than they would offer majority workers.

toward discrimination is 1. Some employers, indicated by the shaded area, would prefer employing women or minorities. Many, who are motivated only by profit and do not care who they hire, cluster around a d_i of zero. The remaining employers, with positive d_i, discriminate against the minority.

This view of employers' tastes for discrimination is obviously oversimplified. The extent to which employers discriminate not only differs from employer to employer, but may also differ according to the nature of the work. A more complete model would specify a set of d_{ij}'s, where the subscript j identifies an occupation. Where the duties of an occupation conform to a view of the minority's appropriate social role (often that of doing menial or servile tasks), there may be discrimination in favor of the minority. For example, some employers prefer having female secretaries and would be offended by having a male worker doing their clerical work. Yet at the same time they prefer not to hire women for executive positions. This preference suggests that many employers have a negative d_{ij} for female clerical workers and a positive d_{ij} for female executives.

The analysis of labor demand from Chapter 4 can be combined with this approach to discrimination to examine employers' decisions about hiring workers from any minority group. The example in this section is for black and white workers, but the analysis applies with minor changes to employers' choices between any two groups. To make the analysis simple, we can, without changing any key results, assume that black and white workers have equal productivity and are perfect substitutes in production. In this case, the typical firm's isoquants are straight lines like Q_1 in Figure 14.2(a), with $0A$ = $0B$. (The assumption of perfect substitutability is an extreme version of the example presented in Figure 4.8(b).)

We assume that employers like those shown in Figure 14.2(a) seek to produce Q_1 at the lowest cost and that they do not discriminate (their d_i equals 0). If we **normalize** the wage of white workers to be equal to 1, and the wage of blacks is w_b, which is less than 1, the budget lines facing such a firm have a slope of $-w_b$. For the same amount of money the firm can hire more blacks than whites. It will do so, minimizing the cost of producing Q_1 by spending the amount indicated by the budget line I_1 and producing at point B. The firm could spend less (on budget line I_0), but it would not be able to produce Q_1. It could spend more (as on I_2) to produce Q_1, but that would be wasteful. Thus, the nondiscriminatory firm will hire only blacks if blacks' wage rates are less than whites', and the two groups are perfect substitutes.

Figure 14.2(b) reproduces the isoquant Q_1 and the budget line I_1. This budget line, however, is no longer relevant if the employer has a positive taste for discrimination, so that its d_i is greater than 0. Each black worker costs the firm w_b in wages, which is less than the white worker's wage of 1. Employers, however, also incur an additional cost of hiring workers because of their prejudice against blacks. The monetary equivalent of this **psychic cost of discrimination** is $d_i w_b$. For the discriminatory firm shown in Figure 14.2(b), the typical budget constraint is steeper, like I, with a slope of $-w_b[1 + d_i]$. If the firm's discrimination coefficient more than offsets the lower wage

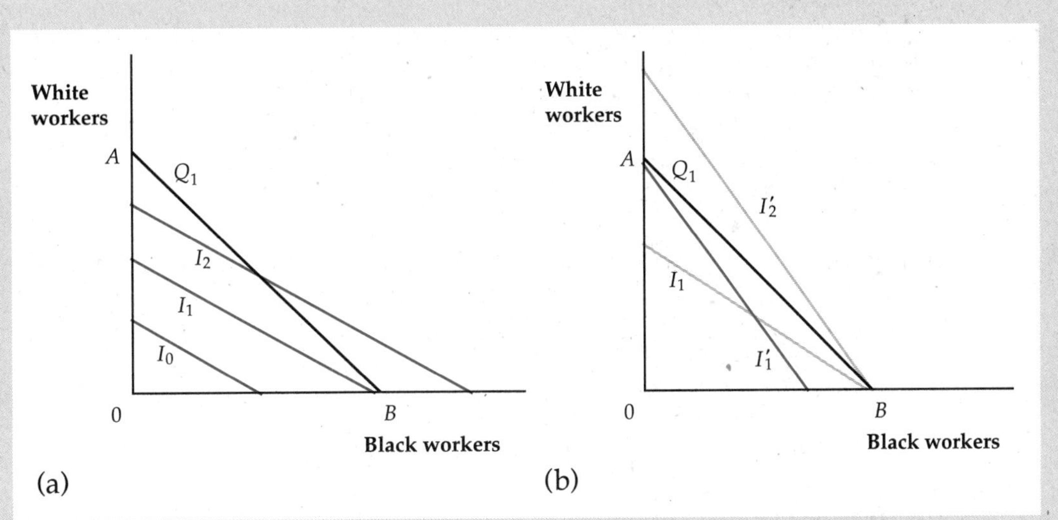

FIGURE 14.2 HIRING DECISIONS WITH DIFFERENT DISCRIMINATION COEFFICIENTS

If equally qualified black workers earn a lower wage, the employer with a discrimination coefficient of 0 in Figure 14.2(a) will minimize costs by hiring only black workers. With a sufficiently positive discrimination coefficient, the employer in Figure 14.2(b) will find his total costs (including psychic costs) minimized by hiring only white workers.

rate paid to blacks, as in the figure, the absolute value of this slope exceeds 1. This firm could still hire 0*B* blacks, but the "cost" would be indicated by the budget line I'_2. The firm instead operates along I'_1 hiring only whites at point *A* and having higher wage costs than if blacks were hired, since $0A = 0B$ and whites' wages are higher than blacks'. The extra monetary cost in terms of wages is more than offset in the employer's mind by the absence of a need to bear the psychic costs of employing minorities. Total "costs," including the employer's appraisal of the monetary equivalent of the firm's tastes for discrimination, are lower than if the employer hired only blacks.

Discrimination by employers based on their own tastes and prejudices implies that they do not maximize money profits. Instead, they maximize utility that is affected by both profits and their taste for discrimination. To some extent, they trade off money profits in order to indulge their tastes about the composition of the work force, by paying higher wages than they need to or accepting less-qualified workers than others whom they could recruit at the same wage.

This theory of discrimination directly contradicts the traditional Marxist analysis, which states that capitalists discriminate against or exploit minorities in order to increase their monetary profits. The present analysis does not deny that some whites make monetary gains as a result of discrimination in employment. Instead, it asserts that the big gainers are the white male workers who get the good jobs that, in the absence of discrimination, would have gone to women or minorities. Nondiscriminating employers like those shown in Figure 14.2(a) also gain, since they can hire equally qualified minority or female labor at a lower wage. One leading economic consultant acknowledged this fact by hiring mostly women for his company, arguing that they were better qualified than the male economists he could find and need be paid no more.

Having seen how the individual employer behaves, we now ask what the market outcomes will be. In particular, what wage differential will arise between blacks and whites? In a competitive labor market the size of the wage ratio, $w_b/1$, between equally competent blacks and whites will depend on two factors: (1) the distribution of employers by their d_i (shown in Figure 14.1), and (2) the size of the minority group. The outcome is depicted in Figure 14.3, which represents the labor market for an occupation in one geographic area. For simplicity, total employment in the occupation is assumed to be constant. We assume, as before, that the white wage is fixed at unity and will not be depressed by a reduction in white employment. This is the equiva-

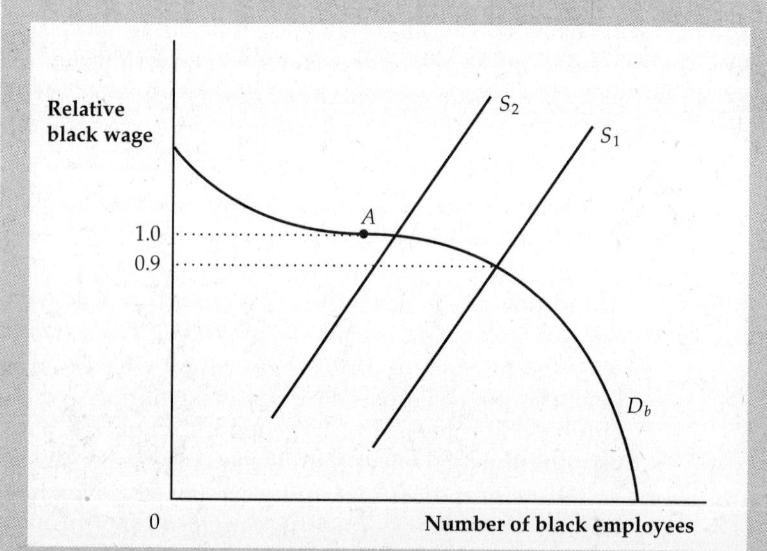

FIGURE 14.3 THE DETERMINATION OF WAGE DIFFERENTIALS WITH DISCRIMINATION BY EMPLOYERS

When tastes for discrimination differ among employers, the relative market wage depends on the location of the supply curve. No matter where the location of this curve, minority workers will be segregated in the workplaces of the least discriminating employers.

lent to assuming that the supply of white labor is perfectly elastic to this labor market. The vertical axis shows the black wage rate, w_b, which, since we have defined the white wage as equal to 1, is equivalent to the ratio of the black wage to the white wage (w_b/w_w).

The demand schedule for blacks, D_b, shows the total number of jobs that will be offered to blacks at each wage, holding the white wage fixed at 1. It is formed from the array of employers by their tastes for discrimination presented in Figure 14.1. As implied by Figure 14.2(a), employers with a 0 or negative d_i will only hire black workers as long as their wage is at or below 1 (the wage paid to whites). The fraction of employers in the shaded area in Figure 14.1 determines the number of black employees hired if $w_b = 1$ where there is no racial wage differential. It thus determines the location of point *A* in Figure 14.3. The D_b curve falls to the right of point *A*, because employers with positive discrimination coefficients can be induced to hire black workers only if blacks' wages are below 1. It falls fairly slowly around point *A* since, as Figure 14.1 is drawn, a large number of employers are profit oriented and have discrimination coefficients near 0. It reaches the x-axis because we have assumed that some employers are so prejudiced that they will not hire the minority group members at any wage. The market wage ratio, $w_b/1$, is determined by the position of the supply curve. If the supply curve is S_1, the wage ratio is 0.9. If the supply curve is S_2, it will be about 1. When the supply of minority workers is larger, their relative wage will be lower. In general, the **market discrimination coefficient** is

$$MDC = \frac{w_w^*}{w_b^*} - 1,$$

where * indicates the market equilibrium wage rate for each of the two groups. This theory predicts that discriminatory pay differentials will be greater where the minority group is a larger fraction of the total population.

Our discussion of search in Chapter 6 suggests one way that lower wages for blacks might arise in a world where only some employers discriminate. If minority workers do not know which employers discriminate against them, the marginal return to each job contact will be lower than it would be in a nondiscriminatory world since each contact has some probability of turning up one of the discriminating employers. With lower returns to searching, blacks will search less and, therefore, have lower expected wages even though there might be sufficient nondiscriminating employers to provide jobs for all the black workers.[6] Once again, however, profit maximization should eliminate this problem. Employers are not passive in the matching process. Rather, nondiscriminating employers still have a strong incentive to compete with each other to hire black workers and will make it widely

[6]Dan Black, "Discrimination in an Equilibrium Search Model," *Journal of Labor Economics* 13: 309–334 (1995).

known that they do not discriminate. Thus, the assumption that black workers cannot avoid wasting resources contacting discriminating employers seems unreasonable.

There are several troubling implications of discrimination theory based on employer preferences. No matter what the position of the supply curve, employers whose taste for discrimination puts them to the left of where the supply curve intersects the demand schedule D_b in Figure 14.3 will hire only black workers. For these employers the market wage differential is larger than is needed to overcome their desire to discriminate. Similarly, those to the right of the intersection point will hire only whites. Thus, discrimination by employers should lead to strict segregation of workers, with some all-black firms existing alongside some all-white firms producing the same product in the same industry. While there is undoubtedly some segregation of workers across firms, the sort of strict separation that employer discrimination should create is not observed.

In addition, as we said earlier, discriminating employers are not profit maximizing. The wage paid to black workers is below their value of marginal product by the amount of the employer's discrimination coefficient. In a competitive industry, however, the maximum profits an employer can earn are 0. Thus, employers who discriminate must be operating at a loss. Other employers to the left of the intersection can hire black labor of standard quality at a below-standard wage. They will be able to produce at a lower cost, expand sales, and eventually drive the discriminators out of business. Thus, discrimination by employers is inconsistent with competitive product markets. Employers with a positive d_i will find that they can earn more on their money by putting it in the bank or into some other activity that does not require them to employ labor.

If it is difficult for competitive firms to discriminate, employer discrimination should be more common in industries where firms have market power. Firms with economic profits could discriminate and still remain in business if they were willing to sacrifice some of their profits in order to sell at the same price as their nondiscriminating competitors. In the extreme case where the firm is a monopolist, it can engage in discrimination by refusing to hire minority workers. The cost of this discrimination would be the reduction in profits resulting from employing majority workers at a higher wage than the wage that would prevail if the firm did not discriminate.

In fact, the evidence on whether monopolistic employers pay lower wages for otherwise identical blacks (or women) is mixed.[7] Perhaps monopolistic

---

[7]Becker, *The Economics*, Chapter 3; Orley Ashenfelter and Timothy Hannan, "Sex Discrimination and Product Market Competition: The Case of the Banking Industry," *Quarterly Journal of Economics* 101: 149–173 (1986); William Johnson, "Racial Wage Discrimination and Industrial Structure," *Bell Journal of Economics* 9: 70–81 (1978).

employers' protected positions are offset by a greater susceptibility to government pressures to offer nondiscriminatory terms of employment, or perhaps other forces are at work. For market power to create discrimination, monopolists must not only dislike employing minority group members, they must actively desire to *hurt* members of this group. The market value of a firm reflects the present discounted value of the profits it will earn in the future. As we have seen, these profits will be lower if the firm discriminates than if it employs minority members. Thus, the market value of the firm will be increased if the firm stops discriminating. If the current owners receive negative utility from employing blacks, they will find that their firm is worth more if it is sold to another owner with a lower d_i. They can invest the proceeds from this sale elsewhere, earn a greater return, and still not have to employ minority members. Thus, for firms with market power to be agents of discrimination in a long-run equilibrium, their owners must receive positive utility from seeing blacks work at lower wages. In this case, they may still be willing to retain ownership of their firm in order to be able to employ blacks.

This analysis is further enhanced by the fact that employment decisions are typically made by managers of a firm rather than its owners, the stockholders. Stockholders probably neither know nor care about the racial composition of their firm's work force. They do care, however, about the price of their stock. Thus, if current managers are lowering the stock price by refusing to employ the lowest-cost labor, they will find themselves vulnerable to a corporate takeover that would replace them with managers who will maximize profits and increase the stock price. Thus, the **market for corporate control** suggests that, even in industries where firms have market power, the long-run outcome will be identical to that in the competitive industry—segregation across workplaces but no difference in wages.

OCCUPATIONAL CROWDING

The data in Table 14.3 show that women are disproportionately employed in certain occupations. Some researchers have sought to explain this fact through a variant of discrimination theory called **occupational crowding.** Crowding is postulated to arise if employers' discrimination coefficients differ greatly depending upon the occupation. Crowding models have been more applied to the labor market for women than for racial minorities. For example, if an employers' discrimination coefficients d_{ij} are large and positive for women in managerial jobs but negative for women in clerical jobs, it might generate crowding. Once again, however, it is difficult for such models to generate wage differences.

Imagine a world with just these two occupations, computational and clerical, as shown in Figure 14.4. We will assume that these occupations require the same abilities and training. In the absence of discriminatory tastes by employers, the supply curve in each market is shown by S_{MF}, and wages are equal at w. With discrimination, employers will not hire women for computational jobs, forcing them into the clerical market. The crowding hypothesis

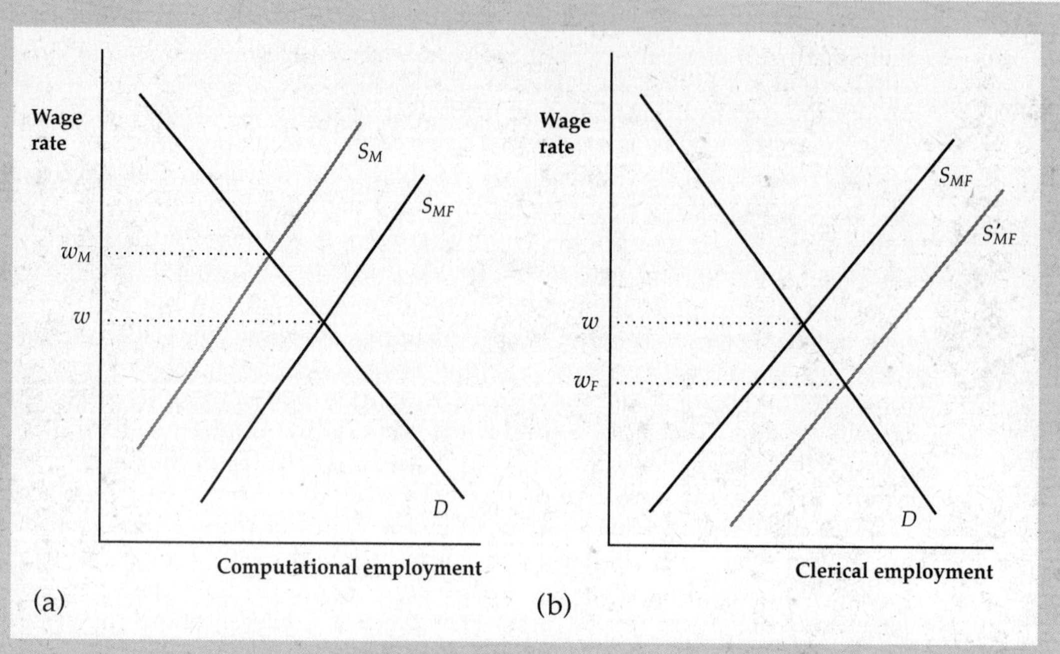

FIGURE 14.4 THE EFFECT OF OCCUPATIONAL CROWDING
In the short run, exclusion of a group from one occupation will shift supply curves and lower the wage of that group. In the long run, mobility by nonexcluded workers will restore the original equilibrium.

assumes that this situation will shift the supply curve in the computational market leftward to S_M, and raise wages to w_M. Occupational crowding supposedly shifts supply in the clerical market out to S'_{MF}, reducing wages to w_F. Thus, it is asserted, women will be stuck in low-paying occupations and will on average receive lower wages than men with the same formal training. Women and men in the same narrowly defined occupation may receive equal pay, but women's wages will be lower in the aggregate because they are crowded into less-desirable occupations by employers' relative distaste for employing them in better-paying occupations.[8] This theory has the obvious prediction that women will receive lower wages than men only because they are in different occupations. The corollary is that men working in occupations that have many female workers will earn less than otherwise identical men working in occupations that have few women.

Upon reflection, there is an obvious problem with this model. Consider the incentives faced by men who, without crowding, would work in the cleri-

[8]Barbara Bergmann, "The Effect on White Incomes of Discrimination in Employment," *Journal of Political Economy* 79: 294–313 (1971).

cal occupation. There is no reason for them to accept lower wages, so they will shift from clerical to computational work, restoring the original supply curves. If the wages would have been equal without crowding, out-mobility by men will continue until they are equal again. Thus, discrimination by employers regarding what jobs they will make available to women will again generate segregation, this time by occupation, but not wage differentials among equally talented workers. For crowding to generate wage differentials, jobs open to women would have to be so limited that they could not absorb the number of women who wanted to work at the wage that would prevail without discrimination. It is not sufficient that some almost exclusively female jobs exist. If *any* jobs contain a significant number of both sexes (and there are many such jobs), then mobility will ensure equal wages for all jobs requiring equal skills. Mobility by men between "male" and "mixed" jobs will ensure that these are rewarded equally, while mobility by women between "mixed" and "female" jobs will bring the compensation of the primarily female jobs up to the overall level.

In addition, if discrimination explains occupational segregation, the question arises as to why some employers don't realize they could gain a competitive advantage by employing minority group workers in jobs from which they have previously been excluded. These employers might even be members of the minority group themselves, if they have access to capital markets. Otherwise, this task would have to fall to less-discriminatory majority-group employers.

Of course, **occupational segregation** can arise from reasons other than discriminatory behavior by employers. For example, as long as women are more likely to leave the labor force for at least part of their adult lives, it pays them not to invest in occupations that require substantial firm-specific training. This behavior leads profit-maximizing employers to structure some occupations to be productive without such investments in order to attract female workers.[9] In addition, if jobs differ in ways other than their wages, systematic group differences in tastes and preferences will lead to different choices regarding occupation even in the absence of discrimination.

STATISTICAL DISCRIMINATION

Even though the theory of occupational crowding accords with the facts about the occupational distribution of workers by sex, it is not very satisfying if women have the same lifetime commitment to the labor market as men. It requires some enforcement mechanism that inhibits individual discriminating employers from realizing that they can make greater profits by hiring the group that is discriminated against. Unless one believes there is massive collusion among employers throughout an economy, such models require some

[9]Peter Kuhn, "Demographic Groups and Personnel Policy," *Labour Economics* 1: 49–70 (1993).

mechanism that makes it difficult for individual employers to depart from the discriminatory norm.

One possibility arises if employers have a differential ability to discern the true productivity of white males as compared to that of minority or female workers. Suppose no employer has a taste either for or against minority or female employees, meaning that every d_{ij} is 0. Employers, however, have more difficulty discovering the true productivity of women or minority workers than of white males. We refer to the outcome of this difficulty as **statistical discrimination.** Its potential effects can be seen in Figure 14.5, which relates the worker's productivity (*VMP*) in a typical occupation to his or her score on a predictor that may be used in screening new employees. We present the analysis for black workers, but a similar presentation could be offered for women. The predictor might be the applicant's score on a test, grades in school, or prior work experience.

We assume that black and white workers are, on average, equally productive in the occupation. Both groups have an average productivity of *VMP**, but productivity varies within each group so that some have higher and some lower *VMP*s than *VMP**. A predictor (e.g., a test) is used in screening applicants. If this test predicts perfectly the ability of a white worker to

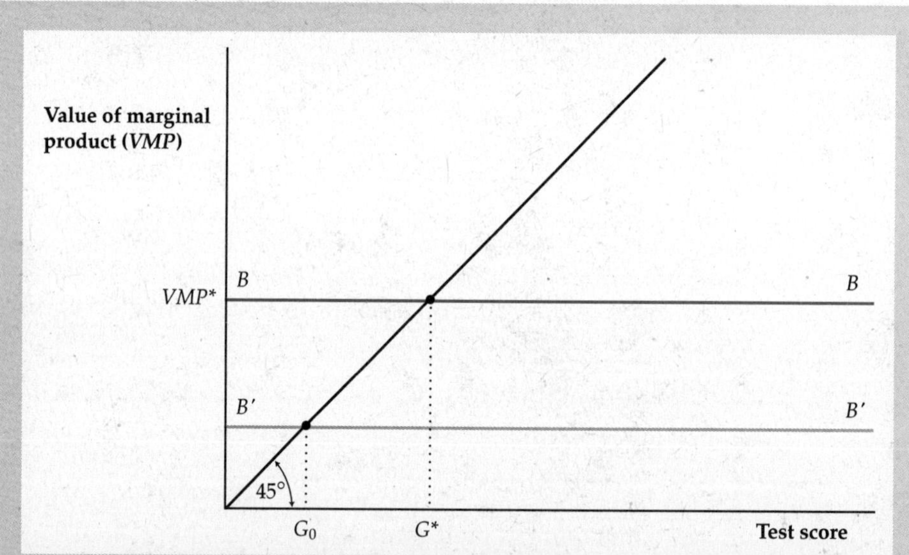

FIGURE 14.5 STATISTICAL DISCRIMINATION

When a test score is less reliable for one group, more able workers will be underpaid and less able workers will be overpaid in that group, but there will be no overall difference in pay. Pay differences will arise if employers are risk averse and must be compensated for the less reliable information available about the group.

perform on the job, the relationship between the test score and *VMP* will be shown by the 45-degree line. Suppose the test is nondiscriminatory in the sense that both black and white workers receive an average score of G^*. The test, however, is such a poor indicator of blacks' productivity that employers cannot distinguish the future productivity of blacks based on their test score.[10] As long as the predictor is more accurate for whites than blacks, the conclusions of this model will hold. If the test provides no information, the relationship between test scores and expected ability among blacks is shown by the line *BB*.

If employers do not mind bearing risks, they will hire blacks in preference to whites when both have below-average scores. Employers know the white will have below-average productivity on this job, but since the test provides no information regarding blacks' performances, their best expectation is that, the black will be average. On the other hand, they will hire whites in preference to blacks if both have above-average test scores. This would imply that, on average, black and white workers would earn the same amount, an outcome that is not consistent with observed wage differences.

Other things being equal, however, employers like most other people are risk averse. If they do not want to bear the risk of hiring blacks who may not be as productive as VMP^*, they will give preference to some whites with test scores below those of blacks. $B'B'$ shows the relation between blacks' test scores and productivity discounted for the risks to employers. Only those blacks scoring below G_0 will be given preference over whites with the same scores. Most blacks will receive lower wages than equally able whites to compensate employers for the risk that the black worker may be less productive, a risk the employer cannot avoid because the test cannot indicate a black person's probable productivity. Even though blacks are as productive as whites on average, blacks will earn less if the indicators used by employers to predict performance are subject to more variability when applied to blacks, *and* employers do not wish to bear the risk this greater variability creates.

Although statistical discrimination has its greatest impact on entry-level wages, its effects may persist much longer. Screening at or shortly after hiring is vital to determining which workers obtain access to the on-the-job training that provides them with a higher path of earnings over the remainder of their working lives. In many instances an individual's productivity is difficult to determine even after many years of employment. This measurement problem was one of the reasons discussed in Chapter 9 as to why piece-rate work is relatively uncommon.

Competition among employers will not eliminate wage differentials that result from a better ability to predict the productivity of white male workers

---

[10]Edmund Phelps, "The Statistical Theory of Racism and Sexism," *American Economic Review* 62: 659–661 (1972); Dennis Aigner and Glen Cain, "Statistical Theories of Discrimination in Labor Markets," *Industrial and Labor Relations Review* 30: 175–187 (1977).

than minorities and women. Only better predictors, or the complete prohibition of the use of information such as tests or previous work records that are less reliable for one group, will eliminate this outcome. Employers will always try to obtain information on prospective employees in order to avoid incurring the cost of training workers with little aptitude for the job. This need gives them very large incentives to develop predictors. Prohibiting the use of information will result in poorer quality matches, on average, and lower national output. Thus, the public policy interest is clear. More and more reliable information about the productivities of various group members will both increase national output and reduce statistical discrimination.

EFFECTS OF TRANSACTIONS COSTS

Even if employers can distinguish perfectly which minority or female workers will perform well there may be inherent costs of hiring these workers that lead to employing them only at a lower wage than white males. Minority workers may have different customs and a different language than employers. The cost to the employer of learning these customs and languages and/or restructuring the workplace so they do not affect operations must be offset by lower wages to maintain a competitive rate of profit. In many cases such restructuring may be impossible or very costly. In most jobs workers need to be able to communicate with supervisors, coworkers, and perhaps the public. It will be especially costly to accommodate members of very small minority groups. If a single worker in a firm speaks only Albanian, for example, it may be prohibitively expensive to provide translators to allow him to function. This **transactions cost approach** suggests that group differences are the result of real differences in worker productivity and will be greatest for small minority groups.[11] Where a minority group is large, it will cost less per worker for employers to learn the language of the minority.

The transactions cost approach can be useful in explaining labor market outcomes for cultural, ethnic, and linguistic minorities. In explaining discrimination against women it is useful only if one resorts to arguments best left to sociologists about women's early-childhood socialization producing cultural differences. The transactions cost approach implies that only if the government explicitly requires equal pay for workers with identical characteristics other than race, language, or sex will it be able to alter outcomes. Without such requirements, employers in competitive product markets will lose out if they do not pay differential wages. With such requirements, employers will attempt to avoid hiring the less-productive group. If they are forced to hire these workers, costs of production will rise and national output

---

[11]Kevin Lang, "A Language Theory of Discrimination," *Quarterly Journal of Economics* 101: 363–382 (1986); George Akerlof, "Discriminatory, Status-based Wages among Tradition-oriented, Stochastically Trading Coconut Producers," *Journal of Political Economy* 93: 265–276 (1985).

will fall. Thus, the public policy debate would have to decide whether the benefits from such a policy would be sufficient to justify the costs.

DISCRIMINATION BY FELLOW EMPLOYEES, UNIONS, AND CONSUMERS

If it is difficult to explain wage differentials as a result of employers' behavior, perhaps the source of discrimination in the labor market lies elsewhere. Suppose that white workers do not like working alongside blacks. In this case they will have to be paid a compensating differential to do so. Particular problems may arise from the relationships between supervisors and their subordinates.[12] Whites may have more intense and persistent prejudice against having a black supervisor than against having black subordinates or coworkers.

If we define the compensating differential that white workers require to work alongside blacks as c, then

$$w_w = w_b + C.$$

Since VMP_b is equal to VMP_w by definition, it is clear that the wages of both groups cannot equal their *VMP*. Paying black workers their *VMP* and white workers a higher wage (by the amount c) would be impossible, since then the average wage would be greater than the *VMP*, and the employer would be taking a loss. Thus, in equilibrium black workers would have to be paid less than the value of their marginal product and less than their white coworkers.

There is some evidence for the U.S. that in 1980, white workers whose work group contained blacks or Hispanics received higher wages, accounting for other differences, than other white workers. Their higher pay might be viewed as a compensating differential to offset the white workers' distaste for working alongside minorities. There was no relationship between male workers' pay and the presence of women in their work group, suggesting that employee discrimination cannot be a source of thc pay differences between men and women.[13]

Once again, however, this outcome should not be stable. Another firm could enter the market, hire the blacks, and make a profit even after raising their wages. Again market forces lead to segregation but not wage differentials. An approximation to this result can arise even within a firm. Different races could be hired to work on different shifts or in different areas of the plant. Thus, for differentials to persist, either black workers must derive positive utility from working in an integrated workplace and therefore be willing

[12]Kenneth Arrow, *Some Models of Racial Discrimination in the Labor Market*, Santa Monica, Calif.: RAND Corporation (1971).

[13]James Ragan and Carol Tremblay, "Testing for Employee Discrimination by Race and Sex," *Journal of Human Resources* 23: 123–137 (1988).

to accept lower wages to do so, or there must be a reason why the two groups have to work together.

One possibility is if blacks and whites are complements in production. For instance, the play *Othello* perhaps requires one white and one black leading actor. In most cases, however, complementarity in production derives from different skills. Perhaps only majority group members have certain skills required in the production process. Thus, employers would have to employ members of the majority group to work alongside minority group members. Once again, however, this outcome should be transitory. It will raise the return to blacks for acquiring the skill in question. Unless there are nonlabor-market barriers to training for blacks, they will eventually acquire the needed skill and be employed in segregated workplaces.

It is easier to see how racial wage differentials can arise from the attitudes and policies of trade unions. As we have seen, when unions negotiate above-equilibrium wages there will be an excess supply of labor to the affected job. Some method must be devised to select workers from this queue. For employers the analysis is similar to that of the nonunion workplace. Profit considerations will lead them to select the most productive workers no matter what their race. For union members, however, the story is different. Their sole interest is to exclude *somebody* in order to restrict supply and raise wages. Since somebody must be excluded, why not make it those against whom they are prejudiced?

Thus, the impact of unions on racial groups will depend on who controls the selection of workers from the queue. Where the employer makes these decisions, impacts should be minor. Where the union has effective control over the labor supply, minority group members may be discriminated against. Since craft unions are more likely to have some control over labor supply, minority workers should fare worse in occupations organized by such unions. Many craft unions have traditionally excluded black members and to some extent still do so, despite various public pressures designed to make them change. For example, among workers admitted to craft union locals in Seattle in 1980, blacks were offered fewer hours of work per year on union jobs and were more likely to be terminated for cause. Blacks in the skilled manual crafts are, therefore, concentrated in the nonunion sectors and have much lower average earnings than do whites. As would be predicted, there is no current evidence that black workers are at a disadvantage in industrial unions, where union control over labor supply is rare.[14]

The overall effect of unionism on black-white earnings ratios can be decomposed into two parts: (1) the extent to which black and white workers are represented by unions; and (2) the effect of unions on the relative earn-

[14]Eugene Silberberg, "Race, Recent Entry, and Labor Market Participation," *American Economic Review* 75: 1168–1177 (1985); F. Ray Marshall, *The Negro and Organized Labor*, New York: Wiley (1965).

ings of those they represent. Table 11.3 showed that blacks are more likely to be unionized than whites. Similarly, Table 13.6 showed that unions increased wages more for black than for white workers after controlling for worker characteristics. This finding is consistent with other studies that have estimated adjusted union wage gaps by race in the U.S. and found that the gap is larger among blacks than among whites, perhaps by about 5 percentage points. With greater unionization and a larger adjusted wage gap, it seems clear that unions in the U.S. raise the black-white earnings ratio on average. Unions benefit blacks partly because of their desire for uniform wages, the equalization hypothesis discussed in Chapter 13. Another part of the difference may result from how unions change the operation of the workplace. Unionization produces a greater reduction in the propensity of otherwise identical black workers to quit a job than it does for whites. This attachment enables black union members to acquire the specific on-the-job training that raises their earnings relative to those of whites with the same total labor-market experience.[15]

The evidence on adjusted union wage gaps for men and women is mixed, but in most studies the gap is about the same.[16] Coupled with the sharply lower extent of unionization among women than men (see Table 11.3), the net effect is that unionism reduces the female-male earnings ratio. As we saw in Chapter 11, there has been a decline in the extent of unionization in the U.S. in recent years. This decline has been more substantial for men than for women. This difference should increase the ratio of female-to-male wages and, indeed, the evidence is that the greater decline in unionism among men has increased the female-male wage ratio by a little over 1 percentage point.[17]

A final possible source of discrimination is **customer discrimination** resulting from a prejudice by consumers against buying products or services produced or offered by sellers from certain ethnic groups or sexes. Prejudice by consumers or buyers is important only in occupations where workers are in direct contact with customers. Buyers of manufactured goods do not know the race or sex of workers in the factory where the goods were made, but they can observe the salespeople who serve them. Consumer tastes operate in both directions. Black consumers may have a more intense preference for buying from black salespeople than white customers have for buying from whites. This preference implies that residential segregation produces segregation in employment in retail trade and services. Nevertheless, consumer prejudice

[15]H. Gregg Lewis, *Union Relative Wage Effects: A Survey*, Chicago: University of Chicago Press (1986), p. 119; Duane Leigh, "Unions and Nonwage Racial Discrimination," *Industrial and Labor Relations Review* 32: 439–450 (1979).

[16]Lewis, *Union Relative*, p. 118.

[17]William Even and David Macpherson, "The Decline of Private-Sector Unionism and the Gender Wage Gap," *Journal of Human Resources* 28: 279–296 (1993).

may lower the relative incomes of blacks even though it operates in both directions. First, the policies of businesses that serve all neighborhoods, such as downtown department stores, may be dominated by the tastes of the white majority. Second, whites have higher per-capita purchasing power, so black influence on retailers' employment policies maybe less than the number of black customers would suggest.

Customer prejudice against a group will result in members of that group being less productive in certain occupations. Unless these are occupations in which innate talents would otherwise have earned rents, the result, once again, will be that minority group members should concentrate in certain occupations. Mobility among majority-group workers that equalizes the net return across occupations for workers of equal skill should, as discussed in Chapter 7, result in wages being equal for these different occupations.

MEASURING DISCRIMINATION

The fact that there are differences in earnings or other labor market outcomes between groups does not provide much guidance for public policy. What we want to know is how much of these differences results from labor market discrimination; how much results from discrimination prior to entry into the labor market (such as denial of access to education); and how much results from nondiscriminatory differences in workers' tastes, preferences, and abilities. Several statistical approaches have arisen to attempt to distinguish these factors. Unfortunately, as we will see, none is entirely satisfactory, leaving a great deal of room for economists, courts, and policymakers to interpret the "facts" according to their own beliefs.

The simplest method used in an attempt to measure the extent of discrimination estimates a statistical equation of the form:

$$w = F(X) - MDC \times R$$

where

R = a dummy or indicator variable that takes the value of 1.0 if a person is in the group against which there is potential discrimination;

MDC = the market discrimination coefficient;

X = a vector including all the observable factors, such as education.

This equation is not, however, a very satisfactory method of measuring discrimination. In effect, the coefficient on R measures only "free floating" discrimination since it imposes an assumption that productive characteristics are rewarded equally for members of both groups. Discrimination, however, may be more subtle. Employers may pay women or minority group members less for each year of schooling, experience, or other characteristics.

Most studies investigating group differences use a more sophisticated technique that also allows rewards for productive characteristics to vary

POLICY ISSUE

BLACKS IN PROFESSIONAL ATHLETICS

The prediction of equal wages will not hold where unusual native talents mean that some workers are more productive in one occupation than in all others. One of the most striking trends in the U.S. labor force has been the growing presence of minorities in professional sports. For example, until the late 1940s there were no blacks in major-league baseball. Until the 1980s no black player was a starting quarterback on a professional football team. Today all of these barriers have fallen. Indeed, blacks account for a far larger share of major-league baseball, basketball, and football players than they do of the population at large. This integration would suggest that any problems of pay discrimination and occupational segregation should now be history.

This observation is almost true in professional baseball. Adjusted for players' productivity (see the Policy Issue in Chapter 5), black players receive the same pay as whites, although they are less likely than whites to play certain positions. There is still substantial segregation by position in football and some apparent salary discrimination even within positions. In basketball, despite the fact that the majority of stars are black, there are substantial pay differences. Depending on the study, white players with the same on-court performance (rebounds, points per game, assists, etc.) are shown to be paid between 10 and 25 percent more than black basketball players.[18]

It is not likely that the source of this differential is the other players (since so many of them are black). While it is possible for the employers to discriminate, many of them are absentee owners who have little contact with the players. We can explain the continuing discrimination in basketball and football, although not its near-disappearance in baseball, as being discrimination by the mostly white customers. White sports fans appear willing to pay more to watch an otherwise equally talented white player. This preference leads team owners, who seek to maximize receipts from attendance and television rights, to bid more for white players, which in turn leads to the observed differential outcomes in this very special labor market.

Some very good evidence of the importance of customer discrimination is shown by the prices customers pay for baseball cards, memorabilia of past players that are traded in open markets. Adjusting for the scarcity of a card and the productivity of the player, cards depicting black players sell for between 10 and 15 percent less than those of white players.[19] Since the only agents in this market are consumers, they must be the source of the discrimination.

---

[18] Lawrence Kahn, "Discrimination in Professional Sports: A Survey of the Literature," *Industrial and Labor Relations Review* 44: 395–418 (1991).

[19] Clark Nardinelli and Curtis Simon, "Customer Racial Discrimination in the Market for Memorabilia: The Case of Baseball," *Quarterly Journal of Economics* 105: 575–596 (1990); Torben Andersen and Sumner LaCroix, "Customer Racial Discrimination in Major League Baseball," *Economic Inquiry* 29: 665–677 (1991).

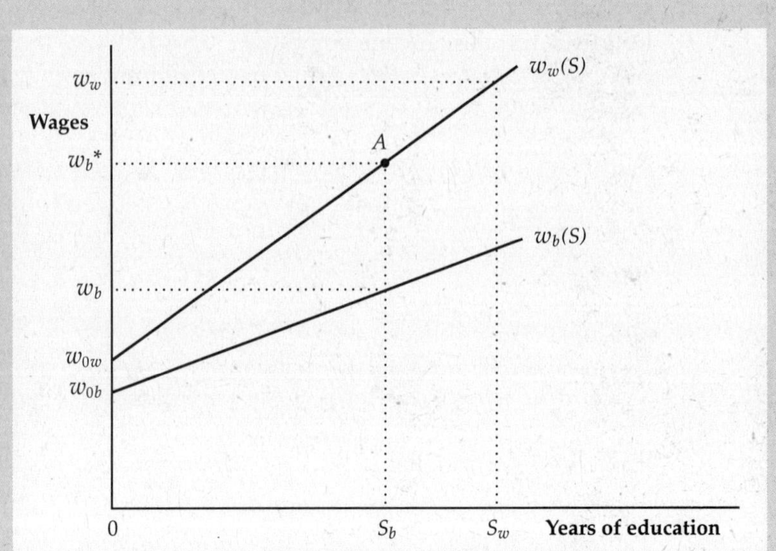

FIGURE 14.6 DECOMPOSING WAGE DIFFERENCES
The difference between black wages w_b and white wages w_w can be decomposed into two parts: what blacks would earn if they were paid the same as whites for their observed characteristics ($w_b^* - w_b$) and an unexplained residual ($w_w - w_b^*$).

across groups.[20] This technique can be understood by referring to Figure 14.6 where we show the relationship between wages and a productive characteristic, for example, education. Here it is assumed that employers pay blacks less than whites independent of any differences in education (w_{0b} is less than w_{0w}). In addition, they reward blacks less for each year of school they attend. The slope of the line showing how wages vary with schooling for blacks $w_b(S)$ is flatter than the slope of the line for whites $w_w(S)$. We also assume that blacks have, on average, less education than whites (S_b is less than S_w). Given this structure, black workers will earn w_b and whites will earn w_w.

The question of interest is how much of the difference between w_w and w_b is due to discrimination. Implicitly, this is the same as asking: What would black workers earn if they were rewarded in the same way as white

[20] Alan Blinder, "Wage Discrimination: Reduced Form and Structural Estimates," *Journal of Human Resources* 8: 436–455 (1973); Ronald Oaxaca, "Male-Female Wage Differentials in Urban Labor Markets," *International Economic Review* 14: 693–709 (1973).

workers?[21] In Figure 14.6 this situation would occur at point A and imply a nondiscriminatory wage for blacks of w_b^*. Thus, the wage differential ($w_w - w_b$) can be divided into a part due to differences in productive characteristics ($w_w - w_b^*$) and a part apparently due to discrimination ($w_b^* - w_b$).

Extension of this **wage decomposition** technique to more than one productive characteristic is straightforward. In general, the relationship between wages and productive characteristics is assumed to be linear. Separate equations relating wages to characteristics are estimated for each group:

$$w_w = \alpha_w + \Sigma\, \beta_{jw} X_{jw}$$

and

$$w_b = \alpha_b + \Sigma\, \beta_{jb} X_{jb}.$$

If we assume that in the absence of discrimination blacks would be paid according to the white relationship, we can calculate their nondiscriminatory wage as:

$$w_b^* = \alpha_w + \Sigma\, \beta_{jw} X_{jb}.$$

These equations hold at the mean values of characteristics and wages for each group. Thus, by a subtle substitution, the difference in average wages between the groups can be written as:

$$\overline{w}_w - \overline{w}_b = (\overline{w}_w - \overline{w}_b^*) + (\overline{w}_b^* - \overline{w}_b).$$

By substitution, this becomes:

$$\overline{w}_w - \overline{w}_b = [(\alpha_w + \Sigma\, \beta_{jw} \overline{X}_{jw}) - (\alpha_w + \Sigma\, \beta_{jw} \overline{X}_{jb})] + [(\alpha_w + \Sigma\, \beta_{jw} \overline{X}_{jb}) - (\alpha_b + \Sigma\, \beta_{jb} \overline{X}_{jb})],$$

which, when we rearrange and cancel terms, becomes:

$$\overline{w}_w - \overline{w}_b = [\beta_{jw}(\overline{X}_{jw} - \overline{X}_{jb})] + [(\alpha_w - \alpha_b) + \Sigma\, (\beta_{jw} - \beta_{jb})\, \overline{X}_{jb}].$$

---

[21]We could ask the reverse question: What would white workers earn if they were paid in the same way as black workers? The general use of the first question reflects an implicit assumption that the relationships prevailing in the majority labor market are what would apply without discrimination. This is probably not too bad an assumption if the minority group is small, but may be increasingly less applicable when it is large enough to cause spillover effects on the market as a whole. More complicated techniques effectively ask for an average of the answers to both these questions. See, for example, Jeremiah Cotton, "On the Decomposition of Wage Differentials," *Review of Economics and Statistics* 70: 236–243 (1988), and David Neumark, "Employers' Discriminatory Behavior and the Estimation of Wage Discrimination," *Journal of Human Resources* 23: 279–295 (1988).

The first part of this equation is typically referred to as the part of the wage difference due to nondiscriminatory differences in productive characteristics, while the second part has been interpreted as the result of discrimination.

There are, however, major problems with this traditional interpretation. Some of them will cause the part of decomposition traditionally attributed to discrimination to overstate the true extent of discrimination, while others will cause it to be underestimated. The first issue involves the factors included in X, the vector of productive characteristics. It is critical that every productive characteristic that might differ between the groups be included. If a characteristic that differs between the groups is omitted, the contribution of the difference in this characteristic to differences in wages will be captured by the constant terms in the equations (the α's), and erroneously show up in our measure of "discrimination." It is clear that we want to control for differences in years of schooling, but that may not be enough. What if one group went to worse schools or earned worse grades? What if the groups studied different subjects? Just as in measuring union wage gaps, it is very hard to account for differences in workers' motivation, inherent ability, and so on.

In effect, the second term in this equation is nothing more than an **unexplained residual.** It *may* represent discrimination, but, on the other hand, it may only represent unmeasured productive attributes. There is no way statistically to differentiate which of these possibilities is the correct explanation. Thus, the unexplained residual has functioned as a sort of Rorschach test for analysts. Those who believe that discrimination must exist see it as a measure of the extent of discrimination. Those who believe that markets work well see it, instead, as a measure of our ignorance. This problem of perception is perhaps best seen by considering results for Jewish Americans. After controlling for measured differences in education, family composition, and place of residence, Jews in the U.S. in recent decades earned 15 percent more than non-Jews.[22] Should this be interpreted as evidence that employers discriminate *in favor* of Jews?

In other contexts, clever statistical techniques enabled us to get an idea of the impact of unmeasured characteristics. We could look at what happened to earnings when workers joined or left unions or switched from private to public employment. Unfortunately for researchers, very few individuals have switched their race or sex, so there is no statistical way to capture the effect of unmeasured characteristics. Researchers have responded by attempting to add an ever-expanding list of attributes to estimates of wage equations used to calculate wage decompositions. As we will see below, these additions have been able to reduce, but not eliminate, the extent of the unexplained difference between groups that might be the result of discrimination.

On the other hand, the traditional wage decomposition makes assumptions that conflict with basic economic analysis. It assumes that all the differ-

[22] Barry Chiswick, "The Skills and Economic Status of American Jewry: Trends over the Last Half-Century," *Journal of Labor Economics* 11: 229–242 (1993).

ences in productive attributes captured in the first term in the decomposition are independent of discrimination. Consider the case of education. As we saw in Chapter 3, workers will decide how much to invest in schooling based on the present value of future returns to education. If the labor market discriminates by paying lower rewards to members of one group, the rational response by those workers will be to invest less in education. Thus, the difference in levels of education or other characteristics could be a result of discrimination even though it is excluded from our measure.

Finally, differences in the returns to characteristics (βs) may not be true discrimination. They would be if the functional-form estimates accurately reflected the market. Frequently, however, this is not the case. As we saw in Chapter 3, for example, the return to an additional year of school or experience depends on how much of these characteristics the worker already has. If blacks have less schooling than whites or women have less experience than men, a nondiscriminatory labor market would, on average, provide them with greater rewards for an additional increment in schooling or experience. Thus, the estimated wage equations will have to have a nonlinear form. If they are instead assumed to be linear, as is typically done, a finding of the same return to education for a group that has less schooling would be interpreted as reflecting an absence of discrimination when, in fact, it provides strong evidence that rewards are *not* equal.

In short, while hundreds of research studies and thousands of court cases have decomposed wages in an attempt to attribute part of the differential between groups to discrimination, problems inherent in the statistical techniques used mean that the results can, at best, be no more than an indication of the actual situation. It is no wonder then that despite years of study, there is still no agreement among economists regarding the extent of discrimination in the economy.

EARNINGS DIFFERENTIALS BETWEEN BLACKS AND WHITES

The data in Table 14.1 imply that in 1992 the unadjusted ratio of earnings of year-round black workers to that of whites was 0.68 for males and 0.91 for females. In Table 14.4 we present ratios of the earnings of black-to-white males based on CPS data for 1993 that have been adjusted for hours worked and two major components of human capital: education and age (which among men closely reflects years of experience in the labor market). If the entire difference in wages were due to differences in education and experience, all the ratios except those in the last row and column in this table would equal 1. Since they do not, we can conclude that wage differences between blacks and whites persist after including education and age among the variables in X. Almost all the ratios, however, exceed the overall average of 0.74 for the year 1993 shown in this table. Even adjusting only for differences in experience and schooling accounts for almost one-third of the 26 percentage point difference (between 1 and 0.74) in wages that was present before the adjustments are made.

TABLE 14.4 BLACK-WHITE EARNINGS RATIOS, FULL-TIME MALE WORKERS, BY AGE AND EDUCATION, 1993

	Age			
Years of Schooling	25–34	35–44	45–54	All ages[a]
0–11	0.78	0.91	0.89	0.97
12	0.81	0.71	0.80	0.76
13–15	0.84	0.83	0.81	0.84
≥ 16	0.86	0.72	0.94	0.81
All	0.77	0.72	0.72	0.74

[a]Includes workers under age 25 and over age 54.

Source: Calculated from Public Use Microsample of March 1994 Current Population Survey.

TABLE 14.5 ADJUSTED BLACK-WHITE EARNINGS RATIOS, 1971, 1981, 1988[a]

	Sex and Years of Experience					
	Males			*Females*		
Year	0–9	10–19	20+	0–9	10–19	20+
1971	0.88	0.78	0.79	0.96	0.92	0.81
1981	0.85	0.80	0.83	0.94	0.99	0.91
1988	0.82	0.84	0.84	0.93	0.94	0.91

[a]Adjusted for differences in education, veteran and marital status, region, urban residence, number of children, and hours worked.

Source: Francine Blau and Andrea Beller, "Black-White Earnings over the 1980s: Gender Differences in Trends," *Review of Economics and Statistics* 74: 276–286 (1992).

The importance of accounting for differences in human capital is shown by the estimates in the last row of Table 14.5. The ratios in this table adjust for hours worked, education, age, and several other factors. When they are compared with those in Table 14.4, it is clear that these additional characteristics (including military experience, marital status, number of children, and urban residence) do not explain much of the wage differential beyond what was explained by education and age alone. Even with all these adjustments, the ratios of earnings of black men to white men in 1988 were between 0.82 and 0.84, indicating that the adjustments account for slightly less than half of the overall difference in pay.

The other half remains unexplained. As such, it is suggestive of the *MDC* against black males. The penalty they face for being black could be as much as 16 to 18 percent of white earnings. On the other hand, the list of factors for which researchers usually controlled when deriving the results in Table 14.5

is very short. We simply do not know how much potential discrimination would have remained had they been able to control for intelligence, quality of school attended, subjects studied, specialization in the military, absenteeism from work, criminal record, health, drug use, work effort, and a host of other factors that might reasonably be assumed to affect wages. Some of these factors might operate against black workers and increase the possible amount of discrimination, while others might work in the opposite direction and reduce it.

Two recent studies that included among the explanatory factors IQ differences as measured by standard tests found almost no unexplained difference in wages among members of different ethnic groups who had the same IQ. This control eliminated over 90 percent of the unadjusted difference in black-white and Hispanic-white wages.

Another interesting finding is that wages for white men tend to be lower in occupations where there are more black men. This is inconsistent with most models of discrimination and has been interpreted as indicative of unmeasured labor quality in these jobs.[23]

Among women the adjusted ratios in Table 14.5 are only slightly higher than unadjusted ratios because differences in human capital investments between women of the two races are small, as are differences in the returns to those investments. Even with these limited adjustments, the market discrimination coefficient against black women (compared to white women) appeared to be less than 10 percent in 1988. Of course, since this comparison is against white women, it excludes any discrimination black women suffered because they were women and not because they were black.

There is substantial evidence that the quality of schooling obtained by the average black worker has historically been inferior to that received by whites. Some evidence shows that training on past jobs raises the rate of return to training on the current jobs for whites but has no impact on the value of current training for blacks. This difference could lead black workers to invest less in training on each job. In addition, a greater loss of training benefits when they change jobs would render black workers less likely to change jobs, with the improvement in earnings that comes from better matches we saw in Chapter 6.[24] The difference in quality helps explain part of the adjusted differences in Table 14.4 for most workers, since the study underlying the table

---

[23] June O'Neill, "The Role of Human Capital in Earnings Differences Between Black and White Men," *Journal of Economic Perspectives* 4: 25–45 (1990); Richard Herrnstein and Charles Murray, *The Bell Curve*, New York: The Free Press (1994); Barry Hirsch and David Macpherson, "Wages, Racial Composition, and Quality Sorting in Labor Markets," Department of Economics, Florida State University, Photocopy (1994).

[24] Peter Orazem, "Black-White Differences in Schooling Investment and Human Capital Production in Segregated Schools," *American Economic Review* 77: 714–723 (1987); Finis Welch, "Black-White Differences in Returns to Schooling," *American Economic Review* 63: 893–907 (1973); Edwin Sexton and Reed Olsen, "The Returns to On-the-Job Training: Are They the Same for Blacks and Whites?" *Southern Economic Journal* 61: 328–342 (1994).

could not standardize for this factor. Also, productivity may differ by race even among year-round full-time workers because of differences in the amount of skills acquired in the past through on-the-job training. Black males who work full-time all year in any given year are less likely to have worked full-time all year for their entire work lives than are white males. As we showed in Chapters 1 and 8, black males' participation rates are lower than whites', and blacks have higher unemployment rates than whites. This means that, at any age, their labor market experience is less. Since experience is related to productivity, otherwise identical black workers have less human capital than white workers at the same age. Racial differences in past participation and unemployment thus induce differences in productivity, even among year-round full-time workers.

Even with adjustments for many characteristics, racial differences in wages between blacks and whites in the U.S. remain substantial. It is important to note that the U.S. is not unique in this problem. In the United Kingdom in 1975, for example, nonwhite immigrants' earnings were roughly 90 percent of those of white workers with the same education and labor market experience. Direct evidence of employers' discrimination is provided by a British study that used pairs of fictitious applications for jobs as accountants. Nonwhite workers were not only less likely to be contacted by employers receiving the applications than were white Britons, but they also fared worse than non-English-speaking white immigrants.[25]

As we suggested earlier, any labor market discrimination by race feeds back into workers' decisions about the amount of human capital it pays to acquire. If the rate of return to a given amount of training acquired by black workers is lower than that for whites, they will invest less in training. Young blacks in the early 1980s were much less likely to have received formal on-the-job training, or to be in an apprenticeship program than otherwise similar whites. Even more important, there is less complementarity between formal schooling and informal on-the-job training among black than among white men.[26] As shown in Chapter 3, this complementarity is an important source of earnings growth over the life cycle.

Wage discrimination can also reduce labor force participation. If there are no racial differences in the reservation wage, labor market discrimination would make it more likely that the market wage will be below the reservation wage for blacks than for whites. This could explain why, as we saw in Chapter 1, labor force participation rates of adult black males are lower than those of whites. This lower participation itself reduces investment in human capital and, thus, produces even lower wages.

---

[25] Mark Stewart, "Racial Discrimination and Occupational Attainment in Britain," *Economic Journal* 93: 521–541 (1983); Michael Firth, "Racial Discrimination in the British Labor Market," *Industrial and Labor Relations Review* 34: 265–272 (1981).

[26] Lisa Lynch, "Race and Gender Differences in Private-Sector Training for Young Workers," Industrial Relations Research Association, *Proceedings* 41: 557–566 (1988); Greg Duncan and Saul Hoffman, "On-the-Job Training and Earnings Differences by Race and Sex," *Review of Economics and Statistics* 61: 601 (1978).

Despite differences in the amount of education and on-the-job training that have been acquired, blacks are no more likely than whites to quit their jobs. This raises the question of why employers fail to invest as much in training black workers as they do in training whites, and why blacks do not invest in their own training. The second question can be answered by pointing to blacks' lower incomes. With low incomes it is harder to borrow to finance investments in human capital than it is for other people. It is not surprising that we observe for a sample of households in the U.S. from 1974 to 1982 that poorer families have higher **rates of time preference** at which they discount future income or consumption. Lower-income people are less willing to sacrifice current low living standards in order to reap higher rewards in the future. The behavior of employers is more difficult to explain. Perhaps, even though economists have shown there are no black-white differences in voluntary quit rates, employers do not perceive the absence of differences. Perhaps, on the other hand, there are differences in the productivity of training dollars invested in the two groups.[27]

The adjusted differences in Tables 14.4 and 14.5 do not account for the occupations in which blacks and whites work, except insofar as they differ in requirements for education and experience. Not adjusting for occupational differences makes sense if we believe that differences in the occupations filled by blacks and whites result from discriminatory actions on the part of employers. It does not make sense if we believe these differences result from different unmeasured abilities or different preferences that lead to different choices. For example, differences in rates of time preference might cause one group to opt for an occupation that paid higher initial wages but had a slower rate of growth over the work life. It is clear that, at least among young people in 1984 in the U.S., even after adjusting for differences in experience and education, blacks were more likely than whites to be in lower-paying occupations.[28]

TRENDS IN BLACK–WHITE EARNINGS DIFFERENCES

Whether discriminatory labor market outcomes have been reduced in the U.S. (and, if so, why) has received a great deal of attention from labor economists since the 1970s. An examination of the adjusted racial earnings differences presented in Table 14.5 for 1971, 1981, and 1988 shows some lessening of unexplained differences between 1971 and 1981 for older workers. Among

[27] Francine Blau and Lawrence Kahn, "Race and Sex Differences in Quits by Young Workers," *Industrial and Labor Relations Review* 34: 563–577 (1981); Andrew Weiss, "Determinants of Quit Behavior," *Journal of Labor Economics* 2: 371–387 (1984); Emily Lawrance, "Poverty and the Rate of Time Preference: Evidence from Panel Data," *Journal of Political Economy* 99: 54–77 (1991).

[28] Paul Gabriel, Donald Williams, and Susanne Schmitz, "The Relative Occupational Attainment of Young Blacks, Whites and Hispanics," *Southern Economic Journal* 57: 35–46 (1990).

TABLE 14.6 BLACK[a]–WHITE EARNINGS RATIOS, 1939–1992[b]

	All Workers		Year-Round Full-Time Workers	
Year	Males	Females	Males	Females
1939	0.41	0.36	0.45	0.38
1955	0.59	0.43	0.63	0.57
1960	0.60	0.50	0.67	0.70
1965	0.57	0.60	0.64	0.71
1970	0.62	0.98	0.69	0.82
1975	0.59	0.91	0.74	0.96
1980	0.60	0.93	0.71	0.95
1985	0.63	0.85	0.70	0.91
1990	0.61	0.81	0.73	0.90
1992	0.59	0.80	0.72	0.92

[a]Nonwhite prior to 1970.

[b]Ratios of medians of wage and salary incomes.

Sources: Bureau of the Census, *Current Population Reports*, P–60, Nos. 23, 37, 51, 80, 105, 132, 156, and 174.

younger workers, earnings differences actually widened a little. Table 14.6 shows that there has been a long and fairly steady trend in unadjusted earnings differences between before World War II and the 1970s. Changing compositions of the labor force mean that this trend was more pronounced among all workers than among year-round full-time workers.

What explains these trends? Part of the convergence of earnings reflects a reduction in occupational segregation. For example, the percentage of blacks in white-collar occupations rose by 24 percentage points between 1960 and 1981. Among whites, the rise during that period was only 7.2 percentage points. Between 1981 and 1994, however, the percentage of blacks in white-collar jobs grew by only 6.5 percentage points, compared to 4.9 among whites. Another factor that may have contributed to the slowing of the rate of convergence in black-white earnings ratios was the increasing return to education and greater variance of earnings that occurred in the 1980s. Increasing returns to education will increases wages more for the group with more education. This result is compounded by the fact that growth in the relative education of young blacks ceased in the 1980s. A greater variance of earnings will reduce the earnings of groups concentrated in the lower half of the income distribution relative to those in the upper half, even if no worker's position in the distribution of earnings changes. Indeed, changes in the structure of wages suggest that the ratio of black-to-white wages would have fallen by 5 percentage points during the 1980s if other changes had not offset this effect. If black educational progress in the 1980s had continued at the same rate as in the previous decade and there had been no change in the return to education or variance of earnings, by 1989 the relative wages of young black males would have been over 94 percent of those of young white men.[29]

THE EFFECT OF GOVERNMENT POLICY

While market forces play an important role in changing the amount of pay discrimination, government may also have a major effect. To what extent has the growth in the black-white earnings ratio been a result of government policies? In the mid-1960s the federal government undertook a variety of new programs that could have affected the earnings and occupational status of blacks relative to whites. The Civil Rights Act of 1964 established the **Equal Employment Opportunity Commission (EEOC),** whose charge was to litigate cases involving unequal pay for equal work or unequal access to promotion.

At the same time, Executive Order 11246 required federal contractors, which includes most large employers, to file **affirmative action plans** showing how they intended to increase the employment and job level of minorities and women. These plans have to be filed frequently and must show how the business or nonprofit agency expects to fill its impending hiring needs. Included in the plan must be information about the **hiring pool,** showing the availability of labor by race, ethnicity, and sex, for the employer's projected vacancies. Both the plan's projected goals and hiring pools are subject to review by the federal government.

The explosion of efforts to equalize labor market outcomes between blacks and whites coincided with a rapid increase in adjusted black-white earnings ratios. Is this correlation or causation? The programs appear to have been partly responsible for the increases in the black-white earnings ratio that occurred between the mid-1960s and 1980. Employers reported that, as a result of these programs, they changed their recruitment practices. Even accounting for changes in the relative supplies of black and white workers, EEOC expenditures were correlated with increased earnings ratios. Industries targeted by the EEOC or affirmative action programs showed especially sharp increases in the earnings ratio. Among firms whose plans were reviewed, those who were induced to set higher goals for hiring and promotion of blacks achieved the greatest gains in the relative employment status of black workers in the late 1970s. Of course, this situation may have

---

[29] Chinhui Juhn, Kevin Murphy, and Brooks Pierce, "Accounting for the Slowdown in Black-White Wage Convergence," in Marvin Kosters (ed.). *Workers and Their Wages,* Washington, D.C.: American Enterprise Institute (1991); John Bound and Harry Holzer, "Industrial Shifts, Skill Levels and the Labor Market for White and Black Males," *Review of Economics and Statistics* 75: 387–396 (1993); James Smith, "Affirmative Action and the Racial Wage Gap," *American Economic Review* 83: 79–84 (1993); David Card and Thomas Lemieux, "Changing Wage Structure and Black-White Wage Differentials," *American Economic Review* 84: 29–33 (1994).

occurred because only firms that anticipated little difficulty in increasing the status of black workers were willing to agree to higher goals.[30]

Having at least partly broken the feedback relationship between labor market discrimination and the acquisition of human capital between the 1960s and 1980, it is possible that government policy may no longer be required. Employers themselves may have sufficient incentives, in the form of a supply of more educated blacks, to maintain the increases in earnings ratios. Having achieved greater representation in white-collar jobs, blacks may also have reduced employers' uncertainty about their productivity (shifted up and tilted the B′B′ line in Figure 14.5), thereby reducing statistical discrimination against them. Alternatively, employers might instead have found their stereotypes reinforced by affirmative action if the minorities they were forced to hire by government pressure proved to be less qualified than other workers hired for the same jobs. When pressures to hire minorities are removed, some employers' d_i might be higher than before the affirmative-action program began.[31]

EARNINGS DIFFERENTIALS FOR HISPANICS AND OTHERS

Table 14.2 shows that the Hispanic work force is nearly three-fourths the size of the black work force in the United States. The unadjusted earnings data in Table 14.1 show that Hispanics, even year-round full-time workers, earn less than whites in general (a group that includes the majority of Hispanics). The unadjusted earnings ratios for these workers are 0.65 for men and 0.79 for women. As with blacks, unadjusted wage differentials are greater among men than among women.

As with blacks, economists have attempted to distinguish the fraction of the wage differential for Hispanics that can be explained by differences in observable characteristics and the part that is unexplained and may be due to discrimination. The first three rows of Table 14.7 present unadjusted and adjusted annual earnings ratios between groups of Hispanics and non-Hispanic whites. Among the dimensions by which these wages are standardized (which are included in the *X* variables) are education, age, ability to

[30]Richard Freeman, "Black Economic Progress After 1964: Who Has Gained and Why?" in Sherwin Rosen (ed.). *Studies in Labor Markets*, Chicago: University of Chicago Press (1981); Jonathan Leonard, "The Impact of Affirmative Action Programs on Employment," *Journal of Labor Economics* 2: 439–463 (1984); Jonathan Leonard, "What Promises Are Worth: The Impact of Affirmative Action Goals," *Journal of Human Resources* 20: 3–20 (1984); James Heckman and Brook Paynter, "Determining the Impact of Federal Antidiscrimination Policy on the Economic Status of Blacks," *American Economic Review* 79: 138–177 (1989); John Donahue III and James Heckman, "Continuous versus Episodic Change: The Impact of Civil Rights on the Economic Status of Blacks," *Journal of Economic Literature* 29: 1603–1643 (1991).

[31]Stephen Coate and Glenn Loury, "Will Affirmative Action Policies Eliminate Negative Stereotypes?" *American Economic Review* 83: 1220–1240 (1993).

TABLE 14.7 UNADJUSTED AND ADJUSTED ETHNIC-WHITE EARNINGS RATIOS, BY SEX, 1979[a]

	Males		*Females*	
	Unadjusted	Adjusted	Unadjusted	Adjusted
American Indian	0.74	0.92	0.89	0.91
Asian Indian	1.13	0.98	1.13	0.91
Chinese	0.89	0.89	1.08	0.97
Cuban	0.79	0.96	0.97	0.98
Filipino	0.79	0.92	1.22	1.01
Japanese	1.05	1.01	1.14	1.07
Korean	0.89	0.82	1.01	0.95
Mexican	0.66	0.98	0.77	0.96
Puerto Rican	0.63	0.95	0.89	1.03
Vietnamese	0.64	0.98	0.89	1.03

[a]Adjusted for differences in education, age, hours worked, marital status, region, knowledge of English, and place of birth.

Source: Leonard Carlson and Caroline Swartz, "The Earnings of Women and Ethnic Minorities, 1959–79," *Industrial and Labor Relations Review* 41: 530-546 (1988), Tables 3, 4.

speak English, and whether or not the worker is native born. This last measure is important because, as we saw in Chapter 7, men working in the U.S. receive a lower return to schooling acquired outside the U.S. than to schooling acquired in the U.S.

The data show that wages of Mexican-Americans, Cuban-Americans, and Puerto Ricans living in the 50 states in 1979 were only slightly below those of non-Hispanic whites after adjusting for numerous differences that affect productivity. Unlike for blacks, for whom observable characteristics explained only roughly half the measured difference, among the three largest Hispanic groups most of the unadjusted differences stem from differences in workers' characteristics. There is relatively little room remaining for possible labor market discrimination against these groups.

Particularly important among these characteristics is fluency in English. Several studies using data from the mid-1970s find that one-third to one-half of the adjustment in earnings ratios stems from differences between Hispanics and non-Hispanic whites in their knowledge of English. The same data show that this difference is especially pronounced in determining which occupations Hispanics enter. In particular, lack of fluency in English has a major effect in keeping Hispanics out of professional and managerial occupations. Thus, as can be seen in Table 14.2, Hispanics are much less common in these occupations than either whites generally or blacks. The importance of language is also shown in a survey of low-skilled Mexican immigrants in Los Angeles in 1986. Being able to read English well raised earnings by the same amount as five extra years of residence in the U.S. (five additional years of country-specific human capital). Among immigrants to Australia, fluency in

English raised both the return to education (from 2 percent to 8 percent per year of schooling) and experience in the local labor market.[32]

In Canada, on the other hand, earnings adjusted for age, education, location, and marital status are the same for English and French speakers.[33] The lack of any difference in adjusted earnings can be attributed, in part, to the large fraction of the population made up of French speakers and, in part, to the fact that a higher fraction of francophone Canadians are fluent in English than is true among Spanish-speaking U.S. residents. Earnings penalties for Canadians who are not fluent in either English or French are, however, significant, equaling 12 percent in the 1980s as compared with 17 percent for Americans and 5 to 8 percent for Australians not fluent in English and 11 percent for Israelis who were not fluent in Hebrew.[34]

Annual data on the earnings of Hispanics that are comparable to those shown in Table 14.6 are only available since 1975 and are shown in Table 14.8. Other data from the decennial censuses of population show that earnings ratios for Hispanics rose between 1959 and 1969, an increase that continued until the middle or late 1970s. The data in the table show that *unadjusted* earnings ratios fell between the late 1970s and around 1990. The decline in Table 14.8 is not, however, reflected in adjusted earnings ratios. The reason goes back to Chapter 7, where we documented the huge growth of Hispanic immigration in recent years and the low initial wages that migrants typically attain. The decline in the unadjusted wage of Hispanics results from a deterioration in their aggregate human capital as new, less-skilled groups entered the U.S. work force.[35]

MALE-FEMALE DIFFERENTIALS

The data on the mean earnings of year-round full-time workers in 1992 in Table 14.1 show that the female-male earnings ratios are 0.67 for whites, 0.82 for blacks, 0.81 for Hispanics, and 0.68 for all races combined. This ratio has

---

[32]Cordelia Reimers, "Labor-Market Discrimination Against Hispanic and Black Men," *Review of Economics and Statistics* 65: 570–579 (1983); Gilles Grenier, "The Effects of Language Characteristics on the Wages of Hispanic-American Males," *Journal of Human Resources* 19: 53–71 (1984); Sherrie Kossoudji, "English Language Ability and the Labor Market Opportunities of Hispanic and East Asian Immigrant Men," *Journal of Labor Economics* 6: 205–228 (1988); Barry Chiswick, "Speaking, Reading and Earnings among Low-skilled Immigrants," *Journal of Labor Economics* 9: 149–170 (1991); Barry Chiswick and Paul Miller, "The Endogeneity between Language and Earnings: International Analyses," *Journal of Labor Economics* 13: 246–288 (1995).

[33]Kossoudji, "English Language Ability;" David Bloom and Gilles Grenier, "The Economic Position of Linguistic Minorities: French in Canada and Spanish in the United States," in Barry Chiswick (ed.). *Immigration, Language and Ethnicity: Canada and the United States*, Washington, D.C.: American Enterprise Institute (1992).

[34]Chiswick and Miller, "The Endogeneity."

[35]David Bloom and Gilles Grenier, "Language, Employment, and Earnings in the United States: Spanish-English Differentials," *International Journal of the Sociology of Language*, in press (1995).

TABLE 14.8 HISPANIC-WHITE[a] EARNINGS RATIOS, 1975–1992[b]

	All Workers		*Year-Round Full-Time Workers*	
	Males	Females	Males	Females
1975	0.70	0.94	0.72	0.86
1980	0.70	0.89	0.71	0.86
1985	0.64	0.82	0.68	0.83
1990	0.64	0.73	0.66	0.78
1992	0.64	0.76	0.65	0.79

[a]Whites include white Hispanic workers. Where data is available on non-Hispanic whites, it lowers the relative ratio by somewhat less than 5 percentage points.

[b]Ratios of medians of wage and salary incomes.

Sources: Bureau of the Census, *Current Population Reports*, P–60, Nos. 105, 132, 156, and 174.

TABLE 14.9 FEMALE-MALE EARNINGS RATIOS IN MANUFACTURING, 1950–1993, SELECTED COUNTRIES

Country	1950	1978	1988	1993
United States	—	0.61	0.71[a]	—
Australia	0.66	0.80	0.80	0.85
France	—	0.77	0.79[b]	0.79
Germany	0.64	0.73	0.73	0.74
Netherlands	0.61	0.76	0.78	0.77
Sweden	0.70	0.89	0.90	0.89
United Kingdom	0.60	0.69	0.68	0.69

[a]1983.

[b]1987.

Sources: 1950, 1993: International Labour Organization, *Yearbook of Labour Statistics*, various issues; 1978: OECD, *Employment Outlook* (1988); 1988: OECD, *Employment Outlook* (1991).

been rising rapidly in recent years, growing by over 1 percentage point a year for all workers between 1989 and 1992. The differences in earnings by sex for the U.S. are not too dissimilar from those in other countries. The last column of Table 14.9 presents the ratios of earnings by sex for manufacturing workers in 1993 in several developed countries. The ratio for the U.S. is higher than that implied by Table 14.1, in part because Table 14.9 already adjusts for some sex differences in occupation by restricting the sample to manufacturing. Pay differences by sex are clearly pervasive across the developed world. Interestingly, female-male wage ratios were (and still are) as low or lower in the former communist countries of Central and Eastern Europe as they are in the West.[36]

Adjusting the earnings ratios in Table 14.9 and those implied by Table 14.1 raises a number of extremely difficult issues. All of them involve distinguishing between sex differences that reflect discrimination and those that would create differences in wages even in the absence of discrimination. Since the educational attainment of women and men in the United States and other developed countries is essentially the same, differences in the amount of education obtained cannot be a major source of nonlabor market discrimination. The quality of the education also probably differs little by sex, since boys and girls generally are in the same classrooms. In the U.S. the only sex difference in educational attainment is that women are more likely to complete high school, whereas men are more likely to obtain college or advanced degrees. Even this difference is much smaller today than it was in the 1960s.

Thus we can rule out differences in amounts of education as an important source of differences in productivity. There are, however, major differences in choice of college major by sex that may contribute to future earnings differentials. Among a sample of students who graduated from college in 1976, a substantial fraction of the lower hourly earnings of women in 1979 was accounted for by their choice of lower-paying college majors. If we only examine starting salaries, the pay difference disappears once differences in mathematics skills are taken into account,[37] since women are not well represented in fields of study requiring mathematical ability and prior training. This situation does not mean that sex discrimination does not affect the earnings of new college graduates. There may be prelabor market discrimination, but those with the same package of skills are treated the same initially.

THE ROLE OF LABOR MARKET EXPERIENCE

A particularly difficult issue in dealing with gender differences in earnings is the role of labor market experience. In presenting the adjusted earnings ratios for black and other minority males in Tables 14.5 and 14.7, only minor

---

[36]Francine Blau and Lawrence Kahn, "The Gender Earnings Gap: Some International Evidence," in Richard Freeman and Lawrence Katz (eds.). *Differences and Changes in Wage Structures,* Chicago: University of Chicago Press (1995); John Ham, Jan Svejnar, and Kathy Terrell, "The Czech and Slovak Labor Markets During the Transition," in Simon Commander and Fabrizio Coricelli (eds.). *Unemployment, Restructuring, and the Labor Market in Eastern Europe and Russia,* Washington, D.C.: The World Bank (1995).

[37]Thomas Daymont and Paul Andrisani, "Job Preferences, College Major and the Gender Gap in Earnings," *Journal of Human Resources* 19: 408–428 (1984); Morton Paglin and Anthony Rufolo, "Heterogeneous Human Capital, Occupational Choice, and Male-Female Earnings Differences," *Journal of Labor Economics* 8: 123–144 (1990); Barry Gerhart, "Gender Differences in Current and Starting Salaries: The Role of Performance, College Major and Job Title," *Industrial and Labor Relations Review* 43: 418–434 (1990).

problems were created by using age as a proxy measure for labor market experience. As we saw in Chapter 1, most males are in the labor force if they are not in school. Age, however, does not measure experience very well for women. Career interruption for child rearing means that, at any given age, married women are likely to have had less labor force experience than men, and, hence, to have made smaller investments in on-the-job training. Estimates for 1982 indicate that the average woman in her late 30s had spent 4 years out of the labor force and not in school, or had lost approximately 2 years of work experience per child. In 1987 the average woman in the labor force had worked about 70 percent of the time since she left school, while the average man had worked over 93 percent of the time since leaving school. This differential was much smaller for younger women, a pattern consistent with a much smaller wage differential for younger workers. With no adjustments, the ratio of female-to-male earnings for full-time year-round workers between the ages of 25 and 34 was 80 percent in 1990 (up from 66 percent in 1955). Among workers over age 45, however, this ratio was around 62 percent in both 1955 and 1990. Among a sample of young women in 1988, the estimated return to actual experience was 5 percent a year, while the estimated return to potential experience (age less schooling) was approximately zero.[38]

Because data on actual work experience are scarce, few studies make the appropriate adjustment for women's intermittent labor market experience. One study that did so included in the vector of explanatory characteristics the actual amount of time a women had spent in the labor force as well as her current tenure with her employer. It found that controlling for experience gave an earnings ratio among whites of 0.77 in 1975. Since the unadjusted female-male earnings ratio among white full-time workers in 1975 was 0.58, the adjustment suggests that perhaps half of the observed pay difference between white women and men can be explained by differences in experience.[39]

Wage differentials might be expected to exist even between men and women who have the same amount of prior experience. A woman who has the same amount of experience as a man is older, on average, and has probably left and then reentered the labor force several times. Thus, her human capital is of an older vintage that may be rewarded less in the labor market. Her work skills may have depreciated during the times she was out of the labor force. Longitudinal data show that women who drop out of the labor

[38] Nadja Zalokar, "Generational Differences in Female Occupational Attainment," American Economic Association, *Papers and Proceedings* 76: 378–381 (1986); June O'Neill and Solomon Polachek, "Why the Gender Gap in Wages Narrowed in the 1980s," *Journal of Labor Economics* 11: 205–228 (1993); Randall Filer, "The Usefulness of Predicted Values for Prior Work Experience in Analyzing the Labor Market Outcomes for Women," *Journal of Human Resources* 28: 519–537 (1993).

[39] Based on Mary Cocoran, "The Structure of Female Wages," American Economic Association, *Papers and Proceedings* 68: 165-170 (1978), Table 1.

force receive a lower real wage upon reentry than they received before they left. The general training they had acquired depreciates when not used, and their firm-specific training is worthless unless they return to their former employer. Even though their wages rise fairly rapidly when they are reemployed, three three-year spells of employment interrupted by periods out of the labor force do not lead to as high a wage rate as one continuous nine-year spell. These losses are especially pronounced if a woman enters and leaves the labor force repeatedly. From the mid-1960s until the early 1980s differences solely in the timing of experience between men and women with identical total experience explains about 12 percent of the total difference in wages between men and women born between 1944 and 1952.[40]

Wage differentials between men and women with the same current job tenure can be explained by rational investments in training together with statistical discrimination. Employers, viewing a woman's chance of staying with the firm as uncertain, will be less willing to invest in her firm-specific training. Thus, years of tenure on the job will reflect a smaller amount of firm-specific training and will produce a lower wage for women than for men.

These effects produce feedback relations among wages, turnover, and investment in training. Wage discrimination may induce greater turnover and a reduced labor force participation rate. These in turn can cause employers to invest less in female employees, which reduces their wages even further below those of males. Pay discrimination would also reduce a woman's incentive to invest in her own general training. In addition, as examination of the formula in Chapter 3 makes clear, any time spent out of the labor force reduces the rate of return to education and causes women to invest less in preparing for the labor market. Similarly, women are less willing to invest in on-the-job training. Both choices reinforce the behavior that produced them and the perceptions of employers.

It is very difficult to solve the chicken-and-egg problem and disentangle these relationships, but its solution could enable us to understand the ultimate cause of observed differentials. One study has shown that women's wages are relatively lower in industries where their quit rates are relatively high. Another study has attempted to solve this problem by using longitudinal data for 1976 to 1979. Women who in 1976 expected to drop out of the labor force received the same wages as otherwise identical women, but lower wages were found to induce a greater subsequent dropout rate. It appears that women's work plans did not affect their wages, but low wages did affect their decisions about staying at work. This striking difference suggests that a major source of the male-female differential is the lower wage offered to

[40] Jacob Mincer and Solomon Polachek, "Family Investments in Human Capital: Earnings of Women," *Journal of Political Economy* 82: S76–S108 (1974); Donald Cox, "Panel Estimates of the Effects of Career Interruptions on the Earnings of Women," *Economic Inquiry* 22: 386–403 (1984); Leslie Sundt, "Two Essays on Women in the Labor Market: The Effect of Time Spent Not Employed and the Determinants of Part-time and Full-time Work," Unpublished PhD Dissertation, MIT (1989); Audrey Light and Manuelita Ureta, "Early-Career Work Experience and Gender Wage Differentials," *Journal of Labor Economics* 13: 121–154 (1995).

women, not their response to that wage in the form of reduced investment in training and a higher exit rate from the labor force.[41]

The tied family migration decisions discussed in Chapter 7 also contribute to observed wage differentials. With lower wages for whatever reason, wives are more likely than their husbands to be the tied migrant and find their wages lowered by a move. Knowing this possibility exists, it is rational for a woman to invest less in specific training that could be rendered worthless in a move. Even if the family does not move, women are often tied by their husbands' jobs to a particular labor market and cannot accept the best job they might otherwise obtain.

The question of tied migration leads to the larger issue of whether marriage hurts a woman's labor market prospects. Most married couples will have children, and, as we discussed in Chapter 1, in most industrialized societies the bulk of child care is provided by wives. Even if a mother continues to work, she will work fewer hours. This fact alone reduces earnings ratios since even among full-time workers, mothers probably have less overtime. Prospects for promotion may be lessened. Because fewer hours are worked, returns to both a woman and her employer from investment in training will be reduced and less training will take place.

Some recent work has claimed to find that men whose wives work earned about 25 percent less than men whose wives stay at home.[42] If it could be established that all or part of these lower earnings was because working wives provided less logistical support to their husbands than wives who were full-time homemakers, this finding would have significant implications for male/female wage differentials. Since almost no working women have nonworking spouses at home, the appropriate comparison should be between working women and men with wives who worked. There is, however, a more straightforward explanation for the negative relationship between a husband's earnings and whether or not his wife works. As we saw in Chapters 1 and 2, there are significant income effects in females' labor supply decisions. Thus, the observed relationship may simply be because women whose husbands earn more are more likely to be out of the labor force. The extent to which a worker's earnings are reduced because his or her spouse also works remains an interesting but unanswered empirical question.

Among a sample of young women in 1980 to 1982, those with young children had lower wage rates, but there was no difference in wages between married women with no children and unmarried women. Moreover, married women's wages did not fall compared to other women after they got married. Among a sample of lawyers, differences in time out of the labor force to care

---

[41] James Ragan and Sharon Smith, "The Impact of Differences in Turnover Rates on Male/Female Pay Differentials," *Journal of Human Resources* 18: 343–365 (1981); Reuben Gronau, "Sex-Related Wage Differentials and Women's Interrupted Labor Careers—The Chicken or the Egg," *Journal of Labor Economics* 6: 277–301 (1988).

[42] L. K. Stroh and J. M. Brett, "Dual Career Dads vs. Traditional Dads: Can We Account for Salary Differences?" Loyola University of Chicago, Institute of Human Resources and Industrial Relations, Photocopy (1994).

for children accounted for over 40 percent of the gap between the earnings of men and women.[43] Marriage itself is not apparently treated by employers as a signal of a lack of attachment to the labor force, but children are.

After all these adjustments are made, however, substantial differences in wages between men and women remain. Part of these may reflect how differences in workers' personality traits are rewarded by employers. One study using data for 1972 found that 6 percentage points of the market discrimination coefficient against women were accounted for by differences in such traits as sociability, desire for domination, emotional stability, and so on. Women are also less likely to be in dangerous jobs and in industries where product demand varies. Since these jobs produce compensating wage differentials, we would expect women to have lower earnings on average. This factor alone eliminated about one-third of the apparent earnings difference in one set of data for 1977. Support for the idea that beliefs matter comes from the fact that women whose views of women's labor market roles were more traditional earned less in later years even after accounting for their human capital and other characteristics. One study of college juniors about to enter the labor market found that women were less likely than men to take risks in their occupation and job choices. Since risky investments always earn higher expected returns than safe ones, this risk-averse strategy will lead to lower average earnings for these women.[44] Clearly, part of the *MDC* against women is produced by sex differences in attitudes. Of course, these differences in traits and in the jobs sought may not be innate, but instead may themselves stem from sex stereotyping (prelabor market discrimination).

As with differences by ethnicity, gender wage differences are not confined to the U.S. In Canada in 1988, the unadjusted earnings ratio for all men and women was 0.65. As in the U.S. roughly half of the pay difference can be accounted for by differences in hours worked currently and by prior labor market experience. In Australia at least a 20 percent pay differential exists between men and women after adjusting for family status (number of children) and experience. Among all workers in the United Kingdom in 1975, the unadjusted earnings ratio was 0.62, remarkably similar to that in the U.S.

---

[43] Sanders Korenman and David Neumark, "Marriage, Motherhood and Wages," *Journal of Human Resources* 27: 233–255 (1992); Robert Wood, Mary Corcoran, and Paul Courant, "Pay Differences among the Highly Paid: The Male-Female Earnings Gap in Lawyers' Salaries," *Journal of Labor Economics* 11: 417–441 (1993).

[44] Randall Filer, "Sexual Differences in Earnings: The Role of Individual Personalities and Tastes," *Journal of Human Resources* 18: 82–99 (1983); Randall Filer, "Male-Female Wage Differences: The Importance of Compensating Differentials," *Industrial and Labor Relations Review* 38: 426–437 (1985); Linda Subich, Gerald Barrett, Dennis Doverspike, and Ralph Alexander, "The Effects of Sex-Role-Related Factors on Occupational Choice and Salary," in Robert Michael, Heidi Hartmann, and Brigid O'Farrell (eds.). *Pay Equity: Empirical Inquiries,* Washington D.C.: National Academy Press; Francis Vella, "Self Discrimination and Human Capital Investment: The Relationship between Gender Roles and Female Labor Market Experience," in Robert Gregory and Thomas Karmel (eds.). *Australian Longitudinal Survey: Social and Economic Policy Research*, Australian National University, Centre for Economic Policy Research (1992).

After adjustments for differences in experience, marital status, and other factors, the earnings ratio was still only 0.85. In 1989 among full-time British workers the unadjusted ratio was 0.79, suggesting that many of the labor market changes that affected women in the U.S. happened in the U.K. as well. There is one particularly intriguing set of results from Israel. Unlike most studies of earnings differences, which rely only on wage data, this research looked at data from firms. It found an estimated male-female pay gap of about 24 percent, but since firm data was also available, the researchers could also look at productivity (output per worker), where they found an estimated male-female gap of between 18 and 25 percent.[45]

In continental Europe the situation is not very different, except that the adjustments to move from unadjusted to adjusted earnings ratios matter less. In Germany in 1981, for example, the unadjusted earnings ratio among a sample of married persons was 0.68. With adjustments, including the time actually spent in the labor force on the two most recent jobs, it rose only to 0.74. In Sweden, with the very high female participation rate shown in Table 1.8, the unadjusted ratio was 0.81 in 1981, but rose to only 0.85 after all adjustments. Especially interesting is evidence for Sweden in 1975, 1980, and 1985 that even among workers receiving piece rate pay for what they actually produced, women's earnings fell as far short of men's as among workers paid by the hour.[46]

TRENDS IN FEMALE/MALE EARNINGS RATIOS

A long and consistent time series of adjusted female-male earnings ratios is not available. In its absence, Table 14.9 shows unadjusted earnings ratios in manufacturing for a number of countries. Each country listed in Table 14.9 shows a sharp increase in the relative earnings of women between 1950 and 1978. The growth in the earnings ratio essentially stops after 1978 except in the U.S., where the ratio in 1978 is the lowest shown in the table.

To examine the American experience, Table 14.10 presents unadjusted earnings ratios in the U.S. for whites, nonwhites, and Hispanics. We will focus on full-time workers, since the figures for all workers are contaminated

---

[45]Morley Gunderson and Craig Riddell, "The Economics of Women's Wages in Canada," *International Review of Comparative Public Policy* 3: 149–174 (1991); Paul Miller, "Gender Differences in Observed and Offered Wages," *Canadian Journal of Economics* 15: 225–244 (1987); Vella, "Self-discrimination;" Antoni Zabalza and Z. Tzannatos, *Women and Equal Pay*, Cambridge: Cambridge University Press (1985); John Ermisch and Robert Wright, "Gender Discrimination in the British Labor Market," *Economic Journal* 101: 508–522 (1991); Judith Hellerstein and David Neumark, "Sex, Wages, and Productivity: An Empirical Analysis of Israeli Firm-Level Data," Photocopy, NBER (1992).

[46]Knut Gerlach, "A Note on Male-Female Wage Differences in West Germany," *Journal of Human Resources* 22: 584–592 (1987); Siv Gustafsson and Roger Jacobsson, "Trends in Female Labor Force Participation in Sweden," *Journal of Labor Economics* 3: S256–S274 (1985); Paul Chen and Per-Anders Edin, "Gender Wage Differentials, Discrimination and Work Effort Across Method of Pay," FIEF, Stockholm, Photocopy (June 1991).

POLICY ISSUE

EQUAL PAY FOR OREGON'S PROFESSORS?

In April 1985 a federal district court handed down a ruling in *Penk et al. v. Oregon State Board of Higher Education*. Twenty-two female faculty members in Oregon's 11-campus public university system filed an individual and class action suit arguing that they had received unequal pay for equal work. They sought back pay totalling more than $20 million.

The case hinged on which adjustments-to-earnings ratios were appropriate. The plaintiffs' expert witnesses adjusted earnings for differences in faculty members' ages, highest degree attained, experience since the degree, and years at the particular campus. Even with these adjustments, the average female-male earnings ratios on the 11 campuses ranged from 0.89 to 0.96. The defendant's expert witnesses also adjusted for the faculty members' specialties, arguing that the university was not responsible for what field students chose to study in graduate school, and there was no reason to expect equal pay across academic specialties. This additional adjustment raised the earnings ratios to approximately 1.00. Once the fact that female faculty are disproportionately located in lower-paying specialties was accounted for, market discrimination coefficients were 0.

The trial judge dismissed the class action component of the suit, arguing that it was appropriate to make the adjustments for specialty. Three of the plaintiffs, all on the faculty of the same college, received small damage awards. The rest received nothing. The adjustments we have been discussing have an impact well beyond understanding how labor markets operate. How the adjustments are made directly affects outcomes of legal actions that often involve large sums of money.

TABLE 14.10 FEMALE-MALE EARNINGS RATIOS IN THE U.S., 1939–1992[a]

	All Workers			*Year-Round Full-Time Workers*		
Year	Whites	Nonwhites	Hispanics	Whites	Nonwhites	Hispanics
1939	0.61	0.53	—	0.61	0.51	—
1955	0.52	0.38	—	0.64	0.58	—
1960	0.49	0.41	—	0.60	0.63	—
1965	0.50	0.53	—	0.60	0.66	—
1970	0.38	0.51	—	0.59	0.70	—
1975	0.39	0.58	0.49	0.58	0.75	0.68
1980	0.45	0.68	0.56	0.58	0.76	0.71
1985	0.50	0.74	0.66	0.63	0.82	0.77
1990	0.55	0.76	0.71	0.69	0.85	0.82
1992	0.51	0.69	0.61	0.70	0.89	0.86

[a]Ratios of medians of wage and salary workers.

Sources: Bureau of the Census, *Current Population Reports*, P–60, Nos. 23, 37, 51, 80, 105, 132, 156, 174, and 184.

by extensive shifts in the ratio of part-time to full-time workers among women. For full-time white workers there is a striking lack of a trend until 1980. Female earnings increased relative to males' between 1890 and 1930, but the period between 1939 and 1980 represents a halt in growth that was resumed only after 1980.[47] Among blacks and Hispanics, this plateau did not exist, and there has been a steady narrowing of pay differentials by sex.

The absence of major changes in unadjusted earnings ratios among whites during the 1960s and 1970s may mask a significant reduction in labor market discrimination against female workers. Comparing changes in unadjusted and adjusted earnings ratios between 1971 and 1981 using CPS data shows that adjusted relative earnings increased by 4 percentage points more than unadjusted ones.[48]

The increase in adjusted ratios in the face of constant unadjusted ratios stems from the revolutionary changes in female labor force participation discussed in Chapter 1. During the 1960s and 1970s the average age of the female labor force fell dramatically, becoming much younger than the male labor force. The huge influx of young women reduced the average experience of female workers and lowered the unadjusted earnings ratio below what it otherwise would have been. It did not affect the adjusted ratio (since differences in experience are accounted for). By the 1980s enough women had been in the labor force for enough time that even the unadjusted earnings ratio increased.

OCCUPATIONAL SEGREGATION AND COMPARABLE WORTH

We saw in Table 14.3 that significant differences existed in the gender ratio of various occupations. During the 1970s and 1980s women entered some traditionally male jobs at unprecedented rates, but in others, gender ratios changed hardly at all. Moreover, men did not enter previously predominately female occupations in great numbers.

Table 14.11 shows changes in the proportion of females in several previously heavily male and female occupations. It is clear that many well-paying occupations are still disproportionately male, while other occupations are disproportionately female. An interesting pattern of the changes emerges from Table 4.11. As a rule, women have entered previously predominately male jobs in large numbers where the occupation involves primarily intellectual work. Where physical labor is involved, the changes have been minimal.

Our analyses in Chapter 7 suggest that mobility by women should have eliminated any occupation-linked differences in earnings. The fact that this has not happened suggests that labor market discrimination against women

---

[47] Claudia Goldin and Solomon Polachek, "Residual Differences by Sex: Perspectives on the Gender Gap in Earnings," American Economic Association, *Papers and Proceedings* 77: 143–151 (1987).

[48] Francine Blau and Andrea Beller, "Trends in Earnings Differential by Gender, 1971–1981," *Industrial and Labor Relations Review* 41: 513–529 (1988).

TABLE 14.11 PERCENT OF FEMALES IN SELECTED OCCUPATIONS, 1970–1994

	Percent Female		
	1970	1980	1994
Previously predominately male with major shift			
Accountants and auditors	24.6	38.1	51.8
Computer analysts and scientists	13.6	22.5	31.4
Marketing managers	7.9	17.6	34.3
Operations researchers	11.1	27.7	41.4
Insurance sales	12.9	23.4	35.1
Physicians	9.7	13.4	21.5
Lawyers	4.7	13.8	24.8
Economists	15.9	30.0	47.4
Previously predominately male with small shift			
Timber cutters & loggers	3.3	2.5	1.0
Automobile mechanics	1.3	1.3	1.0
Aircraft mechanics	6.2	3.3	4.6
Heating and air-conditioning mechanics	1.0	1.0	0.5
Brickmasons	1.3	1.2	0.6
Carpenters	1.1	1.6	1.0
Machinists	3.0	5.0	4.4
Truck drivers	1.5	2.3	4.5
Previously predominately female			
Nurses	97.2	95.9	93.8
Elementary schoolteachers	83.9	75.4	85.6
Librarians	82.1	82.5	84.1
Clothing salespersons	80.2	81.8	80.8
Secretaries	97.8	98.8	98.9
Telephone operators	94.0	91.0	88.8
Bookkeepers	70.1	83.1	91.9
Bank tellers	86.9	91.1	90.4

Source: 1994: *Employment and Earnings,* (January 1995); 1970, 1980: Calculated from public use microsample of U.S. census.

might operate through their relegation to occupations in which the skill requirements are less than in those dominated by otherwise identical males. Gender differences in earnings do not exist if workers are classified by very narrowly defined occupations. Taken together, the evidence shows that roughly 20 percent of differences in pay between men and women are explained by segregation within occupations defined as in Table 14.3.[49]

---

[49] Erica Groshen, "The Structure of the Female/Male Wage Differential," *Journal of Human Resources* 26: 457–472 (1991); Elaine Sorensen, "The Crowding Hypothesis and Comparable Worth," *Journal of Human Resources* 25: 55–89 (1990).

Affirmative action and equal pay laws have not produced an identical occupational distribution for men and women in the U.S. or in other developed economies. Arguing that this result is at least partly because women are concentrated in occupations traditionally regarded as "women's work" that pay relatively little, some have proposed pay scales based on a policy of **comparable worth**. Jobs would be evaluated according to their inherent requirements such as formal and informal training time, unpleasantness, unusual scheduling, and so on, using methods that are now common in constructing pay structures in internal labor markets. Pay would be based on these evaluations, eliminating situations where low-skilled men are paid more than high-skilled women who work in different occupations.

One popular set of evaluations assigns points to various job characteristics and allows employers to base wages on point totals. Figure 14.7 shows how this procedure would apply to state of Washington employees. A linear relationship is constructed between the points assigned to an occupation and its pay level. The squares representing predominately male jobs lie mostly above the line, while the circles for female jobs lie mostly below the line. This relationship shows that male-dominated jobs pay higher wages than jobs with the same evaluation score containing mostly women. A policy offering pay based solely on the job-evaluation score would either raise the pay in "female" occupations or lower it in "male" occupations.

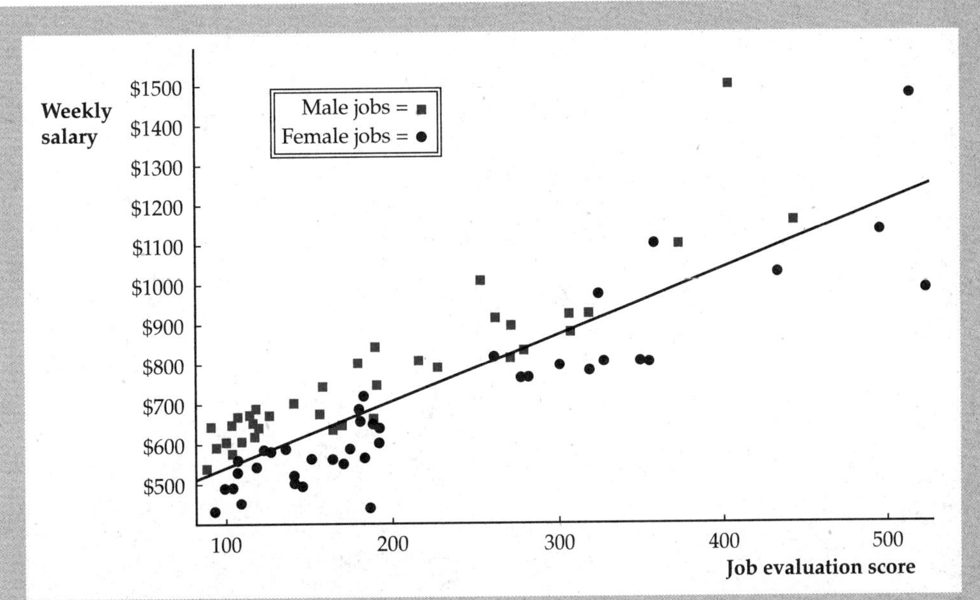

FIGURE 14.7 JOB EVALUATIONS AND SALARIES: STATE OF WASHINGTON
According to the job evaluation scores assigned by the state of Washington, it appears that jobs held primarily by men are paid more than those held primarily by women.
Source: *Fortune* (May 14, 1984), p.134.

Will payment by comparable worth reduce male-female wage inequality? In 1972 Australia instituted a nationwide policy that amounted to a loose system of payment by comparable worth. The unadjusted earnings ratio among full-time workers rose from 0.62 in 1966 to 0.82 in 1984. As in the data for manufacturing shown in Table 14.9, most of the increase came before 1978, that is, shortly after the law became effective. A similar increase occurred in adjusted earnings ratios. After the United Kingdom introduced an equal-pay policy in 1970, one study showed that the unadjusted earnings ratio rose from 0.53 in 1970 to 0.64 in 1984. Research for Canada shows that a comparable worth policy in Ontario had a much larger impact on the public than the private sector.[50]

Comparable worth policies seek an outcome consistent with labor market theories as far back as Adam Smith: Wages should be equal for jobs with similar advantages and disadvantages. There are, however, a number of questions about their adoption. In Chapters 3 and 10 we saw how the labor market determines compensation for various worker and job characteristics. As traditionally implemented, comparable worth policies do not adopt these market-determined rewards. While many of the same characteristics are included in the point totals, their relative importance is determined by "expert" evaluators. Comparable worth is designed not to apply to identical jobs, but merely to jobs defined as comparable. One might require more responsibility while the other involves more heavy lifting. How is the relative worth of these, and hundreds of other characteristics, to be determined? Any imposition of point values will be arbitrary unless grounded in market returns. Yet these returns may incorporate effects of discrimination.

Casual inspection of the heavily female and heavily male jobs in Table 14.11 shows that they differ in many aspects. Several studies have shown that at least half the relationship between the gender composition of an occupation and average wages is eliminated when job characteristics are held constant.[51] Thus, a large part of the wage differences across occupations represents compensating differentials. Women, on average, apparently have lower earnings at least in part because they are in jobs with more attractive working conditions.

---

[50]Robert Gregory, R. Anstie, Anne Daly, and V. Ho, "Women's Pay in Australia, Great Britain, and the United States: The Role of Laws, Regulations, and Human Capital," in Robert Michael et al. (eds.). *Pay Equity: Empirical Inquiries*, Washington D.C.: National Academy Press (1989); Morley Gunderson, "Gender Discrimination and Pay Equity Legislation," in Louis Christofides, E. Kenneth Grant, and Robert Swidinsky (eds.). *Aspects of Labour Market Behaviour: Essays in Honour of John Vanderkamp*, Toronto: University of Toronto Press, (1995), pp. 225–247.

[51]Randall Filer, "Occupational Segregation, Compensating Differentials, and Comparable Worth," in Robert Michael, Heidi Hartmann, and Brigid O'Farrell (eds.). *Pay Equity: Empirical Issues*, Washington D.C.: National Academy Press (1989); David Macpherson and Barry Hirsch, "Wages and Gender Composition: Why Do Women's Jobs Pay Less?" *Journal of Labor Economics* 13: 426-471 (1995).

One disturbing possibility is that adoption of comparable worth will serve to lock women into "female ghettos." If, in fact, the current structure of wages and other job characteristics is not an equilibrium, with women's jobs being less attractive, then mobility should draw women into nontraditional occupations. Adoption of comparable worth would eliminate this incentive and perpetuate the current job structure. If, on the other hand, the current structure is an equilibrium, with the lower wages in some jobs representing compensating differentials for other characteristics, then raising wages in these jobs will lead to more applicants, both male and female. There is no guarantee that, with excess workers to choose from, employers would offer these now more attractive jobs to women.[52] While comparable worth could achieve rapid increases in the female-male earnings ratio, as it did in Australia, the cost to the economy might be substantial. The increases in the adjusted earnings ratio that occurred from the late 1970s through 1989 in the U.S. were due at least in part to conventional antidiscrimination policy. They suggest that the goals of comparable worth can be met without incurring the potentially substantial costs and disruptions it would produce.

SUMMARY

Pay discrimination may arise from the unwillingness of employers, consumers, or fellow employees to hire, buy from, or work with persons of a particular racial or ethnic group or of a given sex. These tastes might induce employers to offer lower wages to the group discriminated against. Firms engaging in discrimination will be at a competitive disadvantage, however, and should eventually be driven from the market. Differences in employer or employee attitudes can, on the other hand, easily lead to segregated workplaces.

Discriminatory outcomes in the labor market may also arise if employers have less ability to use standard methods of relating the background of minority or female workers to their expected productivity on the job. So long as information about the productivity of these workers is poorer than about the productivity of white male employees, differential outcomes will persist even in a competitive economy.

Racial differences in pay exist in the U.S., with unexplained differences of roughly 15 percent between apparently identical white and black workers. These differences may represent the effects of discrimination, or they may be the result of unmeasured differences in productivity. Hispanics receive only slightly lower pay than apparently identical non-Hispanic whites. Relative wages of younger, and especially better educated, blacks in the U.S. rose

[52] Mark Killingsworth, "The Economics of Comparable Worth: Analytical, Empirical, and Policy Questions," in Heidi Hartmann (ed.). *Comparable Worth: New Directions for Research*, Washington D.C.: National Academy Press (1985).

between the mid-1960s and the late 1970s, but haven't increased since around 1980. The general reduction of black-white earnings differentials follows fairly closely the introduction of federal antidiscrimination policies.

In a broad range of developed economies substantial increases have occurred in the earnings of women relative to men: in Europe during the 1970s and in the U.S. mostly in the 1980s. Despite these changes, wage rates of female workers are still well below those of men with the same education and experience. Much of the adjusted pay differential is due to differences in the occupational mix, with women heavily concentrated in occupations in which the returns to experience and education are lower.

QUESTIONS AND PROBLEMS

14.1 Suppose a typical firm has a production function

$$Y = F + 0.8M$$

where Y is output, and F and M are the inputs of female and male labor.

a. Graph the isoquant map associated with this production function.
b. If male wages are 30 percent above female wages, in what proportions would the employer wish to employ men and women? What if male wages are 30 percent below female wages?
c. If the supply of male and female labor to the market is completely inelastic, and all firms have the production function shown above, what would the ratio of female-to-male wages be in equilibrium?

14.2 Let the market price of goods be \$5 per unit and the market wage for all labor be \$15. Suppose that the only available employees are black and that the employer has a discrimination coefficient of 2/3. How many black employees will the firm hire? How much output is lost to the economy due to discrimination by the employer if the firm's production relation is described by the following data?

Number of Workers	Total Product
1	11
2	20
3	28
4	35
5	41
6	46
7	50
8	53

14.3 Awesome Aardvark Associates employs three groups of workers: managers, who are all black male college graduates aged 40; purchasers, who are white female college graduates aged 22; and cage cleaners, who are white high school dropouts aged 16. Managers earn $18 per hour. Using your knowledge of labor market theory gleaned from Chapters 1 to 14 and of empirical evidence on wage differences, what do you expect the wages of purchasers and cage cleaners to be? For each wage, list the factors that contribute to the difference from the wage of managers and the size of the effect produced by the specific factor.

14.4 Examine the ethnic-white earnings ratios in Table 14.7.

a. Some of these ratios exceed 1.00. What does that mean, and how can that happen?

b. Some of the adjusted ratios are less than the unadjusted ratios. What differences between workers in the ethnic group and white workers can be producing this phenomenon?

14.5 Is it fair to account for female-male differences in experience when calculating adjusted earnings ratios? Are sex differences in experience themselves evidence of discrimination by employers, and should employers as a group be held responsible for them?

14.6 Proponents of comparable worth argue that the female-male earnings gap reflects occupational segregation.

a. Would you characterize occupational segregation as a form of discrimination? Why or why not?

b. If comparable worth were imposed nationally in all jobs, what effect would it have on the employment, unemployment, and labor force participation of women?

14.7 Suppose an advanced industrialized economy adopted a policy of "equal pay for equal work" by men and women. Predict the impact of such a policy on

a. investment in general and specific human capital by women and men;

b. birth rates;

c. the probability that a women would enter a nontraditional occupation.

Would your answer to any of the above depend on whether the definition of equal work was derived from a study by "experts" or a wage equation accounting for compensating differentials as discussed in Chapter 10?

14.8 It has been said that "the market is the best friend of any group against which there is prejudice on the part of many members of a society." What reasons would you give *as an economist* to support this assertion?

14.9 What is the evidence regarding whether the ratio of men to women in an occupation (either within a given firm or in the economy as a whole) affects mean wages paid for that job? Suppose you wanted to eliminate any gender effect on wages, what alternative policies could you pursue? Contrast the likely outcomes of these policies with respect to areas other than gender differences in wages.

14.10 Debates over the extent of racial and/or sexual discrimination in the U.S. economy often hinge on the specification of the vector of explanatory characteristics that it is appropriate to include in estimated wage equations. Discuss the possible errors that are introduced by misspecification of this vector. What criteria would you use to select those variables that should be included?

KEY WORDS

affirmative action plan
comparable worth
customer discrimination
differential outcomes
differential treatment
discrimination
discrimination coefficient
Equal Employment Opportunity Commission (EEOC)
hiring pool
labor market discrimination
market discrimination coefficient (*MDC*)
market for corporate control
normalization
occupational crowding
occupational segregation
prejudice
psychic cost of discrimination
rate of time preference
statistical discrimination
taste for discrimination
transactions cost approach
unexplained residual
wage decomposition

15

INEQUALITY OF EARNINGS AND INCOME

THE MAJOR QUESTIONS

- ▲ How do the decisions of workers and firms that we have examined so far interact to create an aggregate distribution of earnings?
- ▲ What is the extent of inequality in this distribution, and how is this inequality measured?
- ▲ How has the extent of inequality changed over time in the U.S.?
- ▲ How does inequality in the U.S. compare to that in other countries?
- ▲ What roles have investment in human capital and changes in the rate of return for such investments played in generating inequality in earnings?
- ▲ How has the apparent change in the relative importance that unions attach to wages versus employment levels affected inequality measures?
- ▲ What impacts have changes in race, ethnic, and sex differentials in the labor market had on these measures?
- ▲ How does the picture of inequality differ if we measure it across families rather than individuals, or if we examine inequality in consumption or utility rather than income?
- ▲ What determines the very high incomes at the upper tail of the earnings distribution?

MEASURING THE SIZE DISTRIBUTIONS OF EARNINGS AND INCOME

Due to a lack of alternative data, much of the evidence we present, as well as much public discussion, relates to the **size distribution** of income, showing the amount of income accruing to people ranked by their total incomes. Total income includes:

1. wage and salary income;
2. self-employment income;
3. income from capital (rents, interest, dividends); and
4. government transfer payments.

Wages, salaries, and self-employment income are clearly determined in the labor market. The other income elements are also closely related to labor market behavior. Life-cycle labor supply decisions and workers' desires to retire from the labor market motivate much of the savings that generate capital income. Income transfers are also either related to life-cycle labor supply (such as Social Security) or are **means-tested** and available only to those whose incomes fall below a certain level. Whether a family's income falls below this level is largely determined by labor market factors such as participation decisions, investments in training, choice of occupation, and discrimination. Thus, except for the people with disabilities, eligibility for many transfer payments is also an indirect labor market outcome.

Unfortunately, distributions of income are not perfect measures of distributions of utility. Other than adjusting for family size, it is difficult to take into account different levels of need, such as if a family has unusually large medical bills. Many forms of income such as employee benefits are also excluded. Some income itself may not be captured in the official statistics if it is earned in the **underground** or **gray economy.**

In the U.S. in 1992, the mean before-tax income of all households was $39,020. Of this amount $24,975 came from wages and salaries; self-employment income contributed $3,170, transfers $6,512, and property income $6,213. Thus payment for labor time was over 70 percent of total income. Moreover, wages and salaries constituted over half the income of every income class above $10,000 total income. (Below $10,000, other income sources such as Social Security and other transfers were more important.) A second way of seeing the importance of earnings in total income is to look at the differences in total family income by number of earners. In 1992, families with no earners had mean incomes of $19,918. Those with one earner had mean incomes of $34,350, and those with two earners had mean incomes of $52,759.

The size distributions of earnings and income have a characteristic shape. Both have a single **mode** (one peak) to the left of the mean and a long tail to the right. In other words, they are positively **skewed** rather than symmetric. Figure 15.1 shows such an earnings distribution for full-time year-round male workers in 1993. The frequencies at low incomes would be larger if part-year workers were included. Annual earnings reflect the interaction of two components: the number of hours worked during the year and the amount earned per hour.

If we had been able to include nonwage compensation (fringe benefits) in Figure 15.1, the entire distribution would have shifted to the right and become somewhat more skewed, since the demand for benefits has an

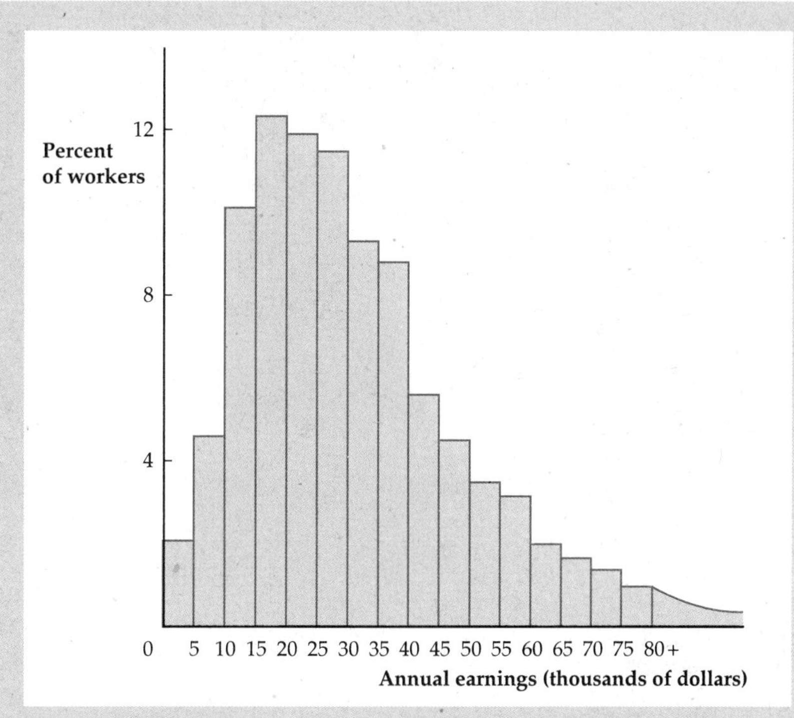

FIGURE 15.1 THE DISTRIBUTION OF EARNINGS OF MALE FULL-TIME, YEAR-ROUND WORKERS, 1993

Earnings distributions do not follow a normal distribution. Rather, they have a positive skew, with the mean earnings greater than the median earnings.

income elasticity above 1.0.[1] If we had been able to capture unreported economic activity, the distribution would again have shifted to the right, but it might have become less skewed since, on average, unreported income is a higher fraction of total income at the bottom of the income distribution.

Underlying much of the interest in the size distribution of earnings or income is the issue of inequality. Ideally, we would like a single statistic that could summarize the extent of inequality reflected in distributions such as those in Figure 15.1 and enable us to make comparisons across societies and over time. Unfortunately, no single measure captures all information of interest. Instead, a wide variety of alternatives has been developed. One

[1]Timothy Smeeding, "The Size Distribution of Wage and Nonwage Compensation: Employer Cost vs. Employer Value," in Jack Triplett (ed.). *The Measurement of Labor Cost,* Chicago: University of Chicago Press (1983).

widely used measure is the **variance** of the logarithms of income (the average squared deviation around the mean of the logarithms). Equivalently, the square root of the variance, the **standard deviation,** is sometimes reported. A problem with both measures is that they suggest a large degree of inequality if there are a few persons or families with extraordinarily high earnings or income.

A measure that avoids this problem is the **relative interquartile range,** which in the case of earnings, E, for example, is calculated as:

$$RIR = \frac{E_{75} - E_{25}}{E_{50}}$$

where the subscripts 75, 25, and 50 denote earnings levels at the 75th, 25th, and 50th (median) percentiles of the distribution of earnings. A higher relative interquartile range shows greater inequality. There is nothing magic about dividing the income distribution into quartiles. Quintiles (the 80th and 20th percentiles) or deciles (the 90th and 10th percentiles) could be chosen instead and might give a somewhat different picture.

A third measure, which takes into account the entire distribution of earnings or income in a population under study, also begins by arranging the population in order from the lowest to the highest earners. A square such as that in Figure 15.2 is drawn with the cumulative fraction of families and income on the two axes. The cumulative share of income accruing to each cumulative fraction of the population is graphed. In Figure 15.2, we have plotted the cumulative percentages of all income received by white families in 1993. In reading the graph, we can see that slightly less than 5.0 percent of all income goes to the 20 percent of families with the lowest incomes. This process produces the **Lorenz curve** $0CA$ in Figure 15.2. Lorenz curves can be plotted for total income or any type of income (such as earnings) and for individuals or families.

Inequality is measured by the **Gini coefficient**, defined as the ratio of the darker shaded area (between $0CA$ and the diagonal $0A$) to the triangle $0BA$. In the case of the distribution shown, the Gini coefficient is 0.422. If each white family received an identical income, the Lorenz curve would coincide with the diagonal, and the Gini coefficient would, therefore, be 0. If all the income were received by one family and all the other families received nothing, the Gini coefficient would be 1.0, because the Lorenz curve would be the edge of the box, $0BA$. Thus, a higher Gini coefficient indicates greater inequality.

None of the many measures of inequality, including some not discussed here, is correct for all purposes. Each provides a different way of summarizing information about the extent of inequality contained in distributions like that in Figure 15.1. Conclusions about the determinants of inequality in earnings or income distributions must be tempered by the recognition that the results may depend upon the measure of inequality used in the analysis. Some changes in the distribution could imply either an increase or a

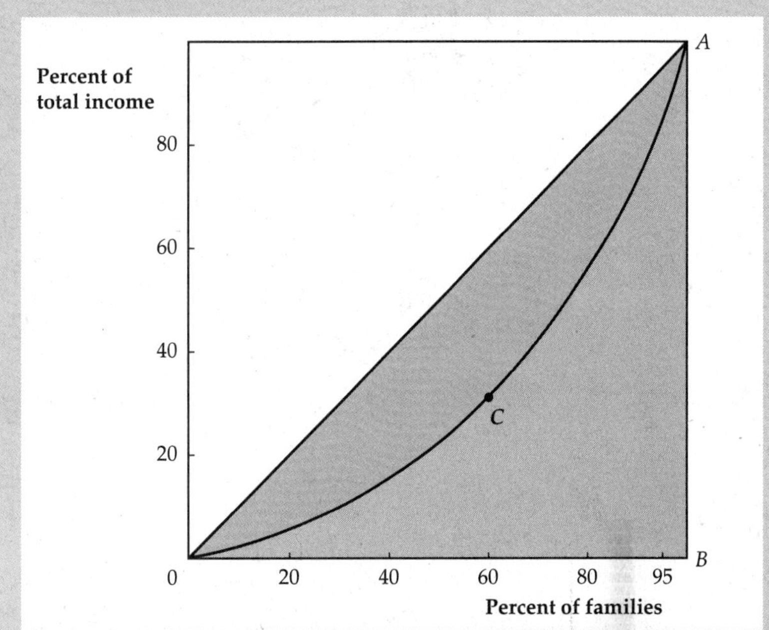

FIGURE 15.2 CUMULATIVE DISTRIBUTION OF FAMILY INCOME, WHITES, 1993

The Lorenz curve shows the cumulative fraction of income earned by each fraction of the population. One common measure of inequality, the Gini coefficient, is the ratio of the shaded wedge to the total area under the 45-degree line.

decrease in inequality, depending on the measure used. In most cases, however, all the measures of inequality will move in the same direction when the distribution of income changes.

LEVELS AND CHANGES IN EARNINGS AND INCOME INEQUALITY

There is substantial inequality in the distribution of earnings in the U.S. Moreover, measured income inequality has increased slightly in the last 25 years. Using data from firms to measure average earnings in an industry, the standard deviation of the logarithms of earnings rose from 0.23 to 0.31 between 1970 and 1987. The same measure applied to average earnings of workers in a large number of companies in three metropolitan areas showed an increase from 0.34 in 1971 to 0.44 in 1990. Finally, the ratio of earnings of workers at the 90th percentile of the distribution to those at the 10th percentile rose from 3.22 in 1970 to 4.35 in 1987. This change appears to have occurred primarily in the 1970s and to result largely from changes in the age structure of the labor force. Among prime-age workers, earnings inequality did not increase and may have fallen in the U.S. during the 1980s. The Gini coefficient for this group remained unchanged at 0.44 between 1982 and 1988, while the standard deviation in log earnings, which is especially sensitive to changes among the rich and the poor, fell from 1.23 in 1982 to 1.13 in 1988.[2]

Growing inequality is reflected in changes in the distribution of income as well as earnings. Table 15.1 shows the distribution of pretax, posttransfer incomes in the U.S. for selected years since 1950. Income inequality fell through the 1960s but has risen since about 1980.

The American experience is hardly unique. Inequality of earnings and income exist in all economies. Although comparable data are hard to obtain, Table 15.2 presents Gini coefficients for household (essentially, family) incomes for several industrialized economies. Inequality in the U.S. in this period was similar to that of other countries. The changes in U.S. inequality since 1970 essentially raised it back to where it had been from 1920 to 1940. In Japan and the United Kingdom, as in the U.S., the dispersion of earnings among manufacturing industries increased between 1975 and the early 1990s. It decreased, however, in France, Spain, Sweden, and Italy. In Germany inequality apparently increased in the early 1980s but remained stable at the end of the decade.[3]

---

[2]Linda Bell and Richard Freeman, "The Causes of Rising Interindustry Wage Dispersion in the United States," *Industrial and Labor Relations Review* 44: 275–287 (1991); Erica Groshen, "Rising Inequality in a Salary Survey: Another Piece of the Puzzle," Federal Reserve Bank of Cleveland Working Paper No. 9121 (1991); Martin Dooley and Peter Gottschalk, "Earnings Inequality Among Males in the U.S.," *Journal of Political Economy* 92: 59–89 (1984); Chinhui Juhn, Kevin Murphy, and Brooks Pierce, "Wage Inequality and the Rise in Returns to Skill," *Journal of Political Economy* 101: 410–442 (1993); Richard Burkhauser, Douglas Holtz-Eakin, and Stephen E. Rhody, "Labor Earnings Mobility and Inequality in the United States and Germany During the 1980s," Syracuse University, Photocopy (1995).

[3]Claudia Goldin and Robert Margo, "The Great Compression: The Wage Structure in the United States at Mid-Century," *Quarterly Journal of Economics* 107: 1–34 (1992); Douglas Hibbs, "Wage Compression Under Solidarity Bargaining in Sweden," in Inga Persson-Tanimura (ed.). *Generating Equality in the Welfare State: The Swedish Experience,* Oslo: Norwegian University Press (1990); Linda Bell and Richard Freeman, "Flexible Wage Structures and Employment," in Morley Gunderson, Noah Meltz, and Sylvia Ostry (eds.). *Unemployment: International Perspectives*, Toronto: University of Toronto Press (1987); Steven J. Davis, "Cross-Country Patterns of Change in Relative Wages," in Olivier Blanchard and Stanley Fischer (eds.). *NBER Macroeconomics Manual* 7: (1992); Katherine Abraham and Susan Houseman, "Earnings Inequality in Germany," in Richard Freeman and Lawrence Katz (eds.). *Differences and Changes in Wage Structures,* Chicago: University of Chicago Press (1995).

TABLE 15.1 PERCENTAGE DISTRIBUTION OF FAMILY INCOMES, 1950–1992

Year	Lowest Fifth	Second Fifth	Middle Fifth	Fourth Fifth	Highest Fifth	Top 5 Percent	Gini Coefficient
1950	4.5	12.0	17.4	23.4	42.7	17.3	0.379
1960	4.8	12.2	17.8	24.0	41.3	15.9	0.364
1970	5.5	12.2	17.6	23.8	40.9	15.6	0.353
1980	5.2	11.5	17.5	24.3	41.5	15.3	0.365
1985	4.7	10.9	16.8	24.1	43.5	16.7	0.389
1990	4.6	10.6	16.6	23.8	44.3	17.4	0.396
1992	4.4	10.5	16.5	24.0	44.6	17.6	0.403

Sources: U.S. Bureau of the Census, *Current Population Reports,* P–60, Nos: 132, 168, and 184.

TABLE 15.2 GINI COEFFICIENTS OF HOUSEHOLD INCOMES, SELECTED COUNTRIES, 1965–1975

Country	Gini Coefficient
United States	0.36
Australia	0.34
Canada	0.34
France	0.38
Germany	0.36
Italy	0.38
Japan	0.30
Sweden	0.29
United Kingdom	0.31

Source: Edward Muller, "Democracy, Economic Development and Income Inequality," *American Sociological Review* 53: 50-68 (1988), Table 1.

INEQUALITY OF CONSUMPTION

Although labor economists are logically interested in earnings inequality, much attention has focused on income inequality because these data are more often available to us. As we have seen, measures of income inequality have increased in the U.S. in recent decades at a faster rate than measures of earnings equality. It is also possible to consider measures of inequality in consumption, the actual goods and services that people buy. Although somewhat less closely connected to labor markets, consumption inequality has a great deal of importance for public policy since it is a better measure of differences in people's utility.

POLICY ISSUE

IN-KIND TRANSFERS AND CHANGING INEQUALITY

Data on levels and trends in income inequality typically include only cash incomes. Excluded are **in-kind transfers** of goods or services that are provided free or subsidized by government. These include food stamps, Medicaid (medical care for the poor), and public housing, as well as other services provided to lower-income families. These transfers grew in the United States from $14.5 billion in 1959 to $282 billion in 1992, a much faster growth than that of cash incomes received by poor families. Does the rapid growth of these transfers mean that the picture of increasing income inequality is false?

The answer to this question depends in part on how we value the transfers. The simplest approach is to use their **market value,** that is the price of the services on the open market. Using this approach, for example, the percentage of families with incomes below the official **poverty line,** which was roughly $14,500 for a family of four in 1992, decreased from about 14.5 percent to 11.7 percent in 1992. This is a smaller decrease in the fraction of families in poverty than the same calculation produced in 1982,[4] suggesting that noncash transfers contribute less to reducing poverty now than they did earlier.

Recall from our discussion of the value of employee benefits and the analysis in Figure 10.5 that the market value overstates how much a family would be willing to pay in cash for the services provided. In the case of Medicaid, a doctor's visit that costs the government $100 may be worth only $40 to the poor person who is the beneficiary of this subsidy. Using the **cash-equivalent value** (the amount the recipient would be willing to pay for the service) to value in-kind transfers reduces their impact on measured income inequality. The percentage of families below the poverty line in 1992 would have been above 11.7, but below 14.5, if in-kind transfers were valued at their cash equivalence.

The size of in-kind transfers makes them important in analyzing income distributions, and accounting for them reduces the amount of inequality in the distribution of income. The reduction is greater if we use a simple method based on their cost than if we account for how the recipients actually value the transfers.

Compared to income inequality, a very different picture emerges when we look at consumption inequality. Measured in this way, inequality is much lower and fewer people are below the poverty level. In addition, this measure shows no increase in inequality or poverty in recent years. In 1972 to 1973, American families in the top fifth of the income distribution had incomes equal to 8 times those of families in the bottom fifth and consumed 4.8 times as much as the poorest fifth of families. By 1988 to 1989 the ratio of

[4] Timothy Smeeding, "Alternative Methods for Valuing Selected In-kind Transfer Benefits and Measuring their Effect on Poverty," Bureau of the Census, Technical Paper No. 51, (February 1984); U.S. Bureau of the Census, *Current Population Reports*, P–60 (1994).

POLICY ISSUE

INEQUALITY AND COMPARISONS OF POVERTY

Is the problem of poverty more or less severe in the U.S. than in other countries? In large part, the answer depends on how poverty is measured. There are two alternative conceptual frameworks. The first derives **absolute measures of poverty** by determining the fraction of the population with an income below the amount needed to purchase some minimum standard of living. The second approach uses **relative measures of poverty** indicating the portion of the population that falls below an income level set equal to a specific fraction of a country's median income (often half of the median).

Increased inequality in a country will increase poverty according to relative measures no matter how wealthy the country. On the other hand, increases in income that shift the entire distribution to the right will not reduce poverty if relative measures are used. The U.S., which has a relatively large degree of inequality but also high absolute incomes at every point in the distribution, looks like a country with a lot of poverty when relative measures are used, but with much less poverty when the measures are absolute. Table 15.3 compares the poverty rate in several countries using a common absolute poverty measure defined as 35 percent more than the official U.S. poverty level and a relative measure equal to 50 percent of the median income of each country.

The differences are striking. Using the relative definition, the U.S. has the highest measured rate of poverty. On the other hand, when absolute measures showing actual deprivation are used, only Canada and Luxembourg among the countries studied had lower poverty rates. Neither absolute nor relative measures are the "right" definition of poverty. Which one is more appropriate depends on the purpose for which it is being used. It is worth remembering, however, that equality of deprivation may be more painful to those at the bottom of a society than inequality of wealth.

TABLE 15.3 ABSOLUTE AND RELATIVE POVERTY RATES

		Percentage Poor	
Country	Year	Absolute	Relative
United States	1986	17.7	17.7
Australia	1987	29.9	15.2
Austria	1987	26.3	8.4
Canada	1987	11.3	11.5
France	1984	29.8	7.6
Germany	1984	30.6	6.6
Italy	1986	42.8	10.4
Luxembourg	1985	13.7	5.6
Netherlands	1987	42.4	5.0
Sweden	1987	34.9	9.1
United Kingdom	1986	35.9	9.2

Source: McKinley Blackburn, "International Comparisons of Poverty," *The American Economic Review* 84: 371–374 (1994), Table 1.

the top quintile's incomes to those of the bottom quintile had risen to 9.8, indicating growing inequality, while the ratio of the consumption expenditures of these two groups remained unchanged at 4.8.[5]

The ratio of rich families' consumption to that of poor families is always lower than the ratio of their incomes because rich families save more of their income. Many poor families are only poor temporarily and will borrow against future income (or spend past savings) in order to maintain consumption. For example, most graduate students are included among the officially poor in the U.S., even though their lifetime incomes will make them among the wealthiest Americans. Incomes increased by 20 percent or more for 34 percent of the poor in the single year between 1990 and 1991.

Differences in levels do not, however, explain the difference in the trend of inequality between income-based and consumption-based measures. What could account for this difference? Statistically, the explanation is easy. In 1972 the average family in the bottom tenth of the income distribution spent about 115 percent of its income, financing some extra expenditures from savings or borrowings. By the 1980s this figure had risen dramatically. Between 1984 and 1989 the typical family in the bottom tenth of the distribution spent 185 percent of its income.

There are several reasons why this change may have occurred. The fraction of the population over age 65 increased from 9.8 percent in 1970 to 12.5 percent in 1990. Since, as we have seen, the average age of retirement fell during this period as well, the share of the population financing consumption from savings accumulated during their working life has grown significantly. This is not, however, the whole story. The pattern of an increasing ratio of consumption-to-income among the poor holds if the group studied is restricted to younger workers or those on public assistance. There is no evidence that savings or access to consumer debt have risen for these groups.

The most likely explanation has disturbing implications for a great deal of empirical work in labor economics. There appears to have been a dramatic increase in underreporting of income among the poorest Americans, making it impossible to determine how much of the change in the income distribution is real and how much results from changes in the accuracy of the data. If the degree of income underreporting among the poor has increased relative to other Americans, many apparent empirical patterns discussed in previous chapters must be reexamined. How much of the increase in measured returns to education is because workers with low levels of education are

[5] Daniel Slesnick, "Gaining Ground: Poverty in the Postwar United States," *Journal of Political Economy* 101: 1–38 (1993); Susan Mayer and Christopher Jencks, "Recent Trends in Economic Inequality in the United States: Income versus Expenditures versus Material Well-Being," in D. Popadimitriou and E. Wolff (eds.). *Poverty and Prosperity in America at the Close of the Twentieth Century*, New York: St. Martin Press (1993).

increasingly understating their incomes? What is the implication of increases in unreported income among the poor for measures of racial differences discussed in Chapter 14?

EXPLAINING THE SIZE DISTRIBUTION AND ITS CHANGES

Even given the data problems, much can be learned by examining the size distribution of income and changes in this distribution over time. The typical shape of size distributions of earnings creates a problem that has concerned economists and statisticians for a long time. Many human characteristics, such as height, are distributed according to the familiar, symmetrical "bell curve" (**normal distribution**). The best evidence is that this type of distribution describes many kinds of ability, including mental ability.

If, however, ability is symmetrically distributed, why should it give rise to a skewed earnings distribution? It is easy to say that inequality arises from unequal ability. The question of interest is why does a symmetric distribution of ability create a skewed distributions of earnings? We are also want to understand what factors make earnings and income in the U.S. less equally distributed now than during the recent past.

HUMAN CAPITAL'S EFFECTS ON EARNINGS INEQUALITY AND SKEWNESS

Suppose that all people have the same ability and that no job has nonmonetary advantages or disadvantages that would produce compensating wage differentials. Under these assumptions, all workers should receive the same earnings unless there were differences in their investment in human capital. To simplify matters also assume that there are no out-of-pocket costs of investing in education and that people do not work in the market while at school. As we saw in Chapter 3, individuals who have access to loanable funds will invest in human capital up to the point where the returns on the investment are equal to the rate of return on equally risky investments in physical capital. What are the implications of such investments for the distribution of earnings?

These few assumptions are sufficient to produce inequality in the distribution of earnings. To simplify the calculations, consider a society made up of three different groups of workers, each of whom works until age 68. Clerks acquire 12 years of schooling and work from age 18 on; auditors attend school for 16 years and enter the labor force at age 22; and economists attend school for 20 years and start work at age 26. Decisions regarding education will ensure that workers in each occupation receive the same discounted lifetime earnings. Yet, because those with more education will have shorter work lives over which to receive these earnings plus compensation for the opportunity costs of attending school, earnings at any age will differ.

TABLE 15.4 HYPOTHETICAL ANNUAL EARNINGS IN THREE OCCUPATIONS REQUIRING DIFFERENT AMOUNTS OF SCHOOLING

	Occupation (Years of Schooling)		
Real Rate of Return (Percent)	Clerks (12 Years)	Auditors (16 Years)	Economists (20 Years)
5	$20,000	$24,922	$30,212
8	20,000	27,738	38,574
11	20,000	31,124	48,498
14	20,000	35,038	61,412

Table 15.4 shows the extent of differences in earnings at any age between 26 and 68 (the ages when all three groups are working), that would be needed to repay the investment in schooling if we assume that clerks earn $20,000 per year. The real rates of return are in the range of 5 to 14 percent which, as we saw in Chapter 3, bracket the real rate of return to college education. Two facts stand out from this table: (1) differences in the amount of investment in human capital produce substantial inequality in the distribution of annual earnings, even for groups with identical lifetime incomes; and (2) the degree of inequality increases when the real interest rate (and, therefore, the required rate of return to schooling) increases.

This simple example shows clearly why there is inequality in the distribution of earnings. It does not, however, explain why there is skewness. To do this we need to explain why relatively few people enter the occupations that require substantial investments in human capital and thus yield high annual earnings. Two explanations are possible. Each depends on the nature of students' demand for schooling and on their ability to finance their investments by borrowing, drawing down savings, or obtaining university or government subsidies (in other words, on the supply of funds that are available for investment in schooling).[6]

One possible case is shown in Figure 15.3(a). All workers are assumed to have equal access to funds at a market rate of interest r_0. Here, however, we assume that students differ in their ability to benefit from schooling so that they have different demand curves for these funds. Again, to keep the calculations simple, assume that the distribution of ability is symmetric, as in a bell curve, but that there are only three types of students. Sixty percent of the

[6] Gary Becker, *Human Capital and the Personal Distribution of Income: An Analytical Approach*, Ann Arbor, Mich: Institute of Public Administration, University of Michigan (1967).

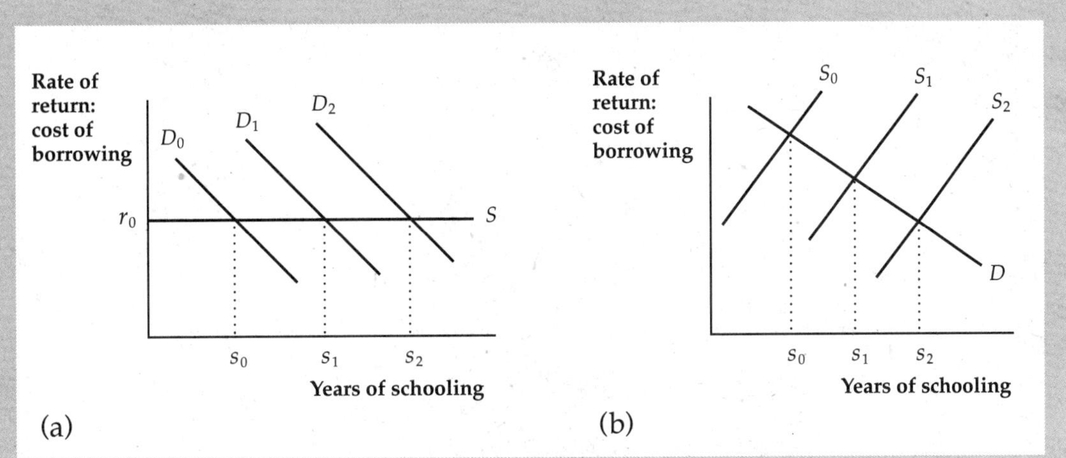

FIGURE 15.3 THE MARKET FOR FUNDS FOR INVESTMENT IN SCHOOLING WITH ABILITY AND LIQUIDITY DIFFERENCES

Differences in levels of schooling can arise because of differences in individuals' ability to benefit from schooling—(Figure 15.3 (a)—or differences in access to funds to finance education—Figure 15.3 (b).

population have average ability, 20 percent fall below average, and 20 percent are above average. Students of high ability will demand more schooling at each interest rate than their less-talented peers. This 20 percent of the population will pick s_2 years of schooling along demand curve D_2. Facing the same cost of funds, the 60 percent of students with average ability will demand s_1 years of schooling along demand curve D_1, while the 20 percent with below-average ability will end up with s_0 years of schooling.

With an interest rate (and rate of return) of 11 percent, and the three levels of schooling (s_0, s_1, and s_2) of 12, 16, and 20 years, respectively, Table 15.4 shows that 60 percent of the work force will earn $31,124 per year, 20 percent will earn $20,000 per year, and 20 percent will earn $48,498 per year. The distribution of earnings implied in this example is shown in the histogram in Figure 15.4. The three bars are connected by a smooth line to allow a better comparison to the actual distribution of earnings presented in Figure 15.1. This figure shows that skewness can be produced by combining the assumption of a symmetric distribution of ability with individuals' utility-maximizing decisions about investment in human capital. Notice that even though educational attainment in each of the top and bottom groups differs from the median by the same amount (four years), the top group's annual earnings exceed the median by far more than the bottom group's earnings fall short of it. The distribution of earnings in Figure 15.4 is not symmetric, but, instead, like all reported earnings distributions, skewed to the right.

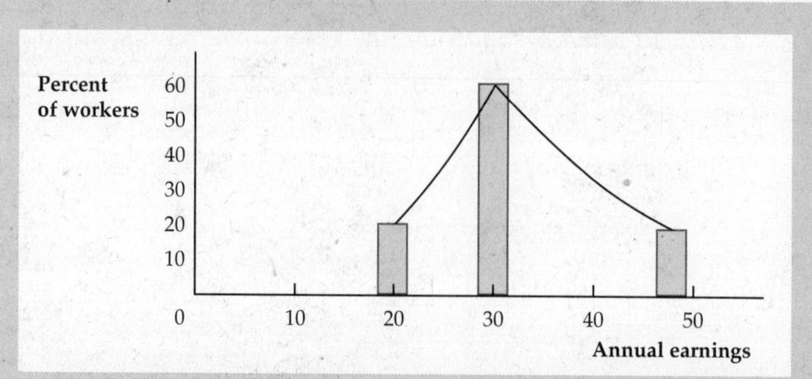

FIGURE 15.4 A SKEWED HYPOTHETICAL DISTRIBUTION OF EARNINGS

The need to produce a competitive rate of return will generate a skewed distribution of earnings even if the distribution of abilities or access to funds in Figure 15.3 is normal and symmetric.

Human capital investments can also explain skewness in the distribution of earnings by differences in the ease of access to borrowed funds among people of equal ability. In Figure 15.3(b) all students are assumed to have the same demand curve for education, *D*, but students from low-income families face greater difficulty in borrowing while their parents have fewer savings to use for their education. The supply curve of funds to finance their education is S_0. Students from better-off families will be able to finance their education more readily. For them the supply curve of funds for education is S_1, or even S_2. If a few people have great difficulty financing education (are on supply curve S_0), most have some difficulty (are on supply curve S_1), and a few find it very easy (are on supply curve S_2), then most people will obtain s_1 years of schooling, whereas a few will obtain s_0 or s_2 years. As with the example in Figure 15.3(a), this dispersion in the amount of schooling obtained will produce skewness in the distribution of earnings. The few people who obtain s_2 years of schooling will have earnings exceeding the median by more than the earnings of those who obtain only s_0 years of schooling fall short of it.[7]

The examples in Figures 15.3(a) and (b) are extremes. In reality differences in both ability and access to funds for investment in education affect the amount individuals are willing to invest in formal schooling. If people

[7]This conclusion will be valid so long as the demand curve in Figure 15.3(b) is not too inelastic. If it is, rates of return on additional amounts of schooling beyond s_0 will fall so fast that the rapid declines in additions to earnings will overcome the tendency toward skewness.

with greater ability to benefit from education also have easier access to funds to finance education, the results will be magnified and the degree of skewness in the distribution of earnings will be relatively large. More concretely, to the extent that students of high ability come from better-off families, or the government offers subsidies to very able students, there will be more skewness in the distribution of earnings. Skewness and inequality will be transmitted across generations to the extent that ability is inherited and/or parents finance their children's education.

These hypothetical examples are obviously artificial, although they illustrate how optimal decisions about the acquisition of human capital can explain the basic facts of inequality and skewness. We have ignored other aspects of investment in human capital, particularly investment in on-the-job training. Even if each worker has made the same investment in formal schooling, differences in the amount of on-the-job training would suffice to produce inequality in earnings. Since schooling and on-the-job training are complements, the inequality that each produces separately is reinforced when they are combined.

THE ROLE OF HUMAN CAPITAL IN PRACTICE

The human capital approach generates several predictions relating inequality in earnings to differences in the amount of investment in schooling and on-the-job training. Substantial study has been devoted to verifying the prediction that greater variation in workers' training will produce more dispersion in earnings. For example, data from nine countries have shown that earnings inequality, as indicated by a measure similar to the relative interquartile difference, is greater in nations where there is more dispersion in the level of formal schooling. Similarly, in the U.S., states in which there is more dispersion in the schooling achieved by adult males also exhibited greater variance in the distribution of adult male earnings. Taken together, differences in schooling and on-the-job training account for a substantial part of the observed inequality and skewness that characterize the earnings distributions.[8]

Additional evidence for the importance of human capital is provided by a comparison of Gini coefficients for the population at a point in time to Gini coefficients for a cohort of workers over its members' work lives. The Gini coefficient for the current income of the U.S. population in 1972 was 0.35, while the coefficient for the lifetime incomes of people alive in 1972 was 0.20. This difference largely reflects the fact that current workers with low levels of experience and human capital from on-the-job training will eventually

---

[8]Barry Chiswick, *Income Inequality,* New York: Columbia University Press (1974); James Smith and Finis Welch, "Inequality: Race Differences in the Distribution of Earnings," *International Economic Review* 20: 515–526 (1979).

become older and more experienced.[9] Accounting for differences in yearly incomes that arise from differences in labor force participation and investments in human capital explains much of the observed inequality in income.

Measures of inequality in the U.S. became smaller when the distribution of schooling attainment became more equal. The distribution of incomes has also shifted in the same direction as the distribution of schooling, although not by as much, since components of income other than wages and salaries are less affected by differences in schooling. Much of the increase in the inequality of earnings in the U.S. during the 1980s is attributable to increasing returns to skill. For example, roughly 60 percent of the increased inequality in wages among industries is explained by the changing demographic and occupational makeup of their workers. The latter is a direct reflection of investment in human capital, while differences across demographic groups relate in part to their differences in human capital investments. The growing dispersion of differences in earnings among occupations accounted for over half the increase in the standard deviation of the logarithms of wages between 1970 and 1990 at the level of individual plants.[10]

One of the originators of the human capital approach claims that when proper adjustments were made, differences in education and experience accounted for over 50 percent of the variance in the logarithms of earnings among workers in the U.S. in 1959.[11] Differences in measured human capital, however, leave unexplained a large fraction of the observed dispersion and skewness of the distribution of earnings. This fact can be vividly seen by examining the distribution of earnings among people whose experience and education are quite similar. In 1984 the median earnings of men in the Cornell University Class of 1960 was $60,000. The mean, however, was over $80,000, and the skewness was such that 1 percent of class members earned more than $500,000.[12] All these men attended the same institution, were about the same age, and nearly all had worked full-time since leaving school. While only some went on to graduate school, and they had different kinds of on-the-job training, one is left with the suspicion that factors other than schooling and on-the-job training must have played a large role in explaining the dispersion and skewness in the distribution of their earnings.

---

[9] Peter Friesen and Danny Miller, "Annual Inequality and Lifetime Inequality," *Quarterly Journal of Economics* 98: 139–155 (1983).

[10] Barry Chiswick and Jacob Mincer, "Time-Series Changes in Personal Income Inequality in the United States from 1939, with Projections to 1985," *Journal of Political Economy* 80: S34–S66 (1972); Bell and Freeman, "The Causes of Rising Interindustry Wage Dispersion;" Groshen, "Employers, Occupations."

[11] Jacob Mincer, *Schooling, Experience and Earnings*, New York: Columbia University Press (1974), p. 134.

[12] *Cornell University Class of 1960 25th Reunion Yearbook*, Gettysburg, Penn.: Herfft-Jones Publishing Company (1985), provided by Sandra Gross.

POLICY ISSUE

TRADE AND INCOME INEQUALITY

The fact that the increase in inequality in the U.S. is largely a result of changes in the relative wages of skilled and unskilled workers has led some to assert that the underlying cause has been an increase in the supply of unskilled labor to the economy. Since, as we saw in Chapter 3, the education level of the domestic work force has been increasing rapidly, any increase in the competition faced by unskilled workers must have come from outside the U.S. One way that this could have happened is if increases in international trade were concentrated among labor-intensive products produced by unskilled workers in countries where wages are lower than in the U.S.

Certainly the U.S. economy has become more open to the rest of the world in recent years. The ratio of imports plus exports to the U.S. GDP increased from 12.4 percent in 1970 to 16.6 percent in 1980 and 26.7 percent in 1994. It is also true that workers who produced products imported into the U.S. typically have at most a high school education. One study estimated that the labor embodied in imports in 1985 increased the effective "supply" of male high school dropouts in the U.S. by between 4 and 8 percent and the "supply" of female high school dropouts by between 8 and 13 percent. Using these figures and historic relationships between the relative wages of various educational groups and their relative sizes, some researchers have concluded that about 20 percent of the 11-percentage-point rise in the relative wages of college graduates relative to less-educated workers could be explained by the unskilled labor embodied in imports.[13]

There are, however, fundamental problems with the trade-based explanation for increases in income inequality. If increases in unskilled labor through imports had raised the relative supply of unskilled workers faster than the relative demand for such workers, the relative prices of products made by unskilled labor should have fallen. In fact, just the opposite has occurred. Neither has the relative amount of skilled and unskilled labor used in manufacturing shifted in a way that is consistent with the import-of-unskilled-labor hypothesis. If an increased supply of unskilled workers through trade were responsible for widening skill differentials in wages, this would have been seen in the U.S. through a shift in industry structure toward industries that are more skill-intensive. Within each industry, however, the rising relative price of skilled labor should have created substitution toward unskilled workers, again just the opposite of what occurred.[14]

---

[13]George Borjas, Richard Freeman, and Lawrence Katz, "On the Labor Market Effects of Immigration and Trade," in George Borjas and Richard Freeman (eds.). *Immigration and the Labor Force,* Chicago: University of Chicago Press (1992); Ana Revenga, "Exporting Jobs? The Impact of Import Competition on Employment and Wages in U.S. Manufacturing" *Quarterly Journal of Economics* 108: 253–284 (1992); David Brauer and Susan Hickock, "Explaining the Growing Gap Between Low-Skilled and High-Skilled Wages," Federal Reserve Bank of New York Research Paper No. 9418 (1994).

[14]John Bound and George Johnson, "Changes in the Structure of Wages in the 1980s: An Evaluation of Alternative Explanations," *American Economic Review* 82: 371–392 (1992); Jagdish Bhagwati and Vivek Dehejia, "Freer Trade and Wages of the Unskilled—Is Marx Striking Again?" in Jagdish Bhagwati and Marvin Kosters (eds.). *Trade and Wages,* Washington D.C.: American Enterprise Institute (1994); Robert Lawrence and Matthew Slaughter, "Trade and U.S. Wages in the 1980s: Giant Sucking Sound or Small Hiccup," *Brookings Papers on Economic Activity 1* (1994); Paul Krugman and Robert Lawrence, "Trade, Jobs, and Wages" *Scientific American* 270: 44–49 (1994).

There is some evidence that increased trade in durable goods such as automobiles has lowered prices to consumers and reduced the ability of unions to obtain above-equilibrium wages. Thus, if union wage increases for unskilled workers in these industries had reduced inequality, international trade may have played a role in concentrated sectors, although it is unlikely to have been a major factor in the overall increase in returns to skill.[15]

That the dispersion of earnings increases dramatically within a cohort as it ages has been shown in several countries including the U.S., the U.K., and Taiwan.[16] Apparently the forces that generate inequality in earnings reinforce themselves as time passes. One possible reason for this pattern is that individual characteristics that cause differences in investment in human capital persist over time. For example, if some workers have lower discount rates, they will invest more in on-the-job training at each age. As a cohort grows older, the differences in human capital will be compounded and earnings will grow even more dispersed. Thus, a partial explanation for the increased degree of inequality in the U.S. in recent years is the fact that the average age of the U.S. labor force has been steadily increasing during this period.

THE EFFECTS OF DIFFERENCES IN ABILITY

It would require great differences in access to capital to explain the dispersion in earnings that actually exists. We must, therefore, examine the role of differences in ability. As viewed by the labor market, *ability* can encompass both genetic differences and differences produced by early childhood experiences. It is difficult to distinguish how much differences in ability affect earnings directly and how much they operate by shifting the demand for investment in human capital. For many purposes, however, such distinctions make little difference.

Although we have been discussing ability in general terms, it is clear that many different kinds of ability can affect earnings. For example, intelligence, creativity, physical stamina, and manual dexterity, among other types of ability, should all matter. If each of the relevant abilities that affects earnings is normally distributed, and if earnings depend on the interactions of several uncorrelated kinds of ability, the logarithms of earnings rather than the earn-

---

[15]George Borjas and Valerie Ramey, "Time-Series Evidence on the Sources of Trends in Wage Inequality," *American Economic Review* 84: 10–16 (1994).

[16]Angus Deaton and Christina Paxson, "Intertemporal Choice and Inequality," *Journal of Political Economy* 102: 437–467 (1994).

ings themselves will be normally distributed.[17] When the logarithm of a variable follows a normal distribution, the underlying variable will exhibit positive skewness. This pattern describes the distribution of earnings quite well.

One indication of ability's role in determining the distribution of incomes comes from studies of **within-group distributions.** When workers are divided into narrow groups according to education level or occupation, the measured degree of earnings inequality increased significantly during the 1970s and 1980s, although the increase in variance of earnings within education/experience/gender groups appears to have halted during the early 1990s.[18]

Surprisingly little attention has been paid to the economics of how ability is translated into earnings. The simplest example is pure piece-rate pay. Consider the example of a factory job where production combines labor *and* capital equipment. Employers must make a competitive return on their equipment if they are to stay in business. Suppose that only one ability (say, manual dexterity) is relevant to this job and that the distribution of this ability across workers is normal (and, therefore, symmetrical). If workers at the far left tail of the ability distribution do not produce enough to cover the costs of capital, supervision, heat, light, and so on, they will not be employed. In this case, although we have assumed a normal distribution of a single ability, the corresponding distribution of earnings has no workers in the left (lower) tail and would have a shape very similar to the overall distribution of earnings in Figure 15.1. A worker who is unfortunate enough to be in the far lower tail of the distribution for every ability of importance in the labor market may be unemployable. In addition, if any single ability (say, intelligence) is relevant to all jobs, a worker could become unemployable by being in the lower tail of this distribution alone.[19]

Some specialized kinds of ability are economically valuable only in a few occupations and may only affect earnings if a worker is in the far right (upper) tail of the distribution. Consider, for example, musical talent. Many children learn to play a musical instrument. Many must at some time consider becoming professional musicians but are discouraged by teachers who feel they lack sufficient talent. Only those in the upper tail of the ability distribution can ever earn a living as a musician. If these workers place a high enough value on the nonmonetary rewards of a musical career or have a sufficient difference in their probable earnings in music and alternative occupations, they will become musicians. People with exceptional musical ability

---

[17] A. D. Roy, "The Distribution of Earnings and of Individual Output," *Economic Journal* 60: 489–505 (1950).

[18] Juhn, Murphy, and Pierce, "Wage Inequality;" John Bound and George Johnson, "What Are the Causes of Rising Wage Inequality in the United States?" *Federal Reserve Bank of New York Economic Policy Review* 1: 9–17 (1995).

[19] Michael Sattinger, *Capital and the Distribution of Labor Earnings*, Amsterdam: North-Holland (1980).

may invest a great deal in training, but the amount of their ability rather than the length and quality of training is the fundamental determinant of their earnings. In general, the best schools and teachers will accept only the most promising pupils.

People with low musical ability will find this lack irrelevant to earnings in other careers and turn elsewhere for employment. Some people in the employed labor force are probably as much below the average in musical talent as Luciano Pavarotti is above the average. Where should we expect to find these musically challenged persons in the earnings distribution of all employed persons? For all we know, they will have average earnings, since our best guess would be that they have average levels of other abilities and musical talent does not play a role in the determination of earnings in the vast majority of occupations.

Clearly, the process of choosing careers to accommodate different talents will produce dispersion in the earnings distribution, even if all abilities were normally distributed and if abilities did not need to be used in combination in any occupation. Very able people would receive high earnings that are partly a return to the training to which their ability gave them access. These earnings are largely, however, a rent to the particular specialized ability.

Neither investment in human capital nor multiplying distributions of underlying abilities can explain the extremely high earnings of many people in the upper tail of the income distribution.[20] Pavarotti earns at least 20 times the income of the average professional singer. This is also true for Jack Nicholson in movies, Steffi Graf in tennis, Michael Jordan in basketball, and a host of other **superstars** in entertainment and professional sports. In these occupations, consumers' demand for excellence plays a large role in the market value of the services of exceptionally talented people. As long as most fans agree that Pavarotti is the best tenor, Jack Nicholson is the top movie actor, and so on, these people will earn rewards that are disproportionately larger than those earned by other people in their specialty who have only slightly less underlying ability. Only when consumers do not agree about who is best or among the best, either because of difficulties in discerning quality differences or because of tastes for different styles of performance, will there be a moderation of the extreme earnings received by the few superstars in a profession.[21]

The homogeneity of consumers' tastes is not sufficient to explain why extreme differences in earnings are found only in certain professions. Why does Madonna earn such fabulous amounts, while the very best house

---

[20]This discussion is based on Sherwin Rosen, "The Economics of Superstars," *American Economic Review* 71: 845–858 (1981).

[21]Melvin Reder, "A Partial Survey of the Theory of Income Size Distribution," in Lee Soltow (ed.). *Six Papers on the Size Distribution of Wealth and Income*, New York: National Bureau of Economic Research (1969), pp. 216–217; Michael Rothschild and Joseph Stiglitz, "A Model of Employment Outcomes Illustrating the Effect of the Structure of Information on the Level and Distribution of Income," *Economics Letters* 10: 231–236 (1982).

painter would probably not receive much more than the average house painter? The answer lies in the interaction of technology and demand. Madonna's product can be sold, through recordings and mass performances in stadiums, to huge audiences and can yield earnings long after she stops performing live or producing new recordings. The house painter's clientele is limited by technology to the few people whose houses she can paint. The technology of reproducing the product expands the market for the performer's services.

Expansion of the market comes at the cost of a reduction in intimacy and perhaps in quality. Some people would rather hear a live concert by a second-tier singer than watch a telecast of a performance by Pavarotti. This quality/quantity trade-off creates a demand for the services of the somewhat less talented, allowing them to earn more than they could in their best alternative occupations. When an expanding market results from an increase in the popularity of the particular service rather than from a change in technology, the number of performers increases. Some people with even less talent (although still from the upper part of the distribution) now find they are able to satisfy some consumers' desires for live performances and earn more than they could in other occupations. The superstars, however, earn even more than before the expansion, as new consumers pay for their services by buying their records, and demand increases for the fixed supply of seats to see their live performances, raising the price they can charge. The fact that more people are now able to earn just enough to justify staying in the occupation rather than accepting employment in the general labor market combines with the higher earnings for stars to create an even more skewed distribution of earnings. This expansion of employment combined with widening income differentials is exactly what happened to the incomes of stand-up comedians in the 1980s and early 1990s as comedy clubs proliferated and the film and "concert" earnings of superstars such as Robin Williams exploded. The threefold combination of consumers' agreement on quality, consumers' preferences for live performances, and the technology that allows the reproduction of stellar performances for a mass audience produces enormous skewness in the distribution of earnings in certain occupations.

THE EFFECTS OF RESPONSIBILITY

In Chapter 9 we discussed how tournaments designed to provide incentives to lower-level executives to work hard while competing for high-level jobs result in large salary differences between executives at different levels of management. Since an optimal tournament contract requires that the size of the prize be inversely related to the probability of winning each round (being promoted), such models can explain a positive skewness in the distribution of earnings. As the number of layers of management in American corporations has declined in recent years, promotion probabilities have been reduced. The decline in the relative number of middle managers should lead to higher rewards for the tournament "winners" who are promoted to top positions. Thus, tournament models could explain an increase in inequality in recent decades.

A related but less-successful model attempts to explain the structure of earnings by the responsibilities required at each level. The dense upper tail of many earnings distributions is explained by this **hierarchical theory** of organization under the following assumptions: (1) managers at each level in an organization supervise a fixed number of people in the grade below them; and (2) the salary of managers in each grade is a constant proportion (greater than 1.0) of the salaries of people they directly supervise. In effect, this means that salaries are related to jobs rather than to individuals. Executives are assumed to be paid mainly for responsibility "and that this criterion of payment is, in principle, quite separate from the criterion of ability."[22]

There are several problems with hierarchical theory as used to explain earnings distributions. Postulating a reward for responsibility implies that people dislike taking it. As we saw in Chapter 10, the fact that many people dislike responsibility does not mean that a compensating differential will necessarily be required to fill jobs involving it. Enough people may enjoy responsibility and authority that no compensating differential needs to be paid. If sufficient people lust after power, such models would predict that supervisors might earn lower incomes than their subordinates.

It seems more reasonable to assume that rewards for position in a hierarchy reflect returns to ability. Top managers have a much greater potential to influence the success of a firm than those at lower levels. In a large corporation the person who wins out over hundreds of competing junior executives to eventually ascend to the presidency must surely have special qualities that account for this rise. A business that is not a monopoly would soon run at a loss if it selected executives without regard to abilities.

The most important difficulty with hierarchical theory is that differences in earnings distributions are equally common in occupations where workers do not operate in hierarchical organizations. Of males who worked 50 to 52 weeks in 1992, 3.2 million (7 percent of the total) had earnings of $75,000 and over, the highest earnings class tabulated. However, only 1.347 million of these were managers and administrators. There were 1.011 million professional workers and 625,000 technical and sales workers with salaries of $75,000 and over. In both of these occupational groups individual ability would seem to be more important than managerial responsibility.

Distributions of earnings with a dense upper tail can be found within groups working in very small organizations. Figure 15.5 shows the distribution of earnings of medical doctors in the U.S. in 1993. Most doctors are self-

---

[22] Lydall, *The Structure,* p. 126, and the discussion on pp. 13–17 and 125–129. The assumptions produce the Pareto distribution of earnings. If we let N be the number of persons with earnings above some given level X, the distribution is given by $N = AX^{-a}$, where A and a are constants. Pareto believed that a was generally in the region of 1.5, but higher values are often found. For an application of both the Pareto and lognormal distributions see Alan Harrison, "Earnings by Size: A Tale of Two Distributions," *Review of Economic Studies* 48: 621–632 (1981).

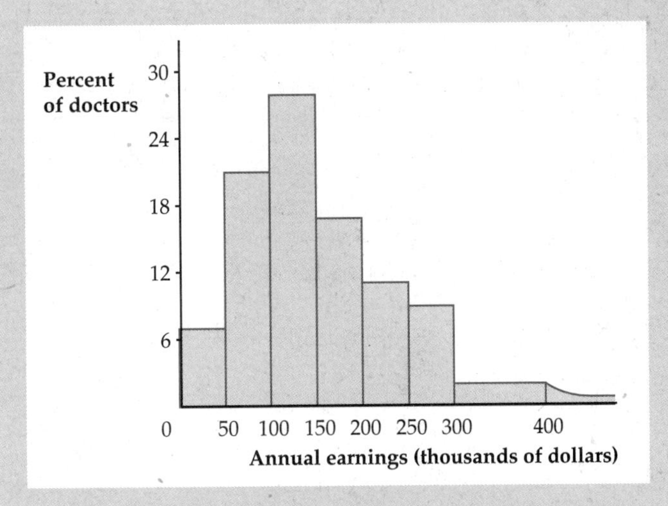

FIGURE 15.5 THE DISTRIBUTION OF EARNINGS OF MDs, 1993

The characteristic skewed distribution of earnings is found even in narrowly defined occupations where most workers operate independently rather than as part of large organizations.

employed or work in small practices with a few other doctors. Very few preside over large numbers of subordinates. The upper tail of doctors' earnings distribution looks very much like that of top managers in large firms with hierarchical structures. This similarity suggests that differences in ability and work effort are better candidates to explain the shape of this earnings distribution than a hierarchical theory.

THE EFFECT OF VARIANCE IN EARNINGS

The distribution of earnings at any time will also be a function of the distribution of workers' attitudes toward risk. Some people are **risk lovers.** In choosing a career these workers will prefer professions such as acting, where although the average income is not unusually high, there is a chance of being extremely successful. Most people, however, are **risk averse.** Other things being equal, they will be attracted to careers like teaching where, despite the absence of the possibility for extremely high rewards, there is income security from year to year. Among occupations overall, as well as the professions, those with greater variation in earnings (some very high and some very low) have higher average earnings.[23] This situation implies that the marginal worker who is drawn into a risky occupation is risk averse and must be paid a compensating differential in the form of higher average earnings in order to induce him to enter an occupation with greater variation in earnings.

Attitudes toward risk can explain the positive skewness in observed income distributions. Figure 15.6 shows three equal-sized occupations that each require the same talents and abilities from workers. Although the distribution of earnings in each occupation is normal, each has a different level of risk as measured by the dispersion of earnings. Since workers are risk averse, they require higher mean earnings in occupations where there is more risk. The aggregate number of workers with each level of earnings will be the sum of the number of workers with those earnings in each occupation. As seen in the figure, even though earnings in each occupation are normally distributed, the aggregate distribution has a marked positive skewness.

FAMILY MEMBERS' EARNINGS AND INCOME INEQUALITY

Family structure, through people's choices about whether and who to marry and through household labor supply behavior, plays a major role in determining how the distribution of individuals' earnings gives rise to the distribution of incomes among families or households. The very fact of marriage will affect the position of individuals in the income distribution and their relative material well-being. While it may not literally be true that "two can live as cheaply as one," there are economies of scale in consumption. In 1992 the official U.S. poverty level for a family of four was $14,355. If, however, this family were to split into two two-person families, each would need an income of $9,443 (for a total of $18,886) to reach the same standard of living. If each parent in this example earned the 1992 minimum wage of $4.25 an hour, the household's income of $17,000 would be well over the poverty line. Divorced and living in two households, however, the same total income would leave each family 10 percent below the poverty line.

There have been significant changes in Americans' living arrangements during the period since 1970 when inequality has apparently increased. In 1970, 72 percent of all households contained a married couple. By 1993 this figure had fallen to 56 percent. The remaining 44 percent of households were either single individuals living alone or single parents with children. Among families containing more than one person, the fraction containing a married couple fell from 88 percent in 1970 to 80 percent in 1993. One study found that between 1969 and 1989 the decline in married couple households as a

---

[23] Pradeep Kumar and Mary Lou Coates, "Occupational Earnings, Compensating Differentials and Human Capital: An Empirical Study," *Canadian Journal of Economics* 15: 442–457 (1982); Richard Evans and Robert Weinstein, "Ranking Occupations as Risky Income Prospects," *Industrial and Labor Relations Review* 35: 252–259 (1982); Orazem and Mattila, "Human Capital, Uncertain Wage Distributions, and Occupational and Educational Choice," *International Economic Review* 32: 103–122 (1991).

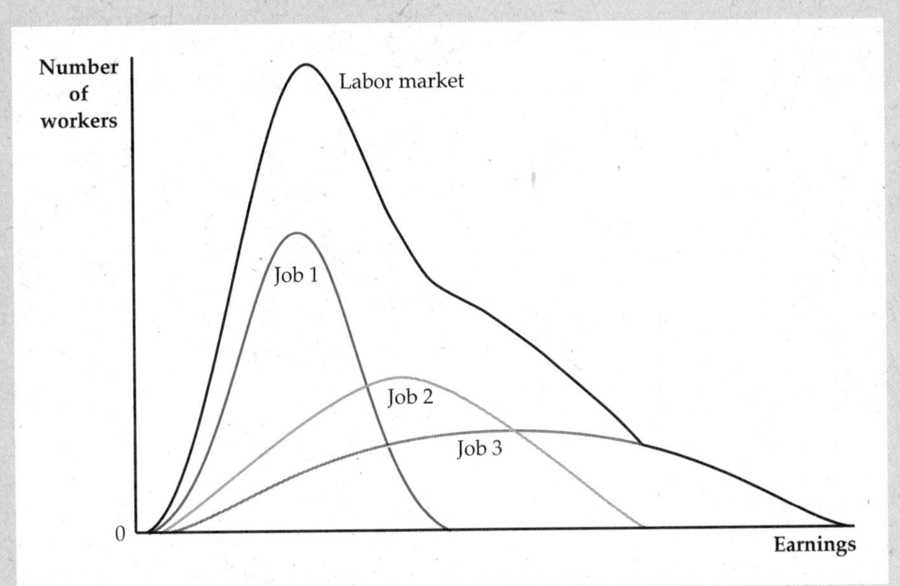

FIGURE 15.6 RISK AND THE EARNINGS DISTRIBUTION
The positive compensating differentials required when the variance of earnings is greater can produce a skewed distribution of overall earnings in the economy.

fraction of all households largely offset the substantial increase in education attainment and resulted in average household income being 10 percent lower than it would have been had the family structure remained unchanged.[24]

In addition to adding another possible worker to the household (and ignoring possible contributions from working children or from other relatives living in a household), there are two ways that marriage will cause the distribution of family income to differ from that of individuals. The first is what demographers call **assortive mating** or the positive correlation between the potential earnings capacity of women and the men they marry. Men with higher earnings potential tend to marry women who also have higher earnings potential. Many students, for example, meet their future spouses in college, thus ensuring that high-income workers tend to marry other high-income workers.[25] Assortive mating will magnify inequality in incomes.

---

[24] Paul Ryscavage, Gordon Green, and Edward Welniak, "The Impact of Demographic, Social and Economic Change on the Distribution of Income," U.S. Bureau of the Census (1991).

[25] See the review by Allen Schirm, "Marital Sorting, Wives' Labor Supply, and Family Income Inequality," University of Michigan, Photocopy (November 1988); Joseph Altonji and Thomas Dunn, "Relationships among the Family Incomes and Labor Market Outcomes of Relatives," in Ronald Ehrenberg (ed.). *Research in Labor Economics*, Vol. 12, Greenwich, Conn.: JAI Press (1991).

An offsetting effect may arise from the income effects on labor supply we discussed in Chapters 1 and 2. The income effect on wives' labor supply is relatively large. Thus, in most industrial societies, a wife whose husband earns more supplies fewer hours to the labor market. A number of early studies from areas as diverse as Israel, Québec, and the U.S. have shown that the effects of household choices about labor supply predominated and spouses' earnings make the distribution of household incomes more equal than the distribution of individual earnings.[26]

These equalizing effects of spouses' earnings are specific to the economy and time being studied. The recent increase in women's participation rates and hours of work have been disproportionately among women from upper-income families since poor women have always tended to work. Adding workers to families at the upper end of the income distribution will increase measured inequality in household incomes. As women's labor market attachment approaches that of men, the only factor linking the earnings and income distributions of married couples will be assortive mating. This tendency will make the distribution of family incomes less equal than the distribution of earnings. The effect of increased female labor force participation on inequality in earnings may be different, however, since even high-earning women may be in the middle of the overall distribution of earnings given new female entrants' relatively young age and lack of experience and the continuing gap between men's and women's earnings.[27]

THE FUNCTIONAL DISTRIBUTION OF INCOME IN AN INDUSTRIALIZED ECONOMY

In addition to the size distribution of income, we are often interested in the **functional distribution of income** showing the fraction of national income derived from various sources. We are particularly concerned with the division of national product or income between workers and owners of property. The functional distribution measures the share of total income going to various factors of production and is not concerned with any subsequent redistribution through taxes and transfer payments. As used here, national income can be defined as output during a particular time period (usually a year)

[26]Reuben Gronau, "Inequality in Family Income: Do Wives' Earnings Matter?" *Population and Development Review* 8: S119–136 (1982); Schirm, "Marital Sorting;" James Smith, "The Distribution of Family Earnings," *Journal of Political Economy* 87: S163–S192 (1979); David Blau, "Family Earnings and Wage Inequality Early in the Life Cycle," *Review of Economics and Statistics* 66: 200–207 (1984); Evelyn Lehrer and Marc Nerlove, "A Life-Cycle Analysis of Family Income Distribution," *Economic Inquiry* 22: 360–374 (1984).

[27]Kathryn Shaw, "Intertemporal Labor Supply and the Distribution of Family Income," *Review of Economics and Statistics* 71: 196–205 (1989); David Betson and Jacques van der Gaag, "Working Married Women and the Redistribution of Income," *Journal of Human Resources* 19: 532–543 (1984).

minus an appropriate allowance for depreciation. In other words, it is the amount a society *could* consume during a given time and still have the same amount of real capital left. If actual consumption is less than this, the difference is an addition to capital that constitutes both savings and investment. For individuals, the concept of income is the same except that it includes financial assets such as money, bonds, and stocks which are claims of some individuals on others that cancel out for an economy as a whole.

In discussing the functional distribution, capital's share of income includes all corporate profits, whether or not they are distributed to shareholders. In measuring the size distribution of income, we only included the part of corporate income distributed to stockholders as dividends. This limitation is imposed by the data, since there is no theoretical reason to include in income dividends that are distributed and then reinvested in buying new shares but exclude retained earnings that are reinvested within the firm.

The property share of income includes the rent of land, interest, and profit. In a modern industrial economy rent on unimproved land is a very small part of total income. Most of what is included as rent in the national income accounts is actually a charge for the use of structures and improvements on the land. We therefore treat the nonlabor share of income entirely as a return to physical capital.

Labor's share of income consists primarily of employee compensation composed of wages, salaries, and supplements to wages and salaries. In Table 15.5, which shows the functional distribution of income in the United States, employee compensation makes up 74 percent of income today. As seen in the table, labor's share has been rising fairly steadily in the U.S. This trend has also occurred in recent years in Canada, the United Kingdom, France, West Germany, and Japan, and between 1948 and 1975 in all 19 developed countries that were examined in one study.[28]

The upward trend in labor's share reported in Table 15.5 overstates the true rise for two reasons. First, all of the increasing share of economic activity performed by the government is improperly counted as part of labor's share because the return on government capital is not included in national output or income accounting, even though governments use capital such as courthouses, schools, and battleships. The entire output of government is attributed to the compensation of its employees. The growth of government thus automatically raises labor's apparent share of national income because of this accounting convention. On the other hand, most of the growth in government activity in recent decades has been in increasing transfer payments. Since these payments do not show up in the functional distribution of income, the impact of the improper recording of government activity on growth in labor's share has been much less than the overall growth of government activity might suggest.

---

[28] Calculated from United Nations, *National Accounts Statistics*, Vol. 1 (1983); Martin Paldam, "Towards the Wage-Earner State: A Comparative Study of Wage Shares 1948–75," *International Journal of Social Economics* 6: 45–62 (1979).

TABLE 15.5 THE PERCENTAGE DISTRIBUTION OF NATIONAL INCOME, SELECTED YEARS, 1929–1993

	1929	1939	1949	1959	1969	1979	1989	1993
Employee compensation	60.3	67.7	66.0	68.7	72.4	72.8	73.4	73.7
Proprietors' income	17.0	16.0	16.7	12.6	9.9	9.4	9.1	8.6
Rental income of persons	5.8	3.6	3.1	3.6	2.3	0.3	0.2	0.5
Net interest	5.6	5.0	1.2	2.5	4.4	7.7	10.6	7.8
Corporate profits	11.3	7.7	13.0	12.6	11.0	9.8	6.7	9.4
	100.0	100.0	100.0	100.0	100.0	100.0	100.0	100.0

Source: Council of Economic Advisors, *Economic Report of the President* (1995), Table B–25.

A second and more basic problem with employee compensation data as a measure of labor's share involves self-employment. Data on proprietors' or self-employment income include both compensation for the labor of self-employed persons and their families and a return on the capital invested in their businesses. To estimate labor's share, the part of self-employment income resulting from labor should be added to employee compensation. As the share of national income from self-employment has declined over most of the period analyzed in Table 15.5, the size of this omission has decreased. Thus, a correct measure of labor's share of income would have grown less rapidly than employee compensation alone. Even after full allowance is made for the labor component of self-employment income, however, estimates of changes in the functional distribution still show a rise in labor's share. We need to allocate self-employment income between labor services and returns on capital. A simple way to do this is to subtract self-employment income from the total national income and calculate what fraction of the remainder is compensation for labor services. We can then assume that self-employment income can be divided in the same proportions. Adding this fraction of proprietors' income to compensation, labor's share would have been 72.7 percent in 1929, 78.6 in 1959, and 80.5 in 1993.

Factor shares are best understood using the theory of input demand we discussed in Chapter 4. In its simplest terms this theory says that labor's share is workers' hourly compensation times the hours of labor used in production, divided by the total output allocated among all factors of production. Capital's share is the return to a unit of capital services times the number of units of capital services used, again divided by the total paid to all factors. As we saw in Chapter 4, the prices or returns to a unit of each factor are typically equal to their marginal products. Under certain conditions, the most important of which is constant returns to scale, the payment of its marginal product to each factor will exactly exhaust the total product. When these conditions do not hold, there is a residual (positive or negative) that alters the share paid to firms' owners.

The income share paid to a factor can vary either because the relative quantity used changes or its relative price (marginal product) changes. Since price changes will cause quantity changes, and shifts in supply or demand curves (quantity changes) will cause price changes, it is often difficult to separate changes in factor incomes into quantity and price components. In the case of labor we have a measure of quantity (hours of work), although it is unsatisfactory if differences in the quality of labor are ignored. In the case of capital it is impossible to obtain physical measures of inputs at an aggregate level (or, frequently, even at the firm level). Research, therefore, is forced to use proxies such as the value of the resources previously invested to produce the capital equipment.

Historical changes in factor shares do not result merely from changes in quantities along a constant production function when prices change. Technological progress is continually shifting the function, permitting the production of more output with given quantities of inputs. As we saw in Chapter 4, such technological progress has generally been labor-saving or capital-deepening, creating a rising capital-labor ratio. Physical capital per worker has increased rapidly by any measure, as we would expect from casual observation of changes in production processes over time. According to one official measure the real value of the stock of business equipment and structures per full-time equivalent employee rose by 1.25 percent per year between 1959 and 1993.[29] Other things being equal, this increase would lead us to expect a rise in property's share of national income since there is now a larger proportion of capital in the input mix. In fact, just the opposite has occurred and labor's share has increased during this period.

There are two plausible explanations for this paradox, both based on the theory of demand for factors of production discussed in Chapter 4. The first possibility is that capital-deepening shifted the economy from point C to point F on a relative demand curve for capital and labor like that shown in Figure 15.7. A relative increase in the amount of capital might have lowered the price of new capital with a given productive capacity relative to that of a given grade of labor. If firms find it relatively difficult to substitute capital for labor, the only way a relative increase in capital could have been absorbed is through a sharp drop in the relative price of capital, from R_0 to R_1. In Figure 15.7, where the axes measure the *relative* price and amount of capital, the ratio of capital income to labor income is shown by the area under the relative demand curve at the going relative factor prices. Before the capital-deepening occurred, the income of capital relative to labor was the rectangle $0R_0CA$. Afterward it is the rectangle $0R_1FB$. The latter rectangle is smaller, showing that, in this example, the fall in the relative price of capital induced by capital-deepening led to a decline in capital's share of national income. In this framework, a reduction in capital's share as more capital is used will occur only when the relative demand curve D has a slope greater than 1.0. The best estimates currently available, however, are that the slope of this relative demand curve is *about* 1.0.

[29] Calculated from the U.S. Department of Commerce, Bureau of Economic Analysis, *Survey of Current Business,* September 1994, and *The National Income and Product Accounts of the United States, 1929–1982.*

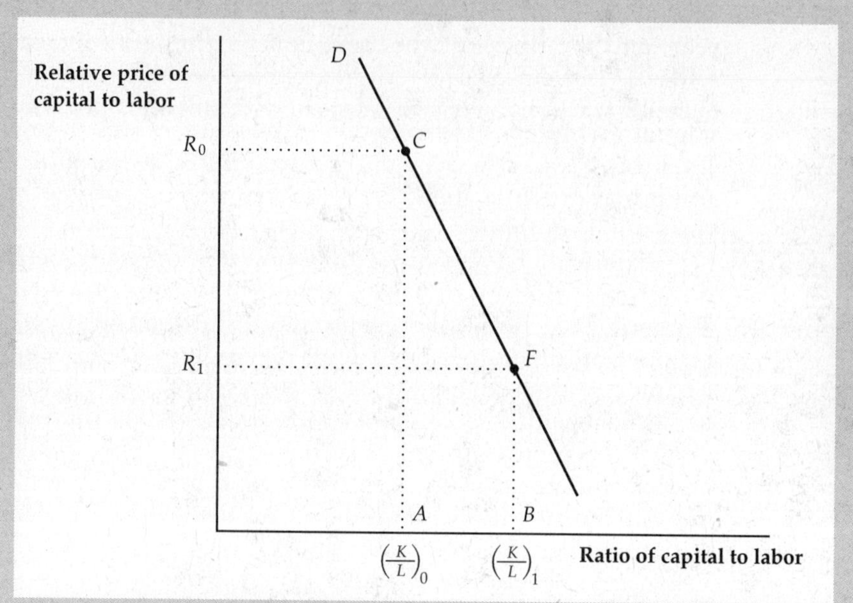

FIGURE 15.7 THE EFFECT OF CAPITAL DEEPENING ON FACTOR SHARES

When it is difficult to substitute capital for labor, the price of capital may have to fall so much for the market to absorb an increased quantity of capital that capital's share of national income will fall.

A second and better explanation, therefore, relies on the complementarity of human and physical capital presented in Chapter 4.[30] Returns on investment in human capital are included in labor income in the national accounts. Even though physical capital per worker has been rising, human capital per worker has probably been rising even more rapidly. If human capital stocks have been increasing faster than physical capital, at constant relative prices the share of national income going to labor (which is composed of both returns to unskilled labor *and* returns to human capital) will have risen. Since we lack precise measures of inputs of human and physical capital, we cannot be sure that inputs of human capital have been rising relative to those of physical capital, but it seems likely, given the rapid growth of technical, professional, and managerial employees as a percentage of the labor force (see Table 3.1). While the real stock of equipment and structures per worker increased by about 1.25 percent a year over the past three decades, the frac-

[30]P. R. Fallon and Richard Layard, "Capital-Skill Complementarity, Income Distribution, and Output Accounting," *Journal of Political Economy* 83: 279–302 (1975), show how complementarity will affect the functional distribution.

tion of workers who had completed high school increased by 2.1 percent a year, and the fraction who were college graduates increased by 3.4 percent a year. Complementarity of human and physical capital implies that the same technological changes that bring new forms of physical capital into use will also increase investment in human capital.

THE EFFECTS OF UNIONS, MONOPOLIES, AND DISCRIMINATION

The discussion so far has treated prices and quantities of inputs into production as being determined by competitive product and labor markets. As the discussions in Chapters 5 and 11 through 14 have shown, this situation is not always the case. Monopoly in the product market affects the return to capital, the quantity of capital used, and the share or national income paid to capital as well as the demand for and compensation of labor (and, therefore, labor's share in national income). The wages of labor are often set above the competitive level by collective-bargaining agreements, with possible effects on both the size and functional distributions of income. Finally, if discrimination exists in the labor market, it will cause wages to diverge from marginal products for some workers and have an effect on earnings distributions that parallels those of unions and monopolies.

THE EFFECTS OF UNIONS

The effect of trade unions on the size distribution of earnings depends on the extent of unionization and the union wage gap at each point in what would have been the earnings distribution in the absence of unions. If union membership is more common among workers who would be in the right tail of the earnings distribution in an economy without unions and those workers achieved the greatest relative wage gain, unionization would increase inequality in the earnings distribution. On the other hand, if unionization is concentrated among what otherwise would be low-wage workers and they achieved the largest wage gain, its effect would be to make the distribution of incomes more equal.

Unfortunately, as with attempts to gauge the true effect of unions on relative earnings, we cannot estimate their true effect on the distribution of earnings because we cannot observe what the economy would look like in the absence of unions. Because of this difficulty, we have to infer the impact of unions from the available evidence. In Chapter 13 we saw that union relative wage gaps are generally higher among laborers than among craft workers. This pattern will contribute to an equalizing effect of unions on income distributions. So, too, will union policies of equal pay for equal work that reduce the dispersion of earnings within plants and within industries organized across many plants. On the other hand, the fact that industries that would pay high wages even in the absence of unions have a higher incidence of unionization and a greater relative wage gap will contribute to unions making the size distribution less equal.

With these conflicting effects, the net impact of unions on earnings inequality requires careful empirical study. The evidence indicates that, overall, unions in the U.S. equalize the distribution of earnings. Wage dispersion is less within unionized plants than in otherwise identical nonunion plants and earnings are more equally distributed in otherwise similar cities and industries in which the extent of unionization is greater. When we account for the incidence of unionism and union wage gaps at different points of the earnings distribution, we find measures of inequality are reduced in the U.S., although one study of this issue in the United Kingdom produced mixed results.[31]

With the decline in the fraction of the labor force belonging to unions (Table 11.5), the importance of this equalizing effect has diminished in the U.S. since the 1950s. One study found that approximately 40 percent of the increase in the relative extent of inequality in the U.S. compared to Canada in the 1980s resulted from the fact that U.S. unions became less equalizing during this period. Declining unionism is one of the many causes for the decreased equality in the distribution of earnings and income since the late 1970s in the U.S., accounting for as much as 20 percent of the increased inequality of earnings.[32]

Since it has long been one of the stated objectives of the labor movement to raise labor's share through collective bargaining, unions should be expected to attempt to affect the functional distribution of income. Whether this attempt has been successful is exceedingly difficult to determine. All the problems that arise in measuring the influence of unions on earnings are compounded in measuring their effects on labor's share, because additional factors affecting property income must also be taken into account. The general conclusion is that no union influence on labor's share can be detected. Analyses that relate changes in the extent of unionization by industry to changes in labor's share of income originating in the industry find no effect in the U.S. and only a weak effect in the United Kingdom. One study for the

---

[31]H. Gregg Lewis, *Union Relative Wage Effects: A Survey,* Chicago: University of Chicago Press (1986), Chapter 10; David Metcalf, "Unions and the Distribution of Earnings," *British Journal of Industrial Relations* 20: 163–169 (1982); Nguyen Quan, "Unionism and the Size Distribution of Earnings," *Industrial Relations* 23: 270–277 (1984).

[32]Richard Freeman, "How Much Has De-unionization Contributed to the Rise in Male Earnings Inequality," in Sheldon Danziger and Peter Gottschalk (eds.). *Uneven Tides,* New York: The Russell Sage Foundation (1992); David Card, "The Effect of Unions on the Distribution of Wages: Redistribution or Relabelling?" NBER Working Paper No. 4195 (1992); John DiNardo and Thomas Lemieux, "Diverging Male Wage Inequality in the United States and Canada, 1981–1988: Do Unions Explain the Difference?, University of Montréal and UC-Irvine, Photocopy (1993).

U.S. that uses more complex methods to account for the nature of production in the union and nonunion sectors finds the same answer. It appears that the gains of unionized labor come mostly at the expense of nonunion labor rather than owners of capital.[33]

There is no contradiction between the findings that unions raise the relative wages of their members but fail to raise labor's share, or that they reduce profits but do not appear to reduce capital's share, even within particular industries where they are powerful. One of management's most common responses to higher union wages is to substitute capital for labor. This substitution means that the percentage increase in the wage bill will be smaller than the increase in the wage rate. Indeed, where the long-run labor demand elasticity is above 1.0 in absolute value, the effect of a wage increase is to *decrease* the wage bill. Even though the rate of return on current capital may be reduced, the substitution of capital for labor may be large enough to produce an increase in outlays on capital services. The combination of these effects may reduce labor's share after all the adjustments to a wage increase have taken place.

THE EFFECTS OF MONOPOLY AND DISCRIMINATION

Monopoly in product markets can also be expected to affect labor's share in the functional distribution of income, but here the direction of the effect is clear. Successful monopolists will earn an economic profit, a profit above the going rate of return on the capital they use, that should decrease labor's share. Strictly speaking, monopoly profit is not just a return on capital. It is a rent arising from the legal or technological position that created the monopoly and prevents other firms from entering the protected market. For this reason increased monopoly profit, unlike higher wages won by unions, does not imply that input proportions would be different from those prevailing if all markets were competitive.

If a competitive industry were suddenly transformed into a profit-maximizing monopoly protected from foreign competition by tariffs and with no fear of government interference, basic microeconomic principles tell us that prices would rise relative to marginal costs. Physical output and the use of all inputs would decline, the *value* of total output could fall or rise, and labor's share of income would decline. The effect on labor's share would be little different if a competitive

---

[33]Clark Kerr, "Labor's Income Share and the Labor Movement," in George Taylor and Frank Pierson (eds.). *New Concepts in Wage Determination*, New York: McGraw-Hill (1957); N. J. Simler, *The Impact of Unionism on Wage-Income Ratios in the Manufacturing Section of the Economy*, Minneapolis: University of Minnesota Press (1961); Keith Cowling and Ian Molho, "Wage Share, Concentration and Unionism," *Manchester School of Economic and Social Studies* 50: 99–115 (1982); Harry Johnson and Peter Mieszkowski, "The Effects of Unionization on the Distribution of Income: A General Equilibrium Approach," *Quarterly Journal of Economics* 84: 539–561 (1970).

industry were to become a regulated monopoly held to some maximum rate of return on its total assets by the regulatory body. In this case, as we noted in Chapter 5, factor proportions might change, with the drop in the relative demand for labor reducing labor's share.

This discussion suggests that a decrease in the extent of monopoly in product markets could explain the historical rise of labor's share in national income. Such a decrease might have resulted from the increased globalization of the economy through freer trade. This trend and, especially, the increased investment in human capital provide the most probable explanations of the slow, steady rise in labor's share of national income seen in Table 15.5.

The effect of discrimination on labor's share will depend on the underlying production function and who is the source of the discrimination. For example, if employers discriminate and pay for their taste for discrimination by accepting a rate of return below the market rate, the impact will be the opposite of a product market monopoly, and labor's share of income will increase. If workers are the source of discrimination, the effects are more difficult to disentangle and depend on whether the increase in the majority groups' income is great enough to offset the fall in the group against whom the discrimination is directed.

SUMMARY

Many forces in the labor market explain the shape of the earnings distribution. The most important are probably differences in training and in ability. Dispersion in the amount of schooling achieved by members of the work force has an important effect on the dispersion of earnings. Moreover, small differences in ability often generate huge differences in earnings, especially in occupations where the worker sells a service that can be replicated for a mass audience. In the U.S. earnings and income inequality have grown since the 1970s, after falling slightly for several decades. A major reason for this increase in inequality is that skills and ability have become more highly rewarded in the labor market. The earnings distribution of individuals differs from that of families due to family composition effects as well as assortive mating and labor supply decisions within the family.

Labor's share of national income shows the fraction of income resulting from production accruing to individuals as workers rather than as owners of property. In the U.S. and other developed countries, this share has been rising during most of the century. The increase has apparently not been caused by the growth of unions, whose workers win their gains primarily at the expense of nonunion workers, leaving labor's share unchanged. It may have resulted from a decline in the extent of firms' market power due to increased international competition. The best explanation is probably that the stock of human capital has grown more rapidly than the stock of physical capital.

QUESTIONS AND PROBLEMS

15.1 From the following data calculate the relative interquartile range, graph the Lorenz curve, and calculate the Gini coefficient.

Number of People	Annual Earnings
30	$5,000
45	8,000
45	12,000
30	16,000
30	20,000
45	25,000
45	35,000
20	50,000
10	100,000

15.2 In a principles of economics class at a large public university in 1988 the median income of the students' families was $70,000. The mean was $100,000, and the distribution exhibited the same skewness and dense upper tail that characterized the income distributions discussed in this chapter. List the factors discussed in this chapter that can affect the income distribution. Which of these affect this distribution, producing its very high median and skewness? Which do not?

15.3 The chapter has demonstrated that the size distribution of income in the United States has become less equal since the early 1970s; yet over this period labor's share of national income has risen, as shown by Table 15.5. Reconcile these two facts.

15.4 We have seen in the text that one possible explanation for an increase in the apparent inequality in incomes is an increasing underreporting of income among those with the lowest level of income. Discuss how this change in the extent of underreporting might affect areas of labor economics discussed in previous chapters.

15.5 Does it matter whether the political debate over poverty is based on an absolute or a relative measure? In particular, could policies designed to reduce poverty according to one measure ever increase it according to the other? How and under what circumstances might this happen?

15.6 How might your understanding and interpretation of the functional distribution of income be affected by whether you are thinking about a single year or about a worker's life time?

15.7 Suppose that the U.S. Congress followed the lead of many European countries and eliminated the taxation of capital gains. What impact would this have on both the functional and size distributions of income? How would your answer differ depending on whether you were talking about the short or the long run?

15.8 Discuss the relationship between individual and family earnings inequality. Which is likely to be more unequal? How has this relationship been changing in recent years?

15.9 We have seen several different reasons why the distribution of earnings might display the positive skewness seen in Figure 15.1. List as many of these as you can. How might you design a research project that would attempt to discover the relative importance of each reason in explaining the amount of skewness that actually exists?

15.10 For which group in each of the following pairs would you expect inequality to be greater? How, if at all, would your answer vary depending on whether you measured inequality using a Gini coefficient, the variance of log earnings, or the interdecile range?
a. Men versus women
b. Individuals versus families
c. The employed versus those not in the labor force
d. Men age 18 to 24 versus men age 70 to 84.

KEY WORDS

absolute measures of poverty
assortive mating
cash-equivalent value
functional distribution of income
Gini coefficient
gray economy
hierarchical theory
in-kind transfers
labor's share of income
Lorenz curve
market value
means-tested transfers
mode
normal distribution
poverty line
relative interquartile range
relative measures of poverty
risk averse
risk loving
size distribution of income
skewness
standard deviation
superstars
underground economy
variance
within-group income distributions

16

The Labor Market over the Business Cycle

THE MAJOR QUESTIONS

- ▲ What are the basic facts that characterize the macroeconomic behavior of labor markets?
- ▲ What happens to wage inflation and unemployment over business cycles?
- ▲ What happens to the duration and incidence of unemployment as aggregate economic conditions change?
- ▲ How can we explain these facts in ways that are consistent with the underlying microeconomic theories and evidence?
- ▲ Can government intervention be useful in altering these cyclical outcomes favorably?
- ▲ How are the behaviors of the labor market we have studied linked to modern study of macroeconomics?

THE FACTS OF LABOR MARKET ADJUSTMENT DURING BUSINESS CYCLES

The Behavior of Labor Market Aggregates

Some of the cyclical behavior of labor markets described and explained in earlier chapters can be summarized as:

1. civilian labor force participation rates decrease in recessions (Chapter 1);
2. hours per worker fluctuate more than employment over the business cycle (Chapter 5);
3. productivity (output per worker hour) falls during recessions (Chapter 5);

4. voluntary mobility (the rate at which workers quit jobs) falls sharply during recessions when an increased fraction of the unemployed are job losers and a decreased fraction are people who have quit their jobs (Chapter 7); and
5. the union wage gap rises in recessions and falls in response to unexpected inflation (Chapter 13).

In this chapter we must first explain why the unemployment rate rises in recessions. While this relationship sounds definitional, it need not be. One can imagine hours per worker falling as rapidly as output so that neither employment nor unemployment changes. The data on unemployment rates at business cycle peaks and troughs in the first column of Table 16.1, however, show that unemployment rises sharply in recessions. Indeed, since World War II the increase in the unemployment rate from the month of the business cycle peak to the month of the trough has averaged over 3 percentage points in the U.S.

We saw in Chapter 8 that some unemployment will exist in a developed economy no matter what macroeconomic conditions prevail. The amount of this structural-frictional unemployment is determined by the composition of

TABLE 16.1 UNEMPLOYMENT, EMPLOYMENT, AND PAY CHANGES, BUSINESS CYCLES, UNITED STATES, 1957–1994

				Unemployment duration		
Peak and Trough Years of Cycle	Unemployment Rate (1)	Unemployment Gap (2)	Employment Population Ratio (3)	Average Length to Date (Weeks) (4)	Percent > 26 Weeks (5)	Hourly Earnings Index, Percentage Change (6)
1957	4.3	0	57.1	10.5	8.4	5.0
1958	6.8	2.5	55.4	13.9	14.5	4.2
1960	5.5	1.1	56.1	12.8	11.8	3.4
1961	6.7	2.3	55.4	15.6	17.1	3.0
1969	3.5	−1.5	58.0	7.9	4.7	6.7
1971	5.9	0.8	56.6	11.3	10.3	7.2
1973	4.9	−0.5	57.8	10.0	7.9	6.2
1975	8.5	3.1	56.1	14.2	15.2	8.4
1979	5.8	0.2	59.9	10.8	8.7	7.9
1980	7.1	1.5	59.2	11.9	10.7	9.0
1981	7.6	2.0	59.0	13.7	14.0	9.1
1982	9.7	4.1	57.8	15.6	16.6	6.9
1989	5.3	−0.7	63.0	11.9	9.9	4.4
1991	6.7	0.7	61.6	13.8	13.0	3.2

Sources: Council of Economic Advisors, *Economic Report of the President* (1992); Robert Gordon, *Macroeconomics*, Boston: Little Brown (1990), Appendix A; and *Monthly Labor Review*, selected issues.

the labor force and the structure of labor market institutions. Since these factors change over time, the level of structural-frictional unemployment also varies over time. We call the level of unemployment where all unemployment is structural or frictional the **full-employment unemployment rate** and define the **unemployment gap**[1] at any time, *t*, as:

$$UGAP_t = URATE_t - U^*$$

where *URATE* = actual unemployment rate, as measured in the CPS, and
U^* = full-employment unemployment rate prevailing at the time.

Although different labor market analysts measure the full-employment unemployment rate differently, and some would disagree with the measure we use, most would acknowledge the need to measure cyclical variations by changes in some form of the unemployment gap. As column 2 of Table 16.1 demonstrates, at some business cycle peaks the unemployment rate has been pushed so low that the gap has been negative and even some structural-frictional unemployment has been temporarily suppressed.

Column 3 shows that the rise in the unemployment gap has been accompanied in most recessions by small decreases in the **employment-population ratio** that measures the ratio of civilian employment to the civilian population age 16 and over. This ratio indicates the ability of the economy to generate jobs. Unlike the unemployment rate, which reflects variations in both employment and labor force participation, cyclical changes in this measure are produced solely by variations in employment. That the unemployment rate rises even though the employment-population ratio falls during recessions shows that the discouraged-worker effect on labor force participation is typically not large enough to absorb the increased number of job losers.

The structure of unemployment also changes over the business cycle. The average duration of current spells of unemployment rises. Using the formula in Chapter 8 relating *URATE* to the duration and incidence of unemployment, and making the assumption that the length of spells to date is a reasonable proxy for the length of completed spells, calculations based on columns 1 and 4 of Table 16.1 show that the incidence of unemployment also rises in recessions. For example, in the boom year of 1979 14.3 percent of those who worked experienced some unemployment while in the recession year of 1982, 20.2 percent of workers were unemployed at some time. Both the extent and duration of unemployment increase during recessions in the U.S. The percentage of long-term unemployed workers, for whom the hardship associated with being unemployed is presumably greatest, increases sharply in recessions, as shown in column 5. Cyclical increases in duration have apparently accounted for a greater proportion of the cyclical rise in unemployment in the recessions since 1980 than in earlier recessions.[2]

---

[1]Michael Wachter, "The Changing Cyclical Responsiveness of Wage Inflation," *Brookings Papers on Economic Activity,* 115–159 (1976), discusses ways of measuring the unemployment gap.

[2]Michael Baker, "Unemployment Duration: Compositional Effects and Cyclical Variability," *American Economic Review* 82: 313–321 (1992).

Column 6 of Table 16.1 shows the annual percentage change in an index of nominal average hourly earnings. This measure of wage rates is adjusted for changes in the amount of overtime hours worked and in the mix of employment by industry. As the table makes clear, there can be periods of relatively high inflation, such as the 1970s, where nominal wage growth increases well into recessions.

POLICY ISSUE

EMERGENCY UNEMPLOYMENT BENEFITS AND HARDSHIP

Except for the recession from 1979 to 1980, in each recession shown in Table 16.1 the U.S. government has enacted emergency legislation extending the maximum duration for unemployment benefits. The announced purpose has been to alleviate the hardship imposed on the increased number of long-term unemployed workers. In several recessions the extensions were for an extra 13 weeks of benefits beyond the 26 weeks to which unemployed workers were normally entitled. In the 1973 to 1975 recession the extension provided for as much as an extra 39 weeks of benefits, while in the 1981 to 1982 recession extended benefits of up to 29 extra weeks were available. During the 1990 to 1991 recession a smaller than usual cyclical increase in the percentage of long-term unemployed workers occurred. As before, Congress passed emergency legislation authorizing extra weeks of unemployment benefits. President Bush disagreed with Congress's actions and took steps to prevent the legislation from taking effect.

Are these emergency benefits necessary to alleviate the problems of people who would otherwise face substantial hardship? Or are they just a transfer to workers who have sufficient other resources to cope with the lost income during their long spells of demand-deficient unemployment?

To the extent that unemployed workers expect cyclical layoffs and have accumulated savings toward this eventuality, they can draw down savings while on layoff. Even if they have no savings, they may be able to borrow while unemployed. If either of these actions occurs, they will treat extended unemployment benefits like any other income flow, spending some and adding the rest to savings. Only if they have no savings and cannot borrow will they spend each dollar received. The evidence suggests that about half of all unemployment benefits go to recipients who do not have sufficient savings, or cannot borrow enough to prevent a drop in spending.[3] Some have interpreted this finding as evidence that workers cannot tolerate the shocks resulting from forcing them to rely on their savings during periods of unemployment. The problem with this logic is that current wages and levels of savings have been chosen by workers who have a rational expectation that unemployment benefits exist and will be extended during recessions. As we saw in Chapter 10, workers would require a greater compensating differential to enter jobs where layoffs were common if unemployment insurance did not exist. Presumably savings behavior would change and workers would accumulate greater resources to fall back on were they no longer to expect extension of unemployment benefits in recessions.

---

[3] Daniel Hamermesh, "Social Insurance and Consumption: An Empirical Inquiry," *American Economic Review* 72: 101–113 (1982).

CYCLICAL RELATIONSHIPS AMONG LABOR MARKET AGGREGATES

The scatter diagram in Figure 16.1 plots the relationship between changes in hourly earnings and the size of the unemployment gap. The pattern of points for the whole period 1954 to 1994 looks almost random, like darts thrown at a board. If, however, we separate the points into two periods, 1954 to 1973 and 1983 to 1994, and 1974 to 1982, and denote the former by dots and the latter by squares, two distinct patterns emerge. The curve *P* fits the first set of points fairly well. The straight line *P*′ provides the best fit to the points from 1974 to 1982. More complex relationships, which account for the effects on

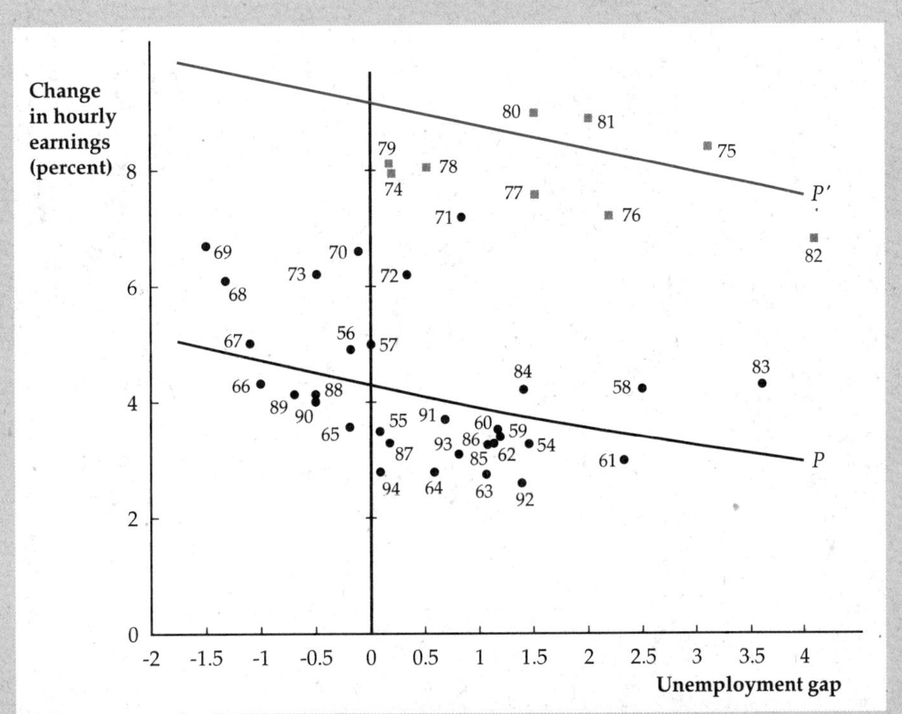

FIGURE 16.1 THE RELATIONSHIP OF CHANGES IN HOURLY EARNINGS TO DEMAND DEFICIENT UNEMPLOYMENT IN THE UNITED STATES, 1954–1994

There is a downward-sloping Phillips curve relating the unemployment gap and rate of wage inflation. This curve shifted up during the 1970s and early 1980s, but now appears to have fallen back to, or even below, its historic position.

wage changes of factors other than the unemployment gap, show a similar pattern.[4]

The relationships between wage changes and the unemployment gap depicted in Figure 16.1 are called **Phillips curves.** Similar curves could be drawn between wage changes and *URATE* with much the same results. It is apparent from the figure that no one curve describes the relationship between wage changes and unemployment in the U.S. since World War II. As we have shown, however, subperiods since World War II can be characterized by separate Phillips curves. Long periods of history in both the U.S. and the U.K., as Phillips showed in his original study, are described fairly well by curves like *P*.[5] In the U.S., there appears to have been a temporary outward shift in the Phillips curve in the 1970s. Interestingly, the points for the 1990s lie increasingly below the curve *P*, suggesting that the historic trade-off between inflation and unemployment may have become more favorable in the current decade.

As in the United States, the Phillips curve seems to have shifted outward in the 1970s for many other countries. In some countries it is not even clear that a downward-sloping relationship like *P′* can be drawn to fit the points characterizing the wage change–unemployment relationship since the early 1970s.[6] Unlike the U.S., however, Phillips curves in many other countries have not shifted back inward since the early 1980s.[7]

EXPLAINING THE FACTS: INFLEXIBLE WAGES

Nobel laureate Robert Solow has observed, "The central question of macroeconomic theory is why do modern capitalist economies respond to disturbances by generating fluctuations in output and employment as well as in relative prices, and not just by generating fluctuations in relative prices."[8] This observation suggests that explaining why unemployment rises during reces-

---

[4] James Medoff and Katharine Abraham, "Unemployment, Unsatisfied Demand for Labor, and Compensation Growth, 1956–1980," in Martin Baily (ed.). *Workers, Jobs and Inflation*, Washington D.C.: Brookings Institution (1982).

[5] A. W. Phillips, "The Relation Between Unemployment and the Rate of Change of Money Wage Rates in the United Kingdom 1861–1957," *Economica* 25: 285–299 (1958), is the original study in this entire area. An historical Phillips curve for the United States is shown in Otto Eckstein and James Girola, "Long-Term Properties of the Price-Wage Mechanism in the United States, 1891–1977," *Review of Economics and Statistics* 60: 323–333 (1978).

[6] Among the many studies of the Phillips curve outside the United States and the United Kingdom are W. Craig Riddell, "The Empirical Foundations of the Phillips Curve: Evidence from Canadian Wage Contract Data," *Econometrica* 47: 1–24 (1979), and for Sweden, Robert Flanagan, "The U.S. Phillips Curve and International Unemployment Rate Differentials," *American Economic Review* 63: 114–131 (1973).

[7] Charles Bean, "European Unemployment: A Survey," *Journal of Economic Literature* 32: 573–619 (1994).

[8] Ian McDonald and Robert Solow, "Wages and Employment in a Segmented Labor Market," *Quarterly Journal of Economics* 100: 1115–1142 (1985).

POLICY ISSUE

THE COLLAPSE OF COMMUNISM, INFLATION AND UNEMPLOYMENT

The shift from P to P' in Figure 16.1 was small and gradual. It followed the "oil shock" that occurred in late 1973 and early 1974 as OPEC sharply increased the price of oil, and thus increased production costs in industrialized economies including the U.S. The collapse of the former communist economies of Central and Eastern Europe illustrates the same phenomenon with much greater magnitude. Prior to the fall of communism, although these economies had numerous problems, very little open inflation or unemployment existed. Table 16.2 shows what happened in the labor markets in six former communist countries between 1990 and 1993.

Differences clearly exist between these countries in whether they were able to prevent severe inflation following the initial liberalization of prices. In all except the Czech Republic, however, substantial increases in unemployment occurred. In terms of Figure 16.1 they would all have moved from a point near the origin to one well off the page.

The unemployment figures would be even larger if they included discouraged workers. Between 1990 and 1992 the labor force participation rate fell by 12 percentage points in Bulgaria and Hungary and 11 percentage points in Slovakia. The decrease was about 6 percentage points in Poland and the Czech Republic. The Polish and Czech decreases were almost entirely among women and may have been a voluntary response when the communist policy of forcing all women to work was abandoned. In the other countries, however, the decline was equally large among men and probably represents hidden unemployment.[9]

These shifts occurred because of the massive collapse of labor-market and other institutions accompanying the fall of communism. Similar drastic and painful shifts occurred at the end of World War I in Germany and Russia, where these changes also accompanied the fall of an old system of government. The sad histories of their cases suggest that the rest of the world would be wise to see that a well-functioning labor market is established in Eastern Europe and the successor states of the former Soviet Union. As evident from the Czech case, government policies providing for rapid privatization and supporting retraining are critical in transition economies. The West must also play its part, however, by ensuring market access for the products of the region's newly privatized and emerging firms.

sions is a major challenge in analyzing labor markets in the macroeconomy. An acceptable theory must also be able to explain the relationship between wage changes and unemployment.

Finally, any theory must address the related question of whether substantial unemployment can reflect an equilibrium in the labor market that will persist for some time. Can a positive *UGAP* be permanent, or will it be of relatively short duration? What are the forces that move the labor market from short-run to long-run equilibrium? These questions are central to a debate in

[9] Tito Boeri, "Unemployment Dynamics and Labor Market Policies," in Simon Commander and Fabrizio Coricelli (eds.). *Unemployment, Restructuring, and the Labor Market in Eastern Europe and Russia,* Washington, D.C.: The World Bank (1995).

TABLE 16.2 UNEMPLOYMENT (U) AND INFLATION (I) IN FORMER COMMUNIST COUNTRIES OF CENTRAL AND EASTERN EUROPE, 1990–1993

	Bulgaria		Czech Republic		Hungary		Poland		Romania		Slovakia	
	U	I	U	I	U	I	U	I	U	I	U	I
1990	1.7	—	0.7	10.0	1.7	29.0	3.5	624.6	—	10.4	1.6	10.3
1991	11.1	338.5	4.1	57.8	8.5	34.2	9.7	76.7	3.0	121.3	6.6	61.2
1992	15.3	79.4	2.6	11.1	12.3	22.9	13.3	46.4	8.4	170.0	11.4	10.0
1993	16.4	84.3	3.5	20.1	12.1	22.5	15.7	35.8	10.2	202.1	12.7	23.3

Sources: International Labor Organization, *Year Book of Labor Statistics* (1994); and International Monetary Fund, *International Financial Statistics*, (February 1995).

macroeconomics that has raged on and off since Keynes's *General Theory* was published in 1936. They are really, however, questions for labor economists, since aspects of labor market behavior are central to answering them.

A simple approach would start with a short-run aggregate labor supply curve, of the sort presented at the end of Chapter 3, and a short-run aggregate labor demand curve, like that discussed in Chapter 4. These are shown in Figure 16.2. We assume that the economy exhibits only structural-frictional unemployment at a real wage rate of w_0 and employment of E_0 when the aggregate labor demand curve is D_0. If a negative shock reduces aggregate demand, shifting the labor demand curve to D_1, the real wage rate should fall to w_1, and employment should fall to E_1.

This simple approach produces a drop in employee-hours when aggregate demand drops, but it produces no cyclical increase in the unemployment rate. Presumably the only unemployment existing at point B is the same structural-frictional unemployment that existed at point *A*. Each worker may be working fewer hours as he moves along his supply curve in response to falling real wages. Some workers will find that w_1 is below their reservation wage, and drop out of the labor force. No one who wants to work at w_1, however, will be denied employment for all the hours they desire.

Under this approach the drop in aggregate demand is met by a combination of decreasing hours and labor force participation. The theory does not explain why changes in aggregate demand should result in changes in unemployment. Because it is clear that recessions are characterized by increases in unemployment and that these increases form an important part of public policy discussions in almost every country, labor economists have devoted a great deal of effort to explaining why business cycles appear to generate fluctuations in employment in modern societies.

Even though employment and unemployment vary over the business cycle, they vary less than product demand and sales. As we saw in Chapter 5, fluctuations in employment will be less than fluctuations in product demand when firms engage in labor hoarding in order to preserve investments in firm-specific human capital or hiring and training costs. At the trough of

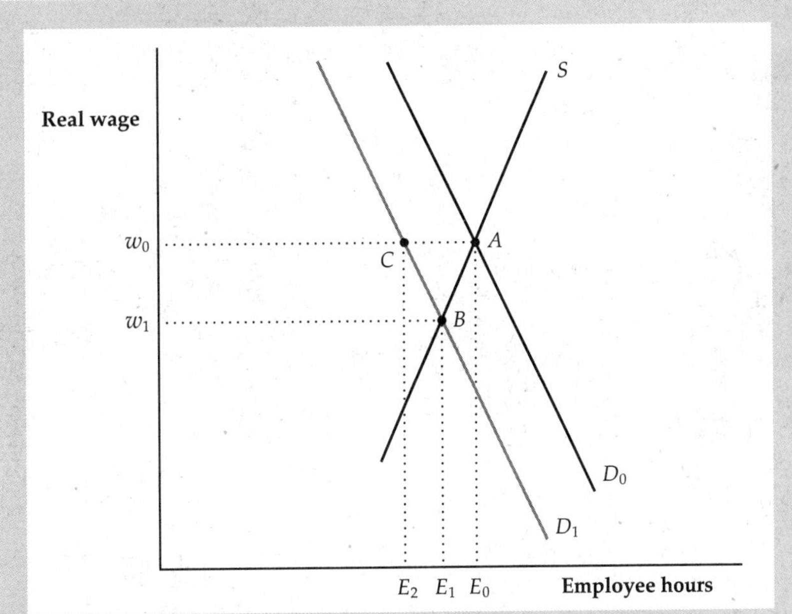

FIGURE 16.2 A NAIVE APPROACH TO CYCLICAL LABOR MARKETS

In a flexible labor market, a drop in demand from D_0 to D_1 will result in a fall in employee-hours worked and wages but should not create an increase in unemployment.

recent business cycles, employment in U.S. manufacturing appears to have been between 4 and 8 percent greater than needed to meet production requirements. This oversupply means that labor productivity varies procyclicly, rising in booms and falling in recessions. The same tendency to hoard labor has been found in Japan, France, Germany, and the U.K. and persists even when variations in hours are taken into account. In Japan employment is much less variable and labor hoarding even greater than in the other economies.[10]

---

[10] Ray Fair, "Excess Labor and the Business Cycle," *American Economic Review* 75: 239–245 (1985); J. Fay and J. Medoff, "Labor and Output Over the Business Cycle," *American Economic Review* 75: 638–655 (1985); A. Aizcorbe, "Procyclical Labour Productivity, Increasing Returns to Labour, and Labour Hoarding in U.S. Auto Assembly Plant Employment," *Economic Journal* 102: 860–873 (1992); H. Odagiri, *Growth Through Competition, Competition Through Growth*, Oxford: Clarendon Press (1992); Robert Hart and James Malley, "Excess Labour and the Business Cycle: A Comparative Study of Japan, Germany, the United Kingdom and the United States," University of Stirling, Department of Economics, Photocopy (1993).

In his *General Theory*, Keynes attributed the fluctuation in unemployment over the business cycle to **rigid wages.** Suppose that the wage in Figure 16.2 were fixed at w_0 and could not fall during a recession. When the demand curve shifted to D_1, employers would demand E_2 employee-hours at point *C*. Since the wage had not changed, workers would still want to supply E_0 hours, and there would be an excess supply of labor equal to $E_0 - E_2$ employee-hours. Of course, this simple graph still does not explain why the excess supply results in some workers being fully employed and others totally unemployed, rather than every worker working fewer hours. The answer can to be found in the trade-off between employees and hours per worker discussed in Chapter 5. We turn now to attempts to explain why real wages might not fall even when there is excess supply of labor.

SLOW ADJUSTMENT—UNIONS AND THEIR EFFECTS

Wages may be rigid downward because of trade unions, in the short run because wages are fixed by collective-bargaining agreements and in the long run because union negotiators resist wage cuts. The British economy was well organized by unions at the time Keynes wrote, and this seems to be the reason he had in mind. Even during the very deep recession of the early 1980s in the U.S., less than 15 percent of the unionized workers who negotiated contracts took nominal wage cuts. Further evidence that union contracts may introduce wage rigidities is provided by the fact that employment levels change more at the time of recontracting, when rigidities should be at their lowest, than they do during the life of a contract. In a sample of 12 industries between 1958 and 1985, 20 percent of the industry change in employment during the prior contract was undone in the first quarter after a new industry-wide contract went into effect.[11]

It is easy to point out that unions might keep nominal wages rigid during long-term contracts and induce rigidity in real wages through COLAs. It is more difficult to construct a theory explaining how this rigidity can persist beyond the length of these contracts. One possibility is if union contracts are **staggered** over time. Both firms and workers may be better off if their contracts do not expire at the same time as everyone else's.[12] Workers care about their relative wages and union leaders must not be seen as winning wage increases less than those obtained by other leaders in past years when prod-

---

[11]Daniel Mitchell, "Shifting Norms in Wage Determination," *Brookings Papers on Economic Activity,* 576 (1985); Mark Bils, "Testing for Contracting Effects on Employment," *Quarterly Journal of Economics* 106: 1129–1156 (1991).

[12]John Taylor, "Aggregate Dynamics and Staggered Contracts," *Journal of Political Economy* 88: 1–23 (1980); and Gary Fethke and Andrew Policano, "Will Wage Setters Ever Stagger Decisions?" *Quarterly Journal of Economics* 101: 867–878 (1986).

uct demand might have been higher. Thus, even workers whose union negotiates during a recession may seek a sufficiently high real wage that employers cannot justify retaining all members of their work force.[13] As we discussed in Chapter 11, this effect is magnified by the fact that seniority rules give most union workers relative certainty that they will not be laid off even if wages are kept above the equilibrium level.

SLOW ADJUSTMENT—THE NONUNION CONTEXT

The most serious difficulty with any theory resting on union wage behavior is that with fewer than 16 percent of American workers belonging to unions in 1994, attributing aggregate fluctuations in employment and wages to union wage behavior is to claim that the tail is wagging the dog. It is possible, but it seems difficult to believe that the relatively small unionized sector is "causing" simultaneous inflation and demand-deficient unemployment economy-wide.

An explanation for wage rigidity in nonunion firms rests on a combination of firm-specific training that ties workers and employers together, and the efficiency-wage hypothesis discussed in Chapter 9. Workers universally regard wage cuts as an affront because they view their wage as a measure of their relative worth and the esteem in which they are held. Nonunion employers, therefore, fear the adverse consequences of wage cuts, including reductions in productivity, increases in quit rates, and formation of unions. This means that when product demand is low, employed and unemployed workers are poor substitutes in production, and the supply price of the unemployed is not relevant to determining the wage level of the employed.[14] If workers' productivity depends on their wages relative to other workers whom they view as comparable, any wage cut in response to a shift in workers' *VMP* schedules when product demand shifts will cause productivity to be reduced even further.

Maintenance of customary wage differentials in nonunion labor markets for motivational (efficiency wage) reasons can produce rigid wages over the business cycle. Since efficiency wages (like union contracts) create a queue of potential employees who are willing to work for a firm at the current wage, it is not necessary for these firms to raise wages in booms to attract additional labor. They can respond instead by lowering hiring standards and selecting

[13]John Taylor, "Union Wage Settlements During a Disinflation," *American Economic Review* 73: 981–993 (1983); Edward Montgomery and Kathryn Shaw, "Long-Term Contracts, Expectations and Wage Inertia," *Journal of Monetary Economics* 16: 209–226 (1985).

[14]George Akerlof, "A Theory of Social Custom, of Which Unemployment May Be One Consequence," *Quarterly Journal of Economics* 94: 749–776 (1980); Janet Yellen, "Efficiency Wage Models of Unemployment," American Economic Association, *Papers and Proceedings* 74: 200–205 (1984).

more workers from the queue. This pattern is consistent with evidence that real wages vary less and employment levels more over the business cycle in high wage industries.[15]

The unemployment that is produced in these models can persist until product demand increases or those customary differentials eventually break down. We saw in Tables 9.1 and 9.2 that many workers hold jobs for a very long time. If customary wage differentials only break down fully when workers who are used to them have died or retired, this evidence suggests that eliminating the persistent unemployment they generate when product demand declines could take a very long time.

THE ROLE OF IMPLICIT CONTRACTS

Rigid wages can also be explained as a result of the theory of long-term employer-employee relations (implicit contracts) discussed in Chapter 9. This theory explains wage rigidity by workers' willingness to supply labor to their employers at a fixed wage that is lower on average than the fluctuating wage that would elicit the required supply of labor at different levels of product demand. When product demand changes, wages remain rigid, throwing the burden of adjustment onto employment. Total labor income varies just as much as if wages were flexible, but the burden is borne by only a few workers, leaving most workers better off.

Employment in firms with well-developed internal labor markets, as in all firms, is buffeted by demand fluctuations for the firm's product. In most industries there are seasonal highs and lows in demand. Moreover, fluctuations in product demand also occur from year to year as aggregate economic conditions change. These variations in product demand can be expected by both workers and firms. Knowing that variation in output is inevitable, firms and workers will structure employment practices in the internal labor market to accommodate this variability.[16]

The structure of such contracts can be seen in Figure 16.3. Product demand varies randomly between the minimum and maximum values shown along the horizontal axis. We assume the average output is halfway between these two values. The firm's wage bill is shown on the vertical axis.

---

[15]Mark Bils and Kenneth McLaughlin, "Inter-Industry Mobility and the Cyclical Upgrading of Labor," NBER Working Paper No. 4130 (1992).

[16]Costas Azariadis, "Implicit Contracts and Underemployment Equilibria," *Journal of Political Economy* 83: 1183–1202 (1975); Martin N. Baily, "Wages and Employment Under Uncertain Demand," *Review of Economic Studies* 41: 37–50 (1974); Herschel Grossman, "Risk Shifting and Reliability in Labor Markets," *Scandinavian Journal of Economics* 79: 187–209 (1977).

POLICY ISSUE

THE SHARE ECONOMY

Other than by exhorting workers to pay less attention to wage differentials when they decide how hard to work or by preventing unions from emulating each other's recent settlements when they negotiate, how might wage rigidity be eliminated? One possibility is to encourage much less reliance on wages, substituting instead much greater participation by workers in sharing profits.[17]

The argument for profit sharing rests on reducing labor costs during times when product demand is low. Suppose workers' compensation includes a fixed wage of $15 an hour and a share of profits averaging 25 percent of their total compensation ($5 an hour), but varying from $0 to $10 over the business cycle. In this case, labor costs could fall by $10 (50 percent of the average compensation) when the economy fell from a cyclical peak to a trough. This reduction in labor costs would induce employers to retain much more of their labor force. Workers would take an effective pay cut without having to renegotiate their contracts. If profit shares or bonuses are sufficiently large *and* flexible, cyclical declines in employment could be totally avoided.

We saw in Chapter 9 that bonuses constitute a substantial fraction of workers' earnings in Japan and Korea. It is also true that overall levels of unemployment are lower and employment fluctuations are smaller in response to equal product market shocks than they are in the United States.[18] Whether the Asian experience could carry over to the U.S. is not clear. The structure of labor relations is very different, as is the extent of internal labor markets. Government protection of large manufacturing firms in which the largest bonuses are paid is extensive in Japan and Korea, with all the costs to consumers this implies. These considerations suggest that one ought not to expect to replicate a Japanese-type system elsewhere. Nevertheless, in the U.S. between 1971 and 1985 cyclical increases in unemployment were accompanied by smaller cuts in employment in firms that had profit-sharing plans than elsewhere.[19] The underlying logic of a share-based compensation is compelling enough that it is hard not to believe that more widespread use of profit sharing would reduce cyclical labor market fluctuations.

The firm has two extreme ways of treating its workers. It can keep employment constant but vary the wage continually, as in an **auction market.** In Figure 16.3 this is shown by movements of the wage bill along *AC*. When product demand is low, increases in it require that employers offer

[17]Martin Weitzman, *The Share Economy*, Cambridge, Mass.: Harvard University Press (1984).

[18]Robert Gordon, "Why U.S. Wage and Employment Behaviour Differs From That in Britain and Japan," *Economic Journal* 92: 13–44 (1982); T. Tachibanaki, "Labour Market Flexibility in Japan in Comparison with Europe and the US," *European Economic Review* 31: 647–678 (1987).

[19]Douglas Kruse, "Profit-Sharing and Employment Variability: Microeconomic Evidence on the Weitzman Theory," *Industrial and Labor Relations Review* 44: 437–453 (1991).

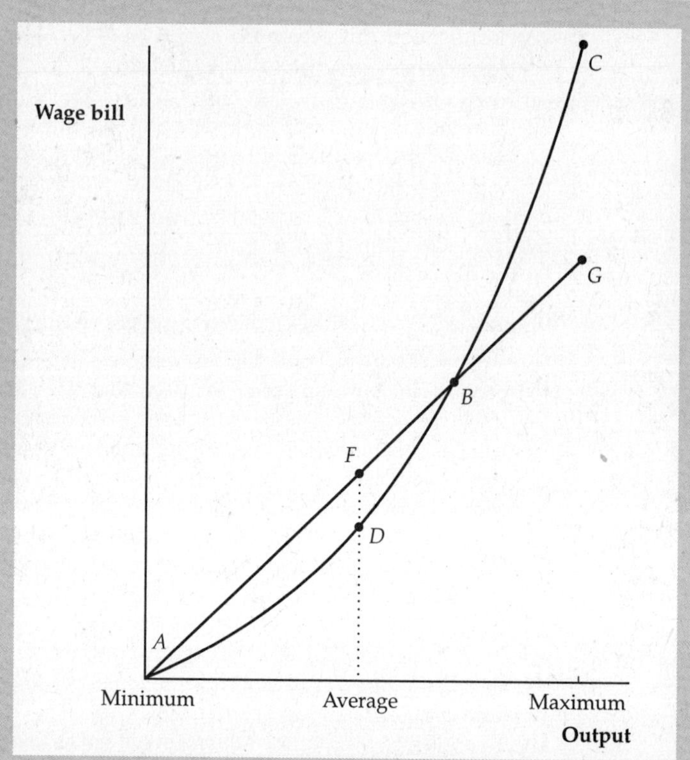

FIGURE 16.3 IMPLICIT CONTRACTS AND WAGE RIGIDITY

Fixing wages but varying employment results in smaller overall variation in the wage bill (along *AG*) than fixing employment by allowing wages to vary along *AC* in response to the tightness of the labor market and workers' alternative opportunities.

only small wage increases to retain workers and stimulate extra hours. Since demand at other firms is also likely to be low, there are few alternatives available to the workers. Because the wage can fall, it can be kept equal to the falling *VMP* as output demand drops without any reduction in employment. At higher rates of output, increased demand requires larger increases in wages. The alternatives open to the typical worker are greater as product (and, hence, labor) demand elsewhere is also probably higher than before. The acceleration of wages as output demand rises implies that the wage bill will also rise increasingly rapidly.

The firm's second choice is to offer an implicit contract that will keep the worker's nominal wage constant at w^*. This will require the firm to lay off workers when product demand falls, since the *VMP* of the marginal worker will now be less than the fixed wage. With a fixed wage, the wage bill varies linearly with employee-hours and is shown by the straight line *AG*.

With a fixed wage and, therefore, a wage bill that varies linearly with output, the average wage bill will be equal to the wage bill at the average level of output, indicated as point *D* in Figure 16.3. If, as is typically assumed, the firm is risk neutral, it will be indifferent between a contract offering a fixed wage w^* and a variable wage if the wage bills are the same on average. Thus, the average wage under the auction contract must also be w^*. This wage is higher than at the average level of output, point *F*, because the rapid increases in wages at high output levels more than offset the relatively small decreases at low output levels.

Given that her average income will be the same across the business cycle, which contract would the worker prefer? Assuming that she is risk averse, the smaller variation in income along the fixed-wage contract *AG* will be more attractive than the larger swings along *AC*. This means that the average worker will prefer fluctuations in employment to fluctuations in nominal wages.

Because output demand is rarely expected to fall more than a fairly small fraction below the average, relatively few workers will be laid off when a fixed nominal wage requires layoffs. All workers, however, would experience wage cuts when output demand fell if wages were flexible. If layoffs are governed by a fixed rule such as seniority, the risk of layoff is extremely low for most workers. Thus their willingness increases to have the burden of fluctuations in output borne in the form of layoffs (of other workers) rather than reduced wages. A survey taken in 1981 reported that 84 percent of employers with hourly paid unionized employees never laid off a senior worker before a junior one. Even among nonunionized firms 42 percent of employers reported that layoffs of their hourly employees were governed strictly by seniority. Another 44 percent reported that a senior worker would be laid off before a junior one only if the junior worker were believed to be significantly more valuable.[20]

Implicit contracts provide one explanation for layoffs in response to fluctuations in product demand. By offering more senior workers the prospect of employment at a high wage, free from the risk of layoff, the employer can induce both younger and older workers to work harder. Output per worker over the years is higher than if wages were cut sufficiently to maintain employment levels in recessions. Younger workers accept the layoffs caused by reduced product demand, knowing that they will soon have enough seniority to be protected from product market fluctuations. The relationship

[20] Katharine Abraham and James Medoff, "Length of Service and Layoffs in Union and Nonunion Work Groups," *Industrial and Labor Relations Review* 38: 87–97 (1984).

reduces the risks of demand fluctuations for most workers and creates a system of incentives that leads to levels of output that are above what they would otherwise be.

The contracting hypothesis is consistent with evidence from U.S. manufacturing that wage rates diverge from the *VMP* in the short run by more than they do in the long run. It is also consistent with evidence that changes in the wage rates of individuals observed in a longitudinal survey from 1976 to 1984 were more closely related to the lowest unemployment rate while they were on their jobs than with current unemployment rates.[21]

For implicit contracts to explain rigid real wages during a recession, we must ask what prevents workers who are laid off from driving down wages by offering to work for less, perhaps at another firm. This failure is explained by **insider-outsider models** based on the fact that workers not currently employed at a firm are fundamentally different from those who are. There is some freedom for current employees to keep wages high even though outsiders are willing to work for less, because the employer would have to incur training and hiring costs to substitute the lower-wage outsiders for the higher-wage insiders.[22] In addition, however, some mechanism must prevent insiders who are about to be laid off from offering to work for a lower wage. In a unionized firm, or any situation where workers can enforce identical actions on their coworkers, collective behavior can prevent this competition and keep the wage rate above the wage that would eliminate demand-deficient unemployment. Government policies that make layoffs expensive may have a similar effect. Otherwise, the contract must be structured so that the welfare of the laid-off worker, including unemployment compensation and the value of leisure, is at least equal to what he would receive while working. In other words, the productivity cost to the firm from lowering incentives for the retained workers must be greater than the wage savings so that the employer will not accept a worker's offer to work at a lower wage.

As yet, no evidence exists to distinguish the effects of insider-outsider behavior from those of other explanations of wages that are too high to clear the market in recessions. The theory predicts, however, that variations in real wages will be procyclical, since the insiders' relative strength is greater in booms because of employers' difficulty in finding replacement workers. This explanation for cyclical unemployment is especially appealing in many European economies, where unions cover a large fraction of the work force.

One difficulty with contract models is that they cannot explain the persistence of high unemployment. When high rates of unemployment have existed

---

[21]James Brown, "How Close to an Auction Is the Labor Market? Employee Risk Aversion, Income Uncertainty, and Optimal Labor Contracts," in Ronald Ehrenberg (ed.). *Research in Labor Economics*, Vol. 5: 189–235 (1982); Paul Beaudry and John DiNardo, "The Effect of Implicit Contracts on the Movement of Wages over the Business Cycle: Evidence from Micro Data," *Journal of Political Economy* 99: 665–688 (1991).

[22]Assar Lindbeck and Dennis Snower, *The Insider-Outsider Theory of Employment and Unemployment*, Cambridge, Mass.: MIT Press (1988).

POLICY ISSUE

INCREASED EXPERIENCE RATING FOR UNEMPLOYMENT INSURANCE TAXES

Another possible explanation for layoffs during recessions is the structure of the unemployment insurance system in the U.S. Unemployment benefits are financed almost exclusively by payroll taxes on employers. These taxes, whose levels are determined by statute in each state, are partly experience rated so that a firm will pay a higher tax rate if it has generated more layoffs (and, therefore, more unemployment benefits) in the past. If the labor market consists of many firms, the imposition of taxes that exactly equalled the benefits paid to each firm's unemployed workers (full experience rating) would have no effect on employment in any firm. In Figure 16.4, when an unemployment insurance system is adopted, the wage, which competitive firms take as given, falls from w_0 to w_1. Workers are now willing to supply their labor at a lower wage rate because unemployment benefits have been added to their total compensation package. The part of their pay that represented a compensating differential for the risk of unemployment is no longer required. Employers' demand curve for labor shifts from VMP_0 to VMP_1^e because the value of each worker to the firm is reduced by the tax that must be paid on his wages. With full experience rating, the tax equals the benefit and *VMP* falls exactly to *B*, leaving employment at E^e. The wage bill is $0w_1BE^e$ while unemployment benefits (and taxes) are w_1w_0AB.

In fact, there is an upper limit on tax rates. Employers who pay the highest tax rate pay less in taxes than is paid in benefits to their discharged workers. In 1978, for example, over 15 percent of employment in six large states was in firms that were likely to have not been effectively experience rated. A number of economists have proposed increasing the degree of experience rating in the taxes that finance this transfer, because an unemployment insurance system financed by taxes that are incompletely experience rated changes the incentives facing a firm and its workers.[23]

Workers will be compensated by unemployment insurance during any layoff resulting from reduced demand due to fluctuations in output. If workers expect this, they will be willing to enter into fixed-wage contracts with firms that have regular, often seasonal variations in output demand at lower wages than they would require from firms in more stable industries. With fewer hours at work, their income from the labor market (wages and unemployment benefits) plus the value of the additional leisure could exceed what they would get from firms where employment is stable but no unemployment insurance and leisure are received. Employers' wage costs per hour worked will be lower and, because of the limit on the payroll tax imposed by incomplete experience rating, this reduction in wages will not be completely offset by higher payroll taxes.

If the firm in Figure 16.4 is not fully experience rated, the wage drops to w_1 as before, but the shift in the labor demand curve is smaller, since the firm's tax payments are less than the compensation its workers receive in unemployment benefits. The firm receives a

---

[23]The data on experience rating are from Robert Topel, "Financing Unemployment Insurance: History, Incentives, and Reform," in W. Lee Hansen and James Byers, (eds.). *Unemployment Compensation: The Second Half Century*, Madison, Wisc.: University of Wisconsin Press (1990). Martin Feldstein, "The Effect of Unemployment Insurance on Temporary Layoff Unemployment," *American Economic Review* 68: 834–846 (1978), among others, has called for greater experience rating of UI taxes.

subsidy from other firms that reduces the shift in its labor demand curve to VMP^i_1. This shift leads it to equate VMP^i_1 to w_1 at point F, expanding employment to E^i and increasing its average production during the year above what it wou.ld otherwise be.

The size of this effect depends on the size of the subsidy, which will be larger the more unemployment the firm generates. Incomplete experience rating induces a shift in production toward firms that exhibit greater fluctuations in output, since their instability is subsidized by taxes on other firms. The average subsidy to firms that receive them is probably about 1 percent of total wages. Employment in firms providing the subsidy is reduced, because their tax bill exceeds the benefits their workers receive. This tax structure also encourages the subsidized firms to increase layoffs. By doing so they can receive a larger subsidy, in the form of the difference between unemployment benefits received by their workers and taxes paid by them, that can be shared with their employees.[24] The net result of the shift from low-variance firms to those with a great deal of instability and the tendency for these firms to increase their layoffs is to raise aggregate unemployment in the economy and make the swings over a business cycle greater. As we saw earlier, the fact that most state unemployment systems in the U.S. provide weak or no compensation for partial layoffs where workers' hours are reduced provides a strong incentive to concentrate hours reductions among full-time layoffs, who will then become eligible for unemployment benefits.

In states where the payroll tax rate reaches a higher maximum, so that more firms are fully experience rated, layoff rates in manufacturing industries are lower. Seasonal fluctuations in manufacturing employment also are greater, other things equal, in those states where the tax structure allows more workers to receive unemployment benefits that do not result in higher taxes for their employers. Removing the ceiling on unemployment tax rates could reduce the layoff rate in manufacturing by one-third.[25]

for a long time, both explicit and implicit contracts should be revised to account for the state of the labor market. In the U.S., union contracts rarely last more than three years. In many other countries, union wages are renegotiated even more frequently. Nonunion wages in the U.S. are changed much more frequently than union wages.[26] The argument that such frequent wage setting would repeatedly ignore the presence of high unemployment is hard to believe. In the face of continuing high unemployment, employers have substantial incentives to break implicit contracts by reducing nominal wages. If employers believe that product demand is stuck at some low level, they can increase profits by breaking the implicit contract and cutting the wage. Unemployment would then fall as employment rises when employers hire

---

[24] Topel, "Financing Unemployment Insurance;" Charles Warden "Unemployment Compensation: The Massachusetts Experience," in Otto Eckstein (ed.). *Studies in the Economics of Income Maintenance*, Washington D.C.: Brookings Institution (1967).

[25] Frank Brechling "Layoffs and Unemployment Insurance," in Sherwin Rosen (ed.). *Studies in Labor Markets*, Chicago: University of Chicago Press (1981); Terrence Halpin, "The Effect of Unemployment Insurance on Seasonal Fluctuations in Employment," *Industrial and Labor Relations Review* 32: 353–362 (1979); Robert Topel, "On Layoffs and Unemployment Insurance," *American Economic Review* 73: 541–559 (1983).

[26] Orley Ashenfelter, George Johnson, and John Pencavel, "Trade Unions and the Rate of Change of Money Wages in the United States," *Review of Economic Studies* 39: 27–54 (1972).

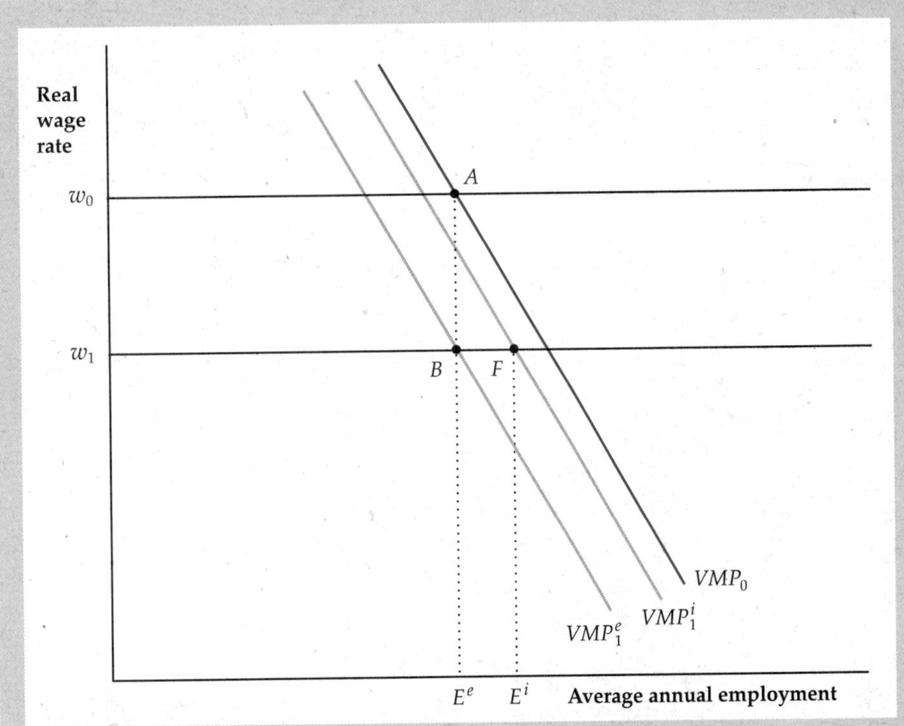

FIGURE 16.4 EMPLOYMENT UNDER PAYROLL-TAX-FINANCED UNEMPLOYMENT BENEFITS

If unemployment benefits are fully experience rated, the shift in the employer's demand curve from VMP_0 to VMP_1^e will result in a wage decrease fully sufficient to pay for the benefits. With less than full experience rating, the shift in the demand curve is smaller, and firms with variability in employment receive a subsidy from more stable firms.

back workers whose real wage cost to them is now reduced. This hypothesis, like the others, implies a faster approach toward the full-employment unemployment rate (faster reduction in cyclical unemployment) than is consistent with the facts.

EXPLAINING THE FACTS: FLEXIBLE REAL WAGES

One problem with all of the explanations for cyclical variation in unemployment rates based on rigid wages is that there is a surprising degree of flexibility in individual wages, even in the short term.[27] Figure 16.5 shows the

[27] This discussion is based on Kenneth McLaughlin, "Rigid Wages?" *Journal of Monetary Economics* 34: 383–414 (1994). See also Ben Craig, "Are Wages Inflexible," Fedreal Reserve Bank of Cleveland Economic Commentary, (April 1995).

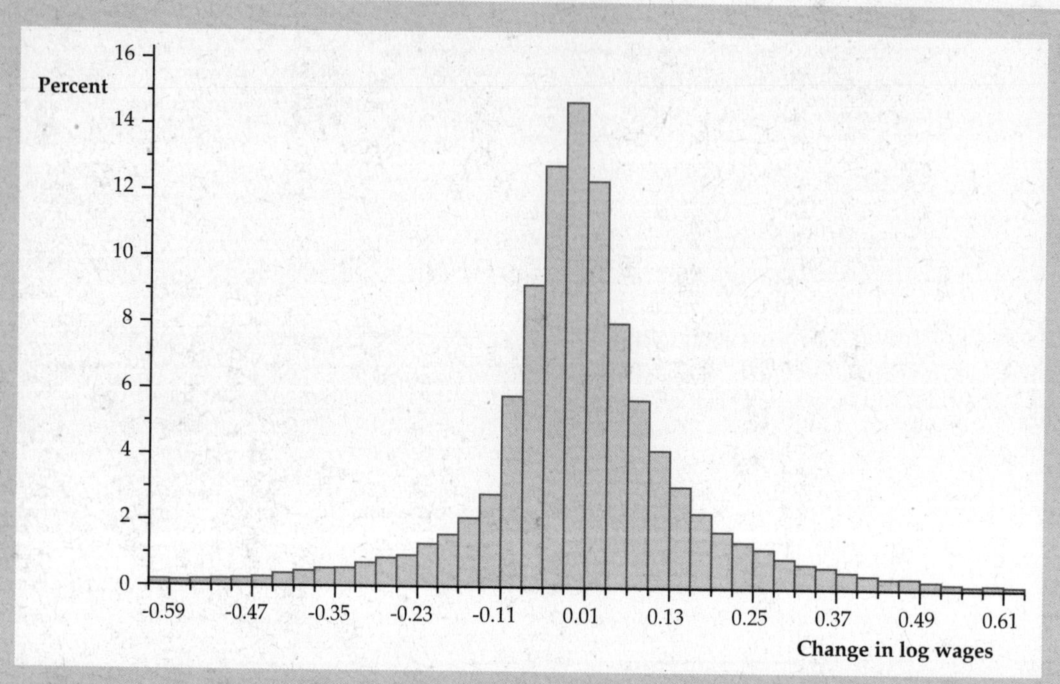

FIGURE 16.5 ANNUAL CHANGES IN REAL WAGES FOR INDIVIDUAL U.S. WORKERS, 1976–1986

Whether measured overall or separately for individuals who remain with or change their employer, a substantial number of workers take real-wage cuts from one year to the next.

year-to-year change in wages in a set of more than 26,000 observations between 1976 and 1986.[28] The variability in this figure is striking. The mean annual real wage growth was 1.9 percent, about the same as the rate of productivity growth in this period. The standard deviation, however, was 15.4 percent and nearly 43 percent of the observations received real wage *cuts*.

This is too large a fraction to have been generated by laid-off workers being forced to take wage cuts on their new jobs. Indeed, wages of workers who remain with the same firm are also highly variable. As would be expected from our discussion in earlier chapters, workers who changed firms experienced greater variability in wages, both with respect to increases and decreases. The increases largely represent the effect of quits by workers with better opportunities elsewhere, while the decreases disproportionately result from employer discharges. Even among those who remain with the same firm, however, 43 percent of the observations involved a real wage cut from the previous year. Indeed, 17 percent of the observations on workers who

[28] The scale on the horizontal axis is the difference in the natural logs of wages in year t and wages in year $t - 1$ multiplied by 100. This is equal to $\ln(w_t/w_{t-1}) \times 100$.

remained with the same firm involved *nominal wage reductions* from the previous year, suggesting that the real wage cuts were not solely due to inflation. Because the wages in this study were self-reported, it is possible that many apparent changes may have resulted from errors in workers' reporting of their wages that did not persist from year-to-year. Several careful strategies designed to investigate the extent of this possible problem all lead to the conclusion that the vast majority of the wage changes are real and that there is, in fact, significant downward flexibility in wages.

There is evidence that real wage rates have been procyclical and varied with business conditions since the mid-1960s, especially when one accounts for differences in the characteristics of employed workers over the cycle. This is true even for wage rates that exclude cyclical variations in the amount of overtime pay. Wages are especially procyclical among low-tenure workers, those for whom the rigid wages produced by the existence of firm-specific training and implicit contracts are less important.[29]

Real wages provide one exception to the generalization we have made in previous chapters that labor markets in the U.S. are more flexible than those in other developed economies. Table 16.3 presents estimates of the aggregate elasticities of employment, weekly hours of work, real wages, and labor productivity with respect to changes in output between 1950 and 1983 for several countries. Real wages are more responsive to output changes in many other countries than they are in the U.S. In particular, the responsiveness of wages to output changes appears to be greater in countries such as Germany, France, Sweden, the Netherlands, and Japan, where there is no pattern of overlapping three-year labor contracts as is common in the U.S. and Canada. It appears that variations in output are reflected relatively more in employment levels (and, therefore, unemployment) in the U.S. than in other countries. This is in line with what we would expect to find given the high fixed costs of hiring and firing imposed by labor markets elsewhere that have created overall higher rates of unemployment in European countries. The Japanese exception, as we have discussed, has to do with high levels of investment in firm-specific human capital and relatively flexible wages created by the bonus system.

Given the extent of short-term flexibility in wages over the business cycle, we must seek explanations for cyclical variations in unemployment that are not based on rigid wages. Several explanations based on flexible wages imply that the apparent instability of the Phillips curve seen in Figure 16.1 reflects movements of a short-run Phillips curve up or down a vertical long-run

[29] Mark Bils, "Real Wages over the Business Cycle: Evidence from Panel Data," *Journal of Political Economy* 93: 666–689 (1985); Michael Keane, Robert Moffitt, and David Runkle, "Real Wages over the Business Cycle: Estimating the Impact of Heterogeneity with Micro Data," *Journal of Political Economy* 96: 1232–1266 (1988); Rebecca Blank, "Why Are Wages Cyclical in the 1970s?" *Journal of Labor Economics* 8: 16–47 (1990); Wendy Rayack, "Fixed and Flexible Nominal Wages: Evidence from Panel Data," *Industrial and Labor Relations Review* 44: 288–298 (1991); Gary Solon, Robert Barsky, and Jonathan Parker, "Measuring the Cyclicality of Real Wages: How Important is Composition Bias?" *Quarterly Journal of Economics* 109: 1–25 (1994).

TABLE 16.3 PERCENTAGE CHANGE IN AGGREGATE LABOR MARKET VARIABLES RESULTING FROM A 1 PERCENT CHANGE IN AGGREGATE OUTPUT: SELECTED COUNTRIES, 1950–1983

	U.S.	Canada	France	Germany	Italy	Japan	Netherlands	Sweden	U.K.
Employment	0.58	0.56	0.47	0.57	0.14	0.33	0.44	0.44	0.47
Weekly hours	0.16	0.11	0.24	0.15	0.24	0.12	0.04	0.01	0.18
Real compensation	0.04	0.02	0.13	0.24	0.13	0.12	0.31	0.24	–0.08
Output per hour	0.24	0.37	0.28	0.28	0.28	0.55	0.52	0.55	0.35

Source: Masanori Hashimoto and John Raisian, "Aspects of Labor Market Flexibility," in Kazutoshi Koshiro (ed.). *Employment Security and Labor Market Flexibility: An International Perspective*, Detroit, Mich.: Wayne State University Press (1992) p. 86.

curve. In the long run, the equilibrium rate of unemployment is determined by the structure of the labor force and by labor market institutions, including the characteristics of workers, firms, and government programs that affect search, mobility, and the duration of unemployment. This rate, the **natural rate of unemployment,** is for our purposes identical to the full-employment unemployment rate. Explanations based on flexible wages imply that the economy may generate some excess unemployment, but that adjustment back to the natural rate of unemployment will be fairly rapid after a shock to aggregate demand.

THE ROLE OF PRICE EXPECTATIONS

Consider a labor market in which employers know the prices of their products, which on average, equal the price level p. Employers thus observe perfectly the real wage involved in employing an hour of labor, w/p. Workers, on the other hand, base their labor supply decisions on imperfect perceptions of real wages, determined by comparing the nominal wage they are offered, w, to a perceived level of consumer prices, p^*, which may not be entirely accurate. This difference in the ability of workers and employers to perceive prices makes sense. Employers, who need only know prices of their products, should have more accurate information than workers, who would need to know the prices of the wide variety of products making up their consumption bundle including the prices of items such as cars and refrigerators that they buy only infrequently. Thus, workers' expectations about inflation may adjust slowly to an increase in the measured rate of inflation. An acceleration of wage and price inflation temporarily leads workers to believe that their real wage has risen, since w (which they know with certainty) rises faster than p^*, where their expectations may be that past prices prevail, at least for some products. Eventually, as their perceptions of inflation catch up to reality, workers become aware that, in fact, their real wage has not changed, although

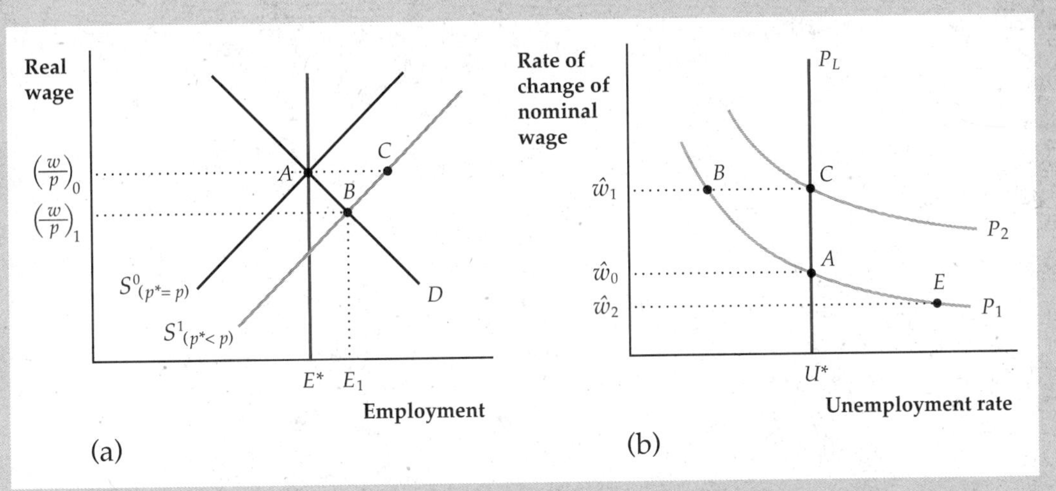

FIGURE 16.6 THE LABOR MARKET AND UNEXPECTED INFLATION
In the short run, unexpected inflation may fool workers and shift the supply curve down in (a), resulting in less unemployment. In the long run, however, workers' expectations will adapt and unemployment will return to the natural level U^* in (b), although at a higher rate of inflation.

as we saw in Chapter 11, the possibility of substitution means that their real utility may have risen.

The labor market depicted in Figure 16.6(a) illustrates these differences. Employers' demands for labor are shown by the usual downward-sloping curve *D*, based on a comparison of the real wage to the *VMP*. Algebraically, the demand schedule is

$$L^d = L^d(\frac{w}{p}).$$

Workers' labor supply is assumed to be upward-sloping but is based on the perceived real wage, which differs from the actual real wage if price expectations are slow to adjust to changes in prices.[30] Algebraically, the labor supply schedule is

$$L^s = L^s(\frac{w}{p^*}).$$

If inflation has been constant for some time, workers' expectations are probably correct, so that $p^* = p$. Labor will be supplied along the curve S^0,

[30]Robert Lucas and Leonard Rapping, "Real Wages, Employment, and Inflation," in Edmund Phelps (ed.). *Microeconomic Foundations of Employment and Inflation Theory*, New York: Norton (1970).

where the actual and perceived inflation rates, $\hat{p}$ and $\hat{p}^*$, are equal. (The ^ denotes the rate of change in a variable.) In this dynamic equilibrium real wages are $(w/p)_0$, and employment is E^*. Wages are growing at some rate $\hat{w}_0$ which, if the economy is in equilibrium in the real market but showing rising prices and wages in nominal markets, will be equal to $\hat{p}$ less any adjustment for substitution possibilities. Unemployment is at the natural rate U^*, and the economy is at point *A* in Figure 16.6(b).

If the rate of price inflation accelerates, perhaps because the government increases the rate of growth of the money supply, nominal wages and prices will rise more rapidly. Workers seeing these changes will think their real wage has risen. They see that w/p^* is higher, even when w/p is the same, because they see the rise in nominal wages without fully perceiving the rise in prices. Because w/p^* has increased, they are willing to supply more labor at any true real wage, such as the equilibrium real wage $(w/p)_0$. The supply curve shifts out from S^0 to S^1. Since employers perceive real wages correctly, this increased supply of labor lowers the real wage employers need to pay and induces an increase in employment. In Figure 16.6(a) this effect is represented by a movement from *A* to *B*. Assuming that the potential labor force remains unchanged, the increase in employment from E^* to E_1 reduces unemployment. In terms of Figure 16.6(b), the increased growth of nominal wages is associated with a decreased unemployment rate. The economy moves from point *A* to point *B* along Phillips curve P_1.

If price inflation continues at the new, higher rate, workers' expectations about inflation will eventually catch up to the reality. P^* will rise, so that w/p^* falls to the true real wage, w/p. With the perceived real wage lower (but equal to the actual real wage) workers will reduce their supply of labor and the supply curve will shift back from S^1 to S^0. Equilibrium will be restored at *A* in Figure 16.6(a) at the initial real wage rate $(w/p)_0$ and the initial level of employment E^*. With the same employment, the unemployment rate also returns to the natural rate, U^*, in Figure 16.6(b). The rate of increase of both wages and prices, however, is now higher. The economy as a whole moves from *B* to *C* rather than returning to *A* in Figure 16.6(b). A temporary increase in employment (and, thus, output) has been purchased at the cost of a higher permanent rate of inflation.

Curves P_1 and P_2 in Figure 16.6(b) are explicitly **short-run Phillips curves**. Curve P_1 reflects the behavior of the labor market before workers' expectations have begun catching up to the acceleration in inflation. P_2 reflects the behavior of the labor market when the price level is accurately perceived. Policymakers cannot force the economy to be at a point like *B* in the long run. Eventually workers' expectations of inflation adjust, and the economy moves back to the vertical **long-run Phillips curve**, P_L. The only choice for macroeconomic policy is the rate of wage (and price) inflation. The natural unemployment rate is determined by the labor market and other institutions that affect structural-frictional unemployment.

The strongest support for this view of the labor market comes from the evidence we have given of the instability of the short-run Phillips curve. The points in Figure 16.1 could not all lie on the same downward-sloping curve. It is hard to avoid the conclusion that the short-run Phillips curve shifted upward in the early 1970s and shifted back down in the mid-1980s, unless one is prepared to argue that there is no meaningful relationship between unemployment and nominal wage inflation even in the short run.

This view of the vertical long-run Phillips curve is called the **expectations theory,** or alternatively the **intertemporal substitution hypothesis.** The former term refers to its basis in the deviation of perceived from actual price inflation. The latter term refers to its dependence on workers temporarily increasing their labor supply in response to short-run changes in perceived real wages. This idea is analogous to the discussion in Chapter 1 of workers substituting effort over the life cycle in response to temporary wage changes. The hypothesis explains cyclical changes in unemployment and nominal wages. It also rationalizes shifts in the short-run Phillips curve. Unfortunately, it predicts that real wages will be countercyclical, falling during booms and rising in recessions, which is apparently inconsistent with recent history.

Evidence covering recent periods also suggests that expectations about price inflation adjust fairly rapidly, although forecasts of price changes do exhibit substantial errors. Surveys of consumers' expectations after the slowdown of inflation in the early 1980s show that took they only a few years to adjust.[31] The unemployment gap was positive, however, until at least 1985. This implies that a theory based on very slow adjustment of workers' expectations about price inflation fails to explain recent facts. It is unlikely that the high rate of unemployment that persisted throughout the 1930s was solely due to workers believing that their real wages had fallen, even though in reality prices fell much more rapidly than wages.[32]

Ignoring the issue of whether workers' price expectations adjust slowly enough to be the source of persistent high unemployment, the theory also requires labor supply to be very responsive to short-run fluctuations in perceived real wages. As we saw in Chapter 1, however, an immense and increasing array of cross-section evidence suggests the actual response is quite small. Studies of time-series data for the U.S. and the U.K. since World War II show that fluctuations in employment and unemployment were not consistent with an increasing supply of labor when expected price inflation lagged behind actual price inflation.[33]

The logic of the expectations argument, on the other hand, is appealing. Clearly workers' inflationary expectations will eventually adjust to reflect past changes in prices. Even if they are fooled for a while, workers are unlikely to

---

[31]Stephen Figlewski and Paul Wachtel, "The Formation of Inflationary Expectations," *Review of Economics and Statistics* 63: 1–10 (1981); Survey Research Center, University of Michigan, *Survey of Consumer Attitudes Redbook* (1982), Table 23.

[32]Albert Rees, "On Equilibrium in Labor Markets," *Journal of Political Economy* 78: 306–310 (1970).

[33]Joseph Altonji, "The Intertemporal Substitution Model of Labour Market Fluctuations: An Empirical Analysis," *Review of Economic Studies* 49: 783–824 (1982).

be fooled forever into believing that their real wage has risen merely because nominal wages have increased. The argument fails to explain the persistence of high rates of unemployment over a long period of time, or to reconcile changes in labor supply with the path of real wage rates over the business cycle. If the Phillips curve is vertical in the long run, adjustment to it—(for example, between points *B* and *C* in Figure 16.6(b)—appear to be fairly slow.

THE ROLE OF JOB SEARCH

An alternative approach based on flexible wages is derived from the search behavior of workers and employers discussed in Chapter 6.[34] Assume that the economy is at the natural rate of unemployment. Employers can maintain work forces of a given size by many combinations of wage offers and hiring standards. By paying more they can attract more applicants and retain employees even if they establish a higher minimum skill requirement. Firms will choose the least-cost combination of wages and hiring standards.

What would happen if, for some reason such as expansionary fiscal or monetary policy, employers find they can charge higher prices for their products? This price hike will increase the *VMP* schedule in each firm. The employer will want to expand employment, but to do so, must either offer higher nominal wages or reduce hiring standards. Either change in the employer's hiring policies will mean that workers will spend less time searching. Employment will therefore rise while unemployment falls. At the same time nominal wages will be increasing. The economy moves leftward along a short-run Phillips curve, such as P_1 in Figure 16.6(b), from a point like *A* to one like *B*. Indeed, the evidence is that matches are made less rapidly during a recession however those that do occur are of lower quality. Comparing a period when the national unemployment rate is 9 percent with one when it is 5 percent to 9 percent, the expected length of time a worker will hold a job accepted during the period of high unemployment is between 20 and 30 percent lower than for jobs accepted during the period of low unemployment.[35]

Recognizing that all firms have raised their wage offers, workers will eventually raise their asking wages. As shown in Chapter 6, this response will lead them to search longer than before. Eventually their asking wage will be rising as rapidly as employers' wage offers. Since labor is no longer a bargain, employers will bring hiring standards back to their equilibrium level. Employment will be the same as before, but wage offers and asking wages will be rising more rapidly than before. The economy will have moved from point *B* to point *C* in Figure 16.6(b).

---

[34] Dale Mortensen, "Job Search, the Duration of Unemployment, and the Phillips Curve," *American Economic Review* 60: 847–862 (1970).

[35] Olivier Blanchard and Peter Diamond, "The Cyclical Behavior of the Gross Flows of U.S. Workers," *Brookings Papers on Economic Activity,* Macroeconomics, (1990), pp. 85–143; Audra Bowlus, "Matching Workers and Jobs: Cyclical Fluctuations in Match Quality," *Journal of Labor Economics* 13: 335–350 (1995).

The result of the search-theoretic approach is the same as that of the intertemporal substitution hypothesis. In the short run, increases in employment are positively correlated with higher growth rates in nominal wages. This approach provides an internally consistent explanation of cyclical fluctuations in nominal wage changes, employment, and unemployment. It also explains why the duration of unemployment decreases in good times.

The search-theoretic approach also explains the strongly procyclical behavior of job quitting. This approach provides a better explanation of cyclical changes in the relationship between job vacancies and employment growth than the intertemporal substitution hypothesis.[36] Like the intertemporal-substitution hypothesis, however, it cannot by itself explain the slowness of adjustments to shocks to the labor market. Why should unemployed workers and employers with vacancies take years to adjust their offered and reservation wages to the changed labor market conditions? It also says nothing about the cyclical behavior of changes in real wages.

The intertemporal-substitution and search approaches are essentially theories of voluntary unemployment. Under the former, workers are counted as unemployed because they choose not to work when their nominal wage fails to rise as rapidly as their perception of price inflation. Under the search approach, cyclical unemployment is observed because workers choose to spend more time searching. The cause of unemployment in both theories is workers' choices about how to spend their time.

It is clear that none of the approaches we have discussed is a wholly satisfactory explanation of the paradox of the labor market in the macroeconomy. Real wages fall during recessions, but unemployment rates increase. The question remains, is this a rational increase so that the observed labor market outcomes represent an equilibrium, or have real wages failed to fall sufficiently to clear the market?

THE TRANSMISSION OF WAGE INFLATION

The discussion in the previous sections has dealt with the microeconomic foundations of macroeconomic adjustment of labor markets. It has not examined how adjustment in one sector of the economy affects other sectors. The importance of this neglect is underlined by the discussion of staggered union-wage contracts. If adjustment in the unionized sector always determined subsequent adjustment elsewhere, the macroeconomic behavior of labor markets could be explained by union behavior even if the unionized sector were only a small part of the economy. When conditions in one labor market produce wage inflation, the result may be wage inflation in other markets if workers fight to maintain customary differentials.

---

[36] Ronald Warren, "Labor Market Contacts, Unanticipated Wages, and Employment Growth," *American Economic Review* 73: 389–397 (1983).

POLICY ISSUE

WHY DID THE NATURAL RATE INCREASE IN EUROPE?

We saw in Chapter 8 that unemployment rates in the European Union have increased steadily in recent decades. As we discussed at the beginning of this chapter, this seems to be the result of a shift in the Phillips curve that increased the natural rate of unemployment. Why did this shift happen in Europe but not the U.S.? Differences in government policies may have played a major role in creating this difference. Curve *P* (for productivity) in Figure 16.7 shows the relationship between a worker's wage relative to the average wage and her position in the distribution of potential wages if she were to work. Given the value of leisure and other income (including unemployment benefits), there will be some acceptance wage w_a below which the worker will not accept a job, choosing instead to remain unemployed (or out of the labor force). As drawn, this wage is low enough that all workers accept their best available job.

Now suppose that the generosity of unemployment benefits is increased and that these benefits are financed by a proportional tax on wages. The impact will be to lower the return for working from *P* to *T* while raising the attractiveness of remaining unemployed from w_a to w_u. Clearly, the impact of this policy will be to increase unemployment, to the level U_u. Now suppose that returns to skill increase. Such an increase will make the *P* and *T* curves steeper, as shown by *P′* and *T′*. This will also serve to increase the fraction of workers who find the highest wage they are offered is below their acceptance wage from U_u to U_u'. As we have drawn Figure 16.7 the deterioration in the relative wage of unskilled workers also makes it attractive for U_a' workers in the world with lower unemployment benefits (who face relative wage curve *P′* and acceptance wage w_a) to refuse their best available job.

The presence of more generous unemployment benefits in Europe should result in higher unemployment there. During recent decades there has been an increase in the value of European benefits relative to those in the U.S. This should have widened the gap in unemployment levels. In France, for example, the 10-percentage-point rise in payroll and personal-income taxes in 1980 is estimated to have increased unemployment rates by 1.5 percentage points. Canada and France, which had the first and third greatest increase in payroll and income taxes between 1965 and 1990 had the third and first greatest increase in unemployment rates during the same period. The U.S., which had the lowest rate of tax increase, also had the smallest change in unemployment rates.[37]

The implication of Figure 16.7 is that the possible increase in inequality in the U.S. seen in Chapter 15 and the greater increase in unemployment in Europe seen in Chapter 8 are reverse sides of the same coin. Increasing returns to skill may have made the U.S. wage distribution more unequal, while in Europe, with its much more generous and long-lasting unemployment benefits, the same structural change in the economy may have had a smaller effect on inequality but substantially increased unemployment. In addition, the evidence for Germany is that shocks to wages and employment are substantially more persistent than those in the U.S., providing further evidence of the difference in labor market flexibility between the U.S. and Euopean economies.[38]

[37] Edmund Phelps, *Structural Slumps: The Modern Equilibrium Theory of Unemployment, Interest and Assets,* Cambridge, Mass.: Harvard University Press (1994).

[38] J. Elmeskov, *High and Persistent Unemployment: Assessment of the Problem and Its Causes,* Paris: OECD (1993); Paul Krugman, "Inequality and the Political Economy of Eurosclerosis," London: CEPR Discussion Paper (1993); Paul Krugman, "Past and Prospective Causes of High Unemployment," in *Reducing Unemployment: Current Issues and Policy Options,* Federal Reserve Bank of Kansas City (1994); Richard Burkhauser, Douglas Holtz-Eakin, and Stephen E. Rhody, "Labor Earnings Mobility and Inequality in the United States and Germany During the 1980s," Syracuse University, (1995), Photocopy.

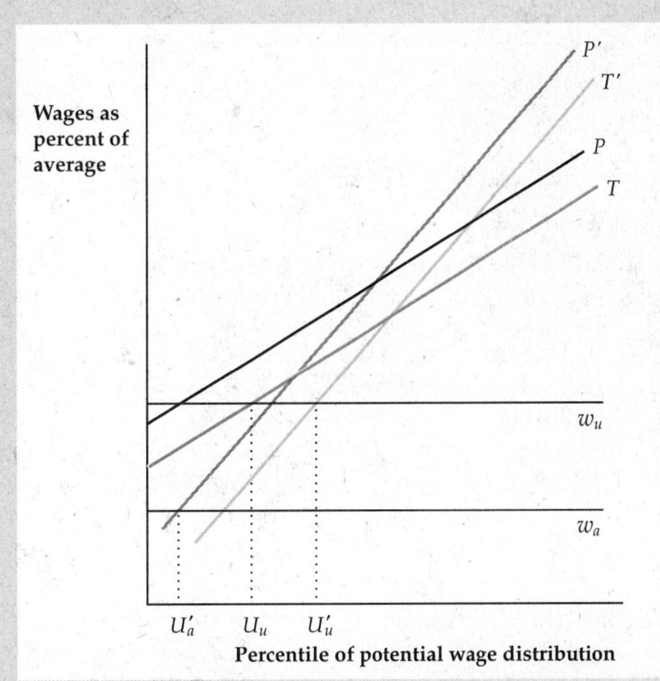

FIGURE 16.7 COMBINED EFFECT OF GENEROUS UNEMPLOYMENT INSURANCE AND INCREASED RETURN TO SKILLS ON UNEMPLOYMENT AND INEQUALITY

An increase in returns to skill will tilt the relative wage curve from *P* to *P′*. This change will have a small impact on unemployment when benefits (and, therefore, acceptance wages, w_a) are low but a significant increase in unemployment when benefits are generous and after-tax wages are reduced to finance these benefits (the intersection of w_u and *T′*). On the other hand, in the first regime inequality will rise more than in the second.

The question is how common these interrelationships are and in which directions these dynamic **wage spillovers** (waves of wage increases across sectors) flow. It is difficult to believe that every worker is concerned about the wages every other worker in the economy receives. Surely there are limits on the directions and magnitudes of wage comparisons, and thus on the size of dynamic spillovers.

The direction of spillovers between nonunion labor markets will depend on the size and direction of labor flows, either actual or threatened. These are induced by changes in customary wage differentials among jobs or labor markets classified either geographically or by skill. Where wages contain a significant return to investment in skills specific to a sector, employers will have substantial room to cut the growth rate of nominal wages in response to a high unemployment rate such as shown at point *E* in Figure 16.6(b).

Where a high-unemployment sector also pays low wages and requires little sector-specific human capital, low unemployment elsewhere that generates more rapid wage inflation will induce the low-paid workers to quit the sector. If, as we suggested in Chapters 1 and 2, the supply of low-wage labor to the market is fairly elastic, employers in the high-unemployment, low-wage sector can reduce the growth of nominal wages only slightly if they wish to retain their workers or hire substitutes for them. Thus, differences in unemployment rates alone do not determine the direction of wage spillovers. Rather, wage increases flow from high-wage to low-wage labor markets when unemployment is low in the former and relatively high in the latter. In the U.S. between 1950 and 1969 wage inflation was especially rapid when high-wage states exhibited relatively low rates of unemployment. Similarly, between 1958 and 1978, wage inflation was more rapid when unemployment in high-wage industries was unusually low relative to unemployment elsewhere.[39] In the nonunion part of the economy the direction of wage spillovers is from tight to loose labor markets only if the tight labor markets pay higher wages than the loose ones.

When the sectors consist of union and nonunion industries, the issue of the spillover direction becomes less clear. Several considerations support the popular belief that unions are a source of general wage inflation, especially when unemployment is above the full-employment unemployment rate. Where the unionized sector is small and the threat of union expansion into unorganized sectors is weak, the principal effect of wage increases in the union sector is on the pattern of relative wages. The general level of wages will be largely unaffected by union gains. Wage increases will be larger in the unionized sector, however, and smaller in the nonunion sector, because of gross employment effects, than they would have been in the absence of unions. The growth of employment in the union sector will be discouraged by the widening difference in relative union wages, while the growth of employment in the nonunion sector will be encouraged. The employment effects of the increased gap will tend to inhibit further wage increases in the union sector.

A greater extent of union organization or a greater threat that collective bargaining will spread to previously nonunion workers, will increase the like-

---

[39] Frank Brechling, "Wage Inflation and the Structure of Regional Unemployment," *Journal of Money, Credit and Banking* 5: 355–379 (1973); Donald Nichols, "Effects on the Noninflationary Unemployment Rate," in Robert Haveman and John Palmer (eds.). *Jobs for Disadvantaged Workers*, Washington D.C.: Brookings Institution (1982).

lihood that union pressures will raise the general level of money wages rather than only distort relative wages. When most workers are organized or subject to a credible threat of organization, an increase in the general wage level could even originate in a fairly small part of the union sector and spread by emulation to other industries or occupations. The larger the wage increases won by unions, the higher will be the wages nonunion employers have to offer their own workers if they hope to remain unorganized. This suggests that wage increases should flow from the union to the nonunion sector.

These arguments are inconsistent, however, with the experience of the economy during inflationary periods, like the late 1960s, when union relative wage gaps were decreasing. During periods of rapid expansion of aggregate demand, nonunion workers, whose wages are adjusted more rapidly than those of unionized employees, receive large increases in nominal wages. When it comes time for unionized workers to renegotiate their contracts, they seek to restore the customary relative wage gap, even though demand conditions may no longer be as favorable. This behavior suggests that the direction of the wage spillover is from increases in the nonunion sector *to* increases in the union sector.

Spillovers of wage increases from union to nonunion industry, and vice versa, are both plausible descriptions of wage inflation transmission. This is the classic chicken-and-egg problem. Did the growth of nonunion wages in the late 1960s spur union wage increases in the early 1970s, or did the union wage increases of the late 1950s induce nonunion employers to raise wages more rapidly in the mid-1960s than market conditions would otherwise warrant? These questions are not easily answered, and the answers undoubtedly vary among economies and over time depending on how collective-bargaining institutions are structured.

Empirical evidence on the issue is somewhat mixed, but the preponderance of data for the U.S. suggests that unions merely react to wage inflation generated elsewhere. One study of the U.S. between 1954 and 1973 found that union wage increases were substantially higher when the relative wage gap in the previous year was smaller, after adjusting for changes in labor market conditions. Nonunion wages were unaffected by the size of the gap. It appears that unions try to restore any decline in their relative wage advantage over nonunion workers induced by wage increases in the nonunion sector. Another study, covering 1956 to 1970, examined all changes in union and nonunion wages not due to variations in price inflation or in the state of the labor market (in the unemployment rate). The remaining variation in wage inflation in the nonunion sector was unrelated to what occurred in the union sector.[40]

---

[40] George Johnson, "The Determination of Wages in the Union and Non-Union Sectors," *British Journal of Industrial Relations* 15: 211–225 (1977); Yash Mehra, "Spillovers in Wage Determination in U.S. Manufacturing Industries," *Review of Economics and Statistics* 58: 300–312 (1976). See also Robert Flanagan, "Wage Interdependence in Unionized Labor Markets," *Brookings Papers on Economic Activity*: 635–673 (1976); and for contradictory evidence, Susan Vroman, "The Direction of Wage Spillovers in Manufacturing," *Industrial and Labor Relations Review* 36: 102–112 (1982).

POLICY ISSUE

REDUCING WAGE PRESSURES THROUGH RETRAINING

Retraining programs have been part of America's labor market policy since the Area Redevelopment Act of 1961. Part of the rationale for these programs, especially in times of low unemployment, has been to remove skill bottlenecks producing inflationary pressures in one sector that could spill over into markets where no such pressures exist, thus raising the aggregate rate of wage inflation. Bottlenecks are likely to be increasingly important in the 1990s, as smaller entering cohorts reduce the fraction of new workers deciding which occupation to enter. These workers are the most responsive to shortages in specific labor markets, and fewer of them will make markets slower to respond to changing relative wages.

The effect of retraining programs is shown in Figure 16.8. The short-run supply of labor to both Sector A and Sector B is assumed to be horizontal up to the point where all workers who have the required industry-specific skills are employed (points *A* in Figures 16.8(a) and (b)). The lack of available trained workers means that labor supply is completely inelastic in the short run above this point. As aggregate demand varies over the business cycle, the demand for labor in Sector A varies from D_L to D_H. When demand is low, there is unemployment in Sector A in the amount $E_1 - E_0$ and no upward pressure on nominal wages. When it is high, there is excess demand for labor and pressures that result in wage and eventually price inflation. For simplicity, we assume that demand is always low in Sector B, and therefore that unemployment always exists in the amount *AC*. Thus, when aggregate demand is high, nominal wage inflation is generated in Sector A even though there is still unemployment in Sector B.

This problem arises because of the existence of industry-specific human capital. Shifting the short-run Phillips curve downward can be achieved by retraining workers from Sector B in the skills specific to Sector A. This retraining would shift the vertical segment of the short-run labor supply to Sector A in Figure 16.8(a) to the right from *S* to *S′* while reducing the supply of labor in Sector B from *S* to *S′* in Figure 16.8(b). Unemployment in Sector B would be reduced from *AC* to *BC*. In periods of high demand, there would still be no unemployment in Sector A, implying that total unemployment is reduced. Wage pressures in Sector A would be removed, since, with the expansion of the supply of trained labor, no excess demand for labor exists in A even when demand is high. Since there are no wage pressures in Sector B even when supply is at *S′* , the rate of wage inflation would be lowered to zero even when demand is high. In times of slack demand, aggregate unemployment would be the same as before the retraining, with the additional $E_1' - E_1$ unemployed workers in Sector A offset by the reduction of unemployment in Sector B. Thus, average unemployment would be decreased during the business cycle, but the variance of unemployment would be higher.

Evidence regarding the impact of retraining programs on the aggregate unemployment rate is mixed. Some studies comparing results across countries find that those with more extensive **active labor market policies** providing retraining seem to have lower unemployment rates. This finding is not universal, however. Since retraining programs raise the welfare of the unemployed, the programs might be expected to weaken the incentives for wage restraint that might lead to unemployment. Such results have been found for Scandinavian countries.[41]

[41] Richard Layard, Stephen Nickell, and Richard Jackman, *Unemployment: Macroeconomic Performance and the Labor Market,* Oxford: Oxford University Press (1991); OECD *Employment Outlook* (1993); Lars Calmfors, "Active Labor Market Policy and Unemployment—A Framework for the Analysis of Crucial Design Features," Paris: OECD Occasional Paper No. 15 (1994).

Clearly when retraining makes sense, it does so not only for society as a whole, but also for individual workers who shift from Sector B to Sector A, where average unemployment is lower, and for the firms in Sector A, where the average cost of labor is lower. Whether there is any role for a government program, therefore, depends on whether the government that sponsors the retraining can identify sectors with skill shortages faster than individual employers and workers, and can train workers more efficiently than the private sector. If so, adjustment to the natural rate of unemployment would be more rapid than if it were left to the free market. There would be less chance of wage pressures in one sector inducing wage increases elsewhere that are not justified by the aggregate state of labor demand. Society would avoid some of the lost resources due to unemployment and the cost of price inflation. If, however, government does not have any special ability to identify and predict shortages correctly, it is merely doing what the private sector would accomplish at least as rapidly on its own. If, as many suspect, the cost-benefit ratio for government training programs is significantly higher than in the private market, the result will be a waste of society's resources to achieve what the labor market would have brought about anyway.

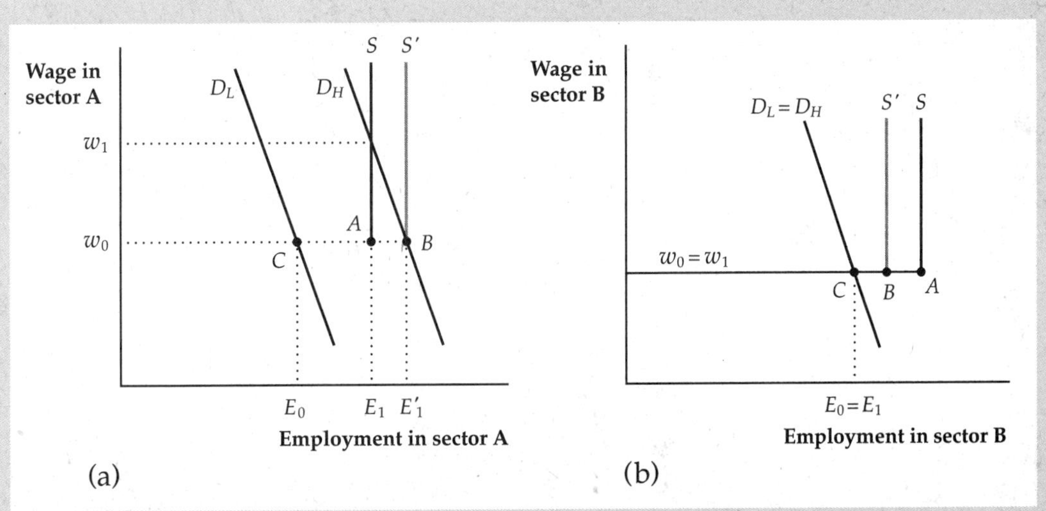

FIGURE 16.8 THE EFFECT OF RETRAINING PROGRAMS ON UNEMPLOYMENT AND INFLATION

Where there are bottleneck and slack sectors, shifting workers from the slack sector to the bottleneck sector through retraining can simultaneously lower average unemployment and inflation rates.

COPING WITH INFLATION IN THE LABOR MARKET

During the 1980s and early 1990s the U.S. has displayed little interest in policies to deal with wage inflation. No doubt this has been partially due to the relatively low rate of wage and price inflation during this time. In large part, however, it is also because Americans have learned from the often serious negative consequences in other countries (and, in earlier years, the U.S.) when governments tried to restrain inflation through a variety of wage and price controls and related policies. These **incomes policies** that affect wages can take a variety of forms. For short periods they often involve a **wage freeze** during which no increases in money wages are permitted. Wage freezes are used mostly during wartime or crises in a nation's balance of payments. The U.S. wage-price freeze of August 1971, for example, was announced in connection with measures designed to improve the balance of payments.

For the longer term most policies have sought to establish guideposts or criteria for acceptable increases in money wages. These are usually based on the trend of average productivity. Examining the formula for unit labor cost:

$$ULC = w \times \frac{L}{Y},$$

it is easy to see that, if the average productivity of labor, Y/L, is rising as some rate g^*, the rate of change in unit labor costs is

$$\widehat{ULC} = \hat{w} - g^*,$$

where $\hat{w}$ = rate of growth of nominal wages.

The wage rate w can rise at the rate g^* and still yield no growth in ULC. If firms set prices at a constant markup over unit labor costs, prices and profit rates can remain constant because the rate of productivity growth "justifies" the growth of wages at the rate g^*. This **justified wage increase** formed the basis of the 3.2 percent guidepost for wage increases promulgated in the U.S. between 1962 and 1966.

When price inflation is already ongoing, the wage criterion may incorporate it and aim to prevent inflation from accelerating. This strategy explains the differences among the 1962 to 1966 wage guideposts of 3.2 percent, roughly the g^* of the time, the 1971 to 1974 pay standard of 5.5 percent, and President Carter's "real wage insurance" proposal of 1979 and 1980, which implied a 7 percent nominal wage criterion.

Wage and price policies induce a number of effects in the labor markets where they are applied. Many of these effects result from employers' and workers' responses to changed incentives imposed on wage-setting mechanisms. Employers of particular groups of workers in short supply will try to find ways to offer wage increases larger than those allowed under the guidelines. They may, for example, increase workers' earnings by scheduling additional overtime work, some of which adds little or nothing to output.

Employers may upgrade workers' job titles, promoting or hiring workers into job classifications above those for which they are qualified, even if they do not alter the workers' actual job duties. Fringe benefits which are, as we saw in Chapter 10, hard to quantify may be increased. Early in the Czech Republic's economic transition from communism, when unemployment rates were very low and wage controls prevented employers from increasing wages fast enough to recruit new workers, some employers even resorted to offering free hairdressers at the workplace to attract secretarial labor. Employers can also compete to attract workers without increasing nominal wages, which are subject to controls, by spending money on better working conditions. Such expenditures must, however, add less to workers' utility than they cost employers. Otherwise, as we saw in Chapter 10, the competitive market would have already provided the working conditions. The impact of wage controls is to force employers needing labor to make inefficient expenditures and may actually increase the rate of inflation in labor costs.

In Chapter 11 we saw that wage and price policies reduce the rate of strike activity. The strikes that do occur, however, can severely affect the likelihood that the policies will be successful in restraining wage inflation. The most important problem is how to settle strikes in which wage demands far exceed those permitted by the wage criteria or guideposts. The economic program of the government conflicts with the right to strike and with the political costs of taking strong action against unions. In both the U.S. and the U.K., important wage settlements in excess of the incomes policy criteria were permitted to go unchallenged or allowed to stand over initial government objections. During the U.S. program of the early 1970s, the board administering the pay guidelines set a goal of a 5.5 percent wage increase (composed of 3 percent productivity growth and an allowable inflation rate of 2.5 percent). Recognizing that there would be hardship cases, the board announced that it would allow increases of up to 7 percent a year to preserve historic relationships or remedy labor shortages. It never could figure out what to do when a union with significant power to disrupt the economy refused to settle for this prescribed increase and, after much internal discussion, approved actual increases of 16 percent for the United Mine Workers and 14.9 percent for longshoremen on the West Coast. When this happens, wage-price policy loses its credibility and must be either discarded or revamped.

By substituting a norm for wage increases in place of the myriad forces that ordinarily determine the size of wage settlements, wage-price policy may merely rotate rather than shift the short-run Phillips curve. Even if the wage norms could restrain wage inflation when aggregate demand is expanding rapidly, establishing a target for wage settlements that workers (especially union members) feel must be attained may lead to wage increases larger than those the unfettered labor market would produce in periods of slack demand. In the U.K., where incomes policies of various degrees of stringency have been applied more often since World War II than in the U.S., the short-run Phillips curve was flatter between 1947 and 1968 during periods when incomes policies were in effect. Nevertheless, on average, these policies did not shift the short-run Phillips curve downward.[42]

Whether the wage norm is specified in percentage terms alone or partly in absolute terms, which would further distort the labor market, does not matter. The wage increases it allows will differ among various industries from those that would arise from free negotiations between management and workers or their union. Because shifts in supply and demand are not uniform across all firms, the effects of the norms eventually become so disruptive that pressures mount to abandon the policies entirely. Consider the industry shown in Figure 16.9. The long-run supply curve S^L of labor to this industry is perfectly elastic, so shifts in demand will eventually have no impact on wages. If the demand for labor in the industry suddenly rises from D to D' but does not change anywhere else, the wage would rise in the short-run relative to wages elsewhere, increasing from w^* to w_1. This effect occurs because the short-run supply of labor to the industry, S^S, is not perfectly elastic. Eventually more workers will be attracted to the industry and wages will return to w^*, with employment rising to E_1. With strict wage-price controls allowing only equal percentage increases in all industries, this adjustment cannot occur. The temporary relative wage increase that would eventually attract $E_1 - E_0$ new workers is forbidden. Instead, there will be a long-lasting shortage of workers equal to $E_1 - E_0$.

The government can avoid this difficulty by making exceptions to its policy in industries where demand is increasing. Making such distinctions is very difficult and subject to immense political pressure. It becomes extremely hard to convince workers in other industries that a government-mandated drop in their relative wage is fair. Most policies have relied, instead, on private responses to shortages of the type we have already discussed.

The record of wage-price policies to date includes few, if any, cases in which increases in nominal wages have been successfully restrained over significant periods. In some cases these policies failed because they were not accompanied by the monetary and fiscal policies required to truly restrain inflation. More often, however, the policies were simply abandoned when politically powerful groups felt that their relative position had worsened, or when the economic dislocations became unbearable.

Do wage-price policies even shift the short-run Phillips curve down, and can they do so without having the curve rebound to an even higher position than its original one after the restrictions are removed? In examining Figure 16.1, the points for the years 1962 to 1966 lie below the short-run Phillips curve P drawn for the years 1954 to 1973 and 1983 to 1990. This simple evidence suggests that the wage-price guideposts of this period might have produced a downward shift in the curve. More detailed consideration of the evidence, however, casts doubt on this conclusion. The overhanging potential labor supply of workers discouraged by the long period of relatively high

---

[42] Richard Lipsey and J. Michael Parkin, "Incomes Policy—A Reappraisal," *Economica* 37: 115–137 (1970).

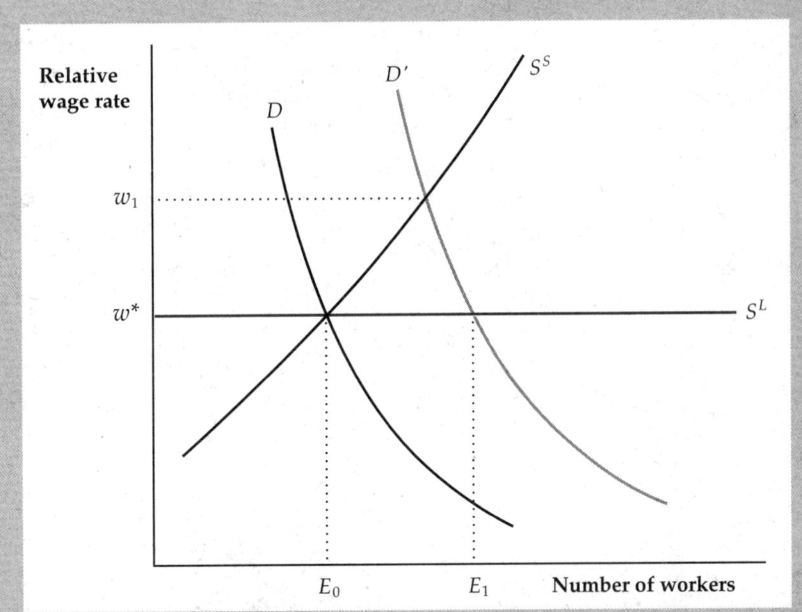

FIGURE 16.9 SHORT- AND LONG-RUN ADAPTATION IN LABOR MARKETS WITH WAGE CONTROLS

When the short-run supply of labor is less elastic than the long-run supply of labor (S^S compared with S^L), temporary wage increases in response to increase in demand will induce more workers to enter an industry and have no long-run effect on wages. Wage controls will prevent this adaptation and create a permanent shortage of labor.

unemployment from 1960 to 1963, and the amount of hoarded labor (see Chapter 5) employed but not fully utilized meant that the degree of slack in the labor market at each unemployment gap during this period was more than the measured gap suggested.[43] Whether the guideposts reduced the rate of wage inflation has not been answered satisfactorily, nor, given the range of other changes occurring at the time, is it likely to be.

Between 1971 and 1974 the Nixon administration imposed a series of four different incomes policies. The brevity of each of the periods prevents inferring from Figure 16.1 whether the policies had any effect on the short-run Phillips curve. Evidence from multivariate regressions suggests that wage

[43] N. J. Simler and Alfred Tella, "Labor Reserves and the Phillips Curve," *Review of Economics and Statistics* 50: 32–49 (1968); Jim Taylor, "Hidden Unemployment, Hoarded Labor, and the Phillips Curve," *Southern Economic Journal* 37: 1–16 (1970). See also the discussion by Paul Anderson, Michael Wachter, Adrian Throop, and George Perry in *American Economic Review* 59: 351–370 (1969).

increases during the first and fourth phases of the policy (the first was a wage freeze) were below what might have been anticipated given labor market conditions. In the periods immediately following these two phases, however, wage increases were above what would have been expected based on the amount of unemployment and price inflation at the time. Although they may have shifted the short-run Phillips curve down temporarily, the Nixon incomes policies were soon nullified by equally large rebounds in the curve.[44]

The broader experience of Western European countries indicates the same overall lack of effectiveness evident in the briefer American experience. In some nations, especially those where the wage-price policy was coupled with effective demand management, nominal wage inflation may have been reduced temporarily at given rates of unemployment. The best example of this reduction is Austria in the mid-1970s, where guarantees to organized labor that job losses would be avoided and restraints on the growth of aggregate demand caused the size of wage settlements to moderate substantially.[45] Other countries, perhaps because of the greater diversity of the economic interests affected by the policies, have been less successful in achieving even a temporary downward shift in the short-run Phillips curve.

Wage-price policies can hope to be effective only when they are accompanied by macroeconomic policies that create an environment for wage restraint by avoiding excess demand for goods and services either by reducing aggregate demand or increasing aggregate supply. To be effective, wage-price policies must shun even the appearance of being less stringently applied to workers in industries with the most economic or political power. Otherwise all workers will abandon their adherence to the policy for fear of seeing their relative pay reduced. More importantly, the policies must be temporary. If not, they will inevitably lead to an increasing inability of wage differences to reflect the state of supply and demand for labor in different occupations, areas, and industries. The labor market will become increasingly unable to allocate workers where their productivity is greatest. This rigidity will reduce, if not eliminate, the mobility that we saw in Chapter 7 is the fundamental way the labor market responds to changing economic conditions.

SUMMARY

There is a short-run inverse relationship between the rate of nominal wage inflation and the rate of unemployment in an industrialized economy. In the long run the rate of wage inflation is determined by the rate of growth of aggregate demand and supply, whereas the long-run equilibrium rate of unemployment is determined by the success of institutions in matching

---

[44] Frank Reid, "Control and Decontrol of Wages in the United States," *American Economic Review* 71: 108–120 (1981).

[45] John Addison, "Incomes Policy: The Recent European Experience," in J. L. Fallick and R. F. Elliott (eds.). *Incomes Policies, Inflation and Relative Pay,* London: George Allen and Unwin (1981).

POLICY ISSUE

"TIPS" FOR REDUCING WAGE-PRICE INFLATION

One modification of wage policies attempts to allow at least some flexibility by enabling a firm to "purchase" the ability to increase wages above the guideline by paying for it through tax penalties. Such policies have been particularly common in the transition economies of Central and Eastern Europe. Such **tax-based incomes policies (TIPs)** were first proposed in the West in the early 1970s.[46] The general form of these proposals is shown in Figure 16.10, a modification of Figure 16.9. Once again the long-run labor supply is perfectly elastic at a wage of w^* but the short-run supply of labor has a positive elasticity.

A typical wage-tax program requires employers to pay a penalty on all wages over a certain level. In practice this penalty is typically progressive and has ranged up to 800 percent in Bulgaria but is more commonly about 100 percent of excess wages over some predetermined wage bill based on changes in employment, productivity, and levels of past wages. Suppose that a constant wage penalty of 100 percent is applied to wages above w^* in Figure 16.10. This increases the effective wage paid by employers above w^* and makes the labor demand curve more elastic. A wage of w_1 will look to the employer like a wage of w_2 with the difference $w_2 - w_1$ representing the amount of the tax payment.

Suppose the demand for labor shifts from D_1 to D_2. Without the excess wage tax, the short-run equilibrium wage would rise to w_2. With the lower elasticity of demand created by the tax, the wage increase is only to w_3. Wages still rise, however, so eventually workers will be attracted into the industry. The policy may slow the speed of adjustment, but it should result in more moderate wage increases and less chance of inflationary spirals created by spillovers.

vacant jobs and unemployed workers. Substantial year-to-year variation in wages exists in the U.S. economy including a significant number of cuts in real and nominal wages. This variability casts doubt on explanations of unemployment gaps resulting from rigid wages. On the other hand, the economy moves back toward the long-run equilibrium rate of unemployment very slowly after unemployment has risen above or fallen below it. The movement toward equilibrium appears to be too slow to be satisfactorily explained solely by theories based on flexible real wage rates.

The transmission of wage increases among labor markets, occupations, and industries provides a potential explanation for this slow adjustment. A wage increase obtained in a tight labor market can influence later wage increases elsewhere, mitigating the effects of looser labor markets.

It is clear that variations in employment are less than would be created by variation in product demand. This smaller variation can be explained by an efficiency wage argument based on the reduction in workers' effort occurring if workers were asked to accept cuts in pay. Another possible explanation is employers' unwillingness to incur the costs of firm-specific training

[46] Henry Wallich and Sidney Weintraub, "A Tax-Based Incomes Policy," *Journal of Economic Issues* 5: 1–19 (1971); Laurence Seidman, "Tax-Based Incomes Policies," *Brookings Papers on Economic Activity*: 301–348 (1978). See also Peter Bernstein, "Inflation Isn't the Bogeyman Now," *New York Times*, September 8, 1991, p. 13.

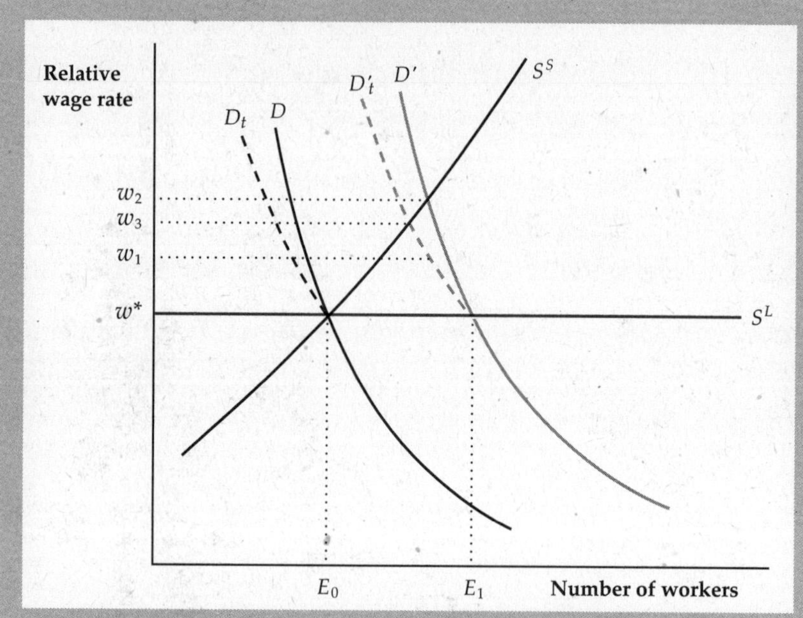

FIGURE 16.10 WAGE RESPONSES WITH A TIP EXCESS-WAGES TAX

An excess-wages tax (one form of tax-based incomes policy) can increase the short-run elasticity of labor demand and produce a smaller temporary wage increase in response to a shift in demand. The long-run equilibrium is unaffected.

for new workers who could be substituted for existing employees whose wages are too high to be justified by their current *VMP*.

Incomes policies such as wage controls can, at best, temporarily reduce the rate of wage inflation at each rate of unemployment, but at the cost of introducing inefficiencies and distortions. The evidence shows that many of these policies have not even succeeded in doing this, and that none have restrained wage increases in the long run. Experimental alternatives, such as a greater reliance on profit sharing as a form of compensation and taxes on excessive wage increases (TIPs), might be more successful.

QUESTIONS AND PROBLEMS

16.1 Use the data in columns 1 and 2 of Table 16.1 to reconstruct a time series on the estimated natural rate of unemployment. Take the data on the unemployment rate in column 1 and redraw the points in Figure 16.1. Comment on the differences between Figure 16.1 and your version.

16.2 Let the supply of labor depend on the *perceived* real wage, w/p^*, so that

$$L^s = 15 + w/p^*$$

where w is the nominal wage rate. Workers' form expectations p^* about the price level p by taking a simple average of prices in the past two periods:

$$p^* = .5 \times p_{-1} + .5 \times p_{-2}.$$

Employers base the demand for labor on the real wage rate (using the *actual* price level), so that labor demand is

$$L^d = 35 - w/p.$$

Assume the price level p has been 1.00 for the last 50 years. In 1996 prices rise 10 percent (to 1.10), and in 1997 they rise again, to 1.25. Thereafter the price level stays at 1.25.

a. Calculate the nominal and real wage rates in 1995, 1996, 1997, etc., through the year 2000, if the labor market reaches an equilibrium based on L^d and L^s each year. Also calculate the level of employment in each of those years.
b. Is the real wage rate higher or lower in 1996, 1997, and 1998 than in 1999 and 2000? How does the path of the real wage rate compare to the level of employment?

16.3 Now ignore the difference between nominal and real wages and let w be the real wage rate. Let the supply of labor be

$$L^s = 15 + w$$

and the demand for labor be

$$L^d = 35 - w + k$$

where k = some number that varies over the business cycle.

a. Let $k = 10$ in good times. What are labor supply, labor demand, and the equilibrium wage rate and employment level?
b. Let $k = 0$ in bad times. What are the equilibrium wage rate and employment level?
c. Assume that labor demand is such that profit-maximizing behavior in bad times allows $k = 5$ if wages are kept at or above 15, but produces $k = 0$ if the wage is less than 15. What is the level of employment in bad times? Is there any unemployment, and, if so, how much? If there is unemployment, why might employers refuse to cut wages and hire unemployed workers?

16.4 We have shown that wage spillovers probably go from the nonunion to the union sector in the United States. How might the direction of spillovers be affected by the relative size of the union sector? How would the direction of spillovers be affected by the structure of collective bargaining, that is, whether craft or industrial unions predominate, and whether wage bargaining is done at the local or national levels?

16.5 There has been very little political pressure to institute wage-price policies in the United States since the early 1980s, undoubtedly because the rate of price inflation has remained at very low levels in the United States. Would such policies be any more or less effective, in the United States and elsewhere in times of decelerating inflation accompanied by fairly high rates of demand-deficient unemployment than at other times? Discuss arguments for and against such policies at different points in business cycles.

16.6 It is observationally true that unemployment increases during a recession. What type(s) of unemployment might we expect to see increase during economic downturns? Why is this observation troubling to a strict neoclassical economist? What violation of normal market working is required for unemployment to increase during recessions? Why might this normal market mechanism fail to prevent the increase in unemployment?

16.7 Do changes in unit labor costs cause changes in the price level, or do changes in the price level lead to changes in unit labor costs?

16.8 What factors are can explain the temporary outward shift in the U.S. Phillips curve during the 1970s? What could account for the fact that it appears to have shifted back toward the origin during the 1980s in the U.S. but not in Western Europe?

16.9 Suppose that the U.S. Congress passed a law that prevented most imports of foreign products. What would be the impact of such a law on American unemployment and inflation rates? Does it matter to your answer where the economy is in the business cycle when the law takes effect?

16.10 Suppose you were in charge of the personnel office in a large firm such as General Motors. How would you design employment contracts so that there was the minimum chance that you would have to lay off workers in recessions? Would your answer be different if you were running Joe's Corner Deli?

KEY WORDS

active labor market policies
auction market
employment-population ratio
expectations theory
experience rating
full-employment unemployment rate
incomes policies
insider-outsider model
intertemporal substitution hypothesis
justified wage increase
long-run Phillips curve
natural rate of unemployment
Phillips curve
rigid wages
short-run Phillips curve
staggered contracts
tax-based incomes policy (TIP)
unemployment gap
wage freeze
wage spillovers

AUTHOR INDEX

Subject Index